The CSS *Arkansas*

ALSO BY MYRON J. SMITH, JR.

The USS Carondelet: *A Civil War Ironclad on Western Waters* (2010)

Tinclads in the Civil War: Union Light-Draught Gunboat Operations on Western Waters, 1862–1865 (2010)

The Timberclads in the Civil War: The Lexington, Conestoga *and* Tyler *on the Western Waters* (2008)

Le Roy Fitch: The Civil War Career of a Union River Gunboat Commander (2007)

The Baseball Bibliography, 2d ed. (4 volumes, 2006)

The CSS *Arkansas*

A Confederate Ironclad on Western Waters

Myron J. Smith, Jr.

McFarland & Company, Inc., Publishers
Jefferson, North Carolina, and London

LIBRARY OF CONGRESS CATALOGUING-IN-PUBLICATION DATA

Smith, Myron J.
　　The CSS Arkansas : a Confederate ironclad on western waters / Myron J. Smith, Jr.
　　　p.　　cm.
　　Includes bibliographical references and index.

ISBN 978-0-7864-4726-8
softcover : 50# alkaline paper ∞

　　1. Arkansas (Confederate ram)　2. Mississippi River Valley — History — Civil War, 1861–1865 — Naval operations, Confederate.　3. United States — History — Civil War, 1861–1865 — Naval operations, Confederate.　I. Title.
E599.A75S65　2011
973.5'25 — dc23　　　　　　　　　　　　　　2011023403

BRITISH LIBRARY CATALOGUING DATA ARE AVAILABLE

© 2011 Myron J. Smith, Jr.. All rights reserved

No part of this book may be reproduced or transmitted in any form or by any means, electronic or mechanical, including photocopying or recording, or by any information storage and retrieval system, without permission in writing from the publisher.

On the cover: The CSS *Arkansas* on the Yazoo River (illustration © 2010 by Daniel Dowdey); *inset* 1862 engraving of the CSS *Arkansas* passing through the Federal fleet (U.S. Naval Historical Center)

Manufactured in the United States of America

McFarland & Company, Inc., Publishers
　Box 611, Jefferson, North Carolina 28640
　　www.mcfarlandpub.com

For Dennie

Contents

Acknowledgments viii
Foreword by George Wright 1
Introduction 5

One •	Beginnings	9
Two •	The Upper River Ironclads	24
Three •	A Frustrating Start, August–December 1861	38
Four •	From Memphis to Yazoo City, January–May 1862	57
Five •	Five Weeks Up the Yazoo, Early May–Late June 1862	80
Six •	Descending the Yazoo, June 25–July 15, 1862	125
Seven •	Morning (Part I), July 15, 1862: Dawn Fight in the Yazoo	151
Eight •	Morning (Part II), July 15, 1862: Running the Gauntlet	178
Nine •	Surviving Farragut's Charge: Night, July 15, 1862	204
Ten •	*Arkansas* vs. *Essex*, Round One: July 16–22, 1862	231
Eleven •	*Arkansas* vs. *Essex*, Round Two: Finale Off Baton Rouge, July 23–August 6, 1862	267

Epilogue 295
Chapter Notes 299
Bibliography 329
Index 343

Acknowledgments

I would like to thank those who have offered insightful comments or suggestions regarding the *Arkansas* on the *Civil War Navies Message Board*. These include Alan Doyle, Tom Ezell, Henry E. Whittle, Ed Cotham, Terry Foenander, Shawn Clark, David Adams, Gary Matthews, and Terry G. Scriber.

From the Vicksburg National Military Park, chief historian Terrence J. Winschel kindly provided assistance and answers to several questions. His work *Vicksburg Is the Key: The Struggle for the Mississippi*, coauthored with William L. Shea, also supplied useful detail.

Ms. Joyce A. McKibben, Collections Management Department, University of Memphis Libraries, and Mr. Wayne Dowdey, History Department, Memphis Public Library, provided assistance during our hunt for information on John T. Shirley and the Fort Pickering construction site.

Special tips of the hat go to three colleagues who have been especially helpful. Their assistance has aided this project tremendously by helping to resolve or nearly so a number of physical issues concerning this ship and her configuration that have eluded historians for 150 years.

Californian George Wright, who prepared the foreword, has been particularly diligent in his study of the *Arkansas* power plant. His cumulative understanding allows us, for the first time, to get a handle on what kind of propulsion unit the armorclad actually operated.

David Meagher, historian and blueprint artist, has significantly advanced our understanding of the size and layout of the *Arkansas*. In a series of thought-provoking communications, this Alabamian gave both solid data and the challenge to dig deeper. His generosity in allowing use of his plans is very much appreciated.

Daniel Dowdey, a commercial artist who specializes in dramatic portraits of Civil War naval vessels, has very graciously provided his support and has allowed us to employ several of his many illustrations of the *Arkansas*, all of which convey the armorclad as she was seen by friend and foe alike.

As usual, the staff of the Thomas J. Garland Library, Tusculum College, was supportive. Special thanks is extended to Charles Tunstall, reference and interlibrary loan librarian, for his diligent pursuit of titles not in Tusculum's collection.

Foreword
by George E. Wright, Jr.

When Jack Smith asked me to do a foreword for this book, I was both flattered and surprised. Smith and I are not old friends or acquaintances. But I quickly realized that we both had "the disease"—a love of research and a desire to solve puzzles. And there are few puzzles more frustrating for the Civil War historian than trying to reconstruct the physical characteristics and operational history of the Confederate ironclad *Arkansas*.

As Jack forwarded draft chapters of his book over the months, I realized that he had the qualities I admire in a researcher: a dogged willingness to track down elusive facts and the intellectual honesty to challenge old assumptions and change direction when new discoveries make older research obsolete. It was a pleasure exchanging ideas and reviewing historical possibilities with him.

The simple truth is that until someone wants to put out millions to excavate the decaying remains of the hull of the *Arkansas*, we'll never be totally sure just how she was constructed or her true potential. But Smith's book, the first devoted exclusively to this ironclad, is going to put events into much clearer focus than previous accounts.

A few comments on "primary sources" would seem in order. The average Civil War historian covering the career of the *Arkansas* is usually dependent upon four "primary" sources: *The War of the Rebellion Records* (army and navy), and the memoirs of three of the ram's officers: Isaac Newton Brown, George W. Gift, and Charles W. Read. The value of the contemporary reports contained in the *Official Records* is universally acknowledged. The postwar recollections of the three Southern officers must be used cautiously. The positive aspect of their memoirs is that they complement one another. Each of the authors had strengths and weaknesses.

Gift must have been a "people person," as his memoirs are full of names and personalities. He also seems to have been an "idea guy." His writings are the most descriptive of "what it was like." Lt. Read is rather poor in terms of remembering names, but a strong student of warfare and tactics. "Action" was his middle name and his recollections are the most trustworthy when he describes them. Surprisingly, perhaps the weakest of the primary memoirs is that of the *Arkansas'* most famous captain, Lt. Isaac Newton Brown. From him you would expect comments upon the place of his warship in Confederate strategy affecting the Yazoo Valley and the Vicksburg campaign. Unfortunately, they are not there and the man has suffered criticism for not offering a broader view of events.

Brown gives the impression of having a strong sense of honor and a driving personality, well able to focus intently upon the job at hand. Where Gift and Read show a certain "diplomacy" in their writings, Brown offers strong opinions on narrow points. He would later foster this image in a correspondence with the Federal naval officer Alfred T. Mahan as the latter prepared the first naval history of the inland river war. It is on record that the pragmatic Lt. (later Cmdr.) Brown frequently bristled over the decisions, comments, or actions of Com. Montgomery, Maj. Gen. Van Dorn, Cmdr. McBlair and Pinkney, and especially the local flag officer, Capt. Lynch, whom, in writing at least, he refused to mention by name. The one general he held the highest regard for was Brig. Gen. Daniel Ruggles, who in the dark early days at Greenwood and Yazoo City provided both support and manpower. Brown was particularly proud of the Missouri and Louisiana soldiers and their officers, who volunteered to ship aboard.

The overriding impression one gathers from the memoirs of these three individuals is of mutual loyalty. In the cases of Read and Gift, one wonders if they may have slanted their views so that they would not conflict with those of Brown or, indeed, the *Arkansas*' growing legend. This is where the present volume may prove most useful to future scholars and Civil War enthusiasts. Smith has gone into the other primary sources, the reports, letters and memoirs of civilians and military personnel serving aboard the *Arkansas* and in the Yazoo and Vicksburg areas during the events of May to August 1862 — and even before. One of the most valuable contributions is a recognition that these individuals made decisions based upon what they thought was going on at the time — not with the omniscience of 150 years of hindsight.

Both sides made serious errors based upon poor information. At the time, numerous Union and Confederate authorities, including even the likes of the Rebel commander at Vicksburg, believed the *Arkansas* was some kind of "superweapon." Coming on the scene as she did within months of the famous *Virginia* (ex–*Merrimack*), the Memphis-built ironclad caused some in the North to suffer from a sort of "ram fever," especially after she escaped destruction time after time. Many inaccurate or partially correct accounts regarding the *Arkansas* had wide distribution in contemporary Civil War era newspapers. These reappear with monotonous regularity in later histories — especially those penned within 50 years of the conflict — and recollections.

My modest contribution to this volume is to attempt to help quantify some of the design characteristics of the *Arkansas*, their impact on her value and how she was manned. Anyone who gets into the subject of this warship quickly discovers that almost everything printed about her disagrees with someone else's analysis. Before going into the biomedical field, I spent a few years as a mechanical engineering designer. I was blessed with an early association with V.H. Pavlecks, one of the grand old men of turbine design, who was tolerant of young engineers but insistent that we "put some numbers" to our ideas. The numbers I've put on the *Arkansas* are of the parametric type — looking at the most extreme reported specifications for the vessel and trying to find which "facts" are the most consistent. This is not easy, as every single major feature of this ship is physically unknown and thus disputed! The lack of blueprints specifically assigned to her and the unavailability of actual wreckage has caused this to be a source of personal frustration — for myself and others — for some time.

We who are interested recently had a break in terms of the possible assignment of physical characteristics to the casemate ironing of the *Arkansas*. In 2007, an excellent survey and artifact recovery program was conducted on the wreck of the Confederate armored battery *Georgia* below Savannah. Data from it regarding the rail hung aboard the battery correlates well with existing information from other contemporary Rebel sources on the nautical use of such protection, as well as the U.S. Navy, which reviewed the effects of gunfire upon similar railroad iron used at Arkansas Post.

Perhaps the most elusive number for *Arkansas* is a solid estimate of her displacement. I have used David Meagher's hull configurations, taken from a contemporary John L. Porter design kept at the National Archives. The draft of the *Arkansas* is quoted in various sources as between nine and 13 feet. Such a four-foot difference could result in an increase in displacement of over 50 percent! Increased draft would also mean more wetted area for hull drag, which would impact speed and fuel consumption. The National Archives and David Meagher's well-known drawings incorporate many well-educated guesses, as do those of other artists and model makers presented through the years, including William E. Geoghegan—famed museum specialist of the Smithsonian Institution—and Cottage Industries. The latter now offers a resin model that, save for the shape of the ram, provides a very visual idea of how makeshift she probably appeared to professional naval eyes at the time.

The officers and petty officers of the *Arkansas* must have viewed their manning problems as a sort of revolving door. There was never enough time to "shake down" the vessel or her crew, which makes her impact even more striking. When all of her physical and manpower attributes and limitations are balanced, it can still be argued that, although she steamed in the *Virginia*'s shadow, the vessel was, in fact, the most successful of the first wave of contractor-built Southern ironclads—something Jack Smith's tale makes abundantly clear.

Before entering the biomedical field, Californian George E. Wright, Jr., was a mechanical engineering designer, working with V.H. Pavlecks, an authority on turbine design. A longtime student of Civil War naval activities, Wright is a department head and medical instructor for Azusa Adult School, the adult and community outreach division of Azusa United School District in Glendora, California.

Introduction

The storm broke in April 1861. At 2:30 P.M. on April 13, Maj. Robert Anderson surrendered his beleaguered Fort Sumter, in Charleston harbor, South Carolina, to the Confederacy. Two days later, U.S. President Abraham Lincoln declared a state of insurrection and called for 75,000 three-month volunteers to quash the revolt. Years of talk, hope, and work spent in seeking a solution to the economic, political, and social differences that divided the North and the South had ended in failure. The most tragic conflict in American history was "on."

The Mississippi Valley west of the Allegheny Mountains lies partly in the North and partly in the South. When the Southern states enacted ordinances of secession, they claimed as their own that portion of the valley lying within their borders and prepared for its military defense. In the North, planners began to formulate a recovery strategy. One military measure envisioned to support such a plan was the construction of a flotilla of armored naval vessels for operation on the great inland rivers. As this strategy unfolded, it forced the South to take notice and respond.

The concept of armored vessels of war, both powered and unpowered, was not altogether a new one. For decades, the Europeans had been active in the experimental development of such craft. First with unpowered "floating batteries," such as the type employed by the French in the Crimea in the middle 1850s, and then the propelled (steam and sail) armored ships *Gloire* (1858) of France, *Warrior* (1859) of the UK, and successor units. In the United States as early as the 1840s, New Jersey engineer Robert L. Stevens persuaded the U.S. government to grant him $250,000 and two years to build an American craft, the "Stevens Battery." Its progress—or lack of same—was keenly watched by interested parties here and abroad, including U.S. senator Stephen R. Mallory. By 1861, the Stevens enterprise was still not, however, completed, though it had already consumed $586,717.84.

When, even before Fort Sumter, the new Confederacy was initially formed by a few—and later all—of the Southern states, it was from the start anything but timid in its approach to new naval thinking. Stephen Mallory, who was confirmed as the Confederate navy secretary on March 4, was keenly aware that Rebel yells alone would not defeat the U.S. Navy in the pending civil conflict. All the guns available on all the warcraft in Southern hands did not then equal the battery of a single Federal sloop-of-war. So it was that, as soon as he was sworn in, the new Confederate navy boss took stock of his situation. The Floridian quickly came to the determination that Richmond would never be the power center for a major sea power. But, by doing a few things well, his new command might be able to extract maximum advantage against the larger Yankee foe.

Within weeks, Secretary Mallory encouraged the development and deployment of commerce raiders, submarines, underwater mines (then known as "torpedoes"), small "mosquito" gunboat flotillas, and amphibious raids. As the war was launched and deepened, the first — most successfully those purchased in Britain and France — caused panic among Union merchants, while the subsurface attacks actually destroyed nearly 50 Federal warships. As James Phinney Baxter put it, Secretary Mallory "staked the success of the Confederate Navy on two well conceived projects: the creation of commerce destroyers ... and the construction of ironclads to break the blockade and carry the war to the enemy."[1] It was, however, in the area of ironclad warship design and operations that the Confederate navy and its chief made their greatest mark and the one that is most germane to this story. These "armorclads," as they were called by Prof. William N. Still, Jr.,[2] would, it was hoped, by their inherent quality, counter the superior number of warships available to the enemy.

The first up was the CSS *Virginia*, built on the hulk of the half-burned USS *Merrimack*. Designed by John Luke Porter and John M. Brooke, the powerful ship had a built up iron-covered box, called a casemate or a shield, affixed to its deck. Protected inside was a battery of heavy guns, while the vessel's machinery was protected in the hold down below. During the late spring and summer of 1861 as the *Virginia* took shape, a huge variety of other developments faced the Southern naval leadership as it struggled not only to create, man, arm, and equip its establishment, but also to develop a defense that would assure protection for the coasts and rivers, as well as ensure logistical viability in the face of a Federal blockade.

Summer was at its height when the Confederate States Navy (CSN) leadership at Richmond first started to worry about the Mississippi Valley. Word was filtering in regarding the North's freshwater naval building, and New Orleans required protection. It was at this time that a steamboat captain arrived with an idea that would eventually — for a brief period a year hence — give the Confederacy naval supremacy on the middle Mississippi River and one or two of its tributaries. Politicians and generals in the area around and just above Memphis, Tennessee (the upper Western river limit of the Confederacy), were keenly aware of Federal plans to sweep down the Mississippi and they knew that some timber-covered warships were even now about to join the Northern war effort from a base at Cairo, Illinois. They would, so reports went, be followed by heavier vessels before Christmas.

At this time, John T. Shirley was a well-known steamboat entrepreneur at Memphis who had already devoted some thought to the creation of an ironclad warship and was in touch on the subject with Primus Emerson, one of the better known Western steamboat builders. After rounding up support from military and civic leaders, he duly arrived at the offices of the Confederate Navy Department with the plans to build two armorclads for river defense. After some discussion and negotiation, Secretary Mallory and leaders of the Confederate congress were able to draft and enact legislation authorizing this construction, a law quickly signed by President Jefferson Davis. By September, Shirley and Emerson were at work on two hulls at Fort Pickering — south of Memphis — that would be named *Arkansas* and *Tennessee*. Only the former would be finished.

The trials and tribulations endured by Shirley and Emerson in construction of the *Arkansas* were just incredible. Both materials and workers were scarce and time and again the timetable for completion slipped. By spring 1862, however, the vessel was sufficiently prepared to allow her launch. Then, with only days to spare, New Orleans was captured and fear for her safety caused the incomplete craft to be towed 300 miles to Greenwood, Mississippi, a hamlet far up the Yazoo River above Vicksburg. Once the *Arkansas* made it to this backwater refuge, progress on her completion and outfitting came almost to a halt. By May, any expectation that she would ever sortie forth under the Rebel banner was almost gone. At this point, Secretary Mallory ordered Lt. Isaac Newton Brown to take over her superintendence, bring her into commission, and take her to war.

The fighting Rebel fleets on the Mississippi prior to July 1862 comprised a handful of wooden rams, gunboats, and four ironclads, three of which were not finished. How Brown achieved his construction goals to finish his in a remote setting is one of the great legends of the Civil War. Equally celebrated is the brief but glorious fighting career achieved by the *Arkansas* against long odds. Every single one of the 23 days of her actual service life was memorable, but several stood out from the others.

First were the two battles of the morning of July 15, one on the Yazoo River and the other with the combined Federal fleet on the Mississippi River above Vicksburg. The passage of RAdm. Farragut's fleet downstream past her that night in a failed attempt to destroy her with concentrated and overwhelming gunfire was spectacularly unsuccessful. Sundry attempts were made to hit her with mortars in the weeks thereafter, even as the tiny number of her surviving crewmen, with contract labor, attempted to make repairs aboard from the three battles. Even as attempts were made also to physically strengthen the craft while she was under fire, the *Arkansas* conducted several short sorties designed to frighten her foes.

On July 22, two Federal vessels launched unsuccessful ramming assaults in another effort to sink the *Arkansas* as she lay at Vicksburg. One, the *Queen of the West*, managed to butt her, causing what turned out to be telling damage. Then sickness and fatigue, to say nothing of wounds, forced many of her officers and crew ashore. The commander of the *Arkansas*, Lt. Brown, had to take sick leave. Illness also sent the boat's chief engineer to the hospital, and he was the one man who seemed able to successfully keep the boat's stubborn engines functioning.

During her brief operational life, the *Arkansas* was subject to the command of an army general, Earl Van Dorn, who regarded the vessel as a "super weapon." When the Federals quit their first Vicksburg campaign at the end of July, he took the opportunity to send troops to recapture the city of Baton Rouge. The *Arkansas*, her repairs not complete, many of her officers not fully recovered, and most of her new crew untrained, was ordered to support the ground attack on Louisiana's capital. As she came within sight of the town, her always-temperamental power plant failed. To prevent certain capture, she was scuttled on August 6.

The *Arkansas*, wrote historian Tom Z. Parrish, "largely eclipsed by the lasting fame of the *Merrimac* and the *Monitor*, has not gained general acceptance in Civil War imagery." Even so, he continued, her "representative significance" has stood out "with cameo sharpness, not lost in the sweep and din of gigantic battles on land."

It is true, as Parrish notes, that her significance as a fighting ship has always been acknowledged. It is not forgotten that the *Arkansas* was the only Confederate casemate ironclad to actually operate, say nothing of achieving victory, on the Mississippi River during the war. Although she held sway over those waters over which she steamed for only a short time, she threw fear into and created consternation among Northerners far and wide.[3]

The physical limitations of this warship, particularly insofar as her power plant was concerned, have likewise not escaped notice. Unfortunately, reliable details concerning her actual size, configuration, armor, propulsion, and ironing, even when known, remain in dispute. Information on her actual length and width, draft, displacement, actual number of crew, ordnance types, her ram, armor thickness, and engine suite remain murky or inaccurate at best or at worst totally unknown. Not until recently have serious efforts been made to complete her story with detailed analysis or conjecture regarding her structure.

The *Arkansas* was "a makeshift vessel with a makeshift crew," wrote her first great profiler, Prof. William Still, in 1958. Despite her rugged frame and weak engines, "she was one of the most formidable" ironclads that the South operated during the Civil War and on the Western waters, and was "probably the most formidable."[4] The *Arkansas* was not only the first casemate Confederate ironclad to fight on the Mississippi, she was also the last. Her time, like a shooting star, was brief but glorious, and she achieved the high-water mark of the CSN on inland rivers. After her, there was no organized Confederate navy on the Western waters to speak of. Although Isaac Newton Brown would attempt to build other ironclads up the Yazoo, he would not be successful before Vicksburg fell to the Federals. Thereafter, only the *Missouri* was finished, way up the Red River at Shreveport, but she came too late to enter the war before Appomattox.

No booklength study of the CSS *Arkansas* has ever been published. This was driven home earlier when I sought information on her for my works on the U.S. timberclad gunboats and the Federal ironclad *Carondelet*.[5] The volume in hand attempts to remedy that situation. It draws upon a wide variety of sources, printed and unprinted, for the information required for a review of the construction and appearance of the vessel and her wartime activities. With the help of numerous contemporary students and enthusiasts, detailed attention is given not only to her combats but also to a review of how the armorclad might have been configured, manned, armored, and gunned.

CHAPTER ONE

Beginnings

In late 1860 and the early months of 1861, political and economic forces on both sides of the Mason-Dixon Line stumbled through the darkness of hatred, mistrust, and slow communications and hastened toward a conflict that would consume the United States. The country in those days was vastly different from what it is today.

The population of the 34 states was 31,700,000 souls, of whom 3.5 million, located mostly in the southern and border states, were slaves. The northern part of the country enjoyed mixed exports of $331 million, while cotton comprised the bulk of the $31 million in goods sent out of the south. When the Confederacy was established between 11 states, its new government would represent a largely agrarian society capable of little heavy manufacture; the 23 states remaining in the Union held a huge advantage in machine facilities, resources, and capital.[1]

In the period between December 20, 1860, when South Carolina seceded from the Union and April 12, 1861, when Rebel forces bombarded Fort Sumter, there was hope in some quarters that the increasing drift to internecine war would moderate and that the North would just agree to let the South become independent. After all, citizens in many walks of life and of various persuasions from the northwest to the northeast and Deep South were dependent upon commerce with one another for their existence. Sadly, however, restraint was not shown and a peaceful Dixie exodus from the North American federation would not be possible.

By February 1, 1861, seven Southern states (South Carolina, Mississippi, Florida, Alabama, Georgia, Louisiana, and Texas) had departed the Union and together created a government for the Confederate States of America at Montgomery, Alabama. Within days, a protempore Congress was established and a provisional constitution was drafted. Just over three months later, on May 20, four more states (Virginia, Arkansas, Tennessee, and North Carolina) had joined the Southern cause. Several border states still teetered (Missouri, Kentucky, Delaware, and Maryland); though, in the end, these remained loyal to the Union. Virginia, regarded as the most important new recruit, provided officers, resources, the only big war industry (Tredegar Iron Works), and, beginning in June, a new capital at Richmond. So it was that, in this springtime 150 years ago, the energized opponents on both sides of the Mason-Dixon line set to work creating or bolstering their political and military establishments, curtailing economic intercourse with one another, and formulating war aims.[2]

Elected to office on February 9, Mississippian Jefferson Davis (1808–1889), the new—and, as it turned out, the only—Confederate president was, according to William C. Davis, a very prudent leader who pragmatically looked to contain current situations rather "than anticipating the uncertain future." During his tenure, the Confederacy would fight a defensive war, protecting her homeland from Federal assault by land or sea.

Davis, who had earlier served as both U.S. war secretary and acting navy secretary (the latter in 1853), looked upon deep sea or amphibious activities as ancillary to ground warfare. Presiding over a new nation that was never a nautically inclined geographical region (except perhaps on the Mississippi), the Southern leader realized that, with the exception of rapidly arriving able officers of Confederate tendency, he lacked watery offensive advantage. The southern partners began with no navy and the small industrial base was incapable of building anything worthy of the name. But as long as blockade runners could slip through a growing cordon of Yankee ships, on the seacoast or the inland streams, and deliver goods to ports for distribution inland, there really wasn't, in most Southern minds, the need for strong fleets.

At the time the war began, some Southern rivers, river mouths, and major harbors were protected by strong forts or shore batteries or both. It was believed that hastily gotten-up gunboats, converted from civilian craft, could augment the forts and protect the rivers and sounds. Numerous guardian forts were, however, in poor repair or not yet constructed and consequently the presidential overview was not universally accepted. On February 15, engineer Maj. Pierre G.T. Beauregard (1818–1893), recently resigned from the U.S. Army and about to become a Confederate brigadier, wrote an op ed in the *New Orleans Daily Delta* stressing the importance of the Mississippi and the need for enhanced defenses for the vulnerable Crescent City.

Many also recognized that it would be impossible for the Confederacy to match the long-established Northern fleet hull for hull. It was hoped that better thinking and a reliance on new technology could help overcome the naval challenge. On February 20, the Confederate Congress established a Navy Department and, five days later, President Davis named the able and knowledgeable Stephen R. Mallory (1813–1873) as navy secretary. Elected to the U.S. Senate from his native Florida in 1850, he had served on the Naval Affairs Committee throughout the decade prior to the war and was long its chairman.

During his time in Washington, Mallory worked to reform and modernize the U.S. Navy, becoming a close student of naval developments abroad, particularly in the area of ironclad warships. He was also quite familiar with a unique experimental American floating battery. In 1842, New Jersey engineer Robert L. Stevens persuaded the U.S. government to grant him $250,000 and two years to build an American craft, the "Stevens Battery." By 1861, the enterprise was still not com-

Jefferson Davis, President of the Confederacy. *Elected to office on February 9, 1861, Mississippian Jefferson Davis (1808–1889), the new—and, as it turned out, the only—Confederate president, had earlier served as both U.S. war secretary and acting navy secretary (the latter in 1853). He looked upon deep-sea or amphibious activities as ancillary to ground warfare and eventually placed the armorclad* Arkansas *under orders of army general Van Dorn. Probably his most effective sea service move was his appointment of Stephen R. Mallory as his navy secretary (Library of Congress).*

pleted, though it had already consumed $586,717.84. In Europe, too, much work was done with the concept of the unpowered armored floating war vessel, particularly in France and Austria. On February 9, 1861, *Frank Leslie's Illustrated Weekly* published a drawing of an unpowered Austrian gunboat, recently employed in the Italian conflict, that, when seen today, bears a striking resemblance to the CSS *Virginia* (ex–USS *Merrimack*).

Keenly supportive of new naval technologies, Mallory, whose appointment was confirmed on March 4, was also aware that Rebel yells alone would not defeat the U.S. Navy. All the guns available on all the warcraft in Southern hands did not then equal the battery of a single Federal sloop-of-war. So it was that, as soon as he was sworn in, the new Confederate navy boss took stock of his situation. The Floridian quickly came to the determination that, by doing a few things well, his new command might be able to extract maximum advantage against the larger Yankee foe.

Secretary Mallory encouraged the development and deployment of commerce raiders, submarines, underwater mines (then known as "torpedoes"), small "mosquito" gunboat flotillas, and amphibious raids. The first—most successfully those purchased in Britain and France—would cause panic among Union merchants, while the subsurface attacks actually caused the loss of nearly 50 Federal warships. As James Phinney Baxter put it, Secretary Mallory "staked the success of the Confederate Navy on two well conceived projects: the creation of commerce destroyers ... and the construction of ironclads to break the blockade and carry the war to the enemy."

Stephen R. Mallory, Confederate Navy Secretary (1813–1873). *On February 20, 1861, the Confederate congress established a navy department and, five days later, President Davis named the able and knowledgeable Stephen R. Mallory as navy secretary. Elected to the U.S. Senate from his native Florida in 1850, Mallory had served on the Naval Affairs Committee throughout the decade prior to the Civil War and was long its chairman. During his time in Washington, Mallory worked to reform and modernize the U.S. Navy, becoming a close student of naval developments abroad, particularly in the area of ironclad warships. He would be a strong proponent of ironclads during his entire tenure at Richmond (Library of Congress).*

It was, however, in the area of the ironclad warship design and operations that the Confederate navy and its chief made their greatest mark and the one that is most germane to this story. These "armorclads" would, it was hoped, by their inherent quality, counter the superior number of warships available to the enemy. "It was fortunate for the infant Confederacy," wrote William C. Davis, "that in Secretary of the Navy Stephen R. Mallory the South had a man well aware of the value of ironclad warships." But actually obtaining any of these was still some months in the future. Now was the time to plan, organize, and acquire.

President Davis signed the Navy Department-enabling legislation on March 16, by which time Secretary Mallory had come up with a rudimentary command structure (based largely upon the U.S. Navy Department). When the war came, some 247 Federal officers resigned their USN commissions and offered their services to the South. A large number of these were appointed officers in the infant Confederate navy and they set to work. For some time to come, the new CSN lacked enlisted personnel, weapons, ships, depots, and supplies. The personnel were unable to resign (without penalty) from the Northern navy and, as was pointed out in a recent study of the CSS *Georgia*, there is no "indication that they wanted to."

On April 13, Brig. Gen. Beauregard compelled the surrender of Fort Sumter, located in the harbor of Charleston, South Carolina. The Federal position simply could not withstand the heavy guns that surrounded it. Interestingly enough, among these were four mounted on an ironclad floating battery built under the direction of Lt. John Hamilton, CSN, son of a former South Carolina governor, who conceived of it with Maj. J.H. Trapier. At the time, the term floating battery was applied to a specific kind of unpropelled, heavily armored and armed vessel—essentially a protected gun platform or unpowered ironclad—like the Stevens Battery. The concept was popularized during the Crimean War when, heavily backed by Emperor Napoleon III, the French navy employed three such craft in the Allied October 17, 1855, assault on Kinburn and at the end of the decade by the Austrians in Italy.

As would later be the case when constructor John Luke Porter and Lt. John Mercer Brooke differed over the parentage of the *Virginia*, there would develop some disagreement between Hamilton and Trapier as to who formulated the idea for this floating battery, with the latter claiming it was he who proposed the concept. In any event, the two men jointly presented their design to the South Carolina Executive Committee. A total of $12,000 in funding was provided by the state on the condition that the project could be completed in under a month. This proviso can be seen as something of a "penalty clause," a more detailed version of which would later be inserted into the contract for the *Arkansas*.

Frank Leslie's Illustrated Weekly provided its readers with a description of what historian David Detzer has called a "remarkably ugly, ungainly craft, like nothing anyone in the city had ever seen." With a length of 100 feet and a 25-foot beam, the structure, with its flat deck looking something like a covered barge or maybe a houseboat, was constructed of heavy pine timbers a foot square buttressed by palmetto logs. Major Trapier later reported slightly different dimensions, stating that the battery was 80 feet long with a 40-foot beam (width) and an 8-foot draft. At the front was a sloping wall almost four-feet thick into which was cut four open windows to serve as gun ports. In a letter to the editors of *Battles and Leaders*, the unit's commander, Col. (then Lt.) Joseph A. Yates commented upon the substantial protection. The wooden wall "was covered with railroad iron, two courses of rails turned inward and outward so as to form a pretty smooth surface." All the iron was bolted together. To safeguard the gunners from plunging fire, a short gable roof was swept back from the top of the wall. Cannonballs were stored below floorboards located just behind the cannon, two each 32-pdrs. and 42-pdrs. As might be imagined, the weight on the front of the craft was tremendous. To keep it on an even keel, the builders left the middle of the deck completely open and at the rear placed thousands of sandbags that, together with the gunpowder they protected, served as a counterbalance.

Originally designed so it could be moved by tugboat to various locations independent of land, this Charleston battery was moored, during Beauregard's shoot, behind a stone breakwater off the western end of Sullivan's Island to enfilade Sumter's left flank from a range of about 2,100 yards. Four giant wedges kept her secure and prevented swaying, while the breakwater protected the hull from ricochets. Yates' gunners fired 470 rounds during the bombardment, while cannon answering from Fort Sumter hit the floating battery repeatedly. Only one Yankee bolt entered, passing "through the narrow angular slope just below the roof." The iron-armored wall of the South Carolinians' floating battery proved that such sloping protection could be effective. Two days after the fall of Sumter, President Lincoln proclaimed the Confederacy to be in rebellion against its rightful government and called for 75,000 militia volunteers to quash it.

Though initially unrealized, a significant opportunity to redress at least part of the South's naval hardware concern was handed to the new Rebel navy just one week following the surrender of Fort Sumter. The big Gosport Naval Base at Portsmouth, Virginia, across the Elizabeth River from Norfolk, was partially destroyed by exiting Federal forces on April 20 to prevent the yard facilities and fleet elements there from falling into the hands of Confederate-leaning Virginia militia. These Southerners arrived just hours before the lead elements of a relief force dispatched by Secretary Welles.

Coming a day after President Lincoln issued a blockade proclamation aimed at closing Southern ports and technically before Virginia was out of the Union, this Northern disaster netted the South the base, the towns of Norfolk and Portsmouth, and nearly every heavy cannon it would deploy on the Atlantic coast and western rivers during the remainder of

Stevens Floating Battery. *In 1842, New Jersey engineer Robert L. Stevens and his brother Edwin A. persuaded the U.S. government to grant them $250,000 and two years to build an unpowered American ironclad craft, the "Stevens Battery." In the years afterward, the work was supported by then senator and future Confederate navy secretary Stephen R. Mallory and others. By 1861, the enterprise was still not completed, though it had already consumed $586,717.84. It would go on to consume $2 million of the Stevens family fortune before it was scrapped in 1881* (Harper's Weekly, May 4, 1861).

Ironclad Floating Battery in Charleston, South Carolina, Harbor. *Fort Sumter (this page and opposite) was the site of the first battle of the American Civil War. U.S. army major Robert Anderson, defender of the fort, ignored calls for surrender from Brig. Gen. P.G.T. Beauregard, CSA. At 4:30, April 12, 1861, the first shot was fired. The Union position simply could not withstand the heavy guns that surrounded it. Interestingly enough, among these were four 42-pdrs. mounted on an ironclad floating battery anchored off the west end of Sullivan's Island. It was built under the direction of Lt. John Hamilton, CSN, son of a former South Carolina governor, who conceived of it with Maj. J.H. Trapier and was known to the designers of the CSS* Virginia *and* Arkansas. *The photograph is a contemporary shot of the floating battery (Miller, ed.,* Photographic History of the Civil War, *volume. 6).*

the year. Professor Still puts the number at 1,198 guns plus 60 thousand pounds of gunpowder. The Gosport takeover also inadvertently made it possible for the insurgents to acquire mountains of supplies and other ordnance materiel, a noteworthy drydock, and manufacturing facilities. Also recovered were the hulks of about 10 U.S. Navy warships, including the recently repaired U.S. frigate *Merrimack*. Editors of the *Richmond Daily Enquirer*, eager witness to the armorclad story, exulted: "We have material enough to build a Navy of iron-plated ships."

As dogwoods bloomed and tulips popped up showing the first signs of spring in Montgomery, Alabama, the idea of the new Confederate navy floating quality over quantity gained additional currency. In an April 26 report to President Davis, Secretary Mallory set forth an initial fleet strategy based upon his long observation of international naval developments. Recognizing that the U.S. had a navy and that "we have a navy to build," the former Florida senator stressed that if the South would pay close attention to the quality of its naval construction and create ships able to well-match any encountered, "we shall have wisely provided for our naval success." To achieve superiority, Mallory hinted that he was about to unleash a revolution. "I propose to adopt a class of vessels," he wrote, "hitherto unknown to naval service." The secretary went on to outline a three-phase approach to his strategy: fast ocean cruisers, such as would be seen in the CSS *Alabama*, to strike the Federal merchant trade;

One: Beginnings

(*Frank Leslie,* The Soldier in Our Civil War)

(Battles & Leaders, *volume 1*)

the introduction of heavy rifled cannon far superior to the smoothbores then common; and armored vessels. Initially, it was hoped that these could be purchased overseas. Together these three elements would constitute a technical surprise that Mallory hoped would reverse the South's waterborne inadequacies.[3]

Within a month of the formation of the Confederacy, the government of the U.S. changed as well. President Abraham Lincoln (1809–1865) came into office and appointed his cabinet, including the Connecticut politician and one-time Office of Clothing and Provisions chief Gideon Welles (1802–1878) as head of the Navy Department, with Gustavus V. Fox (1821–1883) as his assistant. It fell to these men to enhance the Federal fleet and use it to support the U.S. Army and simultaneously strangle the nautical commerce of the South.

As in the South, Union leadership also sought to support a ground war. The U.S. Navy strategy, employing conventional wooden warships in larger and larger numbers, was initially quite conventional, though an emphasis upon ironclad vessels would come. The Northern

Gosport Naval Base. *Located at Portsmouth, Virginia, across the Elizabeth River from Norfolk, this huge facility was partially destroyed by exiting Federal forces on April 20, 1861 to prevent its navy yard and fleet elements from falling into the hands of Confederate-leaning state militia. Coming a day after President Lincoln issued a blockade proclamation aimed at closing Southern ports and technically before Virginia was out of the Union, this Northern disaster netted the South the base, the towns of Norfolk and Portsmouth, and nearly every heavy cannon it would deploy on the Atlantic coast and western rivers during the remainder of the year, including several that made their way aboard the CSS* Arkansas *(Frank Leslie,* The Soldier in Our Civil War*).*

army was, however, the first off the mark in developing a grand war-fighting strategy. Eventually encompassing all of the elements of total war, its plan would be clearly offensive — and feature ironclads.

News of Fort Sumter's surrender on April 13 and President Lincoln's call-up were received in St. Louis, Missouri, where, as in other communities, it received front-page coverage in the local newspapers. One of those reading the coverage was the well-known and wealthy engineer-riverman James B. Eads (1820–1887), who immediately wrote to his friend, a noted Missouri politician and the new U.S. attorney general, Edward Bates (1793–1869). Eads, later made famous by his construction of the steel St. Louis arch bridge, called for aggressive action to defeat the Rebels and suggested he had a plan for "vigorous action" that might prove helpful in wresting the Lower Mississippi away from the South. Bates also believed that the Mississippi could provide a path into the Confederacy and that a naval force should be created to serve on that stream. According to historian Gibson, Bates was "probably the first person to propose to Lincoln" an inland blockade. Eads' letter provided the former congressman with the first thought-out plan suitable for presentation to the president and he determined to do so as soon as possible, asking Eads to come east.

Upon his arrival in Washington, D.C., Eads made his way to the Justice Department, where he and Bates conferred on the engineer's ideas: the Mississippi and its tributaries would be blockaded and then militarily retrieved using, among other resources, a flotilla of gunboats converted from three boats owned by his Missouri Wrecking Company. On April 29, Bates and Eads appeared before President Lincoln and the cabinet to explain the latter's ideas for creating a river navy to aid in a campaign to first blockade and then to recover the Mississippi River Valley employing a huge combined army-navy force. Eads' plan would be sent to the Navy Department for study and would eventually be amalgamated, with others, into a grand Union strategy.

About the same time, Maj. Gen. George B. McClellan (1826–1885), commanding the Department of the Ohio at Cincinnati, sent his superior, the aging hero of the Mexican War and the top Union general, Lt Gen. Winfield Scott (1786–1866), his own elaborate plan for marching upon Richmond, via the Midwest. A veteran of the war of 1812, Scott remained clearheaded, though afflicted, like CSN secretary Mallory, with gout. On May 2, Lt. Gen. Scott, having dismissed the McClelland idea, offered President Lincoln his own detailed strategic blueprint to crush the rebellion. At the heart of his victory formula lay the idea of attacking the Rebels from every side and strangling the South along the Mississippi and its tributaries. These inland river highways would be employed to mount and support amphibious assaults to crush the strong points of the divided parts, eventually reopening the mighty stream to United States commerce. Scott based his strategy on a powerful U.S. Navy coastal blockade and called for a decisive "movement down the Mississippi to the ocean, with a cordon of posts at proper points ... the object being to clear out and keep open this great line of communication."

This was the famous Western river-based "Anaconda Plan." It was often ridiculed and would not be fast or simple to apply. But as this approach gradually unfolded, the bulk of the fighting was concentrated in two major theaters, the East (of the Appalachians) and the West. In the end, Anaconda was, with modifications, followed as the basis of the Union's war-fighting master strategy. The concept had the advantage of being easy for everyone, from private to president, to understand and get behind. "From this time on," wrote T. Harry Williams, "the occupation of the line of the great river became an integral part of his [Lincoln's] strategic thinking." The Confederacy, for its part, devised no real countermeasures to the Union approach and such preparations as could be made to resist the scheme would, in the end, prove useless.[4]

On May 6, the Confederate congress passed an act recognizing a state of war with the United States. The Southern navy was in a desperate spot. Still birthing, it faced a struggle right out of the womb against an opponent that was bigger and stronger and could only be expected to grow larger. Initial efforts by the CSN to acquire vessels, especially iron-covered ones, outside of the south largely failed.

By 1861, significant progress had occurred in Europe, especially France and Britain, regarding the building of ironclad warships. Powered by steam/sail and protected by iron belts, these ships, led by the *Gloire* and the *Warrior*, carried large broadside batteries and were outfitted with rams on their bows. Offensively, these battlers, by their mobility, went beyond the floating batteries employed in the Crimea or at Charleston. The contemporary literature concerning these European vessels, professional and popular, was enormous.

Well versed on these foreign developments, the Confederate navy secretary, on May 10 made perhaps his most famous statement concerning the acquisition of armorclad vessels. "I regard the possession of an iron-armored ship as a matter of the first necessity," he wrote to Louisianan Charles N. Conrad (1804–1878), chairman of the Confederate house of representatives' Committee on Naval Affairs. "Inequality of numbers," he continued, "may be compensated by invulnerability; and thus not only does economy but naval success dictate the wisdom and expediency of fighting with iron against wood, without regard to first cost." Although he may have been thinking of armored vessels in April, this was Mallory's first formal and written message recommending that the congress acquire them.

James Buchanan Eads (1820–1887). *A Mississippi River entrepreneur, Eads was among the first to recommend a concrete plan of action to the Federal government for gunboat warfare along the western rivers. His concept, which envisioned the use of armored vessels, was presented to the U.S. Navy and War departments and, within a few months, resulted in the receipt of contracts to build seven ironclads designed by Samuel M. Pook. Ironically, several of these, including the famous USS* Carondelet, *were built in the same St. Louis area shipyard once operated by Primus Emerson, builder of the CSS* Arkansas *(Library of Congress, Brady Collection).*

A copy of Mallory's letter made its way through back channels to the U.S. Navy Department. Several days after reading it, Secretary Welles wrote to a New Jersey ironmaster, Abram S. Hewitt, saying that the Federal government was not planning to build ironclads. It would be a month before continuing intelligence arriving from Norfolk convinced the national naval leadership that the South was serious. When Mr. Welles, far less up

One: Beginnings 19

Foreign Ironclads for the Confederacy in 1861? *By 1861, significant progress had occurred in France and Britain regarding the building of ironclad warships. Powered by steam and sail and protected by iron belts, these ships, led by the* Gloire *and the* Warrior, *carried large broadside batteries and were outfitted with rams on their bows. Offensively, these battlers, by their mobility, went beyond the floating battery employed at Charleston. Initially, Stephen R. Mallory hoped to purchase one of these, but Confederate agents dispatched to Europe in early May 1861 could not, over the next weeks, arrange a purchase. While this failure unfolded, Secretary Mallory turned to the possibilities of building armorclads in the South (Frank Leslie's,* Illustrated Weekly, *March 9, 1861 [*Gloire*]; Navy History and Heritage Command [*Warrior*]).*

on ironclad matters than his Southern opposite number, sought opinions on the need for ironclads from his naval officers — men like scientist Capt. Charles H. Davis (1807–1877) and John Lenthall (1807–1882), the navy's most renowned naval architect — he was greeted with skepticism. Mid-summer passed before Congress enacted funded legislation allowing Welles to set up an Ironclad Board to study possible oceangoing designs and bid on those deemed most acceptable.

Confederate agents dispatched to Europe in early May, over the next weeks achieved no success in purchasing ironclad warships, even though by 1860 there were, as Professor Roberts notes, some 50 afloat in various nations. While this failure unfolded, Secretary Mallory considered the possibilities of building armorclads in the South. Having inquired that month about the possibility of obtaining iron plating from as far away as Kentucky and Tennessee, he was disappointed, if not surprised, when told that the industrial base was not present to roll what was required.[5]

When, following a fortnight of cabinet debate, the U.S. War Department took over all military projects impacting inland waterways, the navy turned its attention, with varying degrees of alacrity, to questions of blue water campaigns, blockades, raiding, commerce protection, and eventually, as noted, oceangoing ironclads. The first problem facing the generals in implementing the Eads-Scott Anaconda strategy, however, was one of materiel. There were no regular Union gunboats on any of the rivers and Western military officers had no idea exactly what was involved in their creation.

Turning back to the navy for technical help, Maj. Gen. McClellan at Cincinnati was pleased to obtain the services of a veteran advisor, Cmdr. John Rodgers II (1812–1882), who was ordered to the Queen City on May 16. In dispatching the officer, Secretary Welles emphasized that the assignment came with very limited authority. Whatever problems arose under this anomalous permit, Rodgers was expected to work them out with McClellan or local military officers, municipal officials, businessmen, and rivermen. In the end, Western river gunboats were army business, not that of Welles, and they were not to cost or unduly concern the Navy Department.

"Little Mac" immediately dispatched his new naval advisor on a trip up the rivers to visit St. Louis, Cairo, Illinois, at the confluence of the Ohio and Mississippi, and Mound City, just up the Ohio River a few miles. At those places Rodgers was to "obtain all possible information as to the construction of gunboats, floating batteries, etc." The seaman informed his superiors of his itinerary. Secretary Welles now ordered Naval Constructor Samuel M. Pook (1804–1878), presently at the Washington Navy Yard, to head out to Cairo and meet Rodgers. There he would undertake such special duty as the commander, in light of findings from his travels, might desire. Such help would be based upon the designer's not inconsiderable shipbuilding expertise.

Acting under McClellan's authority and with Pook's technical assistance, Rodgers purchased three river steamers for the U.S. Army at Cincinnati. Converted into the gunboats *Tyler, Lexington, and Conestoga*, they would provide the Union with its primary naval strength on the Western waters for the first six months of the war.[6]

It is perhaps ironic that, in those days of national confusion, Lt. Gen. Scott also sent his own man to obtain a picture of Midwest river conditions and the data necessary for gunboat construction, ironclad or otherwise. At almost the same time that Cmdr. Rodgers was headed to Illinois, the army's chief engineer, Brig. Gen. Joseph G. Totten (1788–1864), was travelling up and down the Ohio River putting together a dossier. A veteran of the War of 1812 and Scott's chief engineer during the Mexican War, Totten had commanded the

Corps of Engineers for years and would die on active duty. Totten understood that his superior, Scott, was interested in having gunboats constructed on the Western waters. The 73-year-old had learned that they could be perfectly fitted at any of several river towns and that, if the government pressed the matter, they could be ready in three months. Knowing nothing personally about gunboat construction or conversion, the veteran did not feel comfortable in completing his memorandum until he returned to Washington because he wanted yet another opinion.

To bolster his report's value, the brigadier, while en route back to his headquarters, wrote to the navy's head designer. John Lenthall, a veteran bureaucrat whose knowledge of ship and boat concepts was widely respected. Lenthall's opinions concerning Totten's findings and requirements would carry weight, just as his initial reluctance to endorse the "humbug" of ironclads helped to create a pause before the creation of the Federal Ironclad Board. When his colleague's communication came in on June 1, Lenthall went over to his files and brought out a draught for a gunboat upon which he made a few modifications.

Himself a blue-water design specialist who "felt slight optimism that armed vessels adequate to freshwater conditions in the West could be devised," Lenthall, nevertheless, believed that his design might form the basis for a craft "well adapted to operations on the Ohio and Mississippi Rivers." Others interested in such a project could make necessary modifications. Lenthall sent along his gunboat plans within hours of Totten's return to Washington, complete with written explanations. The designer may also have informed Totten, assuming he had not heard, that Samuel M. Pook, his subordinate and also a top naval constructor, had just gone to Cincinnati.

The army's head engineer completed his Scott report on June 3, the same day that the newly transferred Confederate Navy Department began work at Richmond's Mechanics Institute, newly converted to government use. Although they would probably be modified from the Lenthall plans, Totten thought 10 boats could be had for $200,000 and be ready by November.[7]

Also on June 3, Rebel navy boss Mallory met Lt. John Mercer Brooke, then an ADC to Gen. Robert E. Lee. Among the topics briefly discussed was the possibility of "protecting ships with iron." Brooke later recalled that he right then and there proposed a plan to the secretary for such warship armoring. A veteran of North Pacific exploration, as Cmdr. John Rodgers had been, Brooke was encouraged to begin sketching out rough plans, with figures and cost estimates. The sailor also noted, however, that "it was quite late and he was very tired."

A week later, on June 10, Lt. Brooke was formally ordered to assist the navy by designing an ironclad war vessel "and framing the necessary specifications." Within a few days, Brooke had, as he wrote years later, come up with the idea for a mobile blue-water ironclad battery. Halfway between bow and stern Brooke's vessel featured a prominent, raised casemate, which surrounded the main gun deck. Over the deck was "a light grading, making a promenade about 20 feet wide." The casemate was to be shielded by two-foot thick timber, "plated with three or more inches of iron, inclined to the horizontal plane at the least angle that would permit working the guns." An armored pilothouse would sit before the single smokestack (called a "chimney" in the West), which passed through the top deck

Knowing the design of protected floating batteries such as that at Charleston or those employed in the Crimea during the 1850s, Brooke admitted that there "was nothing novel in the use of inclined iron-plating." Later, when it was time to affix this protection, plates two inches thick cut eight inches wide were bolted through the wood backing and clinched.

The base tier was placed on horizontally, the second vertically. The sides of this "shield," as the lieutenant called it, sloped upwards about 45 degrees and were rounded at the ends. The shield would be pierced for cannon mounted in conventional broadside arrangement along with pivot bow and stern chasers. For additional protection, the sides, which he called "eaves," were to be submerged two feet. The fore and aft portions of the hull upon which the casemate was seated would sit only slightly above the waterline, if that. They would provide additional buoyancy, stability, and speed. Steam from two engines provided the power to turn the single screw, which, together with the rudder, was located below the fantail. A four-foot ram was affixed to the prow.

As the month passed, the Confederate naval leader brought two additional players into the armorclad discussion in order to enhance and help facilitate the initial scheme. Both would also have design roles with later projects, such as the *Arkansas*.

John Luke Porter (1813–1892) was an ex–USN constructor, then at work at the Gosport Navy Yard, who was destined to become the CSN chief naval constructor in January 1864. Porter, who had ranked 8th out of nine naval constructors while in Federal service, would go on to design most of the Confederate armorclads, sending plans to building sites and project supervisors along the East Coast and on the inland waters. Known for his high standards, John McIntosh Kell, the executive officer of the famous raider CSS *Alabama*, afterwards said this of Porter: "To his inventive brain some believe we are indebted for the original idea of the ironclad, brought into service some years later. Porter was a very modest man, of few words, and not being on the 'side of the strongest artillery,' or the winning side, of the Civil War, he died shortly after its close almost penniless."

Former USN chief engineer William P. Williamson (b. 1810), a North Carolinian and father of RAdm. Thom Williamson, USN (1833–1918), had spent his entire professional career as a steam engineer at Gosport, working his way up from apprentice. An associate of naval constructor John Luke Porter, he joined the Rebel navy just 11 days before assignment to the *Virginia* project. By April 1862, he was the CSN's chief engineer. When it turned out that the *Virginia* could be a success, more like her were required. The resulting initial group of nonstandardized vessels (*Virginia*, *Mississippi*, *Louisiana*, *Tennessee*, and *Arkansas*) would all be experimental; no two ended up the same size

John Mercer Brooke (1826–1906). *Noted survey expert and explorer, Lt. Brooke was a close associate of naval scientist Cmdr. Matthew Fontaine Maury. Joining the Confederate navy in 1861, he was an early backer of Secretary Mallory's ironclad concept and a participant in the creation of the CSS* Virginia. *Promoted to commander later in 1862, he became chief of the Confederate navy's Bureau of Ordnance and Hydrography in 1863, a post he held until the end of the war. Brooke is best known for his design of the Brooke Rifle, a cannon similar to the U.S. Parrott (Miller, ed.,* Photographic History of the Civil War*)*.

or shape (though the *Tennessee* and *Arkansas* would have been sisters) and all were built with the materials, machinery, and laborers at hand.

After several meetings, during one of which Constructor Porter showed off his own plans for an iron plated warship, Secretary Mallory agreed to Brooke's concepts; credit for originating certain design details was left for Brooke and Porter to debate, which they did once their ship was scuttled and in the postwar years. Dispatching the lieutenant and engineer Williamson to Gosport to find engines, Mallory complimented Porter by asking him to refine and execute the written plans. When no engines could be found, it was decided to raise the hull of the sunken 3,200 ton *Merrimack*, cut her down to the waterline in a dramatic reconstruction, and use her power plant, even though it had an uneven operating record.

Conversion of the ex–U.S. frigate into the ironclad CSS *Virginia* began on June 23. Three weeks later, on July 18, Secretary Mallory reported to the congress on the progress of conversion, costs, and the vessel's anticipated deployment:

> The frigate *Merrimack* has been raised and docked at an expense of $6,000, and the necessary repairs to hull and machinery to place her in her former condition is estimated by experts at $450,000. The vessel would then be in the river, and by the blockade of the enemy's fleets and batteries rendered comparatively useless. It has therefore been determined to shield her completely with 3 inch iron [actually 4-inch armor], placed at such angles as to render her ballproof, to complete her at the earliest moment, to arm her with the heaviest ordnance, and to send her at once against the enemy's fleet. It is believed that thus prepared she will be able to contend successfully against the heaviest of the enemy's ships and to drive them from Hampton Roads and the ports of Virginia. The cost of this work is estimated by the constructor and engineer in charge at $172,523, and as time is of the first consequence in this enterprise I have not hesitated to commence the work and to ask Congress for the necessary appropriation.

Perhaps the most difficult part of building the new vessel was finding sufficient stocks of good wood and iron fixtures; such would prove the case with all of the Confederate ironclads to follow, including the *Arkansas*. Quality ordnance would also be a challenge.

When the South took over the Gosport navy yard, over a thousand cannon were immediately obtained. Many were worthless. However, Cmdr. Archibald B. Fairfax, the local ordnance chief, soon began to convert a large percentage of the captured 32-pdrs. of 57 and 63 cwt. Efficiency of this traditional weapon was greatly enhanced by rifling them and providing reinforcement of their breeches with strong iron bands. Capt. William Parker, commander of the Confederate States Naval Academy, later called the Fairfax achievement "the most important improvement in our ordnance made during the war." Indeed, many of these cannon, capable of firing 64-pd. shells with an 8-pound powder charge, would be available for transfer from Virginia to posts and vessels all around the Confederacy.

Work on the first great Confederate armorclad was completed in February 1862, and the vessel was commissioned; a month later the *Virginia* steamed into history, fighting an epic battle with the U.S. ironclad *Monitor*.[8]

Having now laid the foundational planks, it is necessary that we move ahead and examine how this brilliant concept for a Southern armorclad was transferred to the Western rivers.

CHAPTER TWO

The Upper River Ironclads

Federalized troops from Illinois occupied the key Mississippi River town of Cairo, at the tip of that state, in late April 1861. The U.S. War Department officially established the Department of the Ohio on May 10 covering the states of Ohio, Indiana, and Illinois. Commanding it, Maj. Gen. George B. McClellan established his headquarters at Cincinnati. Efforts at conciliation in the weeks since Fort Sumter had all failed along the Ohio and Mississippi and it followed that many hostile acts toward civilian steamboat traffic suspected of transporting what was already being called "contraband" were increasingly recorded on both sides.

Fortunately for the North, soldiers were rapidly working on fortifications and artillery positions at Cairo, Illinois. The reporter in town for the *Chicago Daily Tribune* noted on May 19 that batteries had been erected on the Ohio and Mississippi levees for a distance of three miles on each river. Fourteen brass 6-pdrs. and a 12-pdr. howitzer were distributed over the area.[1]

In a full uniform of a type seldom seen in the area, Cmdr. John Rodgers II, who was seconded to an advisory post with the U.S. Army in the West, was sent on an inspection trip to the Mississippi by Department of the Ohio commander Maj. Gen. George B. McClelland. Rodgers duly arrived at Cairo, Illinois, from Cincinnati on May 22. An attentive upstate newspaperman told his readers that "the presence in town of Capt. John Rodgers, U.S. Navy, on a mission that is secret as yet, is reported to have something to do with [a] fleet of gunboats."

Rodgers, a close friend of *Virginia* designer Lt. John Mercer Brooke from their days together exploring the Pacific, had come to the tip of Illinois to visit with the noted entrepreneur James Buchanan Eads and, in fact, to examine several steamboats for possible conversion into river gunboats. One of the vessels under review was a catamaran salvage boat — property of the riverman's Missouri Wrecking Company — named *Submarine No. 7*. The deep-water sailor was not impressed. The Union navy officer traveled back to the Queen City as the month expired. There he found and started conversion on three Ohio River packets, the *A.O. Tyler*, *Conestoga*, and *Lexington*. As their alteration into wooden gunboats (called "timberclads") continued, the previously robust intersectional trade on the Mississippi rapidly washed to a halt.

Most of the many small U.S. registered operators able to exit Southern waters now brought their boats permanently north away from the New Orleans trade. The blockade had a devastating impact; as Louis Hunter has noted, it "was plunged into a depression from which there was little relief until the second year of the war." By the end of May, the St. Louis levee, usually bustling and exciting, was quite. A local reporter told his readers

Cairo, IL, Seat of Federal Naval Power on the Mississippi. *Federalized troops from Illinois occupied the key Mississippi River town at the confluence of the Mississippi and Ohio rivers in late April 1861. Four months later, the first Union timberclad gunboats arrived to serve as the nucleus of the Western Flotilla. The Eads ironclads began to arrive in December for final outfitting. It would only be six months before units from this base had captured Memphis and were above Vicksburg (Miller, ed.,* Photographic History of the Civil War*).*

that it was "quiet as a graveyard; steamboatmen feared a total suspension of business; and grass, it was prophesied, would soon be growing on the wharf."

At the beginning of June, the number of unemployed steamboats on the Upper Mississippi and Ohio rivers represented a buyer's market. At least 150 boats lay idle at St. Louis and another 250 on the Ohio River. At Cincinnati alone, 53 vessels of 300 tons or more were in port by June 4, with that number even higher within the week. Another 40–50 more tied up at Pittsburgh, Wheeling, and other towns. Out of work on the Western waters, many of those in the steamboat industry scrambled to find employment. These included not only boat officers, crews, and dispatchers, but also those in the boat building industry. Riverboat hands travelled from one port to another in search of berths, and craftsmen relocated as well. Allegiance North or South did not often interfere with where one accepted a post.

One of those for whom political sympathy probably played some role in his relocation was Missouri steamboat builder Primus Emerson (1815–1877). A native of Maine who had served his apprenticeship at Cincinnati and then relocated to Indiana, Emerson became one of the West's most famous steamboat builders. From 1836 to 1841, when he moved to St. Louis, Emerson operated what became the important Madison, Indiana, boatyard in partnership with James Howard, who gave it his name upon the partner's departure. Over the next decade and a half, Emerson constructed and repaired boats at a number of Midwestern cities. In 1851, he built a sawmill and small boatyard on the riverfront at Fort Pickering, a former army post below Memphis. There, working as a shipwright and master carpenter in conjunction with designer Sam Gaty, he accepted an order from St. Louis steamboat line proprietor Capt. Joseph Brown to construct the revolutionary *Altona*.

Emerson was unable to complete more than the hull of the *Altona* at Fort Pickering and so, early in 1852, he arranged to have her towed north to St. Louis, where she would be finished. Powered by two engines and five boilers, the side-wheeler was 255 feet long, with a beam of 31 feet and a six-foot draft. Her paddle wheels, called "oral wheels" by rivermen, were her most unique feature. Both had diameters of 32 feet, with 13 foot buckets (blades) of differing widths — 22, 18, 14, and 10 inches. Shortly after entering commercial service on the upstream St. Louis to Altona run in 1853, she turned in the fastest time ever on that route, 1 hour, 37 minutes.

With several colleagues, Emerson was pivotal in the mid–1850s establishment of the Carondelet Marine Railway and Drydock Company, sometimes known as "Emerson's Ways," in the village of Carondelet, then quietly nestled between St. Louis and Jefferson Barracks. The constructor incorporated his yard in 1855, growing it over the next four years into a $150,000 per year operation. When the yard was completed in 1859, it featured Emerson's patented marine railway. Centered on a 50 horsepower steam engine, the railway could pull the largest craft out of the water and had a simultaneous capacity of three big or six small boats.

As the nation slid toward conflict, constructor Emerson, a Yankee by birth and marriage, developed, for whatever reason, strong Southern leanings that became increasingly at odds with those held by his partners. Within two months of the outbreak of war, these views, together with a need for employment, would cause his departure from Carondelet. Ironically, his yard would be leased during the summer of 1861 and used to built Federal warships — including a number of the City Series iron plated gunboats.

By June 10, batteries had been erected on the great river north of Memphis and a complete blockade against upriver traffic was in place. No steamers were allowed to pass without a permit from the local "blockade committee." Along the banks, work was begun on protective fortifications and gun emplacements.[2]

Earlier in the spring, the top Union army officer, Lt. Gen. Winfield Scott, had asked his chief engineer, Brig. Gen. Joseph Totten, to conduct a survey of those nautical requirements in the West needed to support the Anaconda Plan. Totten duly travelled the Ohio River gathering information which, together with input on gunboat designs from the navy's top constructor, John Lenthall, he submitted as a report to Scott on June 3. Satisfied, Scott forwarded the Totten report to the War Department on June 10, with a recommendation that 16 of the Lenthall gunboats be contracted — "each with an engine" — and finished in Western boatyards by September 20. Secretary of War Simon Cameron (1779–1889) quickly digested Scott's report and, next day, shared it with Navy Department secretary Gideon Welles. The secretary of war also provided a copy of the Totten-Lenthall report to the industrious quartermaster general, Montgomery C. Meigs. The latter forwarded a copy to Cmdr. Rodgers via a June 13 covering letter to Maj. Gen. McClellan. While busily modifying his timberclads, the naval officer was asked, along with the recently-arrived naval constructor Samuel Pook, to have as many riverboat construction people as possible look over the Lenthall plans and suggest changes.

To add emphasis, Meigs wrote again to McClellan on June 17 saying that it was vital to get up at least two ironclad vessels; as long as they carried cannon (preferably at least three forward), the pair did not "need much speed" and could be "mere scows." It required the remainder of June for Rodgers and Pook to complete their interviews with builders, captains, and engineers in the Cincinnati area. When they finished, Pook was ready to incorporate all he had learned into extensive modifications of Lenthall's drawings. His boats would be "the first class of vessels designed for war on the rivers."

While the soldiers and citizens on the tip of Illinois awaited the Lincoln gunboats, the locally armed tugboat *Swallow* was active in her attempts to interdict steamers smuggling contraband in the waters around Cairo. Her success caused Southern alarm bells to sound. In Ohio, where the Federals were straining every effort to finish the conversion of their larger gunboats, Confederate spies easily penetrated the building yards and sent reports back South to Richmond and Nashville.

On June 20, Maj. Gen. Gideon J. Pillow (1806–1878), commanding the Army of the Tennessee, wrote to the Confederate secretary of war, Leroy P. Walker, complaining that the *Swallow* was "sweeping the river above my batteries, seizing all the steamboats, completely controlling everything out of reach of my batteries." Could not Walker, Pillow asked, have President Jefferson Davis order a Rebel gunboat to Memphis "as promptly as possible" to halt the *Swallow*'s activity.

Built at Cincinnati in 1849, the tugboat *Yankee* was a large and powerful side-wheeler that spent much of her prewar career assisting oceangoing vessels at the mouth of the Mississippi, as a St. Louis paper later put it, "towing up ships from the Balize." The 297-ton workboat was acquired by the Confederate government at New Orleans on May 9. She was strengthened where possible (Union sources later stated that "she was plated strongly with railroad iron of the T pattern"). Her armament consisted of two 32-pdrs. in pivot. Although she was now christened CSS *Jackson*, the gunboat would continue to be known in many circles as the *Yankee*. Lt. Washington Gwathmey, CSA, was named captain on June 6 and in early July, with a crew of 75, the *Jackson* paddled up to Columbus, where she reported to Maj. Gen. Pillow.

While the *Jackson* steamed north, Cmdr. Rodgers, in consultation with Maj. Gen. McClellan and Naval Constructor Pook, elected to send the timberclads downstream unfinished rather than have them marooned until late fall at Cincinnati by the falling Ohio River. With workmen aboard, the escape of the incomplete gunboats began at 4:00 P.M. on the afternoon of June 24.

Brig. Gen. Gideon J. Pillow (1806–1878). *A Mexican war veteran and Democratic politician, Pillow commanded the Tennessee state militia in early 1861. After Fort Sumter, he commanded and organized the Army of Tennessee and began Volunteer State fortifications at Fort Pillow and Fort Randolph, on the first and second Chickasaw bluffs above Memphis. Once Tennessee joined the Confederacy, Pillow served under Maj. Gen. (and Bishop) Leonidas Polk (1806–1864), the North Carolinian in charge of Confederate Department No. 2. Pillow's later failure at Fort Donelson cost him his military career (Library of Congress).*

It required the remainder of June for Rodgers and Pook to complete their interviews with builders, captains, and engineers in the Cincinnati area relative to the drawings received from Quartermaster General Meigs. Needless to say, information on these drawings and discussions also made its way South via sympathetic rivermen. When the survey of helpful and interested parties was finished, Pook was ready to incorporate all he had learned into extensive modifications of Lenthall's drawings. His boats would be "the first class of vessels designed for war on the rivers."

As a result of this early "naval" action, both actual and reported, political and military leaders in the western Confederacy were able to see a "gunboat gap" developing—and not to their good. The industrial strength of the Northern states and the ability of the Federal government to ratchet up its war machine was well appreciated. The same day that the *A.O. Tyler* steamed away from Cincinnati, the Tennessee legislature, meeting in Nashville, asked the Richmond government to appropriate $250,000 for Western waters naval defense. Over the next couple of weeks, newspapers in the major Southern river towns, including Memphis and New Orleans, launched an editorial campaign demanding the enhancement of the Confederate naval presence on the Mississippi.

On June 25, Capt. George Cable, master of the steamboat *John Walsh*, laid up his boat at Fort Pickering and took passage aboard another to St. Louis to find help in repairing his craft. Arriving at the port two days later, he made his way 10 miles south to the boatyard of his old acquaintance, Primus Emerson. "The circumstances suggest," wrote distant relative Mary Emerson Branch in 1985, "that Cable, using the fiction of repairing the *Walsh* for cover, may have approached Emerson about building boats for the Confederacy."[3]

Drawing upon local input and his own knowledge of naval architecture, Samuel Pook modified the Lenthall gunboat plans at Cincinnati early in July, passing them back, via Cmdr. Rodgers and Brig. Gen. McClellan, to the War Department just after Independence Day. When he put down his pen, the designer had come up with a flat-bottomed, wooden-hulled vessel 175 feet in overall length, 51.6 feet in beam, and 6 feet deep in the hold.

Atop its main deck, Pook drew an oblong rectangular box, the sides of which rose up 8 feet to a flat hurricane deck, 35 degrees on the sides and 45 degrees forward. A single paddle wheel, 20 feet in diameter, would be accommodated in an opening 18 feet wide running 60 feet forward. The casemate, made of oak 8 inches thick on the forward face with 2-inch oak planking elsewhere, was to be pierced for heavy ordnance and to enclose the wheel, engines, boilers, and gundeck. To further guard against shot and shell, Pook wanted iron plates of sufficient thickness placed in suitable positions around the casemate. This could be done, he believed, with 75 tons of charcoal iron plating (13 inches wide by 7½ to 11 feet long) and rail armor (railroad track iron). The armored casemate angles, *New York Times* correspondent Franc B. "Galway" Wilkie noted, would allow the protection to "turn or 'glance off' a missile." This was the same concept employed by the armored floating battery at Charleston during the battle of Fort Sumter and by Lt. John Mercer Brooke's design for the CSS *Virginia*. The armor, when finally placed aboard, would prove far from sufficient: "on the upper deck, there was no armor at all; only water-level combat was envisaged."

With only a few, but significant, modifications to these plans, this overall revision of the Lenthall design accurately foreshadowed the future appearance of the Union's "City Series" gunboats. Historians Fowler and Joiner have also opined that, in addition to modifying Lenthall's concept, Pook crafted his design "more along the recognizable lines of the CSS *Virginia* than of a Union vessel," even though full intelligence details regarding the ex–*Merrimack* were not yet available.

Two: The Upper River Ironclads

The U.S. Congress, on July 17, appropriated a million dollars to the War Department for "gunboats on the western rivers." Responsibility for their construction fell upon the quartermaster general, who was also to account for all project expenditures. Unhappily, and without his approval, orders were later cut for the modification of two additional steamers (one Eads' *Submarine No. 7*) into ironclads and the building of a fleet of mortar boats. That extra work, of course, caused expenditure difficulties.

While the Federals made ready to bid on Western river gunboats, Carondelet boat builder Primus Emerson made his way to Memphis. As his work at Madison and Carondelet was well known up and down the rivers, the constructor was eagerly welcomed into a fraternity of angry and frustrated Southern steamboatmen. Virulently Confederate, some of these men, like Capt. Tom Brierly of the *Ferdinand Kennet*, pledged all profits to the cause while others went further and actually impounded vessels, preventing their return to northern ports.

It is possible that Emerson was cheered on by the fiery oratory of the dashing local Captain Marshall ("Marsh") Miller. It was about this time that Miller took command of the *Grampus No. 2*, a 252-ton sternwheeler originally constructed at McKeesport, Pennsylvania, in 1856. Owned by Thomas Chester of Pittsburgh, the craft, which Miller had painted black, had recently been seized and fitted with a pair of brass 12-pounder cannon. With George Miller as pilot, the *Grampus* became a Confederate navy auxiliary and scout boat, often engaging in cat-and-mouse games with the Federal timberclad gunboats and other Western Flotilla units until scuttled off Island No. 10 in April 1862. More important, builder Emerson now made contact with Capt. John T. Shirley (1823–1873), a well-regarded 20-year veteran of Memphis riverfront business who was well known locally as a maritime entrepreneur, president of John T. Shirley & Co., a philanthropist, and owner of a lovely large home in the city.

Like others who made their fortune on the rivers, Shirley had worked his way up to command of commercial steamboats. By the early 1850s, he was often seen in command of a boat on the Memphis-Napoleon-White River route. In 1856, he was in command of the *James Laughlin*, a 188-ton side-wheeler built at Gallipolis, Ohio, three years earlier. On the evening of September 13, the craft sank, a total loss, at Memphis. The loss of six lives in the disaster may have caused Shirley to go ashore.

The 38-year-old Shirley was in the news back in May 1861 for his important role in securing foodstuffs for the poor in a short-lived program authorized by the city's board of aldermen and administered by former city marshal and police chief William Underwood in his equally brief position as city almoner. Shirley also attempted, without much success, to establish a special "river brigade" for the defense of the Mississippi.

The encounter between Emerson and Shirley, whether by chance based on Shirley's possible earlier use of the builder's Carondelet yard or by arranged introduction, would prove to be fortuitous for Rebel arms. Shirley was well placed to generate business and had a number of influential acquaintances, including 11th District Confederate Congressman David M. Currin (1817–1864) from Memphis, a member of the House Naval Affairs Committee. Other contacts included former U.S. congressmen John DeWitt Clinton Atkins (1825–1908) of Henry County and the 9th District and another former U.S. congressman, John Vines Wright (1828–1908), of McNairy County and the 10th District. Because Memphis was just across the river from Arkansas, Shirley was also friendly with the Razorback State's former U.S. senator Robert Ward Johnson (1814–1879), who was then serving as a delegate to the Confederate congress and would be a Confederate senator within the year.

Within the middle fortnight of the month, Union quartermaster general Montgomery C. Meigs accepted his enhanced gunboat assignment and started to organize that effort with his usual efficiency. The final design details for the Pook craft were completed and entered into the bid stage that would soon have a contractor chosen to actually build the vessels. Even as the technical aspects of the gunboat planning reached their climax, preliminary advertisements were placed in leading Western newspapers announcing the acceptance of bids to build the craft. The first notice appeared in the *St. Louis Daily Missouri Democrat* on July 29:

> Gunboats for the Western Rivers
> Quartermaster General's Office
> Washington, July 18, 1861
>
> Proposals are invited for Constructing Gunboats Upon the Western Rivers. Specifications will be immediately prepared and may be examined at the Quartermaster's office at Cincinnati, Pittsburgh, and this office. Proposals from boat builders alone will be considered. Plans submitted by builders will be taken into consideration.
>
> M.C. Meigs
> QMG U.S.

Once the Pook plans, together with those for engines, were submitted and approved, Meigs signed off on the entire project, specification revisions were made available and the *Daily Missouri Democrat*, on August 1, was paid (as were others newspapers) to adjust its advertisement:

> Western Gunboats
> Proposals for Building Western Gunboats will be received by General Meigs, QM General, Washington City, D.C., until August Fifth when the bids will be opened by him and contracts awarded. Drawings for inspection and specifications for distribution at the office of The Collector of Customs, St. Louis. The bids to be endorsed, "Proposals for Western Gunboats."[4]

As knowledge of what the Federal generals were planning grew, so too did Southern concerns. The summer developments at Cairo and Cincinnati further heightened concern in Rebel circles about the minimal level naval defense of the inland rivers. Pounding out for several months, the drumbeat of editorials demanding waterborne protection intensified. A Southern response to Scott and Eads was deemed essential.

Confederate sympathizers on the south bank of the Ohio River actually saw the Yankee timberclads en route to Cairo in July and spread the word far and wide that there really were big, black inland river gunboats that were not just talk. The concept of the Anaconda Plan, featuring a push by the Federals toward New Orleans via the great streams of the Mississippi Valley, suddenly took on added life.

Meanwhile, Brig. Gen. Gideon J. Pillow's Army of Tennessee was organizing and fortifications were begun by the Volunteer State at Fort Pillow and Fort Randolph, on the first and second Chickasaw bluffs above Memphis. After Tennessee joined the Confederacy, Pillow's command was entrusted to Maj. Gen. (and Bishop) Leonidas Polk (1806–1864), the North Carolinian in charge of Confederate Department No. 2. Hoping to invade the chaotic region of southern Missouri on behalf of the insurrection, Polk ordered his Tennessee general to capture the river town of New Madrid.

On July 26, a grand expedition under Brig. Gen. Pillow departed Memphis aboard six of the South's remaining Mississippi River packets, led by the flagboat *Grampus*, under Capt. Marsh Miller. A stop was made 42 miles upriver at Randolph to add numbers to the regiments already embarked. There was great rejoicing among its local citizens when, on July 28, gray-clad soldiers disembarked from the steamboats onto Missouri soil. It was everywhere expected that these men would take Bird's Point, Cairo or both and if they did not, it would only be because they were "not afforded an opportunity."

Meanwhile, as he sought to strengthen Southern defenses along the Mississippi, Lt. Gen. Polk sent a request to the Confederate Navy Department seeking the services of an experienced naval officer. Such a petition was not unusual, Lt. John Mercer Brooke having earlier served as an ADC to Gen. Robert E. Lee. With more officers available than he could immediately employ, Secretary Mallory was delighted to answer Polk by detailing a highly regarded former Federal sailor. After 27 years in the U.S. Navy, Isaac Newton Brown (1817–1889) of Mississippi, recently arrived at Richmond, had been commissioned a lieutenant in the Rebel navy on June 6. USN Commander Henry Walke, a future opponent, later testified that Brown, whom he had known before the conflict, was "one of the best of the Confederate officers."

Brown's first service for Polk, while still in the Confederate capital city, was to obtain cannon and ammunition for the new Rebel bastions along the Mississippi, especially Fort Pillow. Given the demand for heavy ordnance and heavy projectiles all over the South, this was not an easy task, despite the large quantity of guns available at Gosport. Brown attempted to arrange deliveries and by mid–July, had travelled to Memphis, Tennessee. On July 20, the lieutenant received a request from navy secretary Mallory to dispatch a competent mechanic who could "learn as early as practical the character of the vessels which it is said the enemy is preparing at Cincinnati." The official wanted to know whether the Union boats were steamers or propellers, their size and how they might be armed, and particularly "and whether, and to what extent, they were protected by iron." If they were armored, he wanted to know how thick the armor was and how it was attached. If other boats were being built anywhere else along the upper rivers, it would be important to know and Mallory was prepared to pay for the information.

Brown apparently hired at least one spy who kept his ear to the ground at Cincinnati, and later St. Louis, for information that might help his employer. Perhaps the most important immediately was a brief warning to Secretary Mallory and Gen. Polk that there were, indeed, "extraordinary [Federal] preparations going on the Ohio River in the way of gunboats."

Another naval officer was also sent west about this time to assist Polk, a lieutenant of less seniority than Brown, North Carolinian Jonathan Hanby Carter (1821–1884). While Brown concentrated on procuring ordnance and on the defenses of such river points as Columbus and Fort Pillow, Carter assisted the general by coordinating his activities with those of Commodore George Hollins. He would develop what Polk told the navy secretary was a "knowledge of our wants and how to meet them."

On the Ohio, anyone, whether an actual steamboat builder or not, interested in building a Pook-drawn gunboat for the Union — or purporting to be interested — was free to stop into the customs office at any of the major Northern river ports from Cincinnati to St. Louis and, as Meigs' advertisements promised, see the plans. Although it may be something of a stretch, it is not impossible to believe that knowledgeable and worried Southern river patriots with access may have gained insight from the plans and passed it along to others. Despite the blockade, it was still rather easy to get information back and forth between St. Louis and Memphis. We know for certain that, once construction actually started, intelligence reports were regularly sent.

Memphis steamboat entrepreneur Capt. John T. Shirley was, by all available accounts, a keen student of riverboat design. Now that he was in close association with Primus Emerson, a highly regarded steamboat architect, though perhaps not of the same caliber as Samuel Pook or John Porter, the businessman could offer another way to help the South defend her streams besides his failed effort to set up a "river brigade." Shirley presented a homegrown idea for an iron-protected warcraft.

We do not know exactly what the inspiration was for Shirley's proposal or how exactly it was initially outlined. It is possible that it was based on reports arriving at Memphis from riverboatmen who had participated in the Rodgers-Pook discussions or seen the bid specifications and particulars for Northern gunboat construction shown in Ohio River and other custom houses. Perhaps it was based upon reports on foreign ironclads and warship developments in larger newspapers, particularly those from New Orleans, or on conversations held with Emerson and other Memphis boat builders or engine manufacturers. Maybe it was little more than a riverboat fitted up like one of the Yankee timberclads, though protected by iron rather than wood. It may even have come from some flash, as when Lt. Brooke, upon his first meeting with Secretary Mallory, was able to immediately offer a plan for the iron armoring of a naval vessel. Most likely, however, it was some combination of all of these.

Whatever the source, the idea — when sketched out on paper and shown to interested parties such as Congressman Currin and Lt. Gen. Polk — was deemed worthy of pursuit. Polk, after all, had recently been warned by Lt. Brown of Ohio River Union naval activity. Though he would quibble over providing the manpower necessary to build them, Polk was, and remained, a loyal supporter and advocate of the need for armored gunboats. He would later write to a superior: "The importance of gunboats as an element of power in our military operations was frequently brought to the attention of the Government."

On July 30, the *New Orleans Daily Delta* reported that the Shirley — possibly with Emerson's help — had designed a new type of river vessel plated by iron. Design details were quite vague. According to the newspaper, Shirley's boat "obtained notice from authoritative sources. The iron-plated vessels hitherto built were for sea service. This is designed for operation on the Western Rivers." Also on July 30, as potential builders were being allowed to inspect plans for the City Series gunboats in Midwestern offices and designer Shirley was being lauded by the Crescent City's newspaper, the Confederate navy secretary, Stephen Mallory, who was also troubled at the prospect of Federal brown-water operations, met with a group of naval officers in his Richmond office. It was hoped that they could devise "plans to meet the enemy's gun boats on the Mississippi."

Mallory, Brooke, and several others, including Capt. George Hollins (1799–1878) concluded they should "use tugs and armed vessels ... as well as 'plated batteries'" [i.e., floating batteries on the model of the Charleston craft]. The 62-year-old Hollins, only 20 days into his new berth as commander of the James River defenses, would be sent to New Orleans next day to assume command of naval efforts on the Mississippi. If they knew, which is quite unlikely, no one at Mallory's meeting mentioned anything about Shirley's idea for iron-plated vessels, and a copy of that day's *Daily Delta* would not have been available.

Still, as Raimondo Luraghi indicates in his Confederate navy history, part of the discussion at Mallory's July 30 conference focused upon building "up also in the West a team of ironclads capable of operating not only along the rivers but on the high seas as well." The secretary "did not intend to stay on the defensive" but "hoped to overpower the North by turning the tables against it."[5]

Far away in Washington, D.C., as August began, Quartermaster General Meigs and his staff received the last of seven ironclad construction bids generated as a result of the ads placed in Midwestern newspapers. To the great relief of backers from St. Louis, the low bid was submitted by engineer James B. Eads. He proposed to build between four and 16 boats at a cost of $89,600 a copy and deliver them to Cairo before October 10. If he missed that deadline, he would daily forfeit $100 per boat. Eads signed the official contract two days later and returned west to start his large project. Ironically, one of his first actions upon reaching home was to lease the Carondelet boatyard founded by Primus Emerson.[6]

At the start of the year's eighth month, boat builder Primus Emerson remained in Memphis. He had originally travelled there in June with Capt. George Cable to resolve issues surrounding repairs to the latter's steamer *John Walsh*. While there, the noted constructor reviewed his old haunts at Fort Pickering. After two months, the *Walsh* was no closer to alteration than she had been earlier, leading one of Emerson's later relatives, Mary, to speculate: "Such a prolonged job suggests that Emerson's real concern at Fort Pickering was the practical aspect of constructing an ironclad there, not repairing a steamboat."

As James B. Eads put together his combinations for construction of the City Series gunboats at Carondelet and also a bit later at Mound City, Illinois, riverman John Shirley, like Eads, decided to make the long railroad trip east to sell his concept to the Confederate government. Having gone to the local military headquarters and obtained a letter of endorsement from Lt. Gen. Polk, Shirley boarded a train for Richmond in mid–August. The capital of the South was warm and busy, and still glowed in the aftermath of the victory at First Bull Run. Westerner Shirley, immediately after detraining, repaired to the office of Congressman Currin. Following amenities, the Memphis politician introduced his travel-fatigued guest around to important senators and representatives, presumably including House Naval Affairs Committee chairman Conrad. Many were doubtless excited to hear of his plans as Currin confided that he had already endorsed the plan to the CSN and would be taking Shirley around to meet its chief within a day or so.

Arrangements having been made, Shirley was escorted to the one-time Mechanic Institute, which was now the building of the War and Navy departments, at the corner of Franklin and Ninth streets, on August 17 or 18. Climbing the stairs to the second floor, the Tennessee entrepreneur entered the office of Secretary Mallory, along with Congressmen Currin, Atkins, Wright, and Johnson. When the Floridian came out to shake hands with the entrepreneur and his political allies, the latter all quickly vouched for Shirley "as a fit and suitable person to build vessels at Memphis." The Confederate naval chief was also given Polk's letter, which endorsed Shirley and recommended his plan.

Some time was given over to Shirley, who proposed to construct a pair of ironclad gunboats based on the ideas about his new boats mentioned several weeks earlier by the *New Orleans Daily Delta*. The steamboatman doubtless noted his association with constructor Primus Emerson (which probably did not mean too much to Mallory) and pointed out the role of Memphis as a shipping center. It was probably also pointed out that while not a large number of steamers were built at the town there were a number of skilled laborers engaged in repair work and engine building. Earlier, Mallory may have remembered, a U.S. Navy yard briefly operated there. Strong defenses were being built at Fort Pillow and Randolph, 8–10 miles above the town, and should be capable of defending the construction enterprise from any Federal attack downstream from Cairo.

This meeting for the reader must be reminiscent of that held on April 29 between James B. Eads and the cabinet of President Lincoln, though on a lesser scale. Coming within weeks of his July 30 hurry-up meeting with Brooke, Hollins, and others concerning the defense of the Mississippi, the meeting must have been seen by Mallory as bringing, in the words of historian Luraghi, "manna from heaven." With his best people busy with the *Merrimack* up at Norfolk and no navy yards available to him in the upper half of the Mississippi Valley, Secretary Mallory must have been ecstatic to have a capable representative of private enterprise drop by to offer a viable solution to one of his major worries. Such a craft as Shirley proposed would not only protect the Mississippi, but might also be employed as a coastal or sea boat, perhaps actually making it out into the Gulf of Mexico and maybe as far as Mobile. As the visit drew to a close, it was determined that Congressman Currin would introduce a congressional bill to provide construction funding.

Shirley hung around Richmond as the legislation necessary to fund his vessels unfolded. During this time, he met with naval constructor John Luke Porter or one of his associates

Left: **Lt. (later Cmdr.) Isaac Newton Brown, CSN** (1817–1889). *After 27 years in the U.S. Navy, Isaac Newton Brown was commissioned a lieutenant in the Confederate navy on June 6, 1861. Commander Henry Walke, USN, a future opponent, later testified that Brown, whom he had known before the conflict, was "one of the best of the Confederate officers." The Mississippian spent the first year of the war assisting the Confederate army in the west and supervising the construction of several still-born gunboats, on the Tennessee River and at New Orleans. Following his energetic command of the* Arkansas, *he helped to defend the Yazoo River area from Federal invasion before returning east to command the ironclad CSS* Charleston *at her namesake South Carolina city. After the war, he became a farmer, in Mississippi and then in Texas (Navy History and Heritage Command).* Right: **Commodore George N. Hollins, CSN** (1799–1878). *Before the Civil War, the lieutenant fought Barbary pirates for the U.S. Navy. On June 29, 1861, Marylander Hollins, after "Going South," disguised himself as a woman and took control of the Chesapeake Bay steamer* St. Nicholas, *achieving the first naval victory for the Confederacy. Promoted for his achievement and given command of James River defenses, he met with Secretary Mallory, Lt. John Mercer Brooke, and several others on July 30, 1861, at which time a decision was taken to "use tugs and armed vessels ... as well as 'plated batteries' [i.e., floating batteries on the model of the Charleston craft] to defend the river towns of the west." The 62-year-old Hollins was sent to New Orleans the next day to assume command of naval efforts on the Mississippi, a posting he would hold until after the surrender of Island No. 10 the following year (Navy History and Heritage Command).*

Left: **Charles M. Conrad** (1804–1878). *Grandnephew by marriage of George Washington, Charles Conrad served as a U.S. representative (1849–1850) and senator (1842–1843), as well as secretary of war (1850–1853). Under the Confederacy, he served as a delegate to the Provisional Confederate Congress and as Louisiana representative to the Confederate congress (1862–1864). As chairman of the House Naval Affairs Committee, he was instrumental in obtaining funds for Secretary Mallory's ironclads, including the CSS* Arkansas *(U.S. Army Military History Institute).* Right: **John Luke Porter** (1813–1892). *An ex–USN constructor, Porter was brought into the CSS Virginia project at the Gosport Navy Yard. Destined to become the CSN chief naval constructor in January 1864, he drew most of the plans for the Confederate armorclads, sending sets to building sites and project supervisors along the East Coast and on the inland waters. He is credited with handing Memphis entrepreneur John Shirley the blueprints for the vessel that became the CSS* Arkansas *(Navy History and Heritage Command).*

to develop some basic gunboat blueprints similar in detail to those for the *Virginia*. Porter or his colleague listened closely as Shirley described local Memphis area support and resources, including foundries and labor. Taking Shirley's information, the Confederate draftsmen provided illustrations for a class of armored gunboats that could be built by a workforce that had no warship-building experience. The illustrations featured the new *Virginia*-like concept of a scratch-built casemate ram driven with screw propulsion. The blueprints (which may have been no more than basic specifications and sketches) were drawn up even as lawyers wrote up a construction contract. This was a lock-step process and all involved expected the matter to be expedited as a "done deal."

Although much would be left to the discretion of the builder, Porter's guidelines, according to George Wright, contained two major elements, both of which took into account that Shirley's building crews would have no experience in building warships. First, the vessel would be a pure steamship that did not require skilled sailors. Rather than masts, rigging, or sails, it would employ screw propulsion, with its engines and boilers located below the waterline to reduce their vulnerability in combat. The shape of the hulls, with low freeboard, meant that their seaworthiness (for example, their roll characteristics in swells) beyond rivers was open to speculation. Second, and most important, the new design for the wooden vessels would sheathe the decks above the waterline, the upper hull, and a rectangular casemate (containing four guns) in iron. Armor would shield the ordnance, crew, and machinery. The engines were expected to provide at least the power of contemporary riverboats and hence permit the addition of a stem-mounted iron ram. On the other hand, coal bunker configurations were uncertain, as was the amount of fuel that could be carried.

While Shirley waited for the maritime architects and lawyers, perhaps also enjoying such readily available freshwater seafood as crabs, not found in the Mississippi, Congressmen Conrad and Currin and their colleagues wrote naval legislation for the Confederate congress, then meeting in closed session. A large appropriation of $800,000 for "floating defenses of New Orleans," at the southern end of the great river, was currently under consideration.

Congressman Currin rose on August 19 to voice his support and to ask that additional funds be tacked on "for the construction, equipment, and armament of two ironclad gunboats for the defense of the Mississippi River and the city of Memphis." The defense request received its first and second readings over the next two days. It was then posted to the Naval Affairs Committee. In need of final figures, Congressman Conrad sent a runner over to the Navy Department to pick up Mallory's cost estimates for Shirley's two craft.

Secretary Mallory, who already had an estimate of $160,000 in hand for the Memphis boats, quickly turned it over. On August 23, Congressman Conrad introduced to the house the request for supplemental funding for additional naval expenses. Following his introduction, Representative Currin voiced his support — and requested that an amendment tacking on $160,000 more for the Memphis ironclads be added. There being no objection, both the original bill and its amendment were rapidly passed and forwarded to President Davis. Without comment, the Confederate chief executive signed the naval legislation on August 24. The same day, John Shirley met again with Secretary Mallory to sign a contract, dated from that morning, which specified that, in exchange for a payment of $76,920 per copy, the contractor would deliver two ironclads to the CSN by December 24, Christmas Eve.

The Confederate government pledged to pay the Tennessean in one-fifth installments. The first would come when the frames were completed, the second when decks and planking were finished, the third as the engines and boilers were being installed, the fourth after the engines and boilers were actually in, and the last upon delivery. Shirley's contract was similar to others signed by contractors on both sides of the Mason-Dixon Line during, before, and after the Civil War. As in the 1850s, many shipbuilders, as John Harrison Morrison wrote about the New York yards, accepted work subject to time penalties. In this case, as in most, the procurement of materials and labor was the contractor's responsibility and little help could be expected from the purchaser.

Having been party to its formulation, the Memphis businessman was not surprised that his paperwork contained these stiff penalties for delay. Still, as he later testified, he knew that he would have great difficulty in supplying funds from his own resources to cover expenditures made prior to his tranches. At best, he might be able to come up with about $34,000. Showing no outward worry, Shirley must have been relieved when Secretary Mallory, who understood the scarcity of iron plate and other items in the West, advanced funds. Neither man knew that their arrangement was the same kind of installment and penalty contract (sans any advance) that had been signed for the City Series boats by James B. Eads at Carondelet.

While Shirley was en route back to Memphis, the Confederate naval chief, on August 26, met with old acquaintances Asa and Nelson Tift, who, like John Porter and John Shirley, presented their ideas for ironclads to be used in the defense of New Orleans. Secretary Mallory liked their concept and agreed to fund their proposal, as well as another delivered shortly thereafter by Kentucky boat builder E.C. Murray.

As the summer waned, the Confederate Navy had authorized the building of four big ironclads for defense of the Mississippi. These were exclusive of various wooden craft gotten up under the direction of Capt. Hollins. It was now believed that with a comparatively small number of vessels Mallory's officers could "keep our waters free from the enemy and ultimately to contest with them for the possession of his own." Key to this vision was the *Virginia*, the "ironclad frigates at New Orleans," and "the two plated ships at Memphis."[7]

CHAPTER THREE

A Frustrating Start, August–December 1861

Having obtained a contract from the Confederate Navy Department for the construction of two ironclad gunboats, Memphis entrepreneur John T. Shirley returned home during the first week of September 1861. Met at the railroad station by builder Primus Emerson and a number of other colleagues and commercial well-wishers, the steamboat man perhaps engaged in a bit of joyous camaraderie with his friends, perhaps at one of the city's many saloons, before settling down to the project next day. There was much to accomplish and very little time.

Shirley's first significant meeting was undoubtedly with Emerson, the master builder. At that time, the two men, virtual partners, most likely divided up the task facing them. Shirley as prime contractor would seek out private funding, scour the area for materials, enter into contracts with labor and providers, and generally oversee the work. Emerson as chief constructor would be in charge of the day-to-day operation of actually building the two vessels. Fortunately, Navy Secretary Mallory had advanced some earnest money to serve as seed and investment protection while Shirley sought resources in the West. The premier operational decision faced by the contractor and the builder was where exactly to undertake construction. Neither actually owned a boatyard; and as Memphis, a town with 22,600 black and white residents, was more of a steamboat repair center than an actual construction port, there were no suitable facilities available that were not already in use.

There was some unused riverfront property under the bluff on the plateau at Fort Pickering, an abandoned army post located near a pair of Indian mounds downstream just below the city. The ground was level there and included a pair of rundown sawmills. Emerson had attempted to set up his own construction center there in the early 1850s before leaving for Missouri. A quick inspection was sufficient and the decision was taken to center the ironclad enterprise at that location. Alan Doyle, camp historian of N.B. Forrest Camp 215, Sons of Confederate Veterans in Memphis, tells us that in 1858 his city's engineer, E.W. Rucker, drew a still-extant map showing Fort Pickering "at the southern boundary of Memphis City limits." "It's right next to the current Memphis/Arkansas bridge," Doyle observes, "and now is in the city limits of Memphis."

Shirley immediately moved to rebuild the sawmills and extend them so that they could saw long timber. The machinery also needed to be fixed and enhanced. Fortunately, a third sawmill was also running commercially at Fort Pickering. At least one of the sawmills is shown on the 1864–1865 Fort Pickering map reproduced in the OR *Atlas*.[1]

Shirley and Emerson were just beginning work on the two as-yet-unnamed armorclads

Fort Pickering, TN, 1860s. *Taken from a larger map of the Memphis area ordered drawn by Maj. Gen. William T. Sherman, this segment clearly shows the area south of town where John T. Shirley and Primus Emerson worked to build the armorclads* Arkansas *and* Tennessee. *After the former was withdrawn and the latter burned in early June, the Federal army took over the area and turned it into a giant fortified supply depot (Library of Congress).*

when a military storm further up the Mississippi was unleashed. It was largely understood by both sides at this time that major Confederate efforts made in July and August to advance deep into southeastern Missouri and maybe capture St. Louis or Cairo were over. The Western military leadership North and South reached, almost simultaneously, the belief that this opening phase was finished and that the time had come for some sort of new action along the "Father of Waters."

The opening state of affairs began to change almost as soon as Brig. Gen. Ulysses S. Grant, on orders from his superiors, assumed command at Cairo on August 28. Union military operations in the new District of Southeast Missouri would be backed up by the three timberclad gunboats of Cmdr. John Rodgers' new Western Flotilla, which had just arrived from Cincinnati. As August ended, Federal soldiers began a series of intensive armed reconnaissance marches and small-scale amphibious landings as far down the river opposite Columbus, Kentucky.[2]

At Memphis, the Confederate theater commander, Maj. Gen. Leonidas Polk, was worried. A "student" of the "neutrality" proclaimed earlier by the border state of Kentucky, the Southern general had watched the political situation in that state develop ever since the fall of Fort Sumter. The Cumberland and Tennessee rivers were a natural invasion route into the Volunteer State's heartland; and daily Kentucky's concessions to the North seemed to increase. If the North ever gained control of the heights at Columbus, it would be impossible to dislodge them. Still, the "fighting bishop" tried to hold off. Both sides in the conflict realized that the first to violate Kentucky sovereignty by such an overt act as taking a river-

Memphis in 1862. *At the time the* Arkansas *was under construction at Memphis, the Tennessee city on the Mississippi River was a thriving metropolis and cotton port. Although not a center of steamboat construction, local industry did engage in boat repairs and had the capability of constructing engines and other necessary items. Acquiring sufficient pine wood, sufficient quantities of railroad iron for armor, and, especially, sufficient construction manpower for the Shirley-Emerson project proved more difficult than anticipated* (Harper's Weekly, July 5, 1862).

front community would drive the state into the arms of the other. Sensing that his New Madrid position was untenable, Polk wanted to leave that location and fall back to Union City, Tennessee.

His subordinate, Brig. Gen. Gideon J. Pillow, believed just the opposite and had said so ever since May. The Iron Banks at Columbus, he argued, just had to be fortified, their possession was a point of "paramount military necessity." If the Confederacy held Columbus, it could "close the door effectively against invasion of Tennessee or descent of the Mississippi." So far, Polk had resisted Pillow's argument that taking the town, whatever the consequences, was militarily the correct move and had ignored the pleas of local citizens who did everything in their power, from hanging out Rebel flags to sending him petitions, to change his mind. And then Maj. Gen. Polk started to receive reports that the Federals were planning to move on the town. On September 1, the "fighting bishop" broke down and wrote to Kentucky governor Beriah Magoffin: "I think it of the greatest consequence to the Southern cause in Kentucky or elsewhere that I should be ahead of the enemy in occupying Columbus and Paducah."

Next day, Polk, without informing the Confederate War Department, gave orders for an amphibious advance. He would seize the strategic heights of Columbus before the Yankees. Far from committing an error, the uniformed clergyman, like others, believed the little town with its four brick buildings was "a near perfect place to pot batteries." If it were "properly fortified," no Yankee gunboat or steamer would ever pass.

Confederate forces on eight steamers from New Madrid, escorted by the CSS *Jackson* and the local gunboat *Grampus*, made the short run to Hickman on the evening of September 3. Upon arrival, they landed and occupied the town. The following morning, the same

Three: A Frustrating Start, August–December, 1861

day Brig. Gen. Grant opened his command post at Cairo, 1,500 gray-clad soldiers marched up the east bank of the Mississippi and captured Columbus. The local populace was overjoyed and there was no resistance at either place.

The occupation of the two river towns brought almost as much discord in the South as in the North. The Confederate secretary of war, Leroy P. Walker, ordered Polk to withdraw, and Governor Isham G. Harris of Tennessee asked the same. President Jefferson Davis supported the action: "The necessity justified the action." Davis, like Polk, believed, accurately as it turned out, that the Union was planning to strike first. Within a short time, however, the clergyman would be superseded in departmental command by Gen. Albert Sidney Johnston.

By violating Kentucky's neutrality, the Confederates were seen as aggressors and the Blue Grass State came into the fight on the side of the Union. While Southern generals and politicians debated the action, the press of the North was delighted; "Kentucky Invaded by the Rebels," cheered the *Philadelphia Inquirer* on September 5.

Western headquarters telegraphed the news to President Lincoln that it looked like the Confederates were moving in force into West Kentucky, capturing Hickman, Columbus, Paducah (at the mouth of the Tennessee River) and the river shore opposite Cairo. Ironically on the Confederate side, Maj. Gen. Polk, according to his son William, was determined to make his defense along a line from Columbus down to Fort Pillow, via Island No. 10, the 10th atoll in the Mississippi below its confluence with the Ohio River (which is now part of the Missouri shore). Polk originally considered Paducah's capture, but was unable to proceed further after taking Columbus, which he always regarded as "more important than Paducah." Grant, in transports covered by the timberclads, took the town and the strategic land at the mouth of the Tennessee River on September 6.

Over the next few months, Union and Confederate forces along the Mississippi and Ohio rivers engaged in a series of feints, skirmishes, and other maneuvers. The Union's activities were designed to find a way to capture or outflank Columbus, as it grew into the "Gibraltar of the West." The South had a more simple goal, to hold the Federals back, pouring every resource into their Kentucky fortress while seeking ways to block any Northern advances down the Tennessee and Cumberland rivers.

Collectively, these events would, in both the short term and the long, have an impact upon the construction of the two vessels at Memphis. The need perceived by Maj. Gen. Polk to improve, maintain, and enhance the strength of his command would have direct consequences upon contractor Shirley's efforts to acquire the materials and manpower needed to proceed in a timely manner.[3]

Once Shirley and Emerson established their small armorclad-building yard at Fort Pickering, Emerson set to work preparing the site and repairing and extending the two run-down sawmills already present. This work started, according to Shirley, approximately 10 days after he signed the armorclad contract.

Capt. Shirley, meanwhile, not only worked to consolidate private interim financing, but, employing the money advanced by Secretary Mallory, placed orders for the lumber and other materials necessary to start. It was initially hoped that the project would go smoothly.

We do not know with any certainty the amount of wood Shirley required to create his armorclads. It must have been significant, as both would have wooden hulls and casemates built primarily of pine and oak. In 1880, Henry Hall found, while working on a detailed census, that a single Pennsylvania boat-building yard consumed upwards of 100,000 feet of oak, pine, and poplar (some 20-year-old or more trees) in the construction of every 180 foot steamer. Although the *Arkansas* and *Tennessee* would not have the "wedding cake" superstructure of a typical riverboat, they would have wooden casemates.

In 1861, as in the century and a half since, wood and wood products were a major agricultural product of Tennessee. Due to a significantly increased and heavy demand by commerce, housing, and the Confederate armed forces, however, the necessary amount of easily worked pine timber for the planking was not readily available from local sources. As a result, the pine needed for the deck and hull of the two armorclads had to be ordered from points as much as 104 miles away. As soon as it could be loaded, it would be shipped in by railroad and ox team. Unhappily, we do not know exactly what direction from Memphis it came; pine forests were readily available in Mississippi, Arkansas, and further east in Tennessee. Emerson's relative ease in acquisition suggests that it was brought in from the Razorback State by train and left for pickup at the Memphis and Charleston Railroad depot on the other side of the river. On the other hand, there is a clue that it may have come from Kentucky. Back in 1851 when he first tried to establish a boatyard at Fort Pickering, Primus Emerson told a reporter from the *Memphis Daily Appeal* that it was, frankly, more economical to have sawed timber delivered from Paducah than it was to obtain it from local mills.

Oak for the hull framing, bracing, finish work and other woodwork, and casemate armor-backing, on the other hand, was readily available around Memphis. Its quality was questionable. A few years before Emerson came to Memphis the first time, a survey found that "the oak timber of the West was declared to be less durable and subject to more rapid decay than that used in shipbuilding on the seaboard." Nevertheless, Shirley made arrangements for its provision with five different sawmills. In addition to the one commercially adjacent to the building site, four sawmills were located within a dozen miles. Indeed, one was five miles away and two others three miles off.

Among the latter firms patronized was the Memphis mill of H.D. Connell, at the foot of Adams Avenue, at the river, and the steam sawmill of K.J. and B.L. Winn, on the corner of Mill and Poplar Avenue. Another steam sawmill utilized was that of W.L. and J.B. Griffing at Chickasaw, above the old Navy Yard.

While Capt. Shirley was in Richmond during August, he received some armorclad design specifications from the Confederate Navy Department. The vessel depicted looked very much like the *Virginia*, then under alteration from the former USN frigate *Merrimack*. The less-than-blueprint quality plans taken back West by the contractor were for a pair of vessels each with a casemate and a fairly low freeboard that were sufficiently sophisticated mechanically to operate in coastal, river, or oceanic environments.

Although the Memphis boats would be built as sisters, there were no armorclad building standardizations at this point. George Wright has suggested that there were questions regarding the potential seaworthiness of these boats. Although Maj. Gen. Earl Van Dorn and some aboard the *Arkansas* later openly mentioned plans to push south to New Orleans and Mobile, the ability of a boat of her design to operate openly in the Gulf of Mexico was unknown. With flat bottoms and low freeboard, roll characteristics in ocean swells could not be predicted. Using steam only, such craft were entirely dependent upon their engines and inadequate coal supplies, which would limit them to coastal defense operations.

With the exception of propulsion, Shirley and Emerson were free to improvise as necessity required. So it was that Lt. George Gift later remembered that the *Arkansas* combined the best of the "flat bottomed boats of the West, and the keel-built steamers for navigating in deep water." It would be interestingly observed 150 years later that the shallow draft "diamond" hull designs the two men fashioned would, with their reduced labor and ironing

CSS *Virginia*, ex–USS **Merrimack**. *While Capt. Shirley was in Richmond during August 1861, he received some armorclad design specifications from the Confederate Navy Department. The vessel depicted looked very much like the Virginia, which was then under alteration from the former USN frigate Merrimack. The less-than-blueprint quality plans taken back west by the contractor were for a pair of vessels, each with a casemate and fairly low freeboard, that were sufficiently sophisticated mechanically to operate in coastal, river, or oceanic environments. Although the Memphis boats would be built as sisters, there were no armorclad building standardization at this point. Shirley and Emerson were free to improvise as necessity required. So it was that Lt. George Gift later remembered that the* Arkansas *combined the best of the "flat bottomed boats of the West, and the keel-built steamers for navigating in deep water." She also, famously, was constructed with vertical casemate sides (© 1995 David Meagher. Used with permission).*

requirements, prove more useful than a deep draft straight-sided configuration. Unfortunately, because the *Arkansas* was sunk, Rebel armorclad designers were unable to incorporate lessons of her final configuration into new plans.

Shirley may also have been provided with the latest information and thinking regarding the inclination and thickness of armor plating that his craft, like the *Virginia* and the Federal City Series boats, would feature. Tests would soon be undertaken under the direction of one of his contacts, Lt. John Mercer Brooke, in an effort to determine whether it should be installed vertically upon the casemate or at an incline. Brooke was among the few officers who believed that seaworthiness and other attributes could be enhanced if the armored sides of the casemate rose vertically. As the *Arkansas* would be the only Rebel ironclad built with vertical armored sides, it is reasonable to suggest that Shirley may have had this opinion in hand before he returned to Memphis.

At about the same time as the contracts were let for timber, orders were placed for the iron needed for armor. Some time earlier, navy secretary Mallory had ascertained that the possibilities of rolling armor plate in the West were quite limited. Indeed, the industrial infrastructure needed to extract and process iron was largely nonexistent throughout the South. At this time, what was available was principally located in Virginia. Given that continuing situation, it comes as no surprise some stopgap measure had to be adopted. With the coming of the railroads, local railway companies, North and South, stockpiled extra

Tredegar Iron Works. *Founded in 1833, this Richmond, Virginia, firm functioned until 1952 and is presently a museum. The most famous war materials factory in the Confederacy, it produced all manner of iron products, as well as cannon and other military and naval products. There were several iron foundries in Memphis, including the noted concern Quinby & Robinson, which also produced iron products and artillery and may have helped to supply the CSS* Arkansas *(Alexander Gardner photo, Library of Congress).*

iron rails (known as "T-rails" from their shape), for use in laying new tracks or repairing old ones. This track iron would now have to suffice. T-rails, the reader will recall, were employed with success on the Charleston floating battery back in April. "The navy," William N. Still wrote in his *Confederate Shipbuilding*, "greatly desired railroad T-rails because they were easily rolled into strips of armor plate." It would later be confirmed that the type was efficient, though thicker plate armor when available would be superior.

In building the Western ironclads, both Union and Confederate, the T-rails were not rolled. George Eller notes the following in a post on the *World War II in Color* message board: "Some ships simply used T-rails, despite the recognized fact that they were inferior to rolled plating, though many of the 'City' class ironclads supplemented their plate armor with T-rails in certain locations. One cautionary note: some sources refer to ships being plated with 'rail road iron,' but this does not necessarily mean T-rails. The *Albemarle*, for example, was armored with rolled plates, but the plates had originally been T-rails, so the ship was often mentioned to be armored with railroad iron." Even though it might not be as effective as plate, unmodified T-rails had the advantage of speed. They could be directly applied to whatever backing was planned. The authors of a study on the CSS *Georgia*, upon which it was also employed, have remarked that "without a doubt, it was the most primitive form of iron armoring, but it was effective. *Arkansas*, after all, used this method, and it was one of the most successful of all Confederate ironclads."

Shirley's requisition specified that his railroad iron come in sections 4 inches in diameter. Purchase orders, if employed, were dispatched to an unknown firm in Arkansas and one in Memphis. Plans called for the rail iron to be affixed in rows of dovetailed double thickness. We are uncertain which local firm was chosen as there were at least three or four foundries in town. Only the Western Foundry/A.G. Knapp & Company, dba Quinby & Robinson, was, however, large enough to properly handle the entrepreneur's iron, though two other competitors (Street, Hungerford & Company and Livermore Foundry and Machine Company) may also have been contacted.

Specializing in iron and the manufacture of engines, gears, castings, and "all kinds of machinery," Quinby & Robinson was owned by Knapp and his partners, William A. Robinson and William T. Quinby. Recently, the company had become involved in the manufacture of ordnance and ordnance supplies. Located at the foot of Poplar Street opposite the Exchange Building, its fires could rework the naval iron into the required shape.

The iron that came from Arkansas was brought to the Memphis and Charleston Railroad depot on the other side of the Mississippi and dumped on the ground to await pickup. Two other foundries were likely engaged by Shirley for other fixtures, one for certain. Lt. Gift tells us that the engines were contracted for and built at a foundry on Adams Avenue. There was only one foundry on Adams at this time, the business of S.M. Coates, Founder, located between Adams and Washington avenues.

Another concern likely patronized was the Copper, Tin, and Sheet-Iron Manufactory, owned by C. Richmond, J.W. Woltering, and Peter Gross. Located at 96 Front Street at the old USN rope walk, it specialized in manufacturing chimneys, doors, shutters, and other items "for steamboats, plantations, and distillers." Shirley's armorclads would need smokestacks (called "chimneys" by rivermen) and other light fixtures. Additionally, specialized machinery would be required to punch holes in the railroad iron so that it could be affixed to the gunboat casemates. This drilling equipment was likely manufactured by the Western Foundry and transported to Fort Pickering where it was set up on the building site. Regional firms could not fulfill all of Capt. Shirley's requirements. Contracts were let with certain concerns along the Cumberland River to roll iron into the necessary bolts and spikes needed as fasteners. It would, in the end, take longer than originally anticipated to obtain the needed materials and components. Engines, boilers, drive-shafts, propellers, armor, fasteners, and other items would arrive slowly. It should be remembered that Memphis was a central supply area for Lt. Gen. Polk and the Columbus defenders. That the former riverboat skipper was able to initiate so much business locally was testimony to his drive and patriotism, and perhaps his connections built on years of patronage.

Also in late September, Lt. Isaac Newton Brown, who had been seconded earlier to the staff of Maj. Gen. Polk and was engaged in seeking cannon and other items for the defense of Columbus plus Fort Pillow, came to Memphis on a continuing pursuit of defensive ordnance. It was hoped that a supply of conventional smoothbore pieces available in the town could be rifled. According to Larry Daniel, Quinby & Robinson had, in August, begun construction of a boring machine for the Memphis Arsenal; they had also begun erecting machinery for the rifling of cannon. Brown's visit, on this occasion, was unsuccessful because the capability was not yet in place to perform the task. Lt. Brown would come to the Tennessee community several times more over the next couple of months, but it is unknown whether or not he ever visited the ironclad building site at Fort Pickering. He would later admit in his *Battles & Leaders* contribution that he had heard about the Shirley project, though he did not say when he first learned of it.[4]

October was an extremely busy month for everyone, North and South, concerned with building and operating the Western gunboats. The Union timberclads were extremely active, as were several of the Confederate units of Capt. Hollins river fleet. In addition to the operational activity, work on the competing ironclads progressed. The overwhelming industrial power of the U.S. gave it an early lead.

With over 800 workers employed, Capt. James B. Eads' organizational genius, was, according to the *St. Louis Daily Missouri Democrat*, "exhibited in [a] noiseless and effective manner." Four barges and a steamboat were reported busy hauling timber to Carondelet and Mound City from the locations where Eads had mills at work. There were eight mills, the paper noted, located in Kentucky, Ohio, and Illinois, and 13 in St. Louis alone, all cutting the specified white oak into the various size of lumbered required for the decks and casemates. It was also estimated that, before the enterprise was completed, it would use 15 million feet of wood and 800 tons of iron plating — in addition to bolts, spikes, nails, engines, and boilers. In an effort to remain on schedule, Eads worked his construction gangs in different shifts seven days a week and at night. The project's blacksmith, machine, and coppersmith shops, sawmills, foundries, and rolling mills also functioned 24/7 in different shifts.

October 12 was an important milestone in the Eads gunboat enterprise. Two days after the date for delivery specified in the government contract, the first craft, *Carondelet*, was launched to the delight of a large gathered crowd of onlookers. At 4:00 P.M. that Saturday afternoon, the vessel was, according to the reporter from the *St. Louis Daily Missouri Democrat*, "gradually lowered into the 'father of waters' upon the ways on which it was built, and such was the noiseless, and almost imperceptible manner of the operation, that we found the boat gracefully upon the water and nobody hurt and not even a lady frightened." A rival scribe from the *St. Louis Daily Missouri Republican* was also very enthusiastic. "The launch was conducted in an admirable manner," he testified, "and everything about the Marine Railway worked smoothly."

It was anticipated that the City Series gunboats would all be operational before the first of the year. Although the Federal contractor had some difficulty obtaining his scheduled draws from the U.S. Treasury, he faced none of the project-threatening material, tranches problems, or manpower shortages about to be experienced by Emerson and Shirley. Although the Memphis team of Shirley and Emerson acted with alacrity to get their armorclad building program underway, it almost immediately encountered difficulties. Signing the contract with the Confederate navy and obtaining promises from various suppliers for materials and parts was the easy part. Getting the items delivered and finding the labor to assemble them was something else.

Getting materials to Fort Pickering took time. The schedules of regional railroads were swamped with logistical demands from Confederate generals whose requirements always seemed to take precedence over the two Memphis armorclads. Nevertheless, employing the lumber available, builder Emerson was able to get stocks and ways laid for his two vessels during October and finish their keels by the end of that month. Additionally, a machine shop and forge was built to assist in ironing the vessel while cranes or A-frames were assembled to assist in lowering boilers into the holds and placing engines near their bearers.

Emerson's Fort Pickering construction crew was small, tiny in comparison to that on the payroll of James B. Eads at Carondelet. Skilled ship carpenters, men such as those who had worked for him when he ran the Missouri boatyard, were very difficult to find. Indeed, all skilled labor was at a premium in the wartime economy. Frank E. Smith later commented on the problem. Writing in his "Rivers of America" history of the Yazoo River, he noted "there were not enough skilled carpenters and ironworkers to do the job — too many of the normally small supply in the Memphis area were carrying a rifle in the army."

In addition to marching, many skilled workers in the West were busily helping to throw up or enhance great fortifications at places like Fort Henry, Fort Pillow, and Fort Donelson. The South's faith in land bastions was good for labor. Professor Still puts his finger on the nub of the problem when he observes, "The trouble stemmed from over-mobilization at the beginning of the conflict, which had swept most of the skilled workers into the army. As shipbuilding expanded, and as the ordnance works and other related naval facilities began operating, the need for mechanics and carpenters increased."

Like Eads, Shirley placed help wanted ads seeking carpenters in the major Dixie-leaning newspapers, including those in Nashville, New Orleans, Mobile, Charleston — and even St. Louis. These netted a few responses, but nowhere near the number hoped for. Shirley became desperate for carpenters. He accepted "not only ship carpenters, but house carpenters, and, in fact, every man I could get that could do anything in forwarding the completion of the vessels."

Additionally, the expenses of bringing the men in and maintaining them were high. The laborers working on the Fort Pickering boats knew their own value and were not above demanding that their wages be advanced, oftentimes before work was completed. For several months, Navy Secretary Mallory, in Richmond, had attempted to intercede with the CS Army, corresponding with the War Department in an effort to free up shipwrights and nautical mechanics taken into the ground forces. His counterpart, Secretary Le Roy P. Walker, on August 30, even issued instructions to his military commanders to discharge such men, but immediately met opposition.

As October dragged toward November, the armorclad contractor, in desperation, attempted to obtain carpenters from Lt. Gen. Polk. Army manpower requirements meant that there never seemed to be sufficient men available, so now the man who had warmly recommended Capt. Shirley and his project to the Confederate government was asked for help. It was known that there were many skilled carpenters and machinists available in uniform between Memphis and Columbus, often underemployed, but their commanders would neither transfer them nor loan them out to the project. Shirley petitioned Polk to detail a hundred to work on the vessels. Eight men were provided.

The shotgun approach having failed, Shirley next sent army headquarters a list of 30 carpenters known to him and the regiments to which they were detailed. In the covering letter, Polk was asked to provide these men, but this time he refused to send any. As was the case throughout the Confederacy, military commanders basically refused to release any men they had under arms. In the end, the War Department modified its August order. If the navy or anyone else wanted skilled workmen discharged to aid with their special project(s), it would be necessary to supply substitute soldiers. Throughout the fall, the two boats were lucky to have between 20 and 120 men working upon them. Though he continued to support and advocate the necessity for naval defense, the "fighting bishop" was now more concerned with the bolstering "the Gibraltar of the West."[5]

While construction of the ironclads at Carondelet and Fort Pickering continued, incursions up the Tennessee by one of the Federal timberclads resulted in a new call for armorclad protection of the Confederate upper rivers. The response created greater competition for the limited manpower and resources available to support building of the two ironclads at Memphis that were intended for defense of the Mississippi. It may also help to explain some of the manpower problems faced by contractor Shirley.

On October 11, the Northern timberclad *Conestoga*, based in Paducah, Kentucky, received orders to ascend the Tennessee River and examine a new Confederate position just over the Tennessee state line called Fort Henry. After Gen. Albert Sidney Johnston took charge of Confederate Western Department early in the month, he chose to concentrate his defense on what Brig. Gen. Ulysses S. Grant later described as "a line running from the Mississippi River at Columbus to Bowling Green and Mill Springs, Kentucky." It was Volunteer State governor Harris who sent engineers down the Cumberland and the Tennessee to look for places to erect forts.

Work, which progressed only slowly, was begun on two main upper river defensive positions: one named Fort Donelson (after West Point graduate Daniel S. Donelson, Tennessee's attorney general) on the Cumberland River and the other, 12 miles northwest on the Tennessee River, called Fort Henry (in honor of Gustavus A. Henry, the state's senior Confederate senator). Fort Donelson would be mostly abandoned until October. The *Conestoga* arrived off Fort Henry on October 12 and spent part of the next day reconnoitering its defenses before returning downriver. On the way back, her commander heard rumors that the Rebels were converting three steamers into ironclad gunboats at a point five miles above Fort Henry.

When the *Conestoga* had first begun poking around in the Tennessee River earlier in the fall, Southern leaders were horrified to see that only the unfinished earthworks of Henry offered any protection against the "Linkum gunboats." The Confederate government now took over responsibility for the twin river fortifications, and efforts to finish — or at least improve — them were stepped up. The stories about Rebel gunboats heard aboard the *Conestoga* were not altogether untrue. There was considerable sentiment in some Confederate quarters for the construction of ironclads to defend the upper rivers from the Union's timberclads and the new Carondelet ironclads approaching completion.

Given that there was, indeed, very little coordination between the Confederate army and navy at the command level, particularly in the West, Maj. Gen. Polk, who had earlier supported Shirley's application to Secretary Mallory, decided, in the words of Professor Still, "to form a river defense flotilla" of his own. In late September, Polk informed Navy Secretary Mallory that he had purchased a strong river steamer at low cost and had dispatched it to New Orleans under Lt. Jonathan Carter. When he reached the Crescent City, Carter was to oversee the rebuilding of the craft into a gunboat, which some thought might even become an ironclad. Polk was anxious that, once the boat was finished, Carter would be "permitted to remain on duty in this department." The officer had knowledge of the Columbus region and the general needed "an armed boat under my command to protect our transports" and conduct reconnaissance. The Mississippi theater commander concluded his communication by noting that the vessel in question was nearly ready and hoped that Mallory would return both it and Carter to Kentucky waters.

The craft purchased by the military was the decade-old side-wheeler *Ed Howard*. The 390-ton vessel, constructed at New Albany, Indiana, in 1852, was 280 feet long, with a beam of 35 feet and an 8-foot draft. She had been active on the Nashville-to-New Orleans route before the war. On at least two occasions, she accidentally rammed and sank other packets, a fact which may or may not have had anything to do with her selection or her owner's willingness to sell. When finished, the altered *Howard* was rechristened *General Polk*. Armed with two rifled 32-pounders and a 32-pounder smoothbore, the gunboat, under Lt. Carter, was assigned to the squadron of Commodore Hollins.

So it was that, in addition to Shirley's ironclads and those abuilding at New Orleans,

Building the Federal City Series Class Ironclads. *The Union ironclad building program at Carondelet, Missouri, site of a shipyard previously operated by Primus Emerson, the constructor of the* Arkansas, *was a model of supply and efficiency as compared to the twin-ship effort by Emerson and John T. Shirley at Memphis. Nevertheless, this photograph of the Union project may give the reader some idea as to the appearance of the Fort Pickering operation. Notice the vessels on their stocks and the timber scattered about (National Archives).*

there was now a potential for at least three other Confederate fleets on the Mississippi, that of Commodore Hollins, Polk's, and a new one about to be formed under Capt. James Montgomery, the Confederate River Defense Fleet.

Three days after the *Conestoga*'s visit to the Tennessee, Polk informed Rebel navy secretary Mallory that gunboats like the *Ed Howard* "were indispensable" to Southern protection. The Columbus commander knew of another steamer immediately suitable for the task. He could also identify two others, one on the Mississippi valued at $20,000 and the other on the Cumberland worth $12,000. Having hidden her far up the Tennessee to avoid capture, Capt. Elijah Wood had let it be known to the Army that the big side-wheeler *Eastport* was available for purchase for $12,000. As she was perhaps the largest steamer then plying the Rebel-controlled portion of the Tennessee, the matter of converting the boat into an ironclad was thought to be a relatively easy matter.

On Halloween 1861, Maj. Gen. Polk wired Secretary Mallory giving particulars of Wood's offer and price, offered an endorsement of his need for more boats, and asked the navy to send a voucher. Deeming them "indispensable" to his defense, the general believed that the three could be speedily converted "into armed gunboats." The following morning, Acting War Department Secretary Judah P. Benjamin, after talking to Mallory, wired back authorization for Polk to make the purchase, confirming that the transaction would, in fact,

A Side-Wheel Packet. There was considerable sentiment in some Confederate quarters in the fall of 1861 for the construction of additional ironclads to defend the upper rivers from the Union's timberclads and the new Carondelet ironclads approaching completion. Given that there was, indeed, very little coordination between the Confederate army and navy at the command level, particularly in the west, Maj. Gen. Leonidas Polk, who had earlier supported Shirley's ironclad building application to Navy Secretary Mallory, decided to create his own river defense flotilla. The first unit was a side-wheel packet, the Ed Howard *(similar in layout to the vessel pictured), which was converted into the gunboat* General Polk *(Library of Congress).*

be paid with army money. Within days, Polk ordered the *Eastport* sent to a small boatyard at Cerro Gordo Landing, seven miles below Savannah and 50 miles below Eastport, Mississippi, where, before November was finished, the conversion process would begin. Payment to the boat's owners was delayed. The other acquisitions would follow.[6]

The inability of contractor Shirley to hire sufficient manpower to push his armorclad project to conclusion continued throughout the remainder of 1861. Although both he and builder Emerson made every effort to procure carpenters and mechanics locally, these simply could not be had either from the civilian market or the army. The military was even unwilling to provide guards to watch over the construction site. Still, as the trees lost their leaves, the stocks at Fort Pickering grew full. Framing for the two hulls, given the names *Arkansas* and *Tennessee*, was hammered together. Both the framing and planking was substantial. The hulls for each of the skeletons were (officially) 165 feet long between particulars and 35 feet wide, with an 11.5-foot draft. Their length was actually shorter than any of the City Series ironclads James B. Eads was building for the North in Missouri.

Noted draftsman David Meagher has drawn a set of plans for the CSS *Arkansas*. On that sheet depicting her lines, he has opened a question concerning her overall length with this statement: "Plan based on John Luke Porter drawing for a 180 foot sea-going vessel upon which the *Arkansas* and *Tennessee* were supposedly based. The 165 foot measurement given for the length of the Arkansas was probably the length of keel as opposed to greater measurements derived from the perpendiculars or totaled overall length."

In a personal note to the author, Meagher elaborated on the confusing differences between the Porter sketches and the manner in which Emerson and his Western contemporaries made their measurements. Porter, his colleague Samuel Pook, and others dealing with sailing ships gave the overall length of their vessels along with the between perpendiculars length, not counting bowsprits. "The riverboat people," he continued, measured the length of a vessel from the sternpost to the rudderpost." The extra length projecting behind the rudderpost (anywhere from eight to 30 feet depending upon whether you had a sternwheeler or a side-wheeler) was not taken into account. Ironclads, Meager concluded, "were a lot more cramped than people think, as they do not take in the 24 inches of wood inside most of them had under the outward shape."

Hybrids, the twins would be keeled fore and aft like ocean vessels, with a sharp, somewhat rising, bow and a tapered stern, while their center sections, not keeled, were flat, like the bottoms of Western steamboats. There was no "knuckle" at the waterline. All who saw the *Arkansas* in motion were impressed with how the after modeling of her hull lines created only low drag and permitted good water flow into her twin screw propellers. Also at the stern, there would be a single centerline rudder, secured to the hull by a rudder post and three metal plates on each side.

The following July, in an amazingly accurate contemporary picture written from deserter tales and leaked intelligence reports, the crack *Philadelphia Inquirer* reporter Henry Bentley, imbedded with the U.S. Western Flotilla north of Vicksburg, provided his readers with a detailed profile of the *Arkansas*. Her design, he revealed, was "a combination of the flat-bottomed boats of the West and the keel-built steamers designed for navigation in the ocean or deep inland waters." Bentley's projection of her measurements was off just a bit, giving her length and beam of 180' × 60'. On the other hand, the length at least may have been correct if, as Meager suggests, a J.L. Porter oceangoing blueprint were employed.

Lt. George W. Gift, one of *Arkansas*' officers, labeled his boat an "hermaphrodite-ironclad." He used this term because, instead of completing the craft "with an ordinary rail and bulwark all round," her sides amidships were built up into a casemate, "so as to give an apology for protection to three guns in each broadside."

In keeping with the then in-vogue belief in the naval tactic of ramming, both hulls were to be outfitted with a nine-ton cast iron ram. Each was to extend four feet forward of the stem at the cutwater. It was this cast iron fixture that later caused the *Arkansas* to be called an "ironclad ram," rather than just an ironclad gunboat or sloop. An early report, by an unnamed *Chicago Times* scribe, that was reprinted in the *New York Times* on July 5, 1862, says that the *Arkansas* had "an iron ram, weighing 10 tons, which projects from the bow, two feet underwater."

There has been considerable speculation over the years as to the exact appearance of the vessel's ram. The sketch by crewman Samuel Milliken, one of the only two contemporary drawings known to exist, appears to depict a flattened iron plating covering the extreme edge of the bow and running aft about 10–12 feet. This was probably not the actual appendage, but a layer of boiler iron tacked on to the bow above it as reinforcement. This flat portion of the bow is not the actual ram. Midshipman Dabney Scales' rendering shows a sharp-edged bow, but no ram.

On the morning of July 15, 1862, after the *Arkansas* reached Vicksburg, Federal reconnaissance parties were sent down the Louisiana shore to scout her appearance. A member of one of those teams returned to describe the vessel and its ram to *St. Louis Daily Missouri Republican* reporter William E. Webb: "Her hull rises above the waterline about three feet; her prow runs to a short point, and is vertical from the top to nearly her whole draught of water — evidently intended to butt far below the water and sink her opponent almost instantaneously."

Although the ironclad's ram is usually portrayed as an affixed spike, one current model maker, Old Steam Navy, is currently offering a 26.7-inch long miniature kit showing most of the bow itself sheathed into a projectile. This would be consistent if the vessels employed a large, flat ram covered with 1-inch thick boilerplate over a solid wood backing.

Interestingly, the best description of the rams fashioned for the *Arkansas* and *Tennessee* was provided by RAdm. Henry Walke, whose *Carondelet* would face the *Arkansas* in the Yazoo River on July 15. While writing his memoirs, Walke described the ram of the *Tennessee*, which was found at the Fort Pickering building site after the Battle of Memphis and later exhibited at the Brooklyn Navy Yard. Made of wrought iron, the ram, which Walke depicted in a drawing in his memoirs, had an unusual curve. This confirms contemporary descriptions, including Henry Bentley's, of its having the appearance of a bird's "beak."

Bentley went on to say that the ram of the *Arkansas* was "so made that the entire bow of the boat fits into it like a wedge into a piece of timber." Eight heavy bolts were to be pounded through four to six foot long clasps on each side and would hold the ram to the heavy bow timbers of the stem. In operation, the ram would have ridden at or just below the waterline, being far less vulnerable to gunfire than the boilerplate sheathing above it suggested in the Milliken drawing. Spies let it be known that it was "of sufficient strength to penetrate the hull of any vessel on the river."

In the Yazoo, Walke, having probably already heard some of the tales of the Confederate craft, would fear the ram of the oncoming *Arkansas* and attempt to maneuver his craft away from his enemy. Thereafter, engine difficulties that slowed the *Arkansas* in action, both during her breakout into the Mississippi and later on the cruise to Baton Rouge, would prevent the vessel from fully demonstrating this offensive weapon.

When fully outfitted, the shaped pine, deep-draft hulls, braced by oak and reinforced with iron rails, were expected to support overall displacement of about 1,200 tons. They would have extremely low freeboard (as was initially expected for the *Virginia*) of about a foot. As iron arrived, it was attached to the sides of the hull. Atop the hull of each craft was a long wooden-planked main deck. Drawing directly from the plans Shirley brought back from Richmond, but perhaps also aware of the plans for the City Series boats assembled at his old Carondelet yards, builder Emerson prepared to bolt a protective casemate directly atop this deck, running it for 50 to 60 feet amidships. The casemate sides were constructed from heavy and lengthy oak logs two feet thick, while the solid fore and aft ends were built from foot-thick oak squares across which were nailed 6-inch thick horizontal strips of oak.

Unlike the *Virginia*, or for that matter, any of the other Confederate armorclads, the thick wooden sides of the casemates Emerson was building were not inclined but perpendicular to the water. It is interesting to note that Eads' City Series gunboats under construction for the Union at Emerson's old Carondelet yard had inclined casemate sides. When work began on the *Eastport* a few miles to the east, she too was given an inclined casemate. Some have suggested that Naval Constructor John Porter's original recommendations offered this vertical feature because it would make construction easier for the unskilled laborers it was suspected Shirley might attract to his project. Others believe that this was a modification to the original plan made by builder Emerson, based upon his "knowledge of factors that endowed a riverboat with strength and speed."

We know for certain that Eads made some modifications to his boats and we can surmise that Emerson did the same with the Fort Pickering armorclads. As his relative Mary

Emerson Branch wrote years later, steamboat modification while under construction was a common Western rivers practice that "had evolved over the years in this same innovative, pragmatic way." Like the other Southern armorclads now under construction or soon to be planned out, however, the casemate ends did slope up from the deck at a 35-degree angle. Emerson and Shirley anticipated that their gunboats would only have four cannon each, two per broadside. Consequently, the casemate ends were solid when completed. A flat roof provided cover.

There were, George Wright reminds us, no contemporary reports of a need for "hogging chains" to steady the hulls of the *Arkansas* and *Tennessee*. The casemate framing may have functioned as a "hogging truss," by distributing concentrated loads from her power plant and armament along her longitudinal axis. The longtime student of the *Arkansas'* profile points out that this sort of construction was common on Eastern riverboats. It was also adopted for later Rebel gunboat conversions, including the *Selma* and *Calhoun*.

It is well documented that Maj. Gen. Polk continued to resist requests for help, preferring, perhaps, to concentrate on the *Eastport* and other upper river boats. We know from correspondence between the general and Lt. Brown that the latter was fully engaged in strengthening the defenses of Columbus and Fort Pillow and was not asked, at that point, to assist contractor Shirley. Brown's unflagging activities (which might be one of the reasons he ended up with command of the *Arkansas*) since early summer were bearing fruit. In addition to arranging the acquisition of fourteen 32-pdrs., he had ramrods and carriages built for them locally and manufactured their ammunition at two little shell-making plants he established just for that purpose. A pioneer in mine warfare, he also planned an underwater defense employing "torpedoes." But what, one wonders, about direct assistance to Shirley from the Confederate navy. Commodore George Hollins, whose wooden gunboats were often in the vicinity of Memphis and Columbus that fall, could have been approached by Shirley and asked for some help, if only the temporary detailing of a few men from his boats. There is no record indicating that this avenue was explored.

Work on the Fort Pickering armorclads limped along in November and December. Only a few local carpenters were at work, though the men specially brought in at great expense from Maryland, Alabama, and Virginia apparently performed well. Years later, Emerson was accused by historian Robert Huffstot of being "a man of leisurely temperament, who did not believe in night shifts or Sunday work." Rather than leisure, one could suggest poverty of manpower and resources hindered his work, together with competing interests on the Cumberland and Tennessee.

On December 5, Neil S. Brown (1810–1886), who served as Tennessee governor from 1848 to 1850 before becoming the U.S. minister to Russia, signed a petition to Gen. Albert Sidney Johnston with Maj. Gen. William Giles Harding (1808–1903), a prominent Nashville munitions manufacturer and owner of the Belle Meade plantation. In it, they urgently recommended that a gunboat be purpose built or a steamer converted into a warship for the protection of the Cumberland. Their petition was endorsed by then-governor Harris, who added his voice: "I am deeply impressed with the importance of Confederate gunboats on both the Cumberland and Tennessee rivers...." The petition was presented to the Rebel commander by Mayor Richard B. Cheatham (1824–1877) of Nashville.

Following his visit with Johnston, Cheatham, with an endorsement from the general and a letter of introduction from former Governor Brown, headed off to Richmond to lobby the Confederate government for Cumberland River gunboats. Stops were made at the offices of prominent members of the Rebel congress, as well as those of War Department secretary

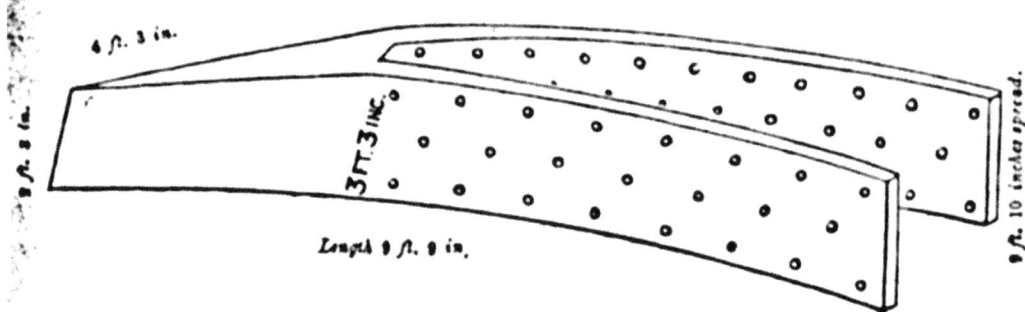

* Dimensions of the beak or ram of wrought iron bolted on the cutwaters of the Confederate rams built at Memphis. One is now lying in the Navy Yard, Brooklyn, New York.

A Ram for the Memphis Armorclads. *There has been much speculation over the years as to the appearance of the iron ram bolted to the stem of the* Arkansas. *This depiction, by RAdm. Henry Walke, shows one seen at Fort Pickering in the days after the June 6, 1862, battle. It was most likely that intended for her sister, the burnt-out* Tennessee *(Walke,* Naval Scenes and Reminiscences of the Civil War*).*

Judah P. Benjamin and Secretary Mallory. Cheatham told Mallory that he knew of at least four steamers that could be readily obtained. Two were valued at $40,000, one at $35,000, and another at $25,000. He was a little fuzzy on their configurations, leaving the naval chief to presume "that these are the ordinary river boats, with the usual exposure of walking beam and boiler on deck."

Given the continued paucity of workers, contractor Shirley was forced to abandon his plans to built both boats simultaneously and to concentrate on just one at a time. Chosen for completion first was the *Arkansas*. The Confederate treasury was late in its contract payments, ironically, just as the U.S. had failed to promptly honor the tranches of City Series gunboat builder James B. Eads. In order to raise the cash to keep going, Capt. Shirley was forced to sell his home.[7]

Having received no local manpower help to speak of from either the army or the navy, Capt. Shirley took the unusual step in early December of writing directly to Secretary Mallory, explaining his difficulties and placing the fate of the whole Memphis armorclad project on the line. If the Richmond official could get Polk to provide mechanics and carpenters, it would be possible to finish both boats within two months.

Meanwhile, the Confederate naval chief had his own problems. In addition to several operational setbacks along the eastern seaboard, the conversion of the *Merrimack* into the *Virginia* was also behind schedule. She should have been "completed by the end of November," wrote William Still over a hundred years later, "but she was far from ready at the end of the year." The building of the *Mississippi* and *Louisiana*, two ironclads at New Orleans, was also running slow. Both needed considerable work with their machinery and ordnance.

During the fall, eight cannon were shipped from Richmond to Memphis for mounting aboard the *Arkansas* and *Tennessee*. As the year ended, it became obvious that they would not be placed aboard the two boats anytime soon. Taking advantage of this delay, the builder of the *Louisiana* petitioned Commodore Hollins for permission to divert them to New Orleans for installation aboard his armorclad. The naval officer granted permission and the guns were sent to the Crescent City by steamer — where they were promptly seized by the army and sent to bolster riverfront fortifications. Elsewhere in the West, in addition to

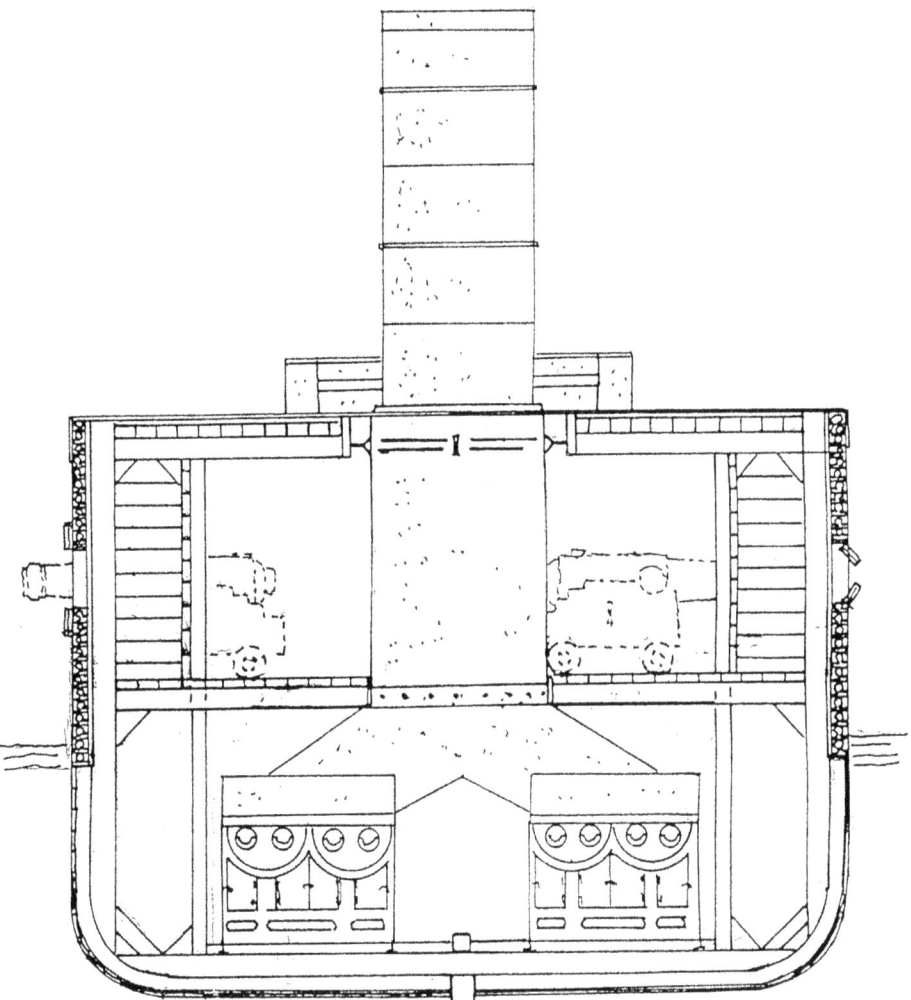

Arkansas Cross Section. *This cross section of the* Arkansas *allows the reader to visualize the location and relationship of the ship's decks, boilers, and stack while appreciating the vertical walls of her casemate (© 1995 David J. Meagher. Used with permission).*

Memphis, the Cerro Gordo conversion also ran into difficulty. At the beginning of December, the Rebel army commander at Columbus wrote to the Navy Department asking that a naval officer be assigned to superintend the alteration of the *Eastport* from a merchant steamer into an ironclad.

On Christmas Eve, the navy secretary replied to John Shirley's plea, enclosing a letter to be hand delivered directly to Maj. Gen. Polk at Columbus. In it, the Confederate cabinet official pointed out that the government had already advanced Shirley funds "to induce the construction of the boats" and was, consequently, vitally interested in their completion. The general, who was then worried over feints being organized by Brig. Gen. Grant at Cairo, was asked to extend the CSN the courtesy of temporarily furloughing men to work on Shirley's boats, a duty he termed "special service." Mallory even agreed to have them paid "the highest current wages."

Reminding Polk that he had initially backed Shirley's proposal, the navy secretary noted his astonishment that the Columbus commander had, so far, been less than helpful. The bishop was also chided: "One of them [Memphis armorclad] at Columbus would have enabled you to complete the annihilation of the enemy. Had I not supposed that every facility for obtaining carpenters from the army near Memphis would have been extended to the enterprise I would not have felt authorized to have commenced their construction then, as it was evident that ruinous delays must ensure if deprived of the opportunity of obtaining mechanics in this way." Unless the men could be detailed "from the forces under your command," Mallory told Polk, "the completion of these vessels will be a matter of uncertainty."

Writing out a cover note, Shirley asked his colleague, the military tailor John H. Waggener, who was visiting Columbus a day or so after Christmas, to personally deliver the communication into Polk's hands. Waggener and his partner, Thomas H. Creek, ran their establishment out of the Ayers Building on 2nd Street. Advertising "Military Uniforms for Officers and Privates, made in the most approved style," Waggener had been patronized by the Columbus commander and many of his officers. "But he was compelled to come away without a reply," Shirley later testified. When Shirley learned that Waggener's mission was fruitless, he immediately penned an ever more urgent appeal and dispatched it, together with a copy of the navy secretary's Christmas Eve letter, to Maj. Gen. Polk via Col. Milton A. Haynes, chief of the Tennessee Corps of Artillery. They "were both returned under cover to me at Memphis, without any sort of reply."

Perhaps hoping that the directness of his communication via Shirley might be softened, Secretary Mallory, writing from afar and without knowledge of Polk's double refusal to accept his communications, took the occasion to inform the general in a separate memo that his earlier request for an *Eastport* building superintendent was being granted. Lt. Brown, already on the scene working on river defenses, was ordered on Christmas Day to take over the construction of all Confederate gunboats on the Tennessee and Cumberland rivers.

Following the visit of Nashville mayor Cheatham, Secretary Mallory, politically persuaded that additional gunboats on the twin Tennessee streams could help Western defense, wrote to Brown with fresh orders. The future commander of the *Arkansas* would now superintend not only the alteration of the *Eastport*, but also choose several new boats to be converted at Nashville. These would come from among four identified by the mayor.

Shirley and Mallory would continue their efforts to pressure Polk into providing skilled laborers through the first quarter of 1862 — all without effect. Indeed, the secretary found himself facing CS Army reluctance to provide labor assistance across the board. Even when President Davis agreed to a plan that would temporarily furlough skilled soldiers to work on navy projects, he left allocation to the discretion of his commanders — down to company level. Faced with continuing shortages themselves, officers would not, as a rule, authorize even short-time transfers. It would take a change in command before a Confederate general determined that the Fort Pickering armorclads should be pushed much harder. By then it was nearly too late.

And so it was that 1861 came to an end. In his *Grant Moves South*, the great Civil War historian Bruce Catton summarized the situation as it applied at Christmas: "1861 was the year of preparation, the year in which a singular tangle of conflicting strategic plans, personal rivalries, and the slowly emerging imperatives of civil war would presently bring forth new opportunities and new actions."[8]

CHAPTER FOUR

From Memphis to Yazoo City, January–May 1862

By the end of 1861, work on the two Confederate armorclads under construction at Fort Pickering, on the Mississippi River just below Memphis, had slowed to a crawl. Although laid down in October, difficulties in obtaining material and labor forced contractor John T. Shirley and builder Primus Emerson to concentrate on finishing one boat ahead of the other. That chosen for completion first was named *Arkansas*.

At the same time, seven Federal (partially) ironclad gunboats being built by James B. Eads at Carondelet, Missouri, and Mound City, Illinois, were nearing completion. Most were long since launched and delivered to the Union naval base at Cairo, Illinois, where they were fitting out under newly assigned commanding officers. As they were readied, a fleet of three wooden gunboats, called timberclads, carried out reconnaissance and patrol missions, occasionally engaging in firefights with watching Confederate vessels.

The incursions of the Union boats, particularly missions up the Tennessee River in the fall, greatly concerned Rebel Gen. Albert Sidney Johnston and his subordinate Maj. Gen. Leonidas K. Polk. In November, the latter sought to establish his own brown-water flotilla. His first move was to arrange for the purchase of a large side-wheeler, the *Ed Howard*, which was converted into the *General Polk*. Another steamboat, the *Eastport*, was also acquired, which he ordered taken to Cerro Gordo for conversion into an ironclad under the direction of his former naval aide, Lt. Isaac Newton Brown. At the same time, contractor Shirley at Memphis was unable to persuade Polk to send him additional mechanics and carpenters to work on the *Arkansas* and her more languid sister, *Tennessee*.

In December, Johnston endorsed a petition from several prominent Tennessee political leaders who wanted more gunboats besides the *Eastport* built on the upper rivers. It was subsequently taken to Richmond by Nashville mayor Richard B. Cheatham, who personally lobbied war secretary Judah Benjamin and navy secretary Stephen Mallory for additional naval protection on the upper Western rivers. While the mayor was en route, the naval chief prepared to write Maj. Gen. Polk asking for men to help build the Memphis armorclads. Always in need of political support and believing that it could be a good thing to have additional gunboats on the upper streams, Secretary Mallory accepted Cheatham's petition and, on Christmas Day, wrote to Lt. Brown ordering him to add to his resume the duties of superintendent of gunboat construction on the Cumberland and Tennessee rivers.

Although he knew that Shirley's building project was behind schedule, as was one for a pair of huge ironclads at New Orleans, the secretary could do little about the impact a new demand for shipbuilders and resources would create for those contractors with projects already underway. After all, not even the New Orleans newspapers seemed all that concerned about the potential danger to the Crescent City, preferring to believe, in the words of the *Daily Crescent* on February 14, that "the only real danger we apprehended comes from the Upper Mississippi."

Although our story concerns the *Arkansas*, a review of Lt. Brown's work with the *Eastport* and the Nashville vessels can prove insightful for the time, a bit later, when he becomes associated with Shirley's ironclad. Some of the traits and accomplishments of his first superintendence would show up again. Mallory's Christmas Day message to Brown would send the lieutenant to Nashville to work with Mayor Cheatham on the selection of suitable craft from among four identified by the politician while in the secretary's office. Brown was deputized to choose boats other than Cheatham's if he found any, but was limited to four total. He was also to notify Richmond of his arrival at the Tennessee capital so that funds could be forwarded to cover the cost of the "important work."

The Richmond cabinet officer anticipated that, at a minimum, the four would have to have their engines and boilers moved below-decks. Brown was allowed to use his discretion as to ordnance and "protection from the shot of the enemy to be adopted." Those and any other alterations were to be made with builders under contracts, with daily forfeiture clauses the same as imposed upon Shirley and Eads. Cheatham had offered his help with the project and Brown was advised to accept, as the mayor's assistance could be important for the procurement of workmen.

At Cerro Gordo since the end of November, Lt. Brown was totally in charge of the *Eastport*'s conversion. While he sketched out plans for a paddle-wheel ironclad, the officer arranged for the enhancement of a nearby sawmill and ordered timbers and lumber cut. Lt. Brown also contracted with a prominent Savannah, Tennessee, carpenter named Hurst to carry out the *Eastport*'s physical reconstruction. Hurst's son, T.M., then a small boy, would later become a Presbyterian minister and would recall aspects of the conversion process for the state historical magazine.

By the end of January, contractor Hurst, with local labor, had removed the superstructure of the *Eastport*, down to her main deck, including her pilothouse, cabins, and siding. He also inserted bulkheads

Lt. Gen. Leonidas K. Polk (1806–1864). *The lieutenant general defended the Mississippi River at Columbus, Kentucky, holding the "Gibraltar of the West" for the South until its March 1862 evacuation. At first supportive of contractor John T. Shirley's proposal to build ironclads at Memphis, as well as the defensive activities of his naval aides, Lt. Jonathan Carter and Isaac Newton Brown, he failed to provide the manpower so desperately required to complete either the* Arkansas *or her sister, the* Tennessee *(Library of Congress).*

and started to erect a slanting timber casemate over about half to two-thirds of the main deck. We might note here that this protective warship structure had numerous names, depending upon who was referring to them: casemate, shield, ark, and Brown's favorite, "gun box," were employed interchangeably. The builder would "put on the armor plate" to the casemate. "She was to be protected by railroad iron," young Hurst remembered; others would later testify that the armor came in sheets stacked adjacent to the building site. To provide an unobstructed gundeck inside the casemate, the boilers were disconnected and positioned for lowering into the hold. Four cannon of unknown type or size were "on the way" to arm her. Unlike the *Arkansas*, there has never been any indication that she would receive a ram.

Riding over to Nashville from Cerro Gordo not long after New Year's, Lt. Brown met with Mayor Cheatham and was escorted down to the levy where he was shown the four boats mentioned to Secretary Mallory. The *C.E. Hillman* and *James Woods* were offered at $40,000, the *James Johnson* at $35,000, and the *B.M. Runyan* at $25,000. Completed at Pittsburg in 1860 for the Cincinnati-Nashville run, the 230-foot, 420-ton side-wheeler *C.E. Hillman* had been involved in a contraband incident back in April and was briefly seized by Union forces at Cairo. She was later released. The *James Woods* was a big 585-ton, 257-foot long side-wheeler constructed by Howard at Jeffersonville, Indiana, in 1860 for the Nashville–New Orleans trade. Constructed by the same builder four years earlier, the 525-ton side-wheeler *James Johnson* was paired on the Crescent City route with the *James Woods*. The two-year-old *B.M. Runyan*, constructed at Cincinnati, was a 230-foot long side-wheeler operated before the war by her owner, Capt. James Miller, on routes from Nashville to both New Orleans and St. Louis.

Lt. Brown took his time inspecting the quartet of steamers identified by Nashville's mayor. It was determined that the *James Woods* and *James Johnson* were suitable and these were purchased. While in Nashville, Brown made arrangements to have made or to take over for both the *Eastport* and these boats a quantity of iron under contract for delivery to John Shirley, contractor for the CSN ironclads abuilding at Memphis. Though he ended up with the armor, the lieutenant subsequently denied Shirley's assertion of consignment poaching.

While Brown and Shirley continued apace on their respective building enterprises, the Union's Western Flotilla, based at Cairo, Illinois, commissioned its ironclads during January 1862. Their arrival permitted Federal military leadership to plan new advances, which were hinted at in the newspapers throughout the month. Interestingly enough, although the craft were accepted they were not yet fully paid for by the U.S. Treasury.

At Fort Pickering, Primus Emerson pushed efforts to ready the *Arkansas*. The casemate was finished and much of the internal woodwork was either started or nearly completed. Unlike other Confederate armorclads, his ram did have exposed wooden decks. The main deck, fore and aft the casemate, was planked, and provided with large white-painted ventilation grates on either end. These could be removed to permit the lowering of coal or supplies.

The type and source of the calking used in her hull and deck seams is unknown. Oakum was the standard, but tarred cotton was known to be used on some steamers. There is reason to believe that the boat's hull was constructed, at least partially, of green timber. Whatever amount of calking was employed, vessels so built were subject to chronic leaking that required constant pumping.

Every Western steamer had a pilothouse for its steering wheel and pilots. The ram was no different, except hers was smaller than most. Years later, when he sought the final resting site of the *Arkansas*, famed novelist Clive Cussler portrayed it as "similar to a pyramid with the upper half cut off."

Located at the forward end of the wood-planked hurricane deck of the casemate and in front of the chimney, the pilothouse/conning tower of the armorclad was very small, probably only about 10–12 feet wide. It rose just a foot or two above the top of that deck. The layout of the *Arkansas* pilothouse was, according to George Wright, a compromise between the need to protect the pilot(s) and watch officers from enemy fire and a need for an elevated position with a good view of the river to the front and sides. Because her casemate was relatively low, the elevation of the pilothouse was too. The pilots aboard the *Arkansas* worked at a disadvantage compared to a contemporary riverboat with its higher wheelhouse. A riverboat pilot could usually distinguish other vessels on a winding river because he could see over medium-sized trees. This was not the case aboard the Southern armorclad; only signs of smoke in the air would warn the men in her pilothouse of an oncoming vessel. Adding further to observation difficulties was a lack of large windows as found in the pilothouses aboard commercial steamers. Wide narrow slits were substituted but these actually limited the ability of the pilots to see or remain oriented. The same sort of pilothouse protection was provided aboard the Union's City Series gunboats and was equally ineffective. In practice, Lt. Brown preferred to stand exposed on the roof of the casemate, believing that he had a better view when the vessel was underway.

Several other features of a riverboat would also apply to the pilothouse of the *Arkansas*. A typical river steamer steering wheel was about 8 feet in diameter with half extending above the deck and half below. The axle of the wheel and its bearings were sited on the deck itself. Though unrecorded, a similar design was undoubtedly installed onboard. A "lazy bench," or small bench, was provided for off-duty pilots; the duty pilot stood behind the wheel.

A variety of levers and cords were positioned overhead in the pilothouse within reach of the pilot at the wheel. At least one commanded the boat's whistle. Some of the cords were attached to the *Arkansas*' bell system. Bells of various sizes and tones were, as on other Western steamboats, hung on the inside walls of the engine room. The interconnecting cables allowed the pilot in the pilothouse to "ring up bells," thus telling the engineer in a nonverbal manner what was needed. The four major bells were an attention bell, a backing bell, a big bell, and a stopping bell.

When the bells were insufficient, the pilothouse and engine room could verbally communicate via a long brass speaking tube strung between the two. In the pilothouse, the speaking tube was located to the side of the wheel and allowed the pilot or the captain to communicate with the engine room, which, in turn, could also contact them. Use of the speaking tube required of its participants good hearing and big lungs. Both ends of the tube were normally "stoppered" and had a small whistle attached. Either the pilot or the captain at their location or the engineer in his could blow through the speaking tube, sounding the whistle on the other end and drawing attention to the need for communication. Thereafter, the parties put their ears to the tube and alternated yelling their messages to each other.

As a last resort, messengers could transmit information and commands. Petty officers, stationed at the hatches, could relay commands from the pilot station to the engine room, say during a battle when noise would make use of the speaking tubes or bells impossible. A similar messenger system could also be employed to transmit orders from the pilot station or captain's location to or along the gun deck.

Four: From Memphis to Yazoo City, January–May, 1862

As she came together, the *Arkansas* presented its workers and visitors with the same simple interior structure common to the other screw-driven Confederate ironclads starting with the *Virginia*. A cutaway of her midships hull would reveal three decks rising from keel to gun deck, upon which the casemate structure was superimposed. Every level was accessible via hatches and ladders. Professor William N. Still has painted the picture. In his classic *Iron Afloat*, the East Carolina University professor emeritus wrote that "the gun deck was that part of the main deck located inside the casemate." As the term indicated, this space held the cannon. Some crewmen, finding this location — one they would soon call "the slaughterhouse" — cooler than their quarters below, slung their hammocks between the great black monsters. They could mess there as well and, with permission, topside.

Still went on to elaborate that the second, or "berth," deck, below the main deck, contained "the crew's quarters and messing spaces" forward, the latter area much smaller than the former. The officers were housed further aft, with their wardroom nearly amidships and their mess behind, near a tiny galley; the captain's cabin was beyond. The dispensary was on the port side and opposite it was the engine room. "Sundry machinery and the boilers were located amidships in the hold," Still says. Indeed, the boilers were centered directly beneath the chimney, while the coal bunkers were probably located forward of them. Also located at each end was a storeroom, magazine, and shell room, all directly below the unarmored decks above.

At Cerro Gordo, Isaac Brown pushed ahead with the *Eastport*, though what exactly was accomplished in what order by builder Hurst's work crews is uncertain, as no plans or descriptions of the conversion process exist. Brown, from his time in Richmond earlier in the year, was probably familiar with plans for the conversion of the USS *Merrimack* into the CSS *Virginia* and may have partially predicated his arrangement upon that alteration. Witnesses who saw the boat after her capture by the Union all agreed that the steamer's original timbers were sound and made of good material, which allowed new planking and other improvements to be simply nailed on or otherwise affixed where needed.

The boilers were dropped into the hold as Secretary Mallory had recommended, but remained to be positioned. The hull was sheathed in oak, which wood was also used to make the fore, aft, and thwartships bulkheads. To protect the engines and boilers, an interior bulkhead was constructed about 4.5 feet back from the outer hull. Atop the main deck, an inclined casemate was erected with placement of the side timbers completed. Gun ports were in the process of being cut. Although the paddlewheels and shafts remained in place, the arms and buckets were taken off. It is probable that wooden armor, similar to that used aboard the Federal timberclads, would cover the wheelhouses and the paddlewheels.

About this time, yet another Confederate nautical force, under control of the army, was authorized for the Western waters. The brainchild of two former riverboat captains, J.H. Townsend and James E. Montgomery, the Confederate River Defense Fleet (CRDF) was created at New Orleans at the beginning of 1862. Employing 14 seized merchant steamers, the new unit was not a part of the Confederate States Navy but a direct creation of the Confederate congress, which funded it to the tune of $1 million.

Once in hand during March to early April, the CRDF vessels, of different sizes, would all be modified along similar lines into rams, craft designed like the Memphis boats and the warships of ancient times to run into other boats. The engines and boilers were lowered as far as possible into the holds and protected by inner and outer bulkheads filled with cotton bales. Cotton bales were also stuffed into every conceivable space for protection, and a few cannon of different caliber were mounted, usually no more than four. Uniquely, the bows were strengthened with railroad iron. Two divisions were created, a northern group under Montgomery's control and a southern under Capt. John A. Stephenson, Townsend's successor. It is the former that will briefly interest us here; Stephenson's division would be destroyed by Flag Officer David G. Farragut (1801–1870) when the USN captured New Orleans at the end of April.[1]

Little success was enjoyed in conversion of the Cumberland River gunboats in the month that followed their acquisition. By the beginning of February, Union forces under Maj. Gen. Ulysses S. Grant and Flag Officer Andrew H. Foote were on the move. The first Northern objective in the West in 1862 was the capture of Fort Henry, on the Tennessee River. It was gunboat reconnaissance of this very same citadel in the fall of 1861 that had encouraged Lt. Gen. Polk to purchase several boats, including the *Eastport*, in the first place. High water, a weak defense, and a determined bombardment caused the bastion to surrender to Foote on February 7.

For the Confederacy, the loss of Fort Henry was nothing short of a disaster. "The Yankees," wrote the editor of the *Atlanta Confederacy*, "have brought their gunboats and forces from Paducah, down the Tennessee River across the entire State of Kentucky, in the most populous and wealthy portion of it, to the Tennessee line." Then they "captured a fortification which our people considered strong which was intended to keep them out of the State of Tennessee." Immediately following the fort's capitulation, the three Union timberclads, *Lexington*, *Tyler*, and *Conestoga*, ascended the Tennessee on a raid designed to sweep Confederate shipping from that stream and, along the way, capture or destroy any Confederate gunboats encountered.[2]

As the three gunboats approached Cerro Gordo Landing, Hardin County, after supper on February 7, they were fired upon by Confederate snipers hidden in the bushes along the east bank of the Tennessee. The *Conestoga* returned fire with her 12-pdr. while a cutter was sent ashore from the *Tyler*. To cover the landing party as it was rowed toward the beach, both the *Tyler* and *Conestoga* turned their heaviest cannon on the woods and brush behind it. Whatever riflemen had greeted them were gone before the shells fell and the boat nosed into the bank. As the *Tyler*'s boat ran into the bank, small-arms fire once more welcomed the Yankee visitors, who retaliated again with cannon. The three gunboats now hove to and launched their cutters, all with heavily armed parties, under the command of Second Master Martin Dun of the *Lexington*. At the levee, they found the large steamer *Eastport*, purchased by Lt. Gen. Polk back in November. They also learned the truth of the rifle fire they had supposedly just been under.

When contractor Hurst's men, working on the Rebel gunboat, received the news of Fort Henry's demise, they quickly made arrangements to sink her if the Yankees came. A man was stationed on the bluff overlooking the river north of town with orders to fire a shot as a signal if they were sighted. At that point, two men would chop a hole in the bottom of the *Eastport* and create whatever other mischief was possible. Once the watchman fired his gun, the timberclads replied, sending two shells his way, one of which penetrated the ground near the shooter's feet. The axmen aboard the *Eastport* started chopping holes in her bottom, but did not linger. In the words of Hardin County historian B.G. Brazelton, "He fled and the men on the *Eastport* fled too, without accomplishing their purpose." Among those hastily departing the scene was Lt. Brown. Although he had turned in a creditable organizational performance in a short period of time, his goal of completing the ironclad was unfinished. Returning briefly to Columbus, he would travel next to New Orleans to help finish the gunboat *Mississippi*.

Four: From Memphis to Yazoo City, January–May, 1862

The U.S. boat crews immediately searched the unfinished warship to determine whether she had been rigged to explode. She turned out to be safe. Her conversion already half finished, the fleeing Rebels had further tried to scuttle her by breaking her suction pipes. A Federal damage control party quickly halted the leaks and kept the boat off the bottom. With an armed guard posted, the three Union gunboats anchored for the rest of the night.[3] The extent of the Union capture was revealed at daylight on February 8. At 260 feet, the steamer was huge. The side-wheeler, partially rebuilt with exposed paddlewheels and an unfinished wooden casemate frame, also had a 43-foot beam and a depth of hold of six feet, three inches. Built at New Albany, Indiana, back in 1852, the *Eastport* already had two high pressure engines and five boilers.

Delighted with this prize, the Federals were also pleased to find large quantities of timber and lumber that the Confederates were employing to finish her, as well as iron plating, lying nearby neatly stacked on the riverbank. Also found aboard were a quantity of documents, including letters and correspondence between Lt. Brown and Secretary Mallory, some of which were yet to be posted. The captured documents and correspondence were later lost, but fortunately for history, some of it was published in the *Cincinnati Daily Commercial* on February 15. The snippets reveal that when Secretary Mallory sent him to Nashville to purchase steamers for conversion into gunboats Brown was to entice the owners into accepting half payment in Confederate bonds. The officer was forced to inform his chief that "the parties wish to sell for cash only." Also, in the opinion of the lieutenant, who was becoming something of an expert on them, "submarine batteries could not be successfully used in the rapid streams of the West." This revelation was contained in one of several notes exchanged with Cmdr. Matthew Fontaine Maury, the "Pathfinder of the Seas."

And then there was the matter of Lt. Brown's request to be relieved. This vignette, not published in any previous account of the *Arkansas*, suggests that the Mississippian not only knew about the armorclads being built by Shirley and Emerson, but actually thought he should have received command, at this point, of the one furthest along. In a letter (the newspaper does not cite a date or recipient) from Brown, perhaps to Secretary Mallory, the former states his request for relief because he understood that he was being denied command of the ironclad advancing under construction at Memphis. Brown had heard that Lt. Gen. Polk was going to give the boat to Lt. Carter, his junior, who commanded the CSS *General Polk* at the time.

A hard charger, Brown was also a man with a strong sense of personal honor, intense in the manner demonstrated by others from the South — and later, by a few in the North when Cmdr. David Dixon Porter was jumped several grades to command the Mississippi Squadron. The lieutenant was extremely and personally insulted by what he perceived as the affront of the reported appointment, "the denying of which at this juncture is an implied disgrace, so far as such an act of denial from a soldier can reflect upon one of my profession. Exigent as the times are, there can be no right in one to decree the dishonor of another." It is perhaps as well that, if his letter were meant for Mallory, it was not delivered. The Confederate naval secretary was about to name the *Arkansas*' commander from among the ranks of unemployed Eastern officers. It was his appointment to make and Carter was not his choice.

Brown's letters and papers were put into a sack and sent aboard the *Conestoga* for delivery to Western Flotilla headquarters at the end of the Tennessee River cruise. The *Tyler*'s men were also to load the wood and metal from shore and otherwise make the vessel ready for a trip to Cairo. She would be towed downstream as soon as the *Lexington* and *Conestoga* returned from however much further up they were able to go.

Two gunboats ascended to Florence, Alabama, before returning to mount an amphibious attack upon Savannah on the morning of February 9. Having attained all that they could at Savannah, the *Tyler* and *Conestoga* returned to Cerro Gordo. There they found that some 250,000 feet of timber, together with nails, machinery, spikes, and other materiel stockpiled for use in finishing the Confederate armorclad were loaded. Just before their departure, a party was sent to burn the local sawmill where the *Eastport*'s lumber was cut. Towing the unfinished Confederate ironclad, the Union raiders returned to Fort Henry the next day. The *Eastport* was forwarded on to Paducah, Kentucky, and later to Mound City, Illinois, where she would be rebuilt into a Federal warship.

As Robert Suhr has noted, the results of the timberclad raid forcibly demonstrated "the potential of the Union Navy on the western rivers." Their voyage "spearheaded the Union advance into Tennessee" and was instrumental in starting a "chain of events that would culminate in the capture of Vicksburg in 1863 and the complete Union domination of the Mississippi River."[4]

February finished out as a dismal time for Confederate arms. Having conquered Fort Henry, Union forces under Grant and Foote headed up the Cumberland River and attacked Fort Donelson. Although assault by the City Series ironclads was a failure, the army investment resulted in the surrender of the position on February 16. Nashville was occupied nine days later. The capital of Tennessee was the first seat of an insurrectionist state to be retaken by the Union. Needless to say, the steamboats *James Woods* and *James Johnson*, identified to Lt. Brown as gunboat candidates by Mayor Cheatham and subsequently purchased, were never a factor, no work on them having even been started. Indeed, on February 23, Charles Gallagher, father of Capt. T.M. Gallagher, who had signed their paperwork but was yet to be paid, set both boats afire to keep them from falling into Union hands.

Meanwhile, on the other side of the South, Confederate forces were forced to abandon Jacksonville, Florida, in the face of an occupation force en route courtesy of the Union's South Atlantic Blockading Squadron. Lacking the capabilities for defense, the Rebels quit the entire region from Amelia Island to Fernandina at month's end and it was occupied on March 4; Jacksonville fell into the Federal bag eight days later.

With its connection to the cross-peninsula Florida Railroad, Fernandina, in particular, was "a choice port to blockade-runners," wrote Paul Calore in 2002. Among the Confederate navy personnel pulled out of the post and reassigned was Baltimore native Commander Charles H. McBlair (1808–1890), who commanded the defensive batteries. Before his posting to Florida, McBlair served on the Richmond station into the fall of 1861. A deep-water sailor innocent of inland experience, McBlair was originally appointed a midshipman in the U.S. Navy in March 1823, moving slowly up the ranks to become a lieutenant in July 1831 and a commander in April 1855. During this time he developed a life-long friendship with RAdm. Charles Henry Davis, who commanded the Union's Western Flotilla from the Battle of Fort Pillow through October and was present off Vicksburg when the *Arkansas* made her run.[5]

The South's loss of control over Tennessee's upper twin rivers meant that Columbus, Kentucky, was effectively outflanked. It was necessary for Rebel forces to withdraw from the "Gibraltar of the Mississippi" and move further south to new positions at Island No. 10. That process was completed during the first week of March, leaving the Confederacy in the West with a defensive line that ran from Corinth, Mississippi, across western Tennessee to the Mississippi.

Four: From Memphis to Yazoo City, January–May, 1862

When the Confederates evacuated the region of the Cumberland and Tennessee, Union forces made ready to pursue. First, however, they paused to regroup and refresh. The Northern gunboat flotilla needed a little time to effect repairs and to address a lingering bluejacket recruitment problem. Outflanked Columbus was not occupied until March 4.

Also as the month began, there was little actual news concerning progress on the Fort Pickering armorclads. Contractor John Shirley and builder Primus Emerson continued to slowly pound the *Arkansas* together. She was still not ready to launch and, without a larger workforce of shipwrights, machinists, and carpenters, the effort continued forward at something akin to a snail's pace. The project originator and his lieutenant were also able to see the effects of the annual spring rise. The great Mississippi's depth was swollen by both local and distant rain and melting snow. Debris was everywhere in the water, swiftly pushed by wind and current and sometimes hidden by fog.

Although there may have been a momentary boost in building site enthusiasm caused by the success of the *Virginia* against the Federal warships at Hampton Roads on March 8 and her valiant fight with the Union *Monitor* next day, it did not translate into accelerated construction. There was also a shortage of iron for protection of the armorclad's casemate. Following the "disappearance" of the original order that Lt. Brown claimed not to have seized, Shirley found iron again "with difficulty." The majority of this acquisition, bought and paid for and now arriving at Fort Pickering, came in 50 to 100 pound lots from all around the South. As soon as it arrived, Shirley sent it to the armor drilling crew.

Even though labor shortages continued to plague the project, Emerson pushed work on the *Arkansas* even as the warming weather of March brought early flowers and buds, as well as flooding. She continued to take precedence over her site-mate. The lumber and other fittings for the *Tennessee* were stacked up adjacent to her scantily clad bottom. Some iron that had arrived for her hull and casemate remained on the other side of the river yet to be retrieved.

Manpower shortages still plagued the *Arkansas* project. The failure of Lt. Gen. Polk to assign military laborers after the loss of the *Eastport* and his Nashville gunboats is, given the loss of the Columbus fortress, perhaps somewhat easier to understand, but remained a significant impediment. At this time, Louisianan Charles N. Conrad, chairman of the Naval Affairs Committee of the Confederate house of representatives, who was greatly concerned with the construction of Rebel ironclads at New Orleans and on the Western waters, became concerned with the possibility "that Memphis might be taken" and that, as a result, the two boats under construction at Fort Pickering "would be captured by the enemy or destroyed by us to prevent their capture."

Conrad, who frequently met with Navy Secretary Mallory, visited the cabinet officer "when the fortifications at Columbus were taken" to determine whether or not the danger to the Tennessee river city "was apprehended." Although the Floridian agreed there was concern, when pressed by Conrad, he admitted that he had not taken any direct action to prevent loss of the two boats. Flabbergasted, the committee chairman suggested that plans be put into place to "send them down to the Yazoo River, where we may probably be able to make a stand and construct some works for protection, or to Vicksburg." The mouth of the Yazoo was about 12 miles above Vicksburg on the Mississippi.

Set atop bluffs overlooking the Mississippi, Vicksburg was an important—later the most important—link between the eastern Confederacy and the trans–Mississippi region. It was, in 1860, the Magnolia State's second largest city after Natchez. The town was a key transportation center, not only because of steamboat traffic the Mississippi and Yazoo Rivers, but also because of a growing network of southeastern railroads. Vicksburg sheltered the terminus for the only trans–Mississippi railroad crossing between Memphis and New Orleans. Trains arriving from Shreveport, Texas, and points west at the riverbank town of De Soto could see their goods transferred across the Mississippi by ferry.

Samuel Carter III, quoting H.C. Clarke's new *General Directory for the City of Vicksburg*, informs us of what Conrad, and possibly Mallory, already knew. Trains of the Southern Railroad of Mississippi puffed east of the bluff-topped community as far as Jackson and then continued on to Meridian. The capital city was also crossed by the New Orleans, Jackson, and Great Northern, the tracks of which snaked north to Canton. There they connected with those of the Mississippi Central, which funneled passengers and freight on to Grenada and hence into Tennessee. Arriving at Jackson, these were passed onto the Memphis & Charleston, a key artery between West Tennessee and South Carolina.

On the great river 40 miles west of the state capital at Jackson, the terraced city held about 5,000 citizens within its limits. That population exploded when one took into account the swampy Delta country and the hilly, stream-possessed areas surrounding the community; but of those 11,156 residents, 9,863 were African-American slaves.

With an increasing number of guns being mounted to command the river, the South intended to make use of the city's natural defenses. Situated atop a hill that rose 200 feet above the Mississippi, the town offered artillerymen the opportunity to sweep the stream below with plunging fire in much the same way the defenders of Fort Donelson had pounded the Western Flotilla back in February. The town on the heights was assisted by the Big Muddy itself, which curved below in a great horseshoe bend. This bend, particularly at the second bend, all but insured that any hostile craft attempting to pass could be greeted with harsh cannon fire. Not only were the bluffs high, but the water was deep. A *Philadelphia Inquirer* reporter, Henry Bentley, later painted the picture, which speaks also to one aspect of the Mississippi herself: "The water 200 yards from the shore directly before the town is over 300 feet deep, and in one place a line 150 yards long has been thrown out without reaching bottom. At every point on the Mississippi where the river sweeps the base of a concave bluff the water is invariably of great depth."

Mallory agreed that Conrad's river planning advice was valid and, with the Louisianan looking on, rang a bell for his secretary, whom he directed to wire the armorclad contractor and order that such preparations be put in place "if Memphis should be threatened."

As part of the reaction to the reshuffling of the Confederate Western military's defensive topography and the aggressive drive south by the Union's Western Flotilla, the Confederate navy now rather quietly opened a naval station at Jackson, Mississippi, inland east of Vicksburg.

A flag officer would soon be assigned to oversee the command and control of CSN operations in the central Mississippi River area. He would be able to travel back and forth between the political capital of the state and Vicksburg easily via the railroad that connected the two cities, running into the latter via a huge bridge over the Big Black River south of town, or the road that ran most of the way almost parallel with it.

Having also been kept apprised of the pace of construction on the two Fort Pickering rams, Secretary Mallory, on March 14, wrote to the War Department secretary, Benjamin, to again seek help. The completion of what he called the "ironclad sloops at Memphis," would be delayed many additional months if mechanics from the army were not detailed to work on her. Extolling the strength of the craft and their potential value in the defense of the Mississippi, the naval chief all but begged his counterpart: "If the commanding

The Port of Nashville. *In December 1861, Confederate theater commander Gen. Albert Sidney Johnston endorsed a petition from several prominent Tennessee political leaders who wanted more gunboats besides the* Eastport *built on the upper rivers. The petition was subsequently taken to Richmond by Nashville mayor Richard B. Cheatham, who personally lobbied War Secretary Judah Benjamin and Navy Secretary Stephen Mallory for additional naval protection on the upper Western rivers. Always in need of political support and believing that it could be a good thing to have additional gunboats on the upper streams, Secretary Mallory accepted Cheatham's petition and, on Christmas Day, wrote to Lt. Isaac Newton Brown ordering him to add to his resume the duties of superintendent of gunboat construction on the Cumberland and Tennessee rivers. Brown was sent to Nashville to work with Mayor Cheatham on the selection of suitable craft, but none could be completed before the loss of Fort Donelson (Miller, ed.,* Photographic History of the Civil War*).*

general at Memphis were ordered to facilitate this important work, we could launch the first vessel within a few weeks."

Benjamin consulted with Confederate president Jefferson Davis and then turned the matter over to Maj. Gen. Pierre G.T. Beauregard, who was the general Mallory was referring to. The hero of Fort Sumter, who remembered the ironclad floating battery used there, had assumed command of the new Army of the Mississippi two weeks earlier. In a note informing Secretary Mallory of this development, Benjamin noted that the chief executive concurred with the urgency of the detail the navy was requesting and "urges immediate action." President Davis' concern over the urgency of the matter was justified. On March 15, elements of the U.S. Western Flotilla rounded to above the head of Island No. 10, just one day after Maj. Gen. John Pope's bluecoats occupied the nearby riverbank town of New Madrid, Missouri. Located near the line separating Kentucky from Tennessee, Island No. 10 was approximately 240 miles below St. Louis, 26 below Hickman, 160 miles above Memphis, and 900 above New Orleans.

Although the western end of the South's defensive line was breached, as long as the Rebels under Brig. Gen. John P. McCowan and, later, his successor, Brig. Gen. William W. Mackall, held the island, the Mississippi River was blockaded. The campaign for this next

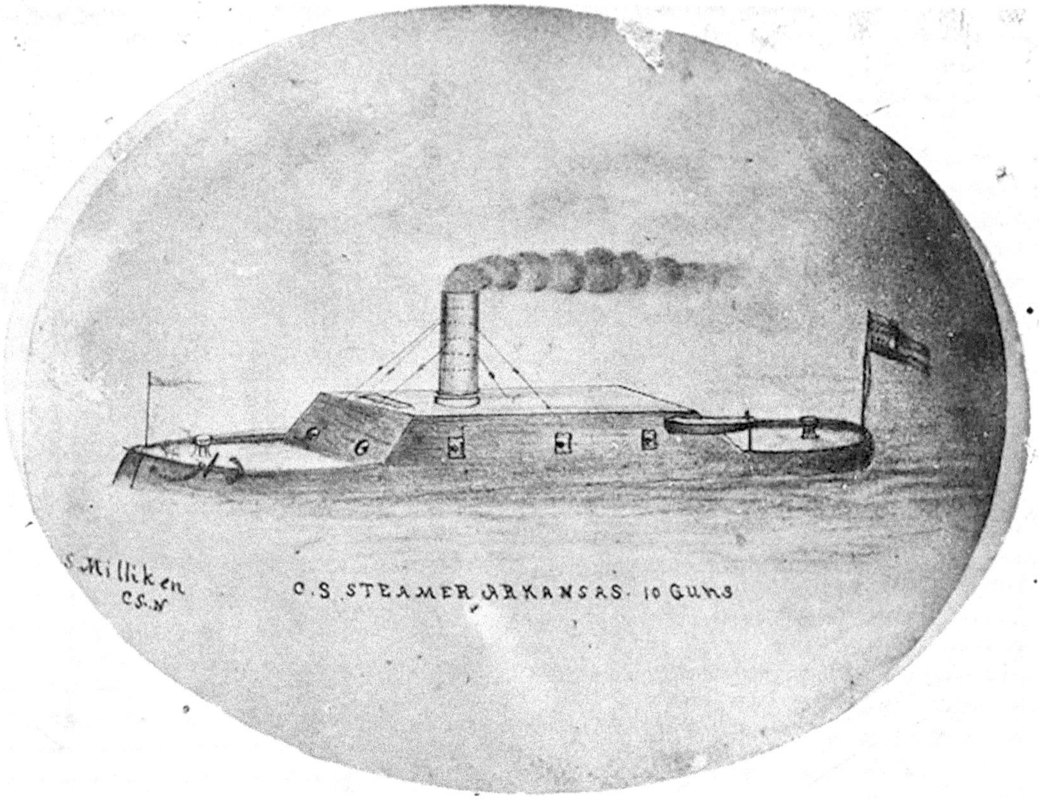

C.S. STEAMER ARKANSAS. 10 GUNS
S. Milliken, C.S.N.

"The Rebel Ram ??? Str Arkansas 10 Guns,
As she Appeared after the fight"

Four: From Memphis to Yazoo City, January–May, 1862

great downstream Confederate citadel commenced in earnest two days later when ironclads, mortar boats, and riflemen launched what turned out to be a two-week-long bombardment of the island's defenders.

In response to Secretary Benjamin's request, Maj. Gen. Beauregard, on March 18, dispatched Lt. John Julius Guthrie (1815–1877) from his command of the Confederate floating battery at Island No. 10 to Fort Pickering "to inspect the state of construction of the two gunboats. He was also to remain as the boat's executive officer to oversee their building and while there, send back a detailed report "of their condition, time necessary to complete them," and any other suggestions he cared to make. Guthrie reported back to Beauregard within a week of his arrival at Memphis. One of the boats, he wrote, had her keel laid and her ribs and framework in place, but "under present prospect, will not be ready to launch in less than six weeks." The other, *Arkansas*, was much further advanced. She would "soon float." About this time, the new captain of the *Arkansas*, Cmdr. McBlair, arrived from Florida. With the armorclad still not launched, it would become his responsibility to hasten her completion.

Both Guthrie and McBlair (as well as later historians) were uncertain of the exact dimensions of important superstructure segments of the boat before them. Plans would later be drawn based upon the officially recognized dimensions of her hull: 165 feet long between the particulars and 35 feet wide, with an 11.5-foot draft (which Lt. Brown later claimed was 13 feet). One set was rendered by the modern naval artist Joe Hinds, another by William E. Geoghegan, famous for his work with the *Carondelet*, and a third by the historian and artist David Meagher. Additionally, powder division master Samuel Milliken and Midshipman Dabney Scales drew sketches which remain the only known contemporary views, though their dimensions are probably not proportional.

In 2006, famed modeler Edward D. Parent undertook to compare the Geoghegan and Hinds sets of plans and the Millken drawing, reporting his findings in the May–June issue of *Seaways' Ships in Scale*. Here we offer a comparison (in feet) of certain key dimensions between Milliken and the three modern sources:

Feature	*Geoghegan*	*Hinds*	*Meagher*	*Milliken*
1. Bottom of hull to top of casemate	20.2	23	21	N/A
2. Casemate height above waterline	11.2	12.4	14.5	17
3. Casemate roof length	84	72	58	64
4. Forward casemate roof length to centerline of chimney	32.7	26.5	21.6	20
5. Fo'csle length of main deck outside casemate	37	37	48	41
6. Fantail length of main deck outside casemate	31	44	51	36
7. Chimney height	17.1	17.7	18.6	24.6
8. Chimney diameter	6.2	5	7	8
9. Broadside gun port spacing (after Brown alteration)	16	16	12	21.4

Opposite, top: **Samuel Milliken Sketch of CSS *Arkansas*.** *Powder division master Samuel Milliken produced a sketch which remains one of the only two known contemporary views of the Confederate armorclad, though its dimensions are probably not proportional (Navy History and Heritage Command).* Bottom: **Contemporary Drawing of the CSS *Arkansas* by Midshipman Dabney Scales.** *Remembered for his heroism in raising the shot-away flag during the armorclad's passage through the Federal fleet above Vicksburg on July 15, Scales apparently drew this sketch before the end of that month. He affectionately refers to his vessel as the "Rebel Rascal." Like the rendering by Master Milliken, it is apparently not proportional (Navy History and Heritage Command).*

In a May 2010 e-mail to the writer, David Meager amplified his figures somewhat. "You can add three or so feet forward, where the stem slopes back, to category # 5," he noted, "and four or five feet" to category #6, "where the stern slopes forward." The artist went on to further elaborate on his plans: "I measured the length of keel to the stem — which is a 'bp' or 'between perpendiculars,' the rudder post and the stem, which in most vessels is timber or timbers almost vertical, but in the *Arkansas* case (like the *Albemarle*, etc.), a lowered angled joint of a stem and the ram support. As this is a narrow bow, like most ferries in a river environment, and not broad like a normal riverboat, I felt it made sense."

As March ended, Maj. Gen. Beauregard, armed with Guthrie's report, contacted Shirley and offered to send him carpenters from his command. Lack of mechanics had retarded work for six months and now all the contractor had to do was identify the men and their units so that Beauregard's adjutants could cut the orders. This was the reverse of the same approach Shirley had originally tried with Polk, but this time and for whatever reason, no list was forthcoming. Perhaps Shirley believed that McBlair, now on the scene with Guthrie, would assume an active superintendence of the project and help speed it to completion, even though such a directive was probably not in his posting orders.

About the time Guthrie made his report, Northern commanders East and West began to exhibit the first symptoms of a war-long political disease known as "ram fever." They were not alone. Startled by the appearance of the mighty *Virginia*, Navy Secretary Gideon Welles, other Washington, D.C., officials, and newspapermen across the Union wrung their hands and raised their voices seeking relief. It would not come easily. The fear was best described a year later by a paymaster on a Federal blockader. A terrible disease that severely attacked commanding officers, it was "supposed brought on by occasional sights of a rebel ironclad passing up and down the river...." Symptoms included "a disposition to gaze long & anxiously...," the frequent mistaking of little river steamers and tugs for rebel ironclads & rams," occasionally mistaking small brown buildings ashore "for the dreaded ram," and "the frequent inquiry on the appearance of a cloud of smoke" ... "do you see the ram?"

In the West, reports of Confederate ironclads on the river disturbed Union military and naval officers far and wide, particularly those with little or no acquaintance with brown or blue water or boats. U.S. Army of the Tennessee commander Maj. Gen. Henry Halleck was the first prominent leader to exhibit the disease when, on March 25, he wrote to the flag officer commanding the Western Flotilla: "It is stated by men just arrived from New Orleans that the rebels are constructing one or more ironclad river boats to send against your flotilla. Moreover, it is said that they are to be cased with railroad iron like the *Merrimack*. If this is so I think a single boat might destroy your entire flotilla, pass our batteries and sweep the Western rivers." Edwin Stanton, U.S. secretary of war, was also bitten by the bug released by the *Virginia*'s triumph. But he had an ace. The noted bridge engineer Charles Ellet, Jr., had earlier suggested that the Federals build rams of their own. On March 27, the cabinet official contacted Ellet: " You will please proceed immediately to Pittsburg, Cincinnati, and New Albany and take measures to provide steam rams for defense against ironclad vessels on the "'Western waters." The next day he wired Ellet at Pittsburg: "The rebels have a ram at Memphis. Lose no time."

In the meantime, and for some weeks to come, Confederate propagandists heralded the building of the two Shirley rams. As late as the end of July, a New Orleans correspondent admitted that, for several months, Federal leaders were drawn to stories of their construction. These were to be "equal to the 'cleaning out' of the Mississippi river, the recapture of New Orleans, and perhaps an excursion to New York and the destruction of that city."

On March 29, Stanton wrote to comfort Maj. Gen. Halleck with a description of Ellet's rams: "They are the most powerful steamboats, with upper cabins removed, and bows filled in with heavy timber. It is not proposed to wait for putting on iron. This is the mode in which the *Merrimack* will be met." Despite the introduction of Ellet's boats, the manifestations of Yankee "ram fever" were exhibited for months to come.

It was another two weeks after Stanton's communication to Halleck before the danger facing the Crescent City was fully appreciated or divulged to its citizens by its own news media. On April 2, for example, the *New Orleans Daily Delta* pondered in print whether the two big star-shaped forts 75 miles downstream would be able to protect the town from the Federal armada now emerging from the Mississippi Passes. This was not a question of "ram fever," but of plain old-fashioned defense against conventional naval gunfire. Indeed, the journal's editor suggested that the greatest concern lay in the possibility that the Federal commander might decide to make a sudden dash past the forts and head directly for the metropolis.

On Thursday, April 3, Lt. Henry K. ("Harry") Stevens (1824–1863) arrived at Memphis and was welcomed as the third-ranking officer of the new ram behind McBlair and Guthrie. After service at Charleston, South Carolinian Stevens, a CSN officer since the previous November, was posted to Memphis on March 31. He would remain with the *Arkansas* throughout her life, from launch to destruction, after which he would serve briefly with Cmdr. Brown at Yazoo City before assuming command of the CSS *J.A. Cotton*. He would be killed aboard that vessel near Patterson, Louisiana, on January 14, 1863.[6]

The Confederates opposing Maj. Gen. Pope's southern thrust were cut off by lunchtime on April 7, about the same time Maj. Gen. U.S. Grant counterattacked at Shiloh in the ferocious battle up on the Tennessee River. Island No. 10 was surrendered to the Western Flotilla on the evening of April 8 and the Mississippi was opened down to Fort Pillow. Three Confederate generals, 4,500 soldiers, and 109 artillery pieces were now taken off the table. "The circumstances as connected with the surrender of this position, with all its guns, ammunition, &c., are," wrote an editorialist for the *Richmond Press* on April 14, "humiliating in the extreme." This Federal success was not only embarrassing but it also heightened concern for the unfinished ironclads Shirley and Emerson were building at Memphis. Three days after the fall of Island No. 10, Com. George Hollins, from his headquarters at Fort Pillow, wired Secretary Mallory regarding the fall of Island No. 10. Mallory telegraphed back from Richmond advising Hollins to use his best tactical judgement in light of developments. "Do not let the enemy get the boats at Memphis," he warned.

Just after his message went out to Hollins, Mallory wired Cmdr. McBlair at Memphis, advising him of the Island No. 10 loss. The sailor was ordered to take the *Arkansas* to New Orleans for completion as soon as possible "if she is in danger at Memphis." The long-delayed armorclad was apparently launched during the first week of April or early in the second, though some sources make it later than that. Whatever day it was, the craft, once its stocks were knocked away, slid into the Mississippi with a great splash. As the ripples dispersed, she could be seen riding with her hull all but submerged and only the main deck and casemate showing.

In the days just after the fall of Island No. 10, Hollins, who had guided CSN fortunes on the upper rivers since the beginning of the year, was recalled to New Orleans to aid in the defense of that city. Command of the few vessels that remained devolved upon Cmdr. Robert F. Pinkney (1812–1878), who had come to the West earlier in the year after commanding the guns at Fort Norfolk, Virginia.[7]

A few days after the Hollins-Pinkney command shift occurred, the regular CSN force above Memphis was replaced by Com. Montgomery's seven vessels from the northern division of the Confederate River Defense Force (CRDF). The creation and deployment of this new naval organization was unknown to both the Federals and those working on the Memphis ironclads.

An army outfit, the northern division of the CRDF was now overseen by West Virginian and Brig. Gen. Meriweather Jeff (M. Jeff) Thompson (1826–1876), the one-time mayor of St. Joseph, Missouri. He had organized a battalion ("The Swamp Rats") of the Missouri State Guard for Rebel service just after Fort Sumter. Eight companies of these troops (three artillery and five infantry) were recruited aboard the CRDF rams and Thompson himself reported aboard Capt. J.H. Hurt's CSS *General Beauregard*.

At about the same time, Secretary Mallory chose his new central Mississippi River flag officer and ordered him West. The move was a lateral (and as it turned out only of eight months duration) shift for a distinguished gentleman of that rank who was bold, but unlucky to say the least. When the Civil War erupted, Captain, later Flag Officer, William Francis Lynch (1801–1865) was one of the most famous officers in the Southern naval service. Like such other officers as Federal Western Flotilla founder Cmdr. John Rodgers, Lynch made his name in the prewar years as an explorer. His major claim to fame came first with some expertise with steam engines, but then grew with an exploring trip to the Jordan River and the Dead Sea in the late 1840s, followed by a similar trip to the African west coast. By the end of the 1850s, Lynch had written official reports on all of his adventures, as well as best selling narratives and even his own autobiography, *Naval Life, or Observations Afloat and on Shore: The Midshipman*.

Resigning his USN commission in April 1861, he joined the CSN and commanded the Aquia Creek Batteries on the Potomac for the next several months. The engagements between his guns and Federal naval vessels represented the Southern navy's opening shots in the rebellion. By October 1861, Lynch found himself the senior naval officer in North Carolina waters and commander of a small squadron of nine light craft called the "Mosquito Squadron."

Charles Ellet, Jr. (1810–1862). *The noted bridge engineer Charles Ellet, Jr., had earlier suggested that the Federals build rams of their own to match those reportedly under construction in the Confederacy. On March 27, 1862, U.S. secretary of war Edwin Stanton contacted him: "You will please proceed immediately to Pittsburg, Cincinnati, and New Albany and take measures to provide steam rams for defense against ironclad vessels on the Western waters." The next day he wired Ellet at Pittsburg: "The rebels have a ram at Memphis. Lose no time." With War Department authority, the visionary ram proponent delivered a fleet that would prove both valuable to the Union cause and controversial (Navy History and Heritage Command).*

Four: From Memphis to Yazoo City, January–May, 1862

On the first day of the month, he won the inaugural CSN naval victory in that area when his boats captured the U.S. steamer *Fanny* in Pamlico Sound. It was his greatest operational success. Outgunned by a larger Federal force descending upon Roanoke Island, Lynch's command was beaten back and then destroyed at Elizabeth City on February 10, 1862.

In fact, all of eastern North Carolina was taken by Northern commanders. A Rebel land commander during the Elizabeth City action, Brig. Gen. Henry Wise, wrote to a colleague that Lynch's combats amounted to "unauthorized intermeddling." It would have been more helpful, the general continued, if Lynch had employed "his boats as tugs for transports instead of vainly trying to turn tugs into gunboats to encounter a Burnside fleet of 60 vessels." Lynch hurried to Richmond after the battle to report to Secretary Mallory. A later historian, John Hinds, harshly wrote that the one-sided battle of Elizabeth City "exposed Lynch for what he was: a man more interested in preserving his own skin and prewar reputation than defending the cause whose uniform he wore." This opinion was shared by at least one contemporary who knew the flag officer, Mrs. Catherine Edmondston. The wife of a plantation owner, she confided to paper that Lynch was a "little great man" who "could not get a house large enough for his dignity."

Because of his academic demeanor and a variety of actions taken while in command of the Mosquito Squadron, Lynch thus managed to earn as many enemies as friends and supporters during the first year of the war. Due to his rank and his supposed knowledge of the requirements of steam propulsion, Secretary Mallory elected to transfer the controversial officer, making him commander of Naval Forces of the West. It would be at least another month before he departed.[8]

Lead elements of the Union's Western Flotilla arrived in the waters above Fort Pillow on April 13. Over the next three days, the Federal mortar boats launched their attack, tossing 13-inch shells 3,800 yards downstream into and around Fort Pillow. On occasion, the big Confederate 10-inch Columbiads, the ones that Lt. Isaac Brown had helped procure for the bluff-top citadel the previous year, returned fire. To the Federals, as Shelby Foote put it, "Fort Pillow was a mean looking place.... Downstream there was a Confederate flotilla of unknown strength, perhaps made stronger ... by the addition of giant ironclads reportedly under construction in the Memphis yards."

On the evening of April 16, Maj. Gen. Pope received an order from Maj. Gen. Henry W. Halleck transferring his army to the Tennessee River. The Union theater commander was then beginning a campaign against the key railroad center of Corinth, Mississippi. The siege of Fort Pillow was to continue and, if the opportunity allowed or the enemy withdrew, a brigade of Indiana troops (1,500 men) left with the flotilla was to land and secure it.

Without a field army to assault the Rebel river defenses, the attack on Fort Pillow settled down into a siege reminiscent of that at Island No. 10 a month earlier. Every day, two or three Federal mortar boats, protected by one or two ironclads, shelled the hilltop citadel. Occasionally, the Confederates fired back, sometimes dropping their bombs relatively near their floating enemy. Thunder from the less-than-hurtful explosions reverberated up and down the Mississippi, while the geysers raised in the flood-swollen waters were sometimes quite spectacular.

At the same time, elements of the Confederate River Defense Force anchored in the stream south of Fort Pillow, near Fulton Landing. Separated from the Federals by Plum Point, the smoke from their chimneys could be seen rising "over the tops of the trees." Transports were seen arriving daily at the bastion from Memphis, 75 miles away.

Completion of the ram downstream at Fort Pickering proceeded "very slowly," opined new arrival Lt. Stevens, "and it seems impossible to get it done faster." On the other hand, even if she were quickly finished, "no great things need be expected of her anyway," he opined. "She is much of a humbug, and badly constructed in many respects." By the time she was launched, the *Arkansas* was, as Stevens noted, far from finished. Still, her hull was covered in iron from her main deck to about a foot below the waterline, as was her main deck fore and aft of the casemate. All of the internal woodwork was finished except for the captain's quarters and the unarmored casemate was erected, though not pierced for cannon. The inner wooden portion of the casemate had a rough finish, lacking the smooth inner surface common to contemporary warships, a finish designed to reduce splintering when struck by enemy fire. Indeed, when the *Arkansas* engaged the combined Union fleets above Vicksburg on July 15, much of this casemate backing did splinter, showering the gun crews with potentially fatal wooden debris.

Cmdr. McBlair and Lt. Guthrie did not share the opinion of Lt. Stevens, but may nevertheless have wondered what might be done to alter the unusual broadside-only ordnance arrangement planned for the vessel. The gun ports had yet to be cut into the casemate and there was still some time. Were there other possibilities? Many folks have pondered this question, including my fellow *Arkansas* student, George Wright who, in a March 17, 2010, letter to the author, outlined two possible modifications: "The first would be the use of a single bow- and stern-chasers with one broadside weapon on each side. If their carriages were of the Marsilly type, *Arkansas* would possess reasonable arcs of fire, but lack the ability to concentrate multiple pieces on a single target. The advantage of this layout was simplicity and a reduction in labor time and materials. Based on early experience of Union river ironclads and their multiple forward batteries, it must have been apparent to Confederate naval officers that single chaser layouts put their vessels at a severe disadvantage in the headon [*sic*] engagements typical on the Western rivers." If the first scheme was out, then an alternative plan to place the single bow and stern chasers on pivot mounts so they could also fire on each broadside might work: "Broadside firepower was greatly enhanced in this scheme, but pivot mounts would not improve fore- and aft-firepower. Two bow and stern chasers were an obvious alternative, but created their own problems. Because of a lack of space or the type of carriages available, two chasers fore and aft left these pieces only able to fire straight forward. We know from the comments of Lt. George Gift, in charge of one of the bow-chasers, that the utility of these weapons suffered from undersized gun ports and very little ability to traverse."

Although the two Adams Street engines, together with boilers and other propulsion machinery, were aboard the *Arkansas*, they had not yet been taken below and mounted. As a result, it was obvious that if the warship was required to quit the waters off Fort Pickering in a hurry, she would need to be towed. Fortunately, the four-bladed hand-made propellers and the drive shafts from New Orleans were in place.

Humbug or not or whether properly pierced for guns, the armorclad remained a significant Confederate asset that needed protection. Stevens was detailed by Capt. McBlair to find a suitable steamboat that could be chartered to tow the armorclad to the Crescent City. The effort was long in bearing fruit, but at last, on April 19, the side-wheeler *Capitol*,[9] an old speed queen, was hired. Once the *Capitol* anchored off Fort Pickering, a growing number of the armorclad's newly recruited complement were quartered aboard, including her cabin and wardroom mess. We are fortunate that a table has been preserved; from it, we can reveal names of personnel who had, or would take, a prominent role in the vessel's history.

In addition to Capt. McBlair and his top two officers, Guthrie and Stevens, a pair of other lieutenants had arrived: John "Jack" Grimball and Arthur Dickson "A.D." Wharton. Four midshipmen were also present: Richard H. Bacot, H.S. Cook, Dabney M. Scales, and C.W. Tyler. Chief Engineer George City and Master's Mate John A. Wilson were also welcome newcomers, as was Virginian Dr. H.W.M. Washington.[10]

It was as well that McBlair had started to receive his officers and to make exit preparations. Not only was the Western Flotilla pounding away on Fort Pillow, but the incomplete armorclads at New Orleans, which were expected to protect the lower end of the Mississippi as the *Arkansas* and *Tennessee* guarded the upper waters, were about to be severely tested. On Good Friday, April 18, mortar-schooners of the U.S. West Gulf Coast Blockading Squadron undertook the bombardment of Forts Jackson and St. Philip, the bastions covering passage to the Crescent City from the Gulf of Mexico.

On April 24, contractor Shirley, according to a quote in William N. Still's *Iron Afloat: The Story of the Confederate Armorclads*, wrote to Maj. Gen. Beauregard assuring him that completion of the rams was within sight. "One of the boats will surely be ready in 15 days," he noted, "and the other in 30 days." It is unknown whether anyone in Richmond knew anything more about the boats than what Shirley had pledged.

Because the mortars failed to crush the forts below New Orleans, the Federal fleet commander, Flag Officer Farragut, also on the 24th, ran his warships past them, eliminating the southern division of the CRDF in the process. For lack of motive power, the *Louisiana* and *Mississippi* were unable to intervene and were neutralized and destroyed. The Federals anchored before New Orleans on April 25, the same day the *Arkansas* was commissioned. The bypassed Louisiana forts surrendered three days later. With the occupation of the Crescent City, the lower end of the Mississippi was effectively opened to the Union almost all the way to Vicksburg.

Although many New Orleans defenders became POWs, a number escaped when the Confederate army

Brig. Gen. Meriweather Jeff (M. Jeff) Thompson (1826–1876). *A West Virginian and one-time mayor of St. Joseph, Missouri, Thompson had organized a battalion ("The Swamp Rats") of the Missouri State Guard for Rebel service just after Fort Sumter. Eight companies of these troops (three artillery and five infantry) were recruited aboard the rams of the Confederate River Defense Force in the spring of 1862. Present with that squadron at the Battle of Plum Point Bend, Thompson, after the defeat of the CRDF at Memphis, would authorize the transfer of some of his men to the ram* Arkansas (Battles and Leaders, vol. I).

Left: **Midshipman Dabney M. Scales** (1841–1920). *Shown toward the end of his life, this Mississippian, a class of '59 USN midshipman, served aboard the CSS* Savannah *before joining the* Arkansas *crew. During the passage through the Union fleet above Vicksburg on July 15, the commander of the forward starboard Dahlgren won fame when he rescued the vessel's national ensign after it was shot away. Elevated in rank, he later served aboard the CSS Atlanta and was 5th lieutenant aboard the famous ocean raider* Shenandoah *(Confederate Veteran 28, 1920).* Above: **Lt. John "Jack" Grimball, CSN** (1840–1923). *This South Carolinian, a former USN midshipman, was commissioned a CSN lieutenant in May 1861 and was initially stationed at Savannah, Georgia. Assigned to the* Arkansas *while Cmdr. Charles H. McBlair was captain, he served Lt. Isaac Newton Brown as chief of the forward starboard battery (one Columbiad and one Dahlgren). Following the loss of the armorclad, he served aboard the steamer* Baltic *and the ocean raider* Shenandoah *(Battles and Leaders, vol. 3).*

evacuated the city. Numerous officers eluded capture, including army Maj. Gen. Mansfield Lovell (1822–1884) and Brig. Gen. Martin Luther "M.L." Smith (1819–1866) plus the navy's Lt. Brown and Lt. Charles W. Read (1840–1890), to name four.

Replacing New Orleans, an inland naval station was opened at Jackson, Mississippi, from which CSN operations in the West would be directed, while every civilian steamer that could depart the town did so as rapidly as possible, all pretty much headed in the same direction. At this time, 41 steamboats wearing the Stars and Bars escaped to or ran further up the Yazoo River, all bound to the Confederacy, as Harry Owens put it, "by national loyalty, self-interest, and circumstances."[11]

Four: From Memphis to Yazoo City, January–May, 1862

Also on April 25, Cmdr. McBlair went to the Memphis telegraph office and wired Secretary Mallory, informing the Richmond official that intelligence had just come in saying that Farragut's fleet had passed the New Orleans forts and "overpowered our boats." It was, Capt. Shirley later noted, "thought that the enemy's fleet was coming up the river."

It was a concern about the proximity of Farragut's fleet, the Memphis entrepreneur confessed, "that led to her [the *Arkansas*] removal." Still, contrary to the image which has come down over the years, old salt McBlair was deliberate in his evacuation planning, if somewhat hurried. McBlair informed Mallory that the *Arkansas* would depart that evening for Yazoo City, a little hamlet up the Mississippi River tributary of that name that nestled in the delta above Vicksburg. A thriving thousand-resident cotton port prior to the war, it was home to several businesses, including Frank Grimme's Mill, one of the largest sawmills in Mississippi. As the war intensified, the town's population and trade shrank.

Still, local steamboats continued to stop at Yazoo City, taking advantage of facilities to make repairs or transfer goods. R.A. Watkinson, Chief Clerk of the USN Bureau of Ordnance and Hydrography and a former area resident, would inform Flag Officer Charles H. Davis in June that "at high water boats carrying a thousand bales come out." And the community was far more accessible by land than might have been imagined.

Maj. Gen. Mansfield Lovell, CSA (1822–1884). *This Mexican War veteran resigned his post as New York City street commissioner to become a Confederate general and defender of New Orleans. He would move on to Vicksburg as commander of the Department of Southern Mississippi and East Louisiana. Succeeded there by Maj. Gen. Earl Van Dorn, Lovell would win praise for his actions at second Corinth in October. Although exonerated by an 1863 court of Inquiry for the loss of the Crescent City, he was given no further formal role (U.S. Army Military History Institute).*

George C. Waterman tells us that roads connected two nearby railroads stops. A planked-over route ran to Vaughan's Station and then a dirt road continued to Canton (25 miles total), northern terminus of the New Orleans, Jackson, and Great Northern. Another road, less improved and less-often employed, went to Bovina Station, on the Southern Railroad of Mississippi connection between Jackson and Vicksburg.

With New Orleans no longer an option, Yazoo City was considered "the safest point, and the one where the work can be most conveniently carried on." All of the materials available for end-game completion of both gunboats would be taken, along with the engines for the *Arkansas* and the *Tennessee*. Also included were cannon and four railroad iron chassis atop which gun carriages would be mounted.

Although Shirley had informed Beauregard a day earlier that he hoped to have the

Tennessee finished in a few weeks, McBlair was not as optimistic. Still, even though the Yankees were pounding on the door up at Fort Pillow, they weren't at Memphis yet (and wouldn't be, as things turned out, for another five weeks). Builder Emerson's men would continue their efforts to hammer the second ram's hull together and maybe they could get it launched and then towed down below. All of the necessary timber was "on the ground, and just out, ready to be put together." All, that was, "except two lots of lumber at the Memphis and Charleston Railroad depot; this was deck plank, etc." If Emerson could not get the *Tennessee* into the water, the naval commander had made arrangements with the city's provost marshal "for destruction of the boat on the stocks when rendered necessary."

Much of the iron for the *Tennessee* remained on the far side of the Mississippi, undelivered and not paid for by Shirley. Steam equipment at Memphis was able to punch holes in a small quantity of acquired T-rails brought across the river from a holding point on the Arkansas shore and would continue to do so right up to the end. Most of the other items comprising the *Tennessee*'s woodwork and interior fittings, including what Shirley called "iron and copper work," was apparently loaded aboard a barge, together with several cannon and other items not left aboard the unfinished *Arkansas*, including a second (disassembled) set of iron-bar drilling equipment. As the *Capitol* took on fuel and last minute departure concerns were addressed, the officers were permitted to post messages to their families.

Cmdr. McBlair initially kept the exact destination of the *Arkansas* a secret from every-

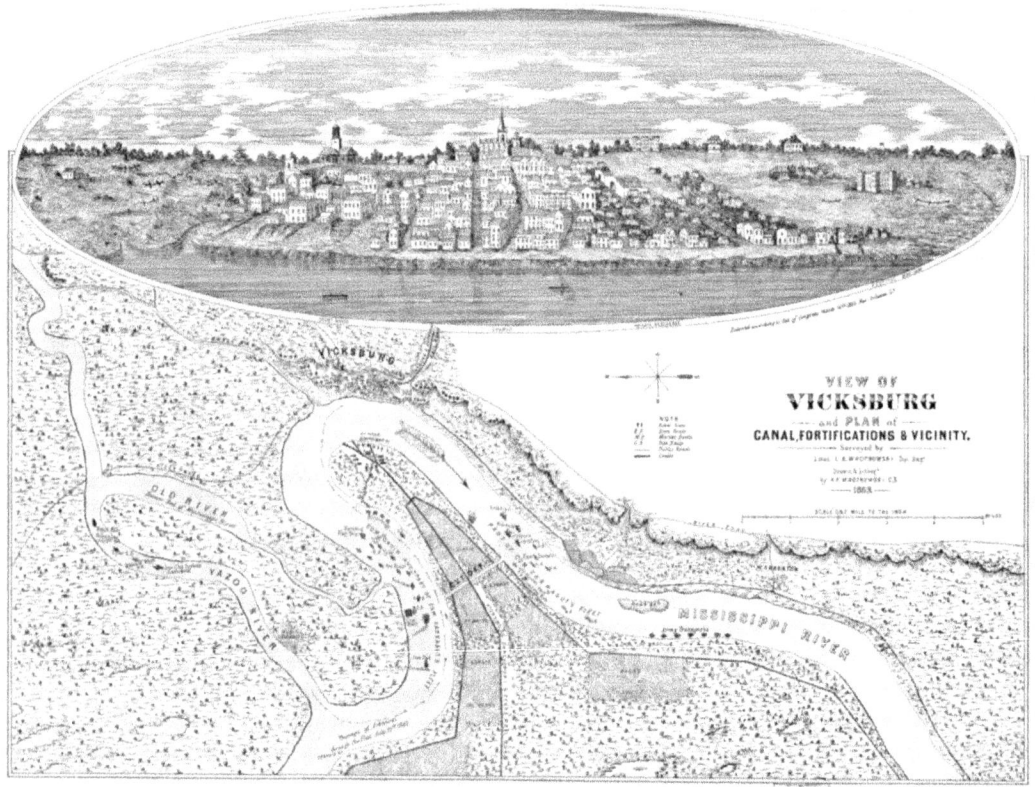

Vicksburg and Environs, 1862. *This contemporary map, upon which is superimposed an illustration of the Terraced City, shows the Mississippi and Yazoo rivers, plus many geographical features and the positions of Union naval elements (Library of Congress).*

one, aside from Secretary Mallory. Writing home at about the same time as his skipper was wiring the Navy Department, Lt. Stevens noted that the crew was "making every effort to move our boat away from here." It was expected that the exodus would commence that day or next, though "where exactly we are to go I do not know." All that Stevens and the others knew for certain was that it was McBlair's "intention to secret the vessel in some swamp until she can be completed." Towing both the *Arkansas* and the support barge, the *Capitol* undoubtedly departed Fort Pickering on April 26 or 27. With several refueling stops, she covered the approximately 300 miles to the mouth of the Yazoo River within several days.

In order that our story be as complete as possible, we should note here that several contemporary Northern newspaper stories indicated that the *Arkansas* and her equipment were removed from Memphis by two steamboats, not just the one. The *Brooklyn Daily Eagle* reported on July 30 that she was sent "up the river in tow of a steamboat, and her machinery, armament, etc followed her in another boat." Earlier, on July 25, Henry Bentley told the readers of the Philadelphia *Inquirer* that she was "taken in tow by two powerful steamboats and guided up the Yazoo, where she would be out of danger."

Probably not wishing to risk the chancy Old River cutoff into the Yazoo, the *Capitol* undoubtedly hauled the *Arkansas* three miles further and entered its regular channel at the mouth, located between Milliken's Bend and Tuscumbia Bend. The pair, with the barge, reached Yazoo City during the first week of May. The side-wheeler would remain, with the ram serving as her receiving ship, providing a place where officers, the few crewmen, and workers could sleep and take their meals.

Sometime later, Franc B. Wilkie, the famed *New York Times* correspondent known to his readers as "Galway" described the local geography. We should see it as contemporaries knew it in order to gain some appreciation of the ordeal about to be faced by the men of the *Arkansas*. A line of hills ran from Vicksburg, wrote Wilkie, and struck the Yazoo about 20 miles above its mouth. These hills were rough, added Chief Clerk Watkinson, throughout surrounding Warren County. The country between the river and the bluffs was alluvial, with swamps and lakes. It was known, said Wilkie, as the "Bottoms" of Mississippi. The rich land up to the riverbank was home to "a half dozen plantations scattered here and there, while along the river and around the lakes are built broad, high levees."

Distances between towns as the crow flies were approximately as follows: Vicksburg to mouth of Yazoo River, 12 miles; Vicksburg to Satartia on the Yazoo River, 32 miles; and Satartia to Yazoo City, 17.3 miles. Above the latter community ran the Sunflower River and Deer Creek. A small trading post was located on the Yazoo at Liverpool Landing, 25 miles below Yazoo City. Prior to the war, it was a thriving steamboat stop and shipping point for cotton. Rudloff Ridge, a towering hill named for its first white settler, dominated the area behind the landing. The town of Greenwood was located approximately 160 miles north of Yazoo City, about three miles below the source of the Yazoo, where it is formed by the confluence of the Tallahatchie and Yalabusha rivers. It, too, was a thriving trading center.[12]

CHAPTER FIVE

Five Weeks Up the Yazoo, Early May–Late June 1862

Towed by the steamer *Capitol*, the unfinished *Arkansas*, together with a barge filled with miscellaneous construction materials, guns, and other equipment, arrived at Yazoo City, Mississippi, during the first week of May 1862. Part of builder Primus Emerson's work force remained behind at Fort Pickering just below Memphis, desperately attempting to build a sister ram, the *Tennessee*, to a point where she could be launched and also towed downstream. That gunboat's frame was completed and workmen raced to plank her. Small quantities of T-rails were brought across the river from a holding point on the Arkansas shore and steam equipment on site continued to drill holes into each bar so that it could be attached to the hull and not-yet-constructed casemate. The laborers would continue to ply their tools right up to the end.

Meanwhile, at Yazoo City, according to prime contractor John T. Shirley, who accompanied the ram, work was resumed on the *Arkansas*. A set of steam drilling machinery removed from the *Tennessee* was taken off the barge and reassembled; operators resumed punching six holes in every bar of railroad iron destined for attachment to the hull. In addition, mechanics worked on her engines. At the same time, the Army Quartermaster Department chartered the 824-ton side-wheel steamer *Magnolia* to provide support. Without a passenger cabin, the 258-foot long cotton freighter might have proven very helpful, but she was chartered for only eight days. This hire, according to Harry Owens, was worth $650 per day.

On or about May 5 or 6, Cmdr. Charles H. McBlair, captain of the *Arkansas*, received a telegram from Mississippi governor John J. Pettus (1813–1867) warning that Federal vessels were coming up the Mississippi and were possibly after his gunboat. Flag Officer Farragut was determined to test the defenses of Vicksburg and, indeed, the Union warships *Iroquois* and *Richmond* left the Crescent City on the latter date, headed toward Baton Rouge, the Louisiana state capital. According to Midshipman Dabney Scales, McBlair was advised by "the big wigs" to take his vessel further on up the narrow, winding stream to the town of Greenwood. Thoroughly alarmed that his "hidey hole" might have been discovered, the Maryland-born commander quickly ordered his lieutenants and contractor Shirley to strike camp and to have everything already taken ashore broken down and loaded back aboard the deck of the *Arkansas*, the *Capitol*, and the barge. This included 400 of the precious punched T-bars that were stacked aboard the latter.[1]

The warning sent to McBlair by Pettus was accurate, if a tad premature. Flag Officer Farragut knew from "a man I had on board ... who is just from Memphis and Vicksburg" that the *Arkansas* had been transferred out of Memphis. From Baton Rouge on May 10 he wrote to Cmdr. Samuel Phillips Lee, who was commanding advance fleet units en route toward Natchez and Vicksburg. Noting that the enemy was just now beginning to fortify Vicksburg and had only about six guns emplaced, he directly referenced the Rebel armorclad: "If it is possible for you to get a gunboat into the Yazoo River a few miles, they may be able to capture or compel the enemy to destroy the ram now building there, which is a thing of the first importance, as they say it will be finished in three weeks."

The *Arkansas* and her equipment barge, in tow of the *Capitol*, departed Yazoo City on May 7, the day before Baton Rouge was occupied by Federal bluejackets. The ram's voyage up the twisting river was made more difficult by the spring rise, which had begun to overflow the entire area. The two boats came to off Greenwood three days later. The gunboat was maneuvered alongside a pier and the barge was tied alongside. The *Capitol* remained as receiving ship and floating barracks. Although her auxiliary service was possible, there is no evidence that the *Magnolia* participated in this transfer. As her charter would by now have been completed, if she did accompany the ram and her towboat to Greenwood, she did not remain with them in further support.

The morale of the workmen and officers who remained behind was down and Midshipman Scales recorded the scene after Capt. McBlair took the governor's advice and retreated upriver: "[T]he move occasioned us the loss of more than a week's time before we could get our workshops and machinery for carrying on the work put up ashore. The river which had been rising for sometime past, now overflowed the whole town.... We had to build scaffolds around the workshops and alongside the vessel, to keep workmen out of the water. Many of them were taken sick and the rest were dissatisfied."

In a letter home written the first night after arriving at Greenwood, Lt. Henry K. Stevens confided that the *Arkansas* "can not now be finished in time to have any great influence on events." He continued: "It will be fully a month more before she can be ready for action." Stevens, like others, was dispirited. "I long to hear how things are going on with the Charleston boats," he sighed. "I wish I had remained there." Over the next three weeks the waters of the Yazoo steadily rose, levies began to break, and the escaping water flooded over her banks. The pier to which the *Arkansas* was tied was submerged and her location relative to the shore grew steadily more distant.

It was during this trying time that the barge, loaded with machinery including the steam drilling apparatus, the drilled iron bars, and several cannon, took on excess water and sank. These contents were scattered across the river bottom by the current. This accident was a near-fatal blow to the armorclad's future, as immediate retrieval appeared impossible. Contractor Shirley immediately sent word to Emerson at Memphis to have the second set of hole-punching machinery broken down and sent to Greenwood, but it would take weeks for it to be delivered. In the end, it wasn't.

Cmdr. McBlair was able to quickly contract with the town of Greenwood for the use of a bell boat, though whether the craft was a steamboat or a large barge is unknown. David Meagher described to the author the type of diving bell employed:

> A diving bell was at least six feet in width at the bottom to allow entry and exit of a diver or divers. It was at least seven feet in height above to allow the divers to stand on a cross member and get a brief rest while their lungs took in fresh air trapped within the bell. The bell was weighted near the bottom to keep this portion always at the bottom and keep the air up and inside. The sides and top were round, as this shape gives the best resistance to pressure. This simple technology had existed since the treasure galleon days. Eads used these bells in his salvage business on the Mississippi.

It is unknown whether the men who dived down on the wrecked barge from the bell boat were crewmen from the *Arkansas* or *Capitol* or contract divers hired in the town.

As May on the Yazoo advanced, the river broke completely through its levees and it became necessary to ferry stores and other supplies to the *Arkansas* by small boat. The distance between the craft and dry land now stretched a distance of almost four miles. The heat intensified, seasonal sicknesses (mostly malaria) arrived, and, whether or not McBlair was able to make any headway with the lost barge, progress on the ram project slowed significantly.[2]

While McBlair and Shirley were being towed up the Yazoo to Greenwood in early May, Capt. Montgomery's Northern Division of the Confederate River Defense Force (CRDF), with Brig. Gen. M. Jeff Thompson embarked, congregated in the waters off Fort Pillow, about 60 miles above Memphis. On May 10, it engaged elements of the Union's Western Flotilla at Plum Point Bend, above the bastion, sinking the City Series gunboats *Cincinnati* and *Mound City*. Both sides claimed victory in the 1 hour, 10 minute engagement. Casualties were light (2 Confederate, 1 Union dead), but, in the end, the blow to Federal prestige would be significant. In one of the few "fleet actions" of the Civil War, the ready Rebel rams sank two of their ill-prepared and superior Union opponents (quickly repaired and returned to service) and, though damaged, all managed to withdraw as planned. Memphis and the *Tennessee* were spared for the moment. "Another month passed away," wrote John

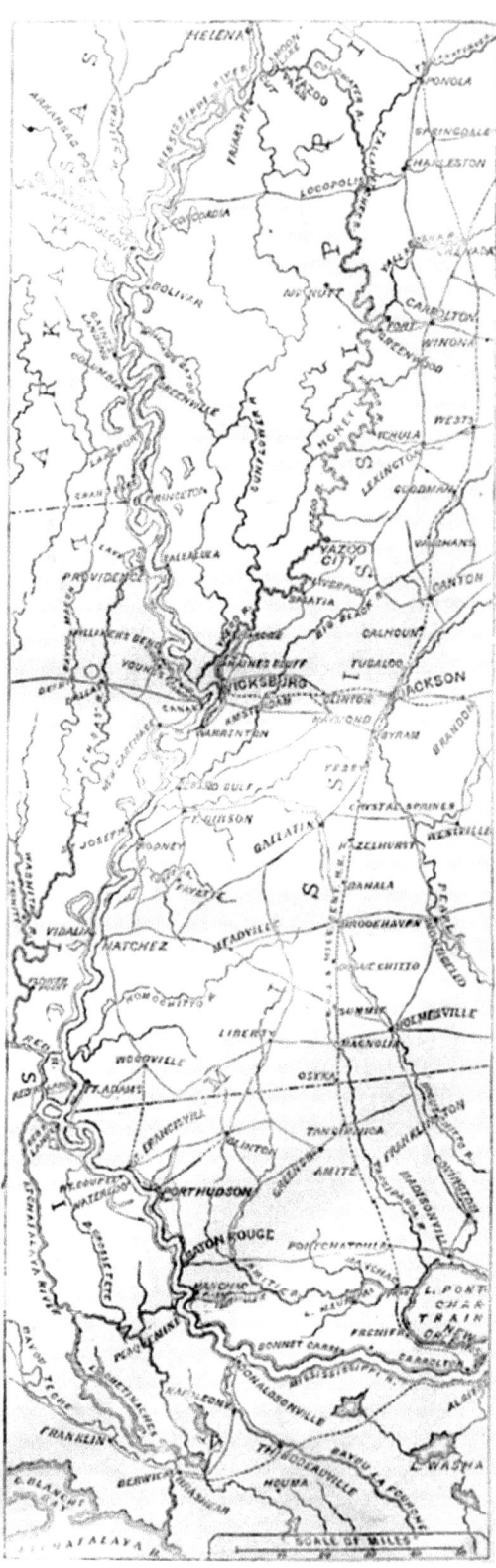

Vicksburg–Baton Rouge–Yazoo River Theater of Operations. *This contemporary map amply places the various towns and geographical locations reviewed in our text, beginning with Grenada in the northeast and running south to Baton Rouge. Among the Mississippi state communities also noted are Greenwood, Canton, Yazoo City, Liverpool, Satartia, and Vicksburg (*Harper's Weekly, *March 28, 1863).*

Five: Five Weeks Up the Yazoo, Early May–Late June 1862 83

Yazoo City Levee, ca. 1939. *This photograph depicts the area near the* Arkansas *completion site. Except for some dredging, little had changed in the years afterwards (U.S. Army Corps of Engineers).*

Abbott, "of languid, monotonous, ineffective bombardment on both sides." Most of the time, the shells went south from the Federal mortar boats, but occasionally, they were dispatched north from the citadel.[3]

"The occupation of Vicksburg," wrote C.S.A. engineer Samuel H. Lockett for the *Battles and Leaders* series, "was the immediate result of the fall of New Orleans." In the weeks following the town's loss, displaced Louisiana regiments made rendezvous and, together with units from Mississippi, headed up to Vicksburg to organize its defense and provide its garrison. Possessed of tall bluffs above the river—some over 200 feet—the town was chosen over Helena, Arkansas, by the leader of the Army of the Mississippi, Gen. Pierre G.T. Beauregard, who so informed the retreating Maj. Gen. Mansfield Lovell. The Creole commander, called the "Napoleon in Gray" by his biographer T. Harry Williams, believed from personal knowledge that the elevated community was the most defensible location that remained in Confederate hands on the entire Lower Mississippi.

Federal warships were also, meanwhile, probing further up the Big Muddy during the rest of the month. Natchez was captured by the USN on May 12, the same day Brig. Gen. Martin Luther Smith, acting under orders from Lovell, assumed command at Vicksburg. Four days later the lead Union naval squadron shelled Grand Gulf, Mississippi. By this time, rumors were rife concerning Confederate ironclad construction both on the Atlantic seaboard and in the Midwest. Additionally, it was also soon known that the first of the Rebel monsters, the *Virginia*, was no more. When the Federals took Norfolk, Virginia, the *Virginia* had been blown up by her own crew off Craney Island to prevent capture, but concern with others remained. One officer, Cmdr. Henry H. Bell, with the Gulf Squadron wrote in his diary: "We must seek this great danger before it hunts us."

The siege of Vicksburg, which would not end until July 1863, officially began on May 18 when the advance division of Flag Officer Farragut's fleet arrived off Vicksburg and demanded the town's surrender. The Confederate post commander, Col. Jason L. Autry, set the tone for the next 13 months in his reply to Cmdr. Lee. "I have to state that Mississippians don't know, and refuse to learn, how to surrender to an enemy," he challenged. "If

The Arkansas and Capitol at Yazoo City. When the Arkansas arrived at Yazoo City, *"the iron of her armor extended only a foot, or a little more, about the water line."* Lt. George W. Gift noted that, even after the bars lost with the barge were salvaged, *"there was not a sufficiency of iron on hand to finish the entire ship."* Bolting the salvaged iron to the armorclad's casemate initially posed a problem, as the drills needed to prepare it were not available. To replace the lost T-rail hole-punching equipment, Lt. Isaac Newton Brown and contractor John T. Shirley came up with an ingenious idea for *"extemporized drilling machines."* The Capitol was maneuvered to the river side of the Arkansas and lashed on. A crane was fashioned forward from hewed tree trunks and fitted aboard the steamboat. Her hoisting engine was rigged via, according to David Meagher, *"a belt drive from a capstan in sort of sawmill fashion,"* to power replacement drilling equipment made on blacksmith forges. The smiths in turn prepared additional iron bars for the casemate, along with other needed items, *"while dozens of hands were doing similar work by hand."* Once the casemate—the side walls of which were vertical and not slanted as here depicted—was armored, the crane was employed to insert the cannon, carriages, and certain other large items and machinery *(*Battles and Leaders, *vol. 3).*

Commodore Farragut or Brigadier-General Butler can team them, let them come and try." Newly arrived Brig. Gen. Smith, commanding Rebel forces in Vicksburg, echoed those sentiments but less flamboyantly.

Interestingly enough, orders were dispatched from Washington on May 19 that required the West Gulf Coast Blockading Squadron to "open the river Mississippi and effect a junction with Flag Officer Davis, commanding (pro tem) the Western Flotilla." Although that directive was yet to be officially received, Flag Officer Farragut arrived below Vicksburg on May 22 aboard the squadron flagship *Hartford*. Accompanying the Northern hero of New Orleans were two more large warships, eight smaller ones, and 1,400 army troops, under Brig. Gen. Thomas Williams, aboard transports. The blue-coated soldiers disembarked and set up

Five: Five Weeks Up the Yazoo, Early May–Late June 1862

camp on the De Soto Peninsula, a finger of land opposite Vicksburg. Williams, in a letter home, reported the general physical situation: "You cannot conceive the flooded condition of the country on both banks of the Mississippi. Water 5 and more feet over the levees. Utter destruction to cotton and other crops. Destruction to cattle and property. Houses almost submerged, abandoned by their inhabitants. One wide desolation, with here and there a spot only above water from here to New Orleans. So I'm told it is above Vicksburg, and yet the June rise of water is to come."

Gazing through long spyglasses, the Union sailors saw formidable defenses that soon totaled 29 guns in seven batteries atop the high bluffs north, south, and behind the city. Brig. Gen. Smith was rapidly building up his force, growing it steadily from the three batteries and five regiments he found only two weeks earlier. The number of heavy gun emplacements were increased, and two, later three, water batteries were situated for a distance of about three miles in front of the town.

Flag Officer David Glasgow Farragut, USN (*Library of Congress*).

The upper batteries, located below Fort Hill, commanded the bend in the river above the city. This location was operated by the newly arrived First Tennessee Heavy Artillery Regiment. Among the units billeted nearby was the 27th Louisiana, which established its base at Camp Tucker, two miles above the city and about a mile back from the river. Her soldiers were able to watch the comings and goings of the Federal navy with ease. The South Fork lower batteries, at the southern end of the town, were manned by the First Louisiana Artillery, while the center batteries, those directly in front of the town, were operated by the Eighth Louisiana Artillery Battalion. Some 3,000 men of a contingent that would eventually total 15,000 soldiers reached the town by rail. Among them was one reassigned naval lieutenant, Isaac Newton Brown, who (although the records do not say) may have initially helped, as he had at Fort Pillow and Columbus, with emplacement of cannon.

Despite the obstacles he faced, Cmdr. McBlair's failure to finish the *Arkansas* led to his relief, and that of his executive officer, Lt. Guthrie. Neither he nor his crew knew that the change was coming, but as surely as the river rose, his days in command of the Western ram might be seen as numbered. It has been said that the sight of the armorclad stranded motionless in the middle of the flooded Yazoo was discouraging not only to her men, but also to the citizens of the town of Greenwood. The more prominent among them reportedly telegraphed directly to the Confederate Navy Department asking that a more "energetic officer" be appointed. Lt. Stevens later wrote that he had heard that the governor of Mississippi had also solicited a change.

While civic request may have had some impact, the impetus for McBlair's removal

USS Hartford. *The siege of Vicksburg, which would not end until July 1863, officially began on May 18, 1862, when the advance fleet division of Flag Officer Farragut arrived off Vicksburg and demanded the town's surrender—which was promptly refused. Interestingly enough, orders were dispatched from Washington on May 19 that required his West Gulf Coast Blockading Squadron to "open the river Mississippi and effect a junction with Flag Officer [Charles H.] Davis, commanding (pro tem) the Western Flotilla." Although that directive was yet to be officially received, the squadron flagship Hartford arrived below Vicksburg on May 22, the same day Richmond decided to appoint Lt. Isaac Newton Brown commander of the* Arkansas *(Library of Congress).*

came from another quarter, old *Arkansas* friend Gen. Beauregard. The reader will recall that it was the theater commander, who now had his hands full some miles to the north with Maj. Gen. Henry Halleck, who had sent Lt. Guthrie to Memphis to report on the ram some weeks earlier.

While large numbers of blue and gray troops made ready to battle at Corinth, Mississippi, the Creole general, on May 19, made another inquiry about the state of the *Arkansas'* readiness. When he learned of her sad state of affairs at Greenwood from Brig. Gen. Daniel Ruggles (1810–1897), his officer in charge of depots and the rear guard, he urged navy secretary Mallory to send the boat new leadership. On May 22, Richmond decided to act and to appoint Lt. Brown as both the armorclad's captain and building superintendent. Secretary Mallory appreciated that Brown was a driving officer who had experience in ironclad construction, even though fortune had thus far prevented him from completing any. Both Charles McBlair and John J. Guthrie were sent relief telegrams on May 24 and ordered back to Richmond.

Unable to persuade the defenders of Vicksburg to hand over their town and frustrated that Brig. Gen. Williams refused to assault it with his small force, Flag Officer Farragut, meanwhile, decided to blockade the town and to fire upon it from time to time "until the battle of Corinth shall decide its fate." The *Hartford* returned to New Orleans leaving Lee and his oceangoing gunboats to watch the bluffs. While the citizens of Vicksburg observed the Yankee navy below their terraced town, events near Memphis were about to come to a head. Com. James Montgomery's CRDF had patrolled the waters around Fort Pillow for almost a month, watching the U.S. Western Flotilla then bombarding the citadel from long range. During much of this time, Brig. Gen. Thompson was away on other command business and his Missourians temporarily on board the river squadron became embroiled in disputes and jealousies with the officers and other crewmen originally assigned to the rams. The "little difficulties" between the factions — as Thompson, nicknamed the "Swamp Fox of the Confederacy," termed the initial incidents — grew into misunderstandings so intense as to destroy the efficiency of the merged crews.

In Vicksburg on May 26, Lt. Isaac Newton Brown, like a number of other Confederate navymen who had exited New Orleans following its capture, was undoubtedly expecting a telegram from Secretary Mallory redeploying him to another post. Each morning he would check with the desk attendant at the Prentiss House, the hotel where he was staying on Levee Street near the river, to see if one had come. Other officers newly in town and hoping for new orders from the Navy Department were Mississippian Lt. Charles W. Read, late acting commander of the gunboat *McRae* who had travelled down from Fort Pillow to recruit sailors for Cmdr. Pinkney. Tennessean Lt. George W. Gift and Louisianan Lt. Alphonso Barbot were just passing through; both were actually en route to the naval station at Jackson.

That day, May 26, the vessels left behind below Vicksburg by Farragut opened a systematic bombardment. It would continue, lasting all day some days, though there was a break at midday for lunch. Most of the civilians who remained in town regularly visited pre-dug bomb shelters. This inauguration of Yankee fire was not initially answered, as the defenders held their fire to conserve ammunition and continued to build their fortification.

Going about his unspecified duties, Lt. Brown may have taken a professional interest in the Federal shoot and watched from some secure location. Not all would have been so dispassionate as a naval veteran. Dr. Ballard quotes the reaction of one Confederate defender who heard the big naval shells for the first time. When they fell, the soldier remembered, they made "such a miserable squawking & scratching & getting along through the wind [as] I never did hear."

Brown's biographer, Charles Getchell, indicates that, at some point during the day, the lieutenant received the not-unexpected transfer wire from Secretary Mallory. Brown himself recalled for *Battles & Leaders* that it arrived two days later. Ripping open the telegram even as the bombs fell, Brown read Secretary Mallory's instructions to proceed up to Greenwood as soon as it was possible. Once there, he was to "assume command of the Confederate gunboat *Arkansas* and finish and equip that vessel without regard to the expenditure of men or money." The lieutenant remembered the armorclad's being under construction at Memphis some months earlier, but "had not heard 'til then of her escape from the general wreck of our Mississippi River defenses."

The Union Navy returned to shell Vicksburg again next day, Brown's 45th birthday. Assuming Getchell is correct, this would also have been the day that the newly empowered naval officer made arrangements for his removal to Greenwood, "more than 200 miles by water north of Vicksburg." Brown would be pretty much on his own out in the Delta. Flag Officer William F. Lynch, an unknown quantity, was not yet present and McBlair still outranked him. Even with the secretary's orders, Brown would have to superintend through the force of his personality and gather support directly from the local population and the Confederate army.

Brig. Gen. Daniel Ruggles, who was about to transfer up to Grenada to establish a special district (within whose lines lay the towns of Greenwood and Yazoo City), would be his closest military contact. Brown and his wife, Eliza, resided to the northeast in Coahoma County; she would later become a refugee in the town. Initiating contact while the general was still in Vicksburg, the navyman learned of Ruggles' continuing interest and received a promise of support.

Communications being what they were during the Civil War, news and orders could be transmitted almost instantaneously over great distances by telegraph when the wires were up or take days or even weeks to arrive. Sometimes one recipient of an order or communication received his notification, while another who was also to have it did not. Time, distance and technology played a role, while military-civilian politics could and also did have an impact upon who knew what when. Dispatches and reports sent between Washington or Richmond and the Mississippi routinely required two to three weeks to arrive, with the situation worse in the Confederacy than in the Union. For example, Chester Hearn tells us that it took until May 8 for Flag Officer Farragut's New Orleans victory report to reach the U.S. Navy Department. Secretary of the navy Gideon Welles in the meantime relied upon reports carried by the *Richmond Daily Examiner* and the *Petersburg Express*. Perhaps surprisingly, the same Rebel newspapers also gave him news of Farragut's progress on the Mississippi—or lack of it.

In Federal circles, another famous naval example of poor order timing involved the dispatch of Capt. Andrew Hull Foote to relieve the first Western Flotilla commander, Cmdr. John Rodgers II. Rodgers, in command of the timberclads en route to capture Paducah back in September 1861, was expected to be in St. Louis where his orders were sent. Thus he did not know of the change until Capt. Foote caught up with him in midstream, climbed aboard the *Tyler*, and told him he was no longer in charge. Such was the case with Brown, McBlair, and, presumably, Guthrie.

Still another failure to properly communicate, coupled with jealousy, threatened to undermine the efficiency of local Confederate defense. At the same time Gen. Mansfield Lovell dispatched Brig. Gen. Smith to command at Vicksburg, Gen. Beauregard, in northeast Mississippi, sent Brig. Gen. Ruggles. By some quirk, Richmond mapmakers had placed Vicksburg in Beauregard's district and the state capital and military department headquarters at Jackson in Lovell's.

When Ruggles arrived at Vicksburg on May 22, not only was Smith present but Lovell had come up from Louisiana as well. To avoid a command dispute, Beauregard advised Ruggles two days later to back off and had the War Department redraw the lines. The crusty Ruggles, a transplanted Virginian originally from Massachusetts, left Vicksburg to Lovell and Smith and established his headquarters at Grenada just as Brown was leaving for Greenwood. The harried Beauregard advised all: "The great point is to defend the river at Vicksburg. The question of who does it must be of secondary consideration."

When Beauregard was sacked by President Jefferson Davis after the battle of Corinth, lesser command changes were also made. Among these was the replacement of Maj. Gen. Lovell as commander of the Department of Southern Mississippi and East Louisiana by Maj. Gen. Van Dorn (after whom a CRDF ram was named), chief of the Confederate Army of the West. Lovell learned of his dismissal just as Rodgers and McBlair did — from his successor, in his case, Maj. Gen. Van Dorn.

The flooding at Greenwood may have prevented McBlair and Guthrie from receiving direct word from Mallory concerning their displacement. If the telegraph wires were down, messages would have had to be conveyed from Vicksburg to Greenwood by steamer, a process that could take several days, despite the fact that numerous craft worked the Yazoo

Five: Five Weeks Up the Yazoo, Early May–Late June 1862

River system. Brown, on the other hand, was in Vicksburg where the telegraph still hummed when he received his new assignment.[4]

Lt. Brown reached Greenwood on May 29 to find his "new command four miles from dry land." Going aboard the receiving ship *Capitol*, he obtained a boat and crew to row him out to the craft. The bearded sailor was shocked further as he approached a structure that might have been described as a nearly derelict. "Her condition was not encouraging," he later confessed in a great understatement. Stepping aboard, Brown was taken to Lt. Henry Stevens, to whom he showed his orders from Mallory to take command, and asked to be directed to the ram's captain. When that worthy was located, the newcomer presented his credentials. As McBlair read the secretary's orders giving Brown, in the words of Stevens, "full authority to take any steps necessary to hurry the completion," he was doubtless flabbergasted.

Brown and McBlair, with contractor Shirley and perhaps also in company with

Top: **Gen. Pierre G.T. Beauregard, CSA** (1818–1893). *The "Hero of Sumter" was transferred west in early 1862, becoming theater commander after Gen. Albert Sidney Johnston was killed at the Battle of Shiloh in April. A friend of the Arkansas project, he consistently sought information on her construction progress and, finding it too slow after the vessel's transfer to Greenwood, requested that Capt. McBlair be replaced. In May, Lt. Isaac Newton Brown was ordered to take over and complete the armorclad without regard to method or cost (National Archives).*

Bottom: **Brig. Gen. Martin Luther "M.L." Smith, CSA** (1819–1866). *Engineer Smith did not become a brigadier until April 1862, even though he built and commanded the Chalmette defenses at New Orleans before racing north to take over command at Vicksburg on May 12. Held POW for seven months after the citadel's capture in 1863, he later served as chief engineer for the Army of Northern Virginia and the Army of Tennessee, before turning his attention to strengthening the defenses of Mobile (US Army Military History Institute).*

Stevens and Guthrie, inspected the *Arkansas*. "The vessel was a mere hull" without armor. Moving inside the dark, un-ironed casemate, lit only by lanterns because no gun ports were yet cut, the group saw that the "engines were apart and guns without carriages were lying about the deck." Pieces of machinery, various supplies, and scrap iron also littered the deck. There was almost no evidence of any work being done. Indeed, only five carpenters were in action and just one blacksmith's forge was in use. Brown was appalled: "things were much less advanced" than had been hoped.

Initially, some minor efforts were made to get things off on a positive note. Early in their rounds, Brown told his companions "of some encouraging successes in northwestern Virginia." In return, he learned that, with the help of the bell boat provided by the town of Greenwood, the river floor had been dragged and most of the iron and some of the other equipment lost from the sunken barge was recovered. The lieutenant's time with the *Eastport* and the New Orleans armorclads, on the other hand, gave him the experience to know that McBride and Shirley were incorrect when they hopefully forecast that it might be possible to raise steam within 10 days. He sensed that it was also "quite out of the question" to get the vessel's armament ready within that period.

Capt. Shirley told Brown that he had since learned that the Confederate government had ordered "that the machinery upon which he depended for fitting the iron at Memphis has been ordered away from there." This was the set he had earlier requested Primus Emerson to forward. Would it be better, when the *Arkansas* was finished, to take her to Memphis without the armor having been fastened to her casemate or risk her on the river without steam, he wondered.

Both men agreed that facilities at Greenwood for completion of the *Arkansas* were simply inadequate. In addition, the Yazoo, recently risen so dangerously high, was beginning to fall. Remaining at this upper town carried the very real danger that the ram would end up grounded high and dry. It was decided that the vessel would be taken back down to a deeper anchorage at Yazoo City "where the hills reached the river" and "where greater facilities exist for getting work done." Taller banks and better-prepared levees also offered greater protection from flooding, even though, as Brown and the men knew, they "were within 50 miles of the Union fleets." None of the men talking over the location options knew that Memphis was about to be captured. In a letter home penned later in the day, Lt. Stevens revealed his boat's upcoming transfer: "We will get off tonight or in the morning."

Brown's reaction to McBlair was not good and grew worse as the day progressed. Discipline, such as it was practiced by the Marylander, was found to be a significant problem, or, as the new chief put it, "difficulty seems to exist as to men working or submitting to proper control." As he listened to a litany of complaints, concerns, and excuses, the lieutenant grew angry with his seemingly lethargic senior. Although he was no longer making the decisions, McBlair was a superior officer due a certain amount of respect. Until his predecessor actually received written orders from Mallory to depart, Brown would tolerate his presence so long as he did not interfere or cause dissention.

Lt. Stevens found the new commander a "pushing man," though he personally wasn't certain "what he will accomplish, but we shall see." The initial opinions of Brown from Shirley, Guthrie, or any of the other men on the scene is not recorded. Stevens was now appointed executive officer succeeding Guthrie, and Brown immediately sent him to Vicksburg with orders to locate and instruct at least three newly arriving CSN junior officers to report aboard the ram at Yazoo City.

Brown wanted immediate and enforceable progress. In a letter sent up to Grenada late in the afternoon, the Kentuckian told Brig. Gen. Ruggles of the upcoming move to Yazoo City and asked him to send there 25 carpenters and five machinists. He also wanted 20 armed volunteers and an army lieutenant to "act under my orders." Those men could not only help with the boat but also act as security and maybe even be trained as marines. After a visit from Lt. Brown, the solons of Greenwood dispatched help the next day. Several men joined the crew, while plantation owners lent slaves. Yazoo River pilot James Shacklett joined the vessel, ready to offer his river knowledge and navigational skills to those of the *Capitol*'s Mississippi pilot, John G. Hodges.

Ropes and grapples from the bell boat continued to drop to the Yazoo floor, retrieving the precious iron and the lost cannon identified by divers. Water was pumped from the hull of the armorclad which, in the past few days, had begun to founder. The same day, Maj. Gen. Halleck's Federal command, including soldiers under Maj. Gen. John Pope, captured Corinth, Mississippi, 93 miles east of Memphis. Coming less than a month after the Battle of Shiloh and the capture of New Orleans. Halleck's success forced Gen. Beauregard, as part of a strategic Confederate withdrawal, to abandon all Mississippi River positions north of Vicksburg.

Under tow of the *Capitol*, the *Arkansas* returned slowly downstream to Yazoo City on the last day of the month. Near her new anchorage "upon the east bank ... about the southern boundary of the small city," was the 283-ton side-wheel gunboat *Mobile*, an ex–Gulf of Mexico tugboat that was ordered to the town for conversion into an ironclad following the loss of New Orleans. There, too, was the famous *Star of the West*, now officially known as the CSS *St. Philip*. Following her failed attempt to reinforce Fort Sumter in January 1861, she was captured off the Texas coast that April 18 by Galveston militia under the command of Col. Earl Van Dorn and impressed into Confederate service.[5]

In early May, as McBlair was taking the *Arkansas* to Greenwood, Southern defenders started work on a defensive log and earthwork raft at Liverpool Landing, about 65 miles up the Yazoo from its confluence with the Mississippi and 22 to 25 miles below Yazoo City. It was designed to block the stream and function, as the *New York Times* later described it, as "a perfect lock against ascending boats." Spanning the river, it was initially protected by two 42-pdrs. mounted on Rudloff Ridge behind the landing, plus one company of infantry. Lt. Brown would soon write to Brig. Gen. Lovell at Jackson asking that a company of artillery and a regiment of infantry move to the raft's defense. Even now this obstruction was strengthened regularly by prefabricated components which were towed downstream from Yazoo City for placement by the *Hartford City* under a 25-day charter valued at $1,000 per day. On more than one occasion, James Oliver Hazard Perry Sessions, owner of the Rokeby Plantation, observed the 150-ton side-wheeler, which Way does not list, "towing two flats" loaded with material for the project.

Going ashore, the armorclad's commander set up his headquarters at the plantation home of Mrs. Lizzie McFarland Blackmore, whose husband was one of those Rebel officers charged with creating the log barrier below Yazoo City. Learning that the force assigned to build and protect it was quite small, Brown dispatched the gunboat *Mobile* to assist in its defense "should the enemy appear." Mrs. Blackmore, in a January 14, 1887, letter to ex–President Davis, told of this meeting and of Brown's solicitation.

While he was ashore, Lt. Stevens established a camp near the river's edge. Tents were set up and cook fires lit. It is likely that hunting parties were dispatched to bring back game; the surrounding area teemed with deer, turkey, raccoons, opossums, squirrels, and other wildlife.

Returning to the levee wearing his construction superintendent's hat, the *Arkansas* captain, as he put it in a letter to Brig. Gen. Ruggles written a few days later, saw to it that "the work of fitting the vessel for service is now actively begun." His exhortation to the men gathered around as to the difficulties lying ahead was not, however, well received. Indeed, as he later noted, it was necessary to be extremely tough and "to assume extraordinary powers both with workmen and officers." Brown's biggest immediate concern was his predecessor, who was still, unhappily, on the scene.

Capt. McBlair and Lt. Guthrie had accompanied the *Arkansas* back to Yazoo City, but, at some point not long after her arrival below, the new captain and the old came nearly to blows. McBlair deeply resented the junior officer's assertions that he had not done his utmost, given the difficulties, to complete the *Arkansas*, and Brown would brook no interference or editorializing as he tried to organize and motivate the handful of available laborers to perform the impossible. As he demonstrated back at the time he was superintending construction of the *Eastport*, Brown was a man who neither suffered fools gladly nor tolerated inferences against his honor. "Even though such was obviously not his intention, "the lukewarmness or inefficiency" of the relieved commander "amounted to practical treason," Brown concluded.

Exercising his "extraordinary powers," the new skipper had his predecessor sent ashore. McBlair did not go gracefully, but the new leader ended the strife dramatically and not without effect upon those watching. As Brown later told Ruggles, "I came near to shooting him and must have done so had he not consented and got out of my way." The lieutenant knew that he was "technically inside the mutiny act" even as McBlair returned to Richmond "to denounce me, no doubt."

The manner in which the lieutenant "got rid of McBlair" was a story told throughout the Confederate Navy for some time to come. Gunner Henry Melvil Doak, who commanded a battery aboard the *Charleston*, one of Brown's later ironclads, remembered after meeting him that this was the man who "had once taken command of the *Arkansas* at Vicksburg by presenting the muzzle of a shot gun at the breast of Capt. Blair [sic]...." Fortunately for all concerned, Brown's energy was needed at Yazoo City and McBlair was judged a poor construction boss who, despite his rank, was expendable. Midshipman Scales, who witnessed the tension between the two captains, compared them in a letter written to his father a few days after the *Arkansas* tied up at Yazoo City: "Captain McBlair is a brave man and a gallent [sic] officer. He would make a very good Commandant of a Navy Yard, where he could have his sub officers, but in a case of this kind, where there are no dockyard appliances at hand, Lieutenant Brown is a superior man, being younger and more energetic."

The lieutenant and not the commander was now fully in charge. A few more malcontents were placed in the local jail and the men who remained appeared ready to begin anew to help finish the ram. Lt. Stevens returned in company with Mr. Read about this time, riding up the river road from Vicksburg via Liverpool Landing. Also, Lt. Gift arrived in a skiff and brought his personal gear and a guitar. Lt. Barbot made his way down from Jackson riding a mule on the leg from Bovina Station; he was joined by Acting Masters Samuel Milliken and John L. Phillips. If possible, Brown now hoped, the *Arkansas* would "hit them hard when ready," perhaps in as little as 20 days.[6]

After Corinth's loss, the evacuation of Fort Pillow and Memphis was ordered by Gen. Beauregard on June 4. Interestingly, the unhappy men from the command of Brig. Gen. Thompson were sent down to Memphis from Pillow aboard a transport. Their captains reported their situation to Thompson, who in turn ordered them to take their men ashore.

He next wired Brig. Gen. Ruggles at Grenada for permission to withdraw. Next day, Thompson's former gunboatmen were sent to the railroad depot to await early evacuation to Grenada. Meanwhile, the CRDF steamed down to Memphis, arriving about midnight. Cmdr. Robert Pinkney and two vessels from the old Hollins fleet, the *General Polk* and *Livingston*, at Fort Randolph, five miles below Fort Pillow, likewise cast off and headed for the Yazoo River.

The *General Polk* was still commanded by Lt. Jonathan Carter, the man whom Lt. Brown once believed a rival for command of the *Arkansas*. Earlier, she had sent her guns ashore to arm the fort. When Pinkney ordered the craft and her consort to flee, the *Polk*'s captain was amazed that no effort was made to take off the cannon installed ashore. Carter stalled his departure and coolly sent his executive officer, Lt. Sardine G. Stone, Jr., formerly of the gunboat *McRae*, ashore to retrieve two cannon that would be put to good use later. The 180-foot-long *Livingston*, also a Hollins squadron veteran, was a year-old New Orleans–built side-wheeler, once a ferry or towboat. She was not much appreciated. One of her midshipman, James M. Morgan, later wrote of her: "There had also been built (from designs by a locomotive roundhouse architect, I suppose) the most wonderful contraption that was ever seen afloat, called the *Livingston;* she carried 6 guns, 3 for'd and 3 abaft the paddle boxes, and she was almost circular in shape. She was so slow that her crew facetiously complained that when she was going downstream at full speed they could not sleep on account of the drift logs catching up with her and bumping against the stern."

When the Federals discovered their enemy's retreat, the Western Flotilla ironclads and rams followed toward the big Tennessee city. On the evening of June 5, per the arrangements made earlier with Capt. McBlair, the *Tennessee* was set alight on her Fort Pickering stocks. Her builder, Primus Emerson, according to a later relative, Mary, disappeared. His location would be unknown until September, when he turned up at Selma, Alabama, to begin work on a new gunboat, the *Nashville*.

There being insufficient coal available for his fleet to retire to Vicksburg, Commodore James E. Montgomery, as he noted in his campaign report, elected to fight when the Union force arrived early the next day. Shortly after midnight on June 6, Gen. Beauregard made both Montgomery and Brig. Gen. Thompson joint commanders of the ram fleet. Montgomery asked if Thompson could provide him with two companies of artillerists and orders were sent to the train station detailing the men to hold themselves in readiness. At dawn, their commander was awakened by a messenger who said the enemy was in sight upriver. Thompson quickly met with Montgomery, who asked that the requested men be hurried to the Fort Pickering landing where a tug would pick them up. Before Thompson's men could make it to the landing, not far from where the embers from the hull of the *Tennessee* still smoldered, the naval Battle of Memphis was fought. It was a Confederate slaughter, witnessed by the general and his men from the riverbank. "Being a little lame," as Lt. Read put it, the ram *General Earl Van Dorn*, the only CRDF unit to survive in Rebel hands, began her escape early. Her consorts were all sunk or captured.

Capt. Isaac D. Fulkerson's (1817–?) ram was a speedy 524-ton side-wheeler was 182 feet long, with a 28.3-foot beam and a 10.7-foot draft. She was protected below decks by cotton bales (hence the term cotton-clad), armed with a single 32-pdr. smoothbore, and heavily reinforced for ramming with a thin iron casemate and an iron ram. Originally constructed at Algiers, Louisiana, in 1853 as Capt. Edward Montgomery's towboat, *Junius Beebe*, for the Good Intent Towboat Company of New Orleans, the boat was one of those seized by the Confederate government at the Crescent City for the CRDF at the beginning of the year.

Battle of Plum Point Bend, May 10, 1862. *In this drawing by RAdm. Henry Walke, units of the Northern Division of the Confederate River Defense Force attack elements of the Union's Western Flotilla above Fort Pillow. Among the Southern vessels involved was Capt. Isaac D. Fulkerson's* General Earl Van Dorn, *pictured just to the right astern of the center ironclad and behind the* General Sterling Price *charging past the tree in the foreground. This is the only depiction we have of Fulkerson's craft, which went on to survive the Battle of Memphis a month later only to be scuttled at the Yazoo River raft in July* (Walke, Naval Scenes and Reminiscences of the Civil War).

The *Van Dorn*, the only one of the CRDF craft that "actually resembled a gunboat," had enjoyed some success in the Battle of Plum Point Bend on May 10, having rammed and badly damaged the Eads ironclad *Mound City*. The ram was joined in the Memphis exodus by Capt. Franklin Keeling's 353-ton side-wheel supply boat, *Paul Jones*. The 172-foot long civilian charter, originally constructed at McKeesport, Pennsylvania, in 1855, had earlier served on the route from New Orleans to Camden on the Ouachita River.

Together the refugees make their way down to the Yazoo. The latter carried a full cargo of powder, shell, cannon balls, and commissary stores removed from Fort Pillow. Two Ellet rams, off to a late post-battle start, made a vain effort to catch them, noting, as reported in the *Cincinnati Daily Commercial*, that the "hull of a new and large steamer, building on the ways, together with the tug *Queen of Memphis*, were fired and burning, as our gunboats passed the ways at Fort Pickering." Although seeing the burning carcass of the *Tennessee* may have been satisfying, Col. Ellet's craft were forced to give up their chase after 35 miles. It was later reported to the Federals that the *General Van Dorn* "hurried down the river so fast she made no stop at Helena but threw out a bottle with the news of the fight at Memphis."

The *General Polk* and *Livingston* reached the vicinity of the Yazoo raft on June 7. It was not, however, deemed prudent to displace the obstructions already laid and so they were not permitted to advance beyond the defenses. The same occurred with the *Paul Jones* when she arrived next day. All three transferred stores, armament, and ordnance supplies over the raft to be brought to Yazoo City. The two Fort Pillow guns retrieved aboard the

General Polk by Lt. Stone were mounted on shore and sailors were sent to help man them. Once she was unloaded, the *Paul Jones* was secreted up the Sunflower River. The *General Van Dorn* arrived a few days later and, like the earlier naval arrivals, was not permitted to pass above the raft. All three boats anchored in the waters below to await new orders upon the arrival on station of Flag Officer Lynch. Although the sailors and their officers lived aboard ship, Cmdr. Pinkney established a camp ashore next to his flagboat, the *Livingston*. None of the trio kept steam up.

Aware of the Confederate ships at the raft, Lt. Brown, as he noted in his June 9 letter to Brig. Gen. Ruggles, determined to offer assistance and to seek with Cmdr. Pinkney a coordinated plan of defense against any marauding Federal gunboats that might go poking their bows up the Yazoo.

Harry Owens tells us that completion of the raft in early June closed the Yazoo to many of the vessels that normally ran on that stream. There were, however, a number isolated above the defense and these continued operations. Several of the stranded steamers were hired by Lt. Brown to take some 400–800 bales of cotton from Yazoo City down to the raft. The bales were to be transferred across the raft to the two gunboats on the other side to use to turn themselves into true "cottonclads" or, if need be, "fireships." The project was to be under the immediate supervision of newly arrived Lt. Read.

Read, and at the last minute, Lt. Brown, rode down to the raft. While the former oversaw the transfer of the cotton, Brown, perhaps in company with Lt. Carter, conferred with Pinkney at the latter's riverbank camp. The lieutenants' superior was asked to have the *General Polk* and *Livingston* moor in a downstream direction, keeping steam up so as to be ready to engage any vessel(s) threatening the raft. Pinkney dismissed their request, indicating to Brown that he and his boats would wait for the anticipated arrival of Flag Officer Lynch, who would inform them all of their duty. Dismayed, Brown and Reid returned to Yazoo City and the *Arkansas*.[7]

Having done what he could for the Yazoo raft and dealt with Cmdr. McBlair, Lt. Brown quickly turned his attention to the prime matter at hand, namely the rapid outfitting of the *Arkansas*. Much remained to be done; as Lt. Gift remembered, "it was fearfully discouraging, but Brown was undismayed." Like contractor Shirley, the naval officer's first requirement was manpower, still largely unavailable. Unlike the civilian, the naval officer was prepared to use his extraordinary powers not only to hire help but also to impress it (a la the old British Navy press gangs) as well. First, however, he would employ traditional American measures. Officers, quite probably Lieutenants John ("Jack") Grimball and Arthur D. Wharton, were dispatched to Jackson and Mobile to open "rendezvous," where, it was hoped, patriotic Southerners would volunteer.

Before actually "shanghaiing" anyone from the surrounding neighborhood, Lt. Brown appealed to the local populace, craftsman and planter alike, and to the army for assistance. "Thanks to the patriotism of the noble people of Yazoo City," he was proud to inform Brig. Gen. Ruggles that he would not require the security detail or the MP officer requested on the evening of his first day in command. Still, it would be helpful if a large detachment of butternut soldiers could be sent to help work on the boat. This request was soon granted. It turned out that dragooning workers was necessary only for a few skilled jobs, including mechanics and blacksmiths.

Indeed, the response of the town and area citizens was more than expected and the lieutenant came to believe that they would help him perform miracles "so long as I shall deserve their support." A number of local planters reassigned field slaves from their own lands to provide unskilled labor, while some sent skilled men who assisted with the forges. Plantation owner Sessions personally provided between seven and ten African Americans to work on the ram. In addition to the men, all manner of blacksmithing and building tools were provided, as was food and certain other necessities. As they arrived, some of the Caucasian workers were assigned quarters with the ironclad's officers aboard the *Capitol*. The slaves apparently returned home at night or at the end of their shifts, though a few may have remained at overseen nearby camps. Numerous citizens, including a few owners or masters who worked side by side with their slaves, volunteered to help out.

Many of those from the community and the military who labored on the *Arkansas* possessed building, blacksmithing and metalworking, carpentry, or other construction skills developed in support of the state's plantation economy. A number had even worked in the boat repair business on the riverfront. Requiring but direction, they hammered, pounded, and otherwise enhanced the gunboat's deck and casemate as though it were a house or barn. To speed the process, Brown ordered activity on the gunboat to continue in shifts, 24/7, without letup or even Sunday rest. Lanterns were strung and pine torches lit to illuminate the night, giving something of a shadowy festive appearance from afar. Trusted hands and volunteers, unskilled in the carpentry arts, fanned out across the region locating and returning with needed supplies and materials. Upwards of 14 blacksmith forges were borrowed from neighborhood plantations. Arriving in wagons, they were erected in a "temporary blacksmith shop" on the riverbank near the *Arkansas* and would be employed to shape required non-armor iron fixtures and machinery parts. At night, their dull red glow could be seen in Yazoo City.

Not far away, several additional tents and lean-tos appeared, including a cook tent and a makeshift hospital. Gunner Thomas Travers reigned over a lean-to where all the ordnance and arms were checked or repaired. Frank Grimme agreed to devote his sawmill fulltime to sawing and fashioning wood for the armorclad. Gangs of African Americans felled trees and ox teams hauled the trunks to the Grimme Mill for sawing, shaping and sundry preparation, returning to the vessel with boards, wooden furniture, shot racks, hatch covers, lifeboats, flag staffs, and other fittings or millwork of appropriate size and shape. Numerous laborers quite literally swung into action almost immediately. Among their first achievements was the piercing of the casemate for additional gun ports. Lt. Brown had decided to enhance the boat's battery from four to ten guns, and, incidentally, thereby change her classification from gunboat to ironclad sloop—though she was still most often known as a ram.

The new captain ordered three window-shaped portholes sawed in each side of the casemate and two in each end face. William E. Webb, a reporter from the *St. Louis Daily Missouri Republican* who would see the *Arkansas* at Vicksburg on the morning of July 15 by using a telescope from a guarded position on the Louisiana shore, later reported: "She mounts three guns on a side, the ports being open just above the bulwark of the hull or three feet above the water." The vertical sides of the casemate, unique among Confederate armorclads, allowed the use of a mixture of artillery with different tube lengths. There has been some dispute over the years as to how close together the gun ports were located, or whether or not they might have been staggered differently on one side than another. Plans by Geoghegan and Hinds, referenced in the previous chapter, show a distance of 16 feet, while Meagher projects twelve.

Recent reviews of all three renderings and the conclusion on armament noted below causes the author to believe that the twelve-foot spacing is the most plausible. A drawn out arrangement would probably have resulted in the broadside guns recoiling into the bow-

and stern-chasers if, as actually occurred, all were in action simultaneously. The new broadside window-shaped openings on the sides were cut large enough to allow a degree of gun traverse. These broadside gun ports would be protected by heavy, locally crafted, hinged iron shutters, with upper and lower halves. Above each gun port was an aperture where a chain ran through the armor to raise the upper shutter. The subscribers of the *Brooklyn Daily Eagle* were told that these "port-holes were made very small and covered by a movable iron door, eight or ten inches thick, so that when the gun is fired and withdrawn, the side of the vessel presents an unbroken wall of iron." The oval gun ports cut into the fore and aft faces of the casemate were another matter. These guns were not kept behind closed iron shutters but rather protruded from oval armored collars bolted to the armor. These were very restricted and Lt. Brown would later admit that they, especially those forward, were too narrow for needed cannon traverse or gun crew visibility.

When the *Arkansas* arrived at Yazoo City, "the iron of her armor extended only a foot, or a little more, about the water line." Lt. Gift also noted that, even after the bars lost with the barge were salvaged, "there was not a sufficiency of iron on hand to finish the entire ship." Bolting the salvaged iron to the armor-clad's casemate initially posed a problem, as the drills needed to prepare it were not available. To replace the lost T-rail hole-punching equipment, Brown and Shirley came up with an ingenious idea for "extemporized drilling machines." The *Capitol* was maneuvered to the riverside of the *Arkansas* and lashed on. A crane was fashioned from hewed tree trunks and fitted aboard the steamboat. Her hoisting engine was rigged via, according to David Meagher, "a belt drive from a capstan in sort of sawmill fashion" to power replacement drilling equipment made on the blacksmith forges. The smiths in turn prepared additional iron bars for the casemate, along with other needed items, "while dozens of hands were doing similar work by hand."

Maj. Gen. Earl Van Dorn, CSA (1820–1863). *A dashing Port Gibson, Mississippi, native, Van Dorn succeeded Maj. Gen. Lovell in command of the Department of Southern Mississippi and East Louisiana. Prior to his Vicksburg command, the successful Mexican War veteran Van Dorn also served at New Orleans, in Texas and Arkansas, and at Corinth. While at Vicksburg, he persuaded President Jefferson Davis to give him tactical control over the* Arkansas *and it was he who demanded that she steam out of the Yazoo in July 1862 and sent her to her end at Baton Rouge in August. Van Dorn later led the Western cavalry command and pulled off the wildly successful raid on Holly Springs in December (Miller, ed.,* Photographic History of the Civil War*).*

Yet more iron was required than just that salvaged from the river or already aboard the ironclad's hull. The nearest commercial foundry was in Vicksburg. This was the Reading and Bros. concern located, according to former resident R.A. Watkinson, chief clerk of the USN Bureau of Ordnance and Hydrography, "on the bank of the river, at the lower end of the town."

Being fully invested with military orders, the owner could not provide much help. His concern was still turning out cannon as quickly as possible. James C. Hazlett, Edwin Olmstead, and M. Hume Parks tell us that, by March 25, Abram B. Reading's company had already cast six 3-inch bronze guns and 14 rifled six-pdr. guns for the Confederate army. Some of these, according to Larry Daniel, were under subcontract to the Memphis concern of Quinby & Robinson.

A call went out across the western parts of Mississippi and Tennessee seeking "iron for the *Arkansas*." This cry for help resulted in the delivery of quantities of various-sized lots from many destinations. All came "to the nearest railroad station," Lt. Brown remembered, "and thence 25 miles by wagons." In addition to railroad T-bars, an interesting assortment of refashionable items was received, including kitchen utensils, bootjacks, fireplace irons, and wrought iron gates. Paul Stevens reports that a Sunday school class in Montgomery, Alabama, gathered miscellaneous scrap iron that was among the items railroaded to the armorclad. The process was not unlike the scrap iron drives of World War II days.

Much of the iron received was in need of punching or reworking by hand into bolts and other items. And reworked it was, both by the *Capitol*'s drills and, as Mrs. Dimitry put it, "by brawny workmen wielding heavy hammers" at the forges, men who "made their mighty strokes ring out in unison with the pulse of their own resolute, hopeful hearts." Over the following days, a single thickness of 4½-inch railroad iron was steadily bolted to the perpendicular almost two-foot thick oak outer side walls of the casemate. These were dovetailed parallel to the waterline with the rail top showing outward and hung the entire length on both sides. Before they were done, workers had pounded almost 700 iron bolts into the two sides of the casemates and another 400 fasteners into the ends.

The forward and aft sloped faces of the casemate was also heavily armored, though as Mahan reports, the iron was bolted on up and down rather than parallel as on the sides. Lt. Brown relates that both ends of the *Arkansas* were "closed by timber one foot square, planked across by six-inch strips of oak." The faces were then "covered by one course of railway iron laid up and down at an angle of 35 degrees." The junctions where the slanted fore and aft faces met the flat roof were guarded with boilerplate "angle iron."

Brown knew that there were limitations to the ram's ends, even if both could be completed as desired. They could deflect "overhead all missiles striking at short range, but would have been of little security under plunging fire." The weakness at the ends of the vertical side casemate walls where they were joined with the sloping end faces was also recognized. The crew would just have to take its chances. If a cannonball impacted directly on the end of the join, it was quite possible that the railroad iron could peel off. The junctions where the vertical side casemate walls joined the flat panels of the roof were, however, covered with bent boilerplate "angle-iron" strips.

The *Arkansas* shared a protection chink with the Eads turtles: the flat top of her casemate. It was generally believed at the time construction began that both the Northern and Southern river ironclad vessels would not be subjected to plunging fire from cannon mounted in high locations. None of the designers gave a thought to mortar boats and schooners — which hadn't been invented when the Union and Confederate armorclads were designed. The designers did, however, take the precaution of covering the roof with half-inch thick boiler iron plate.

Reporter Webb, after having the chance to see the vessel, would tell his St. Louis readers in late July that the *Arkansas* was "protected by railroad T iron, interlapped in such a way as to make it about six inches thick." While they were at it, the workers brought aboard cotton bales to insert in layers along the internal side casemate bulkheads between the gun ports. These were then secured in place, thereby essentially creating a double bulkhead. *Harper's Weekly* on September 6, 1862, told its readers, "The *Arkansas* was plated with railroad iron on the outside, over a planking of six-inch oak; inside that was six inches of condensed cotton on another six inches of oak."

We do not know for certain whether the cotton was contained, as some have suggested, in the usual 500-pound pressed bales or 250-pound unpressed bales. While the latter may have been easily available and could have been "jacked" into the available spaces, it presented something of a fire hazard. The former, on the other hand, offered greater "stopping power" against incoming projectiles or shell fragments but had to first be pressed into shape. "It is not clear how the bales were oriented," George Wright told the author on May 6, 2010. "If placed on their narrow side lengthwise on the vessel's longitudinal axis, the depth of cotton," he noted, "would be about 20 inches." On the other hand, he continued, "if laid on their widest dimension, the bales would have had a depth of about 26 inches." Wright assumed that the bales would be pressed and that they "would have added 36–42 tons" to the boat's displacement, plus the weight of a wooden bulkhead to hold the bales in place."

The idea that the *Arkansas* was being equipped with cotton protection was among the earliest reported by northern newspapermen. As reprinted by the *New York Times*, a reporter from the *Chicago Times* knew by the end of June and informed his subscribers: "Inside of the wooden wall of the hull is a continuous layer of cotton of the thickness of a single bale, compressed by jack-screws into a space of about 18 inches, and inside of that is solid oak again, six inches through." Correspondent Webb, seeing her on the morning of her breakout, also believed this additional protection was added while she was up the Yazoo. He wrote in late July: "The interspace between her outer and inner timbers is evidently filled with compressed cotton." A scribe from the *Brooklyn Daily Eagle* told his readers on July 30 that the interior included "a layer consisting of cotton-bales compressed into about half their ordinary thickness, and held to its place by a lining of oak."

Internal access to the casemate was allowed via 12-rung ladders. These ran up topside from the gun deck through two openings covered by hatches, or what the *New York Times*, in a July 5 report, called "bomb-proof gratings." These passageways were centered fore and aft of the chimney. Similar ladders were also affixed externally to the fore and aft faces of the casemate.

The *Arkansas* also possessed four external bulkheads, two forward and two aft. Those aft in the stern quarter were curved and possessed of scuppers through which aft deck water could be unshipped or lines could be run from ship to shore or ship to ship and attached to the quarterdeck bollards. St. Louis correspondent Webb would be impressed by these. Writing about them on the morning of July 15, he told his *Daily Missouri Republican* readers that, from his observation, "fore and aft, bulwarks about three feet high" could be seen "in front running to a point, and aft having about the usual form. Her stern has two bends, tapering in such a shape as to make it almost impossible for a ball to enter her hull."

Unhappily, time was not on the side of Brown's armorclad. The Yazoo was falling rapidly and the project superintendent and commander did not believe he had time to wait for the iron-bending "apparatus to bend the railway iron to the curve of our quarter and stern, and to the angles of the pilothouse." Though "there was little thought of showing" the vessel's stern, "the weakest part," to the enemy, still it was necessary to provide some protection at this point. The late hour required that, as Lt. Brown admitted, whatever was to be done would be "mostly for appearance sake." The decision was taken to cover those rear bulkheads with two-inch thick strips of iron boilerplate. These were attached with a couple of rows of iron bolts. It is interesting that, like the Eads boats, the *Arkansas* wore her thickest protection on the face of her casemate and sides and her weakest at the stern.

The massive forward bulkheads consisted of, essentially, two straight-line rails. These ran from the apex at the prow back to the corners, port and starboard, of the casemate. Small areas of the main deck, to which they were secured with many bolts, were left outside their protection. Each had openings forward and aft. The bulkhead openings closest to the prow were square in shape and permitted extension outboard of heavy catheads upon which to secure the two iron anchors. The anchor chain ran through those aft. The forward bulkheads appeared far more formidable than those in the rear, perhaps because they did not follow the curve of the bow. Also mounted on the main deck forward, centered between the bulkheads, was a steam-powered capstan. There were bollards on each side inboard of the bulkhead. A small vertical pole called a jackstaff was placed at the prow.

Another vulnerable location for which the machinery could not properly or timely bend iron was the pilothouse or conning tower, a small structure rising about two feet above the top deck in front of the chimney. Brown was forced to "very imperfectly" cover it "with a double thickness of one-inch bar iron," realizing, as Scharf put it, that it remained "in an unfinished state." Two sets of boat davits (secured one leg on the after casemate side and one to the quarterdeck) each held a single gig between them. A flagstaff for the national colors was fitted at the stern.

There has been some discussion over the years as to the paint scheme of the *Arkansas*. After all, the Federal timberclads and City Series ironclads were painted black, as were many other Union vessels. Master's Mate John Wilson, one of the armorclad's crew, confided that his ram was a "dark brown" color, sort of a camouflage scheme that could not be seen at a distance. This observation has been echoed by several later vessel profilers, including Donald Barnhart, Jr., who tells us she was painted a "dull brown" hue. Flag Officer Farragut later called it "chocolate," while Lt. Cmdr. Seth Ledyard Phelps, with Flag Officer Davis, was less descriptive, calling the hue "an earth color." Looking at her from the Louisiana shore on the morning of July 15, William E. Webb of the *St. Louis Daily Missouri Republican* wrote simply "She is painted brown."

Many others, witnesses and later writers, have described the *Arkansas* as being rust colored, suggesting that she was not painted and drew her color from the fact that some of her iron armor spent time in the river while she was stranded at Greenwood. This controversy, like that of the brown paint, has been reviewed by Mark Jenkins on his Website. In all probably, dark brown paint was, as Webb tells us, applied to the ram, the Yazoo City laborers hoping that it would help the *Arkansas* blend with the hues of the Yazoo and Mississippi. However, the quality of the paint's pigment may have been bad. Once applied to the anything-but-new iron, the resulting application, blending with the color of the recovered iron, undoubtedly gave what was the cited rusty appearance. Winston Groom, in his new study, *Vicksburg 1863*, suggests simply that "a mud-brown paint was applied to the finished product but it was defective and within a few weeks, the ship took on a patina of burnished rust." Whatever her color, Flag Officer Charles Davis observed simply that she was "an ugly customer."

As work continued upon the ram's hull and casemate, Lt. Brown next turned his attention to the matter of ordnance equipment, supplies, and the guns that would be fought when the vessel went operational. Lt. Brown would, in the words of Charles Getchell, place "the cannon of greatest combined strength and reliability at the bow and stern to further strengthen the ship for a frontal attack and to help compensate for" weak stern defense.

As with other important components required to run and fight the ship, exactly what kind of guns were placed aboard has been disputed, conjectured, or simply specified without fact over the years. The exact location for the various types has also been disputed. We do know that six of the big cannon were already in hand, or nearly so, along with their percussion locks, as the *Arkansas* lay next to the *Capitol* at Yazoo City. Four came down from Memphis when the ram fled south under Cmdr. McBlair and two others were probably acquired locally. Those immediately available supposedly included two single-banded 6.4-inch Brooke rifles. The total length of these cannon was 141.85 inches, and each, looking much like a Union Parrott Rifle, weighed 9,100 pounds. Shot weighed 80–95 pounds and shells 65, with the range of the former over 2,000 yards. As only between 11 and 14 of these Brookes were actually built before January 1863, it is unlikely, given the time frame, that any made it aboard the *Arkansas*. More than likely, as we note below, the 6.4-inch guns usually listed were, in fact, banded 32-pdrs.

Bearing a superficial resemblance to the Union Rodman gun, there were additionally two 8-inch 64-pdr. smoothbore Columbiads. These were long-barreled cannon normally employed in land fortifications like those at Fort Donelson up on the Cumberland River. Silverstone tells us that the *Star of the West*, riding at anchor not far from the *Arkansas*, carried two of these and so it is possible that she was the source for these pieces. Each of the Columbiads had a total length of 120 inches and weighed 8,750 pounds and may have been among the 69 manufactured at Richmond's Tredegar Foundry beginning in June 1861. Writing almost a century later, Raimondo Luraghi reveals for the lay reader that, "thanks to their perfect fit in the bore, their projectiles had very little 'windage.' They therefore had a remarkable penetrating force and did not need to be elevated much (otherwise Columbiads could not have been used aboard a ship)."

A pair of IX-inch Confederate Dahlgren shell guns were also available. Each of those was 132 inches long and had an approximate weight of 9,200 pounds. Their shot weighed 80 pounds and shells were 73.5 pounds each. The latter projectiles, according to Eugene Canfield, had a range of just over 1,700 yards at 5 degrees elevation. It was anticipated that the four others could be obtained from the Confederate army or perhaps from Cmdr. Pinkney's gunboats. Among those aboard the latter were rifled 32-pdrs. Captured perhaps at Norfolk, these were smoothbore 32s whose inner bores were rifled. They no longer fired cannonballs but elongated rifled projectiles. As their bores were 6.4 inches in diameter, these were undoubtedly the 6-inch guns referred to in accounts of the *Arkansas*. At least three were taken from Pinkney before June 22. Several replicas are today on display, including those at Fort Macon. It is more than likely that two others of these long-barrel pieces were aboard, being mistakenly identified as 6.4-inch Brooke rifles. Those mounted as stern-chasers could fit through the aft-mounted shield and would provide heavy throw weight in the unlikely event the *Arkansas* was forced to flee.

Let us recap the armorclad's heavy ordnance as laid out by various sources. The vessel's commander, Lt. Brown recalled, for *Battles & Leaders*, that the *Arkansas* was armed with two 8-inch, 64-pdr. cannon forward, a pair of rifled 32-pdrs. astern, and two 100-pdr. Columbiads plus a 6-inch rifle in each broadside. This is also the type count given in the CSN ship register reprinted in the Navy *Official Records*. On the other hand, the recollections

Star of the West, *dba CSS St. Philip. Following her failed attempt to reinforce Fort Sumter in January 1861, the side-wheel oceangoing vessel was captured off the Texas coast that April 18 by Galveston militia under the command of Col. Earl Van Dorn. She was thereafter impressed into Confederate service, retreating to the Yazoo River upon the fall of New Orleans. Lt. Isaac Newton Brown would wisely choose not to scuttle her during the breakout of the* Arkansas *from the Yazoo; she would remain up that stream until the following year when she was destroyed to help slow the Federal descent on Vicksburg via the Yazoo Pass (Alfred Waud drawing, Library of Congress).*

of three of the men present with Brown, who have left us writings and also served the guns, disagree with those of their captain. Gift (bow) and Read (stern) point out different type lists, as does Gift's assistant, Master's Mate John Wilson.

Lt. Gift wrote in 1884 that the 10 guns were a mixture of type and size: "two 8-inch Columbiads, one 8-inch shell gun, two 9-inch shell guns, one smoothbore 32 pounder (63 cwt.), and four rife-guns, formerly 32-pounders, but now altered, three banded and one unbanded." Lt. Charles W. Read differs slightly from his colleague, indicating that her "battery consisted of 10 guns — viz: two 8-inch Columbiads in the two forward or bow ports, two 9-inch shell guns, two 6-inch rifles, and two 32-pounders smooth-bores in broadside, and two 6-inch rifles astern." His type list was repeated by J. Thomas Scharf in his Confederate naval history. Wilson's diary records two Columbiads forward and two six-inch rifles astern, with one 9-inch, one 6-inch rifle, and one 32-pounder in each broadside battery.

In 1882, Admiral Mahan wrote that the *Arkansas*' battery "was disposed as follows: in the bow, two heavy VIII-inch Columbiads; in the stern, two 6.4-inch rifles; and in broadside, two 6.4-inch rifles, two 32-pounder smoothbores, and two IX-inch Dahlgren smoothbores." William N. Still, in *Iron Afloat*, does not actually detail the types of cannon employed aboard. However, in his 1958 master's thesis, which forms the base upon which his subse-

Five: Five Weeks Up the Yazoo, Early May–Late June 1862 103

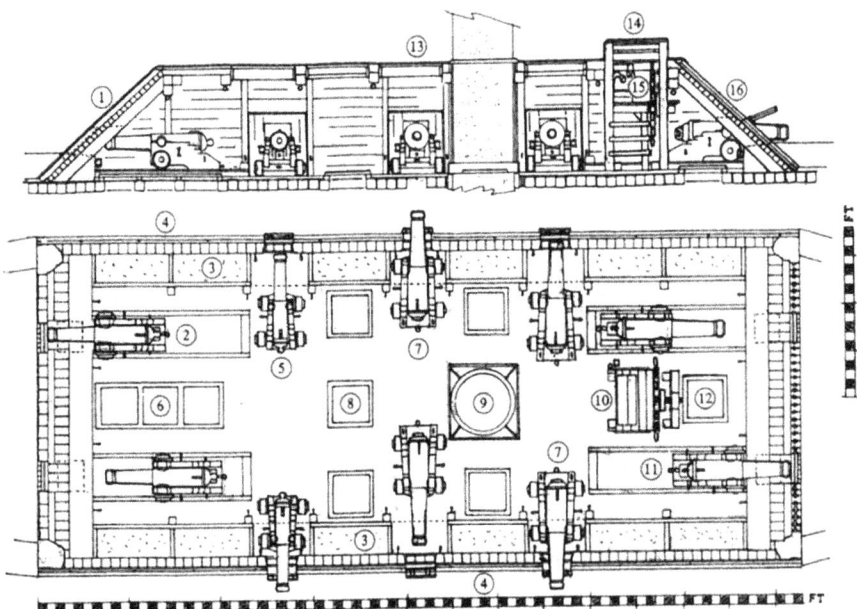

5–5b **David Meagher Casemate Drawing.** *Legend: 1. Boilerplate rear "armor"; 2. Cannon on railway carriage (2); 3. Cotton packing casemate lining; 4. Rail side armor; 5. Cannon (2); 6. Hatches to engines; 7. Cannon; 8. Hatches to fireroom; 9. Smokestack and top of breeching; 10. Pilothouse platform; 11. Cannon on railway carriage (2); 12. Hatch to fore magazine/passage; 13. 1" bar armor atop casemate; 14. 1" bar armor on pilothouse; 15. Speaking tube and bell pulls to engineer; 16. Rail front armor (© 1995 David J. Meagher. Used with permission).*

quent writings on the vessel are based, is specific. With a nod toward Gift's difference, Still agreed with Brown's enumeration. In one of his few errors, Paul Silverstone gives an armament of just eight guns: two 9-inch Dahlgrens, two 8-inch 64-pdr. Columbiads, two 6-inch rifles (either Brooke or rifled 32s), and two 32-pdr. smoothbores. In addition to the 8-inch Columbiads, Raimondo Luraghi tells us there were two 6-inch rifled guns aft and "three more guns on each broadside, among them two 100-pdr. Dahlgrens (one on each side)."

A recent (2006) Internet discussion board, *Civil War Talk*, gives yet another tally. Present, it states, were: "2 × 8 in Columbiads in bow ports, 2 × 6.4 in Brooke Rifles in stern ports, 2 × 6.4 in Brooke Rifles, 2 × 8 in Dahlgren smoothbores and 2 × 32 lb smoothbores in broadside ports." It can thus be seen that nearly every Civil War naval history (book or article) employs one of three officers' counts (with sometimes a slight variation). All agree that there were 10 guns, with at least two of them being forward-mounted Columbiads.

There was not a lot of space within the casemate to mount ordnance. With each casemate wall reportedly as much as 18 inches thick, the effective width of the gun deck was but 32 feet, not the official beam width of 35 feet. Add a 20-inch depth for the pressed cotton believed inserted at Vicksburg prior to the Baton Rouge run and the gun deck became even narrower. The ordnance arrangement is contained within a general casemate interior view prepared as part of a set of plans of the *Arkansas* drawn by the historian and artist David Meagher. His extremely useful illustrations have two apparent ordnance anomalies. The first is the use forward of four Columbiads instead of two Columbiads and two

Dahlgrens. The second is reference to a pair of broadside 6-pounder guns, a weapon long obsolete as a naval cannon, located where it is suspected the vessel hosted 6-inch or rifled 32-pounders (translating into 6.4-inch pieces).

Also available were four one-ton railroad iron chassis, the basis of the standard naval pivot gun carriage system, also transferred from Memphis. Contractor Shirley originally intended to use them with probably the 6.4s and Columbiads. Installed, each iron chassis would serve as a sort of railway over which a gun and its special carriage would move in and out of battery. There was, however, a shortage of wooden carriages to fit atop the chassis or mount the broadside guns.

There were at this time essentially three types of gun carriages in naval use. First was the traditional, some would say ancient, four-wheeled naval truck carriage of the type now required. More recently developed was a variation on that, the Marsilly carriage, plus a chassis and track carriage usually mounted as a swinging pivot. "The commonest mounting of the period," wrote Philip Van Dorn Stern in 1962, "was the naval truck carriage." Elevation was controlled by adjusting a quoin, or sometimes a screw, under the breech of the cannon, while recoil was checked by breeching ropes between the carriage and the hull wall. Made of wood with four wheels, the carriage, usually employed on the broadside, was strengthened by long metal bolts inserted horizontally on the truck's side panel. Gun crew employed handspikes to swing the carriages sideways. Recoil was contained with a breeching rope, attached to the ship's side and looped through a block, that passed through a hole in the cannon's cascable, the rounded projection behind the breech.

The Marsilly carriage, adopted from a French design, had no rear wheels. Its aft section rested directly on the deck, which provided friction to help halt the gun's recoil and was frequently chewed up after multiple firings. A handspike with a roller in its end was used to maneuver the mount; once inserted, several large sailors would push it down, lifting the end of the carriage sufficiently to let the spike roller move. The carriage was otherwise secured to the ship's side in the manner of the truck mount.

The third mount was the chassis and track friction carriage, built from wood and iron, with eccentric axles/wheels and an elevating screw worked by a revolving geared nut. The mount's wheels were located underneath the carriage slightly in front of its trunnion beds. These were often affixed to tracks on the deck that allowed the guns to move (pivot) between, say, forward gun ports and those on the quarter. Such a chassis system, sometimes called pivot mount, was, for example, employed aboard the later Confederate ironclad *Albemarle*.

As part of the maneuvering drill for a chassis-mounted gun forward from the rear of the track, gun crew inserted handspikes into the eccentric maneuvering wheels, putting them in gear. That done, the piece could slide forward along the chassis into battery, its nose sticking out of the gun port. Once in battery, the wheels were locked out of gear until such time as the mount was needed for practice or action.

A bedeviled spurwheel that intersected the elevating screw nut on those carriages that possessed them was attached to one end of a shaft at a right angle to the carriage cheek. The other end of the shaft, with a four-shafted handle, projected out of the right side of the carriage. The gun's muzzle was made to rise or lower by mightily cranking one of the handle braces.

Did the *Arkansas* actually mount the railroad chassis system with which she was originally equipped? Lt. Gift indicated that the two cannon mounted in the bow and the two astern were placed in carriages "mounted on railroad iron chassis; the six broadside guns were on carriages constructed at Canton, Mississippi." This, like the number and type of guns, engines, or boilers, is open to conjecture. Although the chassis gun system Shirley delivered was modern, each mount took up more room than a traditional truck carriage, weighed twice as much when the carriage was fitted, and may have been somewhat more difficult for the uninitiated to master in the short time available for recruit gunnery drill. When Lt. Brown decided to expand the number of guns aboard the *Arkansas*, he may have sacrificed the enhanced carriage system in favor of the traditional if for no other reason than to make more room in a very cramped space.

Having heard that two local construction bosses from Canton, Mississippi, 30 miles off to the southeast, were willing to make the necessary common gun carriages, Lt. Brown sent Lt. Stevens off to seek them out and review their bids. Lt. Gift later wrote that only four carriages were needed; Brown indicated that he received 10. As Gift also indicated that the *Arkansas* did employ her four railroad chassis carriages, that means she already had six carriages before Stevens left for Canton—a discrepancy of two carriages in the stories of Brown and his lieutenant. It is possible that Gift was correct if Brown already planned to take two guns from the *Star of the West*, as they would be turned over with their already-extant carriages, making a total of six in hand.

At any rate, Lt. Gift recalled that both of the carpentry "parties who never saw or heard of such things before" turned out to be genuine. They impressed Stevens and convinced him that they could fashion the required truck mounts. The situation tickled Gift's funny bone then and in years afterwards. When he left for Canton, the XO was doubtful of what he would find. "He made no drawings before his departure," Gift remembered, "not knowing that he could find a party who would undertake the job." Surprised at the men he found (whose names are unknown to this day), Stevens asked a messenger to ride back to Yazoo City and report.

As he dismounted, Capt. Brown and Lt. Gift met the rider, who passed Stevens' message asking for the "dimensions of the guns," which were of "all different patterns." The latter immediately obtained a square and measured the available guns, among which was at least one 32-pdr. smoothbore similar to a rifled model. A saddlebag was found into which Stevens put his drawings along with a note from Brown agreeing to pay the carpenters whatever they wanted to quickly build the mounts. XO Stevens was admonished to watch carefully and give the work his "special attention." The horseman was off to Canton very shortly afterwards.

Construction proceeded rapidly and in just 10 days each contractor built half the number of required carriages from green cypress logs. Stevens returned to the cheers of his comrades at Yazoo City, riding in the first of four large oxcarts that transported the mounts. If, as Brown recalled, there were 10 carriages in those wagons, these quite possibly arrived in sizeable pieces that required final assembly. If Gift was correct and only four were purchased, than one, undoubtedly complete, carriage arrived at the Yazoo City riverbank in each wagon.

It is reasonably certain, as Mr. Meager's casemate drawing shows, that the carriages Stevens had constructed were all of the traditional truck variety rather than the newer Marsilley type. Pleased with the success of his effort, the XO was able to write home to his mother, Sarah F. Stevens, on June 20 that, upon his return, he found "one of your dear letters" had arrived. Even though it is agreed that the chassis system mounts were employed with the bow- and stern-chasers of the *Arkansas*, there is no information that the usual accompanying pivot tracks were fabricated for the vessel or mounted aboard. There was just no room for the necessary swing arcs of such tracks.

Gunner Travers' ordnance lean-to worked without letup once Stevens returned.

Although a quantity of ordnance implements and supplies had come down from Memphis, these were by no means sufficient. A growing stock of implements available or manufactured on the riverbank came to include wrought iron truck and roller handspikes; chocks; gunner's implements; rammers, sponges, and rods; buckets (for water, sponges and tar or grease); elevating bars and pouches' vent covers; worms and worm poles (for cleaning debris from the cannon barrels). It is not mentioned by any of the crew who wrote memoirs whether or not a supply of splinter netting was available to hang in the casemate. A tradition aboard many wooden men-o'-war, its use could lessen casualties. Failure of comment does not mean absence, but that was likely the case.

Working in conjunction with the blacksmiths, Travers probably oversaw manufacture of certain components for the new gun carriages themselves. These might well have included the iron trunnion plates; transoms required to fasten one carriage cheek to the other; iron wheels and eccentric axles (if the chassis were employed); sundry rods; and other fixtures such as I-rings.

Some shells, caps, and fuses for the cannon, along with grape, shrapnel, and small arms ammunition were obtained from the A.B. Reading Foundry in Vicksburg and from Jackson. The exact number and type details are unknown. According to David Flynt, over 100 solid shot arrived from Jackson and Canton, Mississippi. A quantity of needed items arrived by water. "The little 80-ton, 100-foot long sternwheeler *Ben McCulloch*," writes Harry Owens, "was paid $100 per day for transporting ordnance supplies to the *Arkansas* at Yazoo City."

Worse than the scarcity of implements or projectiles, there was no gunpowder. Undismayed, Lt. Brown informed his officers that they would manufacture their own right there at Yazoo City — just as soon as a supply of Louisiana sulphur and Tennessee saltpeter arrived by wagon from the railroad station at Bovina Station. In the meantime, a number of laborers set to work preparing charcoal. *The Encyclopedia of Civil War Artillery* tells us that the gunpowder manufactured during the Civil War comprised saltpeter (75 percent), charcoal (15 percent), and sulphur (10 percent). The combustible ingredient was the charcoal, while the potassium nitrate (saltpeter's chemical name) provided the necessary oxygen supporting combustion. Sulphur changed the gunpowder into the huge volume of gas needed to propel a projectile through the cannon's bore.

The most useful description of the process by which the gunpowder was eventually made at Yazoo City actually appears in a novel, *By Valour and Arms*, the title of which was taken from the Magnolia State motto. This work by the noted Mississippi writer James Street (1903–1954) is a romanticized but nevertheless finely researched and generally well-regarded account of the *Arkansas* that, aside from a few purposeful or non-incident inaccuracies, includes a variety of nonfiction nuggets, including this one:

> Brown was using carbon, saltpeter and sulphur for his coarse powder. The pulverized saltpeter came from Tennessee and they made their own charcoal by burning hemp and willow. The charcoal and sulphur were pulverized in barrels, partly filled with zinc balls and rolled on the ground until the ingredients became a powder. Then the sulphur, charcoal and saltpeter were mixed in barrels made of leather stretched over wooden frames. The mass was worked for two hours and pressed into millcakes, then granulated by hand and pounded into powder. To grade the powder and made it uniform, the Confederates worked it through three sieves and glazed it by putting it in a barrel and revolving it 10 times per minute. Each grain was .31 inch in diameter, the proper size for cannon powder. It was glazed and dried until the grains were smooth, angular, and irregular, but without sharp corners. Each grain was very hard.

By the time of the Civil War, the process of "touching off" a naval cannon had advanced beyond simply applying a slow-burning match to the powder vent at the rear of the piece. Now friction tubes, filled with very fine priming powder (also made at Brown's beachside powder works), were used. Each featured a wire loop attached to a lanyard which when pulled sharply provided the friction necessary to set off the powder in the tube, shooting sparks down to the main charge in the gun chamber and there igniting it. As the supply of powder increased, the carriages were finished and the great guns mounted. Those destined for the chassis were fitted in such a manner as to move freely in and out of battery.[8]

Captain Brown "quickly realized that the unreliability of his handmade engines was his ship's greatest weakness," Paul Stevens confirmed, though there may have been some initial hope for them once they were reassembled and placed below-decks. "We had at first some trust in these," Brown later remembered. The faith would fade with testing.

We know the variety of wood employed in building the Fort Pickering armorclads as well as the iron used in their protection. The ordnance suite is also fairly well established. The greatest unsolved mystery remains the power plants. Detailed contemporary records concerning them were lost and little has been written on this component in the years since. "Speculation" is the single word that best defines the information we have on the propulsion units of the *Arkansas* and the first *Tennessee*. Shirley and Emerson had been free to improvise on their hulls as necessity required — except in the matter of propulsion. Per the designs of John Luke Porter, the engines of their boats would be linked to propellers and not paddle wheels as was common on Western waters. Even knowing that, the layout of the driveline between her engines and propellers is just as much a mystery as are the engines and boilers.

The *Arkansas*, like the *Virginia*, was screw driven; initially, it was hoped that she could also be employed as a coastal or sea boat, perhaps actually making it out into the Gulf of Mexico and then maybe as far as Mobile. On the other hand, as Cmdr. David Dixon Porter wrote Washington from St. Louis in May 1862, the use of propellers on Western boats was not common. They required deep channels when often-times low water level was a navigational problem. If damaged — and the danger from snags, sawyers, and other natural drift was high — the propeller was far more difficult to repair than a paddle wheel.

The paddle wheel dominated on inland rivers because its rugged, simple construction was, in the words of Louis C. Hunter, "admirably adapted to the distinctive and difficult conditions of navigation." These observations were unknown, unappreciated, or ignored in Richmond when Porter provided his drawings to Shirley, more than likely because of a dream for the boats of hybrid river-ocean service. Hunter also reminds us "the relatively small working surfaces of screw propellers on shallow-draft boats would have demanded the development of an entirely different type of engine to supply the high shaft speeds required." There is little evidence that any of the foundries supporting the steamboat industry in the upper Mississippi Valley had the patterns on hand to cast the cylinders or parts needed for direct-driven propeller engines.

The uncertainties and hopes surrounding the potential deployment of the *Arkansas* or her sister strongly suggests that their power plants would be similar in many respects to that of the average Mississippi steamboat. But what *did* they have? Writing about the power plant of the average Western steamboat in 2004, Adam I. Kane observed that, "despite its plain appearance, it was a light, powerful, inexpensive, and easily maintained machine, well adapted to the function it served." When two were employed, they were generally "located near the edge of the hull."

In a detailed report on the *Arkansas* for his readers, the *Philadelphia Inquirer* correspondent Henry Bentley noted in late July 1862 that her engines were "low pressure and of 900 indicated horse power, placed below the waterline and well-protected from hostile missiles." He went on to indicate that her "cylinders are said to be 24-inches diameter and seven foot stroke." The Navy *Official Records* simply indicate that the *Arkansas* and her sister were to be twin-screwed vessels capable of eight mph in still water. Respected warship historian Paul H. Silverstone indicates that the *Arkansas* operated two low-pressure 900 IHP engines.

The Internet forum *Civil War Talk* has posted the following specifics for the armorclad's powerplant: "2 low pressure horizontal direct-acting engines (24" × 7'), 4 boilers, 900 IHP." Tim J. Watt's article on the *Arkansas* in the *Encyclopedia of the Civil War: A Political, Social, and Military History* says "she was powered by 450-horsepower short-stroke screw engines salvaged from a sunken steamer."

The *Arkansas*' power plant has remained a key part of her story for these past 150 years, yet, like other physical attributes, its configuration and performance has also been a subject of controversy. As Brown and his mates ready the great ram for departure down the Yazoo, this seems a fitting point to review her propulsion and perhaps draw a conclusion. No one has made a greater study of the ironclad's propulsion than Mr. George Wright and we largely defer to him, and one or two others, in the discussion here.

Commenting in a string of posts on the *Civil War Navies Message Board* in September 2007 and May, June and September 2009 concerning the difficulties surrounding the determination of the physical attributes and arrangement of the *Arkansas*' power plant, historian George Wright speculated that she carried high-pressure engines. Wright's opinion lines up with the dean of armorclad writers, William N. Still, who earlier deduced the same thing, noting there was "nothing unusual about the engineering installations on board the Confederate ironclads." Still went on to bluntly say that their "engines were generally high pressure, reciprocating, single expansion."

Adding still more weight to the observations of Wright and Still is Adam Kane. In his highly regarded study, the Texan all but describes the situation faced by Shirley and Emerson as they discussed their requirements with the unnamed Adams Street foundry. Given that the hulls of Western boats "constantly altered the alignment of the machinery," Kane noted, "the simple high-pressure engine, not built with anything approaching precision, was more easily adjusted to these frequent changes than a well-made and accurately fitted low-pressure engine."

Lt. George W. Gift, in his description of the *Arkansas*' engines, would note that they were constructed "(or botched, rather)" at the Adams Street foundry. By "botched," we can assume that these were high pressure units made as Kane described, i.e., not "with anything approaching precision." "It would be wonderful if someone actually excavated the wreck of the *Arkansas*," George Wright has suggested. "Her engines are a question mark and it would be interesting to see exactly how they adapted high pressure machinery to twin screws."

In fact, Wright suggests that the armorclad's engines, which were "quite strong," could have been an variation of the type employed aboard civil riverboats. Those low pressure units common to the boats known by Emerson and Shirley were geared to turn their paddle wheels some 20 times per minute. A high pressure engine would be geared up to double the rpms. Wright goes further in his description, noting that from operational experience there were, indeed, two engines each coupled to a separate drive shaft. These would not have been that difficult to construct by a knowledgeable founder. The installation, on the other hand, "would have been complex, with gearing to the drive shafts."

On the other hand, salvage of the ram would allow us to learn the layout of the power plant, Mr. Wright also offered, and conceivably that would tell us, "why her engines on at least one occasion stopped dead top center." Regardless of what exactly comprised the power plant for the *Arkansas*, we know that, aside from the chimney, it was installed below-decks and was far better protected than those of the City Series gunboats built by James B. Eads at Carondelet. On the other hand, a shortage of trained mechanics, tools, and materials together with inadequate construction meant that, as Still puts it, they were "constantly in need of repair." Wright also commented that "if we knew the bore and stroke, we could calculate a theoretical output, and from the layout of the boilers and the grates some idea of how much pressure they could generate and fuel consumption."

The new type of engine Hunter suggested would be necessary for the equipment of a large propeller-driven river steamer might have been, if developed, more efficient than the standard riverboat engine then in use. "Studies in this field," the historian wrote in 1949, "made it clear well before the middle of the century that short strokes and high piston speeds were necessary to reduce condensation losses and obtain maximum efficiency." So it was, Wright told this writer in a March 31, 2010, e-mail, that "the requirements of the *Arkansas*-class ironclads demanded a hybrid engine using tooling and materials common for riverboat engines." Such engines would be "pushed beyond the normal operating range to meet the needs of screw propulsion." History shows (with the second *Tennessee* and the *Albemarle*) that it was perfectly possible to gear up large riverboat engines to drive propellers, though the price was "increased noise, space and losses in efficiency."

It also appears that the engines built in Memphis for the Rebel ironclads were direct-acting. This term does not refer to a specific engine type, but rather to the method of connecting the engine and drive-shaft. Such an engine, which could be used for either paddle wheels or propellers, eliminated various side-levers and transferred power directly to the crankshaft. A connecting rod (piston rod if no connecting rod) linked the piston or piston rod and the crankshaft with a pin.

Another advantage of a direct-acting engine was space. As one of these often weighed 40 percent less than a side-lever engine of the same power, it required an engine room only two-thirds the size. It is also quite probable that these were horizontal-trunk engines. These allowed, as Mike McCarthy later pointed out, "the use of a relatively long connecting rod joined directly to the piston via a hollow trunk that projected through both ends of the cylinder." If properly designed, such power plants were the "most compact of all the direct-acting types."

On the other hand, the use of such engines was not without risks. "The downside of less mass in the engines," George Wright notes, "was less damping of vibration which made critical components like connecting rods and their coupling elements more vulnerable to damage or failure from misalignment or insufficient lubrication." Without a vibration damper or isolator, the proper alignment of the engines on board the Memphis armorclads' engines, shafts and balance of the propellers was critical.

Testimony and tantalizing asides in the memoirs of the *Arkansas*' officers, particularly concerning the vessel's final run down from Vicksburg to Baton Rouge, suggest then the type of engines employed. There is little doubt in Mr. Wright's opinion that the Adams Street foundry — inexperienced with high-speed engines — provided John Shirley with two pairs of high-speed, high-pressure engines with short strokes, direct-acting to the vessel's drive shafts. In this, he agrees with Professor Still, who tells us that the machinery for each included "two horizontal, direct-acting noncondensing engines."

Hidden by the years in a small article on "The Rebel Gunboat *Arkansas*" first published by the *Chicago Times* and then picked up by the *New York Times*—interestingly on July 5, 1862, ten days before the armorclad broke out of the Yazoo—is perhaps the most comprehensive statement concerning the boat's engines. "Two horizontal engines," wrote an unnamed reporter, "working across the hull, furnish power, with a capacity of 48-inches bore and four or five feet stroke, working very fast and at a high pressure." Assuming the correctness of the assertions from the historians and the correspondent, gearing for the engines of the *Arkansas* would also have to have been purpose-built as there would not have been "any off-the-shelf gearing" available. "Mind you, we're getting power to the drive shaft through a gearing system of unknown efficiency," Wright warned this writer. Thus there was most likely no up-ratio gearing that could match engine and propeller speeds.

The size of the two screws carried by the *Arkansas* is also unknown. In the reprinted early report carried in the *New York Times* on July 5, 1862, it was claimed that her "propulsion is achieved by means of two seven-foot propeller wheels, which project from the sides near the stern and are entirely covered by water." "Because of the description of her hull form at the stern, it is likely," George Wright has concluded, "that she could turn 8 or 9 footers. These would be fairly efficient." Maximum propeller speeds were reported by the Northern press at 90 revolutions per minute (rpm), which Wright believes "reasonable for small diameter screw propulsion of the era." There are other propeller mysteries. We know from memoirs and reports that steering while underway could be enhanced by differential thrust from the propellers. We do not know whether this was achieved by reversing one propeller or by simply reducing the speed on one engine to eliminate the balancing thrust to that side. There is no information to indicate whether or not the two propellers rotated in the same direction or were opposed.

The builders of the Memphis armorclads were well aware of the dangers debris in the water posed to the vessels' power plants. Consequently, both were to be outfitted with two "basket-shaped" structures aft (one port and one starboard), fabricated from iron rods, designed to keep flotsam out of the upper arc of the propellers. Those propeller guards aboard the *Arkansas* reportedly worked well.

"The shafts for the two projected ironclads were ordered from Leeds and Company of New Orleans," wrote Raimondo Luraghi in 1996. The 50-year-old foundry of future mayor Charles J. Leeds and his brother Thomas L. was also heavily engaged with both the production of ordnance and the Crescent City armorclad projects and modified and reworked a pair of shafts salvaged earlier from the wrecks of two Lower Mississippi steamboats. Contracting early for this important component from an established firm was a very prudent move. When the builder of the *Louisiana* approached Leeds for shafts, the manufacturer had to decline because they were "making the shafting, of pieces of shafting they had on hand, for the two boats at Memphis." Such a statement suggests that the shafting might have had a basis in components salvaged from other vessels, sunk or broken up.

George Wright points out that "it is unlikely that her drive shafts incorporated gearing, but an extra mass (larger flywheel) to deal with vibration from the connecting rod and referred vibration from the propellers returning up the drive shafts is likely." We do know that neither drive shaft had a "dog clutch," that is, a clutch in which projections on one part fit into recesses on the other part and would have permitted decoupling of the shaft from the engine in the case of engine failure.

Construction of the thrust blocks for the armorclad's drive shafts is unknown. These were specialized bearings used to resist the thrust of the propeller shafts and transmit it to the hull. At least one report concerning the loss of the *Arkansas* at Baton Rouge indicated that her engine "tore loose." If this is true, it may in fact have been a reference to a failure of a thrust block or a failure of the actual engine footings. This would be consistent, Wright believes, "with a torque/resonance issue working on the thrust block or engine bearer, a likely consequence if her drive-line dispensed with the usual oil-filled multi-plate thrust blocks and attempted to carry thrust loads directly from the shafts into the engine and the engine and shaft bearers."

Location of the ship's boilers deep in the vessel's hold for protection from gunfire created unfamiliar problems for the mechanics who normally built and assembled the machinery ordinarily employed on Western riverboats. "Placed near the bow with their doors facing forward," stated Louis C. Hunter, "steamboat furnaces long had the benefit of a draft stimulated by the forward motion of the vessel." Lacking the usual open access to fresh air for combustion, the furnace makers turned to a non-maritime technique. "The simplest method of increasing the draft," Hunter continues, "was to direct the exhaust steam up the chimneys in the manner employed on locomotives." The breechings, sheet iron collectors for exhaust gases from the boilers, were joined and melded into the base of the ironclad's stack (chimney). We also know that the boilers were not adequately lined.

We do not know the dimensions of the boilers the *Arkansas* carried. The maximum boiler pressure reported by Lt. Brown as moving the vessel was 120 pounds per square inch (psi) as she entered Old River on July 15. If this was in fact the case, then her boilers had to have been of relatively small diameter and long in proportion to minimize bursting pressures. Professor Still has written that the boilers "were also quite common — the horizontal-fire-tube-boiler with a double (return) flue." Nor do we know how many boilers the armorclad fired. The number may have been as few as two or, as David Flynt tells us, as high as four. The *Chicago Times* report carried by the *New York Times* on July 5, 1862, says "six boilers supply the steam for the machinery." Were they built new, or, given the big market for used steamboat machinery that existed in those days, perhaps, like the shafts, refurbished from salvage? Whatever their source or number, they were placed in the hold below the waterline, most likely, as in David Meagher's 1995 blueprints, in a side-by-side layout straddling the vessel's keel.

It is likely that the *Arkansas* was provided with a "doctor engine" to drive her feed water pumps. This was a standard auxiliary feature on steamboats of the period. It is also likely that her boilers had an "ash box" as well as a "mud box," the latter for the separation of particulates from the boiler feed water. Bilge pumps were also shipped and would be employed often.

The coal capacity designed into the armorclads is unknown. Given that she made it the 300-plus miles from Vicksburg to Baton Rouge in early August before needing to refuel, it would appear that capacity provided at least that range. Lack of a condenser would increase fuel consumption by 15 to 20 percent. The coal bunkers were most likely located in the hold forward of the chimney, but they may have located in spaces between the hull and the boilers. The coal was loaded in sacks or bushels, terms sometimes used interchangeably, and manually placed into the bunkers. The boiler grates were believed to have been configured to burn coal and would be less efficient if wood, the most common fuel of the West, was consumed instead.

The mass of exhaust steam generated lowered pressure in the furnaces on the exhaust stroke. This caused high pressure air outside the furnace to flow in through the face of the furnace. It also resulted in a repetitive, deep-throated "whuffing" sound not unlike that of contemporary railroad locomotives. All of this enhanced the importance of the vessel's smokestack, called a "chimney" by steamboatmen. The *Arkansas* had a large stack, seven feet in diameter, made from sheets of boilerplate that were attached together with rows of horizontal and vertical iron bolts. Possibly built by the hometown Copper, Tin, and Sheet-Iron Manufactory, it was unarmored and lacked a boiler fan to provide forced draft. Four guy wires or chains (two forward and two aft) led from the top opening to the casemate roof providing support. The vessel's chimney would, during operations, prove a major "weak spot." Any type of damage to its skin would result in an immediate reduction of output from the engines.[9]

Following the Federal naval bombardment of Vicksburg during May 26–28, a shoot that was seen by Flag Officer Farragut as ineffectual, the Union vessels off the town significantly lowered the intensity of their assault. During this time, the fortress was reinforced by the additional Louisiana troops (four regiments of infantry, four companies of cavalry, and an artillery battery) plus four companies of Mississippi soldiers. These were distributed up and down from Walnut Hills to Warrenton to guard against riverborne landings.

Farragut, a blue-water sailor, very much wanted to return to the Gulf, especially now that there seemed little chance that Brig. Gen. Williams' men could do much against the Vicksburg defenses and because the Mississippi was beginning to fall. After consulting with his commanders, the loyal Tennessean elected to steam back down to New Orleans at the end of the month with his heavy ships, leaving six smaller craft to maintain the Federal presence. These little oceangoing craft would lob the occasional shell into town. As the editor of the *Vicksburg Daily Whig* advised his readers on June 5, "As a matter of course, we may expect another bombardment this evening. They generally commence at five o'clock. Admission free, but stand from under."

When news of the *Hartford*'s return to the Crescent City reached the U.S. Navy Department in Washington (including some details first read in the Richmond newspapers), Secretary Gideon Welles was furious, believing that Farragut had given up his mission of effecting a rendezvous with the Western Flotilla at Vicksburg and conquering that city. He certainly did not have his naval commander's letters of explanation, including a request for ironclads. In his correspondence with Washington, the flag officer readily admitted that if the *Arkansas* ever really did come out his wooden vessels would be in great jeopardy. Writing to a friend, he grumbled: "They expect me to navigate the Mississippi 900 miles in the face of batteries, iron-clad rams, etc., and yet, with all the iron-clad vessels they have in the North, they could not get to Norfolk or Richmond." Still, Farragut promised to do his duty.

On June 8, following receipt of a direct redeployment order from Welles, the commander of the West Gulf Coast Blockading Squadron stood back up the river with his heavy men-o'-war. This time he was accompanied by 16 mortar schooners under Cmdr. David Dixon Porter. The huge 13-inch-high trajectory mortars were expected to have an easier time with Vicksburg bluff-top defenses than the guns on the decks of his regular men-o'-war. It would take over three weeks for the Union naval squadron to carefully maneuver its way back up against the current to its previous anchorage below Vicksburg. Indeed, it would take a week just to find sufficient army towboats to bring up the mortar schooners.

In the interim between the Battle of Memphis and the anticipated arrival by the Gulf sailors of their fleet at Vicksburg, the Southern defenders of Vicksburg continued to expand

Five: Five Weeks Up the Yazoo, Early May–Late June 1862

their protections (with civilians building bomb-proof shelters wherever practical) and forces. Brig. Gen. Smith's command would have a total of 16 batteries to greet the second coming of the Federals, including two big 10-inch Columbiads plus 27 smaller 42-pdr. and 32-pdr. cannon. Among the artillery pieces available were the six 6-pdr. smoothbores and two 12-pdr. howitzers of the 1st Kentucky Battery, which, according to one of its sergeants, was "so situated that it commanded the upper part of the river opposite the point. Named for its commander, Robert L. Cobb, Cobb's Battery would welcome the arrival of the *Arkansas* in July.

As June advanced, the Southern naval officers, men, and all the laborers at Yazoo City continued to be engaged on the *Arkansas* from sunup to sundown. Lt. Stevens confessed that "I have not much time for writing [home] now, as my whole day from 5 in the morning until 7 in the evening is taken up, and then I am pretty tired." These travails were unknown at Western Department headquarters at Tupulo. From that Magnolia State town, Gen. Beauregard wrote to Gen. Lovell on June 10: "How is the steam-ram *Arkansas* progressing?" Having long maintained an interest in the vessel, the theater commander was concerned that she, like the ironclad *Mississippi* at New Orleans, would be ready "just one week too late." Lovell's reply, if any, is unknown.

Two days after Beauregard wrote Lovell concerning the Rebel armorclad, a deserter fleeing Vicksburg was taken aboard the Federal flagship *Hartford*. There he told the flag officer that the *Arkansas* was almost completely fitted out and nearly ready for service, perhaps within as little as a week. Fleet Capt. Cmdr. Henry H. Bell, standing next to Farragut, took notes that he later wrote down in his diary (subsequently published in vol. 18 of the Navy *Official Records*). The animated Confederate also told the Union naval officers that the ram's commander was Lt. Brown, CSN. This was the first indication the Yankees received concerning the identity of their opponent. Brown's reputation for industriousness, known to several aboard from their companionship with him in the prewar USN, was appreciated.

Still anchored at Baton Rouge on June 14, Farragut and Brig. Gen. Williams learned of "the destruction by Davis of the rebel fleet of gunboats in sight of the population of Memphis." At Vicksburg, the remaining Union vessels lifted their bombardment; they would hold off for days while awaiting the arrival of their commander and the mortar schooners that had been so successful during the New Orleans campaign. The same day, Confederate president Jefferson Davis wrote to Brig. Gen. Smith at Vicksburg. Greatly concerned about the fate of

Confederate Officers from the CSS *Tacony* and *Atlanta*. *This remarkable group picture of POW Confederate naval officers was taken at Fort Warren, Boston, ca. 1863–1864. Among those posed between the door and right window are two veterans of the CSS* Arkansas, *Lt. Alphonso Barbot (*Atlanta*) and Lt. Charles W. Read (*Tacony*) (Navy History and Heritage Command).*

Vicksburg (not far from his plantation) and the Mississippi, he asked not only about the city's defenses, but also specifically asked, "What progress is being made toward the completion of the *Arkansas*?" As with Beauregard's inquiry of Lovell, no answer has been found.

Temperatures soared above 100 degrees and the men were unprotected from the hot sun during the day. Awnings were everywhere in this part of the South, but none covered those laboring topside aboard the armorclad or working nearby on the riverbank. Anything made of metal or iron exposed to the sun was hot to the touch. Even for those fortunate enough to be required below-decks or within the casemate, there was no escape, as the closed in spaces were equally warm — or warmer. The unrelenting grind of the work and the dogged determination of Lt. Brown took its toll. There was heat exhaustion; more than a few men required timeoff in the shade and there were several desertions.

Because of the summer heat, the great rivers of the Mississippi Valley, as was their cycle, began to fall. The same evaporation that forced the Federal timberclads *Lexington* and *Tyler* to quit the Tennessee River this month now threatened the *Arkansas* as she lay in the stream before Yazoo City. Each morning and sometimes more frequently, Lt. Brown had the Yazoo sounded and sent men to take measurements as far down as the great raft barrier and even the bar at Satartia. The news became increasingly distressful. When there was 20 feet at Yazoo City, further downstream it was only 18. It was calculated that about a fortnight remained before the ram, if she did not move, would be stranded, this time by low water.

On the other hand, Federal concerns with the mere existence of the ram continued to intensify. At Memphis, Lt. Seth Ledyard Phelps, fleet captain of the Western Flotilla, wrote to that squadron's former commander, Flag Officer Andrew Hull Foote, on June 17, in a letter reprinted in Foote's first biography: "Today we have reports that the rebel ram and gun-boat *Arkansas*, of which we have heard so much, sailed down the Yazoo on Sunday last, and is expected to destroy the entire Yankee fleet. The rebels boat that she is another *Merrimack*. We hear nothing from the fleet below Vicksburg."

After the great victory off Memphis, Federal forces occupied that Tennessee city. Both ground and naval forces now assessed their situation and the assets that had come into their hands. Flag Officer Charles H. Davis, commander of the Western Flotilla, ordered those salvageable ex–CRDF vessels repaired and, within days, sent off an expedition to the White River to communicate with a Federal military force headed toward that stream from Missouri. There was also another Union naval force at Memphis, the U.S. Army Ram Fleet. Its founder and commander, Charles Ellet, mortally wounded during the battle of June 6, lingered on, with his brothers and other commanders in attendance at his bedside. Lt. Col. Alfred Ellet took instructions from his dying brother and saw to the needs of his boats and crews. Relations between the Ellets and Davis, always strained, were not improving. Interservice rivalries and personality clashes did not help.

On June 19, at a conference held at the sickbed of Charles Ellet, it was decided that the army's rams would steam off to Vicksburg, acting under the command of Lt. Col. Ellet until such time as the secretary of war, Edwin Stanton, the outfit's ultimate commander, made a decision as to whether to retain the semi-independent fleet or turn it over to Davis. Before sunset, five rams set off toward Helena, seeking both prizes and recruits to enlarge their undermanned crews. Charles Ellet would not see his brother, his son, Medical Officer Charles Rivers Ellet, who was with Alfred, or his beloved rams again; he would die afloat on June 21 while en route to Cairo.

On Friday morning June 20, the *Vicksburg Citizen* published three items of interest.

Five: Five Weeks Up the Yazoo, Early May–Late June 1862

A new commander had been appointed along with a new chief engineer in charge of fortifying the town. Additionally, it was noted that "a Federal naval expedition under Flag Officer Farragut has left Baton Rouge with 3,000 troops under Brigadier General Thomas Williams, reportedly on its way to Vicksburg, with the intention of establishing a base on the De Soto Peninsula ('Swampy Toe') opposite the city."

President Davis had originally determined to appoint his friend Gen. Braxton Bragg (1817–1876) to command the Department of Southern Mississippi and East Louisiana, but Bragg's inconvenient illness forced him to substitute the dashing Port Gibson, Mississippi, native, Maj. Gen. Earl Van Dorn (1820–1863), who, as commander of Trans-Mississippi District 2, had unhappily lost the Battle of Pea Ridge in Arkansas a few months before. Maj. Samuel H. Lockett (1837–1891) was named to oversee continuing preparation of the citadel's defenses.

Bragg replaced the dismissed Gen. Beauregard and Van Dorn would report to him. Davis informed Mississippi governor Pettus of the switch, indicating his hope that the new Vicksburg boss "will answer the popular desire." On June 22, the 10,000 troops of Brig. Gen. Ruggles and Maj. Gen. John C. Breckenridge (1821–1875), the Kentuckian and former U.S. vice president (the nation's youngest), were placed by Gen. Bragg under Van Dorn and ordered to Vicksburg. At the same time, Van Dorn learned for the first time that Farragut's fleet, and probably that of Davis, was "ascending and descending the river toward Vicksburg."

Ruggles anticipated that his "special department" would soon be closed down and advised Lt. Brown. The navyman's ally would, in fact, be ordered to terminate his Grenada operations a week later. Ruggles would command the First District of Van Dorn's Confederate forces from a base at Camp Moore, in Tangipahoa Parish about 25 miles from Baton Rouge.[10]

In addition to the heat, soldiers, sailors, and civilians in the area around Vicksburg were afflicted by insects of all kinds. Fleas, gnats, chiggers (also called redbugs), biting horse flies, houseflies, and ants would plague both sides at Vicksburg during that summer and in 1863. And this was to say nothing about other insect and animal hazards such as bears, panthers, wolves, poisonous spiders and snakes or sweat bees, wasps, and hornets. It was the fabled local mosquitoes that were most dangerous. Malaria and yellow fever rode the insects from the undrained lands and huge swamps of the Delta. Mosquito netting was nonexistent. Most of the laborers and others at the improvised Yazoo City boatyard now growing up on the bank adjacent to the *Arkansas* protected themselves with old fashioned (and usually odorific) home remedies, including lard or other grease thickly applied and even turpentine. Bare skin nevertheless always seemed to show numerous bug welts.

With the mosquitoes came malaria, also known as the ague or "the shakes." It seemed that half the people at Vicksburg, both Confederate and Union, were, or were about to be, stricken with the disease. Sailors aboard the Federal gunboats off the town, Brig. Gen. Williams' soldiers, laborers working on the *Arkansas*, Pinkney's men guarding the raft, Southern troops manning guns or mounting patrols, and the civilians of the local region, in the villages and on the plantations, to say nothing of the African American slaves, suffered equally. Quinine when available was regularly prescribed by medical personnel as a treatment; medicinal whiskey, sometimes mixed with various and sundry tree barks, was also employed.

The disease was not a respecter of rank or cause. For example, Lt. Brown soon "ran a malarial fever," as did an old friend and coming foe, Capt. Henry Walke of the U.S. steam gunboat *Carondelet*, now with the Western Flotilla upstream at Memphis. After arriving at

Vicksburg, Union Brig. Gen. Williams wrote specifically about the problem as it worsened: "Such hot weather as we have here is seldom experienced anywhere, and what is worse, the drying up of the lately overflowed land gives rise to a malarious atmosphere, which is telling alarmingly on the health of the troops. Nearly ½ of my whole force is on the sick list."

Another bothersome irritation was miliaria, also known as prickly heat or heat rash, a skin disease associated with sweating and common in hot, humid conditions. A variety of measures were adopted to combat it by those with medical or homemade remedies, including, according to the *Cincinnati Daily Commercial*, vinegar baths. Most of the *Arkansas* workers just scratched.

In addition to the sickness, Lt. Brown faced yet another command difficulty—finding sufficient crewmen. Inaugural efforts by his lieutenants to ship men at Jackson and Mobile largely failed. Only a few men actually signed articles and returned with the officers. Recruiting sufficient sailors became another big headache. In a March 17, 2010, letter to this writer, George Wright explained that "the ranks and skills sought by Brown for the *Arkansas* can be better understood with a quick review of the pre–War standards of the Federal Navy upon which the Confederate organization was based."

USN sailors were recruited for a period of three years or one cruise. Each was to be 18 years old with a height of 4 feet 8 inches and the ability to pass the rudimentary physical exam where recruited. As we shall see, the captain of the *Arkansas* would be forced to make exceptions to these basic requirements. In general, "line" recruits were classified as Landsmen (newcomers), Ordinary Seamen (3 years experience or reenlistment), Seamen (6 years experience and knowledge of the ship's cordage), or Boy (youth 13–18 years old enlisted with parental permission). There were actually two "staff" enlistments: Firemen and Coal Heavers, both associated with the vessel's power plant.

Although he had sufficient line and warrant officers, e.g., lieutenants, passed midshipmen, surgeons, purser, master's mates, etc., Lt. Brown would always be on the lookout for qualified petty officers, some of whom he inherited and others who would be appointed from the ranks of his most experienced seamen. Only a few were sent aboard from the Jackson naval base. These petty officers were also divided into "line" and "staff" billets, with the latter most often serving as technical personnel for the engines, e.g., assistant engineers. Line petty officers, regular or "leading," included the quartermasters, coxswains, yeoman, cooks, coxswains, and so forth.

Following the Battle of Memphis, the CRDF commander, Capt. James Montgomery, took the surviving crewmen (who were not officially CSN personnel, but army or even civilian) from his cotton-clads by rail to Grenada. There he hoped to obtain funds from either Brig. Gen. Lovell or Ruggles which he would use to pay the men. In addition, the men that Brig. Gen. Thompson removed from Montgomery's boats on June 5 were also en route to Grenada. Ruggles tipped off Lt. Brown that Montgomery's men and maybe Thompson's were available.

After Lt. Stevens returned from Canton, Lt. Brown sent another officer to Grenada to meet with Commodore Montgomery to ascertain whether ex–CRDF crewmen might be persuaded to serve aboard the ram. It was not immediately anticipated that Thompson's soldiers might be available. Accompanied by the *Arkansas* officer, Montgomery and his men travelled to Yazoo City. After their arrival, the sailors met with Lt. Brown, who "tried every way to induce them to join the *Arkansas*." In conversations, as Brown told Ruggles a few days later, "I was led by Commodore Montgomery to believe that I could obtain men from his late command, and I further supposed that they came here from Grenada with the purpose of joining the *Arkansas*." Either there was deception in this case or gross miscommunication.

In his July 1 report to the CSA war secretary, G.W. Randolph, Montgomery admitted the following: "I obtained from General Lovell $30,000 and paid off, on the 21st of June at Yazoo City, the remnant of the upper river fleet." The men were given honorable discharges, even though they still had upwards of three months remaining on their enlistments. Montgomery did not communicate his action to Lt. Brown, who, when he found out about the measure next day, was beside himself with rage. It was too late for the sailor to address the situation with patriotic oratory as the CRDF men, with money in their pockets, were determined to leave this hot and sickly location. "They talk among themselves of going to New Orleans," the angry officer reported to Ruggles. "Many will, I think, attempt to reach Memphis. I think that, with few exceptions they intend to join the enemy." Before that could happen, the lieutenant earnestly hoped that his full-bearded army patron "will cause them to be cared for while making the attempt"— in other words, arrested.

Disappointed because the CRDF fleet "did not give me one man," Brown believed he could "obtain two-thirds of a crew from the Confederate States vessels now in the Yazoo." Having failed to recruit Montgomery's men, he would apply to Brig. Gen. Smith at Vicksburg for transferred soldiers, say 40 or 50. It was now becoming obvious that luck had smiled upon the *Arkansas* at least the matter of her 32 officers. Once McBlair and Guthrie were gone, those who had originally come to Yazoo City and Greenwood with them melded into a cohesive, energetic, and effective unit with those appointed by Brown. Perhaps we might take a moment here to note their duties, as their biographies were presented in footnotes earlier.

Lt. Brown, the captain, would serve topside in battle or in the pilothouse. At the latter post, he would be joined by the boat's pilots, men who, in both Federal and Confederate service, were exposed to the greatest dangers. The chief pilot was John Hodges, with James Shacklett having recently come aboard to help navigate the Yazoo. Three pilots familiar with the Mississippi were also on board: William Gilmore, James Montgomery, and James Brady.

Executive Officer Stevens was second in command. It was his duty, as it had been with first lieutenants for centuries, to oversee the daily functioning of the vessel. He was also in charge of all the gun batteries, which, according to George Wright, "mirrored pre-war French Navy practice, with adaptations for the absence of a quarterdeck." His Gunner, Thomas Travers, was still rather new to his duties. Forgoing tradition, Stevens chose to leave the actual gunnery to his officers and instead served as something of an interior ombudsman, allocating resources, overseeing damage control, and, as necessary, relaying orders received from the captain. The ship's carpenter and any mates, normally a part of the powder division, would be well known by the XO. They would make certain that a ready supply of damage and fire control items were on hand and have ready all the pumps necessary to control leaks.

Stevens' subordinate lieutenants, in addition to miscellaneous shipboard assignments, each held direct command of certain big guns, which were arranged in pairs in divisions that were ordinarily numbered from the bow. There were five divisions aboard the *Arkansas*, though from which Columbiad they were numbered remains a mystery. Thus, Lt. John Grimball was in charge of the forward starboard battery that comprised the forward Columbiad and one Dahlgren. Lt. Gift commanded the forward port battery holding the other Columbiad and Dahlgren. Lt. Charles W. Read oversaw the two rifled 32-pdrs. at the stern. The starboard broadside battery was led by Lt. A.D. Wharton, while Lt. Alphonso Barbot had those in the port broadside battery.

Three of the midshipmen were made assistant gunnery officers and each worked for a lieutenant, serving as the gun captain for a specific mount. Thus the pairs at the casemate guns were Lt. Grimball and Midshipman Dabney Scales, Lt. Wharton and Midshipman Richard Bacot, and Lt. Barbot and Midshipman Daniel Talbott. In place of Midshipman Clarence W. Tyler, who served as aide to Lt. Brown, Lt. Gift had the services of Mater's Mate John Wilson, who kept a diary, excerpts from which were subsequently published in the Navy *Official Records*, Vol. 19.

Each gun crew comprised from 12 to 14 men each, with a powder boy for each. Lt. Gift indicated at one point that 17 men made up his unit. It has been suggested that *Arkansas*' ordnance requirements must have exceeded half of her crew; 120 men were required if all the guns were fully manned simultaneously. This might not have always been the case. Brown and Stevens may have, occasionally and by necessity, followed the prewar U.S. Navy drill manuals, under which broadside gun crews were responsible for guns on both sides of the gun deck. Some hybrid arrangements were also undoubtedly followed. The memoirs of participants indicate that the bow- and stern-chasers, as well as the forward Dahlgren broadside guns, had dedicated crews. During the July 22 fight with the *Essex* and *Queen of the West*, we know for certain that "flying" gun crews were employed for the *Arkansas*' different mounts and all of them were much smaller than those with which she departed the Yazoo. How many gunners the boat had — or for that matter, the total actual crew size — remains in dispute.

Masters John Phillips and Samuel Millikin were in charge of the powder divisions, fore and aft. (Milliken, who liked to paint and draw, has left us the only contemporary sketch of the *Arkansas* by one of her crewmen.) Their duty was to insure that a steady supply of projectiles and powder were available to the gun crews. The pair were assisted by quartermasters, including one named Eaton who passed shells up the ladder from the forward shell room to the berth deck. Men overseen by Phillips and Millikin were also expected to help carry any wounded down to the tender mercies of the surgeon and his mate.

The master-at-arms and his assistant, the boat's police, controlled interior lighting, making certain before action that the galley fire was extinguished and the battle lanterns lit. They made certain that loose gunpowder was promptly swept up or dumped into tubs of water and assisted also with small arms.

Interestingly, there were no Confederate States Marine Corps personnel stationed aboard the *Arkansas*.

The CSMC was established by an act of the Congress of the Confederate States on March 16, 1861, with an initial authorization of 45 officers and 944 enlisted men. Marines provided ship and naval station security, were trained to act as gun crews, and usually comprised boarding or landing parties. Prior to the summer of 1862, when it was broken into squad-sized units and dispersed throughout the South, the CSMC was concentrated on ships and at stations on the East Coast. None of its members were, for example, assigned to New Orleans or Jackson.

Scottish-born chief engineer George W. City ran the propulsion machinery (engines, boilers, and associated equipment). He had one second assistant engineer, Ellison Covert, and five third assistant engineers: Eugene Brown, James Gettis, William Jackson, John Dupuy, and James Doland. None of these men, save the highly regarded City, had any previous experience with machinery aboard naval vessels, especially screw propulsion. Brown,

Five: Five Weeks Up the Yazoo, Early May–Late June 1862

a native of Norfolk, Virginia, was a volunteer from the army whom Gift later called "a young man of pluck and gallantry and possessed of great will and determination."

Two medical men occupied the below-decks sickbay, ex–USN surgeon Dr. H.W.W. Washington and his assistant, Dr. Charles M. Morfit. A third man, name unknown, would serve briefly aboard while the *Arkansas* was at Vicksburg, relieving Washington and Morfit, who were both taken ill. The personnel of the wardroom mess also included the ex–USN paymaster or purser, Richard Taylor.

With the sun beating down and haze everywhere, work neared an end on the project of reclaiming the *Arkansas* from her late May status as a semi-derelict. Her interior was largely finished, an armor coat was hung topside, most of her guns were mounted, the engines were assembled and boilers installed, some supplies were stowed, the *Capitol* was untied, and the officers and a small percentage of the total crew had been shipped. Having overcome shortages and difficulties of every nature, Brown and his men were all but finished with their desperate building project.

Within 34 days of her arrival in the Yazoo and just three weeks after Lt. Brown was ordered to assume her command, John Shirley's realized dream was anchored in the river just off the bank below Yazoo City, ready for her first trial run. As her officers and men admired their work, Lt. Brown admitted that "the *Arkansas* now appeared as if a small sea-going vessel had been cut down to the water's edge at both ends, leaving a box for guns amidships."

It was about this time that Capt. Lynch arrived at Yazoo City from Jackson. The former commander of CSN forces in North Carolina waters, who may have actually seen the CSS *Virginia* before she was destroyed, was very interested in the kind of craft Shirley and Brown had been able to construct. Celebrated as a scholar, the 62-year-old Lynch, accompanied by Brown and Stevens, carefully inspected the *Arkansas*— and was not impressed, comparing her casemate to a "slaughterhouse." After the tour was completed, he took his leave, most likely en route to Liverpool Landing to confer with Cmdr. Pinkney before travelling to Vicksburg to see Maj. Gen. Van Dorn.

Before leaving, Lynch summoned Lt. Read and ordered him to take a message back to Jackson for relay by telegraph to navy secretary Mallory. The young officer hastily set off, though at some point during his ride, he read his superior's comments. "The *Arkansas* is very inferior to the *Merrimac* [*Virginia*] in every particular," the captain wrote. "The iron with which she is covered is worn and indifferent, taken from a railroad track, and is poorly secured to the vessel." Lynch continued, noting that the ram had "boiler iron on stern and counter; her smokestack is sheet iron."

Despite his command's rough appearance, Lt. Brown was exceedingly pleased with his vessel's progress, later claiming that it was "perhaps not inferior under all the circumstances to the renowned effort of Oliver Hazard Perry in cutting a fine ship from the forest in 90 days." Lt. Gift was also generous: "It is sufficient to say that within five weeks from the day we arrived in Yazoo City, we had a man-of-war (such as she was) from almost nothing— the credit for all of which belongs to Isaac Newton Brown, the commander of the vessel." "She was a squat, ugly craft as originally designed," historian Robert Huffstot noted years later. "The necessary compromises and modifications had done nothing to make her more beautiful." Brown, Hufstott noted, was also pleased that he was able to bring the project in at a cost of $79,600, or almost exactly her contract price, an achievement that "made her unusual in this or any other war."

A trial run is just that, a shakedown cruise to learn what works and what does not before it is certified operational. With Capt. Shirley no longer in the picture, the *Arkansas* would not be officially turned over to the CSN in the manner in which the Eads boats were acquired by Capt. Andrew Hull Foote for the USN. Already in possession of the *Arkansas*, those formalities could be dispensed with. Brown's informal situation was, however, far more pressing. With the river stage declining and Federal warships a few hours away, it was necessary only to not prove the armorclad as quickly as possible, especially its power plant, but also to move down to deeper waters.

Either on the afternoon of June 22 or early on the morning of June 23, the *Arkansas* raised anchor and began to slowly float downstream. Master's Mate Wilson later wrote that this departure was actually three days earlier, but we know, from the Navy *Official Records*, that Lt. Brown was still posting letters from Yazoo City on the morning of the 22nd. In a Yazoo City letter to Brig. Gen. Ruggles that day, he suggested that he could obtain three cannon from Pinkney's vessels, which should be employed as fire ships. He also confessed that he had no intelligence concerning the approach of Flag Officer Davis' Western Flotilla from Memphis.

On whichever day she left Yazoo City, the armorclad's great iron beak immediately split the water like a knife and her trim was true. Anyone watching from shore might be excused, as Brown later wrote, for thinking that they saw "a small seagoing vessel ... cut down to the water's edge at both ends, leaving a box for guns amidships." The weather remained hot and hazy. Pressure in the boilers of the *Arkansas* rose steadily to 120 pounds, at which point a gear-controlling lever was thrown. As the Memphis-built engines, assembled and installed with so much care by Chief Engineer City and his assistants, came to life and the big propellers, one under each quarter, began to turn, everyone breathed a sigh of relief. With Lt. Brown at his side, Pilot Shacklett tried the rudder, left and right, finding that the helm answered readily.

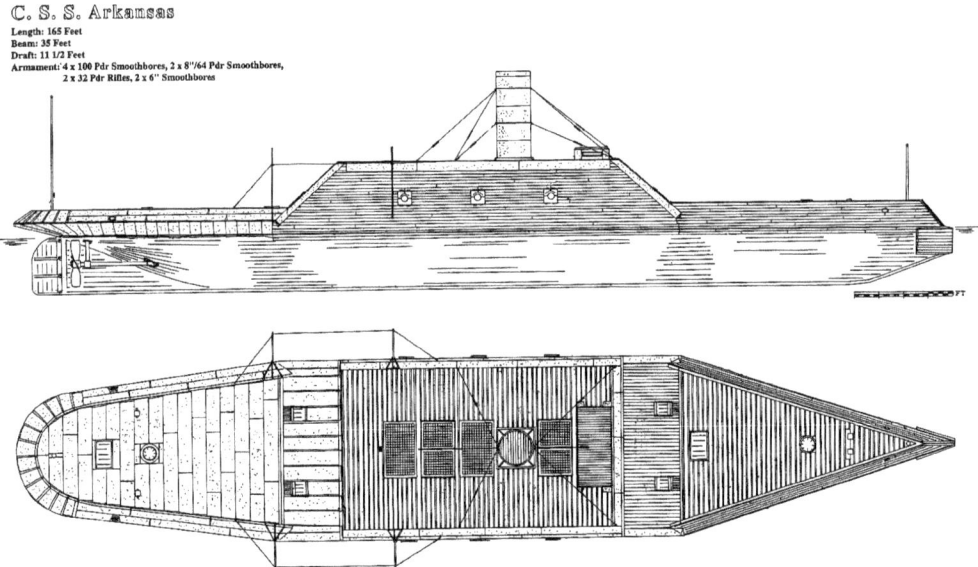

CSS *Arkansas*. *This modern side and top profile clearly reveals the artist's view of decking and hatches and should be contrasted with the drawing of the CSS* Virginia. *(© 1995 David J. Meagher. Used with permission).*

Shakedown Cruise. *The* Arkansas *underway, June 23, 1862. Within 34 days of her arrival in the Yazoo and just three weeks after Lt. Isaac Newton Brown was ordered to assume her command, Memphis contractor John Shirley's dream was anchored in the river just off the bank below Yazoo City, Mississippi, ready for her first trial run. As her officers and men admired their work, Lt. Brown admitted that "the* Arkansas *now appeared as if a small sea-going vessel had been cut down to the water's edge at both ends, leaving a box for guns amidships." Either on the afternoon of June 22 or early on the morning of June 23, the* Arkansas *raised anchor and began to slowly float downstream. The goal for the shakedown of the* Arkansas *cruise was to make it unassisted to Liverpool Landing, where other Rebel gunboats stood guard (without steam up) against any sudden Union naval thrust up the Yazoo. Robert G. Skerrett's noted 1904 painting inaccurately depicts the side casemate walls of the armorclad as slanted rather than vertical. Daniel Dowdey's new illustration provides an excellent broadside profile that corrects Skerrett's casemate depiction. His addition of officers and men on deck lends perspective (top, Navy History and Heritage Command; bottom, © 2010 Daniel Dowdey. Used with permission).*

The goal for the *Arkansas*' first test run was to make it unassisted to Liverpool Landing, where Cmdr. Pinkney's gunboats stood guard (without steam up) at the raft against any sudden Union naval thrust up the Yazoo. Perhaps escorted by the *Capitol* in case of emergency and followed by the *Star of the West*, the untried vessel made steady progress through the river channel. The pounding engines steadily increased the ironclad's speed to eight miles per hour (though it was expected that pace would be halved against a strong current). The components of the powerplant — so far — worked flawlessly, and Brown "at first had some trust in these." Commenting on the pace of the vessel depicted in his drawings, artist David Meagher has commented that "the reason I draw a fast *Arkansas* is that the real ironclad was fast — when her engines worked!"

As the Confederate ram steamed on, her powerplant started to malfunction. "With no insulation on the boilers," remembered Paul Stevens, son of the XO, years later, "they became red hot when fired, running the engine room temperature into astronomical heights." This overheating was caused by the unprotected fire boxes, a problem identified later as the vessel approached the Mississippi, that could, indeed, raise the compartment temperature to 130 degrees. This intolerable situation made it necessary for members of the black gang to frequently come topside for relief.

And then there was the matter of her engines. These, wrote historian Robert Huffstot in 1968, "were prone to hang on dead center." If one of them stopped without warning, the screw of its twin "drove the vessel in a circle despite the rudder." Donald Barnhart labeled the undesired maneuver "a dangerous spin too powerful to be corrected by the rudder." We have no details on this trial run went otherwise. The ram's logbook was, of course, lost and none of the participants thought to write down details other than Master's Mate Wilson, who simply stated the date of departure and the fact that "her general appearance was long and rakish."

We do know, from the logbook of the Federal ram *Lancaster*, that at some point during the trip, the *Arkansas* supposedly ran aground. On the other hand, Henry Bentley of the *Philadelphia Inquirer* later admitted what some suspected. "It is thought that the story of her being aground," he told his readers at the end of July, "was started by him [Lt. Isaac Newton Brown] purposefully to throw our commanders off their guard." If the ram did go aground, this may very well have happened when an engine froze up, stopping unexpectedly on the crankshaft center. It would have demonstrated what Huffstot called "her most fateful peculiarity; namely, that she could not be handled on single screw."

The *Arkansas* was equipped with automatic stoppers that were supposed to halt each engine at the same time. If this did not happen and one engine continued, the remaining screw, as noted, had the power, even against the rudder, to circle her off course. When an engine stopped "top dead center," black gang crews were forced to use metal tools, much like large crow bars, to manually turn the engine's flywheel. This in turn moved the piston away from the cylinder head so that steam could be reintroduced to restart the engine.

With the rivers falling, it was common for vessels of any sizeable draft to get stuck. Flag Officer Farragut's flagship, the *Hartford*, spent some immobile time stuck during her passage up the Mississippi. It would have been a far more serious mechanical matter if the grounding was caused by the boat's engines and not because of a quickly formed islet, a common occurrence on the Western rivers. The *Lancaster*'s log also tells us that "the *Van Dorn* had pulled her off." This part of the report was not possible, as the *Arkansas* was above the great raft and the *Van Dorn* below. Indeed, Capt. Fulkerson's ram was even then near the mouth of the Yazoo keeping watch and prepared to "report on the enemy's proceedings."

More than likely, if she were stuck, it was the *Capitol* or another chartered or civilian steamer that hauled her free.

Lt. Brown's ram was among the assets most dearly treasured by Vicksburg's new commander. Earl Van Dorn was, however, determined that the only major Confederate warship on the Western waters would not uselessly lie as a "force in being" up the Yazoo. She needed to engage the Federal navy quickly. Also on the morning of June 23, Maj. Gen. Van Dorn, accompanied by Mississippi governor Pettus, travelled from Jackson to inspect Vicksburg's defenses. It was a quick trip, but one from which the new department commander gained enhanced appreciation of the citadel's dire situation. Every measure possible must be directed toward preventing the fall of the town — and with it, the Mississippi River.

A key to the city's defense was the First Tennessee Heavy Artillery Regiment, whose veteran cannoneers manned the river batteries on the northern end of town. Back on June 18, Brig. Gen. Smith had ordered it consolidated into four companies: Co. A, Captain Paul T. Dismukes; Co. B; Captain William P. Parks; Co. C, Captain H.T. Norman; and Co. D, Captain John P. Postlethwaite. Also, as part of his stepped-up effort to upgrade Vicksburg's survival chances, Van Dorn telegraphed Richmond on June 23 seeking a naval component. Even as the armorclad slowly made her trial run down the Yazoo, the army commander, unaware of Brown's progress, asked President Davis for permission to take over operational control of the ram for the good of his department's survival. If he could get the *Arkansas* loose on the lower Mississippi, she could not only directly damage the Union war effort in the New Orleans region but also cause Farragut to withdraw from his current anchorage below the Mississippi citadel.

Despite undoubtedly knowing that he was committing a severe affront to interservice protocol (Capt. Lynch should have been the one giving Brown orders), Davis quickly agreed to this measure. Believing Vicksburg faced a dire threat from Farragut's feet, he had orders sent to the boat placing it under direct authority of Van Dorn. Although his command was in the process of moving out, Brig. Gen. Ruggles wanted to make certain that the manpower needs of the *Arkansas* were addressed, even though Montgomery's CRDF crewmen had slipped away. On June 24, he wired Maj. Gen. Van Dorn of his plans to send a large contingent of men to the ram from among Brig. Gen. Thompson's refugee Missouri regiments. Van Dorn did not object.

In his reply to Ruggles sent that evening, Van Dorn, who did not know that Brown was en route toward Liverpool Landing, tried to quickly push the armorclad into action. "Can you send a messenger to the commander of the ram *Arkansas*," he wrote, "and suggest to him to come out, run the fleet, and get behind them and sink transports?" Van Dorn thought that, if the vessel were fast enough, she could easily perform the required task and then steam downriver. "It is better to die game and do some execution," he opined, "than to lie by and be burned up in the Yazoo."

Neither Ruggles or Van Dorn knew that, at 11:00 A.M., the Ellet rams *Monarch* and *Lancaster* had dropped anchor off King's Point, about 4 miles above Vicksburg. They were the first boats from the Union's Memphis-based fleets to arrive in sight of the Confederate fortress city. Going ashore, Lt. Col. Ellet and his 19-year-old nephew, Medical Officer Charles Rivers Ellet, together with Edward Davis, son of the Western Flotilla flag officer, were greeted warmly, apprised of the local situation, and treated to all the stories available concerning the *Arkansas*, including the one about her grounding up the Yazoo.

Per his order from Van Dorn, Brig. Gen. Ruggles sent a messenger to Yazoo City to deliver the commanding general's message. Finding the *Arkansas* had weighed for down stream, the trooper rode on down the river road from Yazoo City next morning until he came up with the armorclad, great clouds of smoke escaping from her thick chimney. She came to once the rider hailed, and Ruggles' message was sent aboard by ship's boat. The horseman was asked to wait for a reply.

As Lt. Brown read Ruggles' letters with the included copies of Van Dorn's dispatches, his frustration rose. Sitting down, he began to write a reply, letting show once more the same concern for his vessel and service (and perhaps his honor and reputation) that he had shown earlier in the year when building the *Eastport*. After recounting his severe disappointment that Montgomery's CRDF "did not give me one man," the ram's captain happily noted that 25 men had arrived that day from Vicksburg, cannoneers from Maj. Henry A. Clinch's 1st Louisiana Heavy Artillery Battalion. They would soon be joined by men from Companies A, E. and G of the 28th Louisiana Volunteers. Capt. William Pratt "Buck" Parks of Company H ("The Arkansas Battery"), 1st Tennessee Heavy Artillery Regiment, was also a volunteer. En route as he was once more to Pinkney's anchorage, Brown anticipated that he would "now soon have a crew." He then hoped that "we shall use our vessel creditably."

Looking back over the dispatches, Brown vented. "I regret to find that by [Van Dorn's] implication," he acidly wrote, "it is thought I would prefer burning the *Arkansas* in Yazoo City to hurling the vessel against the enemy." Perhaps thinking back to the *Polk*, the *Eastport*, and Cmdr. McBlair, he continued: "I have never required prompting in any duties that I have been called upon to perform, and those who have been impatient spectators of my conduct here will not accuse me of being idle." Considering for a moment that his construction difficulties were "only known to those engaged," the sailor went on to assert "that [the reason] I am not yet ready is because I could not perform impossibilities." The work he had accomplished "would have been left under ordinary circumstances." Indeed, "if the army will attack against the same odds as awaits me," he opined, "the war will soon be over."

After jotting a closing sentence to Ruggles thanking him for all "the kind assistance offered and rendered," Brown sealed his communication and had it sent ashore to the waiting rider. As the cavalryman turned away, the *Arkansas* continued toward Liverpool Landing.[11]

CHAPTER SIX

Descending the Yazoo, June 25–July 15, 1862

Following a month of construction travail at Yazoo City, Mississippi, the Confederate ironclad ram *Arkansas* was almost ready for operations. First, however, she had to be proven. On the morning of June 23, she raised anchor and undertook a shakedown cruise, steaming from her "home port" down to Liverpool Landing, accompanied by the *Star of the West* and most likely the chartered side-wheeler *Capitol*. There, just above the defensive raft built early in May, the armorclad would complete her outfitting and, it was hoped, secure additional crewmen.

As the Rebel boats made their way down the Yazoo River, the Federals near Vicksburg were not inactive. On June 24, the two U.S. Army Ram Fleet boats *Monarch* and *Lancaster* dropped anchor off King's Point, about 4 miles above Vicksburg. They were the first boats from the Union's Memphis-based fleets to arrive in sight of the Confederate fortress city and their descent was witnessed by local citizens along the Louisiana shore.

One of those who noticed the rams' passage was 20-year-old Kate Stone, from the large Brokenburn plantation located 20 miles northwest of Vicksburg. Mrs. Stone kept a diary and on June 25, she wrote the following: "Well, we have at last seen what we have been looking for [for] weeks — the Yankee gunboats descending the river. The *Lancaster No. 3* led the way, followed by the *Monarch*. We hope they will be the first to be sunk at Vicksburg. We shall watch for their names. They are polluting the waters of the grand old Mississippi." There, from a pro–Union German refugee, its commander, Lt. Col. Alfred W. Ellet, learned that elements of the U.S. Navy's West Gulf Coast Blockading Squadron were now below Vicksburg. Additionally, news was received that the Confederate ram, about which so many rumors abounded, was up the Yazoo. The informant also told the newcomer that it would be possible to send messengers to the Gulf squadron overland via De Soto Point, a peninsula jutting into a huge horseshoe-shaped bend opposite Vicksburg.

The following morning, Ellet ordered his two vessels to inch down the Mississippi a bit further to Young's Point. From this point, Ellet determined, with the help of the rescued German, to open overland communications with the lower fleet commander, Flag Officer David G. Farragut. Charles Rivers Ellet, by now nicknamed "Little Boy Blue," quickly agreed to lead a party through the two miles of sloughs, marshes, and snake-infested underbrush that separated the two Union squadrons. To further blend in, young Ellet's party would dress in civilian clothes, running the risk of being shot as spies if captured — by either side.

Going ashore, Ellet and the unnamed guide were joined by Edward Davis, son of the

Western Flotilla flag officer, Lt. E.W. Bartlett, and Pvt. William Warren. They were armed only with government-issue navy revolvers. To take advantage of darkness, they began their hike at 2:00 P.M., employing lanterns after dark. Avoiding 500 Confederates in a camp near their path, the five-member U.S. party made it across the peninsula by next morning, hailed a USN cutter, and were taken out to the flagship *Hartford* to see Farragut. There the trek nearly came unraveled, as the flag officer was absent and his remaining officers did not believe the story of their unexpected visitors. Few aboard the big sloop-of-war were able to accept the idea that unarmed U.S. Army vessels could make it all the way to Vicksburg from Memphis undamaged. Even though Lt. Bartlett gave the USN officers a letter from Lt. Col. Ellet, they believed it was a forgery. The ram fleet men were interrogated for three hours as the flagship's officers awaited the return of their commander.

After a three-hour wait, the flag officer came aboard from his inspection tour. When informed of the arrival of Ellet's party, Farragut was delighted. Immediately ordering the men brought to him, he congratulated them on reaching Young's Point and on their earlier success in the Battle of Memphis. He asked if they could get a message to Flag Officer Davis. Farragut was planning to run further up the Mississippi past the Vicksburg batteries. He needed coal and, of equal or perhaps greater importance, he really needed the Western Flotilla to steam down and join him above the Confederate bastion. If the two fleets could link up, he opined, it should be possible to batter Vicksburg into submission. In the meantime, could the U.S. Ram Fleet, he asked, patrol the 12 miles between the city and the mouth of the Yazoo.

While young Ellet's party conversed with Farragut and his officers, the *Monarch* conducted a reconnaissance downstream, returning without damages. The Vicksburg defenses were seen to be quite strong and "seemed to point to a stubborn resistance on the part of the rebel forces."

With letters and messages from flag officers in hand, Ellet and his group recrossed De Soto. Travelling again by night, they picked up several

Lt. Col. (later Brig. Gen.) Alfred W. Ellet, U.S. Army (1820–1895). *Ellet was a captain in the 59th Illinois Volunteer Infantry when, in the spring of 1862, Charles Ellet, Jr., his older brother, formed the U.S. Army Ram Fleet, to which he quickly transferred. When his brother was mortally wounded during the Battle of Memphis, he assumed command of the unit and led it down to Vicksburg. Reporting directly to Secretary of War Edwin Stanton, Ellet was relentless in his support of the efforts of Rear Adm. David Farragut and Charles Davis to eliminate the* Arkansas. *Afterwards, he commanded the reconstituted Mississippi Marine Brigade during operations on the western rivers until 1864, when the unit was disestablished (Library of Congress).*

Six: Descending the Yazoo, June 25–July 15, 1862

deserters en route and reached Young's Point at 9:00 A.M. on June 26. There they reported to an anxious Lt. Col. Ellet, who had heard nothing of his nephew's trip for almost 24 hours. The deserters reported but 13 guns in position at Vicksburg, but their claim was not believed.

After reading a congratulatory communication addressed to him, the ram fleet commander quickly dispatched another boat, the newly arrived *Fulton*, back to Memphis to contact Davis. At the same time, Lt. Col. Ellet, convinced that his young nephew had proven his mettle, gave him command of the ram *Lancaster*. Together the Ellets seized upon the mission of watching the mouth of the Yazoo with alacrity.[1]

Just after 9:30 A.M. on June 26, the *Monarch* and *Lancaster* cast off and headed up to and into the mouth of the Yazoo River on the first Federal reconnaissance of that mysterious tributary. Neither vessel was armed with anything heavier than a musket and, in a pinch, would rely upon their speed to avoid danger or escape back to the Mississippi from any Rebel traps. The black and sluggish Yazoo was found to be about 50 feet deep. In many places, it was too narrow to permit two large steamers to pass if meeting.

The two U.S. rams stopped and made a landing at the confluence of the Yazoo with the Sunflower River, 15 miles below the bar at Satartia. There the Ellets were informed that a small Southern fleet lay at Liverpool Landing, on the east bank about 30–35 miles ahead. Passage up the Yazoo beyond that point was blocked by a large raft made of timber. The nearby Rebel anchorage was protected by several cannon on the overlooking Rudloff Ridge, guns that could rake the river in the vicinity of the raft. The Federals did not know that those guns were currently unmanned. The *Monarch* and *Lancaster* continued cautiously on, their crews wondering what they would encounter.

At Liverpool Landing, Cmdr. Pinkney may have received a visit from the new CSN area commander, Capt. William F. Lynch, who had just arrived from the east to take up his duties at Jackson. Perhaps uncertain of exactly what that worthy required of him and unwilling to accept Brown's earlier recommendations, Pinkney took no significant additional actions for defense of either his boats or the raft barrier.

The *General Polk*, *Livingston*, and *Van Dorn* were still tied to the shore below the protective raft, while the little gunboat *Mobile* was anchored above. Another small vessel, the two-gun 40-ton side-wheeler *St. Mary*, also patrolled above. The first two named were not stationed in midstream facing down the river with a chain linking them as Lt. Brown had originally suggested. Additionally, the trio had no steam in their boilers, even though trees for use as fuel lined the riverbank. Only one real precaution had been taken beyond the earlier stationing of cannon on the bluff ashore. Their guns moved to the fortifications, the cotton armor of the *Polk* and *Livingston* was strengthened with the bales Lts. Brown and Read had delivered at the beginning of the month. The duo were "all oiled and tarred" and otherwise made ready (save keeping steam up) to set alight upon the approach of any Northern vessel(s). In short, they had, in the best tradition of Sir Francis Drake and the Spanish Armada, been readied for use as "fireships."

The Federal vessels, or "hay-plated rams," as the Yazoo City correspondent of the *Jackson Mississippian* labeled them, had no more than departed the Sunflower when news of their incursion was sent by fast rider to Cmdr. Pinkney. The Confederate commander reacted prematurely, one might generously say, though others say outright that he panicked. Perhaps he acted according to his understanding of the recommended fireship strategy and it went awry. Pinkney immediately sent a rider, perhaps Lt. Jonathan H. Carter, captain of the *General Polk*, up along the river road to find the *Arkansas*. Lt. Brown's ship was then about 5–10 miles above Liverpool Landing and was not difficult to locate. Once Carter, or whomever the rider was, had conveyed Pikney's message that two enemy steamers were approaching the raft, Brown immediately called down the *Arkansas*' speaking tube ordering engineer City to increase speed. As the armorclad ploughed ahead, a signal gun was sounded every few minutes to let the defenders and other gunboatmen know that help was on the way.

Perhaps a new rider from downstream brought news that the Ellets were not far off (much closer than expected), the Yankee force was stronger than anticipated (perhaps including ironclads), or it was accompanied by soldiers on troop boats. If the Federal rams could have come within range to engage, it was believed that the defenseless fireships could be rammed and captured like some of the CDRF vessels at Memphis on June 6. In turn, the Confederate vessels, if captured, could have been run into the raft, destroying it and allowing the Ellets to range up and attack the *Arkansas*. Pinkney may also have believed that the current was swift enough that if he could push the "fireships" out into the channel they would somehow round the right-handed point below the bluff and run downstream into the approaching Federals. Perhaps he did not hear Brown's signal or maybe he was, in fact, scared into the preemptive action of scuttling his craft to prevent their capture.

Learning that Cmdr. Pinkney meant to destroy his fleet, a militia squad offered their services to help the sailors remove provisions and other items from the gunboats. These men may have been from Capt. Pierre Grandpre's Sharpshooters, a company of the 8th Louisiana Heavy Artillery Battalion, assigned to the raft's defense. In any event, the officer in charge assured the naval commander that his men would also provide a guard once the materials were ashore. Pinkney wasn't willing to take a chance that any of the goods would be captured and so refused the proposal.

The landing's senior naval officer now ordered the *Polk* and *Livingston* set ablaze and their crews to retire ashore, though none were sent into the protective earthworks to man the gunboat guns mounted there. He also ordered the *Van Dorn* to raise steam and prepare for action. It was possible that this final survivor of the CRDF might escape. The well-lighted CSN gunboats quickly burst into fire and, with the last crewmen ashore, blazed brightly, smoke "issuing from their cabins and hatches." Oil, escaping from the three, some of it burning, spread into the river. As the ropes securing the craft to the shore burned through, they parted, setting the vessels adrift.

At least momentarily, the "fireship" scheme seemed to be off to a good start, even though the *Polk* and *Livingston* were shoved off from shore near the landing rather than at the point below or somewhere in mid-channel. This operational failure turned out to be a big mistake. As the two boats drifted down the river, one of them became entangled with the *Van Dorn*, setting her on fire as well.

Shortly thereafter, the *Arkansas* rounded the point just above the raft. "Capts. Brown and Carter," the *Mississippian*'s scribe reported, "arrived at the scene of this wanton destruction as the boats were fired — too late to save them by their counsels." The sight was, to say the least, heart-wrenching. Flame and smoke shot up from the three wooden gunboats and oil was everywhere on the water. All were starting to settle into the Yazoo.

The armorclad came to just above the raft, not too far from the anchored *Mobile*. Fire and damage control parties were rapidly dispatched in a desperate effort to extinguish the flames. It was quickly apparent that the *Polk* and *Livingston* were gone and that the *Van Dorn* could not be saved. Gone with the cottonclads were all of the supplies and provisions, including crew clothing, that Lt. Brown hoped to acquire for his armorclad. Much-needed small arms, small boats, chains, an anchor, and other items were also lost. Aboard the *Arkansas*, Lt. Charles W. Read raged: "Pinkney had done his cowardly work (all) too well."

Both Lts. Brown and Carter also condemned Pinkney's action in what the *Mississippian* writer labeled as "unmeasured terms." The newspaper went on to note that "Capt. Brown sought to have an interview with him, but could not do so" because his superior's whereabouts now suddenly became unknown. There was general disgust with Pinkney's action by most observers at Liverpool Landing. It was sarcastically expressed in the final paragraph of the newsman's dispatch to his editor: "Nor is it known how much the gallant chief saved of his personal effects, for he certainly saved nothing for his country — but he did heroically manage to have taken ashore, without injury, a pair of pet chickens and a poodle dog."

It was about 1:00 P.M. when, a few miles downstream of the point below Liverpool Landing, the *Lancaster* and *Monarch* came upon a large pool of oil floating on the dark waters of the Yazoo. A little while later, the U.S. rams were hailed by a man in a skiff just outside the slick, paddling for all he was worth. Allowed to come alongside, he was picked up and identified himself as the *Van Dorn*'s carpenter. The new POW explained what had happened upriver. After hearing his tale, the Federal boats cautiously inched up past the left-handed point to within a few hundred yards below the Rebel gun emplacements. All aboard saw the conflagration consuming the Hollins boats ahead and also got "a good view of the *Arkansas*." Aware of the danger they faced, the Ellets ordered their pilots to back down behind the point, at which point the *Van Dorn* blew up, throwing debris everywhere.

Having destroyed without a shot most of the Confederate western navy, the *Monarch* and *Lancaster* rounded to and returned to King's Point, dropping anchor in daylight about 9:00 P.M. As Shelby Foote put it, Ellet was able to report that, as a result of his sortie, "he had destroyed the fag end of Confederate resistance on the western rivers." Believed still under construction, the *Arkansas* was now the only major Confederate warship anywhere on the Western waters and the Yazoo raft was the only obstacle between her and a powerful U.S. Navy flotilla.[2]

The loss of the Pinkney fleet was not a total tragedy. It was true that three relatively weak warships were lost along with a quantity of supplies and provisions. On the other hand, the leftovers, including some additional cannon and a large pool of unemployed sailors, were now, without question, available to Lt. Brown's armorclad. The day after the *Arkansas* arrived at Liverpool Landing, her commander put his officers to work rounding up and bringing aboard all available men and useable items that remained, including cannon. Additionally, Lt. Read and Yazoo pilot James Shacklett were sent downstream to take soundings at the Satartia bar. Riding along the riverbank, the men reached their destination and found that, despite the falling water level, there was sufficient river depth for passage. Reporting back to their vessel, the men conveyed this fact; however, pilot Shacklett opined that, if the depth continued to drop at its present rate, escape to the Mississippi might not be possible.

Lt. Brown next wanted to know whether the raft obstructions could be removed and, if so, how quickly. Lt. Read, George W. Gift, and John Grimball were sent to make a survey. First an interview was held with the military officers responsible for constructing the obstructions in the first place. Proud of their work, they told the trio that it was their professional opinion that the obstructions could not be removed in less than a week. Working from small boats, the three officers conducted their own careful examination and were pleasantly surprised. As they reported back to Brown, it would not take a week to get through the barrier; a passage could, as Read summarized, be secured in "less than half an hour."

On June 27, sixteen Federal mortar schooners, camouflaged and positioned below Vicksburg, opened fire upon the 28 square miles that enclosed the city. Cmdr. David Dixon Porter, afterwards an admiral, later wrote that the shelling had good effect, except "the soldiers in the hill forts refused to stay shelled out, and when the mortars stopped playing on them, they would come back from the fields and again open fire."

Pvt. William Y. Dixon, of Co. G ("Hunter's Rifles") of the 4th Louisiana Infantry camped not far from the river, travelled to the top of a hill with four companions from which they could see both the city and the fleet below. For several hours that evening, they observed the "blazing shells like great balls of fire." Streaking high, they were "continuously rolling up & coming down into the City & among us — making such a smashing & bursting among the canteens, frying-pans & coffee-pots as would make the very D — — himself back his years & Sneeze!" Having seen nearly every flash from Porter's schooners for two hours, they returned to camp, convinced the mighty Mississippi had taken on the appearance of "a vast ocean of flames."

Early the next day, the 13-inch assault was continued and provided some cover as Flag Officer Farragut led his squadron upriver past the bluff-top fortifications. The groups of Rebel guns, "50 yards apart and concealed from view," sent their heavy shells whistling "over the ships, throwing up the water in spouts and occasionally crashing through the vessels' timbers." Confederate chief engineer Maj. Samuel H. Lockett recalled the U.S. Navy's bold upstream charge of June 28. The Union ships "went past our batteries under full headway, pouring into the city broadside after broadside with astonishing rapidity." The Rebel batteries replied "with equal energy."

Professor James Russell Soley afterwards concluded: "No impression of any consequence was made on the forts, nor were the ships materially injured." Having successfully steamed above the town, the oceangoing ships came to in the middle of the stream, where there was about 12 fathoms (72 feet) of water. Most "moored with at least one heavy anchor," reported Henry Bentley of the *Philadelphia Inquirer*, "while some of them have two anchors out."

The U.S. Army Ram Fleet. *The converted 406-ton Ohio River towboat* Monarch *is in the foreground. Having rammed two Confederate vessels during the Battle of Memphis, the victorious side-wheeler, together with the* Lancaster, *arrived off Vicksburg in late June. While guarding the mouth of the Yazoo, the two boats ascended as far as Liverpool Landing on June 26. Their passage caused the surviving Confederate gunboats at that location to be torched (*Harper's Weekly, *July 5, 1862).*

Mortar Schooner Attack. *On June 27, 1862, 16 Federal mortar schooners camouflaged and positioned below Vicksburg opened fire upon the 28 square miles that enclosed the city. Cmdr. David Dixon Porter, afterwards an admiral, later wrote that the shelling had good effect, except "the soldiers in the hill forts refused to stay shelled out, and when the mortars stopped playing on them, they would come back from the fields and again open fire"* (Battles and Leaders, *vol. 2*).

Farragut, in his after-action report to Navy Secretary Welles, was blunt. The forts, he wrote, could be passed in either direction without much damage to the fleet. Unless a large army actually captured the guns, it would, however, be impossible to permanently silence the Vicksburg batteries. Without help from the Federal army and facing the pending fall in the water level of the rivers, it seemed unlikely that the oceangoing ships would ever be able to make a significant impact upon Vicksburg. They might not even be able to accomplish their primary objective of passing the batteries, which Rowena Reed reminds us "was to destroy the Confederate ironclads building up the Yazoo River."

One of the vessels driving upstream that morning was the $98,000, "90-day gunboat" *Wissahickon* of the Unadilla class, built largely of green wood at Lynn, Massachusetts, in late 1861. At 158.4 feet long, with a beam of 28 feet and a 9.6-foot draft, the 691-ton, two-masted, emergency-made schooner was powered in the river by two engines that took their steam from two boilers. Her principal armament comprised one 11-inch Dahlgren smoothbore, one 20-pdr. Parrott rifle, and two 24-pdr. Dahlgren boat howitzers. Her captain was Cmdr. John De Camp, former commander of the USS *Iroquois*. Rather than anchoring with the other vessels of the upper fleet, the *Wissahickon* was ordered to proceed on up to the mouth of the Yazoo where De Camp would keep a lookout for the Confederate ram reported up that river. If he met Lt. Col. Ellet, he was to effect any "concert of action" with him that might prove beneficial to the Federal cause.

At 4:00 P.M., De Camp and his vessel, both veterans of the Battle of New Orleans, "steamed up a little and anchored in company with Colonel Ellet's fleet" above the mouth of the Yazoo. He and the Ellets would picket the stream for some of the next two weeks to, as Henry Bentley put it, "prevent any appearance of gunboats without giving warning to the fleet." Unhappily, this picket would be "removed and the river left entirely unguarded."

The same day Farragut went up past the great Southern bastion, the U.S. Army ram *Fulton* arrived at Memphis with the flag officer's message to the commander of the Western Flotilla. Alerting Washington that his boats were departing immediately, Flag Officer Davis' Pook turtles and other ironclads raised anchor and headed south.

For the next couple of weeks, even after a link-up between Farragut and Davis, the Union warships at Vicksburg would swing to their anchors. Only the tugboats and mortars would see much in the way of action, along with the arriving and departing dispatch and supply vessels. The correspondent of the *Chicago Daily Tribune* called it a time of "monotony and ennui" that "hung like a pall."

It is probable that the thunder of the Vicksburg passage on June 28 could be heard up the Yazoo. The *Arkansas* remained at Liverpool Landing another week. The vessel's battery was completed by the addition of the best pieces previously sent ashore from the *General Polk* and *Livingston*, while other items salvaged from gunboat carnage were also shipped. Most important during these increasingly warm days, a majority of the crews from the sunken gunboats were taken aboard and melded with the men acquired from Vicksburg earlier. Training was intensified even as late outfitting continued. There was no thought of liberty and nothing much for the crew to do in the area if it was granted. The hills surrounding the landing were, even years later, blanketed by "great forest trees, covered with hanging Spanish moss, cane brakes, undergrowth and tangled masses of wild grapes and trumpet vines."

On July 1, Brig. Gen. Daniel Ruggles sent a message to Lt. Brown noting that more help was being sent. In one of the final actions before his headquarters was transferred to Camp Moore, Louisiana, the Grenada-based military commander ordered a detail of 126

Six: Descending the Yazoo, June 25–July 15, 1862 133

men from Brig. Gen. Thompson's command to report to the *Arkansas*. Brown was to telegraph Thompson near Panola, Mississippi.

Shortly after 4:00 P.M., Maj. Gen. John C. Breckenridge and his command marched into Vicksburg, These "Orphan Brigade" soldiers had arrived by train from Tupelo just the day before. Here, according to the historian of the 20th Tennessee, they found Maj. Gen. Smith in command, "with the following troops: 20th and 28th Louisiana Regiments, five companies of Stark's Cavalry, four companies of the 6th Mississippi Battalion, Ridley's Light Battery, and 29 stationary guns, two of which were 10-inch Columbiads, the rest 32 and 42 pounders of the old style."

The same day, the heavy boats of Flag Officer Davis linked up with the Gulf Squadron units above Vicksburg. Thereafter, for the duration of the two units' sojourn above the Rebel city, the Western Flotilla would be colloquially known as "the upper fleet," while Farragut's ocean vessels were called "the lower fleet." One writer, Kevin Carson, has opined that "the arrival of Davis' fleet made Farragut's presence unnecessary, but he lingered on for a while." Flying a blue command pennant, Farragut was the senior officer, while Davis, whose flag was red, was the junior. Chester G. Hearn contrasted the two old friends in his biography of Farragut. "Tall, somber, and thoughtful," he wrote of Davis, "he presented a marvelous contrast to Farragut, who was clean-shaven, short, active, and buoyant."

There was much celebration among the officers and men of the united Union

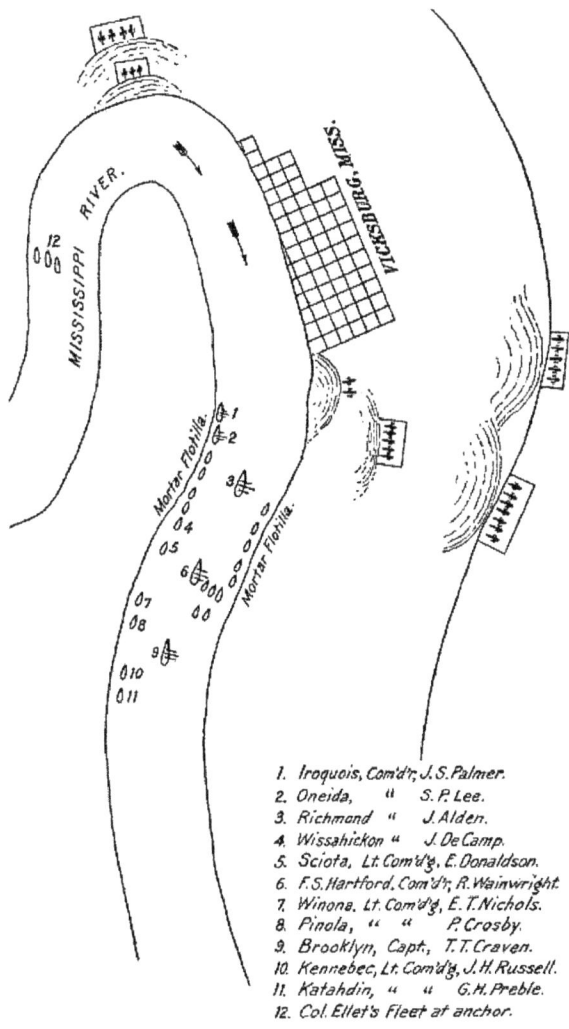

1. *Iroquois*, Com'd'r J. S. Palmer.
2. *Oneida*, " S. P. Lee.
3. *Richmond* " J. Alden.
4. *Wissahickon* " J. De Camp.
5. *Sciota*, Lt. Com'd'g E. Donaldson.
6. *F. S. Hartford*, Com'd'r R. Wainwright
7. *Winona*, Lt. Com'd'g, E. T. Nichols.
8. *Pinola*, " " P. Crosby.
9. *Brooklyn*, Capt. T. T. Craven.
10. *Kennebec*, Lt. Com'd'g, J. H. Russell.
11. *Katahdin*, " " G. H. Preble.
12. *Col. Ellet's Fleet at anchor.*

Farragut Passes Vicksburg, June 28, 1862. *Flag Officer Farragut led his squadron upriver past the bluff-top fortifications where groups of Rebel guns, "50 yards apart and concealed from view," sent their heavy shells whistling "over the ships, throwing up the water in spouts and occasionally crashing through the vessels' timbers." Confederate chief engineer Maj. Samuel H. Lockett recalled the U.S. Navy's bold upstream charge of June 28: the Union ships "went past our batteries under full headway, pouring into the city broadside after broadside with astonishing rapidity." The Rebel batteries replied "with equal energy." Professor James Russell Soley afterwards concluded the following: "No impression of any consequence was made on the forts, nor were the ships materially injured." Farragut, in his report to Navy Secretary Welles, was blunt. The forts, he wrote, could be passed in either direction without much damage to the fleet. Unless a large army actually captured the guns, it would, however, be impossible to permanently silence the Vicksburg batteries (*Navy Official Records, vol. 18).

Farragut Runs by Vicksburg. *Subtitled "On the Memorable 28th of June 1862," this Confederate print depicts the bombardment of Vicksburg when the oceangoing USN ships passed above the city. Prominent on the horizon is the new Warren County Courthouse (left) and St. Paul's Catholic Church (center) (U.S. Army Military History Institute).*

force, with the bluejackets overawed by the appearances of the vessels from their opposite squadrons. The blue-water tars marveled at the squat turtles of the Western Flotilla while the freshwater men marveled at the deep-water men-o'-war. The Confederates were not pleased to see either.

Eliot Callender, a veteran USN participant, has left us a vivid description of what the days were like for the Federals early on during what he called "one of the greatest gatherings of the War":

> The day was ushered in with the echoes of bugle calls, the rat-a-tat-tat of snare drums, the smoke of a thousand camp fires mingling with the morning air. Busy little steam tugs puffed and darted hither and yon across the river. Now and then, the strains of music would be wafted from the deck of one of the big men-of-war, whose frowning batteries were duplicated in the bosum of the river below. Gay colored signal flags would be run up to the mast-head of the admiral's flag ship, and as quickly disappear, as if to exist in the presence of the magnificent American ensign, which floated idly at the stern.... A cloud of black smoke away up the river preceded several additional transports, loaded to the guards with fresh troops. The cheers from the boats were answered with cheers from the shore, and so all day long and into the night, this never-ceasing panorama of life and bustle and beauty moved on.

That evening, several newly arrived soldiers from the 5th (later 9th) Kentucky Regiment, including Pvt. John S. Jackman, were detailed for picket duty on the "steep and rugged bluffs" above the town. He was surprised to find that "though the day had been very hot, the wind swept down the river at night, cold and disagreeable."

Ruggles' message to Lt. Brown was received at Liverpool early on July 4. As soon as he read it, Lt. Brown ordered the *Arkansas* to make a one-day turnaround trip back to Yazoo City. The voyage would be another trial and would also give the armorclad captain a chance to contact Thompson. The *Capitol* and *Star of the West* remained behind.[3]

Lt. Isaac Brown raced ashore the moment the *Arkansas* dropped anchor at Yazoo City on the morning of July 5. At the telegraph office, he contacted Brig. Gen. Thompson, who in turn detailed to the *Arkansas* all of the men — 50 to 60 — from his refugee regiments willing to serve aboard.

Most of the soldiers volunteering to ride the armorclad only as far as Vicksburg were "Show Me State" artillerymen drawn from the three Missouri State Guard 1st Division artillery units: Company A, McDowell Battery (Capt. Drake McDowell, Capt. Samuel S. Harris); Company B, Richardson Artillery (Capt. E.G. Richardson); and Company C, McDonald's Battery (Capt. Robert McDonald). Under Captains Harris and McDonald, with Lt. John D. Parsons of Co. C of the 5th Infantry Regiment and Lt. John L. Martin from Co. F of the 4th Infantry Regiment, the men were dispatched overland to rendezvous with the armorclad after she returned to Liverpool Landing.[4]

The *Arkansas* raised anchor and returned to the Liverpool raft on July 5. The brief trip to Yazoo City not only allowed her commander to contact Thompson, but also gave Chief Engineer City another opportunity to employ the repair facilities of that town to adjust the ram's cantankerous engines.

We do not know for certain what caused the *Arkansas*' continuing engine problems. There is speculation that the poor synchronization of the automatic engine stoppers was at fault. If so, this would have accounted for the fact that when one engine suddenly cut out, the other, powering a few more strokes, caused the boat to circle. Everyone hoped City's modifications would work. If they did not, everyone now knew that the helm, when worked against the push of a single screw, could not hold the ram on her course.

Final outfitting was continued upon the ram. Operational training was stepped up in every department, while a close watch was kept on the depth of the Yazoo. Throughout the oppressively warm days, the men aboard the rust brown Confederate armorclad and her nearby consorts could hear the Federal mortars pounding away at Vicksburg in the distance. Brown's officers grew impatient for battle. Indeed, he later remembered that "the only trouble they ever gave me was to keep them from running the *Arkansas* into the Union fleet before we were ready for battle."

Out on the Mississippi, the Federal fleet continued to shell Vicksburg, with the occasional artillery duel, like that on the 4th of July erupting between the ships and the big guns on the bluffs above. To preserve the precious amounts of coal received by barge all the way from Memphis, many vessels banked their fires and some even took advantage of this opportunity to clean their boilers. It was later reported by some disgusted Northern journalists that none of the upper fleet vessels, as a consequence of the fuel conservation requirement, could "get under way in less than a half an hour from the moment of receiving signal to do so." Even worse, "the sloops-of-war would require two hours at the very lowest estimate."

Occasionally, Union reconnaissance parties landed in the swampy areas below the city, but these were beaten off without difficulty. Writing to his sister from on board the *Iroquois*, Captain's Clerk Edward W. Bacon noted that the Federal sailors "are really starving." The steerage on his ship alone "has eaten in the last Quarter 21 gallons of Beans! No wonder we have scurvy." To remedy the situation, the scribe expected that "tomorrow or the next day we are going to the mouth of the Yazoo to get some fresh grub."

While the two Union fleets lay together, Cmdr. Henry Walke, captain of the *Carondelet*, took the opportunity to have "a heavy timber casemate built over the boilers of his vessel." This bulwark, an improvement upon earlier efforts, would protect the boat's powerplant "from the enemy's shot and shell in her subsequent career." Later, after her encounter with the *Arkansas*, Walke showed the "20 inches of green oak timber" to William E. Webb, a reporter from the *St. Louis Daily Missouri Republican*.

In those days, refugees and Rebel deserters brought Davis a steady stream of details concerning the building of "this devil, the *Arkansas*," up the Yazoo, the mouth of which was only six miles from his anchorage. Many of their details differed. Even as Farragut sought Secretary Welles' permission to leave and continued to discuss the possibility of a downriver departure with Davis, the commander of the Western Flotilla knew that some sort of Confederate naval threat loomed. Davis and his colleagues believed that the ram "was unfinished and aground." "Delta," the imbedded correspondent of the *New Orleans Daily Delta*, a reborn Southern newspaper, told his readers that "the great terror of modern times, 'the Ram,' was discussed in all its ramifications." He went on to agree with others that "there was a good deal of bugaboo in Ram fears."

As July advanced toward the end of its first week, the captain of the Rebel armorclad faced an operational dilemma. What was the best way to actually employ the *Arkansas*? Would it be better for her to remain above the raft obstructions as a "fleet in being," possibly grounding, or moved downstream towards Haynes Bluff and deeper water? With strengthened batteries and cavalry support, it would, the ram captain reasoned, be possible for the armorclad to defend the delta, its cotton and other supplies, plus its many "fine steamers," while backing up Rebel hit-and-run raids he thought should be mounted against Mississippi River traffic. On the other hand, "the now rapid fall of the river rendered it necessary for us to assume the offensive." But should she sally forth against the combined Union fleets, which she might damage but could not destroy?

Brown was cautious and prepared to stay in place. However, if the Confederate government and Maj. Gen. Van Dorn, commander of the Department of Southern Mississippi and Eastern Louisiana and the man whom President Davis had charged with her fate, wished it otherwise, the *Arkansas* would steam to battle. Rumors were flying in Federal circles concerning Brown's state of readiness. Albert H. Bodman, a reporter for the *Chicago Daily Tribune*, remembered that the thought was "hooted down by a large majority" that "scoffed at the bare idea" that the ram might break out.

In 1900, Eliot Callender, who was a Western Flotilla master's mate at the time of the *Arkansas* adventure, noted the source of many stories, employing black-face dialogue in the telling:

> While awaiting the proposed movement of the army, there came to our ears, from time to time, rumors of a Confederate ironclad in course of preparation up the dark recesses of the Yazoo. It was generally from the intelligent contraband, just escaped from the old plantation, that the most vivid details of this mysterious craft were derived. They had all seen it, but apparently from different points of the compass, for their [sic] seemed to be a marked lack of similarity in the descriptions. Combining the accounts would have produced a monster. "Pretty nigh as big as the whole river"; "Guns bigger than any two around hyer"; "Iron a foot thick all ober her and underneath her, and on top of her"; "An as fer the ram, dat was jess the wuss ram agoin — could jess bust de stuffins outer the Rock of Gibraltar"; "An all the lower regions couldn't catch dat boat when she got a move on her — you uns will see some morning and nebber know what you was a seein'."

Given the increasing frequency in these tales from African Americans and a few whites, USN leadership decided there was at least some foundation for them. As early as July 6, navy secretary Welles received a communication from the *Benton* stating that "we are soon to go up the Yazoo to destroy the *Arkansas* and clear the river out." A day later, Henry Bentley, a noted correspondent of the *Philadelphia Inquirer*, told his paper's subscribers "the ram and gun-boat *Arkansas* is finished and ready for active service." He went on to opine "if the *Arkansas* is anything like what those who have seen her represent her to be, she will give our flotilla a good deal of trouble."

Lt. Brown called Lt. Read aside out of the heat on the afternoon of July 8. Explaining briefly what was required and the operational options, Brown ordered his subordinate to ride over to Vicksburg and confer with Van Dorn in person. During his report, Read was to indicate that the *Arkansas* would be finished before another week was gone and Brown needed to know exactly what the general required. Once instructions were received, the lieutenant was to personally reconnoiter the combined Union fleet anchorage above the city. Read rode the 50 or so miles to Vicksburg overnight, arriving early the next day. Upon entering the town, he halted at the headquarters of Col. William Temple Withers, commander of the 12th Mississippi Light Artillery, who received him warmly, fed him breakfast, and escorted him to call on the commanding general.

Maj. Gen. Van Dorn listened closely to the sailor as he detailed Lt. Brown's concerns. He then acknowledged the importance of protecting the Yazoo delta, but then cut to the nub of his own position. The *Arkansas*, he believed, could only protect that tributary during a time of high water. If she were grounded, she could provide no benefit to the war effort. Once more, he emphasized his belief that the armorclad could run by the combined Union fleet above the town, scatter the gunboats "along the lower river in detail," and continue out of the Mississippi to Mobile. Thus orders were issued for the ram to move out immediately and for Brown to carry on "as his judgment should dictate."

Leaving command headquarters late in the afternoon, Lt. Read was escorted by one of Withers' staff officers up along the bluffs to a point abreast the Union flotillas. The foliage was thick and grasping; vines and briars, including blackberries, were everywhere. Obliged to dismount, the two snuck up to a good vantage point, where Read examined the enemy craft with field glasses. The *Arkansas*' lieutenant counted 13 of Flag Officer Farragut's vessels anchored near the east bank of the Mississippi at Tuscumbia Bend in a long line. None had steam up. Nearly opposite the Gulf vessels on the west bank were some three dozen Western Flotilla boats of Flag Officer Davis. These appeared to be maintaining steam. Great sheets of canvas awnings over their spar decks appeared to provide some protection to the men on the vessels of each contingent. From his own experience aboard the *Arkansas*, Read knew that below-decks, especially aboard the Davis ironclads, the sailors sweltered.

The *Arkansas* officer also noticed that "along the Louisiana shore, for a mile or more, lay the army transports, ordnance boats, hospital boats, hay barges and craft of every description." Remarking upon these, Master's Mate Eliot Callender opined, "There was a sample of almost everything in the West that carried a wheel or had a hull, and some of these had little to boast of, in either of these essentials." Some 30 mortar boats were moored below the Davis fleet. As at Island No. 10 and Fort Pillow, six were positioned daily across the peninsula from Vicksburg to undertake a slow, routine bombardment. Because the gunners could not get a clear view through the trees and scrub, spotters were forced to run back and forth calling the fall of the shot. As Read and his companion peered toward the river, a cutter from one of the USN ships landed at the bank nearby. Keeping quite still, the two

Confederates were not discovered. Some hours after arriving, the men returned to Vicksburg.

Taking his leave of Col. Withers and his officers, Lt. Read set out for Liverpool Landing at dusk. By 2:00 A.M. on July 10, he was too fatigued to continue. Stopping at a planter's house, he was given shelter and slept until daylight. Riding on, Read reached the *Arkansas*' advanced anchorage later in the day. There he acquainted his commander with the substance of his interview with Van Dorn, provided the general's written orders, and reviewed the results of his reconnaissance of the enemy. Van Dorn's orders were specific. Brown was to make a passageway through the obstructions large enough to accommodate passage of the *Arkansas* and then sink the *Star of the West* in the opening. He was then to proceed down the Yazoo and out into the Mississippi to battle with the Federals.

As he noted in his September 9 campaign report to the Confederate War Department, Van Dorn left the decision to Brown as to what course to pursue after he reached the city, acknowledging that any attempt to steam out and destroy the lower mortar fleet depended upon the condition of his vessel. Still, the general concluded, he was purposefully making this order imperative in order to get Brown out to the attack. Bowing to these requirements and this command, while realizing that the river stage had fallen to a critical point, Brown had no choice but to proceed.

As Brown and Read conferred, downstream above Vicksburg aboard the USS *Hartford*, Flag Officer Farragut was writing a report to Navy Secretary Gideon Welles submitting his reasons in favor of his withdrawal from the Mississippi for more pressing service in the Gulf of Mexico. His large oceangoing ships were more than 500 miles from the Gulf and the river depth was falling dangerously.

Offering to leave three older vessels at New Orleans, the loyal Tennessean was convinced that all he could do was "blockade" the city of Vicksburg "until the army arrives, which can be done as well by Flag Officer Davis" as himself. The flag officer earnestly believed his squadron could provide greater service elsewhere. Farragut then made perhaps his most inaccurate forecast of the war. "The river is open from one end to the other except this town of Vicksburg," he wrote. The Union naval force "is all-sufficient to keep the river clear, there being no rams or gunboats, except for the *Arkansas*, in the Yazoo, which our vessels are fully able to look out for, but from whence I do not think she will ever come forth." The flag officer had encountered Confederate ironclads, albeit unfinished except for the little *Manassas*, at New Orleans and "his experience had not led him to entertain any high opinion of the enemy rams." Definitely not a victim of "ram fever," Alfred Thayer Mahan was disappointed but not surprised, as he wrote years later, that Farragut "thought little of the single ironclad in his neighborhood."

Just about a week after the ram's return to her lair above Liverpool Landing, Capts. Harris, Martin, and McDonald, with Lt. Parsons, arrived with 60 men from two companies (one contingent of 25 soldiers and the other of 35) of Brig. Gen. Thompson's command. Although many of the Missourians were skilled field artillerymen and some served as gunners with the CRDF, none had ever worked a gun as large as those aboard the *Arkansas*. The crew now totaled 232, some more experienced than others. These included rivermen recruited along the Yazoo, soldiers from Vicksburg, the men from Pinkney's sunken boats, and now the Missourians. Lt. Brown placed the newest volunteers under the orders of Lt. Stevens, who immediately dispatched them aboard the *Star of the West*. There, under the watchful eyes of Lt. Wharton and Barbot as well as their own officers, the Missourians undertook a crash course in big gun drill.

Exercise at the great cannon was an ancient ritual wherein every member of the gun crew played a choreographed role. The basic fundamentals involved for a gun out of battery were cleaning the gun barrel, loading it with powder and shot, ramming those home, placing the gun in battery, and firing. Once the gun was discharged, the entire maneuver had to be repeated, without flaw, as many times as was necessary. Cleaning was known as sponging. A sponge attached to a pole was dipped in water and used to clean out the barrel of the cannon. After firing, any lingering debris was thus removed. Once the barrel was clean, a powder charge contained in a linen bag (lined burned quickly and did not leave residue) was inserted and compressed down with a poled instrument known as a rammer.

Because her projectiles were quite heavy, the *Arkansas*, like other warships of the era, was equipped with simple pulley and sling systems next to each of her big guns. To load one of those after sponging and inserting the powder, a shell was rolled into the sling. Then, lifted by means of the pulley, the sling was maneuvered to the cannon muzzle and the shell was pushed in. It was then rammed back to a position in front of the powder bag. Once the gun's payload was ready, the gun captain yelled "Heave!" Handspikes and brute force caused the carriage wheels to move forward, rolling the piece forward into battery (either directly upon the deck or via a chassis), its nose muzzle poking out of the gun port ready to fire. Once the gun captain adjusted his elevation by means of the elevating screw or quoin, he was ready to "touch off" the cannon by pulling a lanyard. That action set off a friction that ignited the powder and, with a loud noise, emptied the barrel.

The drill was backbreaking and not without some risk. Mostly new hands, but some old, got rope burns, broken fingers, and assorted other injuries. After observing the newcomers for a while with Lt. Stevens, the armorclad's commander was encouraged: "On trial, they exhibited in their new service the cool courage natural to them on land." While the Missourians sweat at the great guns on July 11, the *Arkansas*' coal bunkers were topped off and supplies were stowed.

Last minute touches included a variety of tasks seldom mentioned. For example, the magazines and powder rooms were inspected, small arms and swords were broken out and either stowed in convenient locations or strapped on, fire tubs and water buckets were filled and set about, and late construction details were completed or noted. Dr. Washington made certain that medical items, especially tourniquets, were readied or handed out. Additionally, work was started on opening a path through the raft obstructions.

Out on the Mississippi that day, Captain's Clerk Edward S. Bacon of the *Iroquois* completed a letter to his sister Kate. Noting that his vessel had, in fact, anchored for a few days further upriver where significant quantities of fresh food were obtained from an obliging plantation owner, he failed to mention any news regarding the *Arkansas*. "We have no news," he complained.

Sickness was now facing the Federal sailors in a major way. While on what Bacon called "a little vacation up the river," the fever became more and more severe. Thirty sailors on his ship were down with it on July 10, one of which died and was buried ashore. Other ships were as badly impacted. "We cannot muster a full gun's crew in any of our divisions," the clerk confessed.

Like Farragut, the *Iroquois* sailors and their colleagues aboard other upper fleet vessels were also concerned with the depth of the river. The water, he noted, "is yet steadily falling. If we do not get that army soon, we will retire from Vicksburg in disgrace, defeated not by rebels alone, but by the river too."

Tales concerning the prowess of the Confederate armorclad continued to waft through the Mississippi Valley and were spread east courtesy of numerous Northern reporters and their willing newspaper editors. One wonders what, if any, hand local Southern sympathizers, interested in spreading disinformation, may have played in this dissemination. For example, on July 12, the *Philadelphia Inquirer* published "news from reliable quarters" concerning Brown's craft: "If the *Arkansas* is anything like what those who have seen her represent her to be, she will give our flotilla a good deal of trouble. They say she has a sharp prow, weighing 15 tons, of solid iron and mounts 21 guns of very heavy caliber; that she is so completely covered with double layers of railroad iron that she is perfectly invulnerable from stem to stern."

As residents of the City of Brotherly Love read about her in their morning paper, the time for the *Arkansas*' departure from Liverpool Landing arrived early that Saturday. The Missouri volunteers were ordered aboard from the *Star of the West*, while the last few civilian laborers and mechanics were sent ashore or to the *Capitol*. The raft's defenders finished cutting a passage through the obstruction, completing their effort by early afternoon. "Although the crew was not well trained by any means and the men certainly were not completely familiar with the vessel when they went into the first battle," wrote William N. Still in 1958, "the idea that it was a 'green' crew cannot stand up under careful investigation." Raw it may have been, but these sailors were, in the end, the men who would steam the ram to glory just a few days hence.

The Confederate flag was now raised on the *Arkansas*' aft flagpole, while a small crowd of well-wishers gathered at the shore, soldiers mostly, to see her off. To the cheers of the assembled, the Southern man-o'-war turned her ram into the stream and chugged slowly away. After careful examination of the opening made through the raft, pilot Shacklett steadied his boat, allowing her to chug slowly through. She was followed by the *St. Mary*, which was ordered to accompany her to Haynes Bluff.

Once the *Arkansas* and *St. Mary* arrived downstream of the raft obstructions, Lt. Brown had orders to sink the *Star of the West* in the passage, thus blocking upriver access. Given that the *Star* was a large and valuable ship, an inferior and unnamed smaller vessel was instead selected for sacrifice. Orders were sent to the *Star* to return to Yazoo City. A detail from the *Arkansas* was sent aboard the stranger with axes to cut holes in her bottom. As the water rushed in and the current grabbed hold, she obligingly swung into place and sank to seal the exit.

With great clouds of black smoke rising from their chimneys, the two Confederate warships continued down the placid stream to Satartia, 15 miles above the mouth of the Sunflower River and only about five hours' steaming time from the Mississippi. Few people were seen along the overgrown riverbanks near the village as the gunboat eased to the bank above the notorious bar. After the Pinkney debacle, the locals were naturally suspicious of any gunboat. Additionally, few were likely to be actively about in the heat of another scorching day.

As Lt. Brown wanted his men as ready for battle as possible, he allowed Lt. Stevens all day Sunday to exercise the gun crews and complete their organization. The executive officer, who would assume control of gundeck operations during any action, integrated approximately 160 enlisted sailors into ten gun crews, each under a midshipman, or a mate or both. Each of Stevens' four lieutenants oversaw two guns. Visiting each piece and its crew, the executive officer drew a mark on the trunnion of each cannon. This was on the orders of Lt. Brown, he explained to Gift, Read, Grimball, Wharton, the midshipmen and gun captains. It was expected that only opposing vessels would be engaged and no hillside forts. Thus, if the drill step of adjusting the sights after each shot was eliminated, the time necessary to get off a round would be slightly increased. He left it to his men to do the math and to wonder how many more broadsides or individual shots could thus be executed.

During the afternoon of July 13, Capt. Lynch, who may have conferred with Lt. Brown just before the boat's departure from Yazoo City, arrived from that town to pay her another visit. It is not recorded as to whether or not he took any interest in the ongoing gun drill, but, according to Lt. Read, the easterner did express a desire to ride the ram to Vicksburg, which prospect did not excite the *Arkansas*' commander one little bit. Standing nearby, Lt. Read remembered the Kentuckian's reply to his superior: "Well, Commodore, I will be glad if you go down with us, but as this vessel is too small for two captains, if you go, I will take charge of a gun and attend to that." Lynch supposedly replied, "Very well, Captain, you may go; I will stay."

At that point, Lynch called the other officers over and remarked that he would not be going with them to Vicksburg as earlier thought. He knew that they and their men would all do their duties. The captain hoped all aboard got through the upcoming fight unharmed and lived to see the Confederacy free of Federal invaders. "Then he bade us all goodbye," Read concluded, "and returned to the city." Master's Mate Wilson added that the *Arkansas* was now ready to move "out in compliance with the orders of Captain William F. Lynch, commanding the Confederate States naval forces on the Mississippi and its tributaries." He did not add that he and most of his fellow crewmen were aware of the tremendous odds facing them only a few miles downstream.

After many weeks of "disappointments and crosses," Lt. Gift wrote later, "we had the craft, incomplete and rough as she was, with railroad bars on her hull and sides and ends of the 'gun-box.'" Additionally, there was a crew, mixed as it too was, "with an officer for every gun."

As Capt. Lynch took his leave of Lt. Brown and his men, the telegraph wires between Richmond and Vicksburg were ablaze as usual with messages. As part of a general message to Maj. Gen. Van Dorn, President Davis once more wondered: "What of the gunboat *Arkansas*?" As the general reviewed the inquiry of the chief executive, a courier was en route to Van Dorn's headquarters from Lt. Brown. Riding all night over a distance of 50 plus miles, the messenger was ushered into Van Dorn's presence at midnight and said that the *Arkansas* would arrive at 4:00 A.M. By early morning, the Confederate military commander had completed orders for her reception. Many men were transferred from the outer camps to rifle pits and ravine fortifications near the town.

At that time, it was impossible for anyone standing on the Vicksburg bluffs to tell with certainty down which river a vessel might be descending. Sentinels were, therefore, posted all along the highest points; whenever the smoke of a steamer was seen approaching from the north, an alert would be sent to headquarters. These special lookouts were rivermen who knew the "character of the smoke" emitted by different kinds of fuels (bituminous coal vs. wood) used by steamboats. Every time a signal was received concerning a sighting, an officer would be dispatched from headquarters to note the newcomer's details. Despite this precaution, it was not possible, from a distance, to say whether a boat was coming down the Yazoo or down the Mississippi.

The Federals, too, became increasingly wary. Watching for the ram and conducting logistical missions continued to occupy the vessels of the U.S. Ram Fleet. Flag Officer Davis started planning "to send a gunboat 80 miles up the Yazoo to reconnoiter and prepare the way for an expedition." On one of his trips up the Yazoo, Lt. Col. Ellet's boats were severely handled by Confederate partisans who fired upon them from the banks. As a result, the enterprising officer now armed his craft with light howitzers and riflemen from the 7th Illinois Volunteer Infantry.

While addressing this business in the increasingly warm and sickly week before the *Arkansas* departed Liverpool Landing, Ellet, already sick, became increasingly ill from the same insect-born disease that was afflicting the area's military, naval, and civilian population. For six days of that time, he was confined to bed, leaving direct supervision of flotilla activities to Medical Cadet Ellet. The debilitating weather also drew comment from Flag Officer Davis in a letter home: "The heat exceeds, I think, anything I have ever encountered in the course of my service." Davis was a prewar veteran of duty on and off the South American coast and understood high temperatures.

Flag Officer Farragut, who desperately wanted to take his upriver ships back to the Gulf, was relieved when, on July 13, the powerful upper fleet ironclad *Essex* arrived from the north. Although she was immediately required to replace a burnt-out boiler, the lower fleet commander believed that she could, when ready, spearhead an amphibious force up the Yazoo to seek out and destroy the *Arkansas*. If they were lucky, they could also neutralize any Confederate fortifications along that tributary of the Mississippi. Farragut intended to put this plan before Flag Officer Davis at an early date.

As the Confederate armorclad descended the Yazoo, her departure was betrayed. On the night of July 13/14, two deserters from Capt. Grandpre's Sharpshooters, having stolen a skiff tied to the raft at Livingston Landing and paddled to the mouth of the river, were taken aboard Capt. Thomas Reilly's U.S. Army Ram *Lancaster*. There they reported that the *Arkansas* was en route down the Yazoo and would steam out into the Mississippi the following night. The men were sent as POWs to Lt. Col. Ellet aboard the *Monarch*.

The "breakout" began in the predawn darkness of July 14. The *Arkansas*, accompanied by the *St. Mary*, cast off and, as Lt. Gift recalled, was once more "steaming down the Yazoo River bound for Mobile." Lt. Brown and his officers expected to reach and enter the Mississippi by nightfall and then cruise through the Federal fleet in darkness. All aboard were armed and nervous, anticipating possible fighting. Sand was spread across the gundeck and sprinkled on the several ladders leading up and down.

There were only a few inches to spare when the Confederate ram eased over Satartia Bar. In just two days at the adjacent town, the depth of the river had fallen further. Soundings were now taken regularly and showed the channel to be far more narrow than usual. Pilot Shacklett strenuously worked to keep the *Arkansas* as close to the center of the Yazoo as possible. Where, however, the opportunity arose, he did not hesitate to push her through slack water, usually found in river bends, to conserve fuel. This was a well known tactic long used by steamboat pilots; indeed, the Federal gunboat *Carondelet* had employed the same tactic when approaching Fort Donelson on the Cumberland River back in February. Still, whenever the boat deviated from midstream, the pilots and others always kept a careful eye on the shore, where trees grew almost to the water and the underbrush was exceedingly thick and menacing. Such lookout did not guarantee safety, as any number of obstacles might unexpectedly appear in the river ahead.

At Vicksburg, the word was spread that "the *Arkansas* is Coming!" Drums called Confederate artillerymen and soldiers to their posts. Many eyes eagerly watched from the high bluffs, looking for the first clouds of smoke that would show the *Arkansas* headed closer to the main river. A breeze may have offered some relief from the heat, which remained horrific even for those atop the terraced hills. As the day wore on and she did not arrive, many wondered if the alert concerning the armorclad's imminent appearance had been a bit premature.

Even the commanding general, then composing a telegraphic response to the chief executive, indicated that the ram would be out soon and that he was looking "for her every moment." He went on tell President Davis that the *Arkansas* had had "much to contend with here, but it was deemed better to let her try her strength than to get aground in the Yazoo and be burned up like the rest." Having given Lt. Brown orders to "run the gauntlet," Van Dorn hoped that a successful sweep would allow him to "run to Mobile as soon as out."

At midday on the 14th, the ill Ram Fleet commander received an urgent message from Flag Officer Farragut. Brig. Gen. Williams and Flag Officer Davis had come aboard the *Hartford* to discuss the Confederate warship in light of the intelligence received. It was now necessary to send another, heavier, scouting party up the mysterious tributary to check on her. "Will you come," Farragut wrote, "and we will try and fix up an expedition for the Yazoo."

Unhappily for the determined Southerners aboard her, the *Arkansas* now encountered the first of several problems caused by her power plant. As the ram and *St. Mary* passed opposite the mouth of the Sunflower River, below Satartia and, indeed, less than 45 miles from the enemy, Lt. Brown was informed, probably by Master John Phillips, that half of their gunpowder was all wet. "Steam from our imperfect engines and boiler," wrote Lt. Read years later, "had penetrated our forward magazine and wet the powder so as to render it unfit for use." Just as Brown was considering his options, an *Arkansas* lookout spotted an old abandoned sawmill situated in a riverbank clearing opposite. Fortuitously, the spot was the only sunny opening on the tree-crowded bank for miles.

Deciding to revise the schedule to salvage his powder, the captain of the armorclad ordered her slowly in to shore, where she was made fast to several large cottonwoods growing right at the water's edge. Crewmen then raced ashore and spread tarpaulins over the old tinder-dry sawdust. The powder was then painstakingly hauled ashore and placed atop the waiting sheets. For the rest of the day, until just before sundown, sailors constantly shook and turned the powder in a process not unlike the children's game of blanket toss. Back aboard the armorclad, there was little that could be done to thoroughly dry out the forward magazine, though the heat of the day may have greatly speeded the process.

During the heat, which doubtless caused much suffering and even deeper suntans for the men laboring on the beach, the little *St. Mary* served as picket, prepared to offer whatever assistance she could in the event snooping Northern vessels arrived. If any of the Western Flotilla ironclads showed up, the moored *Arkansas* was doomed. Fortunately, her armor was thick and the Yazoo was narrow; an Ellet ram could not have hurt her, but it would flee seeking help and spoil Brown's surprise.

As the apprehensive sailors toiled ashore, tiny amounts of the powder they were tossing high were tested from time to time; eventually the gunner and his mates were convinced that it was dried to a point where it would reliably ignite. Finally, as daylight slipped away, the bulk of the renewed explosive substance was repackaged and piled into the armorclad's after magazine, which was still dry. With an exhausted crew at quarters and the guns readied, the *Arkansas* cast off and continued downstream. Lanterns hung at key locations on the gun deck and below gave off but murky illumination. As the night deepened, Lt. Brown strove to make up the lost time. He soon found that roving Federal gunboats were not yet as big a worry as the natural dangers of the river, especially bars, snags and overhanging trees.

Left: **Brig. Gen. Thomas Williams, U.S. Army** (1815–1862). *Accompanying Farragut's squadron to Vicksburg were 1,400 army troops aboard transports. The bluecoated soldiers disembarked and set up camp on the De Soto Peninsula, a finger of land opposite the Confederate bastion. A veteran of the Seminole and Mexican wars, Williams later commanded the Federal garrison at Baton Rouge, where he was killed during Breckenridge's August attacks (U.S. Army Military History Institute).* Right: **Flag Officer (later RAdm.) Charles H. Davis, USN** (1807–1877). *Davis commanded the Western Flotilla between May and October 1862. On July 1, his squadron linked up with the West Gulf Coast Blockading Squadron units above Vicksburg. Thereafter, for the duration of the two units' sojourn above the Rebel city, the Western Flotilla would be colloquially known as "the upper fleet," while Farragut's ocean vessels were called "the lower fleet." Calmer in disposition than his blue-water colleague, Davis was later criticized for his perceived admiring attitude toward, and dispositions regarding, the CSS* Arkansas *(Library of Congress).*

Despite the darkness, the interior of the armorclad's casemate remained extremely warm and only partially because of the uninsulated boiler fire boxes below. To help provide some relief, officers and men were allowed, in shifts, to spend some time topside on the cooler upper deck. Some were detailed to keep a lookout for overhanging tree limbs that could tear off the vessel's chimney or crush its boats.

When the *Arkansas* veered toward the bank in a narrow portion of the stream to take advantage of slack water, her chimney almost came to grief. Travelling too fast to stop, the ram nearly ploughed into a thick mass of branches from a huge overhanging tree. Fortunately, Lt. Grimball happened to be on the upper deck and sprang into action as the alarm sounded. Grabbing a rope's-end, he jumped to another tree near the threatening cottonwood and, as Lt. Brown recalled years later with pride and still some wonder, "made it fast." Although a number of branches grazed the chimney, probably leaving small creases and dents, no real damage was done. Once by, the armorclad recovered her daring officer.

Having escaped a potentially disastrous moment, the Confederate vessel anchored under the lee of Haynes Bluff about midnight. Lt. Brown wanted to time his descent into the Mississippi just so in order that he might pass through the Federal fleet at dawn. For the uninitiated, this night would have seemed surprisingly noisy, but for this crew the sounders were normal. The buzz of flying insects, the chirp of crickets, screams from wild animals, including howling wolves, and the croaking from countless bullfrogs prohibited tranquility but could not, by themselves, keep anyone awake. Fear could. The exhausted and anxious crew was given three hours to sleep. A number of them passed up that opportunity to write letters instead or otherwise silently prepare for the ordeal that would surely come later that morning. All knew that, in the words of Lt. George Gift, "we were in for it — yes, in for one of the most desperate fights any one ship ever sustained since ships were first made."

Tired and not sleeping himself, Lt. Brown undoubtedly thanked the captain of the *St. Mary* for his assistance. Returning aboard, he probably sought the patch of top deck space aft the pilothouse and before the chimney where he liked to pace and observe. He may have sat down there to contemplate or, more likely, he simply walked to and fro reflecting upon those things that had passed and trying to anticipate what lay ahead. Neither he nor anyone else on either Rebel boat knew that their adventure was once more being told to a Yankee audience, one which this time would pay greater attention.[5]

Scharf and Cmdr. William D. "Dirty Bill" Porter[6] report that, on this night, two other deserters from Vicksburg went aboard the latter's *Essex*, which was newly arrived after completing repairs to damages incurred during the Battle for Fort Henry back in February. The men reported that the *Arkansas* would assault the Union anchorage within hours or just after dawn on July 15. Porter immediately had the men transferred to the Western Flotilla flagboat, *Benton*, where they repeated their story for Flag Officer Davis. According to a letter from the *Hartford*'s third engineer, John K. Fulton, to his father, Charles C. Fulton, publisher of the *Baltimore American*, these men were sent over to face Flag Officer Farragut.

The deserters from Davis told Farragut, according to Fulton, that the *Arkansas* "meditated an attack on the fleet either that night or the following morning." Yet another refugee butternut from Vicksburg reached Farragut around 10:00 P.M. and said the same thing. The flag officer did not pass the intelligence from that man on to the Western Flotilla, saying, as one officer later remembered, "we had heard that before."

The two squadron leaders, who may not have heard about or from the men taken aboard the *Lancaster*, were reportedly skeptical of the tale told by the Vicksburg men, preferring to believe it "Ram bugaboo." Conserving coal at their anchorage, about six miles from the mouth of the Yazoo, seemed a far more pressing concern. After all, supplies of the black, dirty, bituminous coal were extremely difficult to come by, being forwarded down by barge from Memphis.

As noted elsewhere, stories had been circulating for some time that a powerful warship was abuilding up the Yazoo "equal to the 'cleaning out' of the Mississippi River, the recapture of New Orleans, and perhaps an excursion to New York and the destruction of that city." Thus, historian John D. Milligan reminds us, they were "perfectly aware that the enemy was finishing the *Arkansas* up the Yazoo, but refused to believe that he would dare to bring her out." Davis later admitted that senior Federal officers believed she "was unfinished and aground." David Dixon Porter later opined that, frankly, "they did not believe the Confederates had sufficient resources to build a powerful vessel in such an out-of-the way place." However, Farragut and Davis were, according to Scharf, "moved by the persistency of the two deserters." They agreed to send an exploring expedition to make certain, as New Orleans newspaper correspondent "Delta" put it, "that floating Rams ought to be tied up." Davis, the more concerned of the Union flag officers, undoubtedly took the testimony of the Rebel sailors as confirmation of the necessity for a reconnaissance.

News of the upcoming reconnaissance, though not widespread, began to circulate among the captains of the upper fleet and, because of communications requirements, their clerks as well. Edward S. Bacon, captain's clerk aboard the *Iroquois*, was able to write home a day or so later saying that he had learned that the purpose of the Yazoo scout would be to capture "the splendid river boats secreted up its long and crooked channel and of explaining the myth with which we had so long busied our imagination of the rebel Ram *Arkansas*." Final preparations for Davis' examination of the Yazoo began in earnest on the morning of July 14. Just before 9:00 A.M., Lt. William Gwin,[7] commander of the timberclad *Tyler*, was summoned aboard the Western Flotilla flagboat *Benton* for a strategy session with Davis and Farragut, plus Brig. Gen. Thomas Williams, who had come up the Mississippi with Farragut. The two fleet commanders rather quickly resolved to order a Yazoo River reconnaissance. "The shoalness and narrowness of the stream," wrote Prof. James R. Soley for the *Battles & Leaders* series, "led them to take vessels of the upper squadron in preference to those of the lower."

The general's men were then attempting to build a canal nearby at De Soto Point on the peninsula of that name (also known as "Swampy Toe") across from the city. If completed (it wasn't), it would link Tuscumbia Bend with the Mississippi south of the citadel. While men labored, others established defensive field gun emplacements on the western shore.

The latest intelligence available to the Federals (including Ellet's) indicated that there was, indeed, a raft obstructing passage of the Yazoo about 80 miles from its mouth, with a battery below as additional protection. The *Arkansas* was said to be above the raft and very well protected with a heavy battery of her own. The upper fleet commander, as noted in his son's biography, largely agreed with Farragut that the ram was not yet finished. He did not agree that she would be of little consequence if she were.

When the planning team broke for lunch at noon, Lt. Gwin returned to the *Tyler*. There he informed his lieutenants their craft would soon weigh on a new and special mission. Twenty 4th Wisconsin sharpshooters that Brig. Gen. Williams had offered to provide would be coming aboard shortly. Davis and Farragut, with others from the morning team and without, including Davis' assistant and acting fleet captain Lt. S. Ledyard Phelps,[8] resumed their meeting in early afternoon. It was now agreed that, because of their shallower draft, units from the upper fleet would handle the scout. The *Tyler*,[9] strengthened by U.S. Army riflemen, would handle the reconnaissance. Backup would be provided by one of the Ellet rams, *Queen of the West*,[10] with a 20-man marksman detail from the 13th Massachusetts, as well as an Eads ironclad, the *Carondelet*,[11] that would take station at the mouth of Old River about seven miles from the Mississippi.

Gwin's instruction, as he later told his aide and the boat's signal officer, paymaster Silas B. Coleman, was to take the *Tyler* and *Queen* up the Yazoo looking for the *Arkansas*. If she were underway as the deserters had warned, he was to bring her to action and destroy her with the assistance of the *Queen* and, if need be, the *Carondelet*. As he later confided to Davis with the benefit of hindsight, Farragut would be disappointed for not "begging you to send the ironclad vessels," meaning more than just Walke's lone turtle.

Once the meeting concluded, practical and logistical matters continued to occupy the planners. Davis got off a dispatch outlining his scheme to Navy Secretary Welles. In it, he announced that he was sending the *Tyler* on a reconnaissance up the Yazoo River "preparatory

Six: Descending the Yazoo, June 25–July 15, 1862

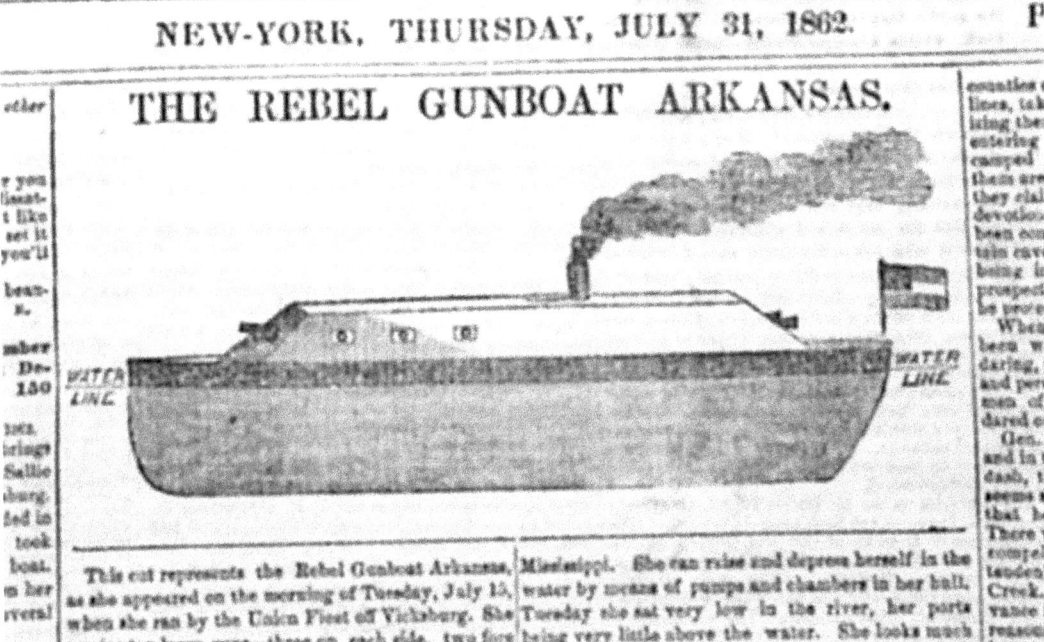

Rumors and Drawings. *Rumors concerning the existence of a powerful Confederate ironclad up the Yazoo River were reported to Flag Officers Farragut and Davis on a regular basis in late June and early July. Correspondents accompanying the Union fleets were also aware of the many stories and sent frequent reports, sometimes accompanied by drawings, to various Northern newspapers. Here is an example of an illustration, drawn from the July 31 issue of the* New-York Tribune.

to an expedition in that direction." Sometime after writing his superior, the flag officer also wrote out orders for Cmdr. Henry Walke, commander of the *Carondelet*, then anchored four miles upstream from the *Benton*. It is uncertain why the hero of Island No. 10 was not involved in the Farragut-Williams-Gwin discussions.

Known as something of a maverick and a great artist, the taciturn Virginian Walke (1808–1896) was, arguments to the contrary acknowledged, one of the most successful and under-celebrated of all Union Civil War naval officers. Entering the fleet as a midshipman aboard the USS *Natchez* in 1827, Walke served in numerous ships and squadrons and, in the process, became a friend of Lt. Brown. He was promoted to the rank of commodore in 1855. One of many officers involuntarily retired by Sen. Stephen R. Mallory's infamous Naval Retiring Board, set up under congressional legislation of that year, he was eventually returned to duty. Like all "restored officers," he was placed on half pay and throughout the Civil War received only 50 percent of the income his rank would ordinarily have provided.

In early 1861, while commanding the store ship *Supply* off Pensacola, Walke elected to remove personnel from the guardian forts and the navy yard rather than allow them to

USS *Winona*. The Arkansas' Lieutenant Charles W. Read counted 13 of Flag Officer Farragut's vessels anchored in a long line near the east bank of the Mississippi at Tuscumbia Bend during his reconnaissance made on the afternoon of July 9. None had steam up. Among them was the Winona, a $101,000 "90-day gunboat" and Unadilla class sister of the nearby Wissahickon, Pinola, and Sciota. Launched at New York City in September 1861, she was commissioned in December of that year. At 158.4 feet long, with a beam of 28 feet and a 9.6-foot draft, the 691-ton two-masted emergency-made schooner was powered in the river by two engines that took their steam from two boilers. Her principal armament comprised one 11-inch Dahlgren smoothbore, one 20-pdr. Parrott rifle, and two 24-pdr. Dahlgren boat howitzers (Harper's Weekly, September 28, 1861).

become POWs. His actions, technically violating previous orders, resulted in his court-martial, a "complementary reprimand," and temporary banishment to the post of lighthouse inspector at Williamsport, New York. Sent west with several other restored officers to serve in the Western Flotilla, Walke was almost a driven man, seeking to restore his reputation. He turned the three timberclads into an effective operational force, becoming a friend of Brig. Gen. Ulysses S. Grant as a result of his actions during the 1861 Battle of Belmont. Transferred to the new Pook turtle *Carondelet* in January 1862, he skippered her at Forts Henry and Donelson before making his reputation by running past Island No. 10 in April.[12]

Walke, now the flotilla's senior operational captain, was not then expecting movement because his ship was "so reduced and debilitated by sickness that she could not fight more than one division of guns." He himself came down with a fever, most likely malaria, during July. It is probable that someone, after the *Hartford* meeting broke up, suggested that the timberclad might require support. The medical situation notwithstanding, Lt. Phelps, "suddenly delivered Davis' "formal, brief, and verbal" orders via steam tug late in the evening. Phelps and Walke, the "restored officer" and *Tyler*'s former commander, were not the best of friends, having been on the outs since early February when the former supposedly refused to obey an order from the latter, his superior. Indeed, as noted earlier, Phelps had little use for Walke or, for that matter, the restored officers captaining the two other Pook turtles that had accompanied the *Benton* down from Memphis.

Phelps may or may not have verbally elaborated on the Davis instructions. Walke, according to his memoirs, "was induced to think" his ship would cruise alone up the Yazoo next morning. Nothing was intimated concerning the possibility that the *Arkansas* was not, as everyone thought, still under construction or "that any other gunboats were to join him." In short, even the captain of the *Carondelet*, who would be the ranking Federal officer on the scene, was either not given, or did not fully understand, the plan Davis and Farragut had worked out with Lt. Gwin.

For his part, Flag Officer Farragut contacted Lt. Col. Ellet, with whom he got on better with than Davis, and asked that he contribute one of his rams to the expedition. Davis and the Ellets had quarreled over possession of salvageable Confederate vessels after the Battle of Memphis, as well as later expeditions. Responding to Farragut's request, Ellet agreed to sent his fastest vessel, the *Queen of the West*, skippered by Lt. James M. Hunter of the 63rd Illinois (for whom no detailed biography exists).

A hero of the Memphis engagement a month earlier, Hunter had commanded the *Queen*'s marines during the big fight; the

USS *Essex*, Drawn by Carpenter's Mate William C. Philbrick. *Flag Officer Farragut, who desperately wanted to take his upriver ships back to the Gulf, was relieved when, on July 13, the powerful upper fleet ironclad Essex arrived from the north. Although she was immediately required to replace a burnt-out boiler, the lower fleet commander believed that she could, when ready, spearhead an amphibious force up the Yazoo to seek out and destroy the Arkansas. If the Union were lucky, they could also neutralize any Confederate fortifications along that tributary of the Mississippi (Navy History and Heritage Command).*

late Col. Charles Ellet, the unit founder, was the ram's commanding officer. After the victory was secured, Hunter took the steamer to Cairo for repairs and, upon her return to the waters off Vicksburg, remained in charge. Ellet told Hunter to follow Lt. Gwin of the *Tyler* next morning "as far as the officer of that boat deems it necessary to proceed for the purposes he has in view." Hunter was to take care that his guns were loaded and his men ready. If Gwin were attacked by the *Arkansas*, the *Queen* was to "dash to her rescue" and sink the armorclad "by running full speed right head on into her." It appears that Hunter did not know that the *Carondelet* would be in the vicinity.

Brig. Gen. Williams, meanwhile, sent orders for the 4th Wisconsin to provide a detail of 20 sharpshooters for the *Tyler*. The men, led by Capt. John W. Lynn, arrived alongside the old gunboat aboard a tug at 10:15 P.M. At the same time, another 20-man detail from the 13th Massachusetts, under Lt. E.A. Fiske, went aboard the ram *Queen of the West*.

It was still dark and as cool as the day would get when the gunboatmen assigned to the reconnaissance prepared to cast off on July 15. Lookouts aboard the craft had to keep a close eye for other units of the combined fleet, anchored as they were in a mixed order. Steam was down on every vessel except those of Gwin, Hunter, and Walke. At 3:55 A.M. that Tuesday, observed the officer of the deck of the USS *Hartford*, the *Tyler* got underway a short distance up the river. Going alongside the *Lancaster*, Lt Gwin requested from Capt. Reilly the services of an experienced Yazoo River pilot. Finally, after an hour's delay, the ram's pilot, Dick Smith, was handed the task.

In the interim, *New York Tribune* correspondent Junius Henri Browne and a colleague made arrangements to accompany Gwin. Unfortunately, the *Tyler* cast off earlier than the agreed upon time, leaving the newsmen behind. It being the middle of the night when the reconnaissance kicked off, it is perhaps understandable that several of the imbedded Western Flotilla correspondents, sleeping on civilian steamers, thought the advance units had departed earlier. Frank Knox from the *New York Herald* actually told his readers that the *Tyler* and *Carondelet* had arrived at the mouth of the Yazoo "about 7 P.M. on the 14th and lay to until morning."

While Lt. Gwin sought a guide, the pokey *Carondelet* actually tripped her anchor at 4:00 A.M. and began slowly steaming up the Mississippi. A half hour later, the ironclad entered the Yazoo. Capt. Walke, an artist ever alert to color and aura, recorded details: "All was calm, bright and beautiful. The majestic forest echoed with the sweet warbling of its wild birds, and its dewy leaves sparkled in the sunbeams."

Finally, at 5:00 A.M., the *Tyler* was also able to depart the fleet anchorage, trailed by the *Queen of the West*. The two arrived at the mouth of the Yazoo 45 minutes later and stood on up, soon catching up with the *Carondelet*. Just as personnel aboard the *Arkansas* did not know they were coming, no one on any of the three Federal craft had so much as an inkling that the dreaded "Rebel ram" lay aground some 10 miles ahead.[13]

CHAPTER SEVEN

Morning (Part I), July 15, 1862: Dawn Fight in the Yazoo

The U.S. Navy and the Confederate States Navy were, in the predawn darkness of July 15, 1862, headed toward an armed confrontation in the Yazoo River — and neither side knew it. For months, rumors had circulated through the Mississippi Valley to friend and foe that the Rebels were building a powerful ironclad ram, named *Arkansas*, on the upper reaches of that Mississippi River tributary.

The previous afternoon, Flag Officers David G. Farragut and Charles H. Davis, commanders respectively of the USN West Gulf Blockading Squadron and the U.S. Army's Western Flotilla, had put in motion a scouting expedition to bring back the latest intelligence concerning the *Arkansas*. Three shallow draft vessels, the *Carondelet*, *Tyler*, and Ellet ram *Queen of the West*, all attached to or under supervision of the latter, were told off and ordered to make the reconnaissance the next morning.

The CSS *Arkansas* was, simultaneously, en route down the Yazoo intent upon striking the combined Federal fleets at dawn. Unhappily for her, a portion of her powder supply became wet from escaping steam and a day-long stop was required to dry and reload the precious commodity. The armorclad fell behind schedule and, when her men turned to at 3:00 am and the mission resumed after a short post-midnight rest near Haynes Bluff, she was still about 12 miles away from the Big Muddy. By lantern light, the men ate a spare breakfast with hot coffee, the immortal navy favorite, and perhaps reviewed their chances. With luck, it might be possible to surprise the Federals just as the sun was rising.

As the vessel gathered way, the men below-decks, working in the dimmest illumination that the gray sky could not aid, made themselves ready. It was expected, at nearly every moment, that they might run into Federal naval scouts. Sand, spread earlier, was refreshed on the gundeck and ladders to keep them smooth against the inevitable flow of battle blood should such a meeting occur. In the continuing heat, the men were stripped to the minimum, only the captain and XO continuing to wear their coats as symbols of professionalism and naval order.

Additionally, the big guns were loaded and placed into battery. In accordance with a decision promulgated earlier, Brown's gunners made certain, using spirit-levels and marking the trunnions, that their pieces were pointed straight and without elevation. When battle came, it was anticipated that no piece would be without a target and all agreed not to "fire until we were sure of hitting an enemy direct." Simultaneously, small arms were handed out and carefully inspected by their recipients. Water buckets were strategically placed, along with basic medical supplies.

USS *Tyler*. *The* Tyler *was one of the three original Western Flotilla gunboats, called "timberclads," converted at Cincinnati from the A.O.* Tyler *in June and July 1861. Displacing 420 tons, she was 180 feet long, with a beam of 45.4 feet and a 6-foot draft. The side-wheeler was powered by two engines and four boilers and was capable of a top speed of 8 mph. Covered all over with various thicknesses of oak, the boat had a crew of 67 and was armed with six 8-inch smoothbores in broadside and a single 32-pdr. stern chaser. This is an excellent full-length profile of the largest timberclad as she lay at anchor in one of the Western rivers. For perspective, note the cutter in the foreground. The exact location and time of this shot is unknown; however, the photograph was found in the Naval Historical Center's collection of the papers of Lt. Cmdr. George M. Bache. As he commanded her in June 1864 and after, it is probable that it was taken then (Navy History and Heritage Command).*

Showing only her dim yellow and green running lights, the Confederate ram steamed on, with Pilot James H. Shacklett keeping her centered in the deep water of the main channel. Unhappily, with the river falling, many natural hazards threatened, chief among them overhanging cottonwood branches and sand bars, which latter could appear or disappear in a stream within hours.

In darkness, at about 4:00 A.M., the *Arkansas* was about three miles below Haynes Bluff when she ran aground on a bar just a couple of inches below the surface that stretched out from the bank. Fortunately, the trap was not as dire as it might have been, even though many crewmen were knocked off their feet by the sudden impact. By shifting the crew from one side of the boat to the other and forcing the screws to churn the water at maximum power, the boat worked her way off within about an hour. This delay made it impossible to burst out at first light into the Mississippi as her captain had planned.

As reported to his readers a few days later by *New York Herald* newsman Frank Knox, the initial miles covered by the three Union vessels were peaceful, with nothing out of the ordinary sighted, even though there was at this time a number of Rebel-employed civilian steamboats up the Yazoo River in addition to the *Arkansas*. The occasional local youth or old man "gazed wonderingly at the 'Linkum gunboats' until they disappeared from sight." A number of African Americans, having first made certain that they could not be seen by their Caucasian masters, came to the bank and "waved hats and branches of trees in token of their delight at our appearance." Knox also reported that one "butternut hero" shouted to the three boats as they passed near him in the river that "the *Arkansas* was coming and would meet them soon." He then retired from sight into "a neighboring canebrake." Whether true or not, the bluejackets dismissed the Southerner's message as a Rebel canard.

Meanwhile, the *Arkansas* was also unable to obtain

USS *Carondelet*. *This center-wheel Pook-designed Eads gunboat was the most famous of seven sister vessels constructed at Carondelet, MO, in 1861. Her first captain was Henry Walke. She displaced 512 tons and was 175 feet long, with a 51.2-foot beam and a 6-foot draft. Although her two engines and five boilers allowed her to be rated with a 9 mph top speed, she was, indeed, the slowest of her class. She was protected by a rectangular sloped casemate that was heavily armored in the bow and, like the* Arkansas, *lightly on the quarters and stern. A total of 251 officers and men made up her crew and she was armed with four 8-inch Dahlgren smoothbores, one 42-pdr., six 32-pdrs., and one each 50-pdr. and 30-pdr. rifle (Navy History and Heritage Command).*

much in the way of local intelligence. Just before sunrise, Lt. Brown decided to stop at the next plantation he came to and send some men ashore to see if its owners knew anything recent concerning Federal dispositions. Shouting down the tube to the engine room, the captain ordered the engines halted. While the *Arkansas* idled in midstream, Lt. Charles W. Read was rowed ashore to conduct interviews. Stepping ashore, he found the place deserted. Everyone, black and white alike, had fled as soon as they saw the craft approaching.

An old African American lady was the only one Read found. On the assumption that she was not worth hurting or freeing, the elderly housemaid was left to guard the house. Assuring her that, in fact, he meant her no harm, the lieutenant inquired after the residents; where were they, he wondered. The guardian held her ground and wouldn't say, putting on an act worthy of a minstrel show. Insisting that he knew they had just left because his men told him the beds of the house were still warm, Read was amazed by the reply, as he later informed Brown and Gift, who recorded the incident. "Dunno," she told Brown's scout, "an' if I did, I wouldn't tell." Read tried to assure the lady, who was referred to as "aunty," that he was not a Yankee. "Don't you see I wear a gray coat?" he asked. She shot right back: "Sartin you's a Yankee. Our folks ain't got none dem gun boats."

Completely baffled and frustrated, Lt. Read returned to the *Arkansas*. The ram soon thereafter resumed her voyage down the Yazoo, no wiser as to what lay ahead. To the east, the gray skies started to retreat, being crowded by hues of yellow and red. Aboard, the men were served coffee ("or an apology therefor," as Gift recalled) and a cold breakfast.

All night at Vicksburg, soldiers and civilians had wondered if the Confederate ram would emerge from the Yazoo this morning, as promised the previous day. Even before daylight, the first of 20,000 spectators began to assemble on the heights above the town overlooking the river bend. They knew that the *Arkansas* had orders to descend the Yazoo and fight her way through Farragut's fleet. Realizing the daring and hazardous nature of the adventure, all were, as Texan Louis S. Flatau wrote, "so anxious for her success." (Flatau was a sergeant with Capt. James J. Cowan's Co. G of the 1st Mississippi Light Artillery and, after the war, would serve as sheriff of Camp County, Texas, and patent a special pistol holster.)

As the sun rose, the Confederate warship was approximately seven or eight miles above the mouth of the Yazoo; Vicksburg was less than five hours' steaming away to the southwest. The day was already quite warm, though otherwise calm. "A dense volume of black smoke, which issued from our funnel, rose high above the trees," remembered Lt. Read. No one was under any illusion that "the enemy would soon be on the lookout for us." There was no necessity to "beat to quarters" or "clear for action." Read, watching from his post inside the aft face of the casemate, could see the crew was ready:

> The men of the *Arkansas* were now all at their stations, the guns were loaded, and cast loose— their tackles in the hands of willing seamen ready to train; primers in the vents; locks thrown back and the lanyards in the hands of the gun captains; the decks sprinkled with sand and tourniquets and bandages at hand; tubs filled with fresh water were between the guns, and down in the berth deck were the surgeons with their bright instruments, stimulants and lint, while along the passageways stood rows of men to pass powder, shell and shot, and all was quiet save the dull thump, thump of the propellers.

Lt. Gift, at the opposite end of the *Arkansas*' casemate from Read, also observed the scene as his man-of-war cleared for action this warming morning. It was, of course, the same throughout the boat and one that would be largely shared, save for the uniform informality, with the Federals downstream:

> Many of the men had stripped off their shirts and were bare to the waists, with handkerchiefs bound round their heads, and some of the officers had removed their coats and stood in their undershirts. The decks had been thoroughly sanded to prevent slipping after the blood should become plentiful. Tourniquets were served out to division officers by the surgeons, with directions for use. The division tubs were filled with water to drink; fire buckets were in place; cutlasses and pistols strapped on; rifles loaded and bayonets fixed; spare breechings for the guns and other implements made ready. The magazines and shell rooms forward and aft were open and the men [were] inspected in their places.

Gift remembered that XO Stevens, a man Brown called "a religious soldier of the Stonewall Jackson type, who felt equally safe at all times and places," was everywhere aboard the craft, "cool and smiling, giving advice here and encouragement there." Many of those sailors, like the Missouri volunteers, who had never stepped foot on a gunboat before—were encouraged, or at least their fear was hidden.

Captain Brown also passed through the ram offering words of support and a few pithy remarks. At one point, he gathered the crew together giving last minute instructions: "Gentlemen, in seeking the combat as we now do, we must win or perish. Should I fall, whoever succeeds to the command will do so with the resolution to go through the enemy's fleet, or go to the bottom." After sparking the men's pep, Brown ordered that if there was a close action that went poorly the armorclad was to be blown up rather than surrendered. His comments finished, the determined leader barked, "Go to your guns!" At that point, he returned "to his post with glass in hand to get the first sight of the approaching enemy."

In any battle, Brown would command from the hurricane deck atop the casemate directly over the bow guns, while Stevens oversaw the whole crew below. While conning the boat, Brown would shout orders to his pilots through a speaking trumpet. This command approach was not uncommon aboard the river ironclads on either side as it provided far greater vision than was available from the pilothouse.[1]

Between 6:00 A.M. (Brown) and 7:00 A.M. (Gwin), the *Tyler* and *Queen of the West*, paralleling the sides of the river right and left respectively, came about three miles in from the mouth of the Yazoo. The *Carondelet*, plodding along roughly in the middle between the two, was a mile and a half further back. There was a light mist, but nothing that really interfered with visibility. Having reached her assigned holding area, the *Carondelet* came to as her two companions churned slowly on. Despite an earlier joyful observation on the morning's wonder by her captain, Cmdr. Henry Walke, there was a slight haze that prevented full forward visibility. This was a good time to pipe his own veteran and well-drilled crew to breakfast.

Meanwhile, the *Arkansas* continued south, expecting to soon encounter the Federal fleet that was known to be ahead but was currently hidden by "the curved and wooded eastern shore." As she steamed along Old River's expanse, her lookouts watching to the left suddenly saw "a few miles ahead, under full steam, three Federal vessels in line approaching." Peering out his porthole, Lt. Gift saw the Federal warships "round a point in full view, steaming towards us gallantly and saucily, with colors streaming in the wind." Because the bow gun ports were too small for wide vision, the men crewing his forward-facing cannon could not see the enemy.

Lt. Brown also remembered the first sighting: "As the sun rose clear and fiery out of the lake on our left, we saw a few miles ahead, under full steam, three Federal vessels in line approaching." In his papers, Acting Master's Mate John A. Wilson later confided that, when Brown saw the trio through his marine glass "lying off a point below," he immediately "headed for them." Simultaneously, the officer of the deck aboard the *Tyler* saw what he thought was smoke from a fugitive Confederate transport—or what newsman Knox called a "foraging tug"—coming down the river about 500 yards ahead. Historian Hartje tells us the former packet was now about six miles up the Yazoo.

Most of the officers and men were at breakfast, but the timberclad's captain, Lt. William Gwin, fastidiously attired as usual in his full uniform, was summoned on deck, where he quickly arrived carrying his telescope. Eliot Callender, then a master's mate aboard the Pook turtle *Cincinnati*, later called Gwin "one of the bravest and truest hearts God ever made."

The same puffs were seen across a point of land aboard the *Carondelet*. Captain Walke, as correspondent Knox later learned, was told by Pilot John Deming that the billowing "was caused by wood smoke and not by the bituminous coal used exclusively by the boats of our fleet." As the small cloud could be from any of the civilian boats known to be operating in the area, no special attention was paid to the distant craft.

Onboard the *Arkansas*, Lt. Brown swiftly notified Lt. Stevens of developments. Orders were passed for the bow gunners to ready their pieces. With 100 pounds showing on the steam gauge, a call was placed over the speaking tube to the engine room requesting an increase to full speed. Bells sounded immediately and the ram surged ahead.

As soon as the timberclad commander saw the interloper rounding the bend above about half a mile away, he ordered gunner Herman Peters to fire a shot across her bow with the 12-lb. howitzer. The unusual tout ensemble of the mysterious craft was very suspicious. "Surely," wrote Junius Henri Browne, "there never was such a queer tug before." If this were a civilian vessel, its captain would know to heave to and await boarding or would round to and make a run for it. In the worst case, this could be the Rebel ram and, if so, it would fight.

The little shell made absolutely no difference to the oncoming stranger. With the haze lifting, the officers assembled on the old gunboat's deck were clearly able to see her house-like shape, her rust brown color, one giant chimney belching forth sparks and black soot, and, most ominously, a sudden puff of smoke at her bow, accompanied by a loud roar. What the officers and men of the timberclad thought was a "river steamboat coming down to give herself up," was, the astonished paymaster Silas B. Coleman remembered, "an ironclad running out guns." Within seconds, a giant projectile passed overhead. This was not a complimentary missile across her bow, but a 64-pound cannon ball that whizzed between the *Tyler*'s tall chimneys, just above the pilothouse, and splashed into the water far astern.

The veterans Lt. Brown and Cmdr. Walke, to say nothing of Lt. Gwin or Hunter, had never fought an ironclad before. Indeed, New Orleans scribe "Delta" tells us that the Union boats were as surprised to actually find the *Arkansas* as she was to find them: "There was common astonishment." He may have been partially correct. Brown expected to encounter the Federals, but perhaps not so soon, while the USN vessels began their expedition clueless as to what they might encounter. Undeterred, the Confederate commander, wearing his cap and also garbed "in full-dress uniform," according to historian Carter, "his tawny beard parted by the wind," ordered colors shown on the stern flagpole and bow jackstaff alike and urged Chief Pilot John G. Hodges to steer the *Arkansas* directly for the *Carondelet*. "I had determined," Brown later revealed, "to try the ram on our iron prow upon the foe, who was so gallantly approaching."[2]

To avoid any loss of speed, the *Arkansas*' bow gunners were ordered to hold their fire. For them, Brown's order may have been just as well: "Owing to the fact that our bow ports were quite small, we could train our guns laterally very little." Initially, as Gift, captain of the port side bow and broadside 8-inch Columbiads wrote later, the ram's bow, because of a slight curve in the channel that affected the course chosen, was "looking to the right of the enemy's line." Before altering course, Pilot Hodges had to steer carefully to avoid grounding.

Lookouts aboard the Union vessels could not immediately discern a flag flying aboard the oncoming enemy. Still, when they saw the huge black guns protruding from the two forward gun ports, everyone from commander to cabin boy quickly figured out that this was, indeed, the "celebrated ram *Arkansas*." Many Northern sailors doubtless reflected that the refugees and deserters encountered earlier were correct after all.

Aboard the *Hartford* next day, young Third Engineer John K. Fulton, son of the proprietor of the *Baltimore American* and a frequent contributor to his father's newspaper, had the opportunity to visit with surviving engineers from the *Tyler* and *Carondelet*. They told him that, initially, the *Arkansas* "had no flag flying, but when she got near, the Stars and Bars were flung to the breeze, and a shot was fired." Paymaster Coleman later remembered that, on board the *Tyler*, "the men sprang to the guns without waiting for the boatswain's whistle; the breakfast things were hastily brushed aside." There would be ship-to-ship action this day. A signal was made to the *Carondelet*, two miles away, that the *Arkansas* was breaking out.

Lt. Gwin immediately stepped up his own rate of fire. Without bow guns that fired directly ahead like those of the *Arkansas* or *Carondelet*, the *Tyler* had to yaw to accomplish this maneuver because her most forward guns had to be angled out of broadside ports. At

Seven: Morning (Part I), July 15, 1862: Dawn Fight in the Yazoo

the same time, riflemen hiding wherever practical shot minie balls at the oncoming monster. Many of the balls hissed into the water alongside and all of those which hit ricocheted like so many pebbles.

The Confederate armorclad also yawed back and forth from side to side as she came on. Capt. Brown knew that the ensuing concussion from the bow guns when fired in this manner would not arrest her forward progress as significantly as would otherwise have been the case. The captains of the broadside guns were authorized to fire only on those rare occasions when one of the enemy was, figuratively speaking, within their crosshairs. This zig-zag tactic permitted the *Arkansas* to gain on the more-distant Eads boat. Both of the iron-covered boats were slow, although Lt. Brown, exercising command from his exposed position outside of the ram's pilothouse, did not immediately know that he was facing his old friend Walke in the *Carondelet*, the pokiest of the seven Northern sister-ironclads. Brown and Walke had been messmates aboard the *Boston* of Com. Lawrence Kearney's prewar China squadron, but neither knew until later that they had faced each other in this engagement.

Her crab-like maneuvers also permitted the *Arkansas* to keep the *Tyler* and the ram *Queen of the West* occupied and away from her own quarter. From the beginning, however, they were regarded as distractions—Brown's primary goal was to "stand for" the *Carondelet*. When he caught up with the Federal ironclad, the Confederate intended to ram her just as the cotton-clads had struck the *Cincinnati* and *Mound City* at Plum Point Bend.

Lt. Gwin's courage (and his forward location in the river) brought the initial wrath of the Southern armorclad down upon the *Tyler*. The lead Federal gunboat, according to paymaster Coleman, "had slowed her engines when the

Lt. William Gwin, USN (1832–1863). *This Hoosier was regarded as one of the most promising junior officers in the Federal service prior to his death. Transferred west from the USS* Susquehanna, *he commanded the Western Flotilla's timberclad division in early 1862, gaining its greatest laurels. A classmate of* Arkansas *officer Lt. George Gift at the U.S. Naval Academy, Gwin later transferred to the flagboat* Benton. *He would be wounded in action at Haines Bluff on December 27, 1862, and die a week later. Always impeccably dressed and gallant in every assignment, had he lived he would undoubtedly have retired an admiral (Navy History and Heritage Command).*

engagement began," allowing the current to take her toward her consorts "then some distance behind." As soon as the Confederate pilot knew he was safe from grounding, the *Arkansas* steered directly for the one-time Ohio River packet. Upwards of the maximum 120 pounds of steam pressure powered her engines and screws as she launched her pursuit, her ram cutting through the water like a knife.

Early in the duel, two of the *Tyler*'s 8-inch shells, with 5-second fuses, struck the bow face of the armorclad's casemate. "The gunnery of the enemy was excellent," remembered Lt. Gift. "His rifle bolts soon began to ring on our iron front, digging into and warping up the bars, but not penetrating." The noise was tremendous as cannonballs tore into the old railroad iron. The *Tyler*'s third shot drew the first blood of the battle out of Gift's division, though it was not seen by the lieutenant, who was occupied with the battle ahead. Indeed, by now the noise and confusion was such that the strike was heard and felt perhaps more than it was visualized.

Lt. Stevens was, however, looking on when one of the Missouri volunteers, 16-year-old immigrant Pvt. Stephen Minton, a member of Gift's port broadside gun crew, stuck his head out of the gun port adjacent to his cannon and was killed by a passing cannonball. Although it did not hit the vessel, the missile whizzed by close enough to decapitate the imprudent sailor. Fearing the sight of the headless corpse might unnerve the men in the vicinity of the tragedy, the XO asked a nearby man to help him toss the body out the gun port. Unhappily, the tar he asked was the victim's brother,

Cmdr. (later RAdm.) Henry Walke, USN (1808–1896). *Known as something of a maverick and a great artist, the taciturn Virginian was, arguments to the contrary accepted, one of the most successful and undercelebrated of all Union Civil War naval officers. Entering the fleet as a midshipman aboard the USS* Natchez *in 1827, Walke served in numerous ships and squadrons and, in the process, became a friend of Lt. Isaac Newton Brown, who he always held in great esteem. Sent west in 1861, he turned the three timberclads into an effective operational force, becoming a friend of Brig. Gen. Ulysses S. Grant as a result of his actions during the Battle of Belmont. Transferred to the new Pook turtle* Carondelet *in January 1862, he skippered her at Forts Henry and Donelson before making his reputation by running past Island No. 10 in April. Successfully avoiding official censure after his fight with Brown and the* Arkansas, *he went on to command the giant* Lafayette *and, after Vicksburg fell, an ocean warship that pursued the Confederate ironclad* Stonewall *(Library of Congress).*

Pvt. Smith Minton. Other men stepped forward to complete the grisly task. (Both lads are buried in Bloomfield Cemetery, Stoddard County, Missouri.)

Every effort was made by the *Tyler* to maintain enough speed to remain ahead of the enemy, now plowing along only 150–200 yards behind. Gwin hoped to reach the "protec-

Seven: Morning (Part I), July 15, 1862: Dawn Fight in the Yazoo

tion" of the *Carondelet* before Mr. Brown smashed his unarmored boat into kindling. Lt. Gift, however, soon got in an opportune and telling shot at Gwin's boat from his huge, black bow Columbiad. With a jerk of the lanyard, a big 64-pd. shell with a five-second fuse was blasted off toward the enemy. Only a few on the gun deck, choking in the huge cloud of discharged smoke, saw the shot smash through the *Tyler*'s wooden bulwark, sending showers of splinters and debris over her decks and striking her engine room "fair and square."

Rebel gunner Gift later wrote that, when it exploded, the Confederate projectile killed a pilot in its flight, burst in the engine room, killed 17, and wounded 14 others. "I think this shell did the better part of the day's work on him," he later opined. "The woodwork and clothes of the survivors were splattered with blood and bits of flesh," David Flynt later wrote. Bodies, he continued, "lay piled in a sickening heap." In fact, the men killed in the blinding flash were Capt. Lynn and six men from the 4th Wisconsin, along with Third Assistant Engineer Oscar S. Davis and Seaman Thomas Jefferson Hood. All of the men were killed instantly but were "horribly mutilated." Six other privates were wounded, along with six seamen, a fireman, and a coal heaver. Additionally, Pilot David Hiner was hit twice by shrapnel and Second Assistant Engineer James M. Walker was slightly hurt.

Unhappily for the pleased Rebel gun commander, his piece recoiled off its chassis. It would require 10 minutes of hard labor before the port bow Columbiad was back in action. However, Gift admitted, Lt. Grimball "made up for it." Grimball, with Robert McCall, whom Gift called "the best gun captain," and "a superb crew" rapidly fired the starboard 8-inch bow gun, which "seemed to be continually going out and recoiling in again."

While the *Arkansas* and *Tyler* were paying their mutual respects to one another, Capt. Walke paced the hurricane deck of the *Carondelet* in front of her pilothouse studying the Confederate's approach with his spyglass. He was not encouraged by what he saw of the ponderous "castle" moving toward him. His glass was powerful enough to allow him to see the messy decapitation of the Rebel Irish sailor.

Although heavily armored on the forward face of her casemate, the *Carondelet* had just over half as much iron on her sides as the *Arkansas* and, interestingly, about the same amount of boilerplate over her stern. As it turned out, Walke had, fortunately, installed a heavy internal bulwark of "20 inches of green oak timber" around his machinery spaces a few days earlier. William E. Webb of the *St. Louis Daily Missouri Republican* told his readers after the fight that, if it hadn't been for the captain's precaution, "we should have had another *Mound City* accident to chronicle," a reference to the White River disaster when another Pook turtle was hit in her steam drum.

Capt. Walke was convinced that he now faced "a powerful gunboat and ram." Northern newspapermen, basing their earlier profiles of the *Arkansas* upon rumor, refugees, and perhaps some deliberate Confederate disinformation, had given her a huge battery. This idea died hard; 20 years after the war, Admiral Porter reported that the *Arkansas* had "a much heavier battery." In fact, the armament of the two craft was similar and throw weight of their similarly arranged batteries different by only seven pounds. An easy comparison is possible, thanks to a chart prepared by Alfred T. Mahan for his first book:

	Carondelet	*Arkansas*
Bow	150	106
Stern	64	120
Broadside	170	165
Total	*384*	*391*

Regardless of the strength of the foe charging down, Walke now shouted orders for his bow gunners to open fire. It was, according to Chester G. Hearn, 6:20 A.M. and the sun, just rising over the hills, had "turned the morning haze to a smoky red."

Unhappily, the initial shot from Walke's three cannon went wide. As the bolts gained accuracy and hit, they seemed to bounce off the Southern monster's casemate. In fact, they threw up big shell fragments and huge iron splinters, which, luckily for the exposed Lt. Brown, flew up and over the top deck. With their "splendid sixty-fours," Grimball and Gift, their captain later recalled, "were now busy at their work, while Barbot and Wharton watched for a chance." As both the *Arkansas* and *Tyler* continued to zig-zag, the other "inquisitive consort" of the *Carondelet* tentatively elected to inspect the Confederate's "boilerplate armor." The *Queen of the West*, according to Lt. Gift, now appeared to "summon courage," as Lt. Hunter "shot up as though he would poke us gently in our starboard ribs." It might also have been possible, according to Still, for the Ellet craft to have "rammed the ironclad head on." If not that, her speed would have permitted her to steam by the Confederate and attack her weak stern.

Divining Hunter's intention, Brown shouted down to Stevens, ordering that the Rebel ram's guns on that side be "trained sharp forward" in their ports. As the Illini soldier started to range up to starboard into a position for ramming, Brown ordered the *Arkansas* to yaw to port, bringing his broadside guns to bear. During that maneuver, Midshipman Scales fired first, quickly followed by Bacot and Wharton. Three shots burst into the water near the unprotected Federal steamer, throwing up huge geysers. The *Queen* quickly turned away and fled toward the *Carondelet*. Correspondent Browne excused Hunter's initial retreat. Noting that her timberclad consort also soon avoided action with the ram, the soldier "thought it proper to imitate her example."

The increasing revolutions of the *Arkansas*' twin screws in the fast waters soon made it evident to the *Tyler*'s captain that his initial evasion plan was not working. The armorclad, steaming slowly but with determination and the help of the current, was nearly on top of him. Now less than 200 yards from the Rebel, Lt. Gwin ordered the *Tyler* to back her engine, round to, and follow Lt. Hunter's *Queen of the West*, already retreating. As the timberclad yawed, gunner Peters' men replied with a broadside, but all of their shot seemed to bounce off their Southern foe. "'Stinkpot' against ironclad ram was suicide," Ivan Musicant put it in 1995. Still, the wooden U.S. gunboat would remain within 200–300 yards of the *Arkansas* for the next six miles.

The *Tyler* then chugged downstream at flank speed attempting to reach the *Carondelet*. Under the personal direction of Gunner Peters, the timberclad's defense was maintained with her aft 30-pdr. Parrott rifle, newly received while under repair at St. Louis. Fire from this lone sternchaser, plus occasional rounds from her broadside guns, would not be enough if the *Arkansas* got any closer.[3]

As the *Queen of the West* and *Tyler* paddled furiously toward him in retreat, Capt. Walke's gunners, many, like him, battling the effects of malaria, attempted to halt the oncoming armorclad. Their efforts were in vain. Shells from the *Carondelet*'s three forward guns and all of her starboard broadside raised huge geysers around the enemy; others clanked harmlessly off or, in the words of the *Brooklyn Daily Eagle* correspondent, "crashed like eggshells" on the armored face of her casemate. The *Arkansas* returned fire. Even as she continued to zig-zag, the ram closed the distance separating herself from the *Carondelet*. About this time, the *Queen of the West* "flew by the *Carondelet* with the words "the *Arkansas* is coming!"

Cmdr. Walke later told Prof. Soley that his command was "raked from stem to stern," being hit forward at least three times. "One shot," he remembered, "glanced on the forward plating, passed through the officers' rooms on the starboard side, and through the captain's cabin." Lt. Read, given the chance to visit forward from his inactive stern chasers, was able to see the *Arkansas*' "shot raking him and making dreadful havoc on his crowded decks." Newsman William Webb was told that all of the furniture in both the captain's cabin and the wardroom was destroyed by the upwards of 16 shots that passed through the two rooms.

As the fireworks continued, the *Tyler* came within "about 100 yards distant on the port bow of the *Carondelet*." When his consort achieved hailing distance, Cmdr. Walke, shouting through his speaking trumpet, ordered Lt. Gwin to speed on down and warn the fleet. Earlier, he had shouted the same request to Lt. Hunter of the *Queen of the West*. Neither of the escorting vessels obeyed Cmdr. Walke's order. Prof. Soley reveals the dilemma now faced by the captain of the *Carondelet*: "It now became a question for Walke of the *Carondelet* to decide whether he would advance to meet the *Arkansas* bows-on, trusting to the skillful management of the helm to avoid a ram-thrust, or would he retreat, engaging her with his stern guns. He chose the latter course." Often criticized in the weeks and years afterward for the decision he took next, Cmdr. Walke, sensing that he was, indeed, a potential ramming target for the *Arkansas*, also swung about. Being a sternwheeler, the *Carondelet* "required room and time to turn around," and so now rounded to and retreated "to avoid being sunk immediately."

Given that the *Arkansas* was twice as fast as his boat, Walke was convinced she would come up with him as he was fighting bows-on and maneuver around until she could thrust her beak into his side. If that happened, his proud vessel would be "sunk in a few minutes." Eliot Callender, speaking to a group of veterans in 1900, wondered if the sick ironclad captain had truly considered "the advantages of being rammed in the rear to being rammed in front." Taking increasingly serious punishment, the *Carondelet* stood down the Yazoo, trying to stay ahead of the Confederate's dangerous ram. The idea that she "sped away," as writers like Kevin Carson have penned, is just plain wrong.

As the helmsman spun his huge wheel, the turtle's gunners were able to bring their pieces into play "bow, broadside, and stern." A Chicago reporter, no doubt briefed by Capt. Walke, told his readers a few days later that the *Carondelet* now "belched forth a whole broadside onto the rapidly-advancing craft." The Union ironclad's shot was, putting it kindly, useless. "Imagine the consternation" aboard as her missiles fell off the *Arkansas* harmlessly into the dark waters. "'At him again,' was the cry, and another broadside was poured into the monster at 50 yards range, but with no more effect than if so many peas had been discharged."

It was at this point, as Capt. Brown later admitted, that one of the Rebel ram's engines again caused difficulty. "In the presence of the enemy," he confessed, " we made a circle, while trying to make the automatic stopper keep time with its sister-screw." The *Carondelet* still was trying to stay ahead of her dangerous foe. She returned fire from her unarmored stern with two aft-mounted sternchases of ancient vintage.

Even though he knew, in the words of historian Chester Hearn, that he "had no business fighting an ironclad with his flimsy wooden gunboat," Lt. Gwin refused to leave Cmdr. Walke to his fate even as the *Queen of the West* appeared to speed away. As the *Arkansas* relentlessly bore down on the *Carondelet*, the *Tyler* stood by her, firing as her guns bore. This did not go unnoticed aboard the *Arkansas*, where Lt. Brown acknowledged that "the stern guns of the *Carondelet* and the *Tyler* were briskly served on us."

For the better part of 60 minutes, the Confederate vessel pursued her Northern enemies in a zig-zag fashion designed, wrote Brown, to keep them "from inspecting my boilerplate armor." It also provided the ram's broadside gunners the opportunity, as their vessel heeled first to starboard and then to port, to get off shots of opportunity. As the hour progressed, the range shrank, becoming much less than the 500 yards which initially separated the combatants. At one point, the armorclad captain, who continued to fight his ship from an exposed position on the hurricane deck, received a severe head contusion; but upon examining the clotted blood he was most relieved not to see any "brains mixed with" it.

The Pook turtle, the principal target of the *Arkansas*, was hit repeatedly, as gun crews on both vessels served their pieces "as rapidly as possible." Many shells from the Columbiads of Lt. Gift and Grimball smashed into the *Carondelet*. Both boats were repeatedly drenched by spray from nearby cannonball splashes. At one time, Capt. Brown thought he could see "the white wood under her armor," not knowing the Federal had no armor aft. Externally and internally the sound of the shared cannonade was horrendous. Continuous smashing noises, accented by the thud and plink of projectiles large and small against the sides, damaged eardrums and made hearing either orders or the screams of the wounded almost impossible.

The gun crews of the three warships (the *Queen* was unarmed) were well drilled (the *Arkansas'* tars having learned more recently than the Federals) and thus were able to function in the chaotic environment. Not only was the sound a distraction for them but the yellow fumes and black smoke from the cannon chocked all three gundecks and made seeing difficult. And that was aside from hits which penetrated the wood and iron protection. Brown's projectiles may have been hitting the new log bulwark Walke had installed just days earlier. In any event, the satisfied Rebel captain knew, as he wrote years later, that it was only a matter of time until he overtook the Eads creation: "No vessel afloat could long stand rapid raking by 8-inch shot at such short range."

For his part, Capt. Walke was extremely frustrated that his cannonballs were having no effect. Next day, he told *St. Louis Daily Missouri Republican* reporter William E. Webb that he attempted to send shots into her only to see them glance off "like water from a duck's back." While the armorclad's bullets repeatedly ploughed into the *Carondelet*'s stern, her missiles and those of the timberclad struck the inclined face of the *Arkansas'* casemate, or sometimes her T-bar-covered perpendicular sides—and just disappeared. "The huge solid shot," wrote the *Daily Tribune* scribe Albert H. Bodman, "flew off like India rubber balls." Watching the fall of shot through his glasses, Lt. Gwin could not see that those from either vessels were doing much good, "though one of them raised the iron on her bow."

As Cmdr. Walke's boat began to lose headway, Lt. Brown doubtless rubbed his hands together believing that his original plan was coming together: "There was a near prospect

Opposite, top and bottom: **Defense of the *Carondelet*.** *After her gunners opened upon the* Arkansas *(top illustration), the* Carondelet, *finding it necessary to withdraw, was badly damaged (bottom illustration). Cmdr. Walke later told Prof. James R. Soley that his command was "raked from stem to stern," being hit forward at least three times. "One shot," he remembered, "glanced on the forward plating, passed through the officers' rooms on the starboard side, and through the captain's cabin." Lt. Charles W. Read, aboard the Confederate ram, was able to see the* Arkansas *"shot raking him and making dreadful havoc on his crowded decks." Newsman William Webb was told that all of the furniture in both the captain's cabin and the wardroom was destroyed by the upwards of 16 shots that passed through the two rooms. Although these two illustrations were originally drawn by RAdm. Walke to illustrate the action at Fort Donelson, they serve as well to show his gundeck during the* Arkansas *fight* (Battles and Leaders, *vol. I*).

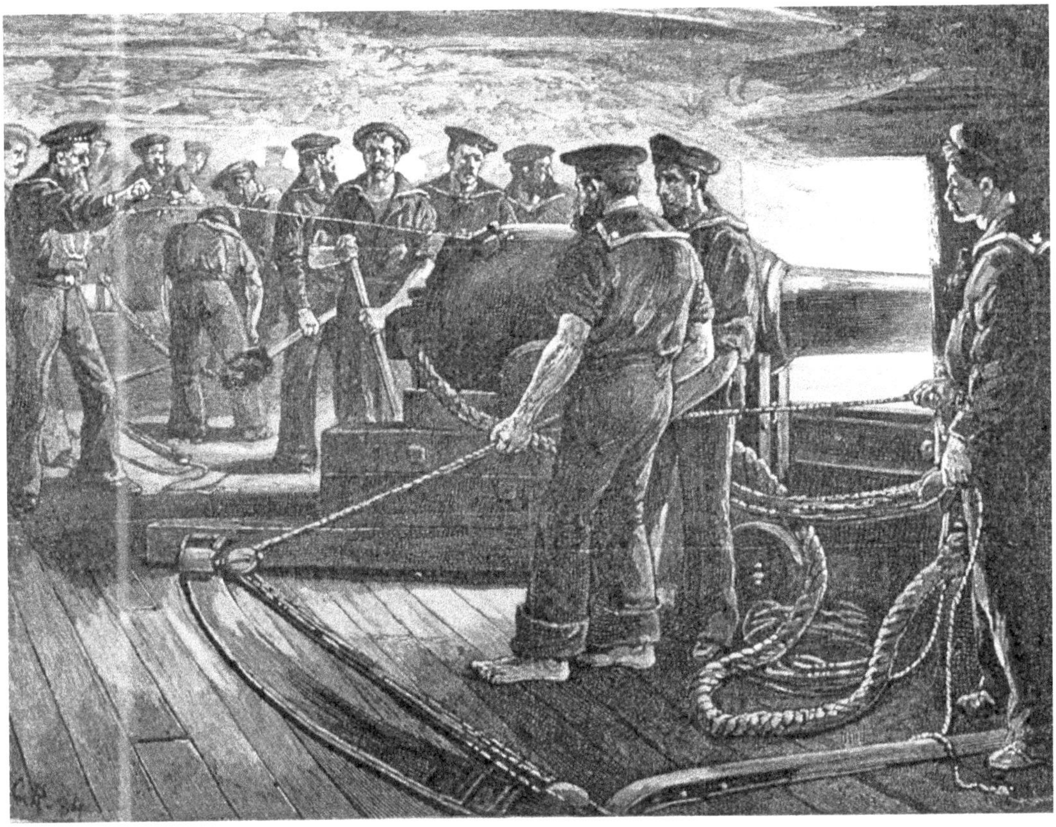

Seven: Morning (Part I), July 15, 1862: Dawn Fight in the Yazoo 163

of carrying out my first intention of using the ram." The stern of the Eads boat was the "objective point" for the prow of the *Arkansas* as the distance between the major combatants steadily shrank from 500 to 50 yards.

The single-minded approach of the *Arkansas* was not made without cost. Aboard the *Tyler*, Gunner Peters and his men were able to blast away at the armorclad, the guns of which remained focused on the *Carondelet*. A moment or so after Lt. Brown escaped the loss of his gray matter, a shell from the timberclad hit the hurricane deck at his feet. The *Tyler*'s shell penetrated into the forward face of the pilothouse and exploded, destroying part of the structure. In the smoke, big chunks of iron cut away the forward rim of the steering wheel and mortally wounded chief pilot John G. Hodges and severely injured pilot Shacklet, the one guide aboard familiar with Old River. As he was carried below, Shacklet, according to Capt. William H. Parker, "had the courage and devotion to exclaim with his dying breath, 'Keep in the middle of the river!'" The blast left two other pilots available to take over, William Gilmore and a Missouri volunteer, James Brady. Both were Mississippi River pilots unfamiliar with the Yazoo. As they were moved below, the two wounded pilots screamed for Brady, Gilmore, and the captain to remain in the middle of the channel.

Lt. Brown, still wanting to smash into Walke's boat, told the new man at the wheel to "keep the iron-clad ahead." Meanwhile, the *Tyler* continued to blaze away. "There is no doubt," Eliot Callender later remarked, "that Gwin's courage and skill saved both his own boat and the *Carondelet*." Within approximately half an hour of their mutual sighting, the *Arkansas* had largely overtaken the *Carondelet*. At least eight Columbiad balls had entered her casemate, smashing everything in their paths. The dead were moved out of the way, near the wounded, whose screams in many cases added to the confusion. The noise of the battle could be heard throughout the Delta. "The fighting up the river from the sound of the guns was something fearful," remembered L.S. Flatau, stationed with his men atop the Vicksburg bluffs, "but we could not see it."

The *Tyler*, keeping pace with the smoking turtle, was now able to intervene again. By this time, the Confederate armorclad was within easy range of the surviving riflemen of the 4th Wisconsin detachment hidden, as best as possible, behind boxes and other temporary barricades on her hurricane deck. The Yankee sharpshooters now unleashed a rapid volley fire at the *Arkansas*. Musketry and individual rifle fire was aimed at her gun ports, portholes—and Lt. Brown, the only human target outside the casemate. Sensing he was no longer just a target for cannonballs, the ram's commander, after almost an hour, finally decided to take shelter below and began to head for the hatch that led down to the gun deck. It was located just behind him, before the chimney. He never made it.

Although Lt. Gwin was unable to see a single man "on her upper deck during the entire engagement," a Wisconsin sharpshooter did and his minie ball found the captain's opposite number just as he reached the passageway ladder. Brown's left temple was grazed and he was knocked unconscious to the gundeck below. Lts. Stevens and Gift thought their valiant commander a casualty and ordered several sailors to carry him to the sick bay, or, as Brown later noted, "a place among the dead." En route, Brown awoke and found that, miraculously, neither the minie ball nor the fall had caused injuries beyond some additional cuts and bruises.

Brushing aside worried hands, but perhaps accepting a drink of brandy, the captain straightened his coat and climbed back up the ladder to his topside post. At this point, the flagstaff of the *Arkansas* was shot away and no effort was made to rehoist the colors. "I ought to have told Stevens to hold off" the gunners "from the iron-clad," the Rebel captain later confessed, "'till they could finish the *Tyler*, but neither in nor out of battle does one always do the right thing." If Brown had done "the right thing," there is little doubt that the timberclad's story would have ended in the Yazoo right then and there.

The *Arkansas*, meanwhile, had further closed the range on the Pook turtle. Repeatedly, her bow guns poured destruction into the enemy. Aboard the *Carondelet*, now seriously hurt by Rebel fire, her stern gunners gamely kept up the pace with their pair of old 32-pdrs. Their aim was "excellent" and many hits were scored on the bow face of Brown's casemate. Lt. Gift recorded a part of his opponent's agony: "The *Carondelet* was right ahead of us, distant about 100 yards, and paddling downstream for dear life. Her armor had been pierced four times by [Lt.] Grimball, and we were running after her to use our ram, having the advantage of speed. Opposite to me a man was standing outside on the port-sill loading the stern chaser. He was so near that I could readily have recognized him had he been an acquaintance. I pointed the Columbiad for that port and pulled the lock-string. I have seen nothing of the man or gun since."

The heat aboard the *Arkansas* was rising, and not just from the fighting. As the battle progressed, the big chimney atop the casemate was increasingly perforated by enemy rounds. Before long, it had difficulty in swallowing sufficient oxygen to keep the boiler fires at their best. On top of that, the unprotected fire boxes themselves warmed up badly, causing black room temperatures to soar to a point where its denizens had to be relieved every fifteen minutes or less. Gradually, the Confederate was losing thrust, and with it the ability to generate ramming speeds.

Unfortunately for the Yankee gunboat across the way, the shots from her lone remaining stern chaser all "seemed to glance off" the surging *Arkansas*. When less than 50 yards apart, the two armored protagonists departed the main channel and entered a treacherous area on the inner curve of the Yazoo near its eastern bank. A great number of willows, broken stumps, and reeds protruded above the dark but more shallow water over a bar not unlike the one further upstream encountered by the *Arkansas* the day before.

The *Carondelet* was badly wounded, having by now taken 13 Confederate rounds in her unprotected stern. St. Louis newsman Webb caught the carnage of a wreck that "in fact, almost defies description." In addition to rounds through the captain's cabin and wardroom that demolished the furniture "generally," "two shots passed through two of the heavy deck timbers; one pounded along and came within an ace of staving in a cylinder head; another passed within three inches of the steam-drum.... One shot went through the casemate, and then bounded along to the stern of the vessel, where it went through ten inches of timber, then five feet of loose timber, and four thicknesses of boiler iron.... On the starboard side, the one and a half inch of iron opposite the boilers was penetrated twice."

Cmdr. Walke, after her steering ropes were cut, leaving no rudder control, rode the crippled vessel toward shallow water. Fortunately for him, Brown could not safely pursue. Pilots Gilmore and Brady, unfamiliar with Old River, had initially followed the steering-deprived *Carondelet*. But knowing shoal water when he saw it, the young Missourian yelled to Lt. Brown that their enemy was headed toward the shallows and warned caution. Recognizing that Walke's draft was less than half of his, the commander of the *Arkansas* knew he could not follow much longer and that ramming his opponent was now out of the question.

"The crippled duck," crowed the refugee *Grenada Appeal* about the Federal gunboat a few days later on July 23, "commenced his favorite dodge of hunting for shallow water, and for this purpose sheered to the left bank of the river." Still, the Confederate commander ordered his craft as close as possible, even as he watched the *Tyler* and the *Queen*, out in deeper water, looking as though they were "awaiting our entanglement." As the Confederate armorclad rushed toward the *Carondelet*, there was a momentary thought aboard the Federal craft that a boarding situation might be at hand. Capt. Walke called for boarders, and a number of crewmen, led by Coxswain John G. Morrison (1842–1897), actually climbed to the hurricane deck via the gun ports, prepared for attack or defense as warranted. Others crowded toward the gun ports, where the smoke of battle made it almost impossible for them to see.

In an entirely fictitious report, the *Philadelphia Inquirer* (and several other Northern newspapers including, the *Louisville Daily Journal*), boldly stated on July 22 that the gunboat's seamen almost succeeded: "Just as the latter [*Arkansas*] was passing over the bar, the *Carondelet* closed with her, intending to board. She succeeded in throwing a grapnel aboard and getting out a plank, when the *Arkansas* opened her steam pipe, throwing hot water across the plank. The *Carondelet* replied in the same manner. While thus engaged, both vessels grounded, and the shock separated them." The *Chicago Daily Tribune* story published the next day is even more heroic and fantastic:

> Finding his guns were doing no service, Capt. Walke had his boarders called away, and into the Rebel craft they poured; but not a man or a passage could be found. The boarders now returned and the guns set to work, but it was so much powder wasted. The *Carondelet*'s stern was now perfectly riddled.... At this juncture, Capt. Walke led a party on the Rebels' deck, but could find no possible way of getting below. The hatches were all secured underneath and the smallest kind of an aperture or hole was nowhere to be found. This discovered, the party returned to give up their boat only when the bottom of the river called for her.

The *Brooklyn Daily Eagle* contributed to the heroics on July 24. An interesting detail was added when its correspondent reported that "their roof was invulnerable," which is wasn't, and that "the rebel crew were as safe from their [the boarders] fury as if they were a thousand miles away."

The actual and momentary opportunity quickly passed. In the smoke and confusion, the gun ports were closed and Morrison led his volunteers back to their guns. A native of Ireland, Morrison received the Congressional Medal of Honor for his bravery under fire.

Brown of the *Arkansas*, who had been, as Walke feared, hoping all along for a chance to ram the Union ironclad, now saw the *Carondelet*'s course becoming quite erratic. It looked like one of Brown's shells had shot away the Federal's steering ropes and despite all Walke's damage-control people could do, the turtle was unmanageable. Rebel balls also cut away a number of the Union craft's steam and water pipes and the steam gauge, while others smashed directly through the captain's cabin, continuing on to clear the steerage cabin and lodge in the new makeshift bulkhead completed around the boilers. Additionally, as noted, one of the two 32-pdr. stern chasers was now knocked out.

With a brief cloud of steam escaping from her gun ports and losing speed rapidly, the *Carondelet* ran inshore closing the trees. A number of the crew, perhaps fearing a boiler would explode, jumped overboard to escape the steam and two men were drowned. Some of these men may have been among Morrison's boarding party, who had probably not all regained the interior of the casemate.

Unable to ram his opponent and advised by his pilots that he could not follow her into the shallow water near the bank, Lt. Brown avoided grounding at the last moment when he screamed, "Hard-a-starboard!" He later remembered closing his enemy, for Alfred T. Mahan. "I found myself going over the tops of the young willows," he told the budding naval historian. "Drawing as the vessel did 13 feet, I feared getting inextricably aground and so ordered the helm aport almost touching the side of the *Carondelet* as the *Arkansas* sheered off." The engines of the Confederate were stopped, allowing the *Arkansas* to slide alongside, as Lt. Read recalled, "with our muzzles of our guns touching him," but actually within about 30 feet of the *Carondelet*. "It would have been easy to have jumped on board," Lt. Gift afterwards remarked.

Simultaneously, Brown called down to Stevens on the gundeck to have the port side guns depressed as far as they would go. Running from cannon to cannon, the XO made certain that the elevating screw of each piece was dialed up to maximum, pushing the muzzle down as far as possible. Then, in passing, a terrible broadside of solid shot, aimed at the bottom of the Northern craft, was loosed in a deafening roar. Master's Mate Eliot Callender indicates that, at this point, the starboard engine of the *Arkansas* had, in fact, quit, while the one on the port side continued to function. This quickly repaired lapse thus "turned her head around and ran her into the woods inside of the *Carondelet*." The Yankee's statement is not backed by other sources and it is not likely that such was a contemporary assessment.

Over a century later, Kevin Carson pointed out how fortunate it was for the hopes of the South that the *Arkansas*, in fact, turned away. "Had the Confederate ironclad followed the Union ship," he wrote in 2006, "they both would have run onto the shoals. That would have ended things for the Confederates right there, but such was not the case."

The blast of the *Arkansas*'s full port broadside was so powerful that her gunners were able to see the *Carondelet* "heel to port and then roll back [to starboard] so deeply as to take water over her deck forward of the shield [casemate]." Despite this blast, Walke's starboard gunners were able to send a partial broadside into the ram as she passed ahead. Some of these cannonballs were seen by Yankee bluejackets to take effect as a pair of holes opened on the enemy's port beam.

Having plastered the Federal boat from the closest possible range, the *Arkansas* continued past on the left (Vicksburg) side of Old River. Changing course, the armorclad steamed back toward mid-channel, giving Lt. Read the first chance to employ his stern chasers. "His rifles 'spoke' to the purpose," effused an appreciative Lt. Gift. From the bow Read and his colleague were able to see their impact upon the *Carondelet* and that "his colors came down." The captain and crew of the *Arkansas* believed and later testified that they had defeated the vaunted *Carondelet*, both actually and formally. "The rascal," boasted the *Grenada Appeal* editor, was seen to "haul down his colors, set a white flag, and desert his vessel."

Bounding down the ladder from the casemate roof, Lt. Brown, convinced of his victory and that his foe had struck, ordered Stevens and his other officers to cease firing. Before word got back along the gundeck, said Lt. Gift, the swinging armorclad gave "Wharton and the others a chance at her with the starboard guns." When news of the ram's victory made its way from mouth to mouth around the ship, the crew was jubilant. "Talk about yelling and cheering," Lt. Gift later wrote. "You should have heard it at the moment on the deck of the *Arkansas* to have appreciated it."

As the *Arkansas* continued to move off, the bow guns of the Eads boat, silent for some time, returned to life and opened up once more. However, at the same time they detonated, the *Carondelet* hit a small unseen stump, and came to a sudden stop. This unintended halt caused all three of her shots to fly wild. Admiral Porter later suggested that the *Carondelet*, in fact, had some success in the exchange. "Two shot holes were observed in the *Arkansas*," he revealed in his *Naval History of the Civil War*, "and her crew were seen pumping and bailing." The colorful naval leader is often remembered for inaccurate details in his stories and this was one of them.

Lt. Brown, who knew that he had "exposed the *Arkansas* to being raked" as she continued on, was overjoyed when his enemy jolted to a standstill. If the *Carondelet* had "fired into our stern when we were so near," he later wrote, "it would have destroyed or at least have disabled us." While Read's stern 32-pdrs. had their practice and pitched a few more rounds on the grounded Pook turtle, Pilot Brady was ordered to steer the armorclad on downriver. The *Carondelet* ran on to the eastern shore bar. Walke's boat, as Brown put it to his superior, Flag Officer William F. Lynch, later in the day, was left "hanging on to the willows."

Indeed, after the armorclad reached Vicksburg, the story was magnified. Walke's vessel became the Western Flotilla flagboat *Benton* and she, in the hurried prose of *Jackson Mississippian* correspondent "Subaltern, "was on the bottom of the river near the shore, careened to one side, and her career ended forever!" Robert G. Hartje, biographer of Vicksburg commander Maj. Gen. Van Dorn, later opined that the *Carondelet* "should have been forced to surrender except that the ironclad [*Arkansas*] could not risk delay."

In 15 minutes, the Confederate seamen had, in the words of Lt. Gift, "thrashed three of the enemy's vessels — one carrying arms as good as ours." Although Cmdr. Walke vehemently protested that he did return fire and that his flag was not down as all of the *Arkansas*' officers later testified, two facts stood out. The heaviest of the three reconnoitering Northern craft was out of action, steam escaping from her as she lay on the bank a mile and a half from the mouth of the Yazoo. There were casualties: Four men aboard were killed and 16 wounded. Ten were missing. "Walke had fired 90 rounds," Jim Miles points out. "He thought he had accomplished everything that could have been expected of him."[4]

The entire close quarters engagement between the *Arkansas* and *Carondelet* was witnessed with uncertainty and alarm from the *Tyler* and *Queen*. It was difficult for their officers and men to tell exactly what was happening, though the Pook boat did suddenly seem to run into the bank. At that point, the *Arkansas* moved toward Walke, coming almost abreast, and fired every gun brought to bear. "Until it was evident that the ram was intent upon continuing her journey down the river," Paymaster Coleman of the *Tyler* remembered, "we considered the capture of *Carondelet* certain."

The contest between the two ironclads was over. It was only the second on record, the first having been that conducted several months earlier between the *Monitor* and the *Virginia*. This time, there was no doubt as to the victor. "It was glorious," opined Lt. Gift. "For it was the first and only square, fair, equal stand up and knock-down fight between the two navies in which the Confederates came out first best." Still, some of the actual facts of the battle would be disputed for years to come. Before moving on, we will pause a moment from the action to consider the outcome of the duel between the *Arkansas* and the *Carondelet*.

Although out of action, *Carondelet* could be repaired. There would be no need, as Walke frankly feared during the heat of battle, for her to be salvaged from the bottom of the channel. As the *Tyler*, *Queen*, and *Arkansas* passed out of sight, the wounded aboard the Eads ironclad were, as it became possible, brought up to the hurricane deck to escape the heat and steam below-decks. During the remainder of the morning, as the Rebel armorclad reached and passed through the combined Union fleet, crewmen aboard the damaged craft were mustered and accounted for, and then they labored mightily to get her back to base.

In these hours, damage control parties made repairs and surveyed the situation. It was found that the gunboat had received 13 "effective shots" and her hull and machinery took "extensive damage." The carpenter reported that 19 beams were cut away along with 30 timbers, three small boats were cut up, the deck pumps were cut away, and davits, pieces of the chimneys, hammock netting, and chunks of the casemate were missing. Three escape pipes were cut away, the engineer added, along with the steam gauge and two water pipes. In short, the boat was a mess, but not an irretrievable one.

With her most significant shot holes patched and as she was soon able to get up steam, the *Carondelet* slowly pulled out of the willows and returned to the main channel. She had not been forgotten. Just after the *Tyler* had anchored and even as the *Arkansas* was passing through the fleet, Lt. Gwin sought aid for the *Carondelet*. The newly arrived *General Bragg* was ordered to steam immediately to the Yazoo and provide help. The assistance of the one-time Confederate warship was not required, as the *Carondelet*, her immediate injuries addressed, was able to rejoin the fleet not long after the *Arkansas* reached Vicksburg. Shortly after her arrival, about 8:30 A.M., the hospital boat *Red Rover* tied up alongside and took off the wounded.

The debate over Cmdr. Walke's handling of the *Carondelet* during her encounter with the *Arkansas* began to rage within days of its occurrence and has continued ever since. Most of the initial indictment came, naturally enough, from the Southern press and Confederate navy officers, who continued it on into the postwar memoir-writing period. It was whispered throughout the Western Flotilla at the time that the commander was ill or, at age 55, no longer in fighting trim. He was, as Ivan Musicant put it, "faulted for 'running away,' as some ignorantly thought." As late as 2003, William L. Shea and Terrence J. Winschel wrote the following: "Walke panicked and lost control of his flotilla."

The former point may certainly have had some impact upon the manner in which Walke chose to engage the *Arkansas*. The *Carondelet*'s captain, a man stung earlier by the navy's retiring board and a court-martial, could admit no error in a third case, even if it might have been caused by illness. What is not commonly taken into account in judgments of his actions during this encounter was the fact that Walke was probably sick. On July 20, he was confined for a fever — doubtless malaria — aboard the *Red Rover* for a period of two days. This disease would continue to haunt him as long as he served on the inland waters. Just how bad this fever was at the time of the *Arkansas* battle or what effect it might have had upon his tactical decisions is impossible to say precisely. This writer believes, however, that it may have been considerable.

Capt. Walke's nemesis, Lt. Cmdr. Seth Ledyard Phelps, failing to acknowledge the possibility of sickness, believed the *Carondelet*'s captain was too old and unfit for his position: "Walke is a brave man and a reliable one when minutely directed as to what is expected of him. He made a fatal error in judgment in the Yazoo when he met the *Arkansas*. Had he kept head to the enemy, the *Carondelet* and *Tyler* would have destroyed him where they met. It was no lack of determination on Walke's part. Younger men are wanted who have the physical energy and habit which will lead them to drill & exercise and discipline their officers and men personally and constantly." On the other side of the coin, Admiral Porter, who also knew Walke and had a favorable opinion of him, deserves here the chance to say some favorable words: "There can be no comparison drawn between the *Arkansas* and her antagonists, for with but one gun she would have been superior to all the *Carondelet* class of gunboats put together and would have been a match for the *Benton*; yet, notwithstanding her inferiority, the *Carondelet* hung on to the last, inflicting all the damage on the ram that she possibly could until her wheel ropes were shot away and she drifted ashore."

The state of his health (and age) aside, two questions regarding fighting are usually raised: (1) Was it a mistake for Walke to avoid fighting the Rebel ram bows-on; and (2) Was the *Carondelet*'s flag struck in surrender? Let us revisit these points one at a time.

In respect to the decision to round to, it is now generally conceded that Capt. Walke erred in judgment. It has been suggested that had Walke elected to engage Brown bows-on he might have stopped the ram — or at least not have been badly damaged. This view is based on the knowledge that the Federal's shot outweighed the Rebel's by 44 pounds, 150–106. Additionally, the thick, specially built armor plating on the forward casemate of the *Carondelet*, designed to battle the heavy guns of land forts, should have proven superior to the old railroad tracks covering the sides of the *Arkansas*.

There is no question that the surprise appearance of the Confederate armorclad — the ram all the newspapers had been speculating upon for some time — and her offensive gunnery was effective. As soon as the *Arkansas* was within range, her shot began raking the *Carondelet* "from stem to stern." The retreat of the *Tyler* and the *Queen of the West* could not have been reassuring. It was, however, the unknown size and shape of ram at the *Arkansas*' bow that concerned Capt. Walke. Early in the fight, before her chimney was perforated causing her progress to be slowed, the twin-screwed enemy was descending upon him at a speed difficult to determine. It was not fast, but it was steady. Having seen the effectiveness of rams at Plum Point Bend and Memphis, Walke was concerned that he not become the victim of one, his proud ironclad sacrificed to the ooze of the Yazoo.

Considerable debate on the captain's decision to round to occupied space on the *Civil War Navies Message Board* in March 2006. One contributor, George Wright, pointed out that, compared to the *Arkansas*, the Union vessel "and her sisters were pigs to steer." Warming, he continued: "Her rudders were normally 'blown' by the current coming out of the wheel. When being backed, you lost this additional flow over the rudders and steering suffered." Not only that, but "speed backing was also penalized."

What Walke may have failed to fully consider, either on July 15 or in later years, was the actual effect a collision between the two boats would have been "in that narrow river." The *Arkansas*, though smaller than the *Carondelet*, was no swift cotton-clad like those fleet Confederate boats at Plum Point Bend or even the somewhat heavier Ellet rams employed at Memphis. Although twice as fast as the *Carondelet* at top speed, the *Arkansas* was still awfully slow, and zig-zagging to boot. Even had she managed to run into the bow of the *Carondelet*, it would have taken a fairly direct hit to sink the Eads craft. In all probability, the Rebel would have succeeded only in shoving the broad-beamed *Carondelet* aside.

In any event, Walke was not prepared, for whatever reason, to accept the enemy's blow, believing it better to join his consorts in withdrawal, perhaps drawing — as he certainly succeeded in doing — the full attention of the *Arkansas* while the *Queen* and *Tyler*, as he ordered, steamed to warn the fleet. On the other hand, as George Wright contends, Walke's first instinct was to keep his command intact: "Logically, the *Carondelet*'s only hope was to run for it and hope that the presence of other Union steamers would cause the *Arkansas* to split her fire."

Despite a ferocious defense of his actions in his memoirs, the hero of Island No. 10 lived long enough to read unfavorable reviews by impartial critics. In 1882, Alfred T. Mahan, whom Walke knew and who had praised so highly his action at Island No. 10, weighed into the debate. In his still-quoted history of the war on Western waters, the future strategic thinker bluntly stated that the loyal Virginian's tactics were "not judicious" because they exposed the weakest part of his craft. "Besides," Mahan continued, "when two vessels are

Seven: Morning (Part I), July 15, 1862: Dawn Fight in the Yazoo   171

Fighting into the Willows. *Lt. Isaac Newton Brown, from his position atop the casemate of the* Arkansas, *ensured a relentless pursuit of the* Carondelet. *When less than 50 yards apart, the two armored protagonists departed the main Yazoo River channel and entered a treacherous area on the inner curve of the Yazoo near its eastern bank. A great number of willows, broken stumps, and reeds protruded above the dark but more shallow water over a bar. The* Carondelet *was badly wounded, having by now taken 13 Confederate rounds in her unprotected stern. Cmdr. Walke — after her steering ropes were cut, leaving no rudder control — rode his crippled vessel toward shallow water. Fortunately for him, Lt. Brown and the* Arkansas *could not safely pursue. The top illustration, drawn by Walke, is relatively accurate, while the lower portrait, from* Frank Leslie's Illustrated Weekly, *is not (top, Walke,* Naval Scenes and Reminiscences of the Civil War, *bottom, Navy History and Heritage Command).*

approaching on parallel courses, the one that wishes to avoid the ram, may perhaps do so by a maneuver of her helm." But when the slowest ship, in this case the *Carondelet*, "has presented her stern to the enemy, she has thrown up the game, barring some fortunate accident."

Just after Mahan, Prof. James R. Soley published a more concise review in his piece "Naval Operations in the Vicksburg Campaign" for the Century Company's *Battles & Leaders* series. The Naval Academy academic readily admitted that the *Arkansas* "was decidedly the superior vessel," better armed and armored. The *Carondelet* was only partially protected and her stern "was not armored at all." He then crushed her commander. "The position adopted by Walke was the one," he concluded, "which, by exposing his weakest point, gave the enemy the benefit of his superiority." When the *Carondelet* presented her unarmored stern armed with two ancient 32-pdrs. and then engaged in an hour-long running fight with the two 8-inch guns carried forward by the *Arkansas*, it was "little short of a miracle ... that she escaped total destruction." To perhaps soften the blow, Soley tells his readers that once the decision was taken, "Walke made a very good fight of it."

Today, most Civil War writers accept the views of Mahan and Soley and kindly refrain from mention of the controversy over the *Carondelet*'s maneuver even in books or articles in which the armorclad's breakout is featured. They prefer to heap well-deserved accolades upon both boats, forgiving the temporary failures of captains who gave exemplary service.

There are many sides taken on the truth of our second question concerning the striking of the *Carondelet*'s flag, and Adm. Mahan found it impossible to resolve them in the 1880s. In his account of the battle, Cmdr. Brown contended that, in passing the grounded Union vessel, he saw "their ports were closed, no flag was flying, not a man or officer was in view, [and] not a sound or shot was heard." Confederate Acting Masters Mate John A. Wilson saw the Federal boat was "compelled to strike her colors," while Lt. Gift noted "the enemy hauled down his colors."

Neither Capt. Walke nor Gwin corroborated this signaling of surrender in their reports to Flag Officer Davis — or even mentioned it. In his story of the *Arkansas-Carondelet* battle of July 23, Albert H. Bodman, the correspondent of the *Chicago Daily Tribune*, wrote in passing that "the flag which still floated from her [*Carondelet*] stern was never to be struck to the Rebels so long as one board floated to hold it up." This particular newspaper account by Bodman was, in general, quite pleasing to Walke. When he wrote his memoirs, the old sailor gave few compliments to anyone therein. This press story was, however, judged as a "tolerably good report."

Later, when the subject became an item of controversy, Walke flatly stated that "the flag of the *Carondelet* waved undisturbed during the battle." It was not until 67 years later that the actual events of this controversy may have been resolved in an obscure personal letter forgotten in a filebox. In 1929, Mr. A.B. Donaldson of Cleveland, Ohio, wrote a letter to secretary of the navy, Charles F. Adams. His uncle, Oliver Donaldson, was a mate and chief carpenter aboard the *Carondelet* in July 1862. According to a testimonial which accompanied his nephew's letter, the late ironclad sailor claimed that the gunboat's colors were shot away during the engagement with the *Arkansas*. When the flag fluttered into the muddy Yazoo, he dived in to retrieve it. Once the Southern monster had passed down and the *Carondelet* was alone in the willows, the rescued bunting was again hoisted to the main and was waving there when the turtle rejoined the fleet. The disputed flag, given to Donaldson after the war, is today at the U.S. Naval Academy Museum.

Interestingly, the deck log of the *Carondelet* notes, among its record of carnage aboard on July 15, that when the *Arkansas* passed the grounded Eads craft, her "flag was down and not hoisted again while in sight." The *Cincinnati Daily Times*, in its coverage of the encounter between the two vessels, told readers, "The hostile boat had a large and beautiful flag at her stern, but the *Carondelet* shot the colors away after the fourth fire, sparing us the mortification of seeing the hateful symbol of defiance flung insolently in our faces as the rebel passed down the river in the teeth of our hapless fleet." No debate ever surrounded its absence.

Cmdr. Walke's reputation did not suffer as a result of this event until years later when Civil War officers wrote their memoirs or offered comments before patriotic groups. The captain's encounter with "the Ram" was written up at the time as "a most gallant exploit" against overwhelming odds. Luckily for him, as a result of the *Arkansas'* escape from the combined Union fleet, official heat fell not on him but upon Davis and Farragut. At the same time, doubtless intrigued by the pile of documents, petitions, and reports taking up space supporting Walke's good works with the Western Flotilla since the time after his court-martial when he was posted west, Secretary Welles decided to include the *Carondelet*'s skipper on the list for advancement. On July 16, Welles mailed Walke word of his promotion to the rank of captain.

Had Welles suspected that Walke had displayed faulty judgment in combat the day before, one might reasonably speculate that the one-time lighthouse inspector's enhanced credentials never would have left his desk. Fortunately for the *Carondelet*'s captain, the same fate that robbed him of glory at Island No. 10 spared him shame in the Yazoo. There was no 24-hour news, the mails moved slowly, Washington offices, often noted for political intrigue, rapidly filled with intelligence of important defeats and advances, and those newspapers that filed dispatches to the Federal City all masked Walke's decision not to fight bows-on, with several actually making him a dime-novel type hero for his supposed boarding exploits.

After rejoining the flotilla, the tars of the *Carondelet* continued to make repairs to their boat. In what was by now a long-standing practice, as one of the newcomers would later remark, many of the musket balls were not dug out but were simply allowed to remain "in the timber and upper works where it is not iron plated" as visible reminders of combat. With Capt. Walke returned from the *Red Rover*, Flag Officer Davis was piped aboard on the morning of July 22 to examine the ironclad's state. Moving around the decks with the visibly weakened Walke, the flotilla leader was aghast at the terrible personnel conditions aboard. As a result of the fever epidemic sweeping the area, one of every two sailors aboard the gunboat was ill.

At noon, a tug came alongside the *Carondelet* with orders that she return upriver for professional repairs, making stops en route at Carlton Landing and Memphis to review matters and communicate with local commanders. At Mound City, her officers and men would be granted personal and sick leave. She would remain in the hands of the carpenters for the next 70 days.[5] When we left her earlier, the Yankee ironclad was disabled in the weeds of a riverbank sandbar. "We had no time to stop and secure our prize," Lt. Gift remembered, "as the enemy would be apprised of our coming and swarm in the river like bees if we did not hurry.... Consequently, we pushed down the river." Lt. Read remembered the boat moving off because she had no pilot and "Capt. Brown considered it unsafe to stop."

Capt. Walke, on the other hand, contended in his memoirs that, if the captains of the *Queen* and *Tyler* had obeyed his orders to speed down earlier to the fleet with a warning,

Farragut and Davis might have had sufficient time to ready their vessels to halt the oncoming *Arkansas*. This view is not widely supported, but one of those who does side with the *Carondelet*'s captain that "sufficient notice of the enemy's approach would have enabled Farragut's men to prepare for battle" is Charles M. Getchell, Jr., the most recent biographer of Lt. Brown.

Later in the day, an excited reporter for the *Jackson Mississippian* would inaccurately tell his readers that the vessel bested by the *Arkansas* was the *Benton*, which was sunk by one broadside. When last seen, the Federal boat "was on the bottom of the river near the shore, careened to one side, and her career ended forever!"

Considering the size of the Federal opposition known to be ahead, Lt. Brown understood that "under the ordinary circumstances of war, we had just got through with a fair hour's work." Quoting his Missouri volunteers, the fight with the *Carondelet* was "'a pretty smart skirmish.'" Now it was time to continue downstream, he hoped first, ridding the river of his pesky wooden opponents. Now the *Arkansas* "turned toward the spiteful *Tyler* and the wary ram." Lt. Brown was belatedly determined "to do the right thing" and get the timberclad, though his chances of catching the Queen *of the West* were slim. Lt. Gwin's champion, Eliot Callender, later asserted that "another *Tyler* and another Commander Gwin would have settled the *Arkansas* then and there." But this did not happen because, in the seaman's opinion, the timberclad's skipper "had a foeman worthy of his steel, in the gallant Brown of the *Arkansas*."

The boats of Gwin or Hunter were never a match for the armorclad and now both "very properly" took advantage of a speed double Brown's to seek the safety of the combined fleet. "Our last view of *Carondelet*," Coleman confessed as *Tyler* and *Queen* left the scene, "was through a cloud of enveloping smoke with steam escaping from her ports and of her men jumping overboard." The commander of the largest of the old wooden Federal gunboats, watching the rust-colored enemy plough back into the channel, knew that he dare not linger or he would die. As Lt. Gwin unashamedly later confessed, "I stood down the river with all speed." Everyone aboard the *Tyler* knew that their salvation lay in speed and perhaps some gallantry. Having deliberately held down speed and lingered off the battle scene to offer any support, her officers knew that the engines of the idling timberclad were not yet churning fully. The *Arkansas*, on the other hand, was charging down on her like a fire-breathing rhinoceros. Frank Bennett later wrote that "with the ram in hot pursuit, they had caught a Tartar!"

Hailing the *Queen of the West*, now some yards ahead, Lt. Gwin, under the terms of Lt. Col. Ellet's orders, requested that Lt. Hunter circle around and, in words more or less similar to Ellet's, run "full speed right head on into" the *Arkansas*. Such a maneuver would allow the *Tyler* to come back up to full speed, while she enjoyed something of a respite from the armorclad's assault. Unhappily, no one from the gallant Ellet family was aboard the *Queen* that day to enforce discipline. The "badly scared" Hunter, stressed earlier by *Arkansas* cannonballs, did exactly the opposite of what Lt. Gwin requested. "He pointed his vessel for the fleet," the timberclad sailors dumbfoundedly observed, "and the last we saw of him, he was making off at the top of his speed."

Gwin was absolutely livid at Hunter's defection and boiled over with rage at the imminent possibility that the perfidy might cause him to lose the *Tyler*. As the *Queen* made off, she was followed, according to Coleman, who was standing near his captain, "by a storm of what the darkey called the 'luwustest kind of language.'" The salty language was later cleaned up when Gwin bluntly informed Flag Officer Davis that Hunter "behaved in a most

Seven: Morning (Part I), July 15, 1862: Dawn Fight in the Yazoo

cowardly and dastardly manner, having deserted us without making an attempt to bring his vessel into action." When next the *Queen* went up against the *Arkansas*, she would be under the personal command of Lt. Col. Ellet.

As Hunter ran away, the *Arkansas* closed and began to fire grapeshot at the timber bulwarks of the *Tyler*. Her pistons pushing as fast as possible, the old gunboat zig-zagged. Her gunners fired every time a cannon was brought to bear, and musketry from the 4th Wisconsin crashed out in almost continuous volleys. Running and weaving like an energized paddlewheel bunny, though nowhere near as fast, the *Tyler* took a pounding. Paymaster Coleman confessed that "things looked squally." The occasional crash of timbers, heard throughout the boat, "seemed to indicate that some vital part would be soon struck."

One of the big missiles from the *Arkansas* smashed the *Tyler*'s steering apparatus. Pilot John Sebastian, with the boat since she first entered service a year earlier, was badly wounded and eventually lost his arm. He refused to leave the wheel until Pilot David Hiner, hurt and relieved earlier, was able to return and — with assistance from *Lancaster* pilot Smith — take over. All *Tyler* hands knew they were fighting for their very existence, no one more so than Lt. Gwin. The Shiloh veteran "was ablaze with the spirit of battle." Some were less convinced of escape than he, as "evidence was accumulating ... that Arkansas' guns were heavy and well served."

About this time, First Master Edward Shaw suggested that the possibility was fast approaching when the timberclad would be so battered she might be forced to surrender. Gwin would have none of it. The vessel might go down, everyone aboard might be killed, but he would sanction no surrender.

After the *Carondelet* went *hors de combat*, the running pursuit of the *Tyler* by the *Arkansas* consumed about an hour. Aboard the timberclad, most of the men had, according to Paymaster Coleman, "practically nothing to do." Their time was occupied watching "the gunners of *Arkansas* as they handled their battery" or rendering "such assistance as was practicable to the wounded encumbering our decks." Occasionally, the pumps were sounded "to see if we had been struck below the belt." Sometimes a few men were able to help out "the crew of our one stern gun working it for all it was worth."

The impact of Confederate shells continued. During the last half hour of the engagement with the armorclad, the *Tyler* ran with her entire after-part full of steam. Until repairs could be made, Gunner Peters and his men fought their stern chaser, despite being almost suffocated by steam escaping from the timberclad's damaged port safe pipe. As demonstrated earlier, the battle between the Union scouts and the Confederate monster was not all one sided. Throughout the steamer race, the *Tyler* peppered the armorclad, shooting away her boats and destroying a hawse pipe. Those were incidental targets, as gun captains and sharpshooters alike focused on her most vulnerable target — the huge chimney atop the hurricane deck and its breechings (the connections between the chimney and the furnaces).

As the *Arkansas* neared the Mississippi, the effectiveness of the *Tyler*'s shot began to tell. With her chimney "shot through and through," smoke poured out the shrapnel and minie ball perforations caused by both the timberclad and, earlier, the *Carondelet*. As the breechings were destroyed, the draft to the armorclad's boilers was largely lost and, along with it, steam pressure to the engines. The steam pressure so necessary to propulsion now dropped steadily from 120 pounds to about 20 pounds, which was barely enough to keep the engines turning. With her speed reduced to about 3 mph (even with the current) and her engines undependable, offensive use of the armorclad's ram became impossible. The armorclad's reduced pace permitted the timberclad "to gain a little on her." While maintaining fire with her stern chaser, the *Tyler* paddled as rapidly toward safety as she possibly could, still far behind the fleeing *Queen of the West*.

The damage to the chimney and breechings of the *Arkansas* had other consequences. As the *Tyler* chased the *Queen* still seeking the safety of the Union fleet, temperatures aboard the pursuing armorclad continued to skyrocket. An incredible 130 degrees was registered in the fire room as raw flame shot out and into the adjacent gundeck, raising temperatures there to 120 degrees.

Even as the great guns roared, Lt. Stevens organized relief parties for the ram's firemen and sent them into the sweltering machinery spaces every 10 minutes. Those they replaced came up, or "in many instances, were hauled up," exhausted. Still, this was the only way, by "great care, steam was kept to service gauge." Capt. Brown was moved by the suffering of the engineers and firemen when, as the *Arkansas* steered for the mouth of the Yazoo, he was able to get below to inspect the engine and fire rooms. Aside from the structural flaw that resulted in the loss of the poorly protected pilothouse and her badly damaged chimney, which reduced draft, the *Arkansas* was holding up as Shirley had dreamed and Brown had hoped. In the main, as Confederate navy historian Raimondo Luraghi opined, "enemy projectiles bounced off her carapace, which, as a whole, held well."

A few decades later, Tennessee soldier Bromfield L. Ridley compared the ram's achievement to legendary USN activities at the start of the 19th century. "Neither Decatur in his feat of burning the *Philadelphia* on Tripolitan shores in 1804 nor Captain Richard Somers in his dare-devil attempts to blow up the Tripolitan fleet was more daring," he wrote, "than Captain Isaac Newton Brown, Commander of the Ram *Arkansas*, in his drive out of the mouth of the Yazoo, 30 miles to Vicksburg, to destroy Uncle Sam's Navy."

The distance from the mouth of the Yazoo to Vicksburg was approximately 10 miles. About halfway between those two points, the combined Federal fleets of Flag Officers Farragut and Davis were anchored, in a somewhat staggered formation, on both sides of the river. Farragut's unit comprised those vessels that had passed the batteries at the end of June, while Davis was present with three operational ironclads, two Pook turtles and the Western Flotilla flagboat, plus several gunboats, some mortar boats and supply vessels. Lt. Col. Ellet had increased his Ram Fleet contingent to four, not including the *Queen of the West*. Except for the latter, the Union vessels were the same as those seen by Lt. Read at the beginning of the month. Looking down the Mississippi toward Vicksburg from the north, the Federal fleet comprised three distinct groups.

Closest to the mouth of the Yazoo off the Mississippi (east) bank were the vessels of the Ram Fleet. Ever since Lt. Col. Ellet and Flag Officer Farragut had first met, Lt. Col. Ellet accepted the duty of maintaining an eye toward the mouth of the tributary. The eight oceangoing ships of Farragut's fleet that successfully passed Vicksburg's batteries on June 28 were anchored next in line below Ellet's boats. Their uneven pattern was also located along the eastern shore. The descending order, as best we can tell from the various sources, was *Pinola*,[6] *Richmond*,[7] *Hartford*,[8] *Sciota*,[9] *Iroquois*,[10] *Oneida*,[11] *Wissahickon*, and *Winona*.[12]

The last contingent anchored along the eastern shore were the river ironclads of Flag Officer Davis, minus the *Carondelet*. The vessels anchored below Farragut's contingent included the *Louisville* and *Cincinnati*,[13] *Benton*,[14] *Essex*,[15] and *Sumter*.[16]

The vessels of the Davis and Farragut flotillas lay three or four abreast. This convenient but unwise formation ensured that "scarcely two" would be able to "fire without pouring their broadsides into some of their own." A large group of miscellaneous Union vessels were anchored or tied up along the western, or Louisiana, bank. These included the transports for Brig. Gen. Thomas Williams' troops, mortar boats, tugboats, a few supply vessels, and several extra craft.

The contest between the *Arkansas* and her Federal opponents was heard, if not seen, by all within the sound of the guns. "In the morning about 5 — I was aroused from my Sleep by the thundering of a 'war dog' up the river," recalled Pvt. William Y. Dixon of Co. G ("Hunter's Rifles") of the 4th Louisiana Infantry, "which we afterwards learned was the bow gun of our little '*Arkansas* Ram.'"

Aboard the units of the Federal fleet, the thunder back up the Yazoo had been heard for some time. The officer of the deck aboard Flag Officer Farragut's flagship, USS *Hartford*, wrote in her log at 7:00 A.M.: "heavy firing heard up the river, supposed to be artillery on shore." In a letter to Flag Officer Andrew H. Foote written on August 29, Lt. Phelps spoke for many when he said that the firing was thought to be upon "guerrillas, bushwhackers, or the like." On the other hand, the Federals could just be shelling the woods. Since the first days of the war, gunboatmen, said the *Tyler*'s Paymaster Coleman, "let off our surplus loyalty by shelling the woods where we thought the enemy might be" even when there was no enemy in sight.

The first direct word on the ram might have come from the frightened captain of the *Queen of the West*, which boat, having led the departure of the three scouts from the scene of action up the Yazoo, was the first to return. Having rushed back to the *Hartford* to communicate with Flag Officer Farragut, Lt. Hunter, in the words of Ram Fleet historian Hearn, "created more confusion by rounding to off the flagship's stern, fouling the anchor chains, and swinging helplessly alongside."

Although Hunter did not initially communicate with Farragut, or anyone else for that matter, the early return of the *Queen* impressed upon everyone watching from any of the Federal vessels that something was amiss. Lt. Phelps, captain of the *Benton*, believed the volume of fire might signify something serious and asked Flag Officer Davis for permission to raise steam. Just how amiss the situation was would soon be revealed to all.[17]

Chapter Eight

Morning (Part II), July 15, 1862: Running the Gauntlet

Three shallow-draft Federal reconnaissance vessels, early on the morning of July 15, had entered the Yazoo River intent upon reaching the Liverpool Landing raft and ascertaining the reported condition of the Confederate ironclad ram *Arkansas* reported lying above that location. They never got anywhere near their destination. Not long after entering the Yazoo, the trio, *Carondelet*, *Tyler*, and *Queen of the West*, was met by the Rebel monster, steaming under break-out orders from Department of Southern Mississippi and Eastern Louisiana commander Maj. Gen. Earl Van Dorn. She was en route down the river preparing to enter into the Mississippi and pass through the Union fleet.

In a spirited engagement lasting over an hour, the *Arkansas* was able to put the *Carondelet* out of action and badly damage the *Tyler*, which retreated downstream to sound a warning. The third vessel, *Queen of the West*, had retired early in the contest to warn Flag Officer David G. Farragut. Hoping to spread the alarm, she could not cleanly round to off the stern of the flagship *Hartford*, but her arrival was another alert that something was amiss upstream.[1] Even as the *Queen*'s Ram Fleet tars tried to properly come to behind Farragut's flagship, as the editor of the *Grenada Appeal* later reported an on board *Arkansas* admission, the *Tyler*'s spurt "gave us [the *Arkansas*] breathing time before the final struggle, which was soon to come."

As the *Arkansas* slowly and laboriously made her way the last few miles to the Mississippi, the smoke cleared from her gundeck. Medical personnel and sailors helped to comfort the wounded or safeguard her dead — 25 in all — while damage control parties plugged shot holes. An inspection by Lt. Brown and Stevens revealed that, although many crewmen were casualties and there had been some damages, the big guns were intact and the iron protection remained intact. As these officers visited the various departments, other men cleared away the worst wreckage and filth. They sought new supplies of ammunition, sanded the decks and ladders once more, and drew water in buckets from the river. Chief Engineer George City oversaw the effort to patch the breeching connections between the furnaces and the perforated chimney. It was determined that, in order to work draft up to a respectable 60–70 pounds, it would be necessary to burn oily substances along with the coal. Greasy barreled salt pork and beef immediately came to mind, though just how much of those victuals was aboard is unknown.

At long last, at 8:30 A.M. according to the timberclad's logbook, the *Tyler* was able to turn out of the Old River channel into the broad Mississippi, heading down Tuscumbia Bend toward De Soto Point. The *Arkansas* continued to tail her. While swinging into the confluence, the Confederate ram sent an occasional cannonball at her heels. "As time passed," the *Hartford*'s yeoman, William C. Holton, later remembered, "the firing neared us, and soon cannon balls could be seen dropping into the river below a bend which hid objects from our view." Once she cleared the bar at the mouth of the Yazoo, the *Arkansas* "felt the river current" of the light-yellow hued Big Muddy and picked up speed.

Peering ahead from his perch atop the earth-colored armorclad, Lt. Brown was unable to catch sight of Vicksburg, now much closer. What he did see, however, was "a forest of masts and smoke-stacks — ships, rams, iron-clads, and other gun-boats on the left side, and ordinary river steamers and bomb-vessels along the right." It appeared, Brown later confessed, "as if a whole navy had come to keep me away from the heroic city." According to Donald Barnhart, Jr., the captain of the *Arkansas* also noticed that the enemy ships "were all at anchor without steam in their boilers; they couldn't move."

Could the *Arkansas* make the intervening eight miles to Vicksburg? "With a partially-disabled engine; with both pilots dead; with one-third of his crew killed or disabled; with his steam run down from 120 pounds to between 30 or 40, owing to the destruction of his furnace draft," the odds facing Lt. Brown were formidable. "There was but one answer to any less daring and gallant heart than his," Master's Mate Eliot Callender opined. "He would make it."

To those watching her approach from the shore, it likewise appeared, as Sgt. Flatau put it, that the Federals "had formed line of battle and had everything in readiness." Watching with the soldiers, the reporter of the *Grenada Appeal* divined a possible Federal strategy to halt the ram. "It seemed to me," he wrote, "that their plan was to form a complete line across the river in the shape of the letter V, the point up stream." The suggestion by the *Appeal*'s writer was wrong. But, if the gallant armorclad commander had cared to reflect more deeply, Scharf later opined, he might have been overawed by the odds facing him: "3,000 men, 300 heavy guns, and a vast squadron ... against a solitary Confederate vessel of 10 guns and 200 men."

In addition to the combined fleet, Brig. Gen. Williams' troops were "spread out with innumerable tents opposite on the right bank." Lt. George W. Gift, captain of the armorclad's port side bow and broadside 8-inch Columbiads, remembered that "batteries of field artillery were run up and several thousands of soldiers prepared to shoot Minie balls into our ports." Everywhere Brown, Stevens, and the rest of the crew looked, except astern, their "eyes rested on enemies." If he now had any doubt concerning his vessel's ability to reach Vicksburg, Lt. Brown reasoned, it was because a number of the officers aboard the ships ahead were prewar colleagues and "valued friends." Like Cmdr. Henry Walke, captain of the *Carondelet*, he knew their mettle and respected many, knowing they would now do their best to send his armorclad to perdition. The same was said of those known by Stevens and the divisional officers.

As the *Tyler* came down the wide river, her paymaster, Silas B. Coleman, oversaw the hoisting of bright colored signal flags as a warning "of the company" she kept. Scharf says the timberclad was actually a half hour ahead of the *Arkansas*, which gave the Federal fleet "sufficient time to prepare for the reception of the unwelcome visitor."

Aided by the current, the two boats approached the Farragut-Davis fleet. "Unaware of the power of the *Arkansas*, some of the Federal officers aboard the other vessels above Vicksburg," Van Dorn's biographer, Robert Hartje tells us, "concluded from the closeness of the chase that the *Tyler* had actually captured the *Arkansas*." A newsman reported that lookouts posted along the riverbank by Flag Officer Davis now "came down like a streak of lightning, screaming, 'The *Arkansas* is coming! The *Arkansas* is coming!'"

Pvt. William Y. Dixon and his companions from Co. G ("Hunter's Rifles") of the 4th Louisiana Infantry had been on picket duty earlier in the morning when they first heard the thunder of the "war dog" from the direction of the Yazoo. Somewhat inland and unable to actually see up the river, they initially thought the sound of the cannonading came from "our light artillery firing into Yankee Transports but we soon learned from a Courier that it was our little 'Ram' trying to butt its way through the Yankee fleet."

All eyes, Union and Confederate, afloat and ashore, now looked in the general direction of the Yazoo as the cannonade above became more rapid. The smoke of several vessels was seen descending toward the confluence of that stream with the Mississippi. Maybe that strange vessel behind the timberclad was nothing to worry about. Perhaps *Tyler*'s commander, Lt. William Gwin, had captured one of the steamers lurking up the Yazoo. Incredibly, Coleman reports, one naval officer remarked, when she first came in sight, "There comes *Tyler* with a prize."

Henry Bentley of the *Philadelphia Inquirer* and several other spectators initially believed her to be "one of the gunboats expected daily from St. Louis." As the vessels grew larger in marine glasses, "the rear boat was distinguished from the others by the large volume of smoke which she poured out," wrote Albert H. Bodman of the *Chicago Daily Tribune*. "As the chimney of the *Arkansas* was known to be seven feet in diameter," he continued, "she was at once pronounced to be the ram."

"All eyes were" noted Bodman, "fixed on the big smoke and it was watched with the most intense interest." Beginning with lookouts and ratings high in the rigging of the *Richmond*, many bluejackets just stared at the oncoming vessels — particularly the "iron creature belching black smoke"—with their mouths open. After all the cannon fire of the last hour and a half, the men aboard the *Tyler* thought the fleet would be prepared to give the *Arkansas* a warm reception. "Not one of the lower fleet," a Northern officer later recalled, "had fires kindled." As the *Hartford* signaled her squadron to raise steam, Captain's Clerk Edward S. Bacon was among those aboard the *Iroquois* tumbled out of bed; he ran to his station to "fight on an empty stomach." The writer later confirmed that "we and several other vessels had several days before hauled our fires in order to save the scanty stock of coal we had."

The blue-water sailors were disabused of their earlier ideas concerning anti-guerrilla shoots as the timberclad and the armorclad drew closer, continuing to exchange fire. The *Brooklyn Daily Eagle* correspondent suggested in his later review of the day that, although "all was confusion and preparation," perhaps this was "on account of the early hour." *Iroquois* clerk Bacon in a letter home next day confirmed that he, too, was able to witness the *Tyler*'s escape. "Backing around the point above us," he wrote, she was "followed by a stranger engaged with her in quite lively style." As soon as the *Arkansas* was identified, "we beat to quarters."

Young Third Engineer John K. Fulton — son of Charles C. Fulton, the proprietor of the *Baltimore American*— had the opportunity, while at his spar deck station aboard the *Hartford*, to observe the oncoming ram for his father's newspaper. He, too, remarked on the fact that most of the vessels of the fleets had their fires banked. "Our objective being," he wrote, "to economize in fuel as much as possible, we having no means to replenish our bunkers should the coal give out." The surprise aboard the Federal warships was soon replaced by hurried preparations for receipt of the unexpected visitor. Lt. Phelps later told treasury comptroller Whittlesey that the "old" *Benton*, thanks to his earlier notice, "smoked vigorously" and was rapidly boosting steam pressure from 30 pounds to the 60 pounds necessary to move.

Eight: Morning (Part II), July 15, 1862: Running the Gauntlet

The Union's Men-o'-War Were Unprepared. *When the* Tyler *sped out of the Yazoo pursued by the* Arkansas, *the vessels of the Union squadrons anchored above Vicksburg were not ready to offer resistance. Although it would be possible for crews to quickly man the big guns, none of the larger blue-water ships could get up steam in time to move. This photograph, from the* Hartford, *suggests some idea of the moment when the Rebel ironclad first appeared (Miller, ed.,* Photographic History of the Civil War*).*

Aboard the *Hartford*, Engineer Fulton also noticed the intense burst of activity aboard the vessels. "Volumes of smoke were soon issuing from the smoke-pipes of the different steamers," he told his father, "as each one was endeavoring to get up steam." Yeoman Holton added that Farragut's warships were "so near together that for one to fire endangered the rest." Forty convalescents onboard the *Richmond*, which was serving as Farragut's hospital ship, were taking the sun on deck and had to be hurried below. A number of others, also ill, remained at their posts, but still, the crew was so debilitated by illness that three of the sloop-of-war's broadside guns could not be crewed.

Master's Mate Eliot Callender, then aboard the *Cincinnati*, reminds us there were Federal civilians with the upper fleet at the time. In addition to the masters, officers, and deckhands of the contract steamboats, there were a host of newspapermen, 10 or 20, he thought, assigned to the transport *J.H. Dickey*, which was anchored near the Louisiana shore:

> As soon as it was evident that the Confederate boat contemplated a raid through the Union Fleet, many conflicting emotions pervaded these brethren. They wanted to see the fight, but duty to the dear ones at home didn't seem to call them to be participants. The key note was struck, when one of them suggested that the *J.H. Dickey* was a great big boat and as such was most likely to call for special attention from the *Arkansas*. Contemplation of this haven of

refuge, which to their excited imaginations was little less than a Providential dispensation, for the *Arkansas* would certainly pay no attention to an insignificant hay barge and under the protection of the covered ends they could watch the fight through the spaces between the boards and push their pencils in that security and peace of mind, so essential to high-grade literary work.

As the *Arkansas* bore down on the huge line of vessels before her, Lt. Brown ordered Lt. Stevens to make fast the gun ports. As the iron shutters clanged shut, the men inside the casemate were shut off from the outside world. The blue and cloudless sky visible to some of them minutes ago turned into darkness. Most of the light now came from lanterns and rays of sunlight sneaking around the port shutters. The men remained largely quiet, moving, if at all, in shadows. The little fresh air available disappeared, quickly to be replaced by a stifling heat, soon to smell of sweat, cordite, and urine.

"On coming in sight of them," Lt. Gift tells us, "the scene was one of intense interest." Peering ahead before his gun port was shuttered, the young Tennessean believed he could see at least "20 pennants flying." "Steam was hurried up on all the river vessels," Gift continued, "and they weighed or slipped anchor, and took up such positions as would enable them to hit us and at the same time keep away from our powerful beak if possible." Support vessels steamed about in uncertainty seeking to flee or hide, "somewhat after the manner of a brood of chickens on the approach of a hawk."

Able to hear but unable to see the earlier fight in Old River, the military and civilian citizenship of Vicksburg had by now turned out en masse to witness the pending fight. While thousands of soldiers lined the tall bluffs back of Cobb's Battery, hundreds of civilians hurried to rooftops, the tallest river-fronting ridges, and the levee to watch and cheer. Samuel Carter quotes an unidentified artillerist with one of the Southern batteries: "We knew the odds against the solitary vessel were overwhelming and, of course, our excitement was almost unendurable."

Units of the Kentucky Orphan Brigade camped inland of the upper batteries heard "firing up the river" about 9:00 A.M. As many men as possible, including Pvt. John S. Jackman of the 5th (later 9th) Kentucky, hustled "up to the bluff to see the cause. Could see a commotion on the upper fleet, which was sending up a dark cloud of smoke, and firing."

It has been estimated that some 20,000 people gathered on Fort Hill and the other hills overlooking the river bend. Despite the smoke and haze of the encounter, at last something of the contest was visible "in as plain view to all of us as though it had been some performance in some great amphitheater prepared for the occasion." A century later, the town newspaper opined that "probably no vessel in history had the hopes of so many people riding with her."[2]

The units of Lt. Col. Alfred Ellet's U.S. Ram Fleet, the closest elements of the Federal combined fleet to the oncoming Rebel armorclad, were, like the other Union craft, caught by surprise and unable to immediately raise steam. A reporter from the *Jackson Mississippian* reported that the prow of one of the Ellet boats was pointed upstream, "while the prows of the other two were inverted from the shore." The *Tyler* passed all of them by, followed by the *Arkansas*.

As they headed downriver, Lt. Brown and his men continued to make final preparations for what lay ahead. Lt. Stevens and the crew stood by in the shuttered casemate, gun crews behind leveled and depressed pieces. As it was hot beyond belief, most persisted in wearing only the barest permissible clothing. There was silence and undoubtedly, shall we say, great concern over what the Union vessels had in store for them. "And we were about to attack him," Lt. Gift worried, "in an unfinished and untried vessel, with engines totally and entirely unreliable."

Although the *Arkansas* got by him, Medical Cadet Charles Rivers Ellet, aboard the *Lancaster*, was determined to "have a go" at ramming her. He ordered the side-wheeler's captain, Thomas O'Reilly, to have his anchor cable cut, allowing the steamer to drift downstream while her engine room crew worked to raise sufficient steam to engage. The officer of the deck wrote hopefully in the deck log concerning a desire "to give her a little of our kind of warfare."

Still unable to make sufficient speed for ramming, the Confederate vessel headed, as the *Chicago Daily Tribune* correspondent Albert H. Bodman recalled, "right for the center" of Farragut's line of big oceangoing wooden warships. Brown, fearful that Ellet's boats would quickly recover and pursue, briefly went topside to reveal his strategy to the armorclad's pilots, who were protected as well as possible in what remained of the pilothouse. "Brady," he shouted to one before returning to the gun deck, "shave that line of men-of-war as close as you can, so that the rams will not have room to gather head-way in coming out to strike us."

Knowing the Mississippi far better than the Yazoo, Missourian James Brady, who had taken over after Chief Pilot John G. Hodges was mortally wounded an hour before, steered for the head of the tall-masted enemies. He would, until they were past, endeavor at all times to keep the *Arkansas* within half a cable's length of each. He would, from time to time, be spelled by pilot William Gilmore, but throughout the ordeal that followed, the plucky armorclad would never be further than 75 yards from her Northern enemies. This close-in maneuver would not , for the most part, allow the Federal warships, several of which towered above the Confederate ram, to depress their huge cannon sufficiently to do great damage. It also increased the possibility that, if the enemy cannoneers missed the *Arkansas*, they would inflict friendly fire damage upon their fellows. This tactic, confessed Mate Callender of the *Cincinnati*, "virtually spiked three-fourths of the guns of the entire fleet." Additionally, it was believed that the U.S. rams would have insufficient room in which to strike effectively. Several of these, according to Cmdr. William D. ("Dirty Bill") Porter, now sought refuge behind the huge ironclad *Essex*.

The fighting did not start immediately upon the entrance of the *Arkansas* into the arena. There was, wrote Gift, "a decided and painful pause." As the armorclad approached the head of the line, her Columbiads came within range, but she did not fire, her captain wanting to wait and make every shot count. Meanwhile, although most could not make steam, the Federal ships prepared to fight. Earlier, some of the flagship's sailors began casting loose the gun tackles, apparently even before receiving orders to do so. It did not take too long, Yeoman Holton recalled, before "all hands were called to quarters."

Crews were "beat to quarters" and the guns manned. It was later reported by Seaman Bartholomew Diggins aboard the *Hartford* that Flag Officer Farragut now "appeared on deck, still in his nightgown and 'much surprised.'" Historian Frank Bennett later opined that the lower fleet commander never "imagined the *Arkansas* would ever venture near a formidable fleet of genuine warships."

There was a young Irishman in the bow gun crew of the Confederate ram who had distinguished himself during the Old River combat. Looking ahead though the tiny slit above his Columbiad, he was overwhelmed by the immense number of vessels he saw ahead. "Holy Mother, have mercy upon us," he exclaimed, "we'll never get through there." Standing near the Irish gunner, but by rank unable to publicly agree, Lt. Gift, watching the changing panorama through a similar opening on the bow port, had his own doubts as to the boat's chances of success. "A half dozen I would not have minded," he said he thought, "but two dozen were rather more than we had bargained for." Still, the *Arkansas* had ventured out "too far to think of backing out; through we must go."

The action was not yet joined when conditions for the men deteriorated beyond the unpleasantries of warm air and darkness. The breechings were failing and again flames from the boiler furnaces escaped, intensifying the heat. As time passed, some of these would even lick the underside of the gundeck, making it decidedly uncomfortable for the many unshod among the gun crews. It is difficult to imagine the vessel steaming on — let along fighting — under such conditions.

Wearing a big No. 6 on her smokestack, the oceangoing gunboat *Kineo*, anchored highest up the river, was, according to Gift, the first Federal vessel to engage the oncoming Rebel warship. It was remembered on the Rebel side that she "came out like a game-cock" and "steamed to the front to take the fire of a great monster." All of the Confederate gun captains knew the *Kineo* as a target of particular interest. Lt. Charles W. Read, commander of the armorclad's stern chasers, had let be known earlier that he believed her responsible for killing his beloved friend and superior, Lt. T.E. Huger, aboard the *McRae* during the Battle of New Orleans.

While the enemy sheered her port helm and came on, "letting fly from her stern guns," Lt. Gift sent his powder boy running aft through the ram's casemate to find and bring back Lt. Read. The *McRae* veteran took the message and returned forward with the youngster, walking "leisurely and carelessly, displaying such remarkable coolness and self-possession." Looking out Gift's gun port, Read saw No. 6 "getting close aboard." His eyes became "as bright and his smile as genuine as if he had been about to join a company of friends instead of enemies." About this time, a tongue of yellow flame erupted from the *Kineo* as a stand of grape was fired at the ports of the *Arkansas* from her 11-inch gun. Because it was too far depressed, however, the little balls mostly all missed, splashing harmlessly into the water alongside the charging Rebel.

The *Kineo*'s blast seemed a signal for the Federals to initiate heavy firing. The quiet but terrible pause that seemed to grip both sides like a spell as the *Arkansas* drove on pursuing the *Tyler* now ended. Aboard the Southern warship, the nerves of all the men "were strung up again and we were ready for the second battle." Just after the Northern gunboat's discharge, Pilot Brady of the *Arkansas* touched his own helm, bringing the Northern "90-day" gunboat directly before the bow of the armorclad. Lt. Brown ordered all guns to fire as they bore. While Read grinned, the gun ports opened and Gift "opened the ball" by sending a big shell into the *Kineo* "through and through." As she passed, the ram's port broadside also shot into the Union gunboat. Undoubtedly damaged, she did not pursue.

The dispatch by the *Arkansas* of her first rounds was almost like a signal to those assembled ashore to pump up the volume of their vocal support. Upon seeing the smoke from her muzzles, L.S. Flatau remembered, "we rent the very heavens with our yells." U.S. Navy records are silent concerning any action between the *Arkansas* and the *Kineo*, because, despite the memory of Lt. Gift, she was not present with Farragut's fleet above Vicksburg. On June 17, Flag Officer Farragut had detailed her to protect the army forces at Baton Rouge. All of the subsequent stories of the *Arkansas* that relied upon Gift's account in naming the *Kineo* are in error. The vessel the lieutenant mistook for the *Kineo* was, in fact, the *Pinola*. Back on April 17, the Unadilla-class gunboats of the West Gulf Coast Blockading Squadron were all required to paint identifying numbers, six feet long, port and starboard near the tops of their smokestacks. The number assigned to *Kineo* was "3," while that assigned to *Pinola* was "6."

There is no written history concerning *Pinola*'s activities this day. Several contemporary accounts mention the battle between the *Arkansas* and *Gunboat No. 6*. The *Pinola*, under her commander, Lt. Pierce Crosby (1824–1899), had initially gained fame for her participation of the river chain below New Orleans in April and it was she who fought the Rebel armorclad this day.

"Bang!" The Southern ram next fired upon the ordnance boat *Great Western* across the stream, while other broadside cannon were loosed against the remaining rams, "who are leaving in every direction." After each cannon discharged, the shutter over its gun port was clanged closed to ward off damage from the enemy bolts and bullets coming her way.

Below Vicksburg, sailors aboard the *Brooklyn* and the other Federal vessels had been hearing reports for about an hour "of distant guns up the river, nearer and nearer." By 7:00 A.M., these reports of heavy guns had grown rapid and orders were now passed to get up steam immediately and prepare for battle.[3]

The *Arkansas* now headed for Farragut's largest warships, the *Richmond* and his flagship, the *Hartford*. "We were the first she had to pass," Cmdr. John Alden, captain of the *Richmond*, later wrote in his ship's journal. The 11-inch gun on the *Pinola* had opened the ball, as they said in those days. Now the *Arkansas* took the floor, so to speak, with any number of partners awaiting her partnership in combat. As she approached to within about 500 yards of the lead enemy ships, the Southern ram became the target for over 100 fleet Union cannon. Within minutes, hundreds of shells and bolts started pounding off her bow and casemate, already dented by the shot of the *Tyler* and *Carondelet*. Huge columns of water cascaded into the sky from near misses while broken shell fragments and spent rifle bullets zinged off her sides, making the iron covering creak, shake, and rattle.

Before she could close the final two ship's lengths to the *Richmond*, the *Arkansas* was subjected to an attack by Ellet's rams. Several had gotten up steam and at least two, including the 169-man *Lancaster*, now sought a collision with the barely moving Confederate armorclad.

While medical personnel attended to the *Arkansas*' casualties, Lt. Brown descended to the gundeck to converse with the Missouri volunteers. Suddenly, an unknown unit of the U.S. Ram Fleet attempted to come at the Rebel warship from her stern. This "feeble attack," the captain observed with pleasure while returning topside, was blown off by Lt. Read's stern rifles.

Almost simultaneously, the *Lancaster*, mistaken by some for the unfinished *Eastport*, steamed across the *Richmond*'s stern and, gathering speed, shot to within 100 yards of the lumbering Dixie warship. On the gun deck of the *Arkansas*, now only a few feet away, gunners at the forward Columbiads could hear the pilot ask Lt. Brown for instructions. "Go through him, Brady," the captain replied, and the young Missourian steadied the craft into the maneuver. Meanwhile, a Southern broadside pounded into her fragile superstructure, shattering it. The collision was saved by Lt. Gift, who wanted to get rid of a shell with a 5-second fuse that was already loaded in his 8-inch gun "before we got to the ironclads." With a yank of the lanyard, the shot was sent on its way. Gift's 64-pdr. projectile smashed through the *Lancaster*'s bulwarks, passed through eight feet of coal, and exploded, cutting off three feet of her mud-drum. The burst and subsequent steam release was catastrophic.

Hot steam and water from the mud-drum filled the Federal ram's barricaded engine room. Gift claims that many of the crew stationed there and a company of sharpshooters seeking protection were instantly killed. Others "came pouring up the scuttles, tearing off their shirts and leaping overboard as soon as they reached the air." The lieutenant's assistant, Master's Mate John Wilson, added that many of those "perished in full sight of the fleet." This was witnessed from the *Richmond* by her captain, Cmdr. John Alden, and many of his crew. "The sight was terrible," Alden recorded in his journal, "as she [was] just in front of us." Years later, one of the *Lancaster* crewmen, Sylvester Doss, recalled how he was "scolded [*sic*] very Bad, my Right sholder [*sic*] broken left Ribbs Broken and my teeth Blowen [*sic*] out." He added that "lots of our crews dide [*sic*] that night by being scolded."

The *Jackson Mississippian* excitedly told its readers that the charging ram "blew up with a tremendous crash! It is thought that not a soul on board the *Eastport* escaped." Third Engineer Fulton, aboard the *Hartford*, probably like other observers aboard vessels not adjacent, couldn't ascertain the origin of the fatal hit on the *Lancaster*. "It is not certain whether this shot came from one of our guns, or from the *Arkansas*," he reported, "as the vessels were much crowded, and in no position for such an encounter."

The log of Ellet's vessel, reproduced in the ORN *Official Records*, notes that two Caucasian engineers were killed outright. At least four other scalded men died later; a number of personnel, including Chief Engineer John Wybrant, were badly scalded or otherwise wounded. So were many that jumped overboard. Of 43 African Americans aboard, most working in the machinery spaces, only six survived. Many of those who fled into the river "never came to the surface again."

A circumstance not understood by all at the time was that the Ellet ram was also a victim of friendly fire, hit numerous times by heavy cannonballs and grapeshot "from our own fleet." At least three cannonballs intended for the *Arkansas* overshot their mark and smashed into the port side of the *Lancaster*. Others smashed her pilothouse, wounding the pilot. The Federal ram was liberally sprayed with stands of grapeshot from both sides.

The *Arkansas* slipped by the motionless *Lancaster*. Unable to stop and render help, Lt. Brown later remembered how his vessel "passed through the brave fellows struggling in the water under a shower of missiles intended for us." Cmdr. Alden saw at least 10 or 12 men in the water, "some swimming and some holding on to the rudder." Although the Federal ram was "shot all to pieces," it remained afloat. As the Rebel warship passed, "a boat was lowered from the *Lancaster* to pick up her drowning men." Sometime later, the *Queen of the West* caught the wreck drifting astern of the *Richmond* and towed her back upstream to her original moorings.[4]

Following her encounter with the *Lancaster*, the *Arkansas* passed the *Richmond*, a vessel nearly as large as the flagship *Hartford*. During her initial approach, the big sloop-of-war held back for fear of hitting the correspondents' headquarter transport, *J.H. Dickey*, just across. But as the ram came close, Alden's ship delivered a tremendous broadside, "without any seeming effect, except one shot struck her on the bow." Aboard the *Hartford*, young Fulton watched the terrible broadside pour toward the *Arkansas*. For a moment, the ram "was lost in the smoke, and eager eyes watched for the smoke to lift in order to get a shot at her."

Lt. Cmdr. Phelps, aboard the *Benton*, wrote that the *Richmond*'s blast "made the iron fly splendidly, whole bars going up 20 feet in the air. The 9-inch shot," he cheered, "riddled the Rebel.... One of her 9-inch Dahlgren shot ploughed through the starboard side of the casemate just aboard the forward cannon, smashing in the bulkhead." Externally, "the blow knocked a great piece out of it"; internally, shanks of iron and wood flew in every direction. One loosened the iron ram while another demolished a hawse pipe. "She never returned the fire at us, until she got astern," wrote Capt. Alden, "when she fired her two stern guns, without doing any damage."

The *J.H. Dickey*, lying near the Louisiana shore, did not escape this exchange. The *New York Times* reported that a cannonball, from either the *Arkansas* or the *Richmond*, sailed through her ladies' cabin and took the top off a rocking chair. Callender of the *Cincinnati* later delighted in recounting what he knew really happened to the contingent of newspapermen, known as the Bohemian Brigade, assigned to that steamer, who earlier had sought safety in a nearby barge:

Federal Ram *Lancaster*. *As the* Arkansas *headed toward the Union fleet on the morning of July 15, this Ellet ram steamed to within 100 yards of her. Lt. Isaac Newton Brown initially wished to ram the Northern craft, but a shell from one of his forward Columbiads hit her mud drum first, with catastrophic effect. Nearly 50 Union men died and the vessel was put out of action. Later, after she was repaired, the* Lancaster *would pass Vicksburg's batteries (Harper's Weekly, April 18, 1863).*

> Down came the *Arkansas* keeping her port battery hot as she passed one after another of the Union Fleet. Paying no attention to the fleet of steamboats on her starboard side, until she came abreast of this hay barge, laden as it was with the brains of a dozen of the leading newspapers of the North evidently figuring it out as an ordnance boat, loaded with ammunition the *Arkansas* let fly her entire starboard broadside at it. Such a crashing of timbers was never heard this side of Pandemonium. The barge doubled up in the middle. The air was full of pine plank and with a yell that would have done credit to Comanche Indians, they jumped through the wreck of falling timbers; onto and up the bank of the river, and struck out for the interior of the State at a rate that no cyclometer that ever has been invented could record.

Once by the *Richmond*, the bow guns astern of her, noted Fulton, "commenced firing on her, and she turned downstream." For her part, the *Arkansas* took the punishment and, rocking to port and starboard, fired her own guns in response. As she staggered forward, her captain remained topside, virtually in plain sight, reportedly firing his side arm at enemy sailors whenever the ram veered close to an opponent.

Thus it was that the *Arkansas* fought her way, as Lt. Brown put it, "within pistol shot" and endured an intense bombardment by the vessels of the stationary Union fleet. Sheets of flame escaped the muzzles of the numerous Northern and Confederate pieces, causing a huge cloud of smoke to blanket the scene. "The smoke from the heavy guns in the still air" soon, Brown confirmed, "began to settle on the water." It was like a cloud bank at sea or a blizzard; for a long time, the only reliable points of aim were the orange tongues of fire from

USS Richmond. *The second largest Federal ship anchored north of Vicksburg, the 2,700-ton Richmond was launched at Norfolk, Virginia, in January 1860 and commissioned 10 months later. With a complement of 260, the sloop-of-war was 225 feet long, with a beam of 42.6 feet and a 17.5-foot draft. Powered by one screw (two engines) and a full suit of sails, her main armament comprised twenty 9-inch. Dahlgren SBs, one 80-pdr. Dahlgren rifle, and one 30-pdr. Dahlgren rifle. As the ram came close, the big ship delivered a tremendous broadside "without any seeming effect, except one shot struck her on the bow." Lt. Cmdr. S. Ledyard Phelps, aboard the* Benton, *wrote that the* Richmond*'s blast "made the iron fly splendidly, whole bars going up 20 feet in the air." The 9-inch shot," he cheered, "riddled the Rebel.... One of her 9-inch Dahlgren shot ploughed through the starboard side of the casemate just aboard the forward cannon, smashing in the bulkhead." Externally, "the blow knocked a great piece out of it"; internally, shanks of iron and wood flew in every direction. One loosened the iron ram while another demolished a hawse pipe. "She never returned the fire at us, until she got astern," wrote her captain, "when she fired her two stern guns, without doing any damage." She is shown here off Baton Rouge a year later (Miller, ed.,* Photographic History of the Civil War*).*

opposition cannon. For however long it lasted, this battle would be enveloped to a point where hardly any living soul could see another.

Although infinitely more confused and deafening aboard the ships, the noise of the *Arkansas*' passage could also be heard on land for miles around. Ever more onlookers crowded the riverbanks of Mississippi and Louisiana to catch glimpses of the epic fight. Gun flashes, reminiscent of lightning from a summer thunderhead, provided visual points of emphasis and reminded many of rolling thunder. Whenever the *Arkansas* appeared through the smoke, the onlookers cheered as if at a "horse race."

Watching from the gun emplacements north of Vicksburg, Lt. Lot D. Young of the 4th Kentucky later gave a sense of the event. It seemed, he wrote, "as if the infernal regions had suffered an eruption, the earth rocked and trembled, the heavens seemed pierced and rent with the roar and thunder of cannon of all sizes." Perhaps the best observation site was Vicksburg's Warren County Courthouse, almost in the center of town. There Confederate

Maj. Gens. Stephen D. Lee, John C. Breckenridge, and Earl Van Dorn watched the developing battle from the cupola. As long as the din continued, everyone knew their lone armored champion survived.

As the hail of Federal response from the various vessels intensified, it appeared to Capt. Brown as though a circle of fire was closing in around his command. Enemies surrounded the *Arkansas* on all sides; all any of her gunners had to do was load and yank the lanyard. Bow, broadside, or stern, the cannon seemed sure of targets. The concussion of heavy missiles striking the ram's sides was continuous, while shrapnel splat-

"**Within Pistol Shot.**" *Once by the* Richmond, *the bow guns astern of her "commenced firing on her, and she turned downstream." For her part, the* Arkansas *took the punishment and, rocking to port and starboard, fired her own guns in response. As she staggered forward, her captain remained topside, virtually in plain sight, reportedly firing his side arm at enemy sailors whenever the ram veered near an opponent. Thus it was that the* Arkansas *fought her way, as Lt. Brown put it, "within pistol shot" and endured an intense bombardment by the vessels of the stationary Union fleet. Sheets of flame escaped the muzzles of the numerous Northern and Confederate pieces, causing a huge cloud of smoke to blanket the scene (*Battles and Leaders, *vol. 3).*

tered off the casemate deck "12 pounds at a time." Shells split into thousands of fragments, while solid shot just seemed to flatten and slide off. "A target for a hundred guns," wrote Adelaide Stuart Dimitry in 1911, "the heavy shot of the enemy pounded her sides like sledge hammers."

At times, the noise within the casemate was so deafening that commands had to be given by prearranged hand signals. "Those who saw the fight say," reported the Brooklyn correspondent, "that a flash of fire denoted the spot where every ball struck, so terrible was the concussion and so strong the resistance." The ram continued to give perhaps better than she received. "Bang! Bang!" went two more guns at the *Great Western*, while, moving down, "she put two balls into the *Champion*," a transport. All this time she continued to punish Farragut's fleet, as her ram bit into the oncoming current and her pumps pushed out unwelcome water.

Lt. Brown now temporarily abandoned his exposed position topside to make an inspection of the gundeck; he particularly wanted to see how the Missouri volunteers were handling their pieces. He, with Stevens, worked to reassure the men that they were going to make it out of this inferno, even though, at that time, both probably had what Brown described as "the most lively realization of having steamed into a real volcano."[5]

When the *Arkansas* approached to within 150 yards of the *Hartford*, her bow Columbiad sang out in a puff of white smoke, then Lt. A.D. Wharton gave her a full salute from the starboard battery. Engineer Fulton aboard the Federal reported that there were "two rifle shots, which passed harmlessly over our heads." The bolts sliced a few halyards and damaged some rigging, but otherwise did no damage. There was a strange silence aboard the flagship:

> Standing on the deck of that boat, with feelings that could be better imagined than described, stood the lion-hearted Farragut, his face rigid with excitement. Beneath him lay the open mouths of thirteen 64's; behind these guns stood the trained crews that had dealt out death and destruction with them at New Orleans. Thirteen captains of those guns stood with lock strings in hand, with arms raised, And waited but for a word. The pale face of the Admiral never changed. The word that every man, from the Executive Officer to the Messenger boy, was crazy to hear, never came.

Like the *Richmond*, the flagship also held back her initial response because "the same broadside which would have hailed on the *Arkansas* would have annihilated the splendid hospital boat *Red Rover*, with her cargo of human freight."

As the ram passed, her earlier complement was finally repaid with 9-inch projectiles from the port battery of the giant sloop, "with what effect could not be seen," reported her captain, Cmdr. Richard Wainwright," as "we were loaded with 5-second shell." In fact, Lt. Phelps, who was watching from the *Benton*, observed that the sloop's rounds "overshot her." The Confederate was beyond before another broadside could be fired. The flagship's one roar was far more effective than her commander initially imagined. Although most of her bolts bounced off the side of the Rebel armorclad, one round penetrated the iron, oak, and cotton toward the rear of the starboard casemate side. Shell fragments killed four men on the 32-pdr. and concussed the gun captain so badly that he was permanently invalided.

While the scrappy vessel passed Wainwright's command, a seaman aboard the *Tyler*, still being followed by the Rebel, suffered that boat's final casualty when a cannonball from the *Arkansas* took his head off. With the *Arkansas'* gun crews yet engaged on all sides, the timberclad was able to scurry behind the ironclad *Essex* and round to under her stern. Amazed at his escape, the officer of the deck aboard the *Tyler* took time to note that their enemy was "receiving the fire of most of the vessels of our flotilla." When the *Arkansas* came by, she would also receive a final dosage from the *Tyler*.

Lying not far from the starboard beam of the *Hartford*, the gunboat and ram *General Bragg*,[6] having raised steam when the armorclad first appeared, now had a chance to strike a blow — but did not take it. The former Confederate ram captured at the Battle of Memphis was newly arrived from above following her rebuilding. Her commander, Lt. Joshua Bishop, one of the officers first assigned to the Western Flotilla in 1861, was ready to slip his anchor cable and had beat his men to quarters. Fearful that his action would "foul the fire of the *Hartford* and *Richmond*," Bishop waited for orders to attack. When they did not arrive, he stayed put. The *Bragg*'s failure to sortie was condemned in naval circles ever after. Admiral Porter, in his *Naval History of the Civil War*, summed up the sentiment: "Had she done this [attacked] she would doubtless have disabled the *Arkansas* by ramming her as the latter vessel was already damaged in her motive power." "Admiral Farragut said next day," Bishop later confided to his diary, "I had lost my promotion thereby." Despite a rather rigid management system, operational initiative — as opposed to inaction — in the face of an enemy had been a U.S. Navy maxim since the days of John Paul Jones.

Lt. Reigart B. Lowry, captain of the Federal gunboat *Sciota*, had heard heavy firing from the direction of the Yazoo River as early as 6:10 A.M. Looking upstream a while later through his telescope, his wonder as to the cause "manifested itself in the appearance of the gunboat Tyler running before and closely pursued by an ironclad rebel ram." Lowry would

Eight: Morning (Part II), July 15, 1862: Running the Gauntlet

Courthouse Vantage Point. *Perhaps the best Southern observation site was Vicksburg's Warren County Courthouse, almost in the center of town. There the Confederates Maj. Gens. Stephen D. Lee, John C. Breckenridge, and Earl Van Dorn watched the developing battle between the* Arkansas *and the Union fleets from the cupola. As long as the din continued, everyone knew their lone armored champion survived (Library of Congress).*

provide the most detailed account of his vessel's participation in the *Arkansas*' fleet-passing breakout of any Northern commander.

The *Sciota* was anchored fourth in line below the Ellet ram anchorage, with her engines under repair and no steam. As the volume and intensity of the bombardment upriver increased, Lt. Lowry ordered his fires lit and steam to be raised as soon as possible. Studying the approach of the *Arkansas*, he saw a construction resemblance between her and the two ironclads Farragut's fleet had faced at New Orleans, the *Louisiana* and *Mississippi*. They were, of course, immobile. The one coming at him "seemed by her movements to trust entirely to her invulnerability for a safe run to the cover of the Vicksburg batteries."

Like the *Pinola*, the principal armament of the *Sciota* was a big 11-inch Dahlgren. As the *Arkansas* came abreast, the monster gun spit a 10-second round into her side, "but the shell glanced off almost perpendicularly into the air and exploded." Lt. Lowry, unable to rapidly reload his great gun, ordered his men to "a brisk fire" against her port broadside gun ports. This fuselage of small arms fire, the commander reasoned, prevented the ram from returning fire "'till after she passed us."

Propelled by the current and her own feeble engines, it took the Rebel warship four to six minutes to pass out of the little gunboat's line of fire. During this time, the *Arkansas* continued to receive Federal largess from every side. Master's Mate John Wilson recalled a shell exploding in front of his gun port, "killing my sponger and knocking down the other men." Watching from the quarterdeck of the *Sciota*, Lt. Lowry "observed one man, in the act of sponging, tumble out of the port, sponge and all, evidently shot by a rifle ball."

At the rear of the casemate, Lt. Read remembered that the armorclad's steam "was now so low we could maneuver with difficulty." On top of this, the boilers had become a great problem, intensifying the fire room heating problem first experienced in Old River. In their haste to fit the boilers and otherwise ready her machinery, the workers had forgotten to line the fire front of the boilers with nonconducting materials. This defect was not noticed at the time and now, whenever a heavy coal fire was put in, "the whole mass of iron about the boilers became red hot and nearly roasted the firemen."

During the breakout, the situation became so bad that the original firemen were overcome and had to be relieved. Lt. Grimball was detailed, as Lt. Stevens had been earlier, to find and rotate replacements. Still, the *Arkansas* "went, fighting our way right and left." As cannonball after cannonball fell off her sides into the water, a newspaper reporter observed: "Steadily but surely she keeps on the way, firing one broadside at the transports and the other at some vessel on the other side. She has nearly run the gauntlet."[7]

For some time now, Lt. Brown had been returned to his broken conning tower, from which he continued to lead his vessel's charge toward Vicksburg. When not peering through

USS *General Bragg*. *The 1,043-ton ex–Confederate side-wheel cottonclad* General Bragg *was captured by Federal forces during the June Battle off Memphis and reconfigured slightly for Union service. The vessel was 208 feet long, with a beam of 32.8 feet and a 12-foot draft. Armament comprised one each 30-pdr. Parrott rifle and 32-pdr. smoothbore, plus a 23-pdr. rifled howitzer. When the* Arkansas *made her run, the gunboat/ram was one of the few Northern vessels with steam up. Her commander, Lt. Joshua Bishop, one of the officers first assigned to the Western Flotilla in 1861, was ready to slip his anchor cable and had beat his men to quarters. Fearful that his action would "foul the fire of the* Hartford *and* Richmond," *Bishop waited for orders to attack. When they did not arrive, he stayed put. The* Bragg's *failure to sortie was condemned in naval circles ever after (Navy History and Heritage Command).*

his telescope, the *Arkansas* captain was shouting commands down the speaking tube or firing his pistol at Union sailors on ships passed. He was entirely exposed not only to Federal cannon but also to hundreds of sharpshooters, any one of whom would have been pleased to have hit him.

Lt. Gift called his superior a hero and said his "man of steel never flinched." Twice he was knocked off his platform by exploding shells, "stunned, with his marine glass broken in his hand, and he received a wound on his temple." Brushing himself off on both occasions, he returned to his post and duty, even as minie balls pattered "all around and about him."

Midshipman Clarence Tyler, Brown's aide and messenger, was not as lucky. He was shot in the head at his post near the captain and badly wounded. Carried below for medical attention, it would be weeks before he returned to duty and, following the demise of the *Arkansas*, he played no further role in the war. Also about this time, a collective gasp escaped the multitude watching from shore. In "the midst of this terrific fire," reported one Southern artilleryman, "we saw the Confederate flag flying over her mast go down."

Midshipman Dabney M. Scales, commanding the forward starboard Dahlgren, heard that the armorclad's battle flag had been shot away. With a nod to Lt. John Grimball at the starboard side bow Columbiad, he scrambled up the forward access ladder to the top deck. Scampering past the pilothouse and chimney, which were "being swept by a hurricane of shot and shell," Scales "deliberately bent on the colors again, knotted the halyards, and hoisted them up." Having displayed, in the words of one lady, "a courage equal to that of the wild, intrepid Beggars of the Sea," it is likely he reentered the casemate aft.

Later, when the flag was knocked down again, Scales started to repeat his action. This time he was restrained by direct order of Lt. Brown. The flag episode was initially understood ashore to have been the work of Lt. Brown himself, but, "we afterwards learned," remembered Sgt. Flatau, that it was Scales that "hoisted the flag, after taking it from Captain Brown's hands." The battle flag of the *Arkansas*, whether the one raised by Scales that was lost (and possibly picked up by a Union craft) or a later one, would become the subject of some controversy in future years.

Meanwhile, below-decks on the Rebel ram, officers and men struggled to keep their cannon supplied with ammunition and firing. Much of the calm distribution of shot and shell to the forward guns was due to the cool actions of a quartermaster's mate named Eaton, who was posted at the head of the ladder leading to the berth deck and provided "a kind of superintendence over the boys who came for powder." Although history does not record his Christian name or allow us biographical detail, Lt. Gift paid him the highest tribute as an example of the determination of the enlisted men:

> Eaton was a character. He had thick, rough, red hair, an immense muscular frame, and a will and courage rarely encountered. Nothing daunted him, and the hotter the fight, the fiercer grew Eaton. From his one eye, he glared furiously on all who seemed inclined to shirk, and his voice grew louder and more distinct as the shot rattled and crashed upon our mail. At one instant you would hear him pass the word down the hatch: "Nine-inch shell, five-second fuse." "Here you are, my lad, with your rifle shell; take it and go back, quick." "What's the matter that you can't get that gun out?" and like a cat, he would spring from his place, and throw his weight on the side tackle, and the gun was sure to go out. "What are you doing here, wounded? Where are you hurt? Go back to your gun, or I'll murder you on the spot. Here's your nine-inch shell." "Mind, shipmate (to a wounded man), the ladder is bloody, don't slip, let me help you."

The next vessel in line was the 1,488-ton second-class sloop-of-war *Iroquois*, the third largest Northern warship present and the one upon which our letter writer, Captain's Clerk

Edward S. Bacon, served. As the *Arkansas* passed her, one of the Federal's heavy shot struck her side, abreast the port side bow Columbiad. The shock knocked down one of its crew, who was taking a cannonball from the shot rack. Rubbing his bruised hip, the sailor grinned at Lt. Gift, shouting they were all very lucky because their enemy could "hardly strike twice in a place."

Hardly had the man uttered his optimism than a shell did, in fact, enter the breach just made and bore into the cotton bale lining on the inside of the bulwark. When securely snuggled, it exploded with tremendous force in a huge cloud of smoke. Fires caught the woodwork, but, fortunately, Lt. Stevens, "ever cool and thoughtful," was unhurt. He ran to the engine room hatch, grabbed the firehose kept there, and "dragged it to the aperture." With the help of an improvised firefighting crew, the blaze was quickly extinguished without the need to sound a general alarm. The effect of this one round was murderous. Lt. Gift, his hair and beard singed and his cap missing, was amazed to find himself alive when all around him, sixteen men, were killed or wounded. Only one other man, a quartermaster's mate named Curtis, survived.

Over on the *Iroquois*, Clerk Bacon, in a message sent home after the fight, remembered that their shot "ricocheted and then struck right amidships, between wind and water." Although the range was not believed to be quite right, the officers, "standing on the poop [deck] of the Flag [ship]," were impressed. They all "cheered right heartily, as did we." Gift, Curtis, and one of the Missouri volunteer captains, were able to get one more 64-pdr. shot down the muzzle of the *Arkansas* portside Columbiad. Before it could be fired, another heavy Federal projectile, this one an 11-inch round from either the *Wissahickon* or *Winona* next in line, entered the casemate just above the port broadside Dahlgren. It loosed a blanket of wood and iron splinters that hit every sailor in the gun crew, killing two men and a powder boy and wounding three others. This time, Lt. Gift's left arm was broken. Master's Mate Wilson was knocked senseless, suffering head and nose wounds. Quartermaster Curtis was again unhurt.

This Northern shot was not finished with the *Arkansas*' forward batteries. The ball "passed across the deck, through the smoke-stack, and killed eight and wounded seven men at Scales' gun," which was being run out at the time. It finally smashed into the other bulkhead, broke in half, and fell to the deck. Once more, Lts. Brown and Stevens sought to contain damages and reassure the men on the gun deck, hurt or not.

The load and shoot routine continued amidst the carnage as men came forward to carry away the wounded and dead, the latter reverently covered with canvas. Others arrived to sweep away the blast fragments, wood, steel, iron, slivers and chunks. Powder boys, sometimes slipping on the blood-soaked decks, ran ammunition and powder bags to the divisions, while gunners shifted between pieces as required. "Blood and brains bespattered everything," remembered Master's Mate Wilson, "whilst arms, legs, and several headless trunks were strewn about." Below, Dr. Washington and his helpers did what they could for the injured.

Steaming past the *Oneida* and approaching the Western Flotilla anchorage, Pilot Gilmore became disoriented, losing his bearings in the blinding smoke of the big guns. Indeed, the black cloud was so thick that it hugged the surface of the river, making it difficult for anyone, Union or Confederate, to see. Fearful that he was steering the armorclad off course, Gilmore rang the ship's bell, causing the *Arkansas* to pause in midstream. As the propellers slowed to their lowest turn rate, the guide ran down the pilothouse ladder to the front of the gun deck. There Lt. Wharton allowed him to take a look out of his gun port while the Columbiad was withdrawn for reloading and so regain his bearings. Onward "through the smoke, the din of shot and the shriek of shell," she continued, firing in every direction. "It was," wrote Ms. Dimitry, "as though the bold heart of the Confederacy beat under her iron ribs!"

Looking upriver at the approaching armorclad, Lt. Phelps, aboard the *Benton*, noted that "some of the smaller vessels with heavy guns gave her very damaging shot. The rail road iron flew from her sides and great holes were made." In the old navy, Phelps had been an even closer friend of Lt. Brown than of Capt. Walke. Flag Officer Davis, standing near Phelps, was also impressed, watching the *Arkansas* defy "danger or interruption." His opinion of Brown's action was very unpolitic. "It was certainly a very exciting and pleasing sight," he wrote, "so far as the gallantry of the thing was concerned."

In a July 19 letter to Comptroller Whittlesey, Lt. Phelps echoed Davis' admiration. "[T]he plucky craft still kept on," he admitted, "never stopping to make fight, having the one object in view to run our fire." Even Flag Officer Farragut, whose flagship was anchored abeam of the *Benton*, though enraged over the successful breakout, would admit to navy secretary Gideon Welles that "she took the broadside of the whole fleet. It was a bold thing." Italian naval historian Raimondo Luraghi later had high praise for the physical success of the *Arkansas*. "Most enemy shot and shell had failed to pierce the casemate," he wrote in 1996, "which, in the main, had resisted well. Those that did, however, caused significant damage, dismounting guns, cracking or smashing gun carriages, and sending splinters flying."

As a result of the few structural penetrations, the interior of the *Arkansas* was now the slaughterhouse the men had earlier feared and Flag Officer William F. Lynch had proclaimed. As the dead were covered and placed out of the way, an increasing number of the wounded or injured required treatment. These were taken below to the sickbay or, if ambulatory, they moved themselves out of the way, with the slightly wounded remaining at their posts.

The heat was intense, upwards of 120 to 130 degrees, while smoke from the cannon and machinery had everyone choking and crying. Soiled clothing was not uncommon. Continuous relief parties spelled the exhausted engine room crew; no one could remain in the black spaces long before he needed to escape back up to the gundeck.

The armorclad's chimney was so perforated that it was nearly impossible to keep up sufficient steam to turn the screws; the Mississippi's current was almost a greater propulsion aid than the boat's own power plant. Admiral Mahan later wrote that "her speed was thereby reduced to one knot, powerless to ram and scarcely sufficient to steer." By now, all of the lifeboats were holed and the wreckage of their frames were dragging along behind.

"It was a little hot this morning all around," remarked Lt. Brown. Nevertheless, his people rallied to their duty. Every officer and man gave without hesitation. "Each one, acting under the eye of Stevens," the commander later beamed, "seemed to think that the result depended on himself." So it was that the Southern armorclad, her cast-iron ram broken and the armor on her sides dented or ominously rattling in many places, slowly continued ahead. Her iron-willed captain and crew were determined to survive the vicious tomahawking of Union cannon shot and rifle fire. Once past the *Wissahickon* and *Winona*, Lt. Brown, sought "a cooler atmosphere" for himself and so returned to his perch atop the casemate.[8]

Looking ahead, Lt. Brown saw that his boat still had to get past the river ironclads of Flag Officer Davis, lying closer to the Mississippi shore. If she made it, the remaining channel to Vicksburg was open. The challenge would prove less daunting than one might think, given that the Northern leader commanded the only ironclad vessels faced during the Mississippi River phase of the breakout.

The *Cincinnati*, *Louisville*, and *Essex* were anchored without steam up. Assigned picket duty, the former lay approximately a half mile lower than the others. "She had barely steam enough raised to turn her wheel over," remembered one of her mates, Eliot Callender. The *Louisville* was repairing from a blacksmith boat moored alongside. The *Essex*, having discovered a burnt-out boiler the night before, was having a new one installed and could not have fired up quickly even if desired. She did manage to fire seven rounds at the *Arkansas*, reportedly hitting her thrice. "One of my shot penetrated her iron covering," Cmdr. Porter later claimed. The former Confederate ram *Sumter*, captured by Flag Officer Davis during the Battle of Memphis, was also under repair, replacing a worn-out water pipe with a new one. Consequently, she, too, was unable to interfere with the Confederate escape. Only the *Benton*, thanks to Lt. Phelps' earlier attention, was able to slip her cable and get underway in time to challenge the embattled Confederate. The refugee *Tyler*, hiding behind the *Essex*, did poke out to loose a broadside as her late antagonist passed by. The timberclad's paymaster, Coleman, paid high tribute to the *Arkansas*, frankly stating that there was "no pluckier exploit in the war" as the *Arkansas* passing through the fleet "without material injury."

U.S. Navy Secretary Gideon Welles (1802–1878). *When embarrassed cabinet official Welles heard and digested the full story of the Rebel armorclad's achievement, he wrote to both Farragut and Davis on July 25 stating the Department's "regret" that the* Arkansas *had slipped through the fleet "owing to the unprepared condition of the naval vessels." That enemy vessel, he ordered, "must be destroyed at all hazards" (U.S. Army Military History Institute).*

From the roof of his casemate, Lt. Brown, without aid of a glass, was able to see "close ahead and across our way, a large iron-clad displaying the square flag of an admiral." She was barely moving and her beam was exposed, offering an easy ramming target, even for a vessel like his, powered as much by the current as by her own machinery. Pilot Brady was ordered to strike the enemy craft amidships. Some believed from afar that the *Benton* was, in fact, the *Cincinnati*, sunk by Confederate rams at Fort Pillow two months earlier, repaired and now present. All eyes turned toward the Federal ironclad as "on comes the *Arkansas*, seemingly like Antes of old, picking up new strength at every step."

As the *Arkansas* descended past Farragut's vessels, the *Benton*'s steam pressure increased gradually — first to 60 pounds, then to 100, and finally to 120. Emitting huge clouds of black, sooty smoke from her twin chimneys, she slipped her cable and inched ahead, barely moving. Davis' flagboat might be able to loose a broadside; she certainly would not be meeting the ram bows-on. Just when it looked like the Rebel might hit her, the *Benton* avoided a collision "by steaming ahead." As she dodged, the *Arkansas* passed

Eight: Morning (Part II), July 15, 1862: Running the Gauntlet 197

under her stern, almost touching. As she did so, Brown heeled slightly to give her his entire starboard broadside.

The ram captain rather imagined that this raking fire "went through him from rudder to prow." The *New York Times* reported that a shot was received by the *Benton* "near the edge of the after part of the larboard side." William E. Webb of the *St. Louis Daily Missouri Republican* was more specific. The Western Flotilla flagboat, he wrote, "got two shots through her port hind-quarter, two in the stern, and two swept the deck.... Several indentations were made in her thickest iron, but the metal was proof to the distance of a mile."

Lt. Phelps later admitted that one of Brown's rifled bolts cut away a stanchion and left a trace on the back of his sack uniform coat. "It was an ugly, whizzing 60-lb. fellow," he remembered. "So much for the favors of my friend Brown," the flag captain lamented. The *New York Tribune* commented further: "A round shot passed so near Capt. Phelps as to take the nap from his coat, without doing him any injury." The marveling scribe opined for his

USS Benton. *The most powerful Federal ironclad on the Western waters in summer 1862, the 633-ton* Benton *was converted by Eads from one of his catamaran snagboats at Carondelet, Missouri, at the same time he was constructing the Pook turtles. Two engines drove a protected stern wheel; however, like the Pooks, the vessel was very slow. With a length of 202 feet, the* Benton *was 72 feet wide and had a 9-foot draft. Her casemate, unlike the* Arkansas *but like the Pooks, had a sloping side; both it and the pilothouse were covered with 2.5 inches of armor. With a complement of 176 crewmen, her armament comprised two 9-inch Dahlgren SB, seven 42-pdr. ex–Army rifles, and seven 32-pdrs. Now she was the only major obstacle still faced by the* Arkansas. *Fortunately for her, she was able to generate sufficient power at the last minute to avoid Lt. Brown's effort to ram her and was powerful enough to largely deflect a parting* Arkansas *broadside (U.S. Army Military History Institute).*

readers: "This is as narrow an escape from propulsion from this planet as usually occurs, and quite as near as any one not enamored of death would desire." More than a week later, in a letter home, Flag Officer Davis told of "the shot that came through us on the 15th." After easily crashing through the *Benton*'s side and decapitating a crewman, it "destroyed the cabin kitchen, Captain Phelps' room, and my own room, finally lodging in the very center of my bed." A damage control party found the shot and turned it over to the squadron commander, who kept it, and hoped "to bring it home with [him] one of these days." The *Benton* did not return the armorclad's greeting, even after she slid past headed downstream. The shots into her from the *Arkansas* were among the last fired by Brown's command during the morning of her breakout.

There remained only the *Cincinnati*, on picket duty, to thwart the passage. Her involvement with the Rebel ram was relived in a 1900 paper by Mate Callender, read before a group of USN veterans in Chicago:

> The *Arkansas*, though badly disfigured, was still in the ring, and having passed all the other boats, made for the lone *Cincinnati*, with no very amiable intentions. The *Cincinnati* gave her bow battery of three nine-inch Dahlgrens; every shot struck her antagonist square on her bow casemates, and all three of these immense solid shot flew up in the air, plainly visible to the naked eye, until they were hardly larger than marbles. The *Arkansas* appeared to have but one of her forward guns in working order, but with that she struck the *Cincinnati* twice, and then started for her with her great steel beak. The *Cincinnati* slipped her anchor, and having so little steam on she drifted quartering down the river toward the Mississippi shore. A long sand bar extended out into the river from this shore. On came the *Arkansas*, with every pound of steam her disabled engines could handle, when within one hundred feet of the *Cincinnati* she ran aground, drawing thirteen feet, while our boat drew only six. Now was the *Cincinnati*'s chance. Oh, for steam to handle that boat! But it was not there. She got in her bow and starboard batteries of nine-inch Dahlgrens and smooth 64's, but not one shot appeared to hurt her antagonist, which was doing its best to get off the bar. Could the *Cincinnati* have run up alongside and boarded, the ram might have changed her colors. But it was not to be. Slowly the ram drew off the bar and swung down stream and was soon around the bend.

Neither Union nor Confederate sources, official or newspaper, refer in detail to the *Cincinnati*'s efforts to block the *Arkansas*. Nor do they mention the ram's grounding.

The Confederate ram had made it to the end "of what had seemed the interminable line, and also past the outer rim of the volcano." Firing level at almost point blank range, the *Arkansas*, despite her injuries, did terrible damage to the vessels of Farragut, Davis, and Ellet. Of the 97 shots fired, only 24 missed their target.

Relieved not to have been sunk, Lt. Brown called all of his subordinate officers topside to get some fresh air and also, for the first time, to take a panoramic look "at what we had just come through." Up the ladders came Lts. Grimball, Gift, Barbot, Wharton, and Read, plus the available midshipmen, including the hero Scales (Midshipman Tyler remained in sickbay), Chief Engineer City and Master's Mate Wilson. "The little group of heroes" closed around Lt. Brown, shouting words of joy and relief back and forth over the noise of the engines. All were undoubtedly shocked to see their chimney "resembled an immense nutmeg-grater, so often had it been struck." Others were cognizant that their pilot, Missourian Brady, like the mortally wounded John Hodges, had shown "the greatest courage and skill in handling this sluggish vessel under such circumstances."

As the men took visual stock and perhaps congratulated themselves, they were not yet fully in sight of Vicksburg. Several may have looked down and seen that "the sides of the ship were spotted as if it had been peppered." Some of the sources of the strange sounds of rattling iron were also noticed. All could see that their small boats "were shot away and dragging." Not knowing if her straining engines would continue to function properly, the *Arkansas* passed around De Soto Point, headed for the Vicksburg landing. As she began to emerge from the smoke, the high bluffs, increasingly more visible in the bright morning sun, were seen to be lined with spectators, who appeared like a dense moving sea of humanity.

Ashore, soldiers from Pvt. William Y. Dixon's unit, Co. G ("Hunter's Rifles"), 4th Louisiana Infantry, had waited patiently above the river "to welcome our little boat with a hearty cheer if it could be so fortunate as to get through the gauntlet of about 50 large gunboats, some carrying as many as 30 guns." All this time, an "awful and thunderous roar" was heard for two miles "up & down the river."

Recovering from her near-fatal encounter with the *Arkansas*, the *Benton* rounded to and, with the *Cincinnati* now tailing, followed the Southern warship, firing their bow guns "as rapidly as she could." Progress was slow; or, as Flag Officer Davis reported, the *Benton* chugged along "at her usual snail's pace which renders anything like pursuit ludicrous." A heavy ball from one of the Federal ironclads passed over the heads of the *Arkansas* officers assembled atop her casemate. "It was the parting salutation," remembered Lt. Brown, "and if aimed two feet lower would have been to us the most injurious of the battle."

As both the *Arkansas* and her pursuers approached the hill batteries in the upper part of the fortress city, Flag Officer Davis and Lt. Phelps considered their strategy. Both men wished to "pursue the rebel to his den," hoping for a chance to destroy him under the city's heavy guns. On the other hand, the two officers also realized that they might fail or be badly damaged by the nine batteries of opposing land cannon ahead or both. Regardless of the outcome, neither Federal ironclad had the motive power required to fight the current and return upstream. If they committed to an attack, it would be necessary for both boats to pass Vicksburg and be forever operationally confined below the town.

While Davis and Phelps considered the options, the *Benton* and *Cincinnati* rounded De Soto Point and became fully engaged with the Confederate batteries below Fort Hill. For fifteen minutes, the ironclads and the First Tennessee Heavy Artillery exchanged rounds noisily. The Volunteer State artillerymen reportedly succeeded in hitting Davis' flagboat five times. One shot penetrated the *Benton*'s shell room, but fortunately for her it did not explode. Two men were wounded.

With so few assets available to keep the Mississippi open between Cairo, Illinois, and Vicksburg, discretion dictated that any plan to pursue the *Arkansas* further be abandoned at this time. The *Benton* and *Cincinnati* gave up the chase, rounded to, and withdrew behind the point, shortly thereafter returning to their former anchorage. Flag Officer Davis had the satisfaction, at least, of knowing that his was only the second Federal vessel to move. Still, as he confided in a letter, "I thought after the morning at Memphis I had done with rams, but here this scamp has come to keep us again in a state of excitement and apprehension."

Aboard the *Cincinnati*, Master's Mate Callender was agog with admiration for Lt. Brown. As he said later, "I respectfully insist that for coolness and bravery, for desperate chances offered and taken, the records of the Civil War will show nothing equal to the raid that morning of the Confederate steamer *Arkansas* through the combined fleets of Admiral Farragut and Flag Officer Davis."

By this time, the *Arkansas* was within sight of Vicksburg and her officers had returned to their duties, telling the men in the darkness below that they had made it. With safety approaching, the vessel was no longer "buttoned up" and crewmen were able to catch glimpses out of the gun ports. For sailors below long in the dark, the light was almost blinding as it danced upon the river. The steeples of churches were seen by many and, more impressively, a large Confederate flag flying atop the courthouse cupola.

As the battered survivor sought the protection of the town batteries and approached the wharf below Jackson Street, someone ran a large pike up through the grating abaft the chimney and hoisted a Southern ensign. R. Thomas Campbell suggests that the glee of the watching throng now became thunderous. "Women cried. Men clapped and cheered. Children danced around and around with one another," he wrote years later. "Flags and old sheets, anything they could get their hands on, were being waved in the morning breeze."

The sound of the firing in the early morning exchange on the Mississippi north of town was heard by officers and men aboard that portion of the U.S. squadron that remained below. Unable to see what was transpiring above, no one knew for certain what was happening until an army officer approached the mortar schooners, tied at the right bank, and passed word that the *Arkansas* was running through the combined fleet. As a result of the news, the lower units, under harassment of Vicksburg's southern guns, withdrew downstream from their advanced positions, during which time the mortar-schooner *Sidney Jones* ran aground and was burned.

Lt. Brown now spied Farragut's lower fleet downriver from the town, "preparing to receive us or recede from us." Damaged, the Rebel armorclad was "not in condition just then to begin a third battle." Moreover, "humanity required the landing of our wounded — terribly torn by cannon-shot — and of our dead." Having returned to his forward post from topside, Lt. Gift took a moment to take stock of the carnage on the gundeck behind him. "A great heap of mangled and ghastly slain lay on the gun deck," he remembered, "with rivulets of blood running away from them." In this slaughterhouse, "brains, hair and blood were all about." Below in the sick bay, 50 or 60 wounded men "were groaning and complaining or courageously bearing their ills without a murmur."

There was great consternation aboard the Federal vessels left in the wake of the Southern armorclad. "Here was the end of the most cool and impudent attack on a fleet of 18 vessels (not to speak of Ellet's Rams, one of which was blown up) that ever could be imagined," opined Captain's Clerk Edward S. Bacon aboard the *Iroquois*— and that by "a little nondescript of only 10 guns." The *Arkansas* had survived the fiery gauntlet. It had taken a half hour to pass the combined fleets; it had been two since the *Carondelet* was spotted in Old River. It was as well that it did not take any longer. As river historian Coombe later noted, "A little longer under fire and the *Arkansas* would have been sent to the bottom of the Mississippi, probably with all hands."[9] "Much of Brown's spectacular success against the Federal Fleet was due to the fact," Coombe opines, "that his enemy was asleep on the watch, with its steam down to conserve fuel." Writing immediately after the war, Northern naval historian Charles Boynton was straightforward in his review. "Her appearance was so sudden, our officers were so conscious of having been caught unprepared, and the success of the bold maneuver was so complete that, for a time," he revealed, "the prevailing feeling was simply astonishment."

Paul Stevens has agreed with Coombe, Boynton, and others who have stated that the Confederate ram's successful passage past the Northern vessels above Vicksburg was due to the lack of steam being up in Farragut's fleet and that of Flag Officer Davis. Without the element of surprise, "in spite of *Tyler*'s 30 minute warning, *Arkansas* would have been destroyed." The great nephew of Lt. Stevens also credits two other factors as contributing

Hot Work! *Her smokestack perforated by Federal shot, the* Arkansas' *steam became "so low we could maneuver with difficulty." On top of this, the boilers had become a great problem, intensifying a fire room heating problem first experienced in Old River. In their haste to fit the boilers and otherwise ready her machinery, workers had forgotten to line the fire front of the boilers with nonconducting materials. This defect was not noticed at the time and now, whenever a heavy coal fire was put in, "the whole mass of iron about the boilers became red hot and nearly roasted the firemen." During the breakout, the situation became so bad that the original firemen were overcome and had to be relieved; replacements were constantly found and rotated. Still, the* Arkansas *"went, fighting our way right and left." As cannonball after cannonball fell off her sides into the water, a newspaper reporter observed that "steadily but surely she keeps on the way, firing one broadside at the transports and the other at some vessel on the other side. She has nearly run the gauntlet" (Frank Knox,* Campfire and Cottonfield, *1865).*

to the Rebel achievement. A second factor, Stevens wrote, "was the fact that each of *Arkansas*' guns had a commissioned officer as gun captain or pointer and that these were all former U.S. naval officers." Thirdly, the sortie past the Federals was made not on the high seas with lots of maneuvering room but on the confined and relatively narrow Mississippi. Shots from the Rebel, made at virtually point-blank range, were telling.

Flag Officer Farragut in particular has been roundly criticized over the years for not being more fully prepared, knowing as he did that a sortie by the *Arkansas* was a distinct possibility. In all honesty, as Musicant reminds us, "For both Davis and Farragut, it was an inexcusable lapse." "Delta" told readers in the Crescent City that they could surely believe that "our folks were chagrined and chopfallen for a moment." To paraphrase and continue Coombe's thought, both flag officers, however, "should have been more prepared for the much anticipated sortie by the Confederate ram down the Yazoo." They "should have alerted the entire fleet, instead of just several vessels — even if one of them was the legendary *Carondelet*."

Some Northern newspapers, unlike those in the South, downplayed the success of the armorclad and, as reported in a headline of the *Philadelphia Inquirer* on July 22, dwelt on

Exiting the Gauntlet. *The* Arkansas *survived her run through the combined Union fleet above Vicksburg, but she paid a heavy price. This contemporary photograph clearly depicts the perforation of her smokestack (© 2010 Daniel Dowdey. Used with permission).*

the "desperate encounter" fought against her. Henry Bentley, the paper's correspondent, wrote three days later that the contest between the *Carondelet* and *Arkansas* "was a brilliant affair, and had it not been that the former ran aground and could not free herself, the Rebel craft would never have passed into the Mississippi River."

"A few more shots were exchanged," wrote Junius Henri Browne, "when the *Arkansas* made off and hastened so rapidly down the river that the *Carondelet*, in her crippled condition, could not follow her." One *Chicago Daily Tribune* reporter, Albert H. Bodman, appreciated the gallant Southern effort: "This unparalleled audacity and boldness elicits unqualified admiration of all. Such a thing never took place before and will probably never take place again!" In penning his biography of Admiral Farragut in 1892, Alfred Thayer Mahan drew a line between appreciation and actual impact. "It was a most gallant exploit," he wrote, "fairly comparable in daring to the passage of the Mississippi forts [at New Orleans in April]." On the other hand, he continued, it resulted "in no decisive effect upon the issues of the war."

For a few weeks, rumors concerning the whereabouts of the Confederate ram were, as Oliver Wood McClinton pointed out many years later, rampant in the North and along the rivers. It was several times reported that she was "seen on its way up the river past Memphis and almost as far South as New Orleans." When the embarrassed U.S. navy secretary Gideon Welles heard and digested the full story of the Rebel armorclad's achievement, he wrote to both Farragut and Davis on July 25 stating the department's "regret" that the *Arkansas* had slipped through the fleet "owing to the unprepared condition of the naval vessels." That vessel, he ordered, "must be destroyed at all hazards."[10]

Chapter Nine

Surviving Farragut's Charge: Night, July 15, 1862

By the end of the 4:00 A.M. to 8:00 A.M. morning watch, the CSS *Arkansas* had participated in two major engagements with elements of the Federal fleet in the waters above Vicksburg. In the first, she had beaten off three Northern scout vessels sent up the Yazoo to discover her lair. Having pursued two of her three enemies into the Mississippi, she encountered the combined fleets of Flag Officers David G. Farragut and Charles H. Davis anchored above the town. These she passed in a second fight, taking all of the punishment the Union craft could dish out while firing her own guns with telling effect. As she rounded De Soto Point and neared Vicksburg, the gallant *Arkansas* was given a rousing Rebel reception, being "received with loud hurrahs from the Confederate soldiers on the heights." The cheering was so loud that it could be clearly heard by Union troops on the peninsula across the river.

Pulled as much by the current as her engines, progress for the *Arkansas* was sluggish. As her engines continued to pound, the loose bearings resonated in a clanking sound when the rods turned. The slow descent of the armorclad gave Vicksburg's military and civilians time to prepare her reception. As she steered toward shore, the roar of battle gave way to the happier echoes of shouts of celebration. The crescendo of welcome was well described in a July 20 letter from Edward G. Butler of the 1st Louisiana Artillery to his in-law, Mrs. Mary Susan Ker of Natchez.

Descending the steps from his vantage point in the cupola of the Warren County Courthouse as fast as possible, Maj. Gen. Earl Van Dorn, commander of the Department of Southern Mississippi and Eastern Louisiana, raced over to the telegraph office to contact Richmond. The passage of the *Arkansas* through the combined fleet had convinced him, as his biographer Arthur Carter has written, that she had shown the Northerners "the invincibility of Vicksburg." "All the vessels of the lower fleet, except sloop-of-war, and all transports have gotten up steam and are off to get out of way of *Arkansas*," Van Dorn wired Confederate president Jefferson Davis. "One mortar boat, disabled and aground, is now burning." Davis passed this early news to navy secretary Stephen R. Mallory. It was also sent to other nearby Southern cities, including Jackson and Mobile.

Texas Sgt. Louis S. Flatau, watching with his battery mates from the bluffs near Cobb's battery, now received new orders from his commander, Capt. James J. Cowan of Co. G, 1st Mississippi Light Artillery. Flatau and his men were ordered to unlimber their 12-pdr. howitzer down at the wharf and ready it to throw canister shot across the ram's forecastle or after deck should any enemy raiding party attempt to board. There was a chance, some believed, that Federal demonstrations might be made.

Nine: Surviving Farragut's Charge: Night, July 15, 1862

Having witnessed the *Arkansas*' charge past the upper Federal fleet, Pvt. John S. Jackman of the 5th (later 9th) Kentucky Regiment and his fellows joined men from other units, such as the 3rd Mississippi, in watching as she "came around the bend." Shortly thereafter, the boat "landed at the levee under our batteries, where there was an enthusiastic crowd assembled to welcome her." It was about 8:30 A.M. when the *Arkansas* slowed, reversed her engines, and eased in toward the wharf opposite the courthouse. As crewmen made ready to throw out lines, Capt. Brown was spotted atop the casemate by growing shoreline crowds, who began chanting his name: "Brown! Brown! Brown."

While the big guns of the upper batteries boomed out a salute, the seldom taciturn commander waved his cap and, legend has it, fired his own pistol into the air, returning the cannon tribute with a single discharge. We cannot say for certain about the pistol but Pvt. William Y. Dixon of Co. G ("Hunter's Rifles"), 4th Louisiana Infantry, actually saw Brown. The soldier wrote in his diary the same day that he was "standing on the bow, waving his cap with one hand & a Confederate Flag in the other."

With blood yet running down his face from a gap in his forehead, the valiant captain, as his boat approached the levee, removed his cap and acknowledged the onlookers. Never at a loss for words, he shouted: "Boys, I never was under fire before, but I am not so scared as I expected to be." Was this bravado? Henry Walke reported in his memoirs that Brown "afterwards stated in private conversation that, when he came in full view of the flotilla, he had no hope of ever seeing Vicksburg!" The response from the soldiers and civilians was overwhelming. "He was welcomed by a continuous cheer from our regiment," 4th Louisiana Private Dixon noted, "that paled the cheeks of the black-hearted Yankees."

Meanwhile, a small rowboat made fast alongside. Maj. Gen. Van Dorn and his aide-de-camp and nephew, Capt. Clement Sulivane, climbed onboard to offer congratulations. His praise on this occasion was later mirrored in his September 9 campaign review, written for the War Department in Richmond. This memorable morning, Van Dorn wrote two months later, "immortalized his [Brown's] single vessel, himself, and the heroes under his command by an achievement the most brilliant ever recorded in naval annals." Entering the casemate in which "the smoke was still rolling around," the two soldiers were appalled by the sight that greeted them. "Altogether, it was the most frightful scene of war," remembered the latter, "that was ever presented to my eyes." And this was from a man present several years later at the evacuation of Richmond.

The armorclad's surviving crewmen, "blackened by gunpowder," were stripped to their essentials and extremely dirty. Only 40 or so were fully fit for duty, but all of the survivors, regardless of their physical state, were still dazed by the magnitude of their triumph, wondering when they would be allowed to sleep or go ashore.

The Confederate sailors had just begun the task of policing the boat; the mangled limbs of men lay about and the bulkhead walls were covered in human gore. "I slipped on blood and flesh as I walked," choked Van Dorn's assistant, "as if on lemon peels." The workforce available for clean-up duty would be further decreased when the Missouri volunteers, who had agreed to serve only as far as Vicksburg, departed.

Before returning ashore, Van Dorn met briefly with Lt. Isaac Newton Brown, commander of the *Arkansas*. The naval officer reported on his engagement out of sight in Old River and of the bravery and dedication of his men, 10 of whom were killed and 15 seriously wounded, plus dozens of others hurt less seriously, including himself. A request was made for new crewmen to replace those lost in battle or, by terms of their enlistments, about to leave. Volunteers were needed immediately to help refuel the vessel and to make emergency repairs. Van Dorn promised to do all that he could and ordered Brown not to undertake immediately any voyage downriver. Hartje tells us the general "ordered the vessel to remain nearby for the next few days until necessary repairs could be made."

Lt. Charles W. Read remembered that it was with "much difficulty that the *Arkansas* was rounded to and secured to the bank in front of the city." Around 8:50 A.M., Maj. Gen. John C. Breckenridge and Vicksburg commander M.L. Smith also boarded, accompanied by their aides and other staff officers, including Brig. Gen. William Preston. As they made their way carefully past the jagged pieces of railroad iron knocked onto the deck and into the interior of the casemate, the scene that greeted them was horrific. Indeed, all of the military men were equally distraught over the ghastly signs of slaughter and destruction, visible, despite some shadow, as sunlight danced through openings both designed and battle-created.

The decks and bulkheads were grimy with dried blood, while huge splinters lay everywhere. Few of the crew saluted or acknowledged "the brass"; many of the dazed and filthy survivors, exhausted by their ordeal, simply sat by their guns awaiting new orders. As Lt. Read recalled, the generals, in meeting with the boat's officers, "complimented us highly and offered us any assistance we required."

Meanwhile, numerous soldiers and civilians gathered on the bank near the wharf to get a closer look at, arguably, the most unusual craft ever yet to dock at their town. These exhilarated men and women desperately strained to catch a glimpse of the city's new heroes. Historian J. Thomas Scharf says they were "frantic with joy." A few of the boldest were able to run up and look inside a casemate gun port — only to recoil at the bloody view beheld.

As Van Dorn conversed with Brown, and Capt. Sulivane silently recorded his thoughts, Sgt. Flatau and several men from his howitzer detachment arrived and entered the casemate to assist with the removal of the dead and wounded. Like Van Dorn's aide, the artilleryman later wrote down his observations of the carnage. They are gripping:

> There was but one gun out of the ten in working order or that could be used. Their carriages were shattered, the embrasures, or portholes, were splintered, and some were nearly twice the original size; her broadside walls were shivered, and great slabs and splinters were strewn over the deck of her entire gunroom; there were but few men of her crew that were not wounded or killed; her gun deck was bloody from one end to the other; her stairways were so bloody and slippery that we had to sift cinders from the ash pans to keep from slipping on the decks and stairways; and the walls were besmeared with brains and blood, as though it had been thrown by hand from a sausage mill.

Able members of the *Arkansas* crew, assisted by military volunteers, removed the dead ashore for burial and helped the seriously injured to Confederate army hospitals. Several of the most grievously hurt, including Pilot John Hodges, were conveyed a little less than two miles east from town out the Baldwin Ferry Road to the plantation home of a Mrs. W. Cox, whose husband was absent in the army. "The scene had such a lasting impact on those who saw it," wrote Farragut biographer James P. Duffy, "that when Brown attempted to locate replacements for his dead and wounded crewmen before he continued downriver, he could find none."

Maj. Gen. Van Dorn and Lt. Brown went ashore to send telegrams reporting the action. Quite pleased with the boat's success, Breckenridge, Smith, and the others disembarked, the former, in particular, asking Brig. Gen. Preston to help find volunteers. The crewmen left behind were given breakfast.

When Commander Brown emerged into view, "the warm, fresh blood still trickling down his furrowed cheeks from his wounded head," the "enthusiasm" of the crowds, writes

Scharf, "became irrepressible." However, the rubberneckers, military and civilian alike, who stood nearby observing the ram and cheering her captain suddenly ran for cover when Federal sharpshooters on the bank across the river began firing at them long-range.

The commander of the armorclad wired Secretary Mallory noting his casualties and outlining the early morning fight "with the enemy's fleet above Vicksburg." Succinctly noting the size of his opposition, Brown confirmed that one ironclad vessel was driven ashore "with colors down and disabled," that a ram had been blown up, another vessel burned, and others damaged. The shot-up smokestack prevented the boat's use as a ram and she was "otherwise cut up, as we engaged at close quarters." His report appeared in several Confederate newspapers, including the *Richmond Whig*.

In addition to the dead and wounded then being transferred ashore, Lt. Brown was faced with the difficulty of replacing his entire health care staff, as both Dr. H.W.M. Washington and his unnamed assistant , too ill to continue, were sent to the Vicksburg city hospital. The armorclad's commander took this opportunity ashore, as Lt. Read remembered, to telegraph "out into the interior of Mississippi for medical volunteers."

Van Dorn, on the other hand, attempted to maximize the publicity to be gained. In a slightly longer wire to President Davis that was also copied to the Navy Department, the district commander, fresh from his visit aboard the *Arkansas*, reported that the armorclad had run "gloriously through 12 or 13 rams, gunboats, and sloops-of-war." Her smokestack was riddled but she was not otherwise, he claimed, "materially damaged." Brown, "her commander and hero," was slightly wounded in the head, but his exploit was "Glorious for the Navy." The whole crew deserved thanks from the nation's chief executive. It was anticipated that the craft's damages would all be repaired quickly and then, with a flair, Van Dorn added: "Ho! For New Orleans."

To Brig. Gen. Daniel Ruggles, commanding the Department of Southern Mississippi and Eastern Louisiana First District from a base at Camp Moore, Louisiana, , Van Dorn announced that the "*Arkansas* came out this morning." After running "the gantlet of the upper fleet of 12 vessels," she was "now safe under our guns." The commanding general went on to excitedly say that she would "attack below as soon as some repairs are made." The local correspondent of the *Mississippian* wired his paper regarding the ram's success, claiming that the "damage done to her is trifling, chiefly to the smoke stack."[1]

Returning aboard, Lt. Brown had the sad task of mustering ashore the Missouri volunteers who had joined his boat up the Yazoo and stayed with her through the great battles that brought her to Vicksburg. Since dawn, four privates had been killed and three wounded. The killed totaled one-fourth of all dead aboard the *Arkansas* that day. Approximately 40 survivors healthy enough to walk were briefly lined up by company behind their Missouri State Guard 1st Division officers. Led by Capt. Samuel S. Harris, these men received Brown's thanks before moving off to help populate the Confederate army artillery units defending the city.

As the Missourians moved off, Lt. Brown found himself with what could only be described as the nucleus of a crew. The remaining few officers and men, the healthy and the many lame, were mustered. All would now be given many new duties, as their captain expressed his hope that the army would soon supply additional men to fill the empty billets. Brown next directed that the *Arkansas* cast off and shift down to the coal depot located below Depot Street, about a mile further on. Here repair work would be continued by the few men still able to get about. If sufficient replacement crewmen could be obtained and patches made quickly enough, Brown "intended trying the lower fleet that evening."

As soon as the engines were cut and the ram tied onto a coal barge, Executive Officer Lt. Henry K. Stevens jumped down on to it and scrambled over to the bank. Ashore, he moved among the men in the crowd that had assembled below the bluff to see this exceedingly strange steamer, explaining his need for help and the opportunity to be part of a glorious enterprise. Seeking a chance to cover themselves in minimal glory, a couple of dozen men were thus convinced to voluntarily help refuel the *Arkansas*—and in the process, get covered with coal dust.

The most strenuous, backbreaking, and filthy immediate effort was coaling the vessel. It had departed the Yazoo very short of fuel; a new supply, carried aboard in the standard bushel format, was obtained from the anchored barges. This was a trial for the exhausted men tasked with the dirty job, but, fortunately, Stevens' "volunteer crew from shore" assisted. As the bushel baskets were emptied, a cloud of coal dust arose above the boat. It settled not only on the men, but over almost everything aboard. It even helped to enhance the mud hue of the armorclad's color scheme.

Meanwhile, there was great embarrassment upstream aboard the units of the Federal fleets. After the "mythical *Arkansas*" had passed victoriously under the guns of Vicksburg, there was within the hour, observed Captain's Clerk Edward S. Bacon aboard the *Iroquois*, "the greatest excitement." He noted in a letter home next day that "everything that could carry a pot and a handful of shavings had 'steam up' and plenty of it, but the *Arkansas* was out of reach."

While Brown and Van Dorn were ashore at the telegraph office, a mortified Flag Officer David G. Farragut began intensive planning for the ram's destruction. Having by this time long since changed from his night clothes into his uniform, the agitated leader received damage reports and was enraged that the *Arkansas* had not been sunk. As Federal fatigue parties repaired damages aboard the naval ships, it was found that some of the auxiliaries had also been hit as well: *J.H. Dickey* (three times), *Champion* (three times), and *Great Western* (once). The reporter from the *Brooklyn Daily Eagle* laid the blame squarely on friendly fire from the warships: "The broadsides from our own vessels did as much damage as the guns of the *Arkansas*."

Farragut now summoned the captains from his surrounding warships to a meeting aboard the *Hartford*. At the same time, a general signal was made for the blue-water warships to get up steam and prepare to get underway. The loyal Tennessean was, as Clerk Edward S. Bacon was told aboard the *Iroquois* later in the day, "A good deal disgusted at the cool impudence displayed in the morning." The blue-water commander also believed his broadsides then "had so injured the Ram as to make her an easy prey."

Led by Cmdr. John Alden and Richard Wainwright, Farragut's captains listened as the flag officer, most displeased by Lt. Brown's escape, both vented his spleen and called for action. Noting that the mortar schooners and other vessels below required enhanced protection and that the river level was still falling, he said it was necessary for the blue-water units above Vicksburg to quickly return below, even if, in the words of one of his biographers, Chester G. Hearn, "it meant losing ships to do it." A plan was tentatively agreed upon and the participants concluded "that the ram had to be taken at all hazards." Once the council of war was over and the captains were piped over the side, the upper fleet commander dictated a message to Flag Officer Charles H. Davis.

He initially blamed himself for not insisting that a larger force inspect the Yazoo. Now, "we must all go down and destroy him." The Gulf Squadron boss wanted his upper river colleague to join him in an all-out, joint, good, old-fashioned line of battle attack on the

Arkansas right under the Vicksburg guns. "We must go close to him and smash him up," he ranted through his pen, continuing: "It will be warm work, but we must do it, he must be destroyed!" Once the blue- and brown-water vessels had steamed by initially, Farragut expected they would be able to round to "and come up again," that way getting two chances to blast the Confederate ram.

About 9:30 A.M., Master's Mate E.J. Allen, bearing a similar message, completed a trek across the De Soto Peninsula to see Capt. Henry H. Bell, who commanded Federal naval forces below the town from aboard the sloop-of-war *Brooklyn*. The flag officer's missive informed his downriver subordinate that the "chocolate color" rebel ram had arrived off Vicksburg and that he would be coming down after her "as soon as we get the steam up." Bell was to stand ready to assist the passage. Meanwhile, Farragut wanted "Renshaw to get the mortars to work." When, a few days earlier, Cmdr. David Dixon Porter had departed the scene for the east with 12 schooners, Cmdr. William B. Renshaw,[2] captain of the *Westfield*,[3] was left in charge of the six from the Gulf Division Mortar Flotilla still remaining below Vicksburg.

Being informed about 7:00 A.M. that the *Arkansas* was attempting to pass the combined fleet above the terraced city, Cmdr. Renshaw had ordered the captains of his mortar schooners to prepare to evacuate their current positions. An hour later, the Confederate ram was seen slowly steaming around De Soto Point, headed to the riverbank under the city. Capt. Bell now gave the departure order, while simultaneously sending a dispatch boat to New Orleans with the news. This was the maneuver of Farragut's downriver fleet seen by Lt. Brown, who could not quite tell if it was "preparing to receive us or recede from us."

Ashore, Brig. Gen. Thomas Williams and soldiers from several Federal infantry regiments camped near the riverbank were able to see the descent of the *Arkansas*, puffing huge clouds of smoke from her injured chimney. The general sent a message to Capt. Bell announcing the Confederate's arrival, while one of the *Brooklyn*'s officers, ashore with the army at the time, also hurried back aboard.

A number of bluecoats on the Louisiana shore grew fearful, and so burned their commissary stores and retreated aboard their transports. These, like the mortar schooners, withdrew nearly out of sight of Vicksburg. The correspondent of the *Jackson Mississippian*, watching from Vicksburg's ramparts, crowed that those hated vessels "were seen heading towards New Orleans and the Gulf as fast as steam could carry them."

Entirely defenseless except for their big mortars, five small Union "bombers" slowly withdrew below the anchorage of the *Brooklyn*, expecting that her big guns would provide them cover. At this point, the escorting *Westfield* returned upstream to assist the sixth schooner, the stranded *Sidney C. Jones*, and to reconnoiter the *Arkansas*. After communicating with the grounded vessel, Renshaw drove his side-wheeler a short distance beyond to get a look at the Rebel armorclad, which by now had moved down to the coaling barges. After observing her with his spyglass, the Union officer was convinced that she was "seriously injured by the conflict with the fleet." He also saw that people were furiously working to coal her.

In an effort to disrupt the enemy craft's refueling process, the captain of the one-time ferryboat ordered the gunners manning his 100-pdr. Parrott to drop a couple of rifle shots on the *Arkansas*. Lt. Brown later remembered that "Renshaw, in the *Westfield*, made very fine practice ... occasionally throwing the spray from his shot over our working party." These near-misses were actually beneficial, however, "sprinkling down the coal dust." Soon thereafter, the *Westfield* moved back down the river so that her captain might report his observations to Capt. Bell.

When, about noon, her coal bunkers were full, the Confederate ram, across the river, moved back out of range of the lower fleet Federals. She tied up at the wharf directly below the middle batteries. Ashore, a road ran almost directly to the middle of town. With her bow pointed upstream, the armorclad docked "where, under less excitement, we hastened such temporary repairs as would enable us to continue the offensive." Immediately, an effort was made to eliminate the dust, polishing all guns, brass, and fixtures while scrubbing the decks, port sills, and sundry other dirty spots.

Under the protection of Vicksburg's water batteries, the *Arkansas* remained an attraction for the curious. Lt. Lot Young of the 4th Kentucky and some of his men took the opportunity to get close and remembered seeing "the monster in her grim and battered condition with numerous holes in her smokestack, made by shots from the enemy's guns." Young was particularly taken with her sailors, whom he labeled "the most daring, despicable, smoke-begrimed looking set I ever beheld, but who were elated at their successful victory."

Cmdr. William B. Renshaw, USN (1816–1863). *This New Yorker entered the USN as a midshipman in 1831. Proceeding up through the ranks, he commissioned the gunboat* Westfield *in January 1862, the only vessel he would ever command. Following his sojourn up the Mississippi, he was charged by Rear Adm. Farragut with the blockade of Galveston, Texas. When the* Westfield *ran aground on January 1, 1863, he determined to destroy it, but was killed in the premature explosion (Navy History and Heritage Command).*

While Cmdr. Renshaw and the butternut soldiers looked over the *Arkansas* from their different vantage points, Flag Officer Davis received Farragut's gung-ho attack message. A more cautionary soul than his opposite number, Davis was not convinced of the value of such an assault. He invited the Tennessee-born deep-water sailor to join him aboard the *Benton* for a reconnaissance of Vicksburg's upper batteries, during which cruise he would "show him the position of the battery" and attempt to talk him out of putting their commands "in all sorts of perilous positions."

Aboard the *Brooklyn*, Renshaw received Farragut's orders to take the *Arkansas* (and the water batteries covering her) under fire. He departed immediately to get his mortars into position and during this interlude, about 10:30 A.M., the *Sidney C. Jones* was destroyed.

Before Cmdr. Renshaw was ready, other Federal forces initiated what would become a regular series of Northern attacks upon the *Arkansas*. Mortar boats attached to the Western Flotilla that in previous

Nine: Surviving Farragut's Charge: Night, July 15, 1862 211

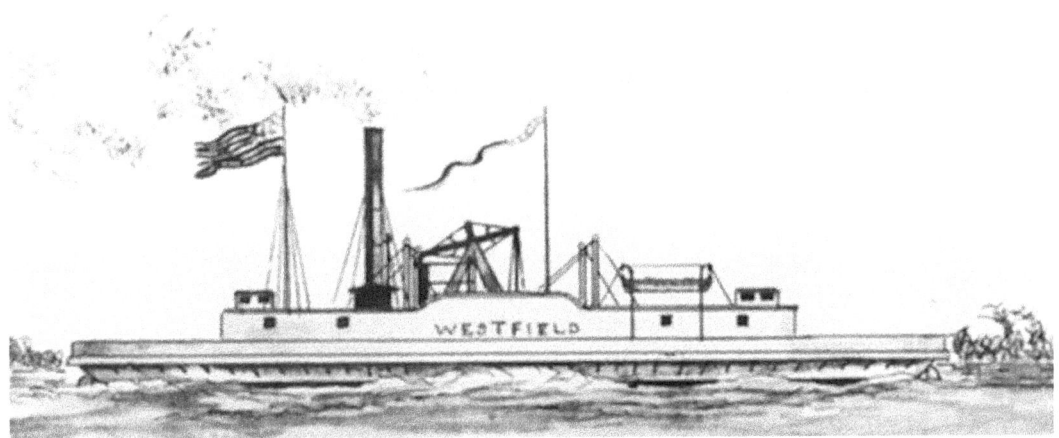

USS *Westfield*. Built for Cornelius Vanderbilt in 1861, this 822-ton side-wheeler was purchased into Federal service in November, converted into a gunboat at a cost of $27,500, and commissioned into service by Cmdr. William B. Renshaw in January 1862. With a length of 215 feet, a 35-foot beam, and a draft of 13.6 feet, the craft was armed with one 100-pdr. Parrott rifle, one 9-inch Dahlgren SB, and four 8-inch Dahlgren SBs. Later on the morning of July 15, Renshaw drove the Westfield *a short distance from her anchorage below Vicksburg to get a look at the* Arkansas, *which by now had moved down to the coaling barges. After observing her with his spyglass, the Union officer was convinced that she was "seriously injured by the conflict with the fleet." He also saw that people were furiously working to coal her. In an effort to disrupt the enemy craft's refueling process, the captain of the one-time New York ferryboat ordered the gunners manning his 100-pdr. Parrott to drop a couple of rifle shots on the armorclad. Her commander, Lt. Isaac Newton Brown, later remembered that "Renshaw, in the* Westfield, *made very fine practice ... occasionally throwing the spray from his shot over our working party." These near-misses were actually beneficial, however, "sprinkling down the coal dust" (Navy History and Heritage Command).*

days had lobbed their shells at Vicksburg in general now prepared to target, as best they could from behind a line of timber, the escaped Rebel armorclad.

While Davis awaited word from Farragut and the firing of his mortar scows, he had the opportunity to speak at length with Lt. William Gwin of the *Tyler* concerning his fight — and that of the *Carondelet* and *Queen of the West*— up the Yazoo earlier that morning. From that interview comes a famous story later repeated in various Northern newspapers. According to Gwin, he was like a man who was chosen by his camping companions to venture out to procure some game for breakfast. "He went out to look for rabbits and prairie chickens," noted the *Brooklyn Daily Eagle* correspondent who broke the tale, "and met a grizzly bear." Rushing back to camp with the bear in hot pursuit, he supposedly, according to the naval officer, "astonished his comrades by an uproariously sarcastic introduction." 'Here boys,' he cried, 'I've fetched the game.'"

Lt. Brown, aboard the Confederate ram, learned that an enemy vessel across the river was "consumed from the effect," one he chose to believe was caused from panic at his arrival. Despite the loss, Bell's vessels below Vicksburg "recovered from their scare and resumed their former anchorage." Several of the armorclad's officers, including Lt. Read, lamented the fact that she could not then sortie. Noting the small size of Bell's force, that Southern officer was confident that, if she had been in condition to maneuver, "she could easily have captured or destroyed that entire flotilla." Donald Barnhart tells us that, still, "her furnaces were kept alight to make it seem that she had her guard up."

Throughout the morning, the *Hartford* and the lower fleet vessels surrounding her prepared for battle. Steam was gotten up and splinter nets were hung along the port sides of the warships. All day long, the little tugs which had accompanied the men-o'-war were kept busy "carrying dispatches from the flagship to the different vessels in the fleet."

Flag Officer Farragut accepted the invitation of Flag Officer Davis and went aboard the *Benton*, as she lay anchored out of range of the Confederate batteries. He was very agitated upon his arrival, "full of going down immediately to destroy the rebel with his fleet," remarked Lt. S. Ledyard Phelps, "going off at once, couldn't waste a moment." Pleasantries were, nevertheless, exchanged between the squadron commanders as the Western Flotilla flagboat raised anchor and commenced her early afternoon scout. To ensure motive power in the current, the big ironclad dropped down stern first below De Soto Point until she came in sight of the town's upper batteries.

When the *Benton* was perceived to be in range, the Confederates began to drop their cannonballs in the waters around her. Great splashes mushroomed up into the air even as the two commanders examined the enemy positions, determining that some of those defenses were new and contained six 6-inch rifled guns. Flag Officer Davis and his visiting counterpart simultaneously debated the possibilities of a close-in joint attack within an hour or so. Observers and spies could not say with certainty that the *Arkansas* was badly damaged; if she were not and chose to fight, the outcome might not be a sure thing for the Federals. It was strongly recommended that Farragut's ships wait "'till near sundown ... when the sun would be in the enemy's eye." The eager Farragut, according to Hearn, fumed with impatience and observed that night "attacks spared ships, but they also spared the enemy."

William Still has written that Davis was as cautious as Farragut was impetuous. He refused to join in the watery charge for fear of his gunboats being sunk. If they were, he could see the loss of the entire upper river back up beyond Memphis. Davis later wrote that his opposite "treated my reason as very cold and repulsive. The contrast between us was very striking, though perfectly friendly."

Although he would not commit his ironclads to passing Vicksburg's cannon, the bewhiskered scholar agreed to use them to draw the fire of the upper defenses while Farragut slipped past. Additionally, he was able to persuade the lower fleet commander to hold off his assault until sundown. It was also proposed that, rather than grappling the ram, a supreme attempt should be made to sink her by cannon fire as the steamers passed its location. To help sweeten the prospect of success, Davis offered to transfer his own "grand ram," *Sumter*, to the lower fleet for the occasion. She could strike the *Arkansas* if the opportunity arose.

The *Benton* remained under fire during the entire time of the Davis and Farragut meeting, which was undoubtedly interrupted by hits or near misses on several occasions. We know for certain that the big steamer was struck once and nearly so at least two other times. The first Rebel shot to strike the *Benton* was the most damaging, entering the exposed and thinly covered casemate rear and killing fireman William Lewis. Two others hit and destroyed the cutter and the launch, both of which were being towed astern. "Steamed upstream," the officer of the deck wrote in the logbook, "and came to the former anchorage at about 1:30."

Returning aboard the *Hartford*, Flag Officer Farragut was now fully determined to proceed past Vicksburg without the Davis ironclads. Taking his fleet back down below the batteries would satisfy three pressing requirements. It would give him a chance to sink the *Arkansas* while, at the same time, removing his ships from their pointless position in the increasingly shallow river above the citadel. Finally, in the event that the Confederate armorclad was not badly damaged and elected to move downriver, the Gulf Squadron could protect the army transports and other vessels now only thinly protected.

From late morning on, as Cmdr. John Alden noted upstream aboard his big sloop-of-war *Richmond*, the "heat was suffocating." About 4:00 P.M., a violent thunderstorm passed through. "It rained about one hour," he remembered, "when it cleared up and the air became much cooler."

All of the schooners were in action by late afternoon, hurling their great 13-inch shells at the enemy positions 3,700 to 4,000 yards distant. As the opportunity presented itself, the watchdog *Westfield* attempted to place "some 8-inch grape among them." Guns from Vicksburg's lower batteries returned fire, but all of their shots fell short, except one, a near miss. The historian of the 20th Tennessee Volunteer Infantry, who was present, recorded his impressions of the mortar fire:

> [W]e were entertained nearly every day and night by shells thrown from the mortar fleet below the city. During the night when one of their mortar guns would fire, we could see the light as it ascended into the skies like a great meteor circling through the heavens with a tail sometimes about 40 or 50 feet long. This was one of the grandest sights I ever witnessed. If this enormous shell should strike the ground before it exploded it would often go 15 feet into the sand and clay. I have seen these shells go into the ground at the roots of good-sized trees, explode, and tear the trees up by the roots, and when they came your direction, you would not know which way to go to get out of the way.

Additionally, Capt. Ormand F. Nims' 2nd Battery, Massachusetts Light Artillery, initially located at Barney's Pont (⅞ of a mile from the heaviest of the Confederate upper batteries) just before Farragut's passage upstream at the end of June, began firing. Its field howitzers, located on the Louisiana shore abreast and partly astern of the mortar schooners, silenced the Confederate sharpshooters firing upon Renshaw's craft from the woods on the opposite bank.

During this time, the U.S. Army transports that had withdrawn earlier returned their men to the abandoned camps on the Louisiana shore across the river from the Rebel fortress. Intense small arms harassing fire was opened upon the Southerners over the wide expanse of water. Huge piles of wood, for possible later use in bonfires, were built at key points along the western shore opposite the ram's lair. Brig. Gen. Williams, privy to Farragut's planning via Capt. Bell, wanted to play his role in events soon to come.

Great geysers of water caused by the mortar shells rose from the water offshore of the *Arkansas*. While the Federals attempted to get her range, engineers aboard the ram checked over her power plant and began to repair her chimney by covering the 60+ shot holes with sheet iron patches. Darkness, when it arrived, prevented completion of the second task.

As workers, under the direction of Lt. Stevens, hammered about him, Lt. Brown was able to prepare a brief report to dispatch to his superior, Flag Officer William F. Lynch, over at Jackson. Reviewing his morning progress in a lengthy paragraph, he concluded his battle summary by stating his belief that "we accomplished all that was possible under the circumstances." Although Brown was the "man of the hour" before the crowds, he appreciated the work and sacrifice of his officers and men and spent considerable ink impressing upon Lynch their great collective "coolness." The "gratifying results of the fight" he attributed "in great part to the excellent arrangements" of Lt. Stevens. The wounded officers and pilots were all praised. His enlisted men "behaved well," as the results of the fights with the craft on the Yazoo and Mississippi "very plainly showed."

Several of the officers gave anonymous interviews to the correspondent of the *Jackson Mississippian*. The correspondent's misnaming of the *Benton* for the *Carondelet* and *Eastport* for the *Lancaster* may, in fact, have come from these men themselves before they were apprised of the actual identities of their opponents. In any event, the reporter, already labeling the steamer as the "immortal *Arkansas*," concluded: "Her injuries will all be repaired by tomorrow, when she will commence the process of 'clearing out' the Mississippi right and left of Vicksburg." On the negative side, the *Arkansas* was, he admitted, "much cut up, our pilothouse is mashed," and there were "some ugly places through our armor." As a result of the chimney being "shot to pieces," she came out of the engagements with but "30 pounds only in the gauge." As a result, "our supposed power as a ram was of no use." It would be necessary of repair the chimney and pilothouse before "going far from here, if possible."

During late morning, Brig. Gen. Preston, responding to Brown's plea for new men, set into motion an effort to gain additional volunteers for the *Arkansas*. Orders and circulars were sent to several of the citadel's defensive batteries, particularly Cobb's and Hudson's (also known as Pettus Flying Artillery), and some of the Kentucky Orphan Brigade regiments seeking artillerists and soldiers willing to serve aboard.

Mississippi Light Artillery Capt. James L. Hoole, of Hudson's Battery (Pettus Flying Artillery), was one of those obtaining a circular and, within a short time, he was able to find 13 men willing to join the armorclad's crew. Then, while trying to actually get the men aboard, Hoole received the runaround. He went to the headquarters of Brig. Gen. Preston and was directed by an aide to Maj. Gen. Van Dorn himself. Van Dorn sent him down to Maj. Gen. Breckenridge, whose adjutant referred him to Lt. Brown. Hoole was unable to obtain a pass to go to the river that evening, being required to wait until the next day.

Lt. W.P. Wallace, from the staff of Brig. Gen. Preston, meanwhile, visited Cobb's Battery, informing its commander, Capt. Frank P. Gracey, that a dozen volunteers were needed for service aboard the *Arkansas*. Twelve men, including Lt. Robert Ballard Mathews, immediately stepped forward; however, Gracey, fearing that the transfer of so many men would decimate his unit, ordered the number halved. Straws were drawn and Mathews was permitted to depart with two sergeants, one corporal, and three privates. Joining them were six volunteer firemen drawn from the 4th Brigade. Not having the difficulty obtaining a pass that Hoole encountered, Mathews and his men reported to Lt. Brown at the wharf. The captain, doubtless delighted to have the services of his artillery-experienced fellow Kentuckians, immediately assigned them to the port bow Columbiad, previously commanded by Lt. George W. Gift.

Mathews immediately let Brown know that he did not have the experience to command such a large piece and asked that he place in charge some officer with a greater knowledge of naval cannon. He offered to serve as a private. Accepting this request, Brown immediately detailed Midshipman Scales, who had taken over the port side forward division of the injured Lt. Gift, to personally command the great gun to which Mathews was assigned. The army lieutenant became a common member of the gun crew.

We do not know exactly how many Orphan Brigade or Mississippi soldiers volunteered and actually served aboard. In fact, of the few troops that actually agreed to serve aboard the ram, only three beyond the artillerymen has received recognition: Caleb Allen of the 6th Kentucky, William Dills and W. Woodward. The latter two were from the 3rd Kentucky and were killed in the battle of July 22. Master's Mate John Wilson later noted that "a few volunteers from a Missouri regiment ashore had come aboard in the afternoon to assist in working our guns." There are no other records to say for certain whether Wilson's Missourians may not, in fact, have been these men from the Bluegrass State.[4]

While the bombers from both squadrons sent their giant mortar shells screaming toward Vicksburg, U.S. Army sharpshooters and artillery batteries on the Louisiana shore opened an incessant fire. Maybe, they hoped, a lucky show would hit the Confederate armorclad or create casualties in the crowds of onlookers who continued to observe comings and goings aboard her from nearby locations.

The rust-colored Rebel boat, whose superstructure wore a new coat of coal dust, lay close under the dull brown bluff and was next to impossible for the Union shooters to actually see. Lt. Gift later noted that, in order to discourage the harassing fire, the *Arkansas* was eventually forced to open fire on them. A half dozen cannon discharges brought relief.

Federal engineers, attempting to assist the fleet in striking the *Arkansas*, set up a range light system[5] abreast of and across from her anchorage. Like a World War II British spotlight attempting to pick up German bombers in the night sky over London, it was supposed to guide the USN warships to the Rebel if Farragut passed after dark.

During this warmup period, Flag Officer Farragut sent his captains last-minute instructions from the *Hartford*. All the orders were aimed at the successful completion of one simple objective: "The ram must be destroyed!" Gunners were instructed to fire solid shot.

Aboard the *Hartford*, as on the others, the bustle of preparation was everywhere evident. There was a unique plan aboard the flagship, however, which the *Cincinnati*'s Eliot Callender later described: "[B]y afternoon an immense anchor was safely triced out on the end of her main yard.... The Admiral's plan was to run up along side the *Arkansas*, and if his broadsides wouldn't faze her, to drop that anchor from its lofty perch, feeling assured that it would carry with it to the bottom of the river all that was left of his gallant antagonist."

Additionally, grappling irons were hung from the crossjack yards. These would be dropped on the *Arkansas* if the opportunity presented. Ashore, Brig. Gen. Williams was told that: "It was the purpose of the Flag Officer to grapple her himself."

There was no rush. Consequently, Union captains were encouraged to drift with the current, taking as much time as was necessary to find the ram's position. If given an opening, any of the vessels should "run into the ram with full force." About 5:30 P.M., the *Brooklyn* moved up and anchored within sight of the flagship above, the easier to see and obey her signals.

The Gulf Squadron warships north of Vicksburg now started to re-form into the same steaming order as that employed on the way up, back on June 28. The eastern column, closest to the Mississippi shore, would be led back down by the *Iroquois*, followed by the *Oneida* and the *Richmond*. The second column was captained by the *Wissahickon*, then the *Sumter*, *Hartford*, *Winona*, *Sciota*, and *Pinola*. The western line was staggered, in order to permit its members to fire at intervals between the vessels of the eastern column. As they went, all were to maintain their positions, keeping a good lookout for signals.

It was anticipated that there would, as before, be a great cloud of smoke caused by all the cannon fire of the eight U.S. ships and the Confederate shore defenses. When that occurred, the flag officer, wrote (perhaps with a nod toward Admiral Lord Horatio Nelson) that "no one will do wrong who lays his vessel alongside of the enemy or tackles with the ram." In keeping with the arrangements made earlier in the afternoon, Flag Officer Davis opened the evening ball at 6:00 P.M., just as sailors aboard both the *Arkansas* and the U.S. vessels were starting the second dog watch.[6] As the ships' bells rang, the *Benton* slipped her chain and dropped down the river, followed by the *Louisville* and *Cincinnati*. It was high summer, "the sun still blazed in its glory," and dusk was still a while off as the Western Flotilla gunboats set off.

During the minutes it took Davis to reach De Soto Point, his mortar boats, under Capt. Henry E. Maynadier (1830–1868) and his assistant, Capt. E.B. Pike of the Corps of Engineers,[7] opened rapid fire on the city, lobbing in the big 13-inch shells as fast as possible. In essence, the 13-inch guns were, to Confederate observers, fired blind from behind woods up around the bend. In fact, the two army captains were not shooting randomly. As they had during previous shoots back up the Mississippi, they had arranged for several steamers to be anchored with a clear view along the opposite bank. By means of signal flags waved from their upper decks, the gunners were kept "fully posted where each shell falls."

Before it became necessary to stop in order not to hit Farragut's ships passing down, Maynadier's men, some of whom were ill, doggedly shelled the enemy. Eventually throwing 80 shot, the little boats were totally exposed as Confederate shell and round shot fell all around them. "Not a man flinched," it was later recorded in the flotilla's logbook.

The three river ironclads poured a heavy fire toward the Fort Hill batteries, which was warmly and eagerly returned. The bluejackets afloat and graycoats ashore would continue to exchange rounds until about 8:15 P.M., when Flag Officer Davis ordered his trio to break off and steam back to their former anchorage.[8]

Having made some extremely basic repairs, engineers aboard the *Arkansas* were able to get up steam late in the afternoon. Unhappily, the ram's chimney had not yet been patched, so the amount of pressure that could be generated was exceedingly limited. The dead and most-seriously wounded were long since removed ashore. Basic cleaning of the interior was complete, though the blood which had dried in splotches could not be removed from either deck or bulkhead. Although the great guns were attended to, there was not time to make more than the most rudimentary fixes to the ripped casemate armor. "As well as we could, we put the ship to rights," remembered one officer, "and the day wore away." The gunners paid particular attention to carriage repair and readying the bow and port side batteries, which were pointed out toward the river. Midshipman Scales had as his special project the familiarization of Lt. Mathews and his men with naval gun drill.

Work was not halted even to celebrate as officers and members of the crew learned that laudatory telegrams had arrived from Richmond. One thanked the men for their "brilliant achievement," while the other "informed Capt. Brown that he had been promoted to the rank of commander." Belatedly, on October 2, the Confederate congress approved a joint resolution, cordially tendering it "to Lieutenant Isaac N. Brown and all under his command, for their signal exhibition of skill and gallantry on the fourteenth [15th] day of July last, on the Mississippi River, near Vicksburg, in the brilliant and successful engagement of the sloop of war *Arkansas* with the enemy's fleet."

The healthy few crewmen remaining aboard the *Arkansas*, together with their officers, were now pretty much all exhausted ("used up" was the usual Civil War term), having been hard at it since well before sunrise. "But there is a limit to human endurance," Lt. Gift reminded his readers in later years. Mealtime had arrived and as the tars messed below a humble supper was served out to the officers and others in the wardroom. Stories and impressions were doubtless exchanged. One of those present, Pilot William Gilmore, reportedly told his colleagues "that he would not again pass through the ordeal of the morning for the whole world." As the meal was finished, "we could do no more," Gift added, "and we rested." In fact, there would be no real rest — not yet.

Not long before dark, another violent thunderstorm, "accompanied by torrents of rain," shook the Vicksburg area. A low cloud ceiling remained after it rolled off and it was suddenly almost sundown, precursor to a much darker night than usual. The Union gunboats above Vicksburg were "observed to be in motion." To the tired men aboard the Confederate ram, it appeared as though "Farragut meant to fight." When a grayclad army officer came aboard and reported that all three Western Flotilla gunboats were moving toward the upper batteries and that intense preparations were being made for getting underway aboard the oceangoing ships above the town, it was "evident that the enemy meant mischief."

The attack of the Western Flotilla ironclads upon the Fort Hill batteries, beginning at 6:00 P.M., turned out to be the beginning of the Federal's mischievous intention. "We had the gratification," wrote Cmdr. Brown, "of witnessing the beautiful reply of our upper batteries to their gallant attack." This would turn out to be close-in work and the fact that no one aboard had a spyglass would not make a difference this night.

A half hour after the pyrotechnics began signal flags shot up the halyards of the *Hartford* ordering the *Brooklyn* and the gunboats below to get underway and "to form second order of sailing." At the same time, four of Cmdr. Renshaw's mortar schooners, and an equal number of Capt. Maynadier's mortar boats above, launched an intense bombardment.

Vicksburg Batteries. *Gazing through long spyglasses, Union sailors saw formidable defenses. Two, later three, water batteries were situated for a distance of about three miles in front of Vicksburg. The upper batteries, located below Fort Hill, commanded the bend in the river above the city. They were operated by the First Tennessee Heavy Artillery Regiment. The South Fork lower batteries, at the southern end of the town, were manned by the First Louisiana Artillery, while the center batteries, those directly in front of the town, were fought by the Eighth Louisiana Artillery Battalion (Miller, ed.,* Photographic History of the Civil War*).*

A "Bomber" Schooner's 13-inch Mortar. *Entirely defenseless except for their big mortars, five small Union "bombers," under the overall command of Cmdr. William B. Renshaw, were available below Vicksburg on July 15. All of the schooners were in action by late afternoon, hurling their great 13-inch shells at the enemy 3,700 to 4,000 yards distant. Guns from Vicksburg's lower batteries returned fire, but all of their shots fell short, except one, a near miss (Miller, ed.,* Photographic History of the Civil War*).*

Between 6:20 P.M. and 6:40 P.M. (depending upon the account), No. 1218 from the *Hartford*'s set of signals went aloft. It required Farragut's ships above Vicksburg to weigh anchor and form line ahead, preparatory to beginning their descent past the town. Some ships, including the *Hartford*, were slower to assemble than others due, says Frank Bennett, to problems involved with "handling such large ships in a swift river."

On the other hand, some, like the *Oneida*, were underway almost immediately, "steaming as necessary whilst the fleet was formed according to the plan for the morning of the 28th ultimo." Within a quarter of an hour or so, the deep-water craft were gracefully taking their positions and moving downstream in two columns. As twilight began, Farragut's columns approached the upper batteries. Flag Officer Davis' vessels, circling in the adjacent waters, had already been "in hot exchange" with the Confederates for 45 minutes, "watching to see them come." It was nearly 7:20 P.M. when the *Iroquois* and *Wissahickon* came abreast of the Western Flotilla gunboats.

Instead of initially holding their fire to allow Farragut's men-o'-war to pass, the upriver ironclads, according to an officer aboard the *Iroquois*, "persisted in firing over our heads to our great annoyance, and danger." As the shadows thickened and fingers of light noted the location of the setting sun, Lt. Phelps later remembered "we even could scarcely tell when the foremost vessel passed the upper battery and saw nothing of the hindmost ones." As the ocean ships continued, assuming "the full weight of metal," Davis ordered his units to stop shooting. The mortars above and below the town had already ceased firing as Farragut's vessels passed the point, fearful of accidentally hitting one of their own. "Owing to our defective fuses," wrote someone in the logbook of the upper mortar flotilla, "we were afraid some might explode too soon." During their shoot, the men of Capts. Maynadier and Pike fired 80 shells, with unknown effect.

As the *Iroquois* and *Wissahickon*, leading the two columns, steamed past De Soto Point — but before the Federal sailors could actually see Vicksburg — Confederate soldiers hiding in a wooded location back from the bank opened upon the Union ships. Capt. James Palmer and the men aboard the former were surprised by their initial reception. The upper batteries, in an effort to

Federal 12-lb. Field Howitzer. *Capt. Ormand F. Nims' 2nd Battery, Massachusetts Light Artillery was initially located at Barney's Point (⅞ of a mile from the heaviest of the Confederate upper batteries) just before Farragut's passage upstream at the end of June. It began firing its field howitzers, located on the Louisiana shore abreast and partly astern of the mortar schooners, across the Mississippi at the same time the big naval mortars attempted to hit the* Arkansas *and the Rebel shore guns. Nims' well-served pieces silenced a number of Confederate sharpshooters firing upon Cmdr. Renshaw's "bombers" from the woods on the opposite bank (Library of Congress).*

drown the man-o'-war in a raking fire, did not have their guns sufficiently depressed to hit anything. Consequently, the Tennesseans' shot and shell all flew over her masts. Captain's Clerk Edward Bacon recorded his impressions: "We were immediately under fire, but the enemy seemed to have been frightened last time [June 28] and replied very poorly, their shot flying over us, as their guns Were not enough depressed. Of course we at once answered with all our port Battery, giving them a dose of 5" [5-second fused] shell and then shrapnel, [and] on we came. Our next shot was from the town which was crammed with musketeers and field pieces."

As the *Iroquois* passed the encampment, she "gave them grape and canister." At some point, she was hit by a 6-pdr. shot from a field gun, which, though not serious, "cut a hole in our bow between wind and water." Mostly, her crew was irritated by the Rebel musket balls, which were "thick as mosquitoes in this Western paradise." Cmdr. Alden later wrote in the journal he kept aboard *Richmond*: "Such a shower of missiles as came around us never was seen before." The big sloop-of-war roared out a broadside of shrapnel. "That was the last we heard of them," Alden noted.

In the twilight, lookouts aboard the *Brooklyn* spied the *Iroquois*, followed by the *Oneida*, passing the head of the Davis line and rounding De Soto Point. From their posts high in the rigging, the Rebel upper batteries across the river at Vicksburg appeared to the observant sailors to be "very lively." Ashore civilians and nonengaged military personnel alike scrambled to find protection wherever possible from this sudden onslaught. Pvt. John S. Jackman of the 5th (later 9th) Kentucky Regiment tells us that he and his company first learned of the upper fleet descent when "one of those long conical shells 2 feet in length, and 10 inches in diameter came shrieking in just over our heads, making something [like] the noise of a man screaming in agony." "Soon," he added, "the fight became general."

When Capt. Bell saw the *Iroquois*, he immediately ordered the *Brooklyn* to move up to the advanced left bank out from the position of Cmdr. Renshaw's mortar schooners. Given that her broadsides could not be brought to bear, she began to play her two bow rifles on the closest Confederate guns. The *Westfield*, on her starboard quarter, did likewise. Both craft eventually assumed positions close-in on the left bank to get out of the way of Farragut's descending columns.

Having been beat to quarters when Davis' duel with the upper batteries commenced, the men of the *Arkansas*, once more stripped to their bare essentials, prepared for what Lt. Gift called a "death struggle." The sun, sinking as it was, partially hid the Federal vessels from the Confederate gunners, though, fortunately, it also hid the rust-colored armorclad against the red bank behind. On the order of Cmdr. Brown, the Southern craft now raised all of what little steam pressure was possible.

Lookouts aboard the *Arkansas* noticed, as the sun sat, a pair of dual-level white lights emanating from across the river. It was determined that this was a U.S. Army range light, "evidently intended to point out our position." Not wishing to cooperate, the armorclad, unnoticed by the bluecoats, shifted her moorings several hundred yards further south into deeper shadow.

As it grew darker Federal troops along the Louisiana shore lit an increasingly larger number of bonfires to help guide the USN vessels. As it turned out, these would, in fact, have the opposite effect, outlining the Union ships for the *Arkansas* gunners.

Farragut's fleet, Gift and his colleagues believed, was coming down to "drag out, and literally mob us" while Davis' ironclads kept the Tennessee and Louisiana gunners ashore occupied. Veterans aboard the *Arkansas* did not have a great deal of confidence in those artillerymen. While the boat was under their guns, "we had as well have been hundreds of miles from there." The land batteries "were perched on the high hills; they were not provided with sights, and if ever they hit anything, it was an accident."

Feisty Cmdr. Brown, having inspected the engine work completed by Chief Engineer George City and his assistants, believed it would be possible for the *Arkansas*, "unfit as we were for the offensive," to give battle. To that end, Lt. Stevens was ordered to get underway and run the armorclad "out into the midst of the coming fleet."

When the oceangoing Union warships from above closed nearer the city, coming fully into range, the eastern column swung left to within 30 yards of the riverbank in order to attack the *Arkansas*. In passing, they would pour rapid broadsides into the Confederate water batteries, hoping to also hit the ram. Pvt. John S. Jackman later noted in his diary that the Federal "fleet vomited forth iron and flame; our batteries thundered, making the earth tremble." He went on to note that "hot shot from the fleet were flying through the air, mimicking the fork-tongued lightning, and the flash of artillery, made the night as light as day." Lookouts aboard the *Arkansas* called out details of Farragut's maneuver to Cmdr.

Brown. He in turn warned Lt. Stevens to get ready. The guns were once more treated to the spirit level; they would fire straight ahead in the same manner as when the boat passed through the combined fleet that morning.

Continuing on down, the *Iroquois* came abreast of Vicksburg where the resistance was more formidable. Volleys of musketry and cannon fire were again answered with grape and shrapnel from her 50-pdr. and two 32-pdrs., though serious damage was yet to be recorded. The 2nd class sloop-of-war continued on, now passing the lower hill batteries, which "raked high over our heads."

From his main deck lookout point, Captain's Clerk Edward S. Bacon believed he saw the *Arkansas* and so informed Capt. Palmer. She was reflected, so he later wrote home, by "the flash of our guns, but she did not seem to fire and appeared dead." It was anticipated that the vessel would turn and attempt to ram the Confederate. At this point, Bacon reports, the vessel's tired "screw suddenly turned more slowly, stopped — and made some effort, and then refused to move." For the next 20 minutes, the *Iroquois* drifted with the current, the "never trustworthy" engines having "failed us in our greatest need."

As the night was deepening, the Confederate fire proved even less effective, and the *Iroquois* captain was able to take "no concern" from it. His guns replied as opportunity presented itself and, as aboard all of the other ships making the run, marines and sailors lined the rails and perched in the tops, attempting to return Rebel musketry with riflery of their own.

This time was terrifying for everyone involved, though some faced the dangers with more courage than others. Clerk Bacon remembers that he "pulled a miserable little powderboy out from under a lot of spars, stowed alongside our smoke stack, who was actually terrified." And, he confirms, "there were a few others who were in a similar state." With her other lookouts unable to see the *Arkansas* in the dark due to the camouflage of her color against a similar background, the Federal ship moved past her, failing to aim any shots specifically in her direction. Bacon later lamented: "Instead of capturing the Ram, we drifted down stream subject to any attack she might wish to make, had she herself not been disabled."

"The darkness which partially shrouded them [the Federals] from the view of the army gunners," remembered Lt. Gift, "completely shut us out from their sight ... consequently, the first notice they had of our whereabouts came from our guns as they crossed our line of fire, and then it was too late to attempt to check up and undertake to grapple with us." The night, in fact, so shielded the Northerners crews aboard Farragut's vessels that the Rebel batteries fired wildly and "we learned to disregard their shot."

The Union vessels continued along in file. As Master's Mate John Wilson later reported, the bow and port side batteries of the Confederate armorclad pumped out shells "when they began passing our line of fire." As each, in turn, would be "punished," as an officer put it, "our men were again feeling in excellent spirits."

By now, the proud *Iroquois* had come abreast of the lower water batteries manned by the Louisiana gunners and what was supposed "might be the ironclad ram." It was impossible, given the color of the Confederate ram and the background of the shore behind her, to tell for certain. In any event, all of these guns opened upon his ship and Palmer returned the compliment with solid shot.

Below the town, Capt. Bell aboard the *Brooklyn* noticed that all of the Confederate land batteries were "in full play." Additionally, so too was the *Arkansas*, "her position being marked before dark, and her fire appearing low down on the water and pointed upstream."

Actually, the ram had moved some yards downriver from where the range light had earlier attempted to point her out.

By the time the *Iroquois* was below the Rebel line of fire, the engine was temporarily repaired and restarted. Thinking he might be able to be of assistance to the *Hartford* behind him, Palmer rounded to and headed back toward the batteries. At some point, he learned that Farragut had slipped by his drifting vessel in the darkness and was, in fact, already anchored below. The *Iroquois* joined her shortly thereafter. The leading vessel of the eastern column that, in the end, did not lead was also very lucky. Despite being under rather heavy fire, no one was killed or wounded aboard and she was not damaged, "with the exception of a 6-pound shell fired from a fieldpiece, left sticking in our side between wind and water."

Per the staggered Federal columns, Cmdr. John De Camp's *Wissahickon*, of the western column, continued the dual with the Rebel armorclad. Like those aboard the *Iroquois*, her "gunners were," wrote Lt. Gift, "guided solely by the flash of our guns, as we were almost invisible in the darkness." It is unknown exactly how the Federal gunboat fought or fared as she swept downstream; Flag Officer Farragut would report next day that a sailor aboard was killed and four wounded.

For now, as the last engine adjustments were completed, the ram's big guns would have to speak from the riverbank. Cmdr. Brown still hoped to move out and give battle, but the craft was not quite mechanically ready.

The *Sumter* slipped by next, firing perhaps not at all. Nevertheless, the Union ram was hit twice below her armor guard and her crew, according to Flag Officer Farragut in a letter to Flag Officer Davis, "had some trouble to stop the leak." This was in contrast to stories in several Northern newspapers, which reported that the *Sumter* "ran into her and tried to knock a hole in her hull, but seemingly might as well have run into a rock."

Cmdr. Lee, the same man who had initially requested Vicksburg's surrender back in May, opened fire on the upper batteries at 7:30 P.M. Emptying stands of grape and 5-second fused shells from her port-side 32-pdrs and his 11-inch Dahlgren, the *Oneida* blasted away at both the entrenched Rebel cannon and butternut infantry, firing from rifle pits dug along the shore. Whether or not Cmdr. Lee viewed the drifting of the *Iroquois* ahead as a purposeful maneuver, he ordered his vessel's engine cut as she passed near the east bank and floated past Vicksburg looking for the *Arkansas* and a wharf boat. The "iron monster," as a diarist aboard called her, was reported to be lying within about 300 yards of the quay. Attentive lookouts did, indeed, spot the wharf boat, and a couple of hundred yards beyond, cannon fire was seen at riverbank level. The Maryland-born captain correctly guessed, alone as it turned out among all of Farragut's captains that night, the location of the dreaded Rebel ram.

As the *Oneida* approached the *Arkansas*, Lee's 50-pdr. Dahlgren rifle began pumping the first of 16 solid bolts toward the enemy gun flashes and, getting closer, two giant sold cannonballs from her 11-inch smoothbore. One of the latter scored a serious hit. Many of the Northern vessels appeared similar in the darkness and smoke. Gift believed it was the *Hartford* that loosed the telling shot, while Lt. Read swore it was the *Richmond*. Neither was armed with 11-inch guns.

The *Oneida*'s 160-lb. solid shot smashed into the port side of the *Arkansas* a few inches above her waterline, forcing her to shudder and shake. Entering the berth deck, the ball ploughed through the dispensary across from the engine room, destroying the ship's medicines, and, in fact, somehow carrying a portion of them into the engine room. Capt. Brown remarked later that, "fortunately, our surgeon, Dr. Washington, was just then away from his medicines." The sickbay was also wrecked.

With a cloud of splinters and iron fragments, the great sphere passed through the engine room, destroyed the berth of Chief Engineer City, and grazed the chimney. More seriously, it dismounted at least one (possibly both) of the engines before careening clear across the deck, imbedding itself so deeply "between the woodwork and the armor" in the opposite side of the casemate that its location could, at dawn, be "told by the bulging protuberance outside." Some of the men called it a "blister."

Lee's missile also caused a serious leak. Lt. Stevens immediately organized a damage control party, which, under the direction of the ship's carpenter, shortly contained that threat with mattresses. Splinters from the side and miscellaneous debris from the bulkheads further damaged the machinery. Admiral Mahan reveals that the *Oneida* also set "fire to her cotton bulwarks," though this is unconfirmed by other sources.

These blows against the hull and engines prevented the armorclad from, as her captain wanted, setting forth to seek battle. But, as his biographer, Charles Getchell, pointed out in 1978, Brown, at the same time, "escaped having his craft rammed by either the *Hartford* or the *Richmond*." This one round not only damaged the *Arkansas* materially but also played havoc among her few remaining crew members. Two men in the engine room were killed and three others were wounded. Topside, Pilot Brady was knocked overboard; luckily, he was able to swim back to shore. And then there was William Gilmore.

Having threatened to avoid any future engagement, the pilot remained below as Farragut's fleet started to pass, eschewing a chance to join Brown, Brady, and the injured Lt. Gift topside. When the *Oneida*'s shell slammed in, it struck him in the middle of the head. Pvt. Tom Hall, who later helped with burials at Vicksburg and had known the Jonesville, Kentucky, native earlier, wrote in the May 1897 issue of *Confederate Veteran* that the shot completely carried "away the upper part of his body and the lower limbs dropped back into the gun room limp." Lt. Gift later noted that Gilmore's mangled body was "collected in pieces" and placed out of the way under a cover.

Continuing to observe the approaching big ship parade from his bridge aboard the *Brooklyn*, Capt. Bell recalled that "darkness and smoke wrapped in all the vessels for a while 'til they began to emerge below." Having completed her passage, the *Oneida* dropped anchor below the town. No one aboard the vessel was hurt and Cmdr. Lee, although he did not say so in his report, had a fairly good idea that he might have struck the *Arkansas*. The boat's diarist was adamant that the *Richmond* was definitely not responsible for any injuries sustained by the Rebel ram.

A check of the *Oneida*'s magazine revealed use of the two solid shot from his 11-inch smoothbores (believed to have been expended "at the ram"), along with six 5-second fused shells and nine stands of grape. The gunners of the 50-pdr. Dahlgren expended 16 bolts and a shell, while the 32-pdrs. shot 10 5-second fused shells, a stand of grape, and two cannonballs whizzing toward unknown targets.

Although mistaken as to the perpetrator of the 11-inch greeting, the gunners of the Confederate ram offered stiff punishment to the *Hartford* of the western column for the sins of the *Oneida*. The gun deck crews of the *Arkansas* were not directly impacted by the damages suffered below. Consequently, the bow and port-side guns were still rapidly, if individually, served on the passing Federal vessels. The Union ships, even those in the outer ranks, were close. Indeed, wrote Cmdr. Brown 20 years later, "So close were these to our guns that we could hear our shot crashing through their sides, and the groans of their wounded." "Incredible as it now seems," he continued," these sounds were heard with fierce delight by the *Arkansas'* people."

Cmdr. Richard Wainwright, in his official report, was succinct regarding the actions of Farragut's flagship once the upper batteries had opened upon her and during her subsequent passage downstream: "We returned their fire as soon as our guns would bear, and continued firing without intermission at batteries, ram, and riflemen until we anchored below the town."

With Lt. Gift topside, Midshipman Scales commanded the forward port battery comprising one of the Columbiads and a 9-inch Dahlgren smoothbore. The latter was most likely the very gun to which army lieutenant Robert Ballard Mathews and his men were assigned earlier in the day. Gift could hear his young colleague distinctly down the pilothouse ladder: "On our gun deck every man and officer worked as though the fate of the nation hung on his individual efforts. Scales was very near, and I could hear his clear voice continually. He coaxed and bullied alternately, and, finally, when he saw his object in line, his voice rose as clear as a bell, and his 'ready! Fire!' rang out like a bugle note."

As the *Hartford* passed, engaging with her port battery, she was struck in the hull several times. Cmdr. Wainwright reported that a 9-inch shell "that did not explode carried away our starboard fore-topsail sheet bitts on the berth deck." This was most likely from the Scales/Mathews piece aboard the *Arkansas*. Wrote an observer from the gundeck: "The rebels seemed, as usual, to concentrate all their fire on the 'Old *Hartford*.'" Yeoman William C. Holton remembered that they never did "discover the ram, which had been secreted behind a huge wharfboat."

Although the sloop-of-war's hull and rigging were not badly cut up, the crew was. Master's Mate George Lounsberry from New York and two ratings were killed, while four sailors or firemen and two marines, including Capt. John Broome, were wounded. Third Engineer John K. Fulton, writing to his father, Charles, proprietor of the *Baltimore American*, later indicated that his friend Lounsberry, a "clever fellow" normally stationed next to him on the spar deck, had been assigned to the flagship's berth deck to replace a sick officer.

Moving slowly, the *Richmond*, next to face the Confederate batteries and the *Arkansas*, "drifted down with the current." Opening initially with her bow guns, the sloop-of-war "soon got the range with our broadside guns when we let them have it." One broadside after another broadside was poured in until the giant warship was below the city. Cmdr. James Alden's official after action report was briefer even than Cmdr. Wainwright's: "Everyone on board behaved well. A careful lookout was kept for the ram as we passed, but owing to the obscurity of the night, we could not make her out." In his journal, Alden later commented upon the difficulty of locating the enemy. "We could not see anything of the rebel ram as we came down," he explained, "although we were not more than 30 yards from the shore, not one on board of us could see her. We must have passed her in the smoke."

In addition to the huge swirling clouds of black smoke that blanketed the combat arena, just as it had that morning, gunners aboard the Union ships were no doubt distracted, to say the least, by the Confederate shore batteries. These poured forth their angry shots in huge quantity and with great rapidity. The sky was alive with shells and bolts, with explosions making the sky red or yellow.

Although only two men aboard were slightly wounded by splinters, the *Richmond* took quite a pounding from Rebel land-based defenders as she passed. Most of this was not serious. At least three 6-pdr. shot hit near gun ports, the port side near the waterline, or the captain's cabin. Five grapeshot struck the side of the ship between gun ports 11 and 13. A

USS Hartford. *Throughout the afternoon of July 15, units of the Federal upper squadron were hastily making preparation to return below Vicksburg at sundown and hoping to destroy the* Arkansas *while en route. A unique plan was put into place aboard the flagship* Hartford, *as an immense anchor was safely triced out on the end of her main yard. Farragut's thought was to run up alongside the* Arkansas *and, if his broadsides wouldn't faze her, to drop that anchor from its lofty perch. If all went right, it would surely carry the armorclad with it to the bottom of the river. Additionally, grappling irons were hung from the crossjack yards. These would be dropped on the* Arkansas *if the opportunity presented itself, perhaps allowing the enemy to be boarded (U.S. Army Military History Institute).*

missile from the *Arkansas*' port-side Dahlgren smashed through the port side into the berth deck under gun port 3 and continued into the ceiling. Yards and rigging were hit and "a large number of bullets struck and lodged in the side."

Cmdr. Brown sensed that his huge opponents could not see him and that in the darkness the *Arkansas* may have resembled just another water battery. Otherwise, he later wondered, "Why no attempt was made to ram our vessel, I do not know. Our position invited it, and our rapid firing made that position conspicuous." Still, the captain of the armorclad also knew that he "had greatly the advantage in pointing our guns, the enemy passing inline ahead, and being distinctly visible as each one for the time shut out our view of the horizon."

As the *Richmond* reached the end of the gauntlet, she received three cheers from the crew of the *Brooklyn*, which salute was returned. The mortar schooners also offered huzzahs thrice, which were also returned. Farragut's largest warships were past the ram's location. "For a long interval the ram did not fire at all," Capt. Bell noted from the *Brooklyn*, "and hopes sprang up that she had been rammed, but at the very close, his fire opened again for one or two broadsides after our vessels had passed."

The Confederate guns attempted to hit the passing Federal vessels with little luck, shooting as best they could in the dark. "The roar of the guns was like an earthquake,"

USS *Iroquois*. *Leading a column in the night passage downstream from above Vicksburg, this 1,488-ton second-class sloop-of-war was the third largest Federal ship present to fight the* Arkansas. *Launched in April 1859 and commissioned seven months later, this sister of the* Oneida *and the famous* Kearsarge *was 198.10 feet long, with a beam of 33.10 feet and a 13-foot draft. Powered by one screw and sails, she had a complement of 123 and was armed with two 11-inch Dahlgren SBs, four 32-pdrs., one 50-pdr. Dahlgren rifle, and a 12-pdr. Dahlgren howitzer. Unfortunately, as she was abreast of the city's defenses, the big ship's engine quit, forcing her to drift downstream out of battle (U.S. Army Military History Institute).*

reported a correspondent from Brooklyn, "and nothing more terrific ever was conceived than this grand artillery duel by night."

Pvt. Isaac A. Walker and his buddies from Co. C ("Rapides Terribles") of the 27th Louisiana Infantry were on guard duty in Vicksburg when the "balls and shells" began to fly around "thick as hale [*sic*]." Though Walker was safe, "we got two men kild." "Sound and fury," as the Shakespearean verse goes.

Shells from passing Union warships set fire to a number of buildings back of the Vicksburg bluff. *Chicago Daily Tribune* reporter Bodman told his readers that the conflagration cast "a lurid glare, giving a reddish tint to the dense volumes of smoke, which rolled up all around and forming with the incessant din of the battle, an effect which must have been seen to be appreciated." "To heighten the grand scene," recorded Pvt. John S. Jackman of the 5th (later 9th) Kentucky Regiment, "some buildings up-town took fire from hot missiles." As a result, "a pillar of flames pierced the very heavens."

Now, only three gunboats were yet to come down. From his location topside with Cmdr. Brown, Lt. Gift was able to see the first of these, the *Winona*, as "she got one of our shots in her outboard delivery." Having sortied fourth in line in the outer column behind the *Hartford*, the *Winona*, Lt. Edward T. ("Bricktop") Nichols commanding, also endured the heavy Rebel fire from numerous batteries and rifle pits. Although her port and starboard howitzers sprayed the enemy rifle pits with shrapnel, she was able to fire her big 11-inch gun only three times before she was blasted in passing by the *Arkansas*. It is not known for

Nine: Surviving Farragut's Charge: Night, July 15, 1862

USS *Oneida*. *The 1,032-ton* Oneida, *sister of the* Iroquois *and also of the famous* Kearsarge, *was launched in November 1861 and commissioned by Cmdr. Samuel Phillips Lee in February 1862. With dimensions and armament identical to her sister, she had two boilers, one less than the* Iroquois. *As the ship approached the* Arkansas *during Farragut's night passage below Vicksburg, Lee's 50-pdr. Dahlgren rifle began pumping the first of 16 solid bolts toward the enemy gun flashes and, getting closer, two giant solid cannonballs from her 11-inch smoothbore. One of the latter scored a serious hit. Many of the Northern vessels appeared similar in the darkness and smoke. Aboard the armorclad, Lt. Gift believed it was the* Hartford *that loosed the telling shot, while Lt. Read swore it was the* Richmond. *Neither boat was, however, armed with 11-inch guns. No useful photograph of the* Oneida, *wrecked off Japan in 1870, has come to hand; however, this profile of the* Kearsarge *will give the reader a good idea of her appearance (Navy History and Heritage Command).*

certain which of the Confederate ram's big guns did the deed, but one of them put a shell into the gunboat's side just above the waterline, destroying the outboard delivery valve chamber and rendering her engines useless. The shot started a heavy leak, necessitating the immediate start of the deck pumps, which could not contain the rush of water.

Meanwhile, two more Southern bolts assaulted the *Winona*. The most telling of the pair was a shell burst above the 11-inch gun that sent shrapnel into the gun crew, killing one man and wounding two others. Hoping to raise the *Winona*'s leak out of the river, Lt. Nichols ran in and pivoted his 11-inch gun to starboard. When this maneuver did not work, he immediately ordered the wheeled port-side howitzer shifted over, along with all of the shot and shell from that side. With the gunboat thus heeled over, the leak was kept just above water, allowing Nichols' vessel to limp down toward the lower fleet's old anchorage below Vicksburg.

Lt. Reigart Lowry drove the *Sciota* into the fire after the *Winona*. To combat the many

USS *Richmond*. Moving slowly, the Richmond *"drifted down with the current,"* until she could face the Confederate batteries and the Arkansas. Opening initially with her bow guns, the sloop-of-war *"soon got the range with our broadside guns when we let them have it."* One broadside after another broadside was poured in until the giant warship was below the city. Cmdr. James Alden's official after action report was brief: *"Everyone on board behaved well. A careful lookout was kept for the ram as we passed, but owing to the obscurity of the night, we could not make her out"* (Top, Navy History and Heritage Command; bottom, U.S. Army Military History Institute).

Confederate sharpshooters concealed in rifle pits along the banks and back in the woods near the upper batteries, he called upon his disabled officers and men for help. The gunboat had a significant percentage of crewmen, hurt or fevered, who did not have the strength to man the big guns but "zealously used their little strength to annoy the enemy by a return fire of musketry."

Initially refraining from the use of his 11-inch gun, Lowry had his 24-pounder howitzers worked rapidly, throwing shrapnel into the butternut troops. These were seen "to burst with good range and effect." A heavy plunging shot from the hill fort "struck under the port bow," grazing the side of the hull but doing no damage.

The *Sciota* came abreast of Vicksburg and continued down. The *Arkansas* was not distinctly seen in the dark, but as the Federal boat passed, she was taken under fire from a battery "at or near the level with the water." A shell from this source, assumed to be the Confederate ram, slammed into her side and continued across, smashing boat davits, timbers, and other items en route. Several grapeshot also passed through the ship without causing harm. The gunboat's surgeon reported only two men wounded and, in due time, she anchored below with Farragut's other vessels. She was duly followed by the *Pinola*, the last of the lower fleet units to return from the squadron anchorage north of Vicksburg.

From start to finish, Farragut's vessels ran the Confederate gauntlet in about an hour. Never again would a squadron under this admiral appear above Vicksburg. When the shooting died down, the Kentucky diarist, Pvt. John S. Jackman waxed eloquently. "As the storm cloud passes, so did this," he wrote. "Soon a perfect silence brooded over the city, and we went to sleep. I hardly think the firing lasted an hour."

After visiting about the boat, Lt. Gift summed up the situation aboard the *Arkansas*: "We had more dead and wounded, another hole through our armor, and heaps of splinters and rubbish. Three separate battles had been fought and we retired to anything but easy repose." He specifically failed to note that the engine room was a mess and that any hope of moving back out into the river would have to wait until after the power plant situation was addressed.

Lt. Mathews, on behalf of his Cobb's Battery volunteers, approached Lt. Stevens to ask if their services were further required. The artilleryman was taken to Capt. Brown, who admitted there was no further need for their services that night and expressed his gratitude for the help. There followed a brief confusion over an alleged unexcused absence. Neither Brown nor the visiting Clifton Rodes Breckenridge (1846–1932), son and aide to the general and a future CSN midshipman (and noted Arkansas politician), had the evening's countersign. Breckenridge agreed to be escort for Mathews and his men ashore that night, agreeing that he would help them clear up the identity matter next morning. Sure enough, word reached the headquarters of Maj. Gen. Breckenridge that "the lieutenant and men who volunteered and went on board the *Arkansas*" had deserted. An investigation was launched down the chain of command through the divisional brigades to the headquarters of Cobb's Battery.

After Mathews, Breckenridge, and the men were ashore, Cmdr. Brown sadly added: "And now this busy day, the 15th of July 1862, was closed with the sad duty of sending ashore a second party of killed and wounded." It consisted, added Master's Mate John William, himself hurt a third time, of eight dead at the guns and 11 wounded, several of the latter mortally. A complete list of the dead and wounded aboard the ram that day was forwarded by Cmdr. Brown to Flag Officer Lynch at Jackson the following morning. It is published in Volume 19 of the Navy *Official Records*. Of the dead in addition to Pilot

Gilmore, William Perry, captain of the forecastle, and two others were regular CSN sailors and one was a fireman; five were Louisiana soldiers; and four were Missouri volunteers.

Damages were minimal to the ships of the Federal lower fleet during their return passage downstream, just as they were on the way up three weeks earlier. Flag Officer Farragut reported that, during the day, five sailors were killed and 16 wounded. He also admitted that, due to the late start, it was too dark "when we got off the town" to see the *Arkansas*. "I looked with all the eyes in my head to no purpose," he confessed. "We could see nothing but the flash of the enemy's guns to fire at." All of the descending Federal vessels were safely anchored below Vicksburg by 9:00 P.M., the "main brace was spliced" and night watches set. Fires in the town caused by exploding shells now intensified and were witnessed from aboard the ships.

At this point, Flag Officer Farragut called all of his captains to a meeting aboard the *Hartford*. Going around the room to see if his subordinates could report success, the Tennessee-born commander was crestfallen when none did. "No one of his fleet saw the ram in their descent," Capt. Bell wrote in his journal, "although everyone was on the lookout for her." Expressing "deep mortification and vexation at his failure," Farragut swore he "would have given his commission to have had a crack at her." He told his assembled captains, in no uncertain terms, that he should not have listened to them or Davis. Failure to kill the ram was caused by holding back from a late morning attack and by the "unlooked for delay in starting" down before sunset. They would have to resolutely go after the *Arkansas*, Farragut was remembered as saying. She had to "be destroyed or she will destroy us." First thing in the morning, scouts would be dispatched to check for visible damage.

Aboard the *Arkansas*, the exhausted crew sought the solace of sleep. Adrenaline had kept them going since the middle of the previous night, but now, for most, the need to collapse had come. As many as possible lay out on the deck or atop the casemate seeking a night breeze. Those who couldn't drop off probably wondered what carnage was ahead. Others, observing the red sky, may only have prayed for rain.[9]

CHAPTER TEN

Arkansas vs. *Essex*, Round One: July 16–22, 1862

The Confederate ironclad ram *Arkansas* survived three stiff fights with U.S. Navy forces on July 15. In the first, she pushed aside the Pook turtle *Carondelet* and pursued two lesser craft out of the Yazoo River into the Mississippi. Upon reaching the great stream, she headed for Vicksburg, running through a combined gauntlet of warships under the command of Flag Officers David G. Farragut and Charles H. Davis. A few hours after docking, she was subjected to an unsuccessful night attack, when that portion of Farragut's fleet encountered above the city in the morning returned below it in the dark.

The successful breakout of the *Arkansas* from the backwaters of the Yazoo was a great morale boost to the South. Citizens and soldiers from Vicksburg to Richmond and Charleston basked in the glory achieved by Lt. (now Cmdr.) Isaac Newton Brown and his determined crew. The opposite was the case throughout the Union. Fanned by stories in Federal newspapers, Farragut, Davis, and navy secretary Gideon Welles, to name three, were stung and embarrassed. Welles would confide in his private diary that "the most disreputable naval affair of the War was the descent of the steam ram *Arkansas* through both squadrons 'til she hauled in under the batteries of Vicksburg."[1]

Following a blustery night, July 16 dawned stormy, wet and still windy. Indeed, great thunderstorms would lash the Vicksburg area throughout the day. Thick clouds offered both lightning and cooling rain.

As was now the case every evening, Rebel pickets were posted along the riverbank below the town to watch for Federal raiders intent upon crossing. The usual practice, according to Pvt. John S. Jackman of the 5th (later 9th) Kentucky Regiment, was to space out the men about 60 yards apart, giving them orders to secret themselves "but watch vigilantly."

At dawn, a Federal reconnaissance party was dispatched down the Louisiana bank to a point where the *Arkansas* could be seen across the water. Among its members were two men from the *Carondelet* who were intimately acquainted with the ram: First Master Edward E. Brennand, who was slightly injured, and Pilot John Deming. The *Arkansas*, wrote William E. Webb of the *St. Louis Daily Missouri Republican*, "keeps up steam and is very busy repairing." The scouts, several of whom may have talked to the reporter, observed nine holes in her side, "none of which, however, seemed greatly to have impaired her fighting qualities." The places where she had been struck by cannonballs "were indicated by bright, glistening spots, and literally dotted with them." Having taken additional notes, the party returned through the rain, went aboard the *Benton*, and reported.

In addition to the visible damage, it appeared, the recon team reported that the Confederate warship was careened "as if to stop the holes in her hull," and her steam pumps were at work. It did not look to the observers, however, as though the ram was in any immediate danger of sinking. A barge lay alongside her for use by carpenters who were repairing her casemate. Perhaps the most startling sight was the chimney of the *Arkansas*. It "was so completely riddled that it could only be repaired by sheathing."

Flag Officer Davis, who had probably had his fill of rams by now, reviewed the Rebel boat's success in a message to Secretary Welles. Although the Bohemian Brigade men of the press were engaging, as Webb had it, in "much speculation in regards to the *Arkansas*," the hero of the Battle of Memphis did not believe that the damaged Confederate posed a significant or immediate problem. "The *Arkansas* is harmless in her present position," he would tell his colleagues, "and will be more easily destroyed should she come out from under the batteries than while enjoying their protection."

At this point, Third Engineer John K. Fulton, writing to his father from aboard the lower fleet flagship, *Hartford*, summed up the Federal situation. "All of Commodore Davis' vessels, except the captured steamer *Sumter*, are," he reported, "still above the city to prevent the ram from going up, and all of our fleet are lying below with steam up, ready for action at a moment's notice."[2]

Following a let-up in the morning rain and not long after Davis heard from his scouts, Flag Officer Farragut summoned Cmdr. Henry H. Bell, captain of the *Brooklyn*, and Lt. Henry Erben (1832–1909),[3] commander of the *Sumter*, aboard the *Hartford* for a conference. The two men were joined by Cmdr. John Alden of the *Richmond*, John De Camp of the *Wissahickon*, and William B. Renshaw, captain of the *Westfield* and commander of the five mortar schooners below the town.

The flag officer's captains were informed that, after dark, he wanted to take the three sloops-of-war, accompanied by the *Sumter*, up and "have another go" at the *Arkansas*. Each was asked his opinion. Cmdr. Bell and Alden were both blunt in their responses. The former favored a day attack because the night was so uncertain and the *Arkansas* so invisible. Alden said the responsibility for combating the Rebel was Davis' because he had the ironclads and departed, promising to do whatever Farragut and Bell determined.

As Cmdr. Bell put it, Lt. Erben, more or less a seconded officer, "remembered that his delivery pipe was broken and could not participate until it was repaired." Farragut immediately ordered that a wagon, with Erben as passenger, be driven across the peninsula to Flag Officer Davis with a request for a replacement. While it was readied, he sat down and wrote a letter to his upper river opposite number for the lieutenant to deliver.

Farragut could not control Davis, so he determined to attempt to persuade him by message to join in or at least support another assault on the *Arkansas*. The urgency was reinforced, he would confess, because he could "see her now very plainly by spyglass." The sight was extremely galling and worrisome, making his mission crystal clear: "she must not have a chance to repair." Although the ram was "getting her steam up," the flag officer could not determine "whether she means to come down or not."

This letter to Davis was the first of several to be exchanged between the two men over the next couple of days. Following a brief summary of the previous night's passage downstream and a request for help in obtaining supplies of coal, Farragut announced his attention to chance another night attack that evening with his three largest vessels. "I will continue to take chances or try to destroy her until my squadron is destroyed," he warmed, "or she is." Maybe, he hinted, it would be possible for Davis to spare Cmdr. William D. Porter and the powerful *Essex* for a night attack. "He could do it," Farragut thought, "without risk of the batteries." Whatever was decided, he closed: "While this is on my mind, I can not rest."

Seeing the waiting Lt. Erben off, Flag Officer Farragut next passed orders for Cmdr. William B. Renshaw to take the ram under fire with the huge 13-inch mounts aboard his flotilla of mortar schooners. Lt. Charles W. Read, an *Arkansas* officer, mistakenly tells us this occurred beginning at 9:00 A.M., but it did not. Unhappily, as Farragut confessed to Flag Officer Davis next day, it was found, by the time the "bombers" were deployed through the rain, that "my mortars cannot reach her or that part of the town without going under fire of the batteries." They would hold off. Meanwhile, every available spyglass remained busy tracking the armorclad's activities.

While workmen from Vicksburg and available crewmen labored to mend the armorclad's damages, halting only when the squalls were most fierce, engineers toiled over the craft's power plant. They were able to get up steam by about 10:30 A.M. and great puffs of black smoke poured out of the colander that passed for a chimney, much to the delight of all Southern witnesses. Northern bluejackets, from Farragut down, were depressed and, not knowing the exhaust represented tests only at this point, became alarmed. Lookouts aboard the *Hartford* and other vessels of the lower fleet saw this activity and cleared for action. Crewmen aboard several of the mortar boats of Flag Officer Davis also saw her "lying close to the shore at Vicksburg this morning with steam up."

In an effort to convince the Federals that his ram was fully operational, Cmdr. Brown had more success than just raising steam. Keeping the Federals on their toes, he conveyed the idea that his craft was not so badly damaged by ordering the *Arkansas* to make several mini-cruises up and down the river during the afternoon. As would be the case for the next week or so, "as soon as smoke began pouring from the ram's well-patched stack," offered historian Robert Huffstot, "one fleet or the other was forced to fire up in answer to the threat." None of her feints progressed far beyond the protection of Vicksburg's cannon.

During the 4:00 P.M.–6:00 P.M. afternoon watch, as recorded in the log of the *Hartford*, "the ram got underway and stood across the river to the point opposite the city." Rounding to, "she stood across to the town." Expecting an attack, the lower fleet flagship, with her consorts, "went to quarters." Shells loaded into broadside batteries were drawn and replaced with solid shot. Having completed her successful De Soto Point sojourn, the *Arkansas* lay to for another stormy night.

Early in the evening, Flag Officer Farragut got off another message to Flag Officer Davis. With foul weather in the offing for another night, it would be impossible for him, as planned, to attack the *Arkansas* "with my three ships only." That being the case, the agitated commander went on to pointedly suggest, along the lines of Cmdr. Alden's earlier expressed thinking, that it was the responsibility of the upper fleet commander, "as you have the ironclad boats," to "cope with the ram better than any wooden vessels."

Warming to his case, the victor of New Orleans went on to outline an audacious plan for a joint attack by the two squadrons the following morning or at whatever "day or hour you suggest." In essence, after meeting off Vicksburg, Farragut's craft would fight the forts, while the *Benton*, *Essex*, and the Pook turtles concentrated on "the destruction of the ram particularly," with the sloops-of-war helping "you occasionally." If this plan were followed, it was believed that the two fleets would be "able to dispose of this ram effectually."

Not long after sunrise on July 17, Flag Officer Davis ordered Capts. Henry E. Maynadier and E.B. Pike to have their mortar boats, anchored at De Soto Point, placed into battery in order to commence an around-the-clock campaign against the ram. From intelligence reports, there was no doubt that she was in range. In a letter home, Davis remarked, as he undoubtedly had to the two army captains, that "we are aiming to destroy the *Arkansas* by the falling bombs."

An effective bombardment was easier requested than done. Of the 130 officers and men assigned to this specialized Northern artillery unit, 100 were ill. The ratio was not quite as high in the gunboats. Aboard the *Benton*, for example, one in four men was sick, while aboard the *Carondelet*, the number was one in two, including Capt. Walke. Still, Maynadier and Pike were able to find about 25 healthy men and finish preparations aboard three boats by noon. As was the case at Fort Pillow back in May, protection was provided by one of the Pook turtle ironclads anchored nearby.

In the meantime, Davis received Farragut's recommendation for a combined attack. His response was as measured as the man himself. Pointing out the possibility of losing the strategic advantages gained on the river since March, the upper fleet commander was equally direct: "I do not think the destruction of the *Arkansas*, without any regard to the consequences to ourselves, would be an object sufficient to justify" the risk. On the other hand, the Western Flotilla boss was "as eager as yourself to put an end to this impudent rascal's existence." To that end, Davis had begun work on his own plan, which could be put into effect sometime after that evening when the *Essex* was able to get up steam. "We should have a good prospect of success to justify our staking upon the hazard of a die all that we have gained," the upper fleet leader penned. That chance would offer itself "without the risk by the patient exercise of vigilance and self-control." This communication was dispatched overland a few minutes before Maynadier's boats set to work.

As the Davis communication made its way across the peninsula, Brig. Gen. Williams was also told that a new operation was afoot. Taking pen in hand, he described it to Maj. Gen. Benjamin F. Butler, commander of the Department of the Gulf: "Another attempt, it is understood, is contemplated today, the ironclads of Commodore Davis to co-operate, and our ram, the *Sumter*, said to be the most formidable. The expectation is that if not destroyed where she lies she will be driven down into Commodore Farragut's fleet and there finished."

While Farragut, Davis, and Williams exchanged communications and the mortar boatmen prepared their mounts, the morning's repair work had already started aboard the *Arkansas*. An observer across the river noted that "he has a long spar rigged across his deck to get out some heavy weight." It was also believed that the ram could "not work his guns or steam." It is probable that this activity revolved around changes that were about to be made to the machinery and armament, or possibly in casemate and deck protection. Master's Mate Eliot Callender of the *Cincinnati* later remembered hearing that she "had but one engine and but four guns that could be served."

While they were at it, the workers brought aboard additional cotton bales to insert in layers along the internal side casemate bulkheads between the gun ports. These were then secured in place, strengthening what was essentially a double bulkhead. *Harper's Weekly* on September 6, 1862, told its readers "the *Arkansas* was plated with railroad iron on the outside, over a planking of six-inch oak; inside that was six inches of condensed cotton on another six inches of oak." The crew of the armorclad, subjected to 13-inch shots from the Union mortar vessels, realized that, if a single round slammed down directly upon their wooden main deck fore or aft of the casemate or on to the lightly covered hurricane deck atop the casemate, they were probably finished. While some may have been fatalistic about their chances, additional topside protection was quickly put in place.

Loose, inch-thick iron bars were laid across the top of the *Arkansas*' exposed outer fore and aft decks, as the vessel's powder magazines and shell rooms were directly below them in the hold. There is no indication any T-bars were found to place atop the casemate roof's boilerplate or on the slanting after shield. How resistant the added deck armor would be was anyone's guess. It has been speculated that a direct hit would probably have penetrated the iron, but its effects might have been localized, minimizing damages below.

The Federals were not the only ones impacted by the current sickly season. According to Lt. Read, when the *Arkansas* started for Vicksburg, most of her seamen, save the Missouri volunteers, "had been on the Yazoo swamps some time, and in consequence were troubled with chills and fever." The ineffectiveness of these sick, together with the wounded removed to hospital earlier, left the ship "very short handed."

Several of the Confederate ram's officers remained aboard in the days after arrival, even though they were sick or hurt themselves. Cmdr. Brown himself continued to suffer with malaria. Though ill to the point of requiring hospitalization, Chief Engineer George City continued to monitor and tinker with the engines along with his assistants. Lt. Gift kept watch and, with Stevens, Grimball, Wharton, and others, helped oversee repairs to the hull and casemate.

As the laborers from town continued to address their shipboard tasks, permission was given to the captain's injured aide, Midshipman Clarence W. Tyler, Third Assistant Engineer William Jackson, and Master's Mate John Wilson to travel to the Cox mansion, 2 miles from town, where, earlier that morning, Pilot Hodges had died. The trio really needed the delayed medical assistance Mrs. Cox, her daughters and her servants could provide. At about the same time, Dr. Washington and Lt. Barbot, who were also ill, were sent to the hospital at Edwards Depot. That facility, which would be burned by Union forces in 1863, was located near the present town of Edwards, two miles west of Jackson and 15 miles east of Vicksburg, on the Alabama & Vicksburg Railroad. Over the next few days, several other officers and assistant engineers would be ordered to the Vicksburg city hospital, including Gunner Thomas Travers.

Wilson remembered his group leaving the *Arkansas* "under a severe shelling from the mortar boats." Lt. Read was another witness who recollected the attack: "As the mortar shells fell with terrible force almost perpendicularly, and as the *Arkansas* was unprotected on upper decks, boilers amidships, a machine and shell room at each end, it was very evident that if she was struck by one of those heavy shells, it would be the last of her. Her moorings were changed frequently to impair the enemy's range, but the enterprising Yankees shelled us continually, their shell often exploding a few feet above decks and sending their fragments into the decks."

Hitting a stationary target the size of the *Arkansas* would not be anywhere near as simple a task as a shore-based gun emplacement, but Capt. Maynadier had been practicing on Southern positions since taking command of the Mortar Flotilla back in February. Consuming at least two hours, his initial bombardment of the Rebel boat was both rapid and surprisingly accurate. "Quite a number [of shells] exploded a few feet above decks, and sent their fragments into the decks," wrote historian J. Thomas Scharf, "and several burst so near under the water as to shake the vessel with earthquake force."

The unpowered Western Flotilla mortar boats — essentially rectangular barges — were about 65 feet long with 25-foot beams. Their sides, pointed at the bow and stern, were each graced with an iron-plated sloped bulwark between six and seven feet high, with those to port and starboard stretched back ¾ of the length. An iron-covered hatch for egress was cut into the stern bulwark. Each bulwark was waterproofed and corked to a height of two feet to allow the craft, which floated at deck level, to survive the tremendous recoil. A canvas covering was available to shield the crew from sun or rain. Occasionally, tents were set up ashore, conditions permitting.

A single iron 17,210-lb., 13-inch seacoast mortar was mounted in the center of the reinforced deck of each boat; the entire Rodman mortar bed carriage weighed 4,500 pounds. This weight, added to the boat's center reinforcement of layers of logs laid at right angles to each other, increased the overall heaviness of each craft to 13 tons. Eight small chambers held the powder and shot; the shells were loaded into the muzzle via a small derrick. The full charge of powder required to launch the giant 204-lb. hollow bullet from an elevation of 41 degrees to its extreme range of 3.5 miles was 23 pounds. Lesser amounts of propellant and elevation would shorten the range. The shells themselves were each loaded with seven pounds of gunpowder and cost $15.

The craft had initially been tested off Cairo, Illinois, on February 9 and the results, witnessed by *St. Louis Missouri Democrat* reporter George W. Beaman, were exciting, promising, and potentially as dangerous for the crews as for the enemy. The noise and concussion from the firing was shocking, made more so by the bulkheads. During one of the trial shots using only a 15-lb. powder charge, "the cap of the gunner was carried away from his head and he was almost taken off his feet."

In practice, the crew loaded the mortar, left through an escape hatch onto the rear part of the deck, and fired the mount by yanking a lanyard, not forgetting to put their hands over their ears and flex their knees against the concussion. The repeated blasts caused the middle of the boats to settle and the ends to rise, thereby causing them to fill with water. After two or three shots, only the buoyancy of the boats' solid timber centers kept them afloat until they could be bailed out. In a letter written years later, found and quoted by J. Thomas Campbell, Midshipman Dabney Scales wrote to Read: "I remember you as you look as watch officer pacing the quarter-deck of the *Arkansas* alongside the levee at Vicksburg under the terrific shelling from the mortar boats. The indomitable coolness with which you watched the great mortar shells as they fell with a shriek and splash in the narrow strip of water between the vessel's magazine and the shore."

During this first session, the 13-inch mortars launched 150 giant shells high into the sky, causing Brown to order two changes of position in an effort to confuse the Northern gunners. Out of range, the Confederate batteries at Vicksburg were helpless to counter the work of Davis' bombers. Still, they made an effort to prevent the mortar schooners and larger vessels of the lower fleet from joining in the bombardment. From atop the hill south of town, the Confederates "fired a few shots" at the largest ships in Farragut's squadron with a single, newly emplaced long-range gun. Several of its balls fell close to the *Richmond*, which, together with the *Brooklyn*, felt compelled to drop 200 yards downstream.

Meanwhile, several Confederate soldiers were captured on the De Soto Peninsula by Brig. Gen. Williams' bluecoats. These men reportedly informed their captors that Maj. Gen. Earl Van Dorn was planning to "land a large body of troops in their rear the same day the ram came." As a result, several Massachusetts batteries were relocated to the shoreline across from the *Arkansas*.

Aboard the *Hartford*, Farragut was now sufficiently composed to author a brief letter to navy secretary Welles. In perhaps the most difficult sentence he ever had to put down on paper, the Flag Officer began: "It is with deep mortification that I announce to the Department that, notwithstanding my prediction to the contrary, the ironclad ram *Arkansas* has at length made her appearance and took us all by surprise." Welles, who doubtless already knew about her breakout from the Richmond newspapers, was given a brief recap and a pledge that no stone would be left unturned in the effort to destroy her.

While his clerk wrote up the unhappy dictation, Flag Officer Farragut went on deck to witness the bombardment by the upper fleet mortar boats and was extremely pleased with Maynadier's effort. According to Paul Stevens, a barge behind the *Arkansas* was sunk. When his report to Welles was finished, the lower fleet commander next wrote to Flag Officer Davis asking that he send it to Washington with his own upriver post, as the mail through Memphis arrived at the capital more quickly than that through New Orleans. Furthermore, he added, "Do tell the captain the shelling is magnificent. They are falling all around him and I expect one to fall on board every moment." These messages were turned over to an orderly for hand delivery.

Cmdr. Alden and Cmdr. Bell were equally impressed, saying so in the logs and journals of their vessels. The shoot so encouraged the former that his *Richmond* steamed back up and fired a single shell from her 50-pdr. Parrott rifle at the one-gun, hill-mounted battery. It "went in amongst them; they skedaddled out of that, and did not come back again as long as we could see."

The day's heat became oppressive for all, including the men aboard the *Oneida*. The diarist aboard complained bitterly that the black room gang was required to keep steam up continuously as the vessel needed to be ready for action instantaneously. The same was true for the other units of the lower fleet.

Later, Farragut again wrote another note to Davis, suggesting that the mortars continuously target the *Arkansas* and saying that a few shells "now and then would disturb the people at work on the ram very much." Aim might need to be adjusted, he warned, "as they generally throw them too far." Dropping a few on the upper fort, under which the ram was hiding, would also be quite helpful. "They are working like beavers on her," he concluded.

The commander of the upriver gunboats received Farragut's messages on both side of the midday meridian. In reply, Davis promised to dispatch newly received supplies of coal overland at night by wagon along with 20 heads of beef, and continued to advise patience, "as great a virtue as boldness." Although Davis cherished his long-standing relationship with Farragut, he was chagrined and a bit angered by his impatience concerning the *Arkansas*. In a letter home, he confided that "my friend the admiral says we are to act 'regardless of consequences.' This is the language of a Hotspur and not of one that hath a rule over his own spirit."

During the night of July 17/18, three Rebel deserters from Vicksburg were taken before Flag Officer Farragut with news regarding the Southern armorclad. Some of this intelligence was new, some confirmed what could be seen by marine glass, and part was speculative. According to the Confederates, the *Arkansas*, in her encounters of July 15, was "perforated in many places" and her ram was knocked off (actually, it was damaged but remained affixed). For the first time, it was learned by the Federals that 10 men had been killed in the three fights, with many others wounded. The captain, they said, was "wounded just over the eye; some thought he would lose it." The pilot and engineer were killed (two pilots died, Chief Engineer George City was ill). The talk on shore, reported the deserters, was that the ram would "try to run the blockade down the river and go to Mobile." Still, it must have been comforting for Farragut to hear that, after Maynadier's mortars began dropping 13-inch shells, "they had to force men on board of her at the point of the bayonet."

Farragut wrote to Davis twice more on July 18. In the first letter, which included the deserter comments and thanks for the cattle, he asked to hear more about "your project as soon as Porter is ready" in order that he might offer any aid possible to the enterprise. As his opinion, he believed that, because of her anchorage, "the ram is easier destroyed than captured." In the second, he noted his difficulties of replenishment from New Orleans and revealed again that if he had a "favorable opportunity" to take another crack at the *Arkansas* he would do so. Lt. Seth Ledyard Phelps, with whom Davis shared Farragut's messages, would later tell a former superior that the lower fleet captain "had apparently only been restrained by our commander and some of his officers, who incessantly watched him, from taking his vessels up under those formidable batteries for the destruction of the one ram."

It was still cool when, early that morning, a volunteer replacement surgeon came aboard the *Arkansas* and reported to Cmdr. Brown, handing over his references. After a quick perusal and handshake, the unnamed stranger from Clinton, Mississippi, near Jackson, was turned over to Lt. Stevens, who took him to the wardroom for breakfast. The newcomer was visibly impressed; the ram now looked her best since before her departure down the Yazoo.

After breakfast, one of the masters took the doctor to the berth deck and gave him a tour, showing him where his station would be in time of action and the arrangements made aboard naval vessels for assisting any wounded. Advised of Dr. Washington's recent experience, the man was told that he would be quite busy during any battle. Men with all kinds of injuries would need his professional help in the worst way. At first, the man "looked a little incredulous," but the seriousness of his post became clear to him a little later when he was shown the still unpatched location of the damaging 11-inch bolt.[4]

About this same time, Capt. Bell, aboard the *Brooklyn*, saw the *Arkansas* lying "snugly against the wharfboat, wagons coming to and going from her." She did not have steam up. Lt. Read reported that the vessel was "cleanly washed down, the awnings spread, and everything was neat and orderly."

As the sun rose higher, the Confederates ashore began to mount a fresh battery of heavy guns atop a 200-foot hill abeam the lower fleet anchorage (estimated distance was 1½ miles). The sloop-of-war fired six shells toward the new emplacement "without their leaving their work." Early in the afternoon, both the *Brooklyn* and *Hartford* dropped downstream. Farragut old Bell it was actually "better for the fleet to lay below the [Diamond] island" should the ram sally forth.

While Farragut's units watched the *Arkansas* from below, the campaign against the armorclad by Capt. Maynadier's mortar flotilla was resumed. Three boats were in battery and, at 8:00 A.M. sharp, launched the first of 80 shells fired on the day.

Aboard the *Arkansas*, the new surgeon was shaken when the first shells began to fall in the water nearby. Never having experienced battle — on land or river — he "became rather nervous." Read remembered that he would stand on the companionway ladder and watch the smoke rising from the Federal mortar boats. The "medico," unlike crewmen and workers who were aboard the day before, was unaccustomed to the psychological chill caused by the shoot, the same fright suffered by Confederates at Island No. 10 and Fort Pillow. When "he heard the whizzing of the shell through the air, he would make a dive for his stateroom," Read noted. The surgeon's reaction was the same every time a shell was fired. Once in a while, however, "when a shell would explode close to us or fall with a heavy splash alongside, he would be heard to groan: 'Oh! Louisa and the babes!'"

Slamming down from on high, the missiles not only scared the ram's new surgeon, but also landed in the water so close to the *Arkansas* that the workmen in the barge alongside were unable to work on her. The huge missiles exploded or landed all around, both in the water and on shore.

Flag Officer Davis was particularly pleased when the armorclad's supporting wharf boat was blown apart on Friday evening. It was lying, he wrote home, "within 300 yards of her; the boat was struck twice and destroyed. If the same good luck would attend us in hitting the *Arkansas*, we would be relieved from anxiety on account of this unwelcome stranger."

The correspondent of the *Mobile Evening News* was similarly impressed when the two shells "entered through the roof and went out at the bottom, sinking the boat." This was a lucky feat, he pointed out, because the mortar boats were "anchored above the bend, behind a point of timber, and not ... able to see the *Arkansas*." Conversely, many missiles were close but near misses, causing huge geysers when the giant shells landed in the river. The water from some of these splashed the men aboard the *Arkansas*, actually cooling them down in the heat. Although "they manage sometimes to come very near sinking" her, Confederate newspapermen marveled that the Federals had, so far, inflicted no damage on the ram. This is not to say they failed to raise dust and debris.

Many of Capt. Maynadier's shots "either fell short or [went] over, sometimes doing damage to buildings on the levee." When one errant 13-incher fell in the river very close to the bow, it killed and surfaced a large number of fish. One of the crewmen, upon seeing them float by, was heard by the captain to exclaim, "Just look at that, will you? Why, the upper fleet is killing fish for the lower fleet's dinner!"

Watching from the *Richmond*, Capt. Alden remarked that Davis' bombers "made some very good shots." Perhaps more important, as Davis observed, "our bombs prevent the work of repair from going on during the day." Much of the attention now given the *Arkansas* had to be accomplished by torch after dark. "But work, under such conditions," the upper squadron flag officer wryly observed, "is not likely to be well and expeditiously done."

Meanwhile, the legend that the *Arkansas* became was building upriver. That day, news of her passage through the combined squadrons reached Brokenburn plantation, 20 miles northwest of Vicksburg, in somewhat embellished form. Upon hearing of the triumph, diarist Mrs. Kate Stone recorded the following: "The ram *Arkansas* has done good work at Vicksburg. It sank several boats and disabled others." Tales of the *Arkansas* traveled even further. "Rumors flew about that it had been seen on its way up the river past Memphis," wrote Oliver Wood McClinton, "and almost as far south as New Orleans." Lt. Phelps told an acquaintance that officials at Helena, Arkansas, were requesting reinforcements to "prevent the Confederate ram from attacking the town."

On the peninsula across from Vicksburg, Brig. Gen. Williams and his men could clearly see the *Arkansas*, which "lies in sight of us." Deserters taken over the past two days all indicated that she would "try to pass down the river to New Orleans and Mobile." "I wish the ram was a sheep," he confided in a letter home to his wife.

The Union bombardment was resumed at 8:00 A.M. on July 19 and was maintained into the evening hours. Over 100 giant shells would fall all around the *Arkansas* and in the city of Vicksburg and, although those aboard were "accustomed to this shelling," each knew that any of these Federal bolts had the potential to destroy their boat. Cmdr. Brown later observed that he knew "of no more effective way of curing a man of the weakness of thinking he is without the feeling of fear than for him, on a dark night, to watch two or three of these double-fused descending shells, all near each other, and seeming as though they would strike him between the eyes."

The ram, according to Capt. Bell, now lay at the levee under the city's batteries, "apparently without steam." By now the mechanics and carpenters, most from Vicksburg and Jackson with a few from as far away as Mobile, had, while working under fire, performed something of a mending miracle. Much (though probably not all) of the armor on the port side casemate was repaired or reattached, the chimney was patched with new iron sheets, and work on the engines was advanced. The damaged pilothouse structure could not be repaired, so it would have to be replaced with a new one.

It was perhaps frustrating to the Federals that, so far, they had not been able to land a round aboard. Finally, near lunchtime, one struck her on the corner of her stern on the starboard side and exploded, though causing little damage. Next day, Flag Officer Davis, while congratulating Farragut on his promotion to RAdm., reported: "We struck the *Arkansas* with our bombs twice yesterday."

The hit on the *Arkansas* was answered by Rebel shore batteries. One round from the Tennesseans manning the upper guns landed so close to the mortar boats that they were forced to cease firing for a while and change position. Another burst along the road network that the Federals called their "contraband telegraph," which led between the anchorages of their upper and lower fleets. Still other Confederate shells exploded directly over the bombers and at least one hit one of the tents the flotilla had set up on the riverbank near where their boats were tied.

Present but not heard of for several days, at some point this Saturday Lt. Col. Alfred W. Ellet, commander of the U.S. Army Ram Fleet, contacted Flag Officer Davis regarding an offensive role for his vessels. Ellet, humiliated by the cowardice exhibited aboard the *Queen of the West* up the Yazoo in the face of the *Arkansas*, wished to vindicate his flotilla. That he and Davis had little respect for one another probably, in his mind, heightened the necessity. Ellet's plan was in keeping with the elan encouraged upon his own officers and Davis by RAdm. Farragut. If the upper fleet ironclads would engage Vicksburg's upper batteries, the lieutenant colonel volunteered to take his best ram down, seek out the *Arkansas*, and "strike the rebel, and if possible, destroy her." If this bold scheme received a response, it is not recorded.

Sometime after 4:00 P.M., the *Essex*, her power plant refreshed, dropped down near De Soto Point and fired a few rounds in the direction of the upper forts and the *Arkansas*. The Confederates afloat and ashore responded, but, as an observer from the *Benton* reported, their shots fell short. A brisk bombardment was launched by the Union's upper fleet mortar bombers at the usual 8:00 A.M. hour on July 20. Their shoot was quite effective and forced the *Arkansas* to shift her billet upriver to a point between the upper batteries.

It is possible that the noise of the mortar firing could be heard by the convalescent crewmen of the *Arkansas* at Cox's plantation. Early in the morning, the men were transferred to the military hospital at Edwards Depot, where they were reunited with Dr. Washington and Lt. Barbot. It was recorded in the logbook of the mortar boat flotilla: "One shot burst under the bows, another almost immediately over her amidships, making her crew, 46 in number, leave for the upper part of the city." It is quite possible that the number of crew identified may have included carpenters and mechanics working on the boat. But maybe not all.

For the past four days, Cmdr. Brown had sought to increase the size of his crew. Maj. Gen. Van Dorn had told him he could have as many as he could recruit "provided the men would volunteer and make application for transfer through proper channels."

During the first 24 hours of victorious enthusiasm, quite a few butternut soldiers and a few working-class riverfront citizens not already enlisted stepped forward and signed articles. Among these, as the casualty figures from the July 22 fight show, were a number of men from the 3rd Kentucky, as well as several additional Louisiana volunteers. Then, as Lt. Read later revealed, they went aboard the *Arkansas* "and saw the shot holes through the vessel's sides, and heard sailors' reports of the terrible effect of shell and splinters, and were made aware of the danger of the mortar shells that fell continuously around the ship." After that, "many found pretexts to go back to their commands; many took the 'shell fever' and went to the hospital."

So it was that Brown's early recruiting successes failed and even he had problems with disciplining the soldiers who remained, some of whom may have been among the 46 leaving. Lt. Read, who had little use for such volunteers, related a story, which most likely occurred during the berthing shift on the 19th:

> We were engaged hauling the ship into a position near one of our batteries; but having but few sailors to haul on the wharf, we were progressing slowly, when Lieutenant Stevens, the executive officer, came on deck, and perceiving a crowd of volunteers sitting on deck playing cards, he said, rather sharply, "Come, volunteers, that won't do; get up from there and give us a pull." One of the players looked up at Lieutenant Stevens and replied, "Oh! Hell, we ain't no deck hands"; and eyeing the man sitting opposite him, was heard to say, "I go you two better."

Just as Flag Officer Davis was getting off a message to RAdm. Farragut, Capt. E.B. Pike came aboard the *Benton* to report that the mortars had struck the *Arkansas* twice more.

During the day, Lt. Col. Ellet, aboard the ram *Switzerland* anchored not too far from the mouth of the Yazoo River above, wrote to Flag Officer Davis inquiring whether "you have given my proposition your careful consideration." It was hoped that the *Arkansas* attack plan he had offered the previous day did not entail so much risk of failure as to prohibit the attempt. Again, the Federal ram chief asked for the favor of a reply, but he was again ignored. A copy of his message was also received by RAdm. Farragut, who undoubtedly viewed it with considerably more favor.

All of the logbooks of the vessels anchored above and below Vicksburg report that this Sunday was among the hottest yet endured. Sickness continued to take a significant toll on Federal sailors, while ashore, troops of Brig. Gen. Williams were dying in significant numbers. This day alone, 10 men died in the 30th Massachusetts Infantry Regiment.

Heat and disease reduced the number of men available to work the mortars of Maynadier and Pike and, consequently, the big guns were not worked between the hours of 11:00 A.M. and 6:00 P.M. It is not reported in Federal records, but there may have been another reason.

Late in the afternoon, Flag Officer William F. Lynch arrived in Vicksburg from Jackson and was welcomed aboard. J. Thomas Scharf tells us that, after a meeting with the ram's weary captain, Cmdr. Brown's superior relieved him "for a few hours to enable him to go ashore and take a dinner and a sound sleep, of which he was in great need and which he had not had for more than week."

It is difficult, given the suicidal orders he issued in early August, for credit to be given to the story about Capt. Lynch that the historian next relates. Capt. Brown, who apparently was not present, later confirmed that "in three days, we were again in condition to move and to menace at our will either fleet, thus compelling the enemy's entire force, in the terrible July heat, to keep up steam day and night."

According to Scharf, once Brown was ashore, Flag Officer Lynch, in temporary command, though probably deferring to Lt. Stevens, ordered the *Arkansas* to depart "up the river beyond the range of the batteries with the intention of destroying the enemy's mortar boats." As the Rebel armorclad became visible aboard the Federal mortar boats and their support steamers, a panic set in and the bombers were quickly towed upstream "at a speed far surpassing that of the Confederate ram."

Given the rapidity of the enemy withdrawal and her own "limited supply of coal," the *Arkansas*, even though she had, as Professor Still remarks, "actually rounded the bend," was forced to give up and return to the city. That evening, the repositioned Union mortar craft resumed their bombardment for about an hour. The bombers could not report anywhere near the success with this shoot that they had enjoyed in the morning. During the day, 63 big 13-inch shells were expended.

Cmdr. Brown returned to the *Arkansas* just after breakfast on July 21 and resumed command. As Flag Officer Lynch departed at 8:00 A.M., the Union mortar campaign was resumed. All morning until noon, shells landed close to the ram, forcing her to shift position on at least two occasions. That afternoon, Brown ordered his vessel to make another attack on the mortar boats, one he intended to press home no matter how far upriver he had to go. As the *Arkansas* ascended the river, the starboard engine quit. The experience was not unlike that suffered up the Yazoo back in June. Fortunately, the vessel had not gone too far, but still, as Brown later wrote, "it was with difficulty that we regained our usual position in front of the city."

Anchored between the two upper forts, Cmdr. Brown continued his best to intimidate the Federals on that Monday, even though his power plant was broken down. "We constantly threatened the offensive," he later noted, "and our raising steam, which they could perceive by our smokestack, was the signal for either fleet to fire up."

The temperature was from 90 degrees to 100 degrees in the shade. Out on the *Richmond*, Capt. Alden remarked that it "was one of the hottest days of the year." By constantly forcing the Federals to prepare for battle or flight, Brown hoped to compel them to raise the siege "for sanitary reasons alone." If more men became ill or the Union coal supply was exhausted, wouldn't they have to quit? At the same time, the captain realized that, if pushed to it in the face of failure, the enemy might well attempt some desperate action to destroy his ship.

Although the *Arkansas* had been able to steam out into the river briefly during the previous two days, her situation today was dire, particularly with regard to personnel. Injury, fear, and illness played havoc with Cmdr. Brown's roster. Daily, more and more of the ram's crew left, the scared soldiers back to their regiments and the sailors, as Lt. Gift put it, "to the hospital, suffering with malarious diseases."

The *Arkansas*, Gift continued, could muster only about 28–30 "seamen, ordinary seamen and landsmen, and I think, but four or five firemen." No more men were to be had and it "was disheartening" to see the ship, "pride of the county, now so deserted." Lt. Read, in his account, is a bit more generous, pegging the number at 41, though Cmdr. Brown indicates that the crew was in the twenties. Many of the younger officers, midshipmen and petty officers, were "used up." In addition to Brown, four or five others remained and they slept in their tiny spaces below with their clothes on ready for any emergency. Sleeping is perhaps too generous a word; they rested "in an atmosphere so heated by the steam of the engines as to keep one in a constant perspiration."

By now, the recruiting situation had become a crisis. The only men willing to come aboard were unemployed drifters and those in ones and twos. The captain, who had applied to military authorities several times before, now made an impassioned personal plea to Maj. Gen. Van Dorn for an immediate draft of soldiers to help fight the boat's big guns. In response, the army commander promised "that the men (needed at the moment) should be sent to me the next day."

As Cmdr. Brown sought redress for his manpower shortage, the Federals were hard at work on new attack plans of their own. The commanders of both the lower and upper fleets were both able to clearly make note that "the ram is anchored between the two upper forts." It was subsequently seen that she "lay against the bank under a battery of six guns, at the upper point of the city."

The mortar bombardment continued as usual during the morning. There really did not appear to be any major program change on either side. The Yankees did not know that the *Arkansas*' engine problems compelled her to remain tied up; the Southerners did not know that, today, the Federals would be ready if she once more attacked the mortar boat anchorage.

Aboard the *Hartford*, RAdm. Farragut, though he did "not feel equal to the undertaking this morning, decided to travel over the De Soto Peninsula in the heat and see his opposite number. Having knowledge of the Ellet offer and no clear idea when Flag Officer Davis' plan involving the Essex might unfold, it was time for a personal conference. In his absence, Cmdr. Bell was given temporary charge of the lower squadron.[5] RAdm. Farragut was piped aboard the *Benton* at 9:00 A.M. There, he and Flag Officer Davis were joined by Farragut's foster brother, Cmdr. William D. "Dirty Bill" Porter and Lt. Col. Ellet. The commanders of the U.S. navy and army fleets would now discuss options for dealing with the *Arkansas*, including Davis' earlier mentioned plan involving use of Porter's *Essex*, and Ellet's ideas.

An observant *Benton* crewman, according to Dana M. Wegner, later recorded his impressions of the arrival of Farragut and Porter. "The epitome of understatement," the lower squadron boss arrived first, dressed in "a plain, unadorned, frock coat. His hair was combed to cover a receding hairline." Porter flamboyantly swept in next, wearing clothes reminiscent of a buccaneer: red flannel shirt, blue trousers, red-line boots turned inside out at the knee, and a black slouch hat. Ellet, like Davis, was dressed in standard-issue uniform.

The sometimes-acrimonious council of war continued for hours. One busy steward was amused by the extroverted Porter. When not animated, Farragut's relative sat "with his feet propped up, drinking large quantities of sherry, pattering incessantly, and flipping a gold coin." Historian Huffstot has observed that he "had been on the shelf along with his boat and was afraid his detested half-brother, David, was getting ahead of him in the glory race." Davis and Farragut concurred early on that Cmdr. Porter should spearhead the attack with the *Essex*. Assuming plans went right, she would, it was later revealed in a *Chicago Daily Tribune* account, draw the *Arkansas* out into the river and grapple her. One of Col. Ellet's rams ascending during this capture would then "butt her from the rear" in an effort to prevent escape. After some further discussion, Davis consented to the inclusion of Ellet's ram, though he was not convinced that the scheme would work.

The Western Flotilla ironclads would "open the ball." The *Benton*, *Cincinnati*, *Louisville*, and *General Bragg* would engage the upper forts, and mortars from both squadrons would occupy the *Arkansas* and any shore defenses within range as soon as the *Essex* came around De Soto Point. Simultaneously, the lower batteries would be engaged by Farragut's big sloops-of-war. Given that they would be steaming upstream and holding their bombardment positions against the current, it was agreed this diversionary fire be their major contribution. Once Porter's ironclad got near the *Arkansas*, her crew would hold her steady with grappling hooks so that Ellet's boat could run into her side.

The ram *Sumter*, already below, would paddle further upstream to hold in a position from which she would be ready for action. "If it became necessary," the newspaper continued, she would be sent to do what she could to assist the *Essex*, perhaps getting a chance herself to ram the enemy armorclad. If the attack were only partially successful and the *Arkansas* was not destroyed, it was hoped, as Lt. Phelps put it, that the assaulting Federal craft could at least "drive him up or down stream to the one squadron or the other." The meeting concluded with a promise by Davis to supply the lower fleet with several Mississippi River pilots. When all was said and done, Cmdr. Porter supposedly "sealed the agreement by saying, 'She's my pigeon, and I am determined to destroy her.'"

Later that afternoon, in anticipation of another possible *Arkansas* sortie and just after the *Benton* summit concluded, Capt. Maynadier received new orders from the *Benton*. Instead of retaining his 13-inchers in bombardment battery, he was to make certain that they were depressed and held in readiness "for the ram should she attempt to pass." The mortars would be used like giant shotguns or those short-ranged cannon of the old sailing navy known as carronades. "A watch was set," someone wrote in the log of the mortar flotilla, "but she did not show up." The *Arkansas* remained anchored between the two upper forts.

The Farragut-Davis agreement suffered its first misunderstanding after dark. The promised pilots had yet to arrive by 10:00 P.M. and, in light of that development, the lower fleet com-

Cmdr. (later Commodore) William D. "Dirty Bill" Porter, USN (1809–1864). *The rascally captain of the U.S. ironclad* Essex *was the son of War of 1812 commodore David Porter, brother of RAdm. David Dixon Porter, and foster brother of RAdm. David G. Farragut. In the USN since 1823, he was scalded by a bursting boiler during the Battle of Fort Henry in February 1862. Laying claim to the* Arkansas *as his special project, Porter attempted to cut her out or destroy her on July 22 but failed. At the beginning of August, he was senior naval officer off Baton Rouge when the Confederate ram appeared. Although she was forced to scuttle when her engines failed, he claimed credit for her destruction. Several disputes led to his spending the remainder of his life on boards and commissions. Interestingly, Maj. Gen. Fitz-John Porter, who was famously court-martialed for his actions at the Second Battle of Bull Run, was his cousin and had two sons who both served the Confederacy (*Battles & Leaders, *vol. 3).*

mander sent a message across the peninsula asking if it would still be necessary for his big ships "to go up and attack her." Or, he continued, "will you drive her down to the lower forts?" Contrary to what Farragut, Cmdr. Porter, or Lt. Col. Ellet understood, Flag Officer Davis believed "the upshot of our conversation today" was different from what his flag captain, Lt. Phelps, called Farragut's "pet idea" of steaming up to attack the *Arkansas*. "We shall either drive her down to you, destroy her, or force her to come up the river," the Western Flotilla commander tardily replied. "In the latter case we are ready for her."

Given the lateness of the hour and the tardiness of the pilots' arrival, Davis begged the admiral "not to think of passing the lower forts." A postscript was added requesting that the admiral inform Lt. Erben that the *Sumter* was expected to do "her whole duty." The upper fleet message, borne by one of the promised pilots named *Seymour*, was delivered aboard the *Hartford* early on the morning of July 22. At 2:40 A.M., RAdm. Farragut sent the man on to Cmdr. Bell with a new order that would be debated long into the years ahead. "We will not pass the forts unless I make the signal to go ahead," the *Brooklyn*'s captain was told. Continuing, he added, "Flag Officer Davis says he will drive the ram down to us or destroy her, and begs me not to pass the forts. So await the signals." Farragut's order was also passed to his other combat captains.

In September, RAdm. Farragut, at the urging of friends, addressed his participation in the July 22 attack. Davis, he said, was confident of being able to destroy the *Arkansas* or push her down to him, "in which case I was to take care of her, and I felt the same ability to destroy or capture her." The admiral believed "the lower fleet were to have no share in the affair until the ram was driven down to us." Cmdr. Porter, having boasted that the *Arkansas* was his special prize and that "he would therefore take or destroy her," plans were laid for the *Essex* and *Queen of the West* to attack the *Arkansas* from above along with the seconded *Sumter* from below. "This I fully impressed, verbally, upon Captain Erben," Farragut wrote, "and told him to take his station at the point above, ready to attack as soon as the *Essex* made her appearance."[6]

Returning aboard the *Essex* the previous evening, Cmdr. Porter had assembled his crew and told them his scheme. They would try to push the *Arkansas* against the rocky levee and then "cut her out" right from under Vicksburg's 60 guns. Any man not willing to follow his plan to challenge her first by ramming and then by boarding was free to transfer to another flotilla boat. None did. His blustery pep talk completed, the great-bearded captain and his men began preparations for implementing the scheme. After the vessel was "coaled," sandbags were packed atop the casemate directly over the boilers. The gun ports of the ironclad would be kept closed as she approached her prey, but when they opened, the *Arkansas* would be blasted not only with regulation projectiles but also "with thousands of common glass marbles intended to blind the ram's sharpshooters at her loop holes."

Porter also organized a well-armed boarding party, explaining that it was his intention to grapple the Confederate ram and swarm aboard to make the capture. The boarders, acting as a prize crew, would then quickly pass hawsers back over to the *Essex*. Once these were tied off, the gunboat would take her in tow downstream to the safety of Farragut's waiting fleet.

These preparations continued past midnight — just finding the hundreds of required marbles was a task — and there was little sleep aboard the ironclad that night. The boat was, as Fourth Master Spencer Kellogg Brown, who was a native of Utica, New York, remembered in a letter to his grandfather, Levi Cozzens, "thoroughly prepared for action, every port being closed, every man and officer, at his station, all ready."

Lt. Col. Ellet chose to make his attack with the *Queen of the West*, which ram had been so ingloriously handled up the Yazoo a week earlier, but was still, despite her age, the best available. A penitent Lt. James M. Hunter of the 63rd Illinois was allowed to remain in command under Ellet's personal supervision. In a lengthy interview with the editor of the *Memphis Bulletin* he would later be able to tell of his ram's participation.

The *Queen*'s crew was reminiscent of Cmdr. Brown's in terms of numbers: 28. All were volunteers, hand-picked by Ellet, including his son, Corporal Edward C. Ellet, of the 59th Illinois Volunteers. To replace his reluctant and insubordinate engineers, the colonel obtained replacements from the *Switzerland* and *Mingo*; a pilot joined from the former vessel. Four 63rd Illinois privates offered to serve as sharpshooters and were welcomed aboard. All of the men were named in the August 4, 1862, *New York Times* account of the attack.

Far below, in the four hours after midnight, the gunboats *Pinola* and *Westfield* placed Cmdr. Renshaw's mortar schooners into position. At 3:00 A.M., all hands in the major units of both fleets were called to quarters and the decks were cleared for action. It was still relatively cool when, at 4:00 A.M., the middle watch turned into the morning watch.

Led by the *Benton*, the *Louisville*, *Cincinnati*, and *General Bragg* arrived off De Soto Point at that hour and dropped anchor. Below, Farragut's sloops-of-war lay with their cables hove short, waiting for Davis' people to begin their shoot. Fifteen minutes later, as recorded in the logbook of the damaged *Carondelet*, the *Essex* started down the river. As she passed the *Benton*, Flag Officer Davis hailed the ironclad, wishing Cmdr. Porter success. The *Switzerland* and *Queen of the West* got underway five minutes later, with the *Queen* continuing down past the line of gunboats.

When the first rays of sunshine were beginning to appear, the upper fleet gunboats started firing upon the Confederate forts. "The cannonading was tremendous and fairly shook the earth," Scharf later recorded. Orange tongues of fire from the great guns matched the slivers of red in the slowly lightening eastern sky. The *Essex* passed slowly below the point twenty minutes later and was greeted by every available gun in Vicksburg's upper batteries. Simultaneously, Cmdr. Renshaw's mortars began launching their 13-inch shells against Vicksburg's lower batteries from a range of 3,700 to 4,000 yards. Their "few shells" did not, in the opinion of the *Chicago Times* reporter, "divert the fire of the enemy." A drum aboard the *Arkansas* summoned her crew to action stations, at 4:00 A.M., as Midshipman Scales recalled on July 31. The great noise and commotion upriver also alerted everyone ashore not already awake. Lookouts and others aboard Farragut's vessels now observed the forts below the upper batteries joining in the defense. "Everything seemed under way again," remembered Lt. Gift, "and it was evident that were soon to have another brush."

At 5:00 A.M., the admiral made signal for his sloops-of-war to get underway and the *Hartford*, *Brooklyn*, and *Richmond* began very slowly to ascend. As they did so, all eyes were turned upstream toward the *Essex*. Yeoman William C. Holton, aboard the flagship, recalled watching "a most sublime picture in naval operations, a lone vessel running the gauntlet of

Opposite, top: **USS *Essex*** (stern view). Bottom: **USS *Essex*** (bow view). *Converted from a large ferryboat, the unique center-wheel powered* Essex *was the best protected Federal ironclad available to upper fleet commander Flag Officer Charles H. Davis. With a length of 159 feet, a beam of 47.6 feet, and a 6-foot draft, this sometimes controversial craft also had a full casemate covered by 3 inches of iron. With a crew of 134, she was armed with three 9-inch Dahlgren SBs, one 10-inch Dahlgren SB, one 32-pdr., and a 12-pdr. howitzer. Under the command of the colorful Cmdr. William D. "Dirty Bill" Porter, the craft made herself a nemesis to the* Arkansas *(top, U.S. Army Military History Institute; bottom, Navy History and Heritage Command).*

Inside View of the *Arkansas* vs. the *Essex*. *The fight at dawn on July 22 between the* Arkansas *and the* Essex *was desperate on both sides. The interiors of both ships were badly lit and both faced serious operational or battle difficulties. The* Arkansas *was woefully undermanned, while the* Essex *spent harrowing minutes stuck ashore under the guns of both the Rebel land batteries and the ram (Abbott,* Bluejackets of '61*).*

some 30 cannon placed in the hillside, raining a shower of shot and shell thickly around her."

The *Arkansas*, meanwhile, was sorely distressed for crew. In his recollection, now available for all to read in Gordon Cotton's *Vicksburg and the War* pictorial, Scales points out that the vessel lacked a sufficient number of enlisted men to man more than two guns. "We did not have a third of the firemen required in that department," he added, "consequently steam was behind hand." Nevertheless, preparations for resistance were made as fires were hastened under the boilers by the three or four available engineers, generating minimal steam pressure. Even if more steam could have been made available, "we did not have enough to heave the anchor up and get under way.

As the *Essex* made her way downstream, Federal observers, again including First Officer Brennand and Pilot Deming from the *Carondelet*, were stationed on the point across from Vicksburg and the *Arkansas*. They were pleased that, as they had reported earlier, the great ram was still moored near the upper forts with her bow headed upstream. Although it was difficult to see detail or activity against the dawn's rising sun, it was possible to tell that the port side of her hull presented an inviting target.

Once Porter was underway, the *Queen of the West* followed. As the U.S. ram passed the *Benton*, Lt. Col. Ellet saw Flag Officer Davis on her deck waving his arms quite vigorously and shouting. Unable to hear over the splash of his craft's big paddle wheels and concerned that the upper fleet commander was offering some kind of warning, Ellet ordered his engines reversed. Drifting close to the ironclad, Ellet heard Davis' repeated calls. Instead of ordering the *Queen of the West* to "Go Back! Go Back!," the flag officer was merely shouting, as he had to Cmdr. Porter earlier, what a newspaper called a "benediction": "Good Luck! Good Luck!" Given their differences dating back to the Battle of Memphis, the colonel was probably surprised that the navy man was actually wishing him *bon chance*. Ellet undoubtedly also realized that by stopping he may now have lost any chance for a coordinated attack with Porter's *Essex*.

Abandoning ceremony and their uniform coats, the *Arkansas*' officers had, meanwhile, joined the jack tars in manning the ram's guns. This mix provided enough men to increase the number of gun crews from two to three. The captain and his XO even helped load the cannon and make certain that a sufficiency of filled water buckets and small arms were available. A plan, probably devised by Cmdr. Brown, was unveiled under which the big gun teams would rotate between the port broadside, the stern, and the forward guns, keeping them all in battery as needed. Rolling fire would be possible if there were not too many casualties.

In a letter to his sister written a week later, XO Stevens indicated his intense pride in this "all-for-one" approach. "One thing that our officers deserve the greatest credit for is they fought the guns themselves," he related, "pointing & firing them in person, not trusting to the men & satisfying themselves with looking on, but actually working like Trojans & giving the advantage [of having] another man at each gun." This was, he continued, "of great benefit when men were so scarce & their example animated the men."

Having passed the upper batteries without damage, the *Essex* steamed down the western bank of the Mississippi at about 5:10 A.M. to a point directly across from the *Arkansas*. Cmdr. Porter's boat, according to Brown, then "made the mistake, so far as her success was concerned," of heaving to port and running at her foe directly across the river's strong current.

We noted in chapter seven how the sailors of the *Tyler*, on patrol up the Yazoo, first reacted when seeing the house-like shape of the *Arkansas*, a great, wide, iron monster with a bow "as sharp as a wedge." If there was another huge, wide, iron colossus on the river at that time, it was the newly arrived *Essex*, "as square across the bow as a float boat or scow." With a beam of 60 feet, the 250-foot centerwheeler had a top speed of only 5.5 knots. Moving across the water, she would have been lucky to make a quarter of that.

Cmdr. Porter's heavily protected ironclad was armed with three 9-inch (forward) and one 10-inch Dahlgren smoothbores, two 50-pounder Dahlgren rifles, and a 32 pounder. These were initially kept silent during her approach. If the marbles were to work as buckshot, they would have to be discharged just as, or a little before, the gunboat bumped into the Rebel armorclad. Although no one aboard the *Arkansas* knew about Porter's marbles, it did not take a genius to see that the *Essex* was intent upon ramming and, if successful, perhaps pushing the Confederate boat completely aground, boarding her, and attempting to make her a prize. Under these circumstances, the Rebels intended to fight for their armorclad as if it were the Texas Alamo, with (at least according to legend) no one surrendering and the last man blowing up the powder magazine.

Cmdr. Brown, seeing both the ironclad and the *Queen of the West* following, easily divined the Union attack plan and reacted quickly, managing, as Midshipman Scales remembered, "by the helm & with the aid of the starboard propeller." "Slackening the hawser which held our head to the bank," Lt. Gift admiringly added, "he [Brown] went ahead on the starboard screw, and thus our sharp prow was turned 'out stream' directly to her to hit against." A collision would "surely cut him down and leave us uninjured."

When the *Essex* reached mid-river, "Grimball unloosed his Columbiad, but she did not stop." As she continued on puffing and snorting "like a mad bull," Lt. Gift emptied his Columbiad as well, "hitting her fair, but still she persevered in sullen silence." Having replied with the bow guns "as long as they could be brought to bear — which was not a very long time," Scales inserts that "their crews had to be shifted to the broadside guns."

With shot and shell from the shore batteries, including three not far behind and above the *Arkansas*, bouncing off her thick protection and her progress unfazed by the ram's bow guns, the *Essex* ploughed across the river intent upon running down her foe — until lookouts and Porter saw the ram's sharp prow extending outward. This, as Lt. Gift put it, "disconcerted the enemy and destroyed his plan." Unhappily for her, this was not enough to save the Confederate vessel from considerable grief. At a range of about 50 yards, the forward gun ports of the *Essex* were raised and her mighty Dahlgrens screamed in anger.

A bolt, identified by Lt. Read as a 10-inch projectile, but by Gift as a 9-incher, struck the *Arkansas* a few inches forward of her "unlucky" port-side bow gun port. The shot broke off the ends of several armor rails, sending them, together with a cloud of iron splinters, inside and wounding a number of men, including Gift. Midshipman Scales later testified that a second Dahlgren shot "struck against the forward edge of one of the broadside ports." It then "glanced in aft in a raking direction over the deck." After crossing diagonally over the gun deck, it split apart against the breach of the starboard after 32-pounder broadside gun. Brown, Stevens, Gift, Read, and Grimball watched in horror as six men died instantly, including two volunteers from the 3rd Kentucky Regiment, and six others were badly wounded.

Yet, as the captain observed, it "left us still half our crew," or 17 men by Lt. Gift's count. It is suspected that, with the vessel now stationary, two or three engine-room men were summoned up into the makeshift gun crews. These now ran from gun to gun as the *Essex* approached. The bow guns and the Dahlgrens were loaded and aimed in rotation,

Ten: Arkansas vs. Essex, Round One: July 16–22, 1862   251

with the men heaving in the shells and pushing the cannon into battery while the officers applied muscle, sighted, and yanked the lanyards.

It was discovered later that the third and final gun fired by Porter at the Confederate ram contained the marbles the Northerners had hoped would serve as antipersonnel shot. After the fight, Gift recorded that over 100 unbroken ones were found on the forecastle, including "'white-allies,' 'chinas,' and some glass marbles." It does not sound outside the realm of reason that these tiny grapeshot were gathered up and later used by their finders for friendly games of the schoolyard variety.

Watching from the *Brooklyn*, Capt. Bell, like his colleagues aboard Farragut's other ships, had no idea how the fight was going. "Both the iron combatants were more or less

Mortar Scow. *Several of these mortar scows, commanded by U.S. Army captain Henry E. Maynadier, were present with the Western Flotilla vessels moored above Vicksburg on July 15. After the* Arkansas *burst through the combined Federal fleet and made it to Vicksburg that morning, Flag Officer Davis ordered that the giant 13-inch mortars concentrate a rain of deliberate fire upon the Confederate ram in an effort to destroy her. There is little doubt that if even one of the giant shells had squarely struck Lt. Brown's boat she would have been finished where she lay (Lossing's* Pictorial Field Book of the Civil War, *vol. 2).*

Marbles as Ammunition. *Cmdr. William D. "Dirty Bill" Porter, USN, captain of the* Essex, *was an original thinker who used India rubber in his armor and who experimented with his own projectiles, among them glass marbles, the same used by schoolboys all over the country. As the* Essex *prepared to attack the Arkansas on July 21, his men scoured the combined Federal fleets, securing every one of the tiny potential projectiles available. When the* Essex *engaged the Confederate ironclad the next day, one of her bow guns would blast her with these "common glass marbles intended to blind the ram's sharpshooters at her loop holes." After the fight, Lt. George W. Gift recorded that over 100 unbroken marbles were found on the forecastle of the Arkansas, including "'white-allies,' 'chinas,' and some glass marbles," looking perhaps not unlike these from an Ohio exhibit. It does not seem outside the realm of reason that these tiny grapeshot might have been gathered up and later used by their finders for friendly games of the schoolyard variety (Cuyahoga Valley National Park, National Park Service).*

enveloped in smoke," he remembered, "we could see but little of them." Fourth Master Brown of the Union ironclad remembered the silence from the enemy vessel in the moments after the bow guns were discharged. "Prior to our striking her she had been firing rapidly," he wrote to his grandfather, "but as we delivered the three round shot from the 9-inch guns in the bow, her men could be seen leaving her and getting ashore, and she no longer returned any fire."

Upstream a few days later, Lt. Phelps, aboard the *Benton*, wrote a former flotilla commander, indicating that "the *Essex*'s shot made big holes in her sides and cries were heard inboard." Porter himself informed Secretary Welles that, after delivering their shot, he and his crew "distinctly heard the groans of her wounded and saw her crew jumping overboard."

In the smoke and carnage, the *Essex* maneuvered to avoid the sharp prow of the *Arkansas*. Orders were desperately passed for engine reverse and full left rudders, which bit hard into the river current. Although she succeeded in missing the outstretched ram, the ironclad's momentum was so great that she could not fully complete a turn and so grazed the Confederate's side before running high up onto the riverbank astern of her "pigeon."

As she passed, "we poured out our port broadside" with, as Lt. Read recalled, "guns depressed." At the same time, XO Stevens and a damage control party worked to clear away "the splinters and broken stanchions, and woodwork, which had been driven the whole length" of the *Arkansas*' casemate. Cmdr. Brown later admitted that when the *Essex* grazed the side of his ram her captain lost another opportunity. In the wake of the decimation and momentary disorder inside the Rebel boat's casemate, had Porter "thrown 50 men on our upper deck, he might have made fast to us with a hawser and, with little additional loss, might have taken the *Arkansas* and her 20 men and officers." The crewmen of the *Arkansas* were ready to repel boarders and as possible, pointed their small arms out her ports and blazed away at their nearby opponent. It is unknown whether the astute captain actually knew, or figured out at the time, that this was his enemy's original plan or, having learned of it for certain afterwards, admitted that it could have worked.

Under Lt. Read's direction, every other available man saw to it that the stern rifles were placed into battery. With these chores rapidly done, says Gift, " we went ahead on our port screw and turned our stern guns on him." The closeness of the contest with the *Essex* may be inferred, Cmdr. Brown suggested 20 years later, from the fact "that several of our surviving men had their faces blackened and were painfully hurt by the unburnt powder which came through our portholes from the assailant's guns."

For 10 long minutes, the *Essex* remained aground, the target of raking fire not only from the guns aboard the *Arkansas*, but from those ashore as well. Shells struck the Federal's casemate and exploded, according to Master Brown, "so near the ports as to throw a continual lurid glare upon the darkened decks." Several cannonballs remained imbedded in her after the fight.

The Northern craft's riflemen also engaged, trying to hit their opposites aboard the Southern ram. In those anxious minutes, the Union ironclad's engines worked furiously, pushing her giant center-mounted paddle wheel to pull her hulk off the beach.

It was during this time that Caleb W. Allen, a volunteer gunner aboard the *Arkansas* from the 6th Kentucky Regiment, reportedly made his mark. According to Edward Porter Thompson, a Federal sailor attempting to enter his gun port between discharges of the big cannon was killed when Allen shot him with a pistol.

Capt. Clement Sulivane, aide-de-camp to and nephew of Maj. Gen. Van Dorn, was having dinner with his friend Maj. Joseph Davis Balfour (1840–1862), a staff inspector general and nephew of President Jefferson Davis, when the upper battery bombardment started. Both men ran to Van Dorn's house, but the commander was gone. They then continued on to the riverbank, running along it toward the firing. Eventually they were stopped by a ravine running into the Mississippi about 50–100 yards below where the *Arkansas* was moored to the bank. By now the firing, they thought, had slackened, just as Fourth Master Brown believed. Wondering why, they looked out, then moved a bit further on. Presently, they saw a steamer that Sulivane recognized as the *Essex* slide slantwise into the soft mud bank just below where they stood. As she came to a stop, a hatch opened and an officer in a USN uniform appeared and looked around. Dawn was just breaking and the emerging bearded man was distinctly visible down to his knee, being "about on a level with us and only about 30 feet away." Amazed, the young officers recognized him from newspaper illustrations as Cmdr. Porter.

Balfour, whom Sulivane later confessed was "the most excitable person I have ever encountered" and "of very little real use because of his total loss of self-command," now decided to stand up and taunt Porter: "[D]ancing about like one possessed, he drew and waved his sword at Porter, crying out: 'Come ashore, you d--n Yankee, and I will give you h---!' 'Go to h---, you d--n negro trader,' replied Porter scornfully. 'I had rather be a negro trader than a d--n negro thief,' bawled back Balfour in a rage. Porter made no reply, but descended his stairway, the trapdoor closed, a bell jingled, and the *Essex* drew away from the bank and turned down the river."

Years later when writing about this encounter, Sulivane elaborated on Porter's attack and what Cmdr. Brown had called a mistake by the *Essex* commander. "But he made a slight miscalculation as to the tremendous power of the water of the Mississippi at that particular point," the captain subsequently learned, "they having rushed against the east bank just above where the *Arkansas* was lying and thence rebounding swiftly down with increased speed and volume."

Although he relived this adventure decades after Brown, Gift, and Read wrote their accounts, Sulivane had not learned of the Rebel ram's prow maneuver out into the stream. He, and probably many others, believed that it was the current that caused the bow of the *Essex* to be "slightly deflected as she reached her mark, and instead of striking the *Arkansas* amidships, she struck her abaft her curvature and thence glanced on down and away from her, only the sides of the vessels colliding."

Cmdr. Porter later claimed that, as he lay thrashing on the beach seeking ways to get a boarding party onto the *Arkansas*, the Confederates drew up "three regiments of sharpshooters and several batteries of field pieces" to attack his boat. He estimated that several of these were less than a hundred feet away, with the soldiers streaming down the bluff. The newcomers supplemented the heavy six-gun battery and riflemen already firing down upon the Union ironclad. Had these butternuts arrived in force, they might have been able to board the *Essex* and capture her. It is almost too juicy to ponder the fate of the river war if that had occurred.

While all of this was going on, the 4th and 5th (later 9th) Kentucky regiments received orders to shift inland away from their picket posts along the riverbank. Before they could withdraw, one of the heavy water batteries started blasting away at the *Essex* over the heads of the men. "The concussion was so great from the balls passing over," remembered Pvt. John S. Jackman, "that we were almost lifted off the ground."

During this time, heavy Rebel shells struck the forward casemate of the *Essex*. Most caused no damage. "After much trouble and cursing," observes Dana Wegner, "Porter was able to back into midstream." Meanwhile, chunks "of shell of all sizes, as well as numbers of splinters, lay upon the deck, and the ricochet shot covered her with one continual foam of water." Jackman tells us that rifle balls "would bounce off, as water-drops from a duck's back."

In September, long after Cmdr. Porter was detached, it would be found during repairs to the *Essex* that her starboard bow had settled. That situation was directly attributed to her "accident" while hanging on the bank next to the *Arkansas*.

As the *Essex* was rounding to, a conical shot struck the casemate on the port side. It penetrated the ¾-inch iron and came halfway through the wooden side before exploding. One sailor was killed and three were slightly wounded. A small piece of shrapnel "grazed my head," the captain admitted, while "another tore the legs of the first master's pantaloons."

Once the *Essex* had backed out, the current swept her downstream. She attempted to head back up, but the water was so swift that she could not. "After hanging there stationary for some minutes, all the batteries pouring their shot upon him," observers watched as "she bore away and stood down the river."

Fourth Master Brown says that Porter, believing that he would be supported, "looked in vain for the promised aid." It is probable that his displeasure was roared for his men and all the world to hear. The ironclad captain would say the same thing, with literary restraint, in his official report. This, shall we say unhappiness, was picked up by the newspapers, including the *New York Times* and the *New York Tribune*. The lower fleet was nowhere to be seen, while Davis' command "looked mere specs in the distance."

Porter's assertion of nonsupport raised a firestorm in September, with both Davis and Farragut telling the Navy Department that Porter was wrong, the former going so far as to press charges in response to comments made by the *Essex* captain in August. The lower fleet gunboats were, Farragut asserted, underway and ready to assist had the admiral "supposed it necessary." Porter, however, "wished the whole credit" and wanted Farragut's help only "in case of urgent necessity."

When he reprimanded his gunboat captains for not attacking the ram, those men actually told him, Farragut said, "that Commodore Porter sent them back and said he only wished them to be within supporting distance, but did not wish them to attack the *Arkansas*." Later, when Porter's nonsupport assertions became an item of controversy, the Gulf squadron leader frankly told Secretary Welles, "I do object to his throwing any share of his failure on me, when I feel assured that it was caused by the unmanagableness of his vessel."

Having abandoned the "pigeon," Porter ordered his helmsman to steer for Farragut's lower fleet, "nearly three miles off and still at anchor." "Still, we were but half way through the danger," the fourth master added. "Lying down on the decks by his order, we received another half-hour's pounding." The escaping *Essex* was a target for every shot, shell, and rifle ball the enemy could throw at her, supposedly about 70 guns in shore batteries, 20 field pieces, and the *Arkansas*' guns.

Far above at the Western Flotilla anchorage, curious eyes were able to take in the smoke, noise, and confusion presented this early morning. Convalescing aboard the hospital steamer *Red Rover*, Cmdr. Henry Walke, captain of the *Carondelet*, was on deck with his marine glass and, as might be expected, took a keen interest in the Federal effort to eliminate his old friend Brown. "I saw our fleet engage the enemy," he later told Flag Officer Davis, "and the *Essex* pass out of gunshot below the rebel batteries some time before the firing between our fleet and the enemy had ceased."

Porter and his men were in action for about an hour, during which their giant craft was struck 42 times but penetrated only twice. The casemate iron was dented in many spots, while the "chimneys, ventilators, and awnings were riddled with shot and pieces of shell." The wheelhouse was often hit, and several wheel-arms were broken. Despite the "perfect storm," only one crewman, Peter White, was killed and three wounded.

About 5:15 A.M., RAdm. Farragut ordered his captains to "Prepare for Action," even as they still held back under his earlier order not to approach the lower Rebel forts until he signaled them to do so. Despite the noisy exchange between the *Arkansas* and the *Essex*, no signal was given. The lower fleet commander had, however, informed Lt. Henry Erben of the *Sumter*, idling above the lower fleet anchorage, that he was expected to "push up to the attack." Like the *Queen of the West*, the *Sumter* was to ram into the side of the *Arkansas*, putting his beak as deeply into her beam as possible. During the fight between the ironclads, the *Sumter* was seen by Capt. Bell to steam "ahead of the fleet about a mile and lay there, steam up."

USS Brooklyn. *Having failed to make the passage north of Vicksburg back on June 28, this huge sloop-of-war remained below the city serving as flagship for the mortar schooners and other vessels that did not accompany Farragut. When reunited with the* Hartford *and the other upriver vessels on the evening of July 15, her powerful battery was added to the Union naval might ready to stop the* Arkansas *should she sortie downstream (National Archives).*

For some unknown reason, future RAdm. Erben, says Chester Hearn, "changed his mind about joining the attack" and did not deliver. So far as is known, the *Sumter* just did not "push up" beyond the point. Neither of his superiors understood at the time why not, but, in the wake of the failed venture, neither seemed too concerned. Davis told Farragut, "I do not understand where the *Sumter* was this morning." Farragut later said simply: "He failed to take his part and never gave me any explanation."

At about 5:25 A.M. when it looked like the *Essex* might be able to claw her way back up the river to reengage the *Arkansas*, RAdm. Farragut signaled the *Brooklyn* and *Richmond* to join the *Hartford* in "Going Ahead." Over the next 10 minutes, the trio steamed up to the position held by Cmdr. Renshaw's mortar schooners. The signal was then made to commence action, but at almost the same time, the *Essex* was seen to be affirmatively moving downstream, at which point, a second flag, "Action discontinue," was raised.

Given the quick up and down of Farragut's action orders to his sloops, Lt. Hunter's quote regarding the *Sumter*'s "if necessary" role to the *Memphis Bulletin* becomes even more operationally revealing. It is quite likely that Erben never actually received orders to engage the *Arkansas* and thus remained out of the fray. His action certainly had no impact on his later promotion.

After the *Essex* steamed south about a mile, the *Queen of the West*, "no doubt the best ram of the Ellet flock," entered the arena with her bow manned by sharpshooters, running

Ten: Arkansas vs. Essex, Round One: July 16–22, 1862

Queen of the West. *After the* Essex *withdrew from her failed July 22 attempt to eliminate the* Arkansas *and had retired downstream about a mile, the* Queen of the West, *"no doubt the best ram of the Ellet flock," as Lt. Isaac Newton Brown labeled her, entered the arena with her bow manned by sharpshooters, running along the western shore under full steam, "regardless of the fire of our upper shore batteries." She, too, was unlucky in her effort to destroy the Confederate ram, although she did butt her severely. Instead of withdrawing south, the unarmored craft steamed back the way she came through a hail of Rebel cannon fire. When she reached the safety of Davis' upper flotilla, the* Queen *was so badly damaged that she resembled a colander. Remarkably, none of her volunteer crew was killed or even seriously hurt (Navy History and Heritage Command).*

along the western shore under full steam, "regardless of the fire of our upper shore batteries." This was the same boat Cmdr. Brown had encountered up the Yazoo a week earlier and he was not impressed. As far as his experience with these federal boats went, "they were all ordinary sheep and equally harmless."

The lengthy interval between the departure of Porter's craft and the arrival of Ellet's, caused by Davis' farewell gesture, gave the *Arkansas* a tiny breather. The ram's mixed officer-rating gun crews were reconstituted into even smaller flying squads that could run between pieces reloading them separately and running them back into battery. Then parties even fewer in number could actually train and fire. In this way, all of the available cannon could be employed as necessary. Cmdr. Brown later claimed he and his busy lads were "as determined and cheerful as they could have been with a full crew on board." One must wonder about the "cheerful" part of that assertion.

An alert eye saw the *Queen of the West* across the water maneuvering to start her "bold dash." Aboard the *Arkansas*, the 17 remaining crewmen — officers and tars alike — rushed over to the other side of the ship and ran out the guns. As the enemy steamer rounded to and began to head in, the starboard Columbiad opened fire, joined almost instantaneously by several other mounts. "We welcomed him as warmly as we could with our scanty crew," Midshipman Scales confessed.

Having successfully halted the charge of the *Essex* by loosening his shorefast, Cmdr.

Brown watched the ripples escaping outward from the bow of his new enemy and sought to ward her off as well. The troublesome starboard engine, still running under minimum power, was thrown into reverse, while that on the port side was pushed forward. The rudder was turned hard over and slowly the bow of the *Arkansas* turned, her ram facing outward toward the oncoming *Queen*. This maneuver would, indicated the chronicler from the *New York Times*, also have the added advantage of concealing "her stern, which, it is stated, was injured a few days ago by the explosion of one of our [mortar] shells."

Foam was escaping from beneath the great paddle wheel of the *Queen of the West* as she passed Louisiana Point. Aboard her, Ellet and Hunter were "astonished to find that the *Essex*, so far as her part of the agreement ... was already three-quarters of a mile below the *Arkansas* ... pursuing her course down the river." In the midst of a galling fire, the Federal ram boatmen decided to continue their mission and engage the Confederate armorclad "single handed." Their boat's great plated bow, protected as it was by extra wood, heavy beams, and cotton, should find its mark.

Lt. Col. Ellet now saw how Brown protected his boat by turning her stern toward shore with her head upstream "so as to use guns on both sides effectively." The soldier attempted to counter Brown's tactic by changing his own course in midstream, hoping to avoid the Confederate's deadly ram. In so doing, the Federal boat lost headway and hit an eddy. The swirling water, in turn, forced the Northern ram to veer into a steeper attack angle and lose additional way. Though slowed, the *Queen* continued on, her engines humming at maximum capacity and great clouds of soot and sparks shooting from her chimneys. "The voices of the rebel gunboat's crew were heard in clamorous blasphemy," wrote the *Times* reporter, "rising in terrible distinctness above the clash and clang of the *Queen*'s machinery."

Seconds before impact, the *Arkansas* staggered Ellet's boat with a ragged broadside from three guns at a range of 50 feet. These shots, when added to concern for the Rebel's jutting prow, caused the *Queen of the West* to swerve just as she hit and to bounce off. "She came into us going at an enormous speed, probably 15 miles an hour," Lt. Gift said later, "and I felt pretty sure that our hour had come."

The *Queen* butted the *Arkansas* "immediately aft the third or last gun on her larboard [port] side." The strike, "though glancing, was a heavy one," that sheared numerous iron bars from her side. Other T-bars "were seen to start from their places and fall half off." As the U.S. ram hit the Rebel armorclad, Lt. Hunter prevented several firemen and deck hands, who had congregated near the wheel-guards during the boat's approach, from jumping overboard.

The beak of the U.S. vessel "made a hole through our side and caused the ship to careen and roll heavily," even though her crew, intimate with her character, knew instantly that no "serious damage had been done" and that they had not received what Midshipman Scales termed "a fair lick." Still, as the blow was struck, a Northern correspondent added, "the blaspheming and terror-stricken wretches" of her crew "were hurled to the larboard-side of their vessel and plunged head-foremost out of her ports to escape." Lt. Hunter later told the *Memphis Bulletin* that four Southern sailors "had jumped ashore" as the *Queen* smashed into the *Arkansas*. He inferred, though he could not substantiate it, that the enemy boat was badly damaged, basing his belief on "the noise and confusion that followed" the collision.

In his *Battles and Leaders* memoir, Cmdr. Brown was contemptuous of Ellet's strike and, by implication, the assertion of the *Times* correspondent. The Rebel ram's captain was adamant that the *Queen* "'butted' us so gentle that we hardly felt the shock." "Had Brown been on board at the time," suggesting that he was not, Chester Hearn believes "he might not have described the 'bump' as 'gentle,' as the engine's connecting rods absorbed the shock." Contrary to Hearn's assertion, Brown was aboard; however, Hearn is correct regarding the actual seriousness of the hit. The butt, reported the *Chicago Times*, "made her tremble from stem to stern."

As her thrust was not clean, the *Queen of the West*, like the *Essex*, also caromed off her beam and was carried by forward momentum up onto the riverbank. There, she too received a salute from Lt. Read's stern guns, though their bolts were, in the opinion of Cmdr. Brown, "probably lost in the immense quantity of hay in bales which seemed stowed over and around him." The Northern press reported that, "in response and in an effort to interfere with the enemy aim," Lt. Col. Ellet "and his brave son discharged their revolvers into the [armorclad's] ports."

The present-day controversy over the battle flag of the *Arkansas* dates from the *Queen*'s sojourn ashore. The bunting, a Confederate 1st National Flag, is allegedly displayed at the National Civil War Naval Museum in Port Columbus, Georgia. Glenn Dedmondt tells us it measures 98" (hoist) by 205" (fly), with seven 7-inch diameter stars in a blue field and three 32⅝-inch bars, two red separated by one white. There is, however, doubt as to whether the artifact is as labeled. Let us here begin the story.

While the *Queen of the West* was stuck in the mud and under fire from all sides, one John P. Skelton, the civilian fourth assistant engineer aboard the Federal boat, jumped over onto the deck of the *Arkansas* and cut her national flag from the halyards of its staff. While folding it to slip into his jacket, he was wounded in a thumb, which was subsequently lost. Scrambling back aboard the *Queen*, he hid it in a barrel of beans as a war souvenir to retrieve later.

As the *Queen* sat with her nose piled into the bank and engineer Skelton was, supposedly, making off with the enemy's flag, Confederate forces continued to shoot at her with everything they had. Once more, butternut soldiers scrambled out of their overhead barricades and started running down the overhanging hills, prepared to swarm aboard and capture the boat. Again, they were too late. "Being more nimble," as Lt. Gift quipped, the *Queen* was able to reverse her engines and back into deep water much more quickly than the *Essex*— a matter of only a few minutes. As the *Queen of the West* wore round, without thought to another ramming attempt, she began to paddle back out into the current. At this point, she received a broadside from the *Arkansas*'s port broadside guns.

Lt. Col. Ellet was faced with a choice. He could separate himself from his command and follow Cmdr. Porter downriver to rendezvous with Farragut. Or he could attempt to rejoin the Ram Fleet, running back upstream against the current and through a hail of shot and shell. The feisty "amphibian" chose the latter course. "I had the undivided attention of the enemy's batteries and sharpshooters," Ellet later wrote to War Secretary Edwin Stanton, and "the consequences were that the *Queen* was completely riddled with balls and very much damaged." Not only was Ellet a target for the Confederate gunners ashore, but as he made his getaway, lurching from many hits, his unprotected boat ran directly into the lines of fire of the *Arkansas*' bow Columbiads.

Joining the land-based batteries, the *Arkansas*' bow guns rained fire upon the *Queen of the West* as she sped away, putting bolts through her upper works and making her look like Swiss cheese. When she was nearly a mile away, Lt. Gift was able to launch one last 64-lb. cannonball at her. He later recollected that it was "the handsomest shot I ever made."

Instead of a straight shot, "I bowled at him with the gun lying level." The projectile "*ricocheted* four or five times before it dropped into his stern. But it dropped there."

Ellet was displeased that neither the *Essex* nor the *Sumter* provided support during his *Arkansas* attack and believed that Flag Officer Davis ceased firing upon the upper forts before he could make it back up past De Soto Point. The *Queen*'s engineers, pilots, and crew were all commended for their "creditable behavior." Only one man was hurt badly when hit in the hand by a splinter. The *New York Times* reporter told his readers in early August that Davis was straightforward concerning the reason his ironclads supposedly did not provide covering fire for the *Queen of the West*. The flag officer, it was printed, "says he never expected to see the ram return and that he forgot that part of the agreement making it obligatory upon him to cover Ellet's retreat."

As the *Essex* approached the Gulf Squadron vessels, her men were ordered on deck to return the chorus of hearty cheers and hurrahs that greeted her arrival. About 5:50 A.M., the *Hartford* came to with her port anchor and 10 minutes later the ironclad passed her stern. At that point, the men aboard the sloops of war "left their quarters."

Meanwhile, the converted side-wheeler *Queen of the West* "was full of steam, and of course so hot as to be scarcely endurable, with shells bursting, one in the pilothouse and another in the engine room, with shot tearing the boat on every side," Ellet informed the secretary, "yet unflinching, every man stood to his post." His praise was highest for Lt. Hunter, whose reputation was redeemed when the Ram Fleet commander attributed to him "in an eminent degree the final escape of the boat and all on board."

As noticed in the logbook of the *Carondelet*, the firing on both sides was over close to half past the hour. At 5:30 A.M., the upper river gunboats returned and anchored in shoal water opposite while the *Louisville* tied up to the coal barges behind Cmdr. Walke's turtle. Long spyglasses revealed the *Essex* "lying below the rebel batteries." The thick wood on the river bend above had long prevented marine glasses aboard Farragut's vessels from seeing their previous anchorage. "We could make out nothing that was going on in" Flag Officer Davis' flotilla, Cmdr. Bell unhappily noted.

From their vantage points across the Mississippi, Davis' observers were unable initially to ascertain against the bright morning sun exactly what or how much damage was done to the *Arkansas*. Later as visibility improved, an "intelligent scout," reported back that she was seriously injured as "Porter's shot tore a long hole in her."

As the *Queen of the West* sped out of range, Cmdr. Brown ordered Lt. Stevens to muster the crew. It was, thankfully for the Confederates, found that no additional men were killed or wounded. The 17 survivors, aided by a few soldiers from shore, moved the dead ashore and sent the most seriously wounded to the hospital. Everyone remaining pitched in to clean ship. Once the main brace was spliced, work was resumed on the engines, which, during this crisis at least, had worked well up until the time the Federal ram struck.

Spirits among the men of the Confederate ram if not high, were, buoyed by their emergence from another big Union assault. Lt. Stevens informed his sister by mail that "never has a naval battle been fought under such circumstances." He allowed himself to boast slightly: "Many of the Enemy's gun-boats were our superiors both in guns & speed & yet we did them more harm than they inflicted on us." Midshipman Scales wrote in his own domestic report, penned a few days later: "We have since heard from the other side of the river that six or eight of our shot penetrated the *Essex*, killing and wounding a good many men."

To the sounds of cheers coming from various-sized crowds once more gathered along the bluffs, Cmdr. Brown went ashore and reported to Maj. Gen. Van Dorn, who in turn wired news of the battle to President Davis. Further impressed by the *Arkansas'* seeming indestructibility, the general added that the enemy failure was "so complete that it was almost ridiculous." He did, however, admit that several men were killed. Brown next wired Secretary Mallory, who in turn reported to President Davis. Brown was apparently rather emphatic about his lack of crewmen, saying that he was "doomed to inactivity by the inability to get them." Davis, in turn, wired Mississippi governor John J. Pettus asking the help of the state government in obtaining additional sailors from among the large unemployed "class of river boatmen and some ordinary seamen on our Gulf coast."

The upper fleet commander met as early as possible with Lt. Col. Ellet and got a good look at the *Queen of the West*. He marveled at how she "is cut to pieces with round shot and grape, but strange to say, though many persons in her small crew were struck, no one was killed and no one ever seriously wounded." When he heard of the exploit, Fourth Master Brown of the *Essex* marveled: "Though built for the business, such was the force of her blow that she stove in her butts and was soon after in a sinking condition." The vivid description of Ellet's wrecked command was provided by the correspondent from the *New York Times*:

> The *Queen* was terribly cut up. Her scape-pipes were cut away and her chimneys riddled. A shell struck an iron safe on her upper deck, and, exploding, demolished it and everything around. A 64-pound shot entered her aft and, traversing the entire length of her cabin, tore all the bedding in the berths over which it passed, and striking the breach of a 32-pounder howitzer, rebounded and wounded Lieut. Hunter in the hip. The rebel balls struck the *Queen* in almost every part but a vital one, and her escape from total destruction under the circumstances seems little less than miraculous.

Lt. Hunter himself, in talking to the *Memphis Bulletin*, added a few other details. The U.S. ram's prow was broken "all to pieces and the timbers on her starboard side were started, and shrank considerably." A shot also passed through her fire grating.

Tuesday was as hot as, maybe hotter than, the three days before. Aboard the *Arkansas*, as on all of the warships and some of the smaller boats of the Federal squadrons, large awnings were spread or, if already up, checked as protection against the sharp rays of the sun. In order for the Western Flotilla mortar boats to be effective, it would be necessary for them to hold off firing until "the thermometer has descended below 140 degrees in the shade." Beginning at 2:00 P.M., Cmdr. Renshaw began to escort his mortar schooners downstream from their advanced position below the citadel. It was finally cool enough between 6:00 P.M. and 8:00 P.M. for Capt. Maynadier's craft to throw 27 shells in the direction of the Confederate ram.

The Confederate sailors wounded in the July 22 assault were taken to infirmaries ashore, along with several more "used up" officers who went to hospital that day and for the next two. Those *Arkansas* crewmen already in medical facilities greeted the ambulatory and heard of the attack by the *Essex* and *Queen of the West*. Master's Mate John Wilson was saddened to learn that so many were killed when the Union ironclad's shot entered his "unfortunate gun port."

The *Arkansas'* officers were not complimentary regarding the support provided to the Confederate ram by Vicksburg's shore batteries. Master's Mate Wilson was especially blunt, indicating that they were of "but small assistance." In fact, he went on to report, one of the 17 surviving crewmen that day "had his arm shattered by a discharge of grape from one of their guns." Lt. Gift added that, under the circumstances, the fact that she beat off the two boats on July 22 "was the best achievement of the *Arkansas*." Sure, they were under the batteries of Vicksburg, but that "did not amount to anything." "I do not believe," he added, "that either [Federal] vessel was injured by an army gun that day." In fairness, the guns of the upper and lower batteries were able to hit both the *Essex* and *Queen of the West*. They could not, however, stop either from making their attacks, nor sink them as they withdrew.

The weather in Richmond that Tuesday was, according to Capt. William Edwards of the 17th South Carolina Infantry, hot and steamy with temperatures in the 90s. Working in his office, Confederate war secretary George W. Randolph dictated a general order of praise recognizing the defense of Vicksburg and the operations of the Rebel ram. "Lt. Brown and the officers and crew of the Confederate steamer *Arkansas*," he praised, "by their heroic attack upon the Federal fleet before Vicksburg equaled the highest recorded examples of courage and skill." He continued that the armorclad's sailors "prove that the Navy ... is entitled to a high place in the confidence and affection of the country."

The entire July episode was labeled "a fizzle" by Lt. Phelps, who, like others in the up-river squadron above the city, blamed RAdm. Farragut for not bombarding the lower forts or independently making certain that the *Sumter* was sent to join the attack. In his July 23 report of the action to Navy Secretary Welles, the Western Flotilla boss spoke in generalities, claiming that the "shot from the *Essex* did serious injury to the casemates of the rebel ram and gunboat." The strike against the Rebel armorclad by the *Queen of the West*, Davis noted, was made with "sufficient force to do her some injury." Of Lt. Col. Ellet, he was praiseworthy, noting that the army man "behaved on this, as on previous occasions, with great gallantry." Secretary Welles would undoubtedly support Stanton's move, a few days later, to nominate Ellet to the rank of brigadier general.

A reading of the Northern newspapers reveals that the press seemed more unhappy with the failed Federal effort than with Cmdr. Brown's defense. "Altogether," wrote a correspondent for the *Chicago Daily Tribune*, "the whole affair seems to have been well planned and most bunglingly executed, but whether from want of proper understanding or proper cooperation remains to be seen."

Some of the nautical reversal, the Midwestern newspaper opined, may have occurred because nearly everyone in the Federal fleet was "indisposed" by the fevers then so prevalent, including Flag Officer Davis, "sick for two weeks past." The *Brooklyn Daily Eagle*, conversely, held the upper river commander responsible, not only for this episode but for the failure of the entire Vicksburg campaign after Independence Day. "Davis, it noted, proved himself an infant in conception and an imbecile in execution from the moment he left Memphis to besiege Vicksburg until he came away with the indelible disgrace of having been whipped and bullied by the *Arkansas* into submission."

Despite a further reduction in the size of his crew and the additional damage taken from the two Federal boats, Cmdr. Brown determined to show both Davis and Farragut of his contempt for their assault upon him. With her faulty engine at least briefly enabled and a battle flag snapping from its staff, the *Arkansas*, at 10:00 A.M. that Wednesday morning, was seen by lookouts aboard the *Brooklyn* to have "moved up the river out of sight, as if meditating something against Davis."

The officer of the deck aboard the *Benton* noted that the Confederate ram was, in fact, making "her appearance around the point." She was taken under fire, but without effect. Would she challenge the Western Flotilla flagboat and the nearby Pook turtles? The correspondent of the *Philadelphia Press* believed she "steamed with difficulty into the middle of the river, in front of the batteries, as an act of bravado, to show the Yankees that she still existed through it all."

"We were in hopes she was coming up" beyond the point, Flag Officer Davis confided in a letter home. That was not to be and, according to Scharf, the *Arkansas* "was seen steaming up and down the river in front of the batteries of Vicksburg" later that afternoon. By evening, she was, according to a note in the diary of Capt. Henry H. Bell of the *Brooklyn*, "under the batteries, upper part of the city, head downriver, steam up." Fourth Master Brown of the *Essex* learned of the episode shortly thereafter. "Not withstanding the shots we gave the ram *Arkansas*," he wrote his grandfather, "she got up steam on the next day and ran up, threatening the upper fleet, drawing their fire, and again returning under her batteries, apparently as vigorous as ever." He concluded: "All honor to the ram!"

Once the Confederate armorclad returned to her lair, her weary survivors began to do what they could to straighten ship. Cmdr. Brown, daily more visibly ill from the effects of malaria, wrote out several reports for Flag Officer Lynch, including the first to contain the names of all the men killed or wounded aboard on July 15 and another listing those who had died the day before. In one of the messages, he also reiterated his belief that his ship had "whipped" whatever Federal ironclad she met up the Yazoo on July 15 and "made it run out of the fight and haul down colors."

The weary Brown could not lay down his pen before taking the opportunity to commend the conduct of his XO, Lt. Stevens, making certain that his superior also clearly understood that all of his officers had "behaved well." Stevens, on the other hand, was a special case who deserved "promotion for his exertions in preparing for and while engaged in battle." The history books do not say so, but quite possibly this praise would, in a few days, lead Lynch to believe that Stevens was, as the army wanted, quite capable of guiding the *Arkansas* downstream into battle without Brown.[7]

The failed July 22 attack upon the *Arkansas* added further to the mortification and

Vicksburg. *During the last week of July, Federal naval forces withdrew from the waters off Vicksburg. "With one ironclad, a handful of guns, and 7,000 troops," National Park Service historian Edwin Bearss opined years later, "the Confederates had regained control of 250 miles of the Mississippi." Maj. Gen. Earl Van Dorn summed up the outcome of the entire Federal effort in a single sentence in his September 9, 1862, campaign review, written for the War Department in Richmond. "With the failure to destroy or take the* Arkansas,*" he concluded, "the siege of Vicksburg practically ended" (U.S. Army Military History Institute).*

general campaign frustration felt by RAdm. Farragut, Flag Officer Davis, Brig. Gen. Williams, and Lt. Col. Ellet after the Confederate ram had avoided destruction at their hands a week earlier. There were, however, other problems, in addition to the Rebel armorclad, that faced these Federal commanders as they attempted to maintain station above and below Vicksburg. The quartet had known for weeks that Brig. Gen. Williams' small group of soldiers encamped on the De Soto Peninsula was numerically insufficient to capture the enemy citadel across the river. Their calls for reinforcement went unheeded.

As July lengthened, the Mississippi revealed more shoal. If the larger oceangoing vessels remained much longer, there was a real chance that they would be grounded. Further, Davis and Farragut found that coal and other provisions were difficult to obtain. The latter, in particular, suffered from logistical problems. His supply chain stretched all the way back to New Orleans and everything sent to him had to travel against the current. Guerrillas and Rebel irregulars constantly harassed the supply steamers of both commanders.

On top of these concerns was illness and death. The "fever-breeding" swamps and the heat brought much sickness and death afloat and ashore. The bluecoats of Brig. Gen. Williams were particularly hard hit, with only 26.6 percent of the 3,000 men available for duty and an average of 10 dying per day. Yeoman Holton, aboard the *Hartford*, remembers that the "malarious fever" was "prostrating a dozen a day. We had a sick list of about 100 men." Only 41 percent of Davis' men were fit for service, with 10–15 cases added to the sick rolls daily. The crews of RAdm. Farragut were also badly affected. Temperatures were normally above 100 degrees from late morning to early evening, though Flag Officer Davis was able to note that, on July 24–25, the thermometer had come down to 90 degrees in the shade, making the weather "delightful."

RAdm. Farragut had, some weeks earlier, requested permission of the Navy Department to retire downstream, which authority was wired from Washington via Memphis on the 18th. Unhappily, these instructions were, as the Gulf Squadron commander admitted, not received before the appearance of the *Arkansas*. After their arrival in Tennessee, the telegram was included with others sent down aboard the regular downriver mail boat. Secretary Welles' withdrawal authority was received at the Federal upper fleet anchorage above Vicksburg on the afternoon of July 22. In the wake of the morning's activities, it was simply dispatched without ceremony across the De Soto Peninsula by courier with the other mail for the lower fleet.

Writing home that evening, Captain's Clerk Edward S. Davis aboard the *Iroquois* observed that "the Ram has steam up this evening and is as well as ever." His family was informed that no further plans were being made to deal with her because orders had been received for "all hands to proceed down the River tomorrow." He concluded that "this move will be a great deliverance."

The next day, Farragut advised Davis that his withdrawal orders were in hand. At the same time, Brig. Gen. Williams informed him that he, too, was pulling out, the sickness being too much a burden upon his small force to sustain. The flag officer wrote to the military man asking him to remain, but he was informed that option was not possible, as the troops were being sent to New Orleans.

Accepting the situation, Flag Officer Davis agreed to a proposal from RAdm. Farragut for the retention of the *Essex* and the *Sumter* in the waters between Vicksburg and Baton Rouge. These vessels, together with several small gunboats from the Gulf Squadron, would be able to maintain a blockade of both the *Arkansas* and the mouth of the Red River, a major Confederate supply artery. Of those two objectives, Davis confirmed that the *Arkansas* remained the more important. "When she disappears from the scene," he wrote, "Porter can go below to Grand Gulf or wherever else he might be wanted."

Cmdr. Porter was advised of this new role in a set of orders from Flag Officer Davis the next day. The bearded commander of the *Essex* was reminded that his was an important duty, not only in blockading the waters between Baton Rouge and Vicksburg, but also in keeping "a careful watch over the rebel gunboat *Arkansas*."

Taking their supplies, the troops of Brig. Gen. Williams boarded their six transports early on July 24, a process that was completed by noon. As the afternoon watch began, the soldiers were heading downstream, followed by the remainder of Farragut's fleet after 2:00 P.M.

After watching a while the smoke from the Union chimneys descend, Maj. Gen. Van Dorn wrote out a wire for President Davis: "The whole of the lower fleet and all the troops have disappeared down the river." He added that Federal newspapers and mail taken from one of the Northern transports, sunk during the evacuation, contained "interesting accounts of the *Arkansas*."

The *Essex* brought up the rear. Some believed there was a possibility that the *Arkansas* might steam down and attempt to interfere with Farragut's withdrawal. Farragut sent instructions to Cmdr. Porter that in the event the ram was seen following he was to raise a special signal by day and two lanterns by night. If these were seen, the oceangoing vessels would "round to to support you." The same message was passed to Lt. Erben aboard the *Sumter*. According to the ironclad's Fourth Master Spencer Kellogg Brown, Porter's boat was placed in back because "she was the best qualified to repel the assault of the rebel ram." To keep the Southern fortifications occupied, Capt. Maynadier's mortar boats took them under fire all afternoon and into the early evening.

Ironically, the same concern over a possible assault grasped the officers of the *Arkansas*. When the fleet was seen to be getting underway, remembered Lt. Read, "we got ready, expecting a general attack." The Federals, however, "steamed away and abandoned the siege." Relieved, the captain of the stern chasers admitted in later years that the ram's crew was "agreeably disappointed." That evening, a detail of 50 men was chosen from among the soldiers of the 4th and 5th (later 9th) Kentucky regiments to report aboard the *Arkansas*. Pvt. John S. Jackman of the latter unit reports that there was genuine fear that the men were being recruited "to make up the crew — and one fellow objected so much he that he ran off."

The following morning, July 25, the Kentucky soldiers reported to the levee ready to go aboard the Confederate ram. Cmdr. Brown indicated, however, that the men would not be required before dark. With no duties, the butternuts moved up town "and took up quarters in a large mansion then vacated.... The boys had piano music and dancing, with plenty of books to read." While Jackman and his fellow soldiers passed their time ashore, the *Arkansas* made another mini-cruise up the river. Like the others before, this one resulted in no action, only serving to reinforce the ram's "fleet-in-being" status.

Also on that Friday, the *Queen of the West* departed for Cairo. Off Greenville, Mississippi, soon to be a hotbed of Confederate antishipping activity, she was taken under fire next day by Rebel irregulars. Her escape pipe was knocked off and her upper works further damaged. One of the army sharpshooters aboard was killed and *New York Tribune* correspondent Junius H. Brown was wounded in the face by a splinter.

Eventually, the battered ram made it to Memphis where Lt. Hunter recounted his boat's adventures for the press. At the same time, engineer John P. Skelton withdrew his prize flag from its hiding spot in a barrel of beans and sent it home to Ohio for preservation. As Cmdr. Brown did not know that the *Arkansas*' flag was missing and so did not report it and Lt. Col. Ellet did not know his man had it, the trophy could be kept secret in a family cedar chest until 1999, when Skelton's grandsons donated it to the National Civil War Naval Museum in Georgia.

The *Arkansas* returned to her anchorage off Vicksburg at 9:00 P.M. The "sweet time" for the 50 Kentuckians detailed to work aboard her was now at an end and the men trooped down to meet her as she put into an area where several coal barges were tied. There they found that the job for which they were wanted "was to coal the boat, which had to be done by carrying the coal some distance in bags." The duty "was through by midnight," after which the men "went back to our house." They returned to their own camps the following morning.

With the U.S. Navy's lower anchorage abandoned, Flag Officer Davis felt obliged to withdraw his own force from the riverbanks above Vicksburg to the mouth of the Yazoo River. Concerned that Mississippi defenses between that point and Helena would now be continuously attacked by squads of Confederate flying artillery and that the sickness afflicting his bluejackets would worsen, the upper fleet commander believed that he, too, must withdraw. By August 1, the Western Flotilla, like the Gulf Squadron, had retired.

The first siege of Vicksburg, begun back in May, was over. "With one ironclad, a handful of guns, and 7,000 troops," Edwin Bearss opined years later, "the Confederates had regained control of 250 miles of the Mississippi." Maj. Gen. Van Dorn summed up the outcome of the entire Federal effort in a single sentence in his September 9 campaign review, written for the War Department in Richmond. "With the failure to destroy or take the *Arkansas*," he concluded, "the siege of Vicksburg practically ended."

Van Dorn's brief comment does not represent the background for the whole picture. Inability of the Union to back its naval commanders with additional troops; confusion and bickering between its officers on the scene; malaria and other tropical illnesses; an incredibly long Federal supply line for the lower fleet; the falling river; and the dawning realization that this would be a long and vicious contest conspired with Van Dorn and Brown to end this campaign. The flamboyant general and the red ironclad, as Dr. Michael Ballard wrote, "bought Vicksburg time, not salvation."

There was much joy from Warrenton in the south and the lower batteries north into the terraced city, the Walnut Hills and the upper batteries, and into the Yazoo country. There was no shooting for the first time since May. As Lt. Read remembered with pleasure, much credit was "given to Brown and the men of the *Arkansas* for making it happen." The captain and his crew, under tremendous pressure for over 60 days, still had much work to do to refit the armorclad. Now, however, it looked like there might be some idle time to finally complete a building task begun by John Shirley such a seemingly long time earlier.[8]

CHAPTER ELEVEN

Arkansas vs. *Essex*, Round Two: Finale Off Baton Rouge, July 23–August 6, 1862

The first siege of Vicksburg, begun in May, ended on July 24, 1862, when the ocean-going vessels of RAdm. David Glasgow Farragut, escorting the troop steamers of Brig. Gen. Thomas Williams, withdrew downstream from the fortress town. Low water, disease, lack of an adequate invasion force, confusion over mission purpose, and failed efforts to destroy the CSS *Arkansas* all contributed to the admiral's decision to leave.

As the deep-water fleet of Union naval ships and transport steamers departed, their rear was protected by the river gunboats *Essex* and *Sumter*. These craft were originally units in the Western Flotilla squadron still anchored north of De Soto Point above the town. The *Essex*, perhaps the most powerful ironclad on Western waters, had failed in a combined attack with the *Queen of the West* upon the *Arkansas* just two days before. Terribly slow, despite the urging of her colorful captain, Cmdr. William D. "Dirty Bill" Porter, she could not buck the Mississippi current and return to her former upper anchorage.

Maj. Gen. Earl Van Dorn, commander of the Department of Southern Mississippi and Eastern Louisiana, was among the thousands of Confederates who watched the Northern departure. In a telegraph to President Davis, he joyously proclaimed, "The whole of the lower fleet and all the troops have disappeared down the river." Within a week, Flag Officer Davis would also be gone from Vicksburg waters, steaming back up to the Federal advanced base at Helena, Arkansas.[1] In the absence of a besieging enemy, the citizens of Vicksburg returned to their lives as lived in the days before Farragut arrived in May. As Lt. Charles W. Read of the *Arkansas* put it, "business to some extent was resumed."

Ever since the Confederate ram had broken out from the Yazoo into the Mississippi more than a week earlier, she had received hardly a moment's peace from the Federals. As her depleted crew attempted to make repairs, she was pummeled by mortar shells from the Western Flotilla, though, fortunately for her, none had scored a direct hit. Northern scouts watched her from the Louisiana shore and reported all activities seen aboard. She sortied occasionally just to convince Farragut and Davis that she was yet battle ready. These tiny cruises convinced the two naval leaders, pushed by the gung-ho Lt. Col. Alfred Ellet, captain of the U.S. Army Ram Fleet, to make another attempt to crush what Davis called "the rascal." It came on July 22 and while not successful, it did cost the Rebel armorclad additional damage and deaths.

Even as the smoke from Farragut's fleet gradually disappeared, the men of the *Arkansas* turned to addressing the needs of the boat. There was much to do, but fortunately an earlier call for carpenters and mechanics proved fruitful. Men from Vicksburg, Jackson, and as far away as Mobile arrived to put right the now-legendary fighting ship. And there was much for them to do.

Great holes and mighty dents still pockmarked the casemate. The railroad T-bar iron armor so laboriously hung while the *Arkansas* was up the Yazoo was loosened in many spots on Brown's "gun box," particularly along the port side. Some of the bars had been knocked off and lay on the deck; others were lost in the river. Observing the *Arkansas* from the wharf and perhaps by rowboat from the river, Cmdr. Brown admitted that many of these "had to be refastened to her shattered sides." Where and as necessary, replacement bars were sought. A few were even found to set upon the casemate roof as protection against plunging shot.

In addition to the armor, the entire matter of the pilothouse had to be resolved. Badly damaged in the fight with the *Carondelet* up the Yazoo and battered since, it could not be repaired. Thus it was removed and "a new one was made." The ram's large chimney was holed during her fight with the *Essex* and *Queen of the West*, though not nearly as badly as during the combats of July 15. Still, it was necessary for the laborers to once more fashion and attach new boiler iron patches.

All of the vessel's officers who penned recollections — Brown, Gift, Read, Wilson — agree that after the July 22 attack by the *Essex* and the *Queen of the West* the vessel's engines were in need of repair. Lt. Brown reports that the attack of the *Queen* resulted in the *Arkansas* receiving just a "gentle bump." Unhappily for her, as Chester Hearn points out, the engine's connecting rods absorbed the shock.

The craft's already-temperamental power plant remained functional, as her mini-cruise on July 23 proved, but Chief Engineer George City — showing, like Brown, the yellow skin of the malaria sufferer — refused to have confidence in it. Consequently, at his urging and with his captain's permission, an overhaul was scheduled to begin on July 24. It is unclear whether or not a full engine overhaul was actually conducted. Later that Thursday, several of the boat's sick officers, including City himself, were sent to the city hospital ashore. Lt. Gift noted that the technician was also "worn out and broken down by excessive watching and anxiety."

Refurbishment of the *Arkansas* continued under the direction of the energetic Lt. Henry K. Stevens and Cmdr. Brown. The latter, increasingly ill and with a high temperature, sought and received permission from Navy Secretary Mallory for a short leave once the upgrade task was "fairly under way."[2]

While Brown and his men, with the contract laborers, worked on the *Arkansas*, the vessels of RAdm. Farragut and Brig. Gen. Williams continued down the river, accompanied by the seconded *Essex* and *Sumter*. This fleet came to off Baton Rouge on July 26. It had been decided some time earlier that Williams' four infantry regiments and two batteries of field artillery would be landed to help garrison the town. These soldiers, many ill from malaria, dysentery, and other maladies, were the same troops that had camped out for a month on the peninsula opposite Vicksburg.

Most of Williams' troops made their way to positions on the eastern side of Louisiana's capital, while a detachment was posted north of town. Offshore, naval protection was enhanced by a pair of blue-water gunboats assigned to coordinate with Porter's upper river vessels. As the 2,000+ bluecoats streamed ashore, the *Essex* and *Sumter* steamed above to inaugurate a blockade of the mouth of Louisiana's Red River. It was believed that two small

Confederate gunboats, the *Webb*[3] and the *Music*,[4] were up that stream and might attempt to sortie forth to contest Williams' occupation.

There has been some speculation and assertion over the past 150 years that the *Arkansas* was not sent forth by Maj. Gen. Van Dorn to act alone, but would, in fact, lead a small task group that included the *Webb* and *Music*. The *Webb* was a powerful tugboat that might have been instrumental in assisting the armorclad if her engines gave difficulty. The two wooden boats were, in fact, up the Red and although several Union captains would believe they saw their smoke on August 5, they did not come out.

The *Kineo*[5] and *Katahdin*[6] were also detached. They were to provide direct liaison and gunfire support to the military command ashore. Once all of the army troops were landed, Farragut proceeded to New Orleans, arriving there on July 28.

Back at the beginning of July, Maj. Gen. Van Dorn, considering ways to divert Union attention from Vicksburg, had begun to formulate ideas for the retaking of Baton Rouge from its small occupying Northern force. If the town could be captured, the supplies emanating from the Red River, 40 miles above, would be secured, along with control of the 268 miles between the Mississippi fortress town and the Louisiana capital. No sooner was planning started than word came in that the Union-held town was being reinforced in numbers that would make an early attack impossible. The bluecoats, continuing to pour in, were turning the town into an armed camp.

And then the *Arkansas* broke out of the Yazoo and, after fighting her way through the combined Federal fleet anchored above, made her way down the Mississippi to Vicksburg. The joyous Van Dorn, believing he had a powerful new hammer, wired Brig. Gen. Ruggles informing him that the ram would be available to "attack below as soon as some repairs are made."

The idea that the ram was some sort of super weapon was not just the opinion in Vicksburg. Back in Richmond, no less of an expert than John Mercer Brooke would write, albeit with a caveat, on August 6 (ironically the day the vessel perished): "I wish we had half a dozen *Arkansas* in the Mississippi, although she is not proof against 11-inch shot."

For the next two weeks Cmdr. Brown attempted to refit his command and find new crewmen. Federal mortars and a daring raid on July 22 unsuccessfully tried to stop him. During this action, Maj. Gen. Van Dorn wrote to Ruggles explaining that operations against the Louisiana town were delayed. On the other hand, theater commander Gen. Braxton Bragg was expected to launch a campaign toward Kentucky that would attract the enemy elsewhere, at which point a contingent of men from Vicksburg could be spared to help reduce Baton Rouge. Other soldiers from the town would be sent to a skirmish line some miles north of Vicksburg.

Although Bragg was yet to start, the withdrawal of Farragut and Williams from the Vicksburg front on July 24 freed up the men and resources needed by Van Dorn to launch the campaign against Baton Rouge. Brig. Gen. Ruggles was informed that about 4,000 men and some artillery would be coming down.

As the Federal troops of Brig. Gen. Williams were landing at Baton Rouge on July 26, Maj. Gen. Van Dorn cut orders for Maj. Gen. John C. Breckenridge to travel with two of the three brigades of his Vicksburg-based division to Camp Moore, Louisiana, not far from the town of Tangipahoa. There he was to join them with Ruggles' forces; Ruggles would assume, by virtue of his seniority, overall command. The combined force was supposed to number about 6,000 men, though many of these subsequently contracted the summer diseases then so wracking the invaders as well as the defenders and general populace of the area.

If the officers aboard the *Arkansas* knew of these developments at this time, there is no public record of that fact. All of their attention was focused upon repairing and upgrading their ram and securing what amounted to a replacement crew. It would have been difficult, however, for the bustle of the town send-off to the troops to have been missed, particularly the band-led formations as they marched to the depot.

XO Stevens wrote to his sister on July 27, noting that "we have lost a good deal of credit by our forced inaction here, but the weakened condition of our crew has compelled us not to seek the enemy." The men carried off the boat following the actions of July 15 and 22 and the holes appearing in her side did nothing to encourage recruitment. Even claims of triumph were proving unhelpful in enticing volunteers: "Whenever he [the Federals] attacked us, we put on a bold front & gave him shot for shot & we flatter ourselves with advantage on our side."

The former U.S. vice president's troop trains, sent by way of Jackson on that Sunday, arrived two days later, about the time most of Farragut's fleet was dropping anchor at New Orleans. In a meeting that night, Breckenridge reorganized his new command into two divisions, one led by Brig. Gen. Ruggles and the other by Brig. Gen. Charles Clark. Earlier, Brig. Gen. Ruggles had received intelligence reports that Baton Rouge was being reinforced with upwards to 7,000 men. These figures were now cut to about 3,000 and thus allowed Breckenridge to contemplate ordering his tiny army to advance on the town.

The same medical and sanitary conditions also faced the Southern field commander as he moved upon Brig. Gen. Williams in the riverfront city. Malaria and dysentery, exacerbated by the hot, humid weather made worse by constant thunderstorms, felled many butternut soldiers. The effective number of fighting men in or approaching Baton Rouge was severely reduced by half on both sides.

Finding himself with only about 3,000 effectives, Maj. Gen. Breckenridge desperately believed he needed a big edge before stepping off. To that end, he wired Van Dorn on July 30 with not only a report on his troop situation but also a request that the *Arkansas* "be sent down to clear the river or divert the fire of the gunboats." There was an implied threat in the

Lt. Charles W. ("Savez") Read, CSN. *A native of Hinds County, Mississippi, this 1860 USNA graduate is depicted in his midshipman uniform. Read served as executive officer and then—following the death of her captain, to whom he was close—commander of the CSN gunboat* McRae *during the New Orleans fight in April 1862. Following the city's capture, he was sent to aid in the defense of Fort Pillow, before his posting to the* Arkansas, *where he commanded the stern chasers. After the* Arkansas *adventure, he assisted in the defense of Port Hudson before transferring aboard the ocean raider* Florida. *He would end the war in command of the CSS* Webb, *undertaking her fabled if unsuccessful attempt to break out to the Gulf of Mexico from Shreveport. He received his nickname from his fellow USNA students in recognition of his horrible lack of achievement in the study of French (Navy History and Heritage Command).*

message that if the ram was not sent to protect his flank, the operation would be cancelled. When this telegram arrived on Van Dorn's desk, he replied: "the *Arkansas* would be ready to co-operate at daylight on Tuesday, August 5." Breckenridge, on the strength of this pledge, departed for Baton Rouge. He would arrive at the Comite River, 10 miles from the town, on August 4. There he would camp, waiting for the armorclad.

Interestingly, Cmdr. William D. "Dirty Bill" Porter, captain of the *Essex*, while cruising between Baton Rouge and the mouth of the Red River, picked up news that "large bodies of rebel troops" were concentrating "in the immediate neighborhood" of Baton Rouge. This intelligence was dispatched to Maj. Gen. Benjamin F. Butler's New Orleans headquarters. Porter also included a scary thought in the same message: "The ram *Arkansas* is still above water, and could, without doubt, if the *Essex* were absent, retake the city." How the Confederate would get past him was not mentioned.

Without a unified command structure, Van Dorn's promise to his Louisiana generals was made with the full knowledge that he would have find a way to get the *Arkansas* committed. There were only two possibilities: to persuade the local naval leadership to sail or to rely upon that already-received special authority from President Davis that had had allowed him to order the Rebel armorclad out of the Yazoo two weeks before. He would rely upon both.[7]

Brig. Gen. John C. Breckenridge, CSA (1821–1875). *After Shiloh and Corinth, the Kentuckian and former U.S. vice president (the nation's youngest), was placed under command of Maj. Gen. Earl Van Dorn in late June 1862. Ordered to Vicksburg, he and his "Orphan Brigade" troops were supportive of the* Arkansas. *In early August, Breckenridge was sent to capture Baton Rouge and requested naval assistance. Van Dorn's decision to send down the unrepaired* Arkansas *led to her loss. After fighting on in lower Tennessee and later in Virginia, Breckenridge became the Confederate war secretary in 1865 (Library of Congress).*

It continued warm and sultry in Vicksburg on the morning of July 31. As the sun climbed higher into the sky, Cmdr. Brown, who had managed by sheer will to so far stay off the sick list, sent a message to the city hospital ordering that all of the officers who were sufficiently recovered to return should report for duty. Refurbishment of the vessel was reaching a final stage and should be completed within a week.

That Thursday afternoon, Cmdr. Brown, his eyes perhaps splotched and his complexion a sickly pale yellow, called upon Maj. Gen. Van Dorn. After reporting upon the progress being made on the *Arkansas*'s repairs, the vessel's captain reminded the general that he had not had but one evening's break in the past two months. Showing the Navy Department permission telegram, Brown informed Van Dorn that he was temporarily turning the boat over to Lt. Stevens in order that he might make a quick trip up to Grenada to see his family. He would be back from the turnaround visit by Tuesday morning, August 5. By then it was hoped that the executive officer, in whom he had the greatest confidence, would have the vessel ready to resume the offense.

It may have been obvious to Van Dorn that Brown was, as Lt. Read put it, "in bad health." Brown's confidence in Stevens may also have convinced the general that the ram was being left in capable hands. Stevens was highly regarded by his colleagues aboard the ram; Lt. Gift later wrote that the XO "was a conscientious Christian gentleman, a zealous and efficient officer in the performance of his duty, he was thorough, consistent, and patriotic. His courage was of the truest and highest type; in the face of the enemy, he knew nothing but his duty, and always did it."

It is possible that Breckenridge's request had yet to arrive. Conversely, it is conceivable that Van Dorn suspected that Brown would object to the boat's being dispatched in an unfinished state and believed Stevens would be easier to convince. In any event, as Edwin C. Bearss later wrote, Van Dorn "did not mention it [the Breckenridge request] to the naval officer."

That afternoon, as Brown headed out of town on the Southern Railroad of Mississippi, the officers most recovered from their convalescent hospital stay began to return aboard the *Arkansas*. These included Midshipman Clarence W. Tyler, Gunner Thomas Travers, and Acting Master's Mate Wilson. Although Engineer City remained behind, Third Assistant Engineer Eugene H. Brown was sufficiently refreshed to come back and take up the duties of acting chief engineer. Unhappily, Lt. Gift tells us that the substitute "never had anything to do with a screw vessel or short-stroke engines." In his recollection, that officer went on to offer a reason why one so unsuited to oversee "the machinery of a vessel of so much importance" was entrusted with the "care and nursing" of the power plant. "Were there not other engineers than Mr. City in the navy," he asked, "and if so, where were they?" There were, he maintained, "dozens of engineers of long experience and high standing at that time in the navy, most of whom were idle at Richmond and other stations."

In addition to the restored officers, the *Arkansas* now received welcome new supplies of victuals, medicines, powder, percussion caps, clothing, and other items. Some of these had come all the way from Mexico via Texas and Louisiana; others had arrived from Mobile and points south and east.

During late afternoon on August 1, Maj. Gen. Van Dorn rode down to the river to meet with Lt. Stevens and see for himself the progress that was being made toward restoring the fighting trim of the *Arkansas*. The commander may have been told about the vessel's untrustworthy power plant, but if so, it is not recorded. After the general was shown around, he thanked the XO for his kindness and took him aside from his officers.

Stevens was told that it would be necessary for the armorclad to go downriver and participate in the forthcoming Southern attack on Baton Rouge. It would be the responsibility of the *Arkansas* to prevent the Union vessels present from interfering with the assault. Stevens hesitated, telling Van Dorn that the campaign should be postponed briefly until all of the boat's repairs were completed and Cmdr. Brown had returned. The district commander was unmoved by Stevens' request and went ashore assuming the naval officer would stand to his assignment with alacrity. The loyal XO, on the other hand, was torn and determined to stall as best he could until he could get a message through to Cmdr. Brown.

Security was a Civil War difficulty for both sides. Before the day was done, Cmdr. Porter was sitting in the great cabin of the *Essex* far below sending off news to RAdm. Farragut at New Orleans. Breckenridge, he told the Gulf squadron commander, was moving on Baton Rouge. He had taken his ironclad off her Red River blockade and placed her above the town to command its rear but he needed help. Porter also learned, even perhaps before CSN Cmdr. Brown, that "the ram is on her way down to aid in the attack." The captain of the *Essex* hoped this news was true. "We will give a good account of her," he boasted. Still, he asked that a gunboat or two be sent to help provide additional support as the *Kineo* and *Katahdin* were under repair or, as he put it, "on the doctor's list."

Leaving the *Arkansas* to Grimball, Gift, and Read, Lt. Stevens traveled to the telegraph office early on August 2 and wired his superior at Grenada telling him of Van Dorn's demand. When he got back on board and had a minute, he wrote a parting letter to his sister: "We [are] ordered off tomorrow and expect a pretty tough time of it, but we will do what we can...." The destination, he revealed, "is Batton-ruge [*sic*]. It is not just to send us in our condition, but I am ready to do what we can."

Following a long journey up from Jackson, the captain of the *Arkansas* had reached his home only hours before. Barely changed out of his uniform, the weakened officer "fell violently ill." Taken to bed and "unable, as I supposed, to rise," Brown was handed his subordinate's message. It had the same effect as an electric shock — or perhaps a very stiff drink of Southern whiskey. Brown dictated a peremptory order to Stevens requiring that the *Arkansas* remain at Vicksburg until he could rejoin her, warning, as Gift later told it, that her "machinery was not reliable." He did not mention that he was quite sick.

Explaining to his horrified family that duty beckoned, Isaac Newton Brown, as Jack Coombe wrote, "pronounced himself cured, packed his kit bags," donned his uniform and had himself taken to the Mississippi Central Railroad station. As he colorfully explained for the *Battles and Leaders* series, "I threw myself on the mail bags of the first passing train, unable to sit up, and did not change my position until reaching Jackson, 130 miles distant."

While Brown traveled south in a railroad baggage car, Lt. Stevens waited upon Van Dorn to show him the commander's wire. The general would have none of it, noting that it would take the *Arkansas* captain at least as long to arrive as it took him to reach Grenada and that the necessary time could not be spared. He may also have suspected that the skipper was not yet recovered from the obvious illness he was suffering when he left town a few days before. Sensing that the acting captain of the ram was dragging his feet, the determined Van Dorn took it upon himself to petition Flag Officer William F. Lynch for an order requiring that the vessel honor his request to sally forth. Capt. Brown later indicated that it was Stevens, not Van Dorn, who wired Lynch; however, Lt. Gift supports the previous view. All three of the *Arkansas*' officers did, however, agree that the general's persistence was "beyond all reason."

A proud and senior product of the old navy, Lynch, the highest ranking Confederate officer in the West, maintained his headquarters at Jackson. Little engaged in combat operations since arriving from the East, he had, nevertheless, been several times aboard the *Arkansas*, even commanding her on a brief mini-cruise two weeks earlier. The Southern flag officer was not impressed with the construction or protection of the armorclad. His relationship with Cmdr. Brown has, in light of the latter's subsequent published denunciation, been a matter of conjecture. He did not have a copy of the captain's letter to his executive officer and may not, in fact, even have known for certain where he was.

Lynch did, however, have Brown's earlier report praising Lt. Stevens as an extremely competent officer, even worthy of promotion. Satisfied with both the validity of Van Dorn's request and Stevens' ability, the flag officer chose not to inform the absent Brown but went ahead and made the decision to order out the *Arkansas*. Stevens received Lynch's directive about Saturday midday and after reading it knew that, despite Brown's message, he had no choice but to obey the flag officer. Lt. Read later put a better face on it: "As no Confederate could refuse to comply with the wish of one so universally loved and respected as General Breckenridge, Lieutenant Stevens consented to go."

Through the remainder of the day, the XO and his other officers worked to make the *Arkansas* as "shipshape" as possible for her upcoming adventure. It is uncertain whether or not the crew was briefed about the mission at this time. Third Engineer Brown fortunately inherited working, if extremely cantankerous, engines that currently functioned well enough to move the vessel down to the coal barges, where she was fueled. Unhappily, as was amply demonstrated over the past three weeks, the power plant's ability to function smoothly continued to be problematic.

To make matters worse, only Chief Engineer City really seemed to understand the screw propulsion system. Neither Virginian engineer Brown nor any of his assistants seemed to have City's ability to caress this temperamental machinery into performing under stress. As Lt. Read remembered, City's helpers were "mostly engineers who had served their time with the simple high pressures engines of the Mississippi river boats." One or two were recently joined navy engineers with no practical experience. The officer summed up: all were "true good men and no doubt did their best" but were equally "incompetent to run such engines as those on the *Arkansas*."

When the always dirty task of coaling was completed, the *Arkansas* returned to her anchorage below the upper batteries. There ammunition and victuals were hoisted aboard and stowed below. Most of the T-rails had by now been replaced or reattached and the chimney was patched.

One of the biggest problems faced by the *Arkansas* during her entire career was an inability to recruit aboard experienced sailors. Those found prior to the July 15 breakout were mostly dead, wounded, or gone ashore before July 22 and, by month's end when Van Dorn made his "request," the crew was still remarkably small. To augment his complement, Lt. Stevens issued a call for volunteers. As everyone in town seemed to have heard that the former U.S. vice president had taken a force into the field, finding a crew was easier this time than it had been earlier. Lt. Read caught the flavor when he wrote later that "no Confederate could refuse to comply with the wish of one so universally loved and respected as General Breckenridge."

By late Saturday, Lt. Stevens had a crew of 242 officers and men. Among the new sailors were a number of cannoneers from the 1st Tennessee Heavy Artillery Regiment. Officers returned from hospital included Gift, Richard Bacot, Dabney M. Scales, Daniel B. Talbott, John A. Wilson, and Gunner Thomas B. Travers. Having prior to July 15 trained and integrated a diverse group of men, the leadership of the boat now organized these recruits, showing them their stations and duties and instituting a new round of drills to ensure efficiency.

At New Orleans during the day, Maj. Gen. Butler sent over to RAdm. Farragut the July 30 communication received from Cmdr. Porter. The Department of the Gulf leader, a political general with a terrible reputation among the local population, was quite frightened that the *Arkansas* might sweep in and take Baton Rouge, which was not fortified on the river side. He warned his opposite number that "if the fleet can not hold the river against the enemy's rams or other boats, the quicker we abandon Louisiana the better!"

At 2:00 A.M. on August 3, the lines were cast off and the *Arkansas* pulled away from the dock, headed down the Mississippi. The hour was chosen in order not to attract attention from the fearful or the unfriendly and to give the ram as much of a head start as possible toward making her destination at the appointed hour. The prevention of desertions could also have been a consideration. Maj. Gen. Van Dorn, who may or may not have seen her off, believed "all damages sustained by the *Arkansas* from the fleets of the enemy had been repaired, and when she left the wharf at Vicksburg for Baton Rouge, she was deemed to be as formidable, in attack or defense, as when she defied a fleet of forty vessels-of-war, many of them iron-clads."

Four hours later, the train bearing Cmdr. Brown pulled into the station at Jackson. The captain of the *Arkansas* asked the ranking CSA quartermaster of the town for a special train, or at least a locomotive and a boxcar, to take him to Vicksburg. He gave as his reason for such an extraordinary application his hope of reaching his command before she departed.

From the supply officer, Brown learned that the *Arkansas*, at Lynch's order, had departed Vicksburg just hours before he arrived in the Mississippi state capital. The commander, "entirely cured by this intelligence," quickly cancelled his request and hopped the next southbound freight, a train headed for Pontchatoula, the closest railhead to Baton Rouge. Maybe he could still catch his ship. As he rode south, the godfather of the Confederate ram seethed. Much of this anger was directed at his superior and later, for *Battles and Leaders*, he would let fly his rage, still so angry that he refused to name Lynch directly:

> Van Dorn had been persistent beyond all reason in his demand, and Stevens, undecided, had referred the question to a senior officer of the Confederate navy, who was at Jackson, Miss., with horses and carriages, furnished by Government in place of a flag-ship, thus commanding in chief for the Confederacy on the Mississippi, sixty miles from its nearest waters. This officer, whose war record was yet in abeyance, had attained scientific celebrity by dabbling in the waters of the Dead Sea, at a time when I was engaged in the siege of Vera Cruz and in the general operations of the Mexican war. Ignorant or regardless of the condition of the *Arkansas*, fresh from Richmond on his mission of bother, not communicating with or informing me on the subject, he ordered Stevens to obey Van Dorn without any regard to my orders to the contrary.

Knowing that the *Arkansas* had a rendezvous approximately 36 hours ahead, Lt. Stevens was relatively confident that the middle of the night departure would permit her to cover the almost 300 miles to Baton Rouge in good time. He was well aware that the power plant would have to function without failure, even if Chief Engineer City was not present to provide the tender care to which the engines were accustomed. Cruising at a leisurely pace with the current, the Confederate armorclad initially performed well, making about 15 miles per hour. Lt. Read remembered that she kept on, largely without incident, throughout the day, "passing many signs of the wanton and barbarous destruction of property by the enemy."

Almost 150 years later, *Arkansas* student George Wright challenged Read's figures as high: "A current speed of 4–5 mph seems more realistic. Her demonstrated speed was in the 7–8 knot range, so top speed with the current could only be about 13 mph." Given that the distance from Vicksburg to Baton Rouge by river was about 265 miles, the time of the ram "under power should have been about 22–24 hours." The remainder of the time necessary to complete the journey would be "expended in coaling and engine repair."

Residents along the riverbank "hailed with exclamation of delight the sight of their country's flag and the gallant little *Arkansas* moving down to chastise the savage foe." The ram tooted her whistle in acknowledgement of every waving crowd, large or tiny.[8] As the *Arkansas* continued downstream in weather often punctuated by thunderstorms, her engines functioned grudgingly and without enthusiasm. Adjustments were made constantly, a number of which involved banging with hammers. The temporary linings of the fireboxes, replaced at Vicksburg, were no more permanent than the engine repairs. It is suspected that one of these may also have burned out during the voyage south, requiring repair.

A number of geographical points, villages and landings were passed, the ram not stopping. These included, early on, Sargent's Point, Palmyra Bend, New Carthage, Hurricane Island and Bend, Big Black Bend, Hard Times Bend, and the landing at Hard Times. After rounding Coffee Point, a stop was made at Grand Gulf, a town Farragut and Williams had spared from the torch back in May and where the Confederates were now mounting batteries overlooking the river. Another halt was called at Bruinsburg, Mississippi, as well as one at Waterproof, Louisiana, where problems were checked. Each stop ate up time and after each the engines were pushed harder to make up the lost minutes. The *Arkansas* skirted Natchez. Even so, Van Dorn later noted in his campaign history, Maj. Gen. Breckenridge was "advised by telegram every hour of her progress toward Baton Rouge" because he was "counting on her co-operation."

On she came. While steaming at night, wire baskets, filled with wood and combustibles, were hung forward and set alight as aboard commercial steamboats. The pilots steered by these fires while special lookouts were posted on the foredeck and atop the casemate to watch out for sandbars, snags, driftwood, and other debris in the water. A floating tree trunk ramming into her hull could be every bit as devastating as any Union shot. Although there was much to worry about, so far there were no significant mishaps. Indeed, the *Arkansas* answered her helm smoothly, her beak occasionally rose from the water, and her chimney draft sucked in air while emitting a nice big cloud of smoke.

As the armorclad approached the Mississippi-Louisiana state line, her engines started to become increasingly unruly, emitting all manner of worrisome sounds and clanking out of the ordinary. Near the mouth of the Red River, Lt. Stevens called a halt to hold a council of war.

"There is reason to believe," George Write has opined, "that her engines were run at too high a speed during her sortie south from Vicksburg." Simultaneously, "the engines may have been insufficiently lubricated at these higher speeds, heating and expanding the bearings." In light of the power plant difficulties being experienced and given that there was no location for a full-scale overhaul between where they were now and Baton Rouge, a decision had to be taken. Was it best for the mission to continue or should it be scrubbed? Stevens officers voiced different opinions, with most concerned that the unfaithful engines would give up entirely.

As the head mechanic, Third Engineer Brown was summoned to give his opinion. "Being zealous for the good repute of his department," Gift later complained, the black room chief "gave it as his opinion that the machinery would hold out." Basing his decision upon Brown's statement, Stevens determined to proceed.

At New Orleans during the day, RAdm. Farragut wrote to Cmdr. Porter urging that the *Essex* continue to patrol near the mouth of the Red River. He did not believe that Breckenridge was descending upon the Louisiana state capital, but was concerned that the flow of "arms, cattle, etc." to Vicksburg be halted. It was his opinion that the *Essex* and *Sumter* could handle the ram between them. If she did get by them and make it to New Orleans, he concluded, "I have an abiding confidence that it will be the last of her, as she will have no forts to shelter her."

Forces ashore at Baton Rouge were also reacting to the approach of the Confederate ram. Brig. Gen. Williams heard an increasing number of rumors that the *Arkansas* would support the Rebel attack when it came. Army scouts reported seeing a huge black smoke cloud approaching down the river from the north. That evening the reconnaissance information was shared with Cmdr. Porter, who believed the billows might signify the approach of the Rebel ram. At the same time, Lt. George M. Ransom (1820–1889),[9] commander of the *Kineo*, also heard the rumors concerning the *Arkansas*, adding that they came to him "in conjunction with other rebel vessels [*Webb* and *Music*] at Red River" that would "act in concert with the land forces." This concern was messaged to RAdm. Farragut, though Ransom admitted that his source on the combined attack did not seem credible. At the same time, an express courier arrived at the camp of Maj. Gen. Breckenridge to announce that the armorclad had passed Bayou Sara and would undoubtedly reach her assigned location on time. Relieved, the Kentuckian ordered that his division commanders lead their men out of camp at 11:00 P.M., prepared to reach the town by, and attack at, daybreak.

Late on Friday afternoon, Engineer Brown asked that the *Arkansas* be halted in order that he and his men could "make all things secure before going into battle." Stevens agreed and the vessel eased into the right bank between Bayou Sara and Port Hudson, Louisiana. While the engineers labored, Lt. Gift and Midshipman Richard Bacot were sent ashore on a quick scout to find out if any of the local inhabitants knew anything about what was transpiring below. "After a deal of trouble," the pair were told that Breckenridge would attack the following morning. The sailors looked at one another in surprise and some disgust. Apparently, the Confederate attack plans had become common knowledge to the local citizenry quite a bit earlier, yet "the important secret could not be entrusted to high officers of the navy until a few hours before they were to cooperate in the movement." Gift and Bacot were also told that the *Essex* was the principal warship guarding Baton Rouge's Union defenders. This "particular enemy" was supported by a few small oceangoing gunboats. The chance to engage Cmdr. Porter again was deemed "very satisfactory" by both officers.

The *Arkansas* got under way again in the dark and continued down past Port Hudson. At this point, as Oliver Wood McClinton later wrote, "the make-shift and hurried construction of the ship appeared." About 1:00 A.M. on August 5, at a point some 15 miles below that town, probably close to Springfield Landing and Island No. 235, or about half way to Baton Rouge, the starboard engine failed.

Engineer Brown hurried up to inform Officer of the Deck Lt. Read that the vessel had to stop and that it would be a while before it could proceed. "I rounded the vessel to," Read later remembered, "and let go the anchor." More precisely, he actually ordered the boat tied up to the bank. All of the engineers were called and began working on the machinery, each with a "different idea of what should be done." Once they decided what to do, the engineers worked feverishly to ready the ram's stopped power plant. It was a dirty, messy, and noisy job carried out in intense heat by lantern light. As the hours passed, it looked less likely that the overhaul would be completed in time. Even if it were, there was growing uncertainty as to whether or not the fix would hold.

"At 4 o'clock, almost to a minute," Lt. Read later told the Jackson newspaper, General Breckenridge opened the attack on Baton Rouge, in heavy fog. The roar of cannon and sharp bark of muskets were distinctly audible aboard Steven's command. The initial and largest Confederate thrust was aimed on the eastern defenses of Baton Route, with a smaller

USS *Katahdin*. Built at Bath, Maine, the $97,500 Gunboat No. 8, the Katahdin, was another "90-day gunboat" of the Unadilla class and built largely of green wood in late 1861. At 158.4 feet long, with a beam of 28 feet and a 9.6-foot draft, the 507-ton two-masted emergency-made schooner was powered in the river by two engines that took their steam from two boilers. Her principal armament comprised one 11-inch Dahlgren smoothbore, one 20-pdr. Parrott rifle, and two 24-pdrs. With her sister Kineo, she was stationed off Baton Rouge during the Breckenridge attack of early August (Navy History and Heritage Command).

USS *Cayuga*. A sister of the Kineo and Katahdin, the $97,500 Gunboat No. 9, Cayuga, was identical to them in all particulars. Built at East Haddam, Connecticut, she had not previously served up the Mississippi but was sent to Baton Rouge when news arrived of the Confederate attack. On August 6, during the advance of the small Federal flotilla toward the Arkansas, Porter then ordered that the Kineo and Katahdin return back downstream to serve as guardships off the city. Cayuga was sent to deliver instructions to the two. Obsessed with the ram, the captain of the Essex, one might generously say, forgot that the Cayuga was dispatched with his command. Later, he would accuse the Cayuga of deserting her station, opening a bitter dispute between himself and these local gunboat captains and others that required some months to resolve (Navy Official Records, vol. 18).

attack that came down on the northern flank. The latter was turned back; however, Brig. Gen. Clark's men hurried in to support and within a few hours, all of the Union troops were being pushed back to the west into the city. During the give and take, Brig. Gen. Williams was killed.

The *Arkansas* was not ready, but the Union squadron was. The *Essex* and *Sumter* stood above the town to offer protection to the Union defenders, while the *Katahdin* and *Kineo* were below ready to provide gunfire support. As the first shots were fired, the *Cayuga*[10] arrived from New Orleans, ready to join in with her 11-inch gun. "[S]oon came the unmistakable boom of heavy navy guns," recalled Lt. Gift, "that plainly told us that we were wanted." The ram needed to make haste, as her "ironsides should be receiving those missiles which were now mowing down the infantry."

Repairs to the starboard engine of the Confederate armorclad were completed about 7:30 A.M. A half hour later, a reconnaissance team was rowed ashore to contact Southern irregulars in the area and seek intelligence on the current disposition of the *Essex* and her consorts. "In feverish haste our lines were cast off and hauled aboard," Gift later wrote. The crew was beat to quarters as the *Arkansas* got underway at 8:00 A.M. and started down the river, stopping a few miles on to pick up her scouts. These informed Lt. Stevens that the "guerrillas" knew of only three operational gunboats below. The captain called down his speaking tube ordering Engineer Brown to open her up.

"Like a war-horse, she seemed to scent the battle from afar," Gift tells us. The *Arkansas* rushed ahead, registering the highest speed "we had ever before witnessed." Letting the engines pound so "was a fatal error." It would have been better if they had been "nursed then by our young and over-zealous engineer," because then, she would have been able to "make her mark on the day's fight." Rounding Free Negro Point, about four miles above Baton Rouge, Lt. Stevens, having stationed himself in Cmdr. Brown's old post atop the casemate, was able to see through dissipating fog the Union flotilla off the Louisiana capital. There were four warships, plus several transports.

Aboard the *Kineo* below, a lookout informed Lt. Ransom that the smoke of a steamer could be seen "moving rapidly down the river toward the bend." From information received the night before, the captain believed the stranger to be the *Arkansas*. Surprisingly, she stopped, he noted, about a mile above Mulatto Bend. He would later report that she stayed there throughout the day, "sometimes apparently moving up a little, then down again." Like Capt. Henry H. Bell of the *Brooklyn*, Lt. Cmdr. Francis A. Roe (1823–1901),[11] who had arrived the day before to assume command of the USS *Katahdin*, also kept a diary. In it, he also observed that the *Arkansas* had made her "appearance down as far as the point of the next bend above and anchored there."

When the *Arkansas* came into view of the Union Navy, Lt. Stevens ordered the guns cleared for action and placed into battery. All around the boat, officers and men alike believed they had been presented with another "chance to make the army and country appreciate us." As the divisions on the gun deck reported their readiness, Lt. Stevens, Pilot James Brady, and Officer of the Deck Gift conferred topside. Brady proposed that the *Arkansas* ram and sink the *Essex* "where she lay." After backing out, she would steam below the wooden gunboats and transports, cutting off their retreat.

The captain agreed to the plan and ordered that anyone not already positioned go to his station immediately. He then rang down to Brown in the engine room seeking half speed. The big propellers began to turn and the engines pounded as the ram moved slowly ahead. In another 100 yards, the boat would make her turn from Mulatto Bend around the head of Free Negro Point into the reach above Baton Rouge and then steam flank speed to the attack. Maj. Gen. Breckenridge had chosen that very location to watch for the craft's intervention — but it never happened.

As the *Arkansas* came toward the point, the starboard engine — the same one they had worked on all night — began to shake. Much clanking, clatter, and an unnatural grinding noise was heard throughout the vessel and then, suddenly, the malfeasant propulsion unit shut down again. As had occurred on several occasions earlier, the portside engine continued functioning at full speed. Before Pilot Brady could gain control with the helm, the ram suddenly turned and ran hard aground, jamming herself among old cypress stumps grouped just under the surface of the river.

Once more, the bone weary engineers, who had gotten little sleep the preceding two nights, faced the hissing, disagreeable machinery. After making their diagnosis, it was determined that several more hours would be required to bring it back on line. They, like Stevens, were not men to surrender if repairs could be made. "Busy as bees," the mechanics again applied their skills, almost in the dark. The engine was torn down and mended "with files and chisels." Later in the afternoon, witnesses aboard the Federal vessels came mistakenly to believe that the Confederate warship was ("judging by smokes") joined by two other steamers, believed to be the *Music* and the *Webb*.

This business with the starboard engine was not only affecting the manner in which the *Arkansas* made war, but was becoming downright embarrassing. There were crowds of admirers on the banks extremely concerned that she not show herself a helpless flop. "Hundreds of people had assembled to witness the fight," Lt. Gift despaired. "In fact," he continued, "ladies in carriages had come to see our triumph. They waved us on with smiles and prayers, but we couldn't go."

Among these well-wishers was a young diarist, Sarah Morgan (1842–1909), and her friends, including her sister Miriam and Lilly Nolan whose father, Dr. John T., owned the plantation seven miles from Baton Rouge where young Sarah was staying. Early that morning, a "guerrilla" had appeared at Dr. Nolan's place to say that the *Arkansas* was lying only a few miles below, on her way to cooperate with Breckenridge's advance. "We all grew wild with excitement," Sarah remembered.

Throwing all reason aside and oblivious to any danger, Misses Morgan and Nolan mounted their saddle horses and started off "in the broiling sun," despite entreaties by their parents that they not leave. The young ladies were followed by a carriage — whose driver was to look out for them — and four other curious lady passengers less equestriennes than the younger two. As they approached the riverbank, the ram came into sight. The excited group jumped down, climbed up the levee, and scampered along it by foot until they reached her, at which point they crossed over to the outer levee — "and there she lay at our feet": "And nothing to her at all. There lay a heavy, clumsy, rusty, ugly flatboat, with a great square box in the center, while great cannon put their noses out at the sides, and in the front. The decks were crowded with men, rough and dirty, jabbering and hastily eating their breakfast. That was the great *Arkansas!* God bless and protect her, and the brave men she carries."

About this time, Federal sailors aboard the vessels off Baton Rouge saw a huge smoke column upriver. The box-like Confederate armorclad was visible once she rounded the point leading into the "stretch," but her progress slowed to a stop. Remaining at their stations in plain sight of their enemy, the Southern crew prayed that Cmdr. Porter would not become curious enough to investigate why they were sitting still in the water, looking for all the world like "a sheer hulk" and making no effort to attack.

Ashore, Confederate soldiers — all of whom were told "The *Arkansas* is Coming!" — awaited for the arrival of the boat many considered to be some kind of super weapon. Federal Maj. Gen. Benjamin Butler later commented to U.S. war secretary Edwin M. Stanton on the morale boost gained by the Southerners from just knowing the ram was approaching. It, he confirmed, "inspired them with the greatest hopes and the utmost confidence in their attack."

Cmdr. Porter and the Union land force commander ashore sent urgent messages by a fast steamer to New Orleans during the battle requesting reinforcements. Determined to have an end to the *Arkansas*, RAdm. Farragut himself led the *Hartford, Brooklyn, Jackson*, and *Westfield* upstream within hours of the message receipt. Sometime later, the diary of a U.S. Marine aboard the *Westfield* became available to the *New York Times*. That day, leatherneck Henry C. Gusley penned in his notebook that his vessel, and the three others, "got under way for Baton Rouge on account of our troops there having been attacked by the infernal ram (*Arkansas*)."

Maj. Gen. Breckenridge was advised regularly throughout the morning fighting concerning the boat's situation. Federal troops mounted a counterattack and, when it became apparent that the armorclad would not appear, the Rebels withdrew from the town. U.S. Lt. Col. Richard Irwin later confirmed that "at 10 o'clock the battle was over."

Union Col. Thomas W. Cahill, who succeeded the fallen Brig. Gen. Williams, remained so jittery, however, that he informed the captain of the *Essex* that it was mandatory that his little squadron remain off the town, lest Breckenridge renew the lulled Southern attack. Upstream, the men of the *Arkansas* watched and waited, perhaps wondering why Porter did not advance, but maybe suspecting he dare not leave.

As Porter readied a fast steamer to take down his preliminary report on the action, he wrote out a brief message in which he characteristically claimed that the *Essex* and *Sumter* had held the advancing Confederates in check, even though a large proportion of his own crew was in hospital and he had borrowed sailors from the *Kineo*. The Confederate ram, he revealed, was "lying behind a point 5 miles above us," even though, he confessed, she had not made an appearance and what he knew of her situation came from information supplied by others. The *Essex*, in turn, was "lying as far up as it is necessary" in order that his big ironclad could protect Cahill's "right wing and keep the *Arkansas* in check." Not knowing that the *Cayuga* was en route, the bearded commander added that if a gunboat were available to take his position he could then attack the enemy boat. When Col. Cahill learned that the high speed supply steamer would be taking naval dispatches to New Orleans, he hurriedly prepared a message for Maj. Gen. Butler. In it, he asked for both ground and naval reinforcements. "The navy is threatened by the ram *Arkansas*," he confided, "which will divert them from our service."

During the afternoon, a courier from Maj. Gen. Breckenridge came aboard the *Arkansas* to give Lt. Stevens a report on the battle ashore and ascertain the reasons for the ironclad's delay. It was emphasized that the Federals were protected by Porter's gunboats. Lt. Charles W. Read, who was present, remembers the captain being told "if we could get down by next morning at daybreak, General Breckenridge would attack again and would probably bag the whole party of Yankees."

One wonders what might have happened had the engine of the *Arkansas* not failed on August 5. Professor Still, like Maj. Gen. Breckenridge and Col. Cahill, believes the *Arkansas* could have made a difference. The scholar opined in his 1958 thesis that "if the *Arkansas* had been able to attack the *Essex* and the gunboats, and drive them from their positions, the Confederates would have been in a much better position to renew the attack, with a good chance of success."

The famed ram could not, however, offer assistance, as she remained "hung up" in the cypress all through the sweltering afternoon. This type of tree is prevalent in the lower Mississippi region, often contributing to steamboat accidents. Indeed, the same sort of cypress obstruction had been encountered by the Federal ironclad *Carondelet* when she grounded during her battle with the armorclad up the Yazoo three weeks before.

To help get the *Arkansas* to a point where she could drift free, Lt. Stevens ordered that all unnecessary items be thrown overboard. Deckhands began with the extra railroad iron that had been added to the decks in Vicksburg to provide increased protection against plunging fire. One of the anchors was placed into a small boat and hauled out some yards into the river, where it was dropped. Men manning the capstan would pull it in to help free the boat.

Up until the time in late afternoon when his courier returned from the river, Maj. Gen. Breckenridge hoped that he could still have the cooperation of the *Arkansas* and would be able to renew his attack. When he learned that she lay disabled and helpless on the right bank, the Kentuckian knew the ball was over. The sick and dispirited Confederate military force disengaged and returned to the Comite River, headed toward Port Hudson. Interestingly, the retreat was well covered. "The Hudson Battery ... and Cobb's one piece,"

Breckenridge afterwards reported, "played their parts well." Both units had supplied temporary crewmen to the *Arkansas* back on July 15 and 16.

Out on the river, the Confederate armorclad was sufficiently lightened by 5:00 P.M. The anchor was hauled up and the *Arkansas* floated free. It was almost dark when the engine was fixed, but, before it was engaged, Engineer Brown took Lt. Stevens aside and warned that this repair could no more be guaranteed than the previous one. Given that engine's several failures, the Virginian did not think it would last much longer. To test the power plant, it was suggested that the ram, in need of refueling, return back upstream a short distance (less than two miles) to a stockpile of coal seen on the way down on the riverbank at John Bird's plantation. It was agreed that once the boat arrived the crew would coal her through the night "and be ready for hot work in the morning."

Drifting out into the stream, the *Arkansas* got underway, rounded to, and started back up the river. No one aboard knew that below, off Baton Rouge, Cmdr. Porter and the captains of the other Union gunboats were maturing a plan to battle the Confederate warship the following morning. According to Loyall Farragut, the captain of the *Essex* told his officers, "That fellow keeps me uneasy, and, after I get my breakfast tomorrow, I will go up and destroy him."

The little coal depot was sighted at Mulatto Bend Landing just above the cypress trap. As the armorclad drew abreast of it and headed toward shore, the starboard engine failed again. This time the crank pin of its connecting rod, which steamboatmen called a "wrist," broke completely in two. Once more the *Arkansas* went into the bank in a crippled state. Happily, it was realized, even as she tied up, that once more the vessel was not without resources, though often quite primitive, and resourcefulness. One of Engineer Brown's black room associates also happened to be a blacksmith and there was a forge aboard (possibly having been shipped back up the Yazoo in June). The forge was carried onto the bank and set up. After several hours, a new crank pin was manufactured and Engineer Brown was able to inform Lt. Stevens that the pin was "finished and the parts thrown together." Once the "wrist" was fitted, the power plant was fired up — and the machinery turned as it should. Although the engine was functional again, there were no promises.

As the Confederate engineer-smith worked in the light of his fire to forge a new part, down the river the Federal gunboat *Cayuga* took position in the river above Baton Rouge. It was her job to provide "warning of the movements of the ram." Her captain sent a note to Lt. Cmdr. Roe of the *Katahdin* saying that if the *Arkansas* sallied forth he would engage her, buying the others time to come up and join in the engagement.

Aboard the other Union boats, according to a later report in *Harper's Weekly*, the Union officers wondered why the "nondescript, or 'What is it?' as [P.T.] Barnum would term it," had failed to come down. It was concluded that "as the mountain would not go to Mohammed, Mohammed would go to the mountain" shortly after first light.

By 3:00 A.M., the *Arkansas* was once more under way and headed down the river, her smoke unseen by the *Cayuga* because of the darkness. As she again approached Free Negro Point, the engines suffered another failure — though exactly what it was this time is not clear — forcing the craft to stop once more.

Stevens and his divisional officers were now desperate. It was clear that the engines could not be depended upon and only a fool could believe that Cmdr. Porter would not strike as soon as it was light enough to fight. Suspecting that the enemy would appear not long after sunrise, the captain concluded that his own attack would have to be shelved in favor of the best possible defense.

Forge. *As the* Arkansas *drew abreast of a little coal depot at Mulatto Bend Landing above Baton Rouge on August 5 and headed toward shore, her starboard engine failed. The crank pin of its connecting rod, which steamboatmen called a "wrist," broke completely in two. The armorclad went into the bank in a crippled state. Happily, it was realized, even as she tied up, that the vessel was not without resources—though these were often quite primitive—and resourcefulness. One of the acting chief engineer's black room associates also happened to be a blacksmith and there was a forge aboard (possibly having been shipped back up the Yazoo in June). The forge, perhaps similar to this one shown on the deck of the U.S. monitor* Saugus, *was carried onto the bank and set up. After several hours, a new crank pin was manufactured and Lt. Henry Stevens was informed that the pin was "finished and the parts thrown together" (Library of Congress).*

While Engineer Brown attended to the power plant, the whole crew slaved at hauling the armorclad into a "gap in the bank," where she was secured, stern in, bow pointed upstream. Perhaps reminding the professional blue-water sailors aboard of an electric eel hiding in its lair, the *Arkansas* presented her most dangerous "points to the river," much as she had at Vicksburg when Porter and Ellet attacked. There she would remain as long as possible, hoping that "good engineers could be obtained, and the engines put in proper order."

Once the *Arkansas* was tucked into her little inlet, Lt. Stevens made certain that she was ready for any eventuality. Here she was invulnerable to ramming and her unarmored waterline was only minimally exposed. Full use of the bow-chasers and the forward broadside ordnance was retained, while the necessity of simultaneously manning all of her broadside guns was eliminated.

If concern over an attack from the river was minimized, there still remained danger from the shore. A land attack by Union troops could be met by her stern chasers while her after-cladding with boilerplate was expected to be resistant to musket balls and field guns. The chance that men at her stern-chaser ports could be hit by Union riflemen appeared the greatest danger. Lt. Stevens, in choosing this position, may also have believed that troops from Breckenridge's command would provide cover. In any event, it should be possible to maintain position until the engines were repaired or help arrived from out of the Red or elsewhere.[12]

The Federal squadron weighed anchor from its Baton Rouge anchorage either late in the morning watch or into the forenoon watch (between 7:00 A.M. [Read], 8:00 A.M. [Gift/Porter/Roe], or 9:00 A.M. [Ransom]) on August 6. Over at Dr. Nolan's plantation, Sarah Morgan noted that the weather was cloudy with rain threatening. Also that morning, the *Grenada Appeal* reported that a new armorclad, the *Richmond*, was descending the Yazoo. Heavily armed, she was supposedly "made from the *Star of the West*."

Aboard the *Arkansas*, Lt. Stevens was already in conference with his officers preparing contingencies. The boat was safe where it was for the time being; but if the engines could be repaired, she could sortie forth.

A few minutes later, a lookout stationed forward sang out, "Ship ahoy!" All eyes looked down the river to see the huge *Essex*, the *Sumter*, and the newly arrived *Cayuga* headed toward them, "very slowly" against the current. Lt. Gift estimated, "at a rate not to exceed two miles per hour."

Initially, the *Kineo* and *Katahdin* remained off Baton Rouge "to guard the right flank of the army in case of attack." Lt. Cmdr. Roe of the latter noted in his diary that "the small ram *Sumter* was disabled and could do nothing." Confiding further to his notes, Roe noted that when the *Essex* came within approximately two miles of the *Arkansas* she "opened a sort of desultory fire." Porter, her captain, found the enemy "of such formidable appearance" that he signaled for the two army support gunboats to come up as well.

When the supplemental Union task group was about a mile above the town, white smoke was seen rising from the eastern edge of Baton Rouge, leading the ranking Federal naval officer to suspect that Breckenridge was launching another assault. Porter then ordered that the *Kineo* and *Katahdin* return back downstream to serve as guardships off the city. In order to convey the order, the *Cayuga* came about and steamed down to within hailing distance of the *Katahdin*. Meanwhile, the *Essex* advanced less than half a mile toward the enemy, and "her fire was only occasional at that great distance." It required time for the gunboat to complete her down-and-back task.

Obsessed with the ram, Porter, one might generously say, forgot that while he was exchanging rounds with the *Arkansas* the *Cayuga* was delivering his command. Later, he would accuse the *Cayuga* of deserting her station, opening a bitter dispute between himself and these local gunboat captains and others that required some months to resolve. Some have suggested that his problem stemmed from the fact that either the *Cayuga* did not signal her departure or Porter did not see the flags in her halyards announcing her maneuver.

The latest engine repairs being made aboard the *Arkansas* were still not finished. Steven's officer call took on a more serious and defensive tenor as the *Essex* hove within half a mile and opened fire with her three 9-inch bow guns. These initial rounds, all solid shot, fell short. Ashore, Sarah Morgan and her friends heard a tremendous roar. "From the two volumes of smoke," she jotted down, "judge it was the *Arkansas* and the *Essex* trying their strength at a distance." This time, the diarist's mother succeeded in keeping her daughter from "going to the levee to see the fight," though two of her acquaintances did sneak off alone in a buggy.

As the *Arkansas*' leadership team concluded its conference, Engineer Brown came up from below to announce "in a loud voice: 'The engines are in good order, sir!'" Indeed, according to Lt. Read's account in a Jackson newspaper, Brown went so far as to say "they would last half a day." The news, which would turn out to be premature, was electric and the whole crew cheered. Despite the short term engine life projection, the boat need no longer be considered a floating battery huddled against the bank for protection. The just agreed upon plan to fight her so was immediately junked.

Pilot Brady's earlier plan to attack Porter first was resurrected. The *Arkansas* would ascend the river a few hundred yards, round to, increase speed until abreast of the pokey *Essex*, and then turn and send her beak deep into the Federal's side. This tactic was similar to that Cmdr. Brown had hoped earlier to employ against the *Carondelet*. After pulling out of the enemy, the powerful Confederate armorclad would endeavor to catch and dispatch her smaller consorts. Like the *Tyler* and *Queen of the West* up the Yazoo, neither was a match and might already have begun to flee. The Union ram *Sumter* did not attack on July 22 and there was no particular reason to believe she would do so now without the *Essex*.

Once the officers broke from their huddle and returned to their stations, Stevens went down to the gun deck to give the *Arkansas* men a quick pep talk. Alluding to all they had survived since July 15, he indicated they were about to engage in the "battle for the supremacy of the river." Although their boat was brought to bay by a larger force, he expected everyone aboard to meet their responsibility "as men and patriots," helping him to "fight it out as long as we could swim."

The boilers of the ram were now stoked, and pressure built and smoke billowed from the chimney. Climbing back up to the pilothouse minutes after his talk, Lt. Stevens ordered the lines cut and pulled on the engine room bell rope signaling Brown to engage the engines. The twin screws began to slowly turn and the *Arkansas* inched out into the river. "The pleasant sensation of again being afloat and in possession of the power of locomotion was hardly experienced," Gift recalled 20 years later, "before our last and final disaster came."

After the Confederate armorclad slid out into the wider expanse of the Mississippi and completed rounding to, Lt. Stevens called for "full speed" ahead. About 300 yards into her charge, "the port engine went ahead fast and the starboard engine stopped." Once more and for the last time, the *Arkansas* experienced her peculiar power plant problem. Again, one engine had stopped "on the center" at the wrong time and wrong place, or, as Lt. Gift put it, "broke down and would not move." As usual when this occurred, as Cmdr. Brown had noted months earlier, the vessel rocked heavily and turned around, "despite the rudder."

The *Arkansas* now thrust in toward the riverbank, "her stern down." As she did so and within the space or a minute or two, her starboard engine also failed. She now began to drift toward the enemy with the current, totally helpless. Soon, however, the ram grounded on the infamous group of cypress knees along the right bank, captured with her stern pointed downstream. In a letter to his father written on August 13, Lt. John Grimball admitted that, after the boat "succeeded in getting into the bank, we were not lying in such a good position." The iron, he added, "was so thin toward them that every shot would have gone through her."

The captain of the *Katahdin* reported seeing that the ram "backed into a bend in the river and did not come out." An officer aboard the *Arkansas* conceded that the vessel was now "immovable and her guns could not be brought to bear upon the Federal fleet."

The boat's specific driveline problems seemed to concentrate not only in her automatic shut-offs but also in her highly stressed connecting rods and pins. The power plant failures on this occasion were both laid to broken connecting rods. If one had snapped, "that could have been attributed to misalignment," wrote Charles G. Hearn a century later. "[B]ut as both failed, a case can be made" that the power plant as a whole had been disarranged, most probably by the July 22 "butt" received from the *Queen of the West*. Repair crews brought to Vicksburg in the days after the attack were not able to remedy the damages before Van Dorn ordered her south. In fact, an *Arkansas* crewman later told the contemporary historian of the U.S. Ram Fleet that the ram's fate was, indeed, sealed when the *Queen* hit and skewed the engines. Although we have no proof, the additional stress subsequently placed upon her connecting pins and rods as a result of the butt by the Ellet boat almost certainly exceeded anything John Shirley and Primus Emerson expected.

"The stern guns being in my division," Read recalled, "I opened as soon as they bore." The 32-pdr. projectiles fell short of the *Essex*, which boat was tentatively returning fire with the same effect from below. Acting Master's Mate Wilson happily observed that all of Cmdr. Porter's missiles fell "short and out of range."[13] While Read's rifles fired off "a few rounds," Lt. Stevens conferred once more with Engineer Brown. The despairing black room chief informed his captain that the engines were both now beyond repair and that neither he nor his men could do anything more with them.

Stevens, with his officers and probably most of the crew, realized that the *Arkansas* was powerless to resist the oncoming *Essex*. Even if Engineer Brown had been able to once more work on the power plant, the iron protection over the stern was so thin that it would have been easily penetrated by Porter's Dahlgren bolts. Additionally, as Lt. Gift later revealed, a group of "mounted home guard" were reportedly coming up the river to try to cut off the ram's retreat. The end, they knew, had come. Cmdr. Brown had the greatest of admiration for his XO, calling him "as humane as he was true and brave." Knowing the ball was over, Capt. Stevens, recalled the officer standing next to him at the time, "did not call a council of war, but himself assumed the responsibility for burning the ship."

Interestingly, in a letter to Clement Stevens in September, the acting captain admitted to first polling his colleagues. Stevens wrote: "After she broke down the second time, I called on the officers to give me their opinions in writing as to the course that should be pursued." Once these were in hand, the commander weighed his options: "It was a hard thing to have to destroy the vessel, but in her condition, she must have fallen into the hands of the enemy, without the greatest cowardice on their part or a miracle in our defense. Had I protracted the defense, the enemy could have selected their positions & torn us to pieces at their leisure, when we must have blown up vessel & all hands or risked their getting on shore under a concentrated fire. The only thing is that the vessel had such a reputation that just then wonders were expected of her." Gift could long "recollect the look of anguish he gave me and the scalding tears which were running down his cheeks when Lt. Stevens announced his determination." To keep the *Arkansas* out of enemy hands, she had to be destroyed.

A sailor was sent to Lt. Read telling him to cease firing. Lt. Cmdr. Roe of the *Katahdin* believed that, so far, no more than "20 shots were fired on both sides." Orders were passed for his men and the rest of the crew to abandon ship, taking with them stocks of small arms and ammunition. Once ashore, Gift, Grimball, and Wharton would form the men up into a temporary skirmish line and also prepare them for escape into the interior as quickly as possible. Lt. Read, with Midshipmen Bacot, Scales, Talbott, Acting Master's Mate Wilson, and Gunner Travers, remained behind to assist the captain in firing the boat.

As the rest of the crew of the *Arkansas* went over the side, the demolition party set to work. It was later reported that the engines and other machinery were smashed with axes. More than likely, rather than pounding away at the metal parts of the propulsion units, the men severed the steam, water, and pump lines leading to and away from them. Lt. Stevens may have taken some pleasure in personally confronting the source of his frustration as he tossed hand grenades into the black spaces. Unhappily for him, one of the little bombs went off prematurely, burning his hands.

The thin side bulkheads were smashed open in various spots. Bales of compressed cotton used as armor reinforcement between the guns were torn out and cut open. All of the wardroom and cabin bedding was ripped to shreds. As these acts of official vandalism were completed, torches were applied. Wilson, under Stevens' direction, lit up the wardroom and cabins, while the others dropped fire on the cotton and other combustibles. The fore and aft magazines were also opened and cartridges and powder were spread about. Each of the cannon was shotted and run out in battery, as loaded shells were stashed around the gun deck ready to detonate when reached by flames from below.

As the boat began to blaze, the strong current successfully loosened the grip of the cypress on her hull and she started drifting out into the river. Her officers escaped over the side, though not before Midshipman Scales had once more, as at Vicksburg, securely fastened the colors to the mast. Lt. Stevens, assisted by Wilson, was the last to leave. Both men literally jumped into the stream and swam ashore. These volunteer firebrands, together with the earlier-departing crewmen, landed "with our side arms and no other clothing than what we had on, which, being our fighting rig, was rather scanty."

Although the logbook was lost, the XO, as he told his brother, had managed to stuff into his tunic the written opinions asked of his officers regarding the necessity for the armorclad's destruction. "A truer friend to the South, a cooler or braver man than Lieutenant Stevens never lived," remembered an admiring Lt. Read, who resentfully added, "though there were not wanting newspaper editors and other bombproof critics to defame him as a coward and a traitor."

The surviving officers and crew were mustered a distance up the high levee. It was just about 10:00 A.M., some 20 minutes since the *Essex* had opened fire. An inspection of all present showed that, other than Stevens, there were no casualties suffered during the evacuation. Two men did desert, "both mess-room men from New Orleans." There were a number of others who were missing. Safe positions were now chosen from which to watch the end.

The excitement of the morning prevented young Sarah Morgan and her friends from remaining at home. Not knowing exactly what they would find, they headed down a mile-and-a-half long lane toward the river. Upon reaching the levee, they found a large group of men standing about talking or "wringing their hands and crying." The local girls had come upon the *Arkansas* crew. They were "dirty, half-dressed, some with only their guns, others, a few, with bundles and knapsacks on their backs, grimy and tired, watching what appeared to be a boat on fire. "Several of the men surrounded the girls, though most remained scattered in small groups along the levee road. "We found ourselves in the center of two hundred men," Morgan recorded.

Several of the officers were pointed out, including Lt. Stevens, the boat's unnamed doctor, and an unnamed midshipman, "the only ones who possessed a coat in the whole crowd." "You could only guess" most were officers, "for a dirtier, more forlorn set I never saw." Two officers made such impressions upon Miss Morgan that she has left us physical descriptions. Lt. Read was dressed "in rough sailor pants, a pair of boots, and a very thing and slazy lisle undershirt." That was all he had on, except for "an old straw hat." The lady was particularly taken by a "handsome Kentuckian," whom she learned was Midshipman Daniel Talbott. She quickly found out that he was a U.S. Naval Academy graduate. When they were introduced, she found him "charmingly picturesque in his coarse cottonade pants, white shirt, straw hat, black hair, beard, bright eyes and rosy cheeks." Read repeatedly blushed and tried to explain away the crews' state of undress, remarking that they were prepared to fight, not meet five young ladies.

As their ship made her last run, some of the men, perhaps including her new officer friends, told their stories. Having lost everything but his pants and undershirt, one veteran of the CSS *Virginia* mourned the loss of his "commission appointing him there." Another was a Frenchman, who laughed, "*Me voilà*, I have saved my gun, *et puis* the clothes that I stand in!" Others related the past 24 hours of their boat's history. Yesterday, the men said, their engine had broken down and they had worked all day to repair it, had sat by their guns all night, and this morning had started to meet the *Essex* when the other engine failed.

The sailors went on to reveal that "each officer wrote his opinion that it was impossible to fight her with any hope of success under such circumstances and advised the captain to abandon her" and that they had all resolved to do so. Meanwhile, several shots had been exchanged with the Federal ironclad across the point. Orders were passed for the crewmen to "take their side arms." The sailors thought, when they were assembled together, that they were going to board the *Essex*, but instead they received the order to fire the boat and go ashore, "which was done in a few minutes."

Down the river, lookouts aboard the *Essex*, *Sumter*, and *Cayuga* all saw the *Arkansas* float free of the cypress. When she was back in the stream, the current turned her around and sent her south, as though she was advancing toward them. Maj. Gen. Van Dorn, in a colorful phrase, suggested in his September 9 campaign history that "with every gun shotted, our flag floating from her bow, and not a man on board, the *Arkansas* bore down upon the enemy and gave him battle." It was now about 10:00 A.M. and in the time since the three Federals had begun shooting long range at the Rebel ram they had yet to score a hit.

The *Essex* and her consorts continued to remain at respectable distances (largely out of range) even after the *Arkansas* launched her unmanned charge. The cautious ironclad continued to loft shells at the approaching Southern craft as she bore down from above. Fourth Master Spencer Kellogg Brown, in a letter home next day, told his grandfather that "the second shell we fired caused her crew to desert her, and a moment after she commenced burning."

As she neared the Federals, her battle flag streaming in the breeze, flames shot out of her casemate and decks. Her cannon discharged as the fire reached the gun deck, while the independently placed shells, according to Miss Morgan, "exploded one by one beneath the water, coming up in jets of steam." After all hands were ashore, Lt. Read later told the *Jackson Mississippian*, the *Essex* "fired upon the disabled vessel most furiously." Believing the exploding shells were aimed by Southern gunners (when, in fact, no one was aboard),

Cmdr. Porter, who had boasted he would take the enemy alone, "began to pour shell into her."

None of the Federal commanders knew they faced a ghost ship. At the same time, they also believed that the *Music* and *Webb*, which were never present and must therefore also be considered "spirits," had "fled," as Maj. Gen. Butler characterized their departure, before the Federal boats' arrival.[14]

Observing from the levee, Lt. Stevens and his crew, together with the girls from the Nolan plantation, watched the *Essex* and her consorts, "crowded with men," cautiously "turn the point and watch her burn." Shells continued to randomly explode aboard the doomed armorclad and the enemy vessels were seen to back off cautiously as she swayed down toward them.

There were a number of sick and hurt among the ram's survivors. With the clouds threatening an imminent downpour, it was now decided that all of the assembled men would trek back up the lane to the Nolan place, the ladies giving over their carriage to the infirm. As they departed, eyes took final glances at the *Arkansas*, "a mere wreck, still burning." Ms. Morgan walked home with Mr. Talbott "and each of the others with some one else." Most of the crew did not see the *Arkansas* blow up, in what Cmdr. Porter called "a tremendous explosion." Watching from the protection of his pilothouse, the captain of the *Essex* later proudly told his superiors, "There is not now a fragment of her left."

Lt. Cmdr. Roe, skipper of the USS *Katahdin*, which was headed back to Baton Rouge, also saw the *Arkansas*'s destruction and believed Porter's task group had won a "bloodless victory." Of course, "the timely arrival of the *Cayuga* and our approach in force no doubt had a good moral effect," he opined in his after action report, "as the ram was badly managed and made a poor fight." He, too, did not then know that the armorclad was unmanned, though, as he revealed in his diary, it was eventually discovered that the blazing vessel was "deserted and left by her people."

Aboard the *Kineo*, Lt. Ransom had a different take on the reason behind the Confederate's destruction, admitting in his message to RAdm. Farragut that by the time the action was over "it has been ascertained, I believe, that she had suddenly become helpless there, by some failure of her engines, and seeing our approach so formidable to her in her crippled condition, doubtless, they set her on fire and abandoned her. At about 1 o'clock, her magazine exploded, and the ram *Arkansas* was extinct." This was the version subscribed to by Maj. Gen. Butler, who reported it so in his General Order No. 57, which was published in the *New Orleans Picayune* of August 9.

"It was beautiful," Lt. Stevens later told Van Dorn, who included the naval officer's comments in his official campaign review. "While the tears stood in his eyes," the general added for effect, the sailor further added that "when abandoned by commander and crew," the vessel took on a life of her own, "dedicated to sacrifice, fighting the battle on her own hook."

"A few minutes later, a Confederate ensign floated down across the *Essex*'s bow, " recalled Eliot Callender of the *Cincinnati* in 1900. "For the first time in its history, it had trailed in the presence of an enemy." As other debris settled over the river, the *Essex* steamed up and sent a boat ashore. Numerous chunks of debris were picked up for souvenirs. Fourth Master Spencer Kellogg Brown sent his grandfather "a little cotton from the inside bulwarks of the *Arkansas*—also a fine splinter."

Approximately 10 of the ram's crew that had not yet departed the levee were taken prisoner. Cmdr. Porter later reported finding several wounded Confederate tars. These were "conveyed 4 miles inland by carts belonging to a planter by name of Bird." The POWs were interrogated over a period of several days, some by no less an inquisitor than Farragut himself. The admiral reported to Secretary Welles four days later from New Orleans that he had "catechized" all of them "very closely." The tales told by the Southern sailors were virtually identical in particulars concerning the breakout from the Yazoo and the number of killed aboard, the fact that the boat was commanded at this time by Stevens and not Brown, and that they were en route to Baton Route to cooperate with Breckenridge.

Most important, the Southern prisoners all agreed that the engines were the cause of their vessel's demise and that, although the *Music* and *Webb* were sent for, they did not arrive. The *Arkansas*, they confessed, had to be run ashore because she was "perfectly unmanageable." Stevens ordered his men to go ashore and set the boat ablaze. This was "as we suspected," Lt. Cmdr. Roe and some of the other Federal gunboat captains believed.

When the *Essex* returned to Baton Rouge, her captain telegraphed the secretary of the navy to announce that he had attacked and destroyed the *Arkansas*. He also wrote out a report for RAdm. Farragut in which he claimed that rounds from his bow guns disabled the ram's rudder and actually set her cotton stuffing alight. Prof. William Still has suggested that, at the time of the action, "Dirty Bill," who could not see that the *Arkansas* was abandoned and fired by her crew, may have been justified in his initial belief. When the true fate of his enemy became known, actually within a few hours, his continued assertion "that it was still true" he had destroyed her "was unwarranted."

Porter's account was widely published in Northern newspapers and embellished by some. By late summer, the tale resembled the product of that old saying about telling one person something at the head of a line of 20 others and seeing how it was different when it reached the last person. Here for example, is an excerpt from an account that appeared in *Harper's Weekly* on September 6. It recognized that the *Arkansas'* engines were not functioning and she was immovable:

> The *Essex* ran past the *Arkansas* to a part of the river where there was a reach of some length, and opened on her formidable antagonist at 500 yards with three guns loaded with solid shot. One of these took effect right under the port in the starboard bow of the *Arkansas*, and split in two from the force of the concussion. Cmdr. Porter then ordered the same gun to be loaded with an incendiary shell of his own invention, and, without moving the gun to take a new aim, the shell was fired, entering just where the solid shot had struck. Immediately, a jet of flame was shooting upward from the *Arkansas*, and in a short time, the entire vessel was on fire.

Once the group of Confederate escapees ashore reached the refuge offered by members of the planter families, the men were given refreshments and advised that as Dr. Nolan was on parole he could not offer aid or refuge. However, it was intimated that if the staff received orders "they might do as they please as women could not resist armed men!" That said, the crew of the *Arkansas* spent the night of August 6 in a sugar house, eating better than they had in weeks. Charles Roland tells us that "they chose to order and the entire group partied until the following day, with each young woman appropriating an officer, naming him Miriam's, Ginnie's, or Sarah's, as if he belonged to her."

News from Baton Rouge reached Vicksburg on the morning of August 7. Maj. Gen. Van Dorn wired Richmond to say that Breckenridge had captured large amounts of stores and burned the Union camp. The *Arkansas*, he told the commander in chief for the first time, was "ordered to cooperate." Unhappily, she was attacked by the enemy and though fighting well and inflicting heavy damages, she "was then blown up by crew, all of whom escaped." In endorsing the telegram, President Jefferson Davis wrote: "Read with deep

Eleven: Arkansas vs. Essex, Round Two: Finale Off Baton Rouge

The Battle That Wasn't. *As a result of her engine failures, the* Arkansas *was destroyed by her own crew on August 6, 1862. Cmdr. William D. "Dirty Bill" Porter, captain of the USS* Essex, *later stated that it was the action of his command which directly destroyed the Confederate armorclad. His version was picked up by Northern newspaper reporters and spread widely. Despite evidence to the contrary given by surviving Rebel crewmen, Confederate officials, and even Federal captains, this belief continued for some time (*Harper's Weekly, *September 6, 1862).*

regret for loss of *Arkansas*." The loss of the *Arkansas* was also reported by the *Grenada Appeal* on August 8. It was said she "got aground on a bar while going down the river, and that, to save her from falling into the hands of the enemy, she had been blown up and entirely destroyed."

RAdm. Farragut arrived off Baton Route aboard the *Hartford* at noon that day. He was accompanied by the *Brooklyn* and several smaller gunboats, including the *Westfield*. No sooner had his task group dropped anchor than Cmdr. Porter rushed aboard with information that his *Essex* had sunk the *Arkansas* the day before, following the army's repulse of Breckenridge's attack. At the same time, he handed over the written account he had composed the previous afternoon.

Listening to his subordinate, whose account he did not then have any reason to doubt, Farragut was ecstatic. By mid afternoon, once his subordinate had departed, the Gulf squadron commander busily dictated a new report on the matter of the *Arkansas* for transmittal to Navy Secretary Welles. It began: "It is one of the happiest moments of my life that I am enabled to inform the Department of the destruction of the ram *Arkansas*, not because I held the ironclad in such terror, but because the community did." The message also confirmed Porter's claim to have single-handedly sunk the enemy warship.

Porter would continue to boldly state, to his superiors and colleagues, military and naval, in the press and to the Navy Department, Congress, and other political entities, that he alone had "attacked the rebel ram *Arkansas* and blew her up." As the true facts of the action, which Lt. Cmdr. Roe called "no fight at all," became known, most in the USN, save his brother RAdm. David Dixon Porter, backed away from their support of the officer's story.

Farragut insisted that while Porter did not destroy his enemy the presence of his little task force caused it and hence he was entitled to the glory he claimed. In a private July 20 letter quoted in his son's appreciation, the admiral confessed that, although he was pleased the *Arkansas* was destroyed, "My delight would have been to smash her in *Hartford* style." Or, in short, to have had a chance to end her himself.

Aboard the *Westfield*, U.S. Marine Henry C. Gusley heard of the whole incident differently, carried out by other players. Writing in his notebook, later obtained by the *New York Times*, the leatherneck observed that "the two gunboats lying here, the *Kineo* of Farragut's fleet and the iron-clad *Sumter* of Davis' fleet, went up to engage the rebel ram and, after a running fight, compelled the crew to blow her up to prevent her falling into our hands."

With the *Arkansas* sunk, there was no other significant Confederate naval force in the vicinity to cause worry. Consequently, Farragut now decided to return to New Orleans the next morning, leaving several additional gunboats to help the army ashore. The admiral departed "with a light heart, that I have left no bugbear to torment the communities of the Mississippi in my absence." In his biography of Farragut, Alfred T. Mahan also noted that the "disappearance from the waters of the Mississippi of the last hostile vessel capable of offensive action" released the Gulf squadron commander from either remaining on the river himself or maintaining there "a large force during the unhealthy season."

Having failed in his efforts to reach the *Arkansas* before her end, Cmdr. Isaac Newton Brown arrived at the headquarters of Maj. Gen. Breckenridge, several miles from Baton Rouge toward Port Hudson, during the afternoon. The naval officer was briefed by the general, though that leader did not know the details surrounding the loss of the *Arkansas*. Perhaps she had run ashore in the early morning fog. In any event, the soldier was probably careful not to assert, as he did later, that the campaign failed because the ram provided no support.

The former U.S. vice president noticed that his guest still suffered from the illness that had taken him from his quarterdeck in the first place. Breckenridge insisted that Brown stay the night with him in his own tent, even giving the fighting seaman his own cot, while he slept on the floor.

Knowing that they had to reach safety before Union cavalry patrols cut them off, Lt. Stevens appropriated several wagons during the day to take the *Arkansas* men away from the Nolan plantation. Sarah's mother, also quite taken with Lt. Read, gave him $20 to help him buy new clothes once he reached his destination. The diarist, knowing nothing about sailors, and two of her girlfriends ran after the wagons, handing out bottles of gin "to help them along." Sarah remembered "a rough old sailor received mine with a flood of thanks." Others of the plantation staff offered food, including meat and bread. In many ways, the first 24 hours after the loss of the ship was the best her crew experienced.

Among the men who were separated from this main group at the levee, but not captured, were eight sailors, three of the lieutenants, and Chief Pilot Brady. Most of these men reached Port Hudson, 20 miles upriver, in company with elements of Breckenridge's army. Brady, though, continued to the north, attempting to find the Stevens party, which he also believed was headed toward Tangipahoa.

Eleven: Arkansas vs. Essex, Round Two: Finale Off Baton Rouge

Brown departed the Breckenridge camp early on August 8 intent upon finding his men. He suspected that they would attempt to either reach the railhead at Tangipahoa or escape via Port Hudson. The road to Clinton, Louisiana, 40 miles north of Baton Rouge, would take him to the former location, which he considered the most logical escape route for a large group of seamen wishing to return to naval headquarters at Jackson. Riding onto the grounds of a plantation near Clinton, 20 miles from the Breckenridge headquarters, Cmdr. Brown, escorted by two cavalrymen provided by Brig. Gen. Daniel Ruggles, encountered Pilot Brady. The two men had to have been delighted to meet. As Brady related the fate of the *Arkansas* in great detail, her captain was relieved to know that she did not run ashore in the fog.

Her demise, Brady pointed out, was caused by "defects in the machinery, which no one on board could remedy or guard against." Brown was aware that his engines were defective and was fearful of possible consequences as a result. But no one could, he later wrote, "think they would so soon have ruined everything." Even if he had made it to the boat before its departure, Brown knew that "I could not have, by my presence, averted the wearing out of the engine." That was small consolation.

Brady went on to tell his commander how his party, "seeking food and protection," approached a camp of Southern irregulars not far from the beach where they had landed from the armorclad. The irregulars refused to give any assistance and rode away, leaving the men to fend for themselves.

As they had for the past 36 hours, the larger of the two contingents of ex-*Arkansas* crewmen marched to the northwest. Most walked, but several found horses and the hurt and ill continued in wagons. In sun, thunderstorms, and the darkness of night, they crossed the Comite and Amite rivers, always headed northwest. Stevens finally led his men into Camp Moore, near Tangipahon, about 70 miles away from the river. There they were joined by Cmdr. Brown. Reunion came the better part of two days following the loss of their boat. The naval refugees boarded a train and returned to Jackson, Mississippi, where they arrived on August 9. Lt. Read was interviewed the same day by a reporter from the *Jackson Mississippian*, whose concise report was printed in the next day's edition.

Cmdr. Brown's account of meeting Pilot Brady, sent initially to Breckenridge, was printed in the *Richmond Dispatch* on August 26. Many of the officers and men wrote letters home. Meta Grimball, the mother of John, received his missive at her South Carolina home and wrote in her diary on August 19:

> We have received a long letter from John giving an account of the 3 engagements in which he was in the *Arkansas* they were most brilliant and the vessel did wonderfully for the Machinery evidently was not of sufficient force to make the vessel effective. The Majestic way in which she moved was as fast as she could go. The end of this was naturally the destruction of the vessel. We are now most anxious to hear from John he sent us a drawing of the vessel and which he wishes photographed and we saw by the Papers that the last engagement of the poor Arkansas ended in her being blown up by her own crew they all escaped to the shore.

Cmdr. Brown returned to his interrupted leave. Having heard that Breckenridge might be preparing an attack on New Orleans, Maj. Gen. Butler elected to concentrate his forces at the Crescent City and evacuated Baton Rouge on August 18–19. At Jackson, Flag Officer William F. Lynch agreed to provide a naval contingent to supplement a Confederate artillery defense being set up at Port Hudson.

Several weeks later, most of the surviving crew of the *Arkansas*, led by Lt. Stevens, traveled to Port Hudson. When Cmdr. Brown, who had earlier prepared artillery sites at

Columbus and Fort Pillow, arrived to assume command, his tars were already hard at work assisting in the creation and fortifying of a defensive bastion to guard Vicksburg from the south.

Thoughts of the *Arkansas* never left these men and several would travel with Cmdr. Brown back up the Yazoo during the months ahead to work on new gunboats for the Confederate navy. But that is another yarn for another book.[15]

Epilogue

The 23-day operational career of the CSS *Arkansas* was over. For a period of just under a month, she was, as Admiral Alfred T Mahan wrote, the "most formidable Confederate ironclad that had yet been equipped on the Mississippi" and the one most feared by the North.

Although she was never defeated, unreliable engines doomed her to an early end. Her short career and loss had a major impact upon both the Union and the Confederacy. The end of what David Flynt has called a "hero ship" would be remembered in poem and song for years to come, as in this verse from 1911:

> And her brave banner sparkled prouder
> Till the fire had reached her powder;
> In her loudest peal of thunder
> Went the Queen of Battle down.

News of the ram's destruction reached both Richmond and Washington within 48 hours; it would take longer to filter through the rest of the divided country. For example, as late as August 9, the *Memphis Bulletin* was reporting that "the *Arkansas* has made a trip up the Mississippi to within 50 miles of Helena." In his memoir of his presidency, Jefferson Davis summed up the Southern lament that he had first wired to Maj. Gen. Earl Van Dorn with his "regrets" of August 8, 1862. Her demise was "a sacrificial offering to the cause she had served so valiantly in her brief but brilliant career."

When he heard of the loss of the *Arkansas*, the chief of the Confederate ordnance office, Col. (later Brig. Gen.) Josiah Gorgas, whose wife later became librarian of the University of Alabama, wrote a reflective August 11 entry in his journal: "The brilliant passage of the *Arkansas* thro' the enemy's fleet three weeks ago, destroying several of them, made us hope much of her. Had she lived, N. Orleans might have been re-taken. With her dies all hope of re-conquering the Mississippi."

Given his high hopes for her, Stephen Mallory was distraught over the armorclad's loss. He wrote his London naval agent, Cmdr. James D. Bulloch, on August 8 saying it was hard for him to bear her demise "with equanimity." A few weeks later, the vessel's destruction, coupled with several other reversals, caused the Confederate Navy Department minister to be attacked by his political opponents in the Confederate congress. In a letter to his wife on August 31, the ironclad visionary defended himself and the construction of the *Arkansas*: "Knowing that the enemy could build 100 ships to our one, my policy has been to make such ships, so strong and so invulnerable, as would compensate for the inequality in numbers. With the *Merimac* [sic], the *Arkansas*, the *Mississippi*, the *Louisiana*, etc., I revolutionized the naval warfare of the world, astonished all people by showing what could be done...."

Maj. Gen. Earl Van Dorn has received much criticism over the years for dispatching the ram to Baton Rouge. His latest biographer, Arthur Carter, writes of it: "It was equally foolhardy to send the *Arkansas* to Breckenridge's aid, since the vessel's condition virtually ruled out any chance it could complete her mission of destroying the enemy gunboats." In the end, he was so worried that the Confederate attack on Louisiana's capital might be cancelled, "he assented to Breckenridge's request for the ram." The Kentucky-born field general and former U.S. vice president placed the blame for his failure upon the armorclad. As the *Richmond Daily Dispatch* reported on August 14, "General Breckenridge has issued a congratulatory address to his army. He claims to have gained a complete victory by land at Baton Rouge — the most essential fruits of which, however, are lost by the failure of the *Arkansas* to co-operate. All accounts agree in saying that the Yankees were beaten to and into the river."

It has been speculated that the *Arkansas*, had she not been lost, might have, at least temporarily, been able to remove and prevent reestablishment of "the ever-tightening" Federal blockade of the Mississippi. Others took that argument further, suggesting that she might even have been able to alter somewhat the outcome of the war by helping to keep Maj. Gen. Ulysses S. Grant from capturing Vicksburg the following year. John Mercer Brooke wrote, albeit with a caveat, on August 6 (ironically, the day the vessel perished): "I wish we had half a dozen *Arkansas* in the Mississippi." As Oliver Wood McClinton suggests, it would be "interesting to speculate what the outcome would have been had the South been able to launch and utilize more such ships, such as her sister ship, the *Tennessee*."

McClinton's observation deserves some attention. Richmond had never intended for the *Arkansas* to work alone and had assumed prior to June that she would be supported by her sister, the *Tennessee*, as well as other Confederate gunboats, either from the squadrons of Commodore Hollins or Montgomery. The two *Arkansas*-class vessels were supposed to meet the challenge of James Eads' Carondelet-built City Series boats. In a fleet action, Shirley's boats would take on these Union ironclads while Hollins or Montgomery dealt with, say, the timberclads or anything else (the fact that the Battle of Memphis blew up that idea in practice is outside this theoretical discussion). The Memphis twins were more heavily armed and better protected in their ordnance and machinery spaces than the Eads craft (save perhaps the separate *Benton* conversion) and faster than any of them. If the machinery had worked as hoped, either would have been more maneuverable than their Northern enemy. The rams mounted at their bows would have conceivably been of great value.

None of this was to be fully realized, as the *Tennessee* was not completed. A taste of possibility was provided in the contest with the *Carondelet* in the Yazoo. While a powerful opponent even for the seagoing frigates and sloops on temporary assignment above Vicksburg, the *Arkansas*, with her feeble power plant, was, in the end, unable to stand alone.

The three weeks of glory enjoyed by the *Arkansas* were wrecked by Van Dorn's willfulness, the weakness of her contrary power plant, and the loss of the gifted black room boss George City, who alone seemed able to make the engines function (nearly) as they should. As Frank E. Smith wrote years later, "For want of an engineer, another Confederate dreadnought had been lost, and with it the last chance to stop the Federal gunboats on the Mississippi."

Still, the successes enjoyed by the *Arkansas* provided lessons that had an impact upon both sides as they jockeyed for triumph in the Mississippi Valley. "The North could not win the war so long as Confederate ironclads could be built in shallow waters," observed

Howard J. Fuller in 2008, "and launched to threaten Union gunboats penetrating into the South."

Professor Still observed the same thing earlier when he noted that, because the *Arkansas*, like the *Virginia*, was destroyed by her own side and not the enemy, the Confederate navy retained faith in the value of building armorclads. Consequently, Secretary Mallory took heart and pressed ahead to further implement his visionary decision that the South required more of these vessels. Fuller went on to opine that, just as new classes of monitors were needed by the USN on the East coast, so too "would even lighter-draft ironclads of superior armor-crushing armament and impregnability be needed to bolster Union combined operations in the West."

Until new vessels appeared, "the North was as much on the strategic defensive there as it was in the East." Fortunately, what remained of the Confederacy's already weak industrial base beyond the Allegheny Mountains insured that here, too, the few boats started (only the *Missouri* was finished, if one doesn't count those at Mobile) would have been mostly powered by engines that insured grief.[1]

In November 1981, famed novelist and maritime explorer Clive Cussler and an associate conducted an examination of the known and supposed wreck sites for the South's Mississippi River ironclads. The men conducted interviews with local residents and reviewed the available evidence, including a 1927 account that a few miles north of Baton Rouge a Civil War wreck was found by the Thompson Gravel Company. Cussler concluded that what remained of the *Arkansas* rested on the west bank of the Mississippi at Sunrise, Louisiana, "deep under the levee on a north/south heading about a mile and four tenths south from the auto and railroad bridge just below Free Negro Point, 230 yards below Mile 233." The expedition was summarized both on a Website and in a popular work on underwater salvage.

There is very little chance that what may remain from the hulk of the *Arkansas* will ever be recovered. What endures, however, is the incredible tale of her backwater construction and her glorious, if brief, operational career. Speaking to a group of Union naval veterans in 1900, a former USN sailor, Eliot Callender, sounded the theme that exists today:

> I know of no more interesting event of the War than the career of the Confederate ram *Arkansas*, and while the incidents connected therewith may not touch our pride, I trust there is no soldier or sailor of the late War that cannot appreciate bravery and gallantry whether exhibited by friend or foe. We were Americans all, before the days of the Civil War, and, Thank God, we are Americans all to-day.[2]

Chapter Notes

Introduction

1. James P. Baxter III, *Introduction of the Ironclad Warship* (Cambridge, MA: Harvard University Press, 1933; repr., U.S. Naval Institute, 2000), 222.
2. William N. Still, Jr., *Iron Afloat: The Story of the Confederate Armorclads* (Columbia: University of South Carolina Press, 1985).
3. Tom Z. Parrish, *The Saga of the Confederate Ram Arkansas: The Mississippi Valley Campaign, 1862* (Hillsboro, TX: Hill College Press, 1987), 141.
4. William N. Still, "The History of the C.S.S. *Arkansas*" (master's thesis, University of Alabama, 1958), 57.
5. Myron J. Smith, Jr., *The Timberclads in the Civil War: The "Lexington," "Tyler" and "Conestoga" on the Western Waters, 1861–1865* (Jefferson, NC: McFarland, 2008) and *The USS "Carondelet": A Civil War Ironclad on Western Waters* (Jefferson, NC: McFarland, 2010).

One: Beginnings

1. E.B. Potter and Chester W. Nimitz, *Sea Power: A Naval History* (Englewood Cliffs, NJ: Prentice-Hall, 1960), 247–251.
2. James M. McPherson, *Battle Cry of Freedom: The Civil War Era*, vol. 6, *The Oxford History of the United States*, ed. C. Vann Woodward (New York: Oxford University Press, 1988), 252–260, 276–307; E. Merton Coulter, *The Confederate States of America* (Baton Rouge: Louisiana State University Press, 1950), 19–32; Bruce Catton, *The Coming Fury* (Garden City, NY: Doubleday, 1961), 214–215; William C. Davis, *Look Away: A History of the Confederate States of America* (New York: Free Press, 2002), 55–77; Raimondo Luraghi, *A History of the Confederate Navy* (Annapolis: Naval Institute Press, 1996), 2–9.
3. Mark M. Boatner III, *The Civil War Dictionary* (New York: David McKay, 1959), 54–55, 225–226, 503–504; David J. Eicher, *The Longest Night: A Military History of the Civil War* (New York: Simon and Schuster, 2001), 140; New South Associates, *C.S.S. Georgia: Archival Study* (U.S. Army Corps of Engineers, Contract Number DACW21-99-D-0004, January 31, 2007) http://sav-harbor.com/Cultural%20Resources/CSS_Georgia_Archival_Study.pdf?CFID=5719029&CFTOKEN=b794a43d13065f5e-928D3131-D60D-557F-44FBC05168261FF4> (accessed May 1, 2010); Davis, *op. cit.,* 92; McPherson, *op. cit.,* 314–315; Joseph T. Durkin, *Confederate Navy Chief: Stephen R. Mallory* (Chapel Hill: University of North Carolina Press, 1954; repr., University of South Carolina Press, 1987), 63–64, 150, 153–154; "Stephen Russell Mallory," in *The Political Graveyard: Index to Politicians,* http://politicalgraveyard.com/bio/mallory.html (accessed September 11, 2009); Rodman L. Underwood and Stephen Russell Mallory: *A Biography of the Confederate Navy Secretary and United States Senator* (Jefferson, NC: McFarland, 2005), 54–56, 77–87; Luraghi, *op. cit.,* 4, 7–8, 65–67; William N. Still, Jr., *Iron Afloat: The Story of the Confederate Armorclads* (Columbia: University of South Carolina Press, 1985), 9–11; Still, *Confederate Shipbuilding* (Athens: University of Georgia Press, 1969), 8–10; William C. Davis, *Duel Between the First Ironclads* (Garden City, NY: Doubleday, 1975), 8–9; J. Thomas Scharf, *History of the Confederate Navy from Its Organization to the Surrender of Its Last Vessel* (New York: Rodgers and Sherwood, 1887, repr., New York: Fairfax, 1977), 17; U.S. Navy Department, *Official Records of the Union and Confederate Navies in the War of the Rebellion,* 31 vols. (Washington, D.C.: GPO, 1894–1922), Series II, vol. 2, 42, 51–69, 174, (cited hereafter as ORN, followed by a comma, the series number in Roman numerals, a comma, the volume number in Arabic, a colon, and the page in Arabic); ORN, II, 1: 783; U.S. War Department, *The War of the Rebellion: A Compilation of the Official Records of the Union and Confederate Armies,* 128 vols. (Washington, D.C.: GPO, 1880–1901), Series I, Vol.1: 17, 43, 63, 191, 250 (cited hereafter as OR, followed by a comma, the series number in Roman numerals, a comma, the volume number in Arabic, a colon, and the page in Arabic); Alfred Roman, *The Military Operations of General Beauregard in the War Between the States, 1861 to 1865,* 2 vols. (New York: Harper & Brothers, 1884), I, 422; *New Orleans Daily Delta,* February 15, 1861; James P. Baxter III, *Introduction of the Ironclad Warship* (Cambridge, MA: Harvard University Press, 1933; republished U.S. Naval Institute, 2000), 222, 225, 237; James Chester, "Inside Sumter in '61," in *Battles and Leaders of the Civil War,* ed. Robert V. Johnson and Clarence C. Buell, 4 vols. (New York: Century), 1884–1887, repr. Thomas Yoseloff, 1956), I, 66–67 (cited hereafter as *B&L,* followed by a comma, the volume number in Roman numerals, a comma, and the page numbers); David Detzer, *Allegiance: Fort Sumter, Charleston, and the Beginning of the Civil War* (New York: Harcourt, 2001), 198–200; *Frank Leslie's Illustrated Weekly,* February 9 and 16, March 30, April 27, 1861; *New York Herald,* April 13, 1861; W.A. Swanberg, *First Blood: The Story of Fort Sumter* (New York: Charles Scribner's Sons, 1957), 205–206; E. Milby Burton, *The Siege of*

Charleston, 1861–1865 (Columbia: University of South Carolina Press, 1970), 22–23; *Richmond Daily Enquirer*, April 22, 1861; John S. Long, "The Gosport Affair," *Journal of Southern History* 23 (May 1957), 155–172; John Niven, *Gideon Welles: Lincoln's Secretary of the Navy* (New York: Oxford University Press, 1973), 340–345. President Davis and members of his family, incidentally, owned a plantation that bordered the Mississippi River below Vicksburg. Among the first to support Mallory's ironclad acquisition concept was former USN lieutenant and fellow Floridian John Mercer Brooke (1826–1906), who wrote to the new navy secretary on May 6 suggesting it might be possible to get one from France through the Union blockade by wooden ships (John Mercer Brooke, *Ironclads and Big Guns of the Confederacy: The Journal and Letters of John M. Brooke*, ed. George M. Brooke, Jr., Studies in Maritime History (Columbia: University of South Carolina Press, 2002), 16). In something of an ironic preview to a part of our story, historian Baxter later noted that "inclined sides became the characteristic feature of Confederate ironclads." In the case of the *Arkansas*, her sides were not inclined but those of her opponents, especially the *Essex* and *Carondelet*, were (Baxter, *op. cit.*, 223).

4. Boatner, *op. cit.*, 50, 254, 303, 524–525, 728–729, 900–901; Edward Townsend, *Anecdotes of the Civil War in the United States* (New York: D. Appleton, 1884), 56; OR, I, 51: 338–339, 369–370, 386–387; Timothy D. Johnson, *Winfield Scott: The Quest for Military Glory* (Lawrence: University Press of Kansas, 1998), 226–228; T. Harry Williams, *Lincoln and His Generals* (New York: Alfred A. Knopf, 1952; repr. Vintage, 1962), 16; Bern Anderson, "The Naval Strategy of the Civil War," *Military Affairs* 26 (Spring 1962), 15; Anderson, *By Sea and By River: The Naval History of the Civil War* (New York: Knopf, 1962), 33–34; Richard Webber and John C. Roberts, "James B. Eads: Master Builder," *The Navy* 8 (March 1965), 23–25; Elmer L. Gaden, "Eads and the Navy of the Mississippi," *American Heritage of Invention & Technology* 9 (Spring 1994), 26–27; John D. Milligan, *Gunboats Down the Mississippi* (Annapolis: Naval Institute Press, 1965), 3–4; Gideon Welles, *The Diary of Gideon Welles, Secretary of the Navy Under Lincoln and Johnson*, ed. John T. Morse, Jr., 3 vols. (Boston: Houghton, Mifflin, 1911), I, 242; *St. Louis Daily Missouri Democrat*, May 10, 1861. A recent review of the Anaconda and later Union plans is by Brian Holden Reid, "Rationality and Irrationality in Union Strategy, April 1861–March 1862," *War in History* 1 (March 1994), 25–29.

5. Richard Hill and John Keegan, *War at Sea in the Ironclad Age* (Smithsonian History of Warfare; New York: Harper, 2006), 32–36; Baxter, *op. cit.*, 98–99, 110–111, 223–226; ORN, II, 1: 740–743; ORN, II, 2: 67–69; Still, *Iron Afloat*, 10; Niven, *op. cit.*, 364–365; Underwood, *op. cit.*, 87–90 ; Luraghi, *op. cit.*, 90–91; Scharf, *op. cit.*, 43; Durkin, *op. cit.*, 152–154; William H. Roberts, *Civil War Ironclads: The U.S. Navy and Industrial Mobilization* (Baltimore: Johns Hopkins University Press, 2002), 9; "Charles Magill Conrad," in *The Political Graveyard: Index to Politicians*, http://politicalgraveyard.com/bio/conrad.html (accessed September 11, 2009). Given the lag in Federal initiation of an ironclad imperative, John Ericcson's short time construction of the USS *Monitor* becomes the more remarkable. Capt. Davis temporarily assumed command of the Western Flotilla on May 9, 1862. In the antebellum period, Davis developed an enviable reputation, like the first leader of the army's Western Flotilla leader, Cmdr. John Rodgers, as a scientific officer. Born in Boston, he earned a degree from Harvard University, becoming superintendent of the Nautical Almanac Office located there. With sea service during the expedition to capture the filibuster William Walker in Nicaragua and with the South Atlantic Blockading Squadron, Davis was confirmed in his command in June 1862, only to be himself succeeded in command of the unit, re-formed as the Mississippi Squadron, by David Dixon Porter in October (effective July). Constantly on duty ashore and afloat, he would die at his desk as superintendent of the Naval Observatory. Our profile of Rear Adm. Davis is taken from William B. Cogar, *Dictionary of Admirals of the U.S. Navy*, 2 vols. (Annapolis: Naval Institute Press, 1989), I, 41–43, and Charles Henry Davis, *Life of Charles Henry Davis, Rear Admiral, 1807–1877* (Boston and New York: Houghton, Mifflin, 1899). Well-known naval architect John Lenthall was chief of the Bureau of Construction, Equipment and Repair from 1853 to 1871. During this time, he compiled a large collection of ship plans for blue-water vessels. In 1991, the Library of the Philadelphia Maritime Museum released the 52-page booklet *John Lenthall, Naval Architect: A Guide to Plans and Drawings of American Naval and Merchant Vessels, 1790–1874: With a Bibliography of Works on Shipbuilding ... Collected by John Lenthall (b. 1807–d.1882)*.

6. OR, I, 53: 490–491; ORN, I, 22, 277–280, 284–286; Charles Dana Gibson, with E. Kay Gibson, *Assault and Logistics*, vol. 2, *Union Army Coastal and River Operations, 1861–1866* (Camden, ME: Ensign, 1995), 160; Edwin C. Bearss, *Hardluck Ironclad: The Sinking and Salvage of the Cairo* (Baton Rouge: Louisiana State University Press, 1966), 12–13; Milligan, *op. cit.*, 5–6; Robert E. Johnson, *Rear Admiral John Rodgers, 1812–1882* (Annapolis: Naval Institute Press, 1967), 156–157; Donald L. Canney, *The Old Steam Navy*, vol. 2, *The Ironclads, 1842–1885* (Annapolis: Naval Institute Press, 1993), 47; William B. Cogar, *Dictionary of Admirals of the U.S. Navy*, 2 vols. (Annapolis: Naval Institute Press, 1989), I, 150–152; Myron J. Smith, *The Timberclads in the Civil War: The "Lexington," "Conestoga," and "Tyler" on the Western Waters* (Jefferson, NC: McFarland, 2008), 40–96. Bostonian Samuel Moore Pook started working at the Brooklyn Navy Yard in 1825 as a shipwright's apprentice. Named a naval constructor (the last of the great designers of U.S. wooden sailing warships given that title) in 1841, he built, among others, the sloops-of-war *Preble* and *Saratoga*, the frigates *Congress* and *Franklin*, and the steamers *Merrimack* and *Princeton*. In 1852, he rebuilt "Old Ironsides," the U.S. frigate *Constitution*. Interestingly, the obituary in the *Times* does not mention Pook's Western service. His son, Samuel H. Pook, designer of such noted clipper ships as the *Red Jacket*, also labored at the Brooklyn yard (*New York Times*, December 4, 1878; Howard I Chapelle, *The History of American Sailing Ships* (New York: W. W. Norton, 1935), 129; Chapelle, *The Search for Speed Under Sail* (New York: W.W. Norton, 1967), 362–363).

7. Boatner, *op. cit.*, 843–844; OR, I, 3, 1: 164–165; OR, I, 3, 2: 814–815; Lenthal to Totten, June 1, 1861, Records of the Office of the Quartermaster General, U.S. National Archives and Records Service, Record Group 92 (cited hereafter as QMG Records); Totten to Scott, June 3, 1861, QMG Records; OR, I, 51, 1:157–160, 164–168; OR, I, 52, 1:164–167; Still, *Armor Afloat*, 3; David D. Porter, *Naval History of the Civil War* (New York: Sherman, 1886; repr., Secaucus, NJ: Castle Books, 1984), 268; John D. Milligan, "The First American Ironclads: The Evolution of a Design," *Missouri Historical Society Bulletin* 22 (October 1965), 3–13; Milligan, "From Theory to Ap-

plication: The Emergence of the American Ironclad War Vessel," *Military Affairs* 48 (July 1984), 126; *St. Louis Daily Democrat,* June 5, 1861.

8. ORN, II, 2: 77–78, 90. 92, 174, 783; Brooke, *op. cit.*, 17; Luraghi, *op. cit.*, 43, 48, 93; Underwood, *op. cit.*, 92–93; Davis, *op. cit.*, 9–10; John Mercer Brooke, "The Plan and Construction of the Merrimac," *B&L*, I, 715–716; Brooke, "The *Virginia* or *Merrimac:* Her Real Projector," *Southern Historical Society Papers* 19 (January 1891), 3–5; Brooke, *Ironclads and Big Guns,* 22; John Taylor Wood, "The First Fight of Iron-Clads," *B&L*, I, 693–694; John McIntosh Kell, *Recollections of a Naval Life, Including the Cruises of the Confederate States Steamers Sumter and Alabama* (Washington, D.C.: Neal, 1900), 130; William H. Parker, *Recollections of a Naval Officer, 1841–1865* (New York: Charles Scribner's Sons, 1883; repr. Annapolis: U.S. Naval Institute Press, 1985), 207; Brian T. Clayton, *Guide to the John Luke Porter Papers, 1860–1993,* Manuscript Collection, East Carolina Manuscript Collection, Special Collections, Joyner Library, East Carolina University, 2003, http://digital.lib.ecu.edu/special/ead/findingaids/0850/#histnote (accessed August 25, 2009); *Papers of Thom Williamson,* Special Collections: Manuscripts, Old Dominion University Libraries, 2008, http://www.lib.odu.edu/special/manuscripts/williamson.htm (accessed August 25, 2009). Porter, who also had a plan, and Brooke debated into long after the war over who deserved credit for the original design. Although the exact glory was never attributed, the latter won most of the laurels. In the end, the three shared in the *Virginia*'s triumph. Porter in Gosport oversaw construction with Williamson also there working on the power plant; Brooke stayed in Richmond securing iron and ordnance. For a full review outside the scope of this work, see John Mercer Brooke, "The *Virginia* or *Merrimac,*" 3–34, and John W.H. Porter, *A Record of Events in Norfolk County, Virginia* (Portsmouth, VA: W.A. Fisher, 1892), 327–334; Still, *Iron Afloat,* 14–15. Porter and Brooke both receive excellent and lengthy biographical treatment in consecutive chapters of Carl D. Park's *Ironclad Down: The USS "Merrimack"-CSS "Virginia" from Construction to Destruction* (Annapolis: Naval Institute Press, 2007), 12–37. There is little in Civil War literature, other than a profile in Park's work, regarding Chief Engineer Williamson. Former naval officer Tom H. Wells was not impressed with his skill or leadership (or for that matter, with Porter's) and said so in his *The Confederate Navy: A Study in Organization* (Tuscaloosa: University of Alabama Press, 1971), 97–107. Statistics on the rebuilt *Virginia* are found in Paul Silverstone, *Warships of the Civil War Navies* (Annapolis: Naval Institute Press, 1989), 202.

Two: The Upper River Ironclads

1. Charles Henry Ambler, *A History of Transportation in the Ohio Valley* (Glendale, CA: Arthur H. Clark, 1932), 248; James Monaghan, *Civil War on the Western Border, 1854–1865* (Boston: Little, Brown, 1955), 130–132; Edwin C. Bearss, *Hardluck Ironclad: The Sinking and Salvage of the Cairo* (Baton Rouge: Louisiana State University Press, 1966), 12; Rodman L. Underwood, *Stephen Russell Mallory: A Biography of the Confederate Navy Secretary and United States Senator* (Jefferson, NC: McFarland, 2005), 98; John W. Allen, *Legends and Lore of Southern Illinois* (Carbondale: University Graphics, 1978), 288–289; T.K. Kionka, *Key Command: Ulysses S. Grant's District of Cairo* (Shades of Blue and Gray Series; Columbia: University of Missouri Press, 2006), 49; *Chicago Daily Tribune,* May 21, 1861; U.S. Navy Department, Naval History Division, *Civil War Naval Chronology, 1861–1865* (Washington, D.C.: GPO, 1966), 12–13; S. Chamberlain, "Opening of the Upper Mississippi and the Siege of Vicksburg," *Magazine of Western History* 5 (March 1887), 611–613; Milford M. Miller, "Evansville Steamboats During the Civil War," *Indiana Magazine of History* 37 (December 1941), 363; *Cincinnati Daily Commercial,* May 8, 1861; *New York Evening Post,* May 11, 1861; *Evansville Daily Journal,* May 14, 1861. According to the Valley of the Shadows Resource Center's 1861 timeline, the river blockade was officially launched on May 13, almost a month after President Lincoln had ordered establishment of a coastal blockade (*Valley of the Shadow Homepage,* http://valley.vcdh.virginia.edu/reference/timelines/timeline1861.html, (accessed September 1, 2006).

2. U.S. Navy Department, *Official Records of the Union and Confederate Navies in the War of the Rebellion,* 31 vols. (Washington, D.C.: GPO, 1894–1922), Series I, Vol.22, 279 (cited hereafter as ORN, followed by a comma, the series number in Roman numerals, a comma, the volume number in Arabic, a colon, and the page in Arabic); *Chicago Daily Tribune,* May 22, 1861; Bearss, *op. cit.*; Edwin C. Bearss, *Hardluck Ironclad: The Sinking and Salvage of the Cairo* (Baton Rouge: Louisiana State University Press, 1966), 13; Louis C. Hunter, *Steamboats on the Western Rivers: An Economic and Technological History* (Cambridge, MA: Harvard University Press, 1949), 548; *Memphis Daily Appeal,* July 17, 1851; *St. Louis Daily Democrat,* June 5, 1861; *St. Louis Daily Missouri Republican,* January 12, 1877; *Memphis Daily Avalanche,* September 10, 1873; Myron J. Smith, Jr., *The Timberclads in the Civil War: The "Lexington," "Conestoga," and "Tyler" on the Western Waters* (Jefferson, NC: McFarland, 2008), 48–68; Mary Emerson Branch, "Prime Emerson and Steamboat Building in Memphis," *West Tennessee Historical Society Papers* 38 (1984), 69–72; Branch, "A Story behind the Story of the *Arkansas* and the *Carondelet,*" *Missouri Historical Review* 79 (April 1985), 313–316; Frederick Way, Jr., *Way's Packet Directory, 1848–1994: Passenger Steamboats of the Mississippi River System Since the Advent of Photography in Mid-Continent America* (Athens: Ohio University Press, 1983; revised ed. (Athens: Ohio University Press, 1994), 17. In August, the government purchased the *Submarine No. 7* and Eads converted her into the powerful flotilla flagship USS *Benton.* In a blot on his otherwise brilliant and patriotic record, conveniently forgotten, Eads, as a part owner of the Missouri Wrecking Company, was later accused of conflict of interest in the *Benton* conversion matter (Donald L. Canery, *The Old Steam Navy,* vol. 2, *The Ironclads, 1842–1885* (Annapolis: Naval Institute Press, 1993), 44). Rodgers, who served as construction superintendent and commander of the timberclads, was initially superintendent of the City Series ironclads; ironically, Lt. Isaac Newton Brown would, six months later, be named both building boss and skipper of the *Arkansas.*

3. Charles Wright Wills, *Army Life of an Illinois Soldier,* comp. Mary E. Kellogg (Washington, D.C.: Globe, 1906), 20; Jay Slagle, *Ironclad Captain: Seth Ledyard Phelps and the U.S. Navy* (Kent, OH: Kent State University Press, 1996), 116–117; John D. Milligan, *Gunboats Down the Mississippi* (Annapolis: Naval Institute Press, 1965), 8; Branch, "The Story Behind the Story of the *Arkansas* and the *Carondelet,*" 316; Bearss, *op. cit.*, 15–16; Meigs to McClellan, June 13, 1861, QMG Records; Meigs to McClellan, June 17, 1861, Montgomery C. Meigs Papers, Library of Congress (cited hereafter as Meigs Papers); *Cincinnati*

Daily Commercial, June 25, 1861; *Philadelphia Inquirer,* June 26, 1861; *St. Louis Daily Republican,* June 28–29, 1861; *Memphis Daily Avalanche,* June 26, 1861; *New York Times,* July 3, 1861; U.S. War Department, *The War of the Rebellion: A Compilation of the Official Records of the Union and Confederate Armies,* 128 vols. (Washington, D.C.: GPO, 1880–1901), Series I, Vol. 52, Part 1, 164 (cited hereafter as OR, followed by a comma, the series number in Roman numerals, a comma, the volume number in Arabic, any part number in Arabic, a colon, and the page in Arabic); OR, I, 52, 165, 167–168; ORN, I, 22: 285–287, 319, 791–792; ORN, II, 2: 117; Smith, *The Timberclads,* 68–69; William N. Still, Jr., *Iron Afloat: The Story of the Confederate Armorclads* (Columbia: University of South Carolina Press, 1985), 15; Donald L. Canney, *The Old Steam Navy,* vol. 2, *The Ironclads, 1842–1885* (Annapolis: Naval Institute Press, 1993), 48; Robert E. Johnson, *Rear Admiral John Rodgers, 1812–1882* (Annapolis: Naval Institute Press, 1967), 159. The *Jackson* did not survive a year in service (U.S. Navy Department, Naval History Division, *Civil War Naval Chronology, 1861–1865,* 6 vols. in 1, rev. ed.; Washington, D.C.: GPO, 1966), 253–254, 269; R. Thomas Campbell, *Confederate Naval Forces on Western Waters* (Jefferson, NC: McFarland, 2005), 15–16; J. Thomas Scharf, *History of the Confederate Navy from Its Organization to the Surrender of Its Last Vessel* (New York: Rodgers and Sherwood, 1887, repr., New York: Fairfax, 1977), 242–244, 263). Information on the armor plating aboard the *Jackson* comes from a *St. Louis Daily Democrat* story of September 5, 1861, published several days later. Powerful Pennsylvania senator Simon Cameron received his cabinet position as a payoff for his support in Lincoln's 1860 campaign. Ineffective and embarrassing, he was packed off as soon as possible (to Russia as ambassador, 1862–1866). Reelected to the Senate in 1867, he remained in that body through Reconstruction. The efficient and politically adroit Meigs (1816–1892) was named QMG on May 15, 1861, and held that post through the war, winning appointment as a brevet major general in July 1864. His name would appear often in support of the Western river war. He was also brother-in-law to postmaster general Montgomery Blair. A Mexican war veteran and Democratic politician, Pillow commanded the Tennessee state militia at the time of Fort Sumter. His later failure at Fort Donelson cost him his military career (Mark M. Boatner III, *The Civil War Dictionary* (New York: David McKay, 1959), 115, 542, 653–654). Emerson's name is occasionally spelled Emmerson, but we will use the single "m," per the writing of Mary Emerson Branch. Engineer Totten, incidentally, was the father-in-law of ex–USN lieutenant Henry Kennedy Stevens, whose exchange he would arrange in November. Stevens joined the CSN and eventually became executive officer of the CSS *Arkansas* (Margaret Alexander Carr, "Lieutenant Henry Kennedy Stevens, CSN: Warrior of the CSS *Arkansas,*" *UDC Magazine* 65 (June-July 2002), 16).

4. OR, III, 2: 819–820; *U.S. Statutes at Large* 12 (July 17, 1861), 261–263; *St. Louis Daily Missouri Democrat,* July 20, August 1, 1861; Robert J. Rombauer, *The Union Cause in St. Louis in 1862* (St. Louis, MO: Nixon-Jones, 1909), 222; William E. Geoghegan, "Study for a Scale Model of the USS *Carondelet,*" *Nautical Research Journal* 17 (Summer 1970), 147–148, 155; *New York Times,* December 31, 1861; John D. Milligan, *Gunboats Down the Mississippi* (Annapolis: Naval Institute Press, 1965), 14; Smith, *The Timberclads,* 85; George W. Gift, "The Story of the Arkansas," *Southern Historical Society Papers* 12 (January–May 1884), 210; *Memphis Daily Appeal,* May 26, 31, June 14, 1861; *Memphis Appeal,* September 10, 1873; *Memphis Daily Avalanche,* May 31, June 1, August 16, 1861; Canney, *op. cit.,* 52; Johnson, *Rear Admiral John Rodgers, 1812–1882,* 160–161; William M. Fowler, Jr., *Under Two Flags: The American Navy in the Civil War* (Annapolis: Naval Institute Press, 2001), 134–135; Gary D. Joiner, *Mr. Lincoln's Brown Water Navy: The Mississippi Squadron* (Lanham, MD: Rowman & Littlefield, 2007), 25; John L. Mitchell, *Tennessee State Gazetteer and Business Directory for 1860–1861* (Nashville: John L. Mitchell, 1860), 125; Way, *op. cit.,* 240. The Memphis almoner's program limped on voluntarily for five additional weeks before ending; during its brief span 260 people received assistance (*Memphis Daily Appeal,* July 9, 1861). In her review of Shirley's content-light *Memphis Appeal* obituary, one source points out that it "just says what a grand fellow he was and how everyone who knew him liked him" (Joyce A. McKibben, reference librarian, University of Memphis, "Re: Ask a Librarian: John T. Shirley," personal e-mail, June 29, 2009). Shirley was not listed in contemporary Memphis city directories from the 1850s to 1861, nor does his name appear in the several postwar Tennessee state histories, several of which contain extensive biographies of prominent Volunteers. Prewar Democrat state legislator Currin served in the Confederate congress from the 11th District (and died in office) (Charles A. Miller, comp., *Official and Political Manual of the State of Tennessee* (Nashville: Marshall & Bruce, 1890), 177; "David Maney Currin, Sr.," in *The Political Graveyard: Index to Politicians,* http://politicalgraveyard.com/bio/curren-currin.html [accessed September 11, 2009]). Atkins was a member for the 9th District. He had served in the U.S. Congress from 1857 to 1859 and would again (1873–1883) (Miller, *loc. cit.;* "John DeWitt Clinton Atkins," in *The Political Graveyard: Index to Politicians,* http://politicalgraveyard.com/bio/athon-atkins.html [accessed September 11, 2009]). John V. Wright served in the U.S. Congress from 1855 to 1861 and as a postwar justice of the Tennessee Supreme Court (Miller, *loc. cit.;* "John Vines Wright," in *The Political Graveyard: Index to Politicians,* http://politicalgraveyard.com/bio/wright5.html [accessed September 11, 2009]). Johnson served as a U.S. congressman from 1847 to 1853 and as a senator from 1853 to 1861 ("Robert Ward Johnson," in *The Political Graveyard: Index to Politicians,* http://politicalgraveyard.com/bio/johnson7.html [accessed September 11, 2009]).

5. John Mercer Brooke, *Ironclads and Big Guns of the Confederacy: The Journal and Letters of John M. Brooke,* ed. George M. Brooke, Jr., Studies in Maritime History (Columbia: University of South Carolina Press, 2002), 27; ORN, I, 22: 792; OR, I, 7: 924; OR, I, 52, 2: 122; *New Orleans Daily Delta,* July 30, 1861; Scharf, *op. cit.,* 45; Branch, *op. cit.,* 318; Raimondo Luraghi, *A History of the Confederate Navy* (Annapolis: Naval Institute Press, 1996), 104; Boatner, *op. cit.,* 405; "Isaac Newton Brown," in *Register of Officers of the Confederate States Navy, 1861–1865* (Washington, D.C.: GPO, 1931), 23; "Jonathan Hanby Carter," *Register of Officers, loc. cit.,* 31; Charles M. Getchell, Jr. "Defender of Inland Waters: The Military Career of Isaac Newton Brown, Commander, Confederate States Navy, 1861–1865," (master's thesis, University of Mississippi, 1978), 7–13; Getchell, "Isaac Newton Brown of Navarro County, Texas," TXGenWeb Project, http://www.txgenweb6.org/txnavarro/biographies/b/brown_isaac_newton.htm (accessed July 13, 2009); "Jonathan Hanby Carter, Surry County's Civil War Sailor," *Free State of Patrick: Surry County North Carolina History,* http://www.freestateofpatrick.com/sccwr.htm

(accessed October 4, 2009); Henry Walke, *Naval Scenes and Reminiscences of the Civil War in the United States on the Southern and Western Waters during the Years 1861, 1862 and 1863, with the History of That Period Compared and Corrected from Authentic Sources* (New York: F.R. Reed, 1877), 302; Jay Carlton Mullen, "The Turning of Columbus," *The Register of the Kentucky Historical Society* 64 (July 1966), 211, 214. Commodore Hollins would command Confederate naval forces on the upper Mississippi through April 1862 when he returned to New Orleans and hence to a war-ending career serving on various boards of inquiry. During his time on the lower Mississippi, Hollins spent over $250,000 on seven wooden paddle wheel gunboats, "not the kind of ships needed to confront the forthcoming threat" (ORN, II, 1: 472; Underwood, *op. cit.*, 98–99; Luraghi, *loc. cit.*; James M. Merrill, *Battle Flags South: The Story of the Civil War Navies on the Western Waters* (Rutherford, NJ: Fairleigh Dickinson University Press, 1970), 68–69). An Episcopal bishop, Lt. Gen. Polk, a relative of President James K. Polk, was later killed during the Atlanta campaign (Boatner, *op. cit.,* 657–658). The espionage communication between Mallory and Brown was captured at Cero Gordo, TN, and published in the *New York Times* on February 25, 1862. Brown and Carter were both veterans of the prewar U.S. Navy, the latter with many years fewer service, having graduated in 1846 with the first class from the new Naval Academy at Annapolis. Carter would enjoy more early active service than Brown, but nothing as glorious as the latter's cruise in command of the *Arkansas.* Carter's claim to fame was his close association with the CSS *Missouri,* an armorclad he was ordered to construct in Texas beginning in the fall of 1862 and which would be the last Rebel inland ironclad to surrender in 1865. See particularly Katherine Brash Jeter, ed., *A Man and His Boat: The Civil War Career and Correspondence of Lt. Jonathan H. Carter* (Lafayette: Center for Louisiana Studies, University of Southwest Louisiana, 1996); Jeter, "Against All Odds: Lt. Jonathan H. Carter, CSN, and His Ironclad," *Louisiana History* 28 (Summer 1987), 265 (263–288). We should probably note here a bit of terminology. During the Civil War (as before and after), the ranking officer for a group of ships was referred to as "commodore" or "flag officer." While either a captain or a lieutenant could command a ship, the commanding officer of any ship, regardless of rank, was referred to as "captain" or "commander." The commanding officer of a naval yard or base was called a "port captain" (David J. Eicher, *The Longest Night: A Military History of the Civil War* (New York: Simon and Schuster, 2001), 138.

6. Bearss, *op. cit.*, 18–20; Johnson, *Rear Admiral John Rodgers, 1812–1882,* 161–163; Branch, *op. cit.,* 319.

7. ORN, II, 1: 248, 454–455, 780–782; ORN, II, 2: 152; *Journal of the Congress of the Confederate States of America, 1861–1865,* 7 vols. (Washington, D.C.: GPO, 1904), I, 371, 396; Hunter, *op. cit.,* 106–107, 316; Underwood, *op. cit.,* 100; Luraghi, *op. cit.,* 57, 107, 118–119; Scharf, *op. cit.,* 303; George Wright to this author, March 17, 2010; Branch, "Prime Emerson and Steamboat Building in Memphis," 73; Still, *op. cit.,* 16, 62; Still, *Confederate Shipbuilding* (Athens: University of Georgia Press, 1969), 11. Shirley's contract still exists and is found in Controller's Contracts, U.S. Treasury Department, Collection of Confederate Records, Record Group 365, National Archives, Washington, D.C.; it is also reprinted in William N. Still, "The History of the C.S.S. *Arkansas,*" (master's thesis, University of Alabama, 1958), 137–140. Grandnephew of George Washington by marriage, Charles Conrad served as a U.S. representative (1849–1850) and senator (1842–1843), as well as secretary of war (1850–1853); Walter Chandler, "The Memphis Navy Yard: An Adventure in Internal Improvement," *West Tennessee Historical Society Papers* 1 (1947), 68–72; John Harrison Morrison, *History of New York Ship Yards* (New York: Wm. F. Sametz, 1909), 153. Shirley, like Eads, would have great difficulty in obtaining his payment tranches. At one point, according to Lt. Gift, he would need to sell his home in order to raise working capital. Although Eads would receive full compensation of the funds appropriated for the construction of the *Arkansas* and her sister, only $138,000 would actually be paid (Gift, *loc. cit.;* ORN, II, 1: 435–436).

Three: A Frustrating Start, August–December 1861

1. U.S. Navy Department, *Official Records of the Union and Confederate Navies in the War of the Rebellion,* 31 vols. (Washington, D.C.: GPO, 1894–1922), Series II, Vol.1, 779–780, 782 (cited hereafter as ORN, followed by a comma, the series number in Roman numerals, a comma, the volume number in Arabic, a colon, and the page in Arabic); Raimondo Luraghi, *A History of the Confederate Navy* (Annapolis: Naval Institute Press, 1996), 118; John L. Mitchell, *Tennessee State Gazetteer and Business Directory for 1860–1861* (Nashville: John L. Mitchell, 1860); Mary Emerson Branch, "A Story Behind the Story of the *Arkansas* and the *Carondelet,*" *Missouri Historical Review,* 79 (April 1985), 318; J. Thomas Scharf, *History of the Confederate States Navy* (New York: Rodgers and Sherwood, 1887, repr., New York: Fairfax, 1977), 303; George W. Gift, "The Story of the *Arkansas,*" *Southern Historical Society Papers* 12 (January–May 1884), 49. A complete report on Fort Pickering as it was found and built up by the Federals appears in U.S. War Department, *The War of the Rebellion: A Compilation of the Official Records of the Union and Confederate Armies,* 128 vols. (Washington, D.C.: GPO, 1880–1901), Series I, Vol. 49, Part 2, 898–901 (cited hereafter as OR, followed by a comma, the series number in Roman numerals, a comma, the volume number in Arabic, any part number in Arabic, a colon, and the page in Arabic); John Preston Young and A.R. James, *Standard History of Memphis, Tennessee: From a Study of the Original Sources* (Knoxville: H.W. Crew, 1912), 337, 341; Alan Doyle, "Ram *Arkansas*/Fort Pickering," Civil War Navies Message Board, October 16, 2009, http://history-sites.com/cgi-bin/bbs53x/cwnavy/webbbs_config.pl?read=3516 (accessed October 16, 2009).

2. ORN, I, 22: 319; Robert E. Johnson, *Rear Admiral John Rodgers, 1812–1882* (Annapolis: Naval Institute Press, 1967), 164. From a humble and inauspicious beginning, U.S. Grant (1822–1885) rose to become the North's generalissimo and later served two terms as president (1869–1877) (Mark M. Boatner III, *The Civil War Dictionary* (New York: David McKay, 1959), 352–353).

3. Ulysses S. Grant, *Personal Memoirs of U.S. Grant,* 2 vols. (New York: C.L. Webster, 1885–1886; repr., 2 vols. in 1, New York: Penguin Books, 1999), I, 264–267; Joseph H. Parks, *General Leonidas Polk, C.S.A.: The Fighting Bishop* (Baton Rouge: Louisiana State University Press, 1962), 179–182; Jefferson Davis, *Rise and Fall of the Confederate Government,* 2 vols. (New York: D. Appleton, 1881), I, 385, 391; Thomas L. Connelly, *Army of the Heartland: The Army of Tennessee, 1861–1862* (Baton Rouge:

Louisiana State University Press, 1967), 51–52; William M. Polk, *Leonidas Polk, Bishop and General*, 2 vols. (New York: Longmans, Green, 1915), II, 17–29; William P. Johnston, *The Life of Gen. Albert Sidney Johnston* (New York: D. Appleton, 1878), 292; Bruce Catton, *Grant Moves South* (Boston: Little, Brown, 1960), 48–49; E Merton Coulter, *The Civil War and Readjustment in Kentucky* (Chapel Hill: University of North Carolina Press, 1926), 54–56; ORN, I, 22: 301, 317, 321; OR, I, 3: 151–152, 683; OR, I, 4: 179–192, 196–198; Stanley F. Horn, *The Army of Tennessee* (Indianapolis: Bobbs-Merrill, 1941), 44; Myron J. Smith, Jr., *The Timberclads in the Civil War: The "Lexington," "Conestoga," and "Tyler" on the Western Waters* (Jefferson, NC: McFarland, 2008), 96–106; *Philadelphia Inquirer*, October 3, 1861; Steven E. Woodworth, *Nothing but Victory: The Army of the Tennessee, 1861–1865* (New York: Alfred A. Knopf, 2005), 36–40; Jean Edward Smith, *Grant* (New York: Simon and Schuster, 2001), 118; Edward Conrad Smith, *The Borderland in the Civil War* (New York: Macmillan, 1927), 118–119, 301; E.B. Long, "The Paducah Affair: Bloodless Action That Altered the Civil War in the Mississippi Valley," *The Register of the Kentucky Historical Society* 60 (July 1972), 255, 257–260, 262; *St. Louis Daily Democrat*, September 7, 1861; *Chicago Daily Tribune*, September 11, 1861; Bruce Catton, *This Hallowed Ground: The Story of the Union Side of the Civil War* (Garden City, NY: Doubleday, 1956), 70; *Chicago Daily Tribune*, September 7, 12, 1861. Gen. Johnston (1803–1862) had been offered a commission as second in command to Union lieutenant general Scott but did not receive it before casting his lot with the South. He would be mortally wounded at Shiloh in April 1862 (Boatner, *op. cit.*, 440). Despite the fact that Southern forces were not advancing on the town, Grant's decision to take Paducah was one of the best he made during the entire war. Its capture guaranteed the future southbound invasion route down the Tennessee River to the Union. It also prevented any major Confederate threat to Southern Illinois or Northern river transportation from Louisville to Cairo.

4. ORN, II, 1: 578, 780–783, 785–786; ORN, II, 2: 86, 174; Mitchell, *op. cit.*, 144, 152, 160–161, 172, 182; *Memphis Daily Appeal*, May 29, 1851; Luraghi, *op. cit.*, 119–120; Branch, "The Story Behind the Story of the *Arkansas* and the *Carondelet*," 323; Branch, "Prime Emerson and Steamboat Building in Memphis," *West Tennessee Historical Society Papers* 38 (1984), 71; George Wright to this author, March 17, 2010; Isaac Newton Brown, "The Confederate Gun-Boat *Arkansas*," in *Battles and Leaders of the Civil War*, ed. Robert V. Johnson and Clarence C. Buell, 4 vols. (New York: Century, 1884–1887, repr., Thomas Yoseloff, 1956), III, 572; John Preston Young and A.R. James, *Standard History of Memphis: From a Study of the Original Sources* (Knoxville: H.W. Crew, 1912), 340–341; New South Associates, *C.S.S. "Georgia": Archival Study*, U.S. Army Corps of Engineers, Contract Number DACW21-99-D-0004, January 31, 2007, http://sav-harbor.com/Cultural%20Resources/CSS_Georgia_Archival_Study.pdf?CFID=5719029&CFTOKEN=b794a43d13065f5e-928D3131-D60D-557F-44FBC05168261FF4 (accessed May 1, 2010); Larry Daniel, "The Quinby & Robinson Cannon Foundry at Memphis," *West Tennessee Historical Society Papers* 27 (1973), 19, 21; Harriet Castlen, *Hope Bids Me Onward* (Savannah, GA: Chatham, 1945), 64–65; William N. Still, Jr., *Iron Afloat: The Story of the Confederate Armorclads* (Columbia: University of South Carolina Press, 1985), 94–98; Still, *Confederate Shipbuilding* (Athens: University of Georgia Press, 1969; repr., Columbia: University of South Carolina Press, 1987), 50; Henry Hall, *Report on the Ship-Building Industry of the United States* (Washington, D.C.: GPO, 1884; repr., New York: Library Editions, 1970), 188; George Eller, "Armor," *World War II in Color*, December 3, 2007, http://www.ww2incolor.com/forum/archive/index.php/t-5644.html (accessed October 6, 2009); Charles M. Getchell, Jr., "Defender of Inland Waters: The Military Career of Isaac Newton Brown, Commander, Confederate States Navy, 1861–1865" (master's thesis, University of Mississippi, 1978), 19–20; John Sanders, *Memoirs of the Military Resources of the Valley of the Ohio* (Washington, D.C.: C. Alexander, 1845), 7. Larry Daniel tells us that at least three city foundries forged cannon early in the war: Street, Hungerford & Company, Livermore Foundry & Machine Company, and Quinby & Robinson" (Daniel, *op. cit.*, 18).

5. ORN, II, 1: 783; *St. Louis Daily Missouri Democrat*, September 18, 21, October 14, 1861; *St. Louis Daily Missouri Republican*, September 21 and October 13 1861; David W. Miller, *Second Only to Grant: Quartermaster General Montgomery C. Meigs* (Shippensburg, PA: White Mane, 2000), 125; Rodman L. Underwood, *Stephen Russell Mallory: A Biography of the Confederate Navy Secretary and United States Senator* (Jefferson, NC: McFarland, 2005), 100; Branch, "The Story Behind the Story of the *Arkansas* and the *Carondelet*," 320; Frank E. Smith, *The Yazoo River* (Rivers of America; New York: Rinehart, 1954; repr., Jackson: University Press of Mississippi, 1988), 94; Still, *Iron Afloat*, 141–142; Luraghi, *loc. cit.* On October 1, Confederate naval forces under Flag Officer William F. Lynch captured the Federal steamer *Fanny* in Pamlico Sound. This was the first CSN success in North Carolina waters and the first capture of a Union man-o'-war by Southern warships. Transferred west later, Lynch would order the *Arkansas* to her doom at Baton Rouge. His profile appears below.

6. ORN, I, 22: 365–366, 371–372, 430, 792–794; ORN, II, 1: 783; OR, I, 3: 531; OR, I, 7: 306; Still, *Iron Afloat*, 42; Charles E. Pearson, and Thomas C. C. Birchett, *The History and Archaeology of Two Civil War Steamboats: The Ironclad Gunboat U.S.S. "Eastport" and the Steamer "Ed. F. Dix"* (Baton Rouge: Coastal Environments, 2001), 53–56; Ulysses S. Grant, *Personal Memoirs of U.S. Grant: A Modern Abridgment* (New York: Premier, 1962), 80; Peter Franklin Walker, "Building a Tennessee Army: Autumn, 1861," *The Tennessee Historical Quarterly* 16 (June 1957), 113; Kenneth R. Johnson, "Confederate Defense and Union Gunboats on the Tennessee River," *The Alabama Historical Quarterly* 64 (Summer 1968), 40–42; Benjamin F. Cooling, *Forts Henry and Donelson: The Key to the Confederate Heartland* (Knoxville: University of Tennessee Press, 1987), 29, 42; Katharine Brash Jeter, "Against All Odds: Lt. Jonathan H. Carter, CSN, and His Ironclad," *Louisiana History* 28 (Summer 1987), 265–266; Jay Slagle, *Ironclad Captain: Seth Ledyard Phelps and the U.S. Navy* (Kent, OH: Kent State University Press, 1996), 135–136; Frederick Way, Jr., *Way's Packet Directory, 1848–1994: Passenger Steamboats of the Mississippi River System Since the Advent of Photography in Mid-Continent America* (Athens: Ohio University Press, 1983; revised ed. Athens: Ohio University, 1994), 140, 182–183; Paul H. Silverstone, *Warships of the Civil War Navies* (Annapolis: Naval Institute Press, 1989), 244; William N. Still, *Confederate Shipbuilding* (Athens: University of Georgia Press, 1969), 16–17; Craig L. Symonds, *The Civil War at Sea* (Santa Barbara, CA: ABC/CLIO, 2009), 95.

7. ORN, I, 22: 806, 809–810, 813; ORN, II, 1: 248, 763, 779–780; Isaac N. Brown to Leonidas Polk, September 24, September 27, November 4, December 4,

1861, Isaac Newton Brown Papers, Records Relating to Confederate Naval and Marine Personnel, U.S. War Department Collection of Confederate Records, Record Group 109, National Archives, Washington, D.C.; *New York Times,* July 5, 1862; *St. Louis Daily Missouri Republican,* July 22, 1862; Branch, "The Story Behind the Story of the *Arkansas* and the *Carondelet,*" 322; Still, *Iron Afloat,* 68–69; Luraghi, *loc. cit.*; Castlen, *op. cit.*, 64–65; Henry Walke, *Naval Scenes and Reminiscences of the Civil War in the United States on the Southern and Western Waters During the Years 1861, 1862 and 1863, with the History of That Period Compared and Corrected from Authentic Sources* (New York: F.R. Reed, 1877), 302–303; *Philadelphia Inquirer,* July 25, 1862; Scharf, *op. cit.,* 303; Brown, "The Confederate Gun-Boat *Arkansas,*" *loc. cit.*; Robert S. Huffstot, "The Brief, Glorious Career of the C.S.S. *Arkansas,*" *Civil War Times Illustrated* 7 (April 1968), 20; "Neil S. Brown," in *Tennessee, The Volunteer State, 1769–1923,* by John Trotwood Moore and Austin P. Foster, 2 vols. (Chicago: S.J. Clarke, 1923), I, 749–750; "Major General William Giles Harding," in *Norwich University, 1819–1911: Her History, Her Graduates, Her Roll of Honor,* 3 vols., comp. William A. Ellis (Montpelier, VT: Capital City Press, 1911), II, 127–128; "Richard Cheatham," *Biographical Directory of the United States Congress, 1774–Present,* http://bioguide.congress.gov/scripts/biodisplay.pl?index=C000341 (accessed September 29, 2009); Silverstone, *op. cit.,* 202; David Meagher, "C.S.S. *Arkansas*" (Chart, 1995); "C.S.S. *Arkansas,*" Modelmaker.com, http://www.modelshipmaster.com/products/civil_war/index.htm (accessed September 15, 2009). The casemate of the *Arkansas* had other names, including "shield," and "gunbox," the latter favored by Lt. Brown when he was in command. When he took over the boat on the Yazoo, Brown had additional two gun ports cut into the fore and aft ends of the closed casemate, thereby allowing the boat's battery to grow from four guns to ten (Gift, *op. cit.,* 49).

8. ORN, I, 22: 811–813; ORN, II, 1: 780–783; OR, I, 7: 789; OR, I, 52, 2: 286–287; Stephen R. Mallory to Leonidas Polk, December 25, 1861, Confederate Naval Papers, Mississippi River, Area File 5, U.S. Navy Department, Office of Naval Records and Library, Naval Records Collection: Record Group 45, National Archives, Washington, D.C.; Underwood, *loc. cit.*; Scharf, *op. cit.,* 304–305; Still, *Iron Afloat,* 142; Still, *Confederate Shipbuilding,* 24; Still, "Confederate Behemoth: The C.S.S. *Louisiana,*" *Civil War Times Illustrated* 16 (November 1977), 20; Ron Field and Richard Hook, *The Confederate Army:, 1861–1865: Tennessee and North Carolina* (Men-at-Arms; Oxford, England: Osprey, 2007), 15; Bruce Catton, *Grant Moves South* (Boston: Little, Brown, 1960), 110.

Four: From Memphis To Yazoo City, January–May 1862

1. U.S. Navy Department, *Official Records of the Union and Confederate Navies in the War of the Rebellion,* 31 vols. (Washington, D.C.: GPO, 1894–1922), Series I, Vol.22: 615, 812–813 (cited hereafter as ORN, followed by a comma, the series number in Roman numerals, a comma, the volume number in Arabic, a colon, and the page in Arabic); ORN, II, 1: 406; George Wright to this author, March 17, 31, 2010; *New Orleans Daily Crescent,* February 14, 1862; J. Thomas Scharf, *History of the Confederate States Navy* (New York: Rodgers and Sherwood, 1887; repr., New York: Fairfax, 1977), 303–305; Charles M. Getchell, Jr., "Defender of Inland Waters: The Military Career of Isaac Newton Brown, Commander, Confederate States Navy, 1861–1865" (master's thesis, University of Mississippi, 1978), 28–29; William N. Still, Jr., *Iron Afloat: The Story of the Confederate Armorclads* (Columbia: University of South Carolina Press, 1985), 42, 62–63, 97–98; Charles W. Read, "Reminiscences of the Confederate States Navy," *Southern Historical Society Papers* 1, no. 5 (1876), 356; Jay Slagle, *Ironclad Captain: Seth Ledyard Phelps and the U.S. Navy* (Kent, OH: Kent State University Press, 1996), 292–293; Myron J. Smith, Jr., *The Timberclads in the Civil War: The "Lexington," "Conestoga," and "Tyler" on the Western Waters* (Jefferson, NC: McFarland, 2008), 37–38; Frederick Way, Jr., *Way's Packet Directory, 1848–1994: Passenger Steamboats of the Mississippi River System Since the Advent of Photography in Mid-Continent America* (Athens: Ohio University Press, 1983; revised ed., Athens: Ohio University Press, 1994), 63, 243, 240, 35; Clive Cussler and Craig Drago, *The Sea Hunters: True Adventures with Famous Shipwrecks* (New York: Pocket Books, 1996), 104; T.M. Hurst, "Some Tennessee Historical Notes," *Tennessee Historical Magazine* 7 (April 1921), 134; Charles E. Pearson, and Thomas C.C. Birchett, *The History and Archaeology of Two Civil War Steamboats: The Ironclad Gunboat U.S.S. "Eastport" and the Steamer "Ed. F. Dix,"* Baton Rouge: Coastal Environments, 2001), 57–58, 63–65. Maj. Gen. Polk had great hopes for the *Eastport* which he had "ordered to be purchased and converted into a gunboat," but as time drew on and the Federal menace grew, he recognized that it would be "too late to be of any service" (U.S. War Department, *The War of the Rebellion: A Compilation of the Official Records of the Union and Confederate Armies,* 128 vols. (Washington, D.C.: GPO, 1880–1901), Series I, Vol. 7: 924 (cited hereafter as OR, followed by a comma, the series number in Roman numerals, a comma, the volume number in Arabic, any part number in Arabic, a colon, and the page in Arabic); OR, I, 52, 1: 37–38; Robert Burpo, "Notes on the First Fleet Engagement in the Civil War," *American Neptune* 19 (October 1959), 267–268; Michael L. Gillespie, "The Novel Experiment: Cottonclads and Steamboats," *Civil War Times Illustrated* 22 (December 1983), 34–36; Jack D. Coombe, *Thunder Along the Mississippi: The River Battles That Split the Confederacy* (New York: Bantam, 1996), 122–123). Tennessean Farragut joined the USN of his father, Commodore David Porter, in 1810, rising through the ranks to command of the West Gulf Coast Blockading Squadron. He remained in control of that unit through the end of 1864, also winning the Battle of Mobile Bay. He became the first full U.S. admiral in July 1866 (Mark M. Boatner III, *The Civil War Dictionary* (New York: David McKay, 1959), 275–276).

2. Carole Bucy, *A Path Divided: Tennessee's Civil War Years* (Nashville: Tennessee 200, 1996), 7; *Atlanta Confederacy,* n.d., quoted in the *Macon Daily Telegraph,* February 10, 1862; ORN, I, 22: 537, 782; Pearson and Birchett, *op. cit.,* 58; Getchell, *op. cit.,* 29–30; Smith, *The Timberclads,* 189–224; Spencer C. Tucker, "Timberclads Attack Up the Tennessee," *Naval History* 16 (February 2001), 27; Edwin C. Bearss, "A Federal Raid Up the Tennessee River," *The Alabama Review* 17 (October 1964), 261–262, 268; *Cincinnati Daily Gazette,* February 17, 1862.

3. *Philadelphia Inquirer,* February 10, 1862; *St. Louis Daily Missouri Republican,* February 10, 1862; *St. Louis Daily Missouri Democrat,* February 10, 1862; *Memphis Avalanche,* February 12, 1862; *Memphis Daily Appeal,* February 12, 1862; *Chicago Daily Tribune,* February 10, 1862;

Cincinnati Daily Gazette, February 17, 1862; ORN, I, 22: 572, 574–575; 782; OR, I, 7: 153–154, 591; Smith, *op. cit.,* 230; Bearss, *op. cit.,* 262–263; Getchell, *op. cit.,* 35; Pearson and Birchett, *op. cit.,* 60; Slagle, *op. cit.,* 163–167; Tucker, *op. cit.,* 28–29; Paul H. Silverstone, *Warships of the Civil War Navies* (Annapolis: Naval Institute Press, 1989), 249; Donald Davidson, *The Tennessee,* vol. 2, *The New River, Civil War to TVA* (Rivers of America; New York: Rinehart, 1948), 23; B.G. Brazelton, *A History of Hardin County, Tennessee* (Nashville: Cumberland Presbyterian, 1885), 63–64; Kenneth R. Johnson, "Confederate Defenses and Union Gunboats on the Tennessee River," *The Alabama Historical Quarterly* 64 (Summer 1968), 50–52.

4. ORN, I, 22: 572–573, 578, 583–585, 643, 782–783; OR, I, 7: 153–156, 600, 858, 864–867, 894; *Cincinnati Daily Commercial,* February 15, 1862; *Cincinnati Daily Gazette,* February 13, 17, 1862; *Florence Gazette,* January 22 and February 12, 1862; *Memphis Avalanche,* February 12, 1862; *Richmond Dispatch,* February 12, 1862; *New York Times,* February 13, 1862; *Tuscumbia Constitution,* n.d., quoted in *Memphis Appeal,* February 13, 1862; *Chicago Daily Tribune,* February 12, 1862; *Harper's Weekly,* March 1, 1862; Bearss, *op. cit.,* 264–265; Slagle, *op. cit.,* 165–176; Smith, *op. cit.,* 231–240; Tucker, *op. cit.,* 28–30; Johnson, *op. cit.,* 53–60; Davidson, *op. cit.,* 23–24; Pearson and Birchett, *op. cit.,* 61–62; Robert C. Suhr, "Converted River Steamers Dubbed 'Timberclads' Gave the Union Navy an Important Presence on Southern Waters," *America's Civil War* 11 (July 1998), 25; Steven R. Davis, "Workhorse of the Western Waters: The Timberclad *Tyler.*" *Civil War Times Illustrated* 44 (February 2005), 38.

5. Smith, *op. cit.,* 240–260; Way, *op. cit.,* 243; Paul Calore, *Naval Campaigns of the Civil War* (Jefferson, NC: McFarland, 2002), 112; Paul Taylor, *Discovering the Civil War in Florida: A Reader and Guide* (Sarasota, FL: Pineapple, 2001), 94; Martin K. Schafer and D. Schafer, *Jacksonville's Ordeal by Fire: A Civil War History* (Jacksonville: Florida, 1984), 58; ORN, I, 12: 617–618, 840–843; OR, I, 6: 403–404; OR, I, 53: 214; Bucy, *loc. cit.;* "Charles H. McBlair," *Register of Officers of the Confederate States Navy, 1861–1865* (Washington, D.C.: GPO, 1931), 119; Terry Foenander, "Charles H. McBlair," *Confederate Naval and Marine Corps Personnel,* http://www.tfoenander.com/csnindex2.htm (accessed October 6, 2009). Following his relief from the *Arkansas,* McBlair served as chief of artillery for the Confederate army's Department of Middle and East Florida until 1864 when he was assigned to the Mobile Squadron and CSS *Tuscaloosa.* After the Battle of Mobile Bay, he was named commander of the Charleston, SC, naval base. After the war, he worked as a clerk in a Washington, D.C., railroad office (Robert J. Driver, Jr., *Confederate Sailors, Marines, and Signalmen from Virginia and Maryland* [Westminster, MD: Heritage, 2007], 206; Charles H. Davis, *Life of Charles Henry Davis, Rear Admiral, 1807–1877* [Boston: Houghton, Mifflin, 1899], 11; Foenander, *loc. cit.*). About the only bright spot for Confederate ironclads during the month was the commissioning of the CSS *Virginia* (ex–*Merrimack*) under Capt. Franklin Buchanan. The South had high hopes for the giant ram. Secretary Mallory wrote to her new commander on February 24, seven days after commissioning: "Could you pass Old Point and make a dashing cruise in the Potomac as far as Washington, its effect upon the public mind would be important to our cause. The condition of our country, and the painful reverses we have just suffered, demand our utmost exertions" (ORN, I, 6: 777).

6. OR, I, 7: 426–427, 437; OR, I, 52, 2: 286–287; ORN, I, 22: 677, 680–683, 838; ORN, I, 23: 227; ORN, II, 1: 722–723; ORN, II, 2: 244; *New Orleans Daily Delta,* April 2, July 22, 1862; *Philadelphia Inquirer,* July 25, 1862; David Flynt, "Run the Fleet: The Career of the C.S. Ram *Arkansas,*" *The Journal of Mississippi History* 51 (April 1989), 111 (full article 107–132); David Meagher to this author, May 23, 2010; William F. Keeler, *Aboard the U.S.S. "Florida," 1863–1865* (Annapolis: Naval Institute Press, 1968), 66–67; Still, *op. cit.,* 63; Gene D. Lewis, *Charles Ellet, Jr.: The Engineer as Individualist, 1810–1862* (Urbana: University of Illinois Press, 1968), 186; Chester G. Hearn, *Ellet's Brigade: The Strangest Outfit of All* (Baton Rouge: Louisiana State University Press, 2000), 5–19; Edward D. Parent, "The New *Arkansas* Kit by Old Steam Navy," *Seaways' Ships in Scale* 17 (May-June 2006), 48, 51; Marshall S. Legan, "The Confederate Career of a Union Ram," *Louisiana History* 33 (Summer 2000), 278–279; John D. Milligan, "Charles Ellet and His Naval Steam Ram," *Civil War History* 9 (1963), 124–125; George C. Gorham, *Life and Public Services of Edwin M. Stanton,* 2 vols. (Boston and New York: Houghton, Mifflin, 1899), I, 292–294; Samuel H. Lockett, "The Defense of Vicksburg," in *Battles and Leaders of the Civil War,* ed. Robert V. Johnson and Clarence C. Buell, 4 vols. (New York: Century, 1884–1887, repr., Thomas Yoseloff, 1956), III, 482–483; Scharf, *loc. cit.;* Cynthia Elizabeth Mosely, "The Naval Career of Henry Kennedy Stevens as Revealed in His Letters, 1839–1863 (master's thesis, University of North Carolina at Chapel Hill, 1951), 274, 293–298; Margaret Alexander Carr, "Lieutenant Henry Kennedy Stevens, CSN: Warrior of the CSS Arkansas," *UDC Magazine* 65 (June-July 2002), 16–17. North Carolinian Guthrie was the one officer immediately available to Beauregard who had some idea of what might be expected of armorclads having commanded the floating battery *New Orleans* at Columbus and removed her to Island No. 10. He remained with the *Arkansas* until the end of May when, together with Cmdr. McBlair, he was transferred back to the Richmond naval station. The following year, he commanded the ironclad *Chattahoochie* (lost to a boiler explosion). Guthrie was then sent to superintend the Halifax, NC, navy yard where he assisted with the materials requirements of the famous armorclad *Albemarle.* After the loss of the latter to Lt. Cushing's torpedo in 1864, Guthrie commanded a blockade runner and finished the war as naval aide to North Carolina's governor. He died a hero attempting to rescue the crew of the stricken USS *Huron* off the North Carolina coast in November 1877 (Smith, *op. cit.,* 175, 184–185, 193, 261; Driver, *op. cit.,* 135; Still, *loc. cit.;* Terry Foenander, "Confederate Naval and Marine Corps Personnel," *U.S. Civil War Navies: A Collection of Articles, Muster Rolls and Images of the Union and Confederate Naval Services,* http://www.tfoenander.com/csnindex.htm (accessed October 8, 2009); *Raleigh (NC) News and Observer,* June 17, 1928; Robert G. Elliott, *Gilbert Elliott's Albemarle: Ironclad of the Roanoke* (Shippensburg, PA: White Mane, 1999), 238, 245, 299; Samuel Carter III, *The Final Fortress: The Campaign for Vicksburg, 1862–1863* (New York: St. Martin's, 1980), 18). Clarke's Vicksburg city directory, like that for Memphis, has been posted, at least partially, on the World Wide Web. See H.C. Clarke, comp., *"General Directory for the City of Vicksburg* [1860]," Rootsweb.Ancestry.Com, http://homepages.rootsweb.ancestry.com/~holler/dir1860.htm (accessed November 1, 2009).

7. Marylander Pinkney entered the USN as a midshipman in 1827 and rose to the rank of captain by 1860. After

resigning to join the CSN as a commander in April 1861, he was posted first to Norfolk and then was sent to Jackson, MS, and command of the CSS *Livingston*. Second in command to Commodore Hollins at Island No. 10 and Fort Pillow, he departed the latter point when it was abandoned and withdrew south. Following the sortie of the *Arkansas,* Pinkney would be posted to Savannah, GA, and promoted to the rank of captain. In April 1864, he would command the naval defenses of North Carolina and oversee the deployment of another noted armorclad, the *Albemarle.* He would finish the war as a flag officer at Fort Fisher and as a commander in the naval brigade organized by Adm. Rafael Semmes.

8. ORN, I, 6: 763; OR, I, 23: 210, 699; Boatner, *op. cit.*, 837–838; M. Jeff Thompson's colorful story is told by Doris Land Mueller in her *M. Jeff Thompson: Missouri's Swamp Fox of the Confederacy* (Columbia: University of Missouri Press, 2007); William F. Lynch, *Naval Life, or Observations Afloat and Ashore: The Midshipman* (New York: Charles Scribner, 1851); Jaxon B. Autry, "William Francis Lynch (1801–1865)," The Latin Library, http://www.thelatinlibrary.com/chron/civilwarnotes/lynch.html (accessed October 29, 2009); John W. Hinds, *Invasion and Conquest of North Carolina: Anatomy of a Gunboat War* (Shippensburg, PA: Burd Street, 1998), 116; Hinds, *The Hunt for the Albemarle: Anatomy of a Gunboat War* (Shippensburg, PA: Burd Street, 2001), 17, 23; Catherine Devereux Edmondston, *Journal of a Secesh Lady: The Diary of Catherine Ann Devereux Edmondston, 1860–1866,* ed. Beth G. Crabtree and James Welch Patton (Raleigh, NC: Division of Archives and History, Dept. of Cultural Resources, State of North Carolina, 1979), 482 ; U.S. Navy Department Library, "Lieutenant William Francis Lynch and the U.S. Navy Expedition to the River Jordan and the Dead Sea: A Select Bibliography," Navy Department Library, http://www.history.navy.mil/library/manuscript/lynch_bib.htm (accessed October 29, 2009). Elliott, *op. cit.,* 19. Following his tenure at the Jackson station, Lynch returned to command Confederate naval forces in North Carolina. In 1864, where he promptly became embroiled in controversies with the builder, Gilbert Elliot, and captain, Cmdr. James W. Cooke, of the famous armorclad *Albemarle.* Later, he compiled a history of the CSN and commanded at Fort Fisher. He died six months after Appomattox, leaving a widow and two children. Interestingly, one of his friends, the Richmond newspaper editor Edward A. Pollard, in his postwar history, inaccurately gave the flag officer credit for building the *Arkansas,* claiming that a refugee steamer up the Yazoo "was razed by Com. Lynch and the construction of the ungainly Arkansas begun" (Elliott, *passim*; Autry, *loc. cit.*; Edward A. Pollard, *The Lost Cause: A New Southern History of the War of the Confederates* (New York: E.B. Treat, 1866; repr. New York: Gramercy, 1994), 325).

9. Built at the Howard yards at Jeffersonville, IN, in 1854, the 448-ton *Capitol,* according to a note in *Way's Packet Directory, 1848–1994,* "had the name in her day of being the fastest boat in the world." The side-wheeler was 224 feet long, with a beam of 32 feet and a six-foot draft. Her two engines received steam from six boilers and she had steady prewar employment on the New Orleans-Bayou Sara and then the New Orleans to Memphis trade. When war came, she was hauling ice to Tennessee from Upper Mississippi during the summers.

10. South Carolinian John Grimball (1840–1923), a former USN midshipman, was commissioned a CSN lieutenant in May 1861 and was initially stationed at Savannah, GA. Following the loss of the *Arkansas,* he served aboard the steamer *Baltic* and the ocean raider *Shenandoah.* Following service on the Richmond station, Alabamian Wharton (1840–1900), who was appointed a CSN lieutenant in February 1862 after four years' midshipman service in the USN, was posted to the *Arkansas,* followed by a year in Texas as commander of the *Harriet Lane* and *W.H. Webb.* He joined the crew of the *Tennessee II* at Mobile Bay in February 1864 and was captured by Farragut's fleet that August. He finished the war as a POW. Richard Bacot (1842–1915) of South Carolina became a USN midshipman in 1859, keeping that rank when he joined the CSN in 1861. He arrived at Memphis in April 1862 after service at Savannah and aboard the CSS *Resolute.* Following the loss of the *Arkansas,* he returned east to serve aboard the CSS *Chicora, Charleston,* and *Neuse.* Virginian Henry S. Cook (1845–ca. 1907) was three years older than Bacot, but became a USN midshipman the same year as his messmate. After the *Arkansas,* he later served at Wilmington, NC, and Charleston, SC, and aboard the CSS *Raleigh* and *Fredericksburg.* Dabney M. Scales (1841–1920) from Mississippi, another Class of '59 USN midshipman, served aboard the CSS *Savannah* before joining McBlair's crew; he later served aboard the CSS *Atlanta* and was 5th lieutenant aboard the *Shenandoah.* North Carolinian Clarence W. Tyler (1844–?), a prewar college student, transferred to the CSN from the 18th North Carolina Infantry and was commissioned a midshipman. After service at Savannah, he was transferred to Memphis. Wounded on July 15, he saw no further active service. One of the most important men aboard was George W. City (1836–?), the boat's 1st assistant engineer. A native of Washington, D.C., he joined the CSN at Richmond in August 1861, eventually serving aboard the CSS *Virginia* (ex-USS *Merrimack).* Sent to Memphis in April, he later served at the Savannah station and aboard the CSS *Macon.* Another important person was Master's Mate John A. Wilson, who had transferred to the CSN in February from the 1st Maryland Infantry. Sent to Memphis from Richmond, he joined the crew of the crew of the *Capitol* in April. Wounded during the July 15 engagement with the Federal fleet, he later served on the James River and aboard the CSS *Rappahannock.* Having joined the CSN in 1861 after five years as a surgeon in the USN, Dr. H.W.M. Washington (1838–?) was first assigned to the Richmond station. Later, during his stint aboard the *Arkansas,* he found himself, with the ram's former lieutenants Guthrie and George W. Gift, assigned to the gunboat *Chattahoochee.* Sick during much of 1864, he also served aboard the *Fredericksburg* of the James River Squadron. Terry Foenander ("Confederate Naval and Marine Corps Personnel," U.S. Civil War Navies: A Collection of Articles, Muster Rolls and Images of the Union and Confederate Naval Services, http://www.tfoenander.com/csnindex.htm (accessed October 8, 2009).

11. ORN, I, 23: 5–7, 10–11, 62–63, 69–70, 84, 667–668, 698; OR, I, 6, 809–817, 853; OR, I, 10, 2: 107–108; ORN, II, 1: 798; *St. Louis Daily Missouri Democrat,* April 8, 18, 1862; *New York Times,* April 8, 27, 1862; *New York Herald,* April 26 and May 10, 1862; *Chicago Daily Tribune,* April 8, 12, 26, 28, 1862; *New Orleans Daily Delta,* April 19, 25, 30, 1862; *Richmond Daily Dispatch,* April 23, 28, May 14–15, 1862; *Richmond Press,* April 14, 1862; *Petersburg (VA) Express,* April 26, 1862; *Harper's Weekly,* May 10, 17, 1862; Larry J. Daniel and Lynn N. Bock, *Island No. 10: Struggle in the Mississippi Valley* (Tuscaloosa: University of Alabama Press, 1996), 128, 130, 132; J. Thomas Scharf, *History of the Confederate Navy from Its Organization to the Surrender of Its Last Vessel* (New York: Rodgers and

Sherwood, 1887, repr., New York: Fairfax, 1977), 143, 248; Moseley, *op. cit.*, 303–304; Shelby Foote, *The Civil War, a Narrative: Fort Sumter to Perryville* (New York: Random House, 1958), 379; John Kendall, *The History of New Orleans* (Chicago: Lewis, 1922), 251–258; other helpful accounts of the capture of New Orleans are Chester G. Hearn, *The Capture of New Orleans, 1862* (Baton Rouge: Louisiana State University Press, 1995) and H. A. Trexler, "The Confederate Navy Department and the Fall of New Orleans," *Southwest Review* 19 (Autumn 1933), 88–102; Michael B. Ballard, *Vicksburg: The Campaign That Opened the Mississippi* (Chapel Hill: University of North Carolina Press, 2004), 29; Still, *op. cit.*, 100; Way, *op. cit.*, 71; Terry Foenander, "Confederate Naval and Marine Corps Personnel," U.S. Civil War Navies: A Collection of Articles, Muster Rolls and Images of the Union and Confederate Naval Services, http://www.tfoenander.com/csnindex.htm (accessed October 8, 2009); Pinkney's biography is in Driver, *op. cit.*, 268; Harry P. Owens, *Steamboats and the Cotton Economy: River Trade in the Yazoo-Mississippi Delta* (Jackson: University of Mississippi Press, 1990), 44. Among the vessels scuttled at Island No. 10 to prevent capture was the *Grampus*, the speedy little gunboat of Capt. Marshal "Marsh" Miller that builder Emerson had first seen at Memphis the previous year. Albert H. Bodman, the famous correspondent for the *Chicago Daily Tribune*, could hardly hold back his joy. Acknowledging that she and her commander had been woven into romantic legend, the reporter summed up: "[T]he reality strips off the romance. The *Grampus* is a dirty little tow-boat, which one 32-pdr. shot would tear to pieces; her commander a poor devil, fleeing for his life through swamps and marshes" (*Chicago Daily Tribune*, April 11, 1862). Mexican War veteran Lovell resigned his post as New York City street commissioner to become a Confederate general and defender of New Orleans. He would move on to Vicksburg and win praise for his actions at second Corinth in October. Although exonerated by an 1863 court of inquiry for the loss of New Orleans, he was given no further formal role. Engineer Smith did not become a brigadier until April 1862, even though he built and commanded the Chalmette defenses at New Orleans before racing north to take over command at Vicksburg on May 12. Held POW for seven months after the citadel's capture, he later served as chief engineer for the Army of Northern Virginia and the Army of Tennessee, before turning his attention to strengthening the defenses of Mobile. A native of Hinds County, MS, Lt. Read was an 1860 USNA graduate who served as executive officer and then, following the death of her captain to whom he was close, commander of the CSN gunboat *McRae* during the New Orleans fight. Following the city's capture, he was sent to aid in the defense of Fort Pillow. After the *Arkansas* adventure, he assisted in the defense of Port Hudson before transferring aboard the ocean raider *Florida*. He would end the war in command of the CSS *Webb*, during her fabled attempt to break out to the Gulf of Mexico from Shreveport. He was awarded the Confederate Congressional Medal of Honor (Boatner, *op. cit.*, 494; 773; R. Thomas Campbell, *Sea Hawk of the Confederacy: Lt. Charles W. Read and the Confederate Navy* (Shippensburg, PA: Burd Street, 2000); *New York Times*, January 26, 1890).

12. ORN, I, 23: 227; ORN, II, 1: 782, 798; *Philadelphia Inquirer*, July 25, 1862; *Brooklyn Daily Eagle*, July 30, 1862; Moseley, *op. cit.*, 305; William N. Still, Jr., "Confederate Shipbuilding in Mississippi," *The Journal of Mississippi History* 30 (Fall 1968), 294–295; George C. Waterman, "Notable Naval Events of the War," *Confederate Veteran* 7 (January 1891), 61; *New York Times*, January 19, 1863; Rodman L. Underwood, *Stephen Russell Mallory: A Biography of the Confederate Navy Secretary and United States Senator* (Jefferson, NC: McFarland, 2005), 106; *Biographical and Historical Memoirs of Mississippi, Embracing Authentic and Comprehensive Accounts of the Chief Events in the History of the State, and a Record of the Lives of Many of the Most Worthy and Illustrious Families and Individuals* (Chicago: Goodspeed, 1891; repr. Spartanburg, SC: Reprint Co., 1978), 206–208; Jim Ewing, "Liverpool Landing: Mississippi Byways," Yazoo County, MSGenWeb, http://www.rootsweb.ancestry.com/~msyazoo/Liverpool_Landing.htm (accessed January 4, 2010). During the last week of April, a shipment of nine naval cannon without carriages destined for New Orleans was held up at Mobile. Mississippi governor John J. Pettus wired the Crescent City's commander, Maj. Gen. Benjamin Lovell, who had transferred to Jackson, MS, on April 28, asking if he wished the guns diverted to Vicksburg. An affirmative answer was received (OR, I, 6: 653). CSN Lt. Isaac Brown, who went to New Orleans to work on ironclad projects following the loss of the *Eastport*, was ordered to Vicksburg about this time. We do not know if he was tasked to install the Pettus cannon or form a special naval battery for the upcoming defense of the citadel (Getchell, *op. cit.*, 35–36; Scharf, *op. cit.*, 306). During the great earthquakes of 1812, the Mississippi shoved away from its old flow and cut a new route. Thereafter called Old River, the ancient bed became, in fact, a navigable lake created by the cutoff from the Mississippi. The Yazoo flowed into this lake at its north curve and comingled with it for about 10 miles. Then, at a narrow strip of land which separated it from the "Big Muddy," it broke through into the Mississippi at a point three miles south of its new mouth and some 12 miles north of Vicksburg.

Five: Five Weeks Up the Yazoo, Early May–Late June 1862

1. U.S. Navy Department, *Official Records of the Union and Confederate Navies in the War of the Rebellion*, 31 vols. (Washington, D.C.: GPO, 1894–1922), Series II, Vol. 1: 615, 781–782, (cited hereafter as ORN, followed by a comma, the series number in Roman numerals, a comma, the volume number in Arabic, a colon, and the page in Arabic); ORN, I, 18: 471–474, 744; Jack D. Coombe, *Thunder Along the Mississippi: The River Battles That Split the Confederacy* (New York: Bantam, 1996), 129–130; Rodman L. Underwood, *Stephen Russell Mallory: A Biography of the Confederate Navy Secretary and United States Senator* (Jefferson, NC: McFarland, 2005), 106; Harry P. Owens, *Steamboats and the Cotton Economy: River Trade in the Yazoo-Mississippi Delta* (Jackson: University of Mississippi Press, 1990), 46; David Flynt, "Run the Fleet: The Career of the C.S. Ram *Arkansas*," *The Journal of Mississippi History* 51 (May 1989), 109; Charles M. Getchell, Jr., "Defender of Inland Waters: The Military Career of Isaac Newton Brown, Commander, Confederate States Navy, 1861–1865" (master's thesis, University of Mississippi, 1978), 40; William N. Still, Jr., *Iron Afloat: The Story of the Confederate Armorclads* (Columbia: University of South Carolina Press, 1985), 63; Frederick Way, Jr., *Way's Packet Directory, 1848–1994: Passenger Steamboats of the Mississippi River System Since the Advent of

Photography in Mid-Continent America (Athens: Ohio University Press, 1983; revised ed., Athens: Ohio University, 1994), 303–304. Pettus, the wartime governor of Mississippi, was refused amnesty and died a fugitive in Arkansas in 1867 ("John J. Pettus," in *The Political Graveyard: Index to Politicians,* http://politicalgraveyard.com/bio/pettitt-pezzulo.html [accessed September 11, 2009]). Baton Rouge had a population of less than 5,500 at this time. The town, as remembered by Lt. George W. Gift, was "situated on a 'reach,' or long, straight stretch of river, which extends three or four miles above the town" (George W. Gift, "The Story of the *Arkansas,*" *Southern Historical Society Papers* 8 (January–May 1884), 208).

2. ORN, I, 18: 478; ORN, II, 1: 781; Getchell, *loc. cit.;* Cynthia E. Moseley, "The Naval Career of Henry Kennedy Stevens as Revealed in His Letters, 1839–1863," (master's thesis, University of North Carolina, 1951), 307; Coombe, *op. cit.,* 152; Flynt, *op. cit.,* 110; Isaac Newton Brown, "The Confederate Gun-Boat *Arkansas,*" in *Battles and Leaders of the Civil War,* ed. Robert V. Johnson and Clarence C. Buell, 4 vols. (New York: Century, 1884–1887, repr., Thomas Yoseloff, 1956), III, 572; David Meagher to this author, May 20, 2010; Silas B. Coleman and Paul Stevens, "A July Morning with the Rebel Ram *Arkansas,"* U. S. Naval Institute Proceedings 88 (July 1962), 91; Still, *Iron Afloat,* 63–64. For many years, it has been a part of the *Arkansas* liturgy that Cmdr. McBlair was not up to the task of completing the construction of the armorclad from this point. Perhaps he was more active that has been reported — or his unmentioned executive officer, Lt. Guthrie, was acting for him. Whether by intention or not, at least one Confederate brigadier general actually all but said that one of the men was efficient while recapping his own tenure in command of Vicksburg's defense. In his official August 1862 report of Vicksburg's defense, Brig. Gen. M.L. Smith wrote the following: "It was reported that the contractor had virtually suspended work; that mechanics and workmen were leaving; that supplies were wanting; finally that a very considerable quantity of iron prepared for covering her had been sunk in the Yazoo River. Steps were taken to promptly furnish mechanics and supplies and a bell-boat being obtained and sent up to the spot, the prepared iron was soon recovered. It was fortunate that *soon after this* Captain Brown was assigned to the duty of completing the boat" (emphasis added). U.S. War Department, *The War of the Rebellion: A Compilation of the Official Records of the Union and Confederate Armies,* 128 vols. (Washington, D.C.: GPO, 1880–1901), Series I, Vol. 15: 7 (cited hereafter as OR, followed by a comma, the series number in Roman numerals, a comma, the volume number in Arabic, any part number in Arabic, a colon, and the page in Arabic). Cmdr. Samuel Philips Lee was eventually promoted to the rank of captain, going on to command the North Atlantic Blockading Squadron as an Acting Rear Admiral. On October 19, 1864, he became the last commander of the Mississippi Squadron, successor organization to the Western Flotilla (Dudley Taylor Cornish and Virginia Jeans Laas, *Lincoln's Lee: The Life of Samuel Phillips Lee, United States Navy, 1812–1897* (Lawrence: University Press of Kansas, 1986), 140; Johnny H. Whisenant, "Samuel Phillips Lee, U.S.N.: Commander, Mississippi Squadron (October 19, 1864–August 14, 1865)" (master's thesis, Kansas State College of Pittsburg, 1968), 12–20; "Samuel Phillips Lee," in *Dictionary of Admirals of the U.S. Navy,* 2 vols., by William B. Cogar (Annapolis.: Naval Institute Press, 1989), I, 96–97).

3. ORN, I, 23: 14–19, 54–57, 669, 677; OR, I, 10: 888–890; *Cincinnati Times,* May 16, 1862; *St. Louis Daily Missouri Democrat,* May 17, 1862; *Memphis Daily Appeal,* May 13, 1862; Coombe, *op. cit.,* 122–124; Eliot Callender, "What a Boy Saw on the Mississippi River," in *Military Essays and Recollections: Papers Read before the Illinois Commandery, Military Order of the Loyal Legion of the United States,* vol. 1 (Chicago: A.C. McClurg, 1891), 60–63; Henry Walke, *Naval Scenes and Reminiscences of the Civil War in the United States on the Southern and Western Waters During the Years 1861, 1862 and 1863, with the History of That Period Compared and Corrected from Authentic Sources* (New York: F.R. Reed, 1877), 245–272; *New York Herald,* April 26, 1862; Walke, "The Western Flotilla at Fort Donelson, Island Number Ten, Fort Pillow and Memphis," in *Battles and Leaders of the Civil War,* ed. Robert V. Johnson and Clarence C. Buell, 4 vols. (New York: Century, 1884–1887, repr., Thomas Yoseloff, 1956), I, 446–449; John S.C. Abbott, *The History of the Civil War in America,* 2 vols. (New York: H. Bill, 1863), I, 272–273; Davis, *op. cit.,* 223–227; Robert Burpo, "Notes on the First Fleet Engagement in the Civil War," *American Neptune* 19 (October 1959), 265–273; Michael L. Gillespie, "The Novel Experiment: Cottonclads and Steamboats," *Civil War Times Illustrated* 22 (December 1983), 34–39; R. Thomas Campbell, *Confederate Naval Forces on Western Waters* (Jefferson, NC: McFarland, 2005), 88–91; Edwin C. Bearss, *Hardluck Ironclad: The Sinking and Salvage of the Cairo* (Baton Rouge: Louisiana State University Press, 1968), 57–63; H. Allen Gosnell, *Guns on the Western Waters: The Story of the River Gunboats in the Civil War* (Baton Rouge: Louisiana State University Press, 1949), 89–91; E.B. Long, "Plum Point Bend: The Forgotten Battle," *Civil War Times Illustrated* 11 (June 1972), 4–11; Alfred T. Mahan, *The Gulf and Inland Waters,* vol. 3, *The Navy in the Civil War* (New York: Scribner's, 1883), 45; Jack D. Coombe, *Thunder Along the Mississippi: The River Battles That Split the Confederacy* (New York: Bantam, 1996), 122–125; Jay Monaghan, *Swamp Fox of the Confederacy: The Life and Military Service of M. Jeff Thompson* (Tuscaloosa: University of Alabama Press, 1956), 52; Spencer C. Tucker, *Andrew Foote: Civil War Admiral on Western Waters* (Annapolis: Naval Institute Press, 2000), 196; John D. Milligan, *Gunboats Down the Mississippi* (Annapolis.: Naval Institute Press, 1965), 64–67; Jay Slagle, *Ironclad Captain: Seth Ledyard Phelps and the U.S. Navy* (Kent, OH: Kent State University Press, 1996), 219–225; Henry R. Browne and Symmes E. Browne, *From the Fresh Water Navy, 1861–1864: Letters of Acting Master's Mate Henry R. Browne and Acting Ensign Symmes E. Browne,* ed. John D. Milligan, Naval Letters Series, vol. 3 (Annapolis: Naval Institute Press, 1970), 74–77.

4. ORN, I, 18: 8, 473, 478, 492–493, 498–499, 502, 507, 704–705, 708, 725, 783, 810; ORN, I, 25: 120; OR, I, 15: 647, 741–742; OR, I, 23: 699–700; Stephen R. Mallory to Charles H. McBlair, May 24, 1862, in McBlair File, in ZB Files, U.S. Navy Department, Navy Department Library, Washington, D.C.; P G.T. Beauregard to Daniel Ruggles, May 19, 1862, Ruggles Papers, 1862–1865, Archives and Library Division, Mississippi Department of Archives and History, Jackson, MS; Coombe, *op. cit.,* 137–140; Moseley, *op. cit.,* 308; Samuel H. Lockett, "The Defense of Vicksburg," *B&L,* III, 482; Flynt, *loc. cit.;* Thomas Williams, "Letters of General Thomas Williams," *American Historical Review* 14 (January 1909), 318; Isaac Newton Brown, "The Confederate Gunboat *Arkansas,*" *B&L,* III, 572; Owens, *op. cit.,* 46; Chester G. Hearn, *Admiral David Glasgow Farragut: The Civil War*

Years (Annapolis: Naval Institute Press, 1998), 127; Samuel Carter III, *The Final Fortress: The Campaign for Vicksburg, 1862–1863* (New York: St. Martin's, 1980), 56; Ballard, *op. cit.*, 32–34, 39–41; Robert G. Hartje, *Van Dorn: The Life and Times of a Confederate General* (Nashville: Vanderbilt University Press, 1967), 182–183, 187–188; T. Harry Williams, *P.G.T. Beauregard: Napoleon in Gray* (Baton Rouge: Louisiana State University Press, 1955), 156; Arthur B. Carter, *The Tarnished Cavalier: Major General Earl Van Dorn* (Knoxville: University of Tennessee Press, 1999), 75; Gustavus W. Smith, *Confederate War Papers* (New York: Atlantic, 1884), 97; William C. Davis, *Duel Between the First Ironclads* (Garden City, NY: Doubleday, 1975), 153–154; Christopher Martin, *Damn the Torpedoes: The Story of America's First Admiral, David Glasgow Farragut* (New York: Abelard Schuman, 1970), 207; Still, *Iron Afloat*, 63–64, 66; Still, "Confederate Shipbuilding in Mississippi," *The Journal of Mississippi History* 30 (Fall 1968), 293; Getchell, *op. cit.*, 40–41; Getchell, "Isaac Newton Brown of Navarro County, Texas," Navarro County TXGenWeb, http://www.txgenweb6.org/txnavarro/biographies/b/brown_isaac_newton.htm (accessed October 19, 2009); Charles W. Read, "Reminiscences of the Confederate States Navy," *Southern Historical Society Papers* 1 (May 1876), 349; Alfred Roman, *The Military Operations of General Beauregard in the War Between the States, 1861–1865*, 2 vols. (New York: Harper & Brothers, 1884), I, 370; Campbell, *Sea Hawk of the Confederacy* (Shippensburg, PA: Burd Street, 2000), 47; Mark M. Boatner III, *The Civil War Dictionary* (New York: David McKay, 1959), 712; Myron J. Smith, Jr., *The Timberclads in the Civil War: The "Lexington," "Conestoga," and "Tyler" on the Western Waters* (Jefferson, NC: McFarland, 2008), 105; Allen C. Richard, Jr. and Mary Margaret Higgeinbotham Richard, *The Defense of Vicksburg: A Louisiana Chronicle* (Williams-Ford Texas A&M University Military History Series; College Station: Texas A&M University Press, 2003), 48; Brown later recalls receiving his order on May 28; Getchell, his biographer, indicated it was May 26. Brown wasted no time in steaming up to Greenville, racing from Vicksburg up the Yazoo as quickly as possible. Although his steamer's passage was undoubtedly fast, it could not have been made, as Brown remembered it, in the day between the time the lieutenant received Mallory's telegraph message and the time he arrived at the site of the marooned armorclad (Brown, *loc. cit.*; Getchell, *op. cit.*, 40; Campbell, *Sea Hawk of the Confederacy*, 48). Tennessean George Washington Gift (1833–1879) entered the USN in 1846 but resigned in 1852 to enter the banking business in Sacramento, CA. He returned east in 1861 to join the Confederate Army, but was commissioned a CSN lieutenant in March. Escaping New Orleans, he was assigned to the *Arkansas*. Following the loss of the ram, he found himself aboard the gunboat *Chattahoochee*, with Lt. Guthrie and Dr. Washington. Following duty at Mobile, AL, Wilmington, NC, and Charleston, SC, he was placed in command of the *Chattahoochee*, later serving at Savannah. After the war he resided at Memphis, worked in China to recruit laborers for the Arkansas Emigration Company, and returned to California to become editor of the *Napa City Reporter*. After escaping from New Orleans, Lt. Alphonse Barbot (dates unknown), who had originally joined the USN in 1838 and moved to the CSN at the outbreak of the war, was posted to the Jackson station and reassigned to the *Arkansas*. He then served aboard the ironclad *Atlanta*, was captured, held as a POW, exchanged, and became captain of the *Fredericksburg* (Terry Foenander, "Confederate Naval and Marine Corps Personnel," U.S. Civil War Navies: A Collection of Articles, Muster Rolls and Images of the Union and Confederate Naval Services, http://www.tfoenander.com/csnindex.htm [accessed October 8, 2009]).

5. OR, I, 15: 5–6, 747; ORN, I, 18: 647; Moseley, *op. cit.*, 308; George C. Waterman, "Notable Naval Events of the War," *Confederate Veteran* 6 (January 1891), 61, 170; Still, *Iron Afloat*, 139; Ballard, *op. cit.*, 34–36; Flynt, *loc. cit.*; Adelaide Stuart Dimitry, "The Queen of the Mississippi," in her *War-Time Sketches Historical and Otherwise* (New Orleans: Louisiana Printing Co. Press, 1911), 11 (11–15); H. Allen Gosnell, *Guns on the Western Waters: The Story of the River Gunboats in the Civil War* (Baton Rouge: Louisiana State University Press, 1949), 101–104; Shelby Foote, *The Civil War, a Narrative: Fort Sumter to Perryville* (New York: Random House, 1958), 550; Frank Ellis Smith, *The Yazoo River*, Rivers of America Series (New York: Rinehart, 1954), 95; Isaac Newton Brown, "The Confederate Gunboat *Arkansas*," *B&L*, III, 572; Peter Cozzens, *The Darkest Days of the War: The Battles of Iuka and Corinth* (Chapel Hill: University of North Carolina Press, 1997), 16–67. The Navy Official Records volume that includes a directory of Confederate warships states that the *Mobile* had four guns, all 32-pdrs., in February 1862. Silverstone points out that the craft, with three masts, was once an oceangoing ship, built in Philadelphia in 1860, while Way confirms her eastern pedigree by not mentioning her in his directory of Western steamers (ORN, II, 1: 260; Paul Silverstone, *Warships of the Civil War Navies* (Annapolis: Naval Institute Press, 1989), 230). Two days after her capture by Van Dorn, the 10-year old New York-built *Star of the West* was moved to New Orleans where Louisiana's governor changed her name. The old name persisted and she remained at the Crescent City as a hospital ship until just before Farragut captured the town. Fleeing to Vicksburg with millions of dollars in gold and silver, she continued on to Yazoo City where Brown found her. The 1,172 ton vessel was 228.3 feet long, with a beam of 32.7 feet, and was armed with two 68-pdrs. and four 32-pdr. smoothbores. Rigged as a sidewheeler, she also carried two masts for sails (Jack D.L. Holmes, "Star of the West," in *Handbook of Texas Online*, http://www.tshaonline.org/handbook/online/articles/SS/qts5.html (accessed November 8, 2009); ORN, II, 1: 265; "Star of the West," in *The Ships List*, http://www.theshipslist.com/ships/descriptions/ShipsSS.html (accessed November 8, 2009); Silverstone, *op. cit.*, 232). The two larger cannon aboard the *Star* may, in fact, have been wearing their British designation while aboard the former merchantman. "The 64-pdr. differed in no material particular from the English 68-pdr., except that the US gun had a bore of eight inches," states the UK-based Global Security organization in its Internet article on naval armament, "Old Steam Navy: Armament," GlobalSecurity.Org, http://www.globalsecurity.org/military/systems/ship/steam6.htm (accessed November 10, 2009).

6. Getchell, *op. cit.*, 43, 127; ORN, I, 18: 647–648; ORN, I, 18: 648; ORN, I, 19: 132; *New York Times*, August 1, 1862; Flynt, *loc. cit.*; Still, *Iron Afloat*, 64; Bruce Catton, *Grant Moves South* (Boston: Little, Brown, 1960), 371–372; Owens, *op. cit.*, 40, 47; Jefferson Davis, *Jefferson Davis, Constitutionalist: His Letters, Papers, and Speeches*, 10 vols., ed. Dunbar Rowland (Jackson, MS: Little & Ives, 1923), X, 516–517; Claude E. Fike, ed., "Diary of James Oliver Hazard Perry Sessions of Rokeby Plantation on the Yazoo River, January 1862 to June 1872," *Journal of Mississippi History* 39 (August 1977), 245. Lt. Guthrie

later attended the ironclad *Albemarle* from the naval base at Halifax, NC. Cmdr. McBlair was posted to Mobile for duties aboard the gunboat *Morgan*. Shortly thereafter, Flag Officer Franklin Buchanan, former commander of the armorclad *Virginia*, sent him to Selma, AL, to concentrate full time on the completion of the *Huntsville* and *Tuscaloosa*. Work on these projects also faltered as Buchanan devoted available resources to the *Tennessee II,* namesake of the vessel destroyed on the stocks at Memphis (Maurice Melton, *The Confederate Ironclads* (Cranbury, NJ: Thomas Yoseloff, 1968), 205). Samuel Milliken (dates unknown) was transferred to the ram from the Jackson station; after her loss, he was posted to the Charleston station, where he served two years. Alabamian John L. Phillips (dates unknown) also got his start at Jackson and aboard the *Arkansas*. Later, he saw duty with the Mobile Squadron and skippered the CSS *Webb* on the Red River until relieved by Lt. Charles W. Read on March 31, 1865 (Terry Foenander, "Confederate Naval and Marine Corps Personnel," U.S. Civil War Navies: A Collection of Articles, Muster Rolls and Images of the Union and Confederate Naval Services, http://www.tfoenander.com/csnindex.htm [accessed October 8, 2009]).

7. ORN, I, 18: 648; OR, I, 10, 1: 912–914; OR, I, 52, 1: 38–40; *Cincinnati Daily Commercial,* June 8, 1862; Coombe, *op. cit.*, 130–132; "Capt. Isaac D. Fulkerson, C.S.N.," Fulkerson Organization home page, http://www.fulkerson.org/isaacd.html (accessed October 13, 2009); Charles W. Read, "Reminiscences of the Confederate States Navy," *Southern Historical Society Papers* 1 (1876), 343–344, 348; Owens, *op. cit.*, 40–41, 45, 47; Campbell, *op. cit.*, p 49; Silverstone, *op. cit.*, 227, 245; James M. Morgan, *Recollections of a Rebel Reefer* (Boston: Houghton Mifflin, 1917), 61; John D. Milligan, "Charles Ellet and His Naval Steam Ram," *Civil War History* 9 (1963), 128–130; Mary Emerson Branch, "Prime Emerson and Steamboat Building in Memphis," *West Tennessee Historical Society Papers* 38 (1984), 75; J. Thomas Scharf, *History of the Confederate Navy from Its Organization to the Surrender of Its Last Vessel* (New York: Rodgers and Sherwood, 1887, repr., New York: Fairfax, 1977), 244–245; Way, *op. cit.,* 180, 364; Katherine Brash Jeter, "Against All Odds: Lt. Jonathan H. Carter, CSN, and His Ironclad," *Louisiana History* 28 (Summer 1987), 266; Chester G. Hearn, *Ellet's Brigade: The Strangest Outfit of All* (Baton Rouge: Louisiana State University Press, 2000), 44. Alabamian Stone (ca. 1842–1900), a USN midshipman 1857–April 1861 when he joined the CSN, was posted to New Orleans and the *McRae*. Sent to the *General Polk*, he went to the Jackson station after her loss and was then posted to the ocean raider CSS *Florida*, 1862–1864 (Terry Foenander, "Confederate Naval and Marine Corps Personnel," U.S. Civil War Navies: A Collection of Articles, Muster Rolls and Images of the Union and Confederate Naval Services, http://www.tfoenander.com/csnindex.htm (accessed October 8, 2009).

8. ORN, I, 18: 648; ORN, I, 19: 3, 57, 132; ORN, I, 23: 210, 227; ORN, II, 1: 248; OR, I, 15: 763; Brown, *op. cit.,* 572; Read, *op. cit.,* 349–351; *New York Times,* July 5, 1862; *St. Louis Daily Missouri Republican,* July 22, 1862; *Brooklyn Daily Eagle,* July 30, 1862; Fike, *loc. cit.*; Gift, *op. cit.,* 49, 211; Flynt, *op. cit.,* 111, 114; Gosnell, *op. cit.,* 104–105; Still, *Iron Afloat,* 65; Still, "Confederate Shipbuilding in Mississippi," 294–295; Moseley, *op. cit.,* 309; Harriet Castlen, *Hope Bids Me Onward* (Savannah, GA: Chatham, 1945), 76; Coleman and Stevens, *op. cit.,* 91–92; Campbell, *Sea Hawk of the Confederacy,* 51; Alfred T. Mahan, *The Gulf and Inland Waters,* vol. 3, *Navy in the Civil War* (New York: Scribner's, 1883), 98–99; Scharf, *op. cit.,* 307–308; Silverstone, *op. cit.,* 202, 232; Raimondo Luraghi, *A History of the Confederate Navy* (Annapolis: Naval Institute Press, 1996), 174–175; "Coastal Ironclads: C.S.S. *Arkansas,*" *Civil War Talk,* http://civilwartalk.com/Resource_Center/CS/Confederate_Navy/coastal-ironclads-c-s-s-arkansas-a104.html (accessed November 10, 2009); *Harper's Weekly,* September 6, 1862; U.S. Navy Department, Bureau of Ordnance, *Ordnance Instructions for the United States Navy* (Washington, D.C.: George W. Bowman, 1860), 52, 164–165; Dimitry, *op. cit.,* 11–12; Getchell, *op. cit.,* 50–51; George Wright to this author, March 17 and May 6, 2010; David Meagher to this author, May 2, 23, 2010; Edward D. Parent, "The New *Arkansas* Kit by Old Steam Navy," *Seaways' Ships in Scale* 17 (May-June 2006), 48, 51; Larry J. Daniel, "The Quinby & Robinson Cannon Foundry at Memphis," *West Tennessee Historical Society Papers* (1973), 27–28; William N. Still, "The History of the C.S.S. *Arkansas*" (master's thesis, University of Alabama, 1958), 47–50; Waterman, *op. cit.,* 61; Ian Drury and Tony Gibbons, *The Civil War Military Machine: Weapons and Tactics of the Union and Confederate Armed Forces* (New York: Smithmark, 1993), 132–133; Daniel Barnhart, Jr., "Junkyard Ironclad," *Civil War Times Illustrated* 40 (May 2001), 31–35, 37; Mark F. Jenkins, "Mysteries and Controversies: The Color of the *Arkansas,*" *Ironclads and Blockade Runners of the American Civil War,* http://www.wideopenwest.com/~jenkins/ironclads/mysteries.htm (accessed November 18, 2009); Winston Groom, *Vicksburg 1863* (New York: Alfred A. Knopf, 2009), 153; Charles H. Davis, Jr., *Life of Charles H. Davis, Rear Admiral, U.S.N.* (Boston: Houghton, Mifflin, 1899), 263; James C. Hazlett, Edwin Olmstead, and M. Hume Parks, *Field Artillery Weapons of the Civil War,* rev. ed. (Champaign: University of Illinois Press, 2004), 61–62; Edwin Olmstead, Wayne E. Stark, and; Spencer C. Tucker, *The Big Guns: Civil War Siege, Seacoast, and Naval Cannon* (Bloomfield, Ontario, and Alexandria Bay, NY: Museum Restoration Service, 1997), 125–126; "Brooke Rifles and Smoothbore Guns, *The Encyclopedia of Civil War Artillery,* http://www.cwartillery.org/ve/brooke.html (accessed October 13, 2009); "Dahlgren Guns and Rifles," *The Encyclopedia of Civil War Artillery,* http://www.cwartillery.org/ve/dahlgrens.html (accessed October 13, 2009); "Rodmans and Confederate Columbiads," *The Encyclopedia of Civil War Artillery,* http://www.cwartillery.org/ve/rodman.html (accessed October 13, 2009); "Dahlgrens, Brookes, and Parrotts," *Ironclads and Blockade Runners of the Civil War,* http://www.wideopenwest.com/~jenkins/ironclads/ironguns.htm (accessed October 13, 2009); Paul Branch, "Armament of Fort Macon," *The Fort Macon Ramparts, Spring 1996,* http://www.clis.com/friends/armament.htm (accessed October 13, 2009); Eugene B. Canfield, *Civil War Naval Ordnance* (Washington, D.C.: GPO, 1969), 7, 13, 20; Owens, *op. cit.,* 40, 47; "Gunpowder," *The Encyclopedia of Civil War Artillery,* http://www.cwartillery.org/glossary/glossarygz.htm (accessed October 13, 2009); Philip Van Dorn Stern, *The Confederate Navy: A Pictorial History* (New York: Bonanza, 1962), 65; Edward Henry Knight, *Knight's American Mechanical Dictionary,* 3 vols. (Boston: Hurd and Houghton, 1876), II, 1035; Edward Simpson, *A Treatise on Ordnance and Naval Gunnery, Compiled and Arranged as a Text-Book for the U.S. Naval Academy,* 2nd ed. (New York: D. Van Nostrand, 1862), 35–99, 152–182, 204–213; Gosnell, *op. cit.,* 107; Edward W. Very, *Navies of the World* (New York: John Wiley and Sons, 1880), 292–295; James Street, *By Valour and Arms* (New York: Dial, 1949),

157–160; Ernest Dumas, "James Howell Street (1903–1954)," *The Encyclopedia of Arkansas,* http://www.encyclopediaofarkansas.net/encyclopedia/entry-detail.aspx?entryID=5680 (accessed October 14, 2009). Reading's foundry was also known as the Vicksburg Foundry and was listed by H.C. Clarke in his 1860 city directory. See H.C. Clarke, comp., *"General Directory for the City of Vicksburg* [1860]," Rootsweb.Ancestry.Com, http://homepages.rootsweb.ancestry.com/~holler/dir1860.htm (accessed November 1, 2009) and Michael A. Rosen, "Historical Aspects and Black Powder Manufacturing," *The Encyclopedia of Civil War Artillery,* http://www.civilwarartillery.com/disarm/blackpowder.htm (accessed November 20, 2009). I have found the most helpful guide to Civil War naval cannon, carriages, and gun drill was Simpson's USNA textbook, written during the conflict. It is now a Google book: http://books.google.com/books?id=_5gtAAAAYAAJ&printsec=frontcover&dq=treatise+on+ordnance+and+naval+gunnery#v=onepage&q=&f=false>.

9. ORN, I, 23: 83; *Philadelphia Inquirer,* July 25, 1862; George Wright to this author, March 17, 2010; David Meager to this author, May 13, 2010; *New York Times,* July 5, 1862; Louis C. Hunter, *Steamboats on the Western Rivers: An Economic and Technological History* (Cambridge, MA: Harvard University Press, 1949), 160, 167, 177; Adam I. Kane, *The Western River Steamboat* (College Station: Texas A&M University Press, 2004), 70–71, 118–119; "Coastal Ironclads: C.S.S. *Arkansas,*" *Civil War Talk,* November 4, 2006, http://civilwartalk.com/Resource_Center/CS/Confederate_Navy/coastal-ironclads-c-s-s-arkansas-a104.html (accessed September 29, 2009); Tim J. Watts, "The *Arkansas,*" in *Encyclopedia of the Civil War: A Political, Social, and Military History,* ed. David Stephen Heidler, Jeanne T. Heidler, and David J. Cole (New York: W.W. Norton, 2000), 74–75; Still, *Iron Afloat,* 62, 101; Gift, *op. cit.,* 49; George Wright, "C.S.S. *Arkansas* Engine," Civil War Navies Message Board, September 2, 2007, May 8, 2009, http://history-sites.com/mb/cw/cwnavy.cgi?rev=3376, and June 3, 2009, http://history-sites.com/cgi-bin/bbs53x/cwnavy/webbbs_config.pl?read=2321 and <http://history-sites.com/mb/cw/cwnavy/index.cgi?rev=3383, and http://history-sites.com/mb/cw/cwnavy/index.cgi?rev=3458> (accessed September 29, October 1, 2009); Luraghi, *op. cit.,* 119–120; Mike McCarthy, *Iron and Steamship Archaeology: Success and Failure of the SS Xantho* (New York: Kluwer Academic, 2000), 13–14; Jeff Joslin, "Leeds & Co., New Orleans," *Old Wood-Working Machines,* http://www.owwm.com/MfgIndex/detail.aspx?id=1490 (accessed September 29, 2009); Brown, *op. cit.,* 575; Flynt, *op. cit.,* 114.

10. ORN, I, 18: 241, 502, 506–507, 519–522, 534, 649, 705–706, 709; ORN, I, 23: 137; OR, I, 17, 2: 40; OR, I, 15: 497, 753–754, 758, 761–763, 766, 768, 770; OR, I, 17, 2: 599, 606, 612, 622, 897; OR, I, 52, 2: 323; Moseley, *op. cit.,* p 309; Carter, *op. cit.,* 56, 59; *Vicksburg Daily Whig,* June 5, 1862; *Vicksburg Citizen,* June 20, 1862; Williams, *op. cit.,* 320; Flynt, *loc. cit.;* Milligan, *Gunboats Down the Mississippi,* 79; Chester G. Hearn, *Admiral David Glasgow Farragut: The Civil War Years* (Annapolis: Naval Institute Press, 1998), 134–138, 140; Loyall Farragut, *Life and Letters of Admiral D.G. Farragut* (New York: D. Appleton, 1879), 269; James M. Hoppin, *Life of Andrew Hull Foote, Rear-Admiral, United States Navy* (New York: Harper & Brothers, 1874), 344; Lockett, *op. cit.,* 483; Ballard, *op. cit.,* 44–45; Hartje, *op. cit.,* 183–184, 188–189. North Carolinian Bragg commanded major Rebel forces at Shiloh and Corinth. When Bragg took over the Army of Tennessee from Beauregard, he was replaced in northern Mississippi by Maj. Gen. Sterling Price. After a failed invasion of Kentucky, he besieged Chattanooga and Knoxville, before becoming military advisor to the CSA president in February 1864 (Boatner, *op. cit.,* 78–79; Louis S. Flatau, "A Great Naval Battle," *Confederate Veteran* 25 [October 1917], 459; Edward Porter Thompson, *History of the Orphan Brigade* [Louisville, KY: Lewis M. Thompson, 1898], 862–869; Steven E. Woodworth, *Nothing but Victory: The Army of the Tennessee, 1861–1865* [New York: Alfred A. Knopf, 2005], 217). Prior to his Vicksburg command, successful Mexican War veteran Van Dorn also served at New Orleans, in Texas and Arkansas, and at Corinth. After fighting at Corinth II, he led the Western cavalry command and pulled off the raid on Holly Springs in December 1862 that ruined the North's Chickasaw Bayou attempt to take Vicksburg from the north. He was killed by an unhappy husband as the result of a domestic liaison (Boatner, *op. cit.,* 867; Stanfly F. Horn, *The Army of Tennessee* (Indianapolis, Bobbs-Merrill, 1941), 453). Kentuckian Breckenridge was not only the U.S. vice president but also a former congressman. After Shiloh and Corinth, he was sent to Vicksburg and later led the Baton Rouge attack that resulted in the loss of the *Arkansas.* Fighting on in lower Tennessee and later in Virginia, he became the Confederate war secretary in 1865 (Boatner, *op. cit.,* 82–83). There is little resource material available on Lockett, who was highly regarded in his time, being a Confederate engineer not only for the defenses at Vicksburg, but also later at Mobile and Pensacola. After the war, he served with the Egyptian army as well as on engineering projects in the Midwest and in South America. He taught at both Louisiana State University and the University of Tennessee-Knoxville, and from 1883 to 1884, worked on setting up the Statue of Liberty at New York City (*Collection Guide, Samuel Henry Lockett Papers, 1820–1972,* Wilson Library, University of North Carolina home page, http://www.lib.unc.edu/mss/inv/l/Lockett,Samuel_Henry.html [accessed November 19, 2009]).

11. Williams, *op. cit.,* 324; OR, I, 7, 2: 324; OR, I, 15: 510, 767; OR, I, 52, 1: 40; ORN, I, 18: 589, 649–650; ORN, I, 19: 67, 132; ORN, I, 23: 242, 699–700; *Philadelphia Inquirer,* July 25, 1862; Isaac N. Brown to Daniel Ruggles, June 22, 1862, Confederate States of America, Navy, Confederate Naval Papers, Mississippi River, Area File 5, U.S. Navy Department, Office of Naval Records and Library, Naval Records Collection. Record Group 45, National Archives, Washington, D.C.; *Cincinnati Daily Commercial,* July 17, 1862; Brown, *op. cit.,* p.572; Read, *op. cit.,* 350; Flynt, *op. cit.,* 112–113; Hartje, *op. cit.,* 188–189; Campbell, *op. cit.,* 50; Gift, *op. cit.,* 207; Robert S. Huffstot, "The Brief, Glorious Career of the C.S.S. *Arkansas,*" *Civil War Times Illustrated* 7 (April 1968), 23; George Wright to this author, March 17, 2010; David Meagher to this author, May 28, 2010; Myron J. Smith, Jr., *The USS "Carondelet": A Civil War Ironclad on Western Waters* (Jefferson, NC: McFarland, 2010), 123; Coleman and Stevens, *op. cit.,* 92; John E. McGlone III, "The Lost Corps: The Confederate States Marines," *U.S. Naval Institute Proceedings* 99 (November 1972), 69–73; Milligan, *op. cit.,* 80; Barnhart, *op. cit.,* 35 Guy Hasegawa, "Quinine Substitutes in the Confederate Army," *Military Medicine* 172 (June 2007), 650–655; Michael J. Klag et al., "Miliaria," in John Hopkins Family Health Book (New York: HarperCollins, 1999), 1308; "First Tennessee Heavy Artillery Regiment," Tennesseeans in the Civil War Project, http://www.tngenweb.org/civilwar/csaart/hartl.html (accessed January 23, 2010). Capt. Parks (1843–

1907) was involved after the war in Arkansas' Populist movement, attended several national conventions and stood for office. His proudest recollection was of his service aboard the Confederate armorclad (Charles Rector, "William Pratt 'Buck' Parks," in The Encyclopedia of Arkansas History and Culture, http://www.encyclopedia ofarkansas.net/encyclopedia/entry-detail.aspx?entryID= 1733> [accessed January 23, 2010]; Arkansas Gazette, June 14, 1907; May 16, 1911). Pilot Brady (1844–1886), a Missourian, has been confused with Ordinary Seaman James Thomas Brady (1839–1908), who served aboard the C.S.S. Virginia ("James Thomas Brady," ZoomInfo Business People Information, http://www.zoominfo.com/people/ Brady_James_60547976.aspx (accessed January 16, 2010); Kendall Haven, "Meet James Brady," in Voices of the American Civil War: Stories of Men, Women, and Children Who Lived Through the War Between the States (Greenwood Village, CO: Libraries Unlimited, 2002), 118).

Six: Descending the Yazoo, June 25–July 15, 1862

1. U.S. Navy Department, *Official Records of the Union and Confederate Navies in the War of the Rebellion*, 31 vols. (Washington, D.C.: GPO, 1894–1922), Series I, Vol. 18: 727 (cited hereafter as ORN, followed by a comma, the series number in Roman numerals, a comma, the volume number in Arabic, a colon, and the page in Arabic); ORN, I, 19, 585–584; ORN, I, 23: 242; U.S. War Department, *The War of the Rebellion: A Compilation of the Official Records of the Union and Confederate Armies*, 128 vols. (Washington, D.C.: GPO, 1880–1901), Series I, Vol. 15: 498 (cited hereafter as OR, followed by a comma, the series number in Roman numerals, a comma, the volume number in Arabic, any part number in Arabic, a colon, and the page in Arabic); *New York Times*, July 1, 6, 1862; *Brooklyn Daily Eagle*, July 3, 1862; Warren D. Crandall and Isaac D. Newell, *History of the Ram Fleet and the Mississippi Marine Brigade* (St. Louis, MO: Buschart Brothers, 1907), 86–88; Chester G. Hearn, *Ellet's Brigade: The Strangest Outfit of All* (Baton Rouge: Louisiana State University Press, 2000), 44–46; John D. Milligan, *op. cit.*, 79–80; Kate Stone, *Brokenburn: The Journal of Kate Stone, 1861–1868*, ed. John Q. Anderson (Baton Rouge: Louisiana State University Press, 1955; repr., 1995), 122; David Flynt, "Run the Fleet: The Career of the C.S. Ram *Arkansas*," *The Journal of Mississippi History* 51 (May 1989), 112.

2. ORN, I, 23: 242–243; ORN, II, 1: 265; OR, I, 15: 515; *New York Times*, July 3, 1862; *Philadelphia Inquirer*, July 25, 1862; Charles W. Read, "Reminiscences of the Confederate States Navy," *Southern Historical Society Papers* 1 (May 1876), 351; R. Thomas Campbell, *Sea Hawk of the Confederacy* (Shippensburg, PA: Burd Street, 2000), 52–53; Hearn, *op. cit.*, 46–47; *Philadelphia Inquirer*, July 16, 1862; *Jackson Mississippian*, July 12, 1862, quoted in J. Thomas Scharf, *History of the Confederate Navy from Its Organization to the Surrender of Its Last Vessel* (New York: Rodgers and Sherwood, 1887, repr., New York: Fairfax, 1977), 338–339; Hosea Whitford Rood, *Wisconsin at Vicksburg* (Madison, WI: Wisconsin-Vicksburg Monument Commission, 1914), 285; Harry P. Owens, *Steamboats and the Cotton Economy: River Trade in the Yazoo-Mississippi Delta* (Jackson: University of Mississippi Press, 1990), 47–48; Shelby Foote, *The Civil War, a Narrative: Fort Sumter to Perryville* (New York: Random House, 1958), 548; Myron J. Smith, Jr., *The USS "Carondelet": A Civil War Ironclad on Western Waters* (Jefferson, NC: McFarland, 2010), 123; William N. Still, "The History of the C.S.S. *Arkansas*" (master's thesis, University of Alabama, 1958), 58–60. The tiny gunboat *St. Mary*, built at Plaquemine, LA, earlier in the year, was 89.6 feet long, with a beam of 15.2 feet and a draft of 5.1 feet. She would be captured by the Federals a year later (Frederick Way, Jr., *Way's Packet Directory, 1848–1994: Passenger Steamboats of the Mississippi River System Since the Advent of Photography in Mid-Continent America* (Athens: Ohio University Press, 1983, revised ed., Athens: Ohio University Press, 1994), 10). In his August 16 report to President Jefferson Davis, Navy Secretary Stephen R. Mallory indicated that Pinkney had "been sent before a court-martial for trial" (*Navy Annual Report, 1862*, http://www.cs navy.org/mallory,aug62.htm (accessed November 19, 2009); James Russell Soley, "Naval Operations in the Vicksburg Campaign," in *Battles and Leaders of the Civil War*, ed. Robert V. Johnson and Clarence C. Buell, 4 vols. (New York: Century, 1884–1887, repr., Thomas Yoseloff, 1956), III, 554–555). Pinkney was not convicted, but rather given new commands, eventually including the North Carolina command earlier held by Flag Officer Lynch. After the disaster, the locals supposedly renamed Rudloff Ridge to Battle Ridge. Jim Ewing, "Liverpool Landing: Mississippi Byways," Yazoo County, MSGenWeb, http://www.rootsweb.ancestry.com/~msyazoo/Liver pool_Landing.htm (accessed January 4, 2010).

3. ORN, I, 18: 464, 585–586, 608–611, 650–651, 727, 798; ORN, II, 1: 242; *Chicago Daily Tribune*, July 23, 1862; *Philadelphia Inquirer*, July 25, 1862; Read, *loc. cit.*; Campbell, *op. cit.*, 53–54; Samuel H. Lockett, "The Defense of Vicksburg," in *B&L*, III, 483; William Y. Dixon, *Diary*, June 21, 1862, *William Y. Dixon Diary*, Louisiana and Lower Mississippi Valley Collections, Louisiana State University Library, Baton Rouge; Soley, *op. cit.*, 554; Still, *op. cit.*, 61; Barnhart, *loc. cit.*; Charles H. Davis, Jr., *Life of Charles H. Davis, Rear Admiral, U.S.N.* (Boston: Houghton, Mifflin, 1899), 258; Jay Slagle, *Ironclad Captain: Seth Ledyard Phelps and the U.S. Navy* (Kent, OH: Kent State University Press, 1996), 150–251; Smith, *USS "Carondelet,"* 122; Paul Silverstone, *Warships of the Civil War Navies* (Annapolis: Naval Institute Press, 1989), p.54; Flynt, *op. cit.*, 112–113; James P. Duffy, *Lincoln's Admiral: The Civil War Campaigns of David Farragut* (New York: John Wiley, 1997), 127–133; Chester G. Hearn, *Admiral David Glasgow Farragut: The Civil War Years* (Annapolis: Naval Institute Press, 1998), 142–151; Arthur B. Carter, *The Tarnished Cavalier: Major General Earl Van Dorn* (Knoxville: University of Tennessee Press, 1999), 77; Milligan, *op. cit.*, 81; Kevin Carson, "21 Days to Glory: The Saga of the Confederate Ram *Arkansas*." *Sea Classics* 39 (July 2006), 40; Jim Ewing, "Liverpool Landing: Mississippi Byways," Yazoo County, MSGenWeb, http://www. rootsweb.ancestry.com/~msyazoo/Liverpool_Landing. htm (accessed January 4, 2010); David Dixon Porter, *Naval History of the Civil War* (New York: Sherman, 1886; repr., Secaucus, NJ: Castle Books, 1984), 248; W.J. McMurray, *History of the Twentieth Tennessee Volunteer Infantry, C.S.A.* (Nashville: Publication Committee, 1904), 216; John S. Jackman, *Diary of a Confederate Soldier: John S. Jackman of the Orphan Brigade*, ed. William C. Davis (Columbia: University of South Carolina Press, 1990), 47–48; Rowena Reed, *Combined Operations in the Civil War* (Annapolis: Naval Institute Press, 1978; repr., Lincoln: University of Nebraska Press, 1993), 216. At this

time, the weather was extremely warm throughout the Mississippi Valley. The 4th of July at St. Louis, for example, "passed tamely" due largely to the fact that the "day was intensely hot" causing a "want of spirit" (*Chicago Daily Tribune,* July 9, 1862). Lt. Commanding Phelps, captain of the Western Flotilla flagboat *Benton,* whose biography is provided in footnote 8 below, was, like many naval officers, a prolific letter writer. One of these, particularly helpful to this account of the *Arkansas,* was a July 19 missive sent to his long-time mentor and friend, U.S. treasury comptroller Elisha Whittlesey (1783–1863), a former Ohio congressman (1823–1838). The Phelps-Whittlesey correspondence is located in the library of the Westen Reserve Historical Society in Cleveland, OH, and was employed by Jay Slagle in his vital profile of Phelps. Indeed, Whittlesey (1783–1863) was the first comptroller of the U.S. Treasury (1849–1857, 1861–1863) ("Elisha Whittlesey," in *Biographical Directory of the United States Congress, 1774–Present,* http://bioguide.congress.gov/scripts/biodisplay.pl?index=W000431 (Accessed January 4, 2010); Eliott Callender, "Career of the Confederate Ram *Arkansas,* Given before the Farragut Naval Veterans Association, Chicago," in *Speeches of a Veteran,* (Chicago: Blue Sky, 1901; repr., Charleston, SC: BiblioLife, 2009), 46). Callender served in the Western Flotilla/Mississippi Squadron for three years, entering as a landsman and departing as an Acting Ensign and captain of the tinclad *Marmora.* The Peoria, IL, resident presented a number of talks on Civil War naval activities before the Chicago navy veterans group in 1900; they were collected and published in a small 158-page volume (only 25 copies were printed) that is now offered as an on-demand book ("Eliot Callender," in "Peoria County Biographies," Rootsweb, http://freepages.history.rootsweb.ancestry.com/~historyconnection/Peoria/Bio/04.htm [accessed April 10, 2010]).

4. Capt. Samuel Stanhope Harris (1836–1899), the senior horse artillery officer serving aboard the *Arkansas,* was a medical doctor from Jackson, MO, who joined the Missouri State Guard in early 1861 as first lieutenant of Co. A of the 2nd MSG Cavalry. He moved on to command of McDowell's Battery and later his own unit, Harris' Missouri Light Artillery. He would later serve under Col. Colton Greene in the Camden campaign and in Greene's June 1864 antishipping campaign from southeast Arkansas. He also served in Price's Missouri invasion of fall 1864. He resumed his medical practice after the war (Scott K. Williams and James McGhee, "Missourians Aboard the C.S.S. *Arkansas,*" Sons of Confederate Veterans, Missouri Division, *Missouri Units,* http://www.missouridivision-scv.org/mounits/cssark.htm [accessed December 1, 2009]). McDonald was elected captain in July 1861, as was Scott Countian Martin; Parsons, from Perry County, arrived in September. A roster of Missouri State Guard Personnel, 1861–1862 is found on Chris and David Long, *Civil War Battle of Wilson's Creek (Battle of Hills),* http://www.chrisanddavid.com/wilsonscreek/roles/SOLDIERSMSGL-R.html (accessed December 1, 2009).

5. ORN, I, 18: 635–636, 652, 675, 729; ORN, I, 19: 132; ORN, I, 23: 235; OR, I, 15: 15; *St. Louis Daily Missouri Republican,* July 22, 1862; *Philadelphia Inquirer,* July 25, 1862; *Chicago Daily Tribune,* July 23, 1862; *Jackson Mississippian,* July 17, 1862; *Columbus (GA) Daily Enquirer,* July 23, 1862; Williams and McGhee, *loc. cit.;* James McGhee, "Units of the Missouri State Guard, 1861–1862," *Confederate Links: Missouri Divisions and Commanders,* http://www.mogenweb.org/mocivwar/confederates.html (accessed December 1, 2009); Isaac Newton Brown, "The Confederate Gun-Boat *Arkansas,*" *B&L,* III, 572–573; Read, *op. cit.,* 352–353; Foote, *op. cit.,* 550; M. Jeff Thompson, *The Civil War Reminiscences of General M. Jeff Thompson* (Dayton, OH: Morningside House, 1988), 168–169; Scharf, *op. cit.,* 309–310; Brown, *op. cit.,* 572; Callender. *op. cit.,* 45–48; Alfred T. Mahan, *Admiral Farragut* (New York: D. Appleton, 1892), 190–191; Hearn, *Admiral David Glasgow Farragut,* 152, 154; George W. Gift, "The Story of the *Arkansas,*" *Southern Historical Society Paper,* 8 (1884), 49–50; Harriet Castlen, *Hope Bids Me Onward* (Savannah, GA: Chatham, 1945), 65–67; Hartje, *op. cit.,* 200; John L. Martin, "A Great Naval Battle," *Confederate Veteran* 28 (March 1923), 93; George C. Waterman, "Notable Naval Events of the War," *Confederate Veteran* 6 (January 1891), 61–62; Flynt, *op. cit.,* 114–115; H. Allen Gosnell, *Guns on the Western Waters: The Story of the River Gunboats in the Civil War* (Baton Rouge: Louisiana State University Press, 1949), 107; Still, "The History of the C.S.S. *Arkansas,*" 56–57, 59–64; Still, *Iron Afloat,* 61–63; Smith, *USS "Carondelet,"* 123–124; Edward W. Bacon, *Double Duty in the Civil War: The Letters of Sailor and Soldier Edward W. Bacon,* ed. George S. Burkhardt. (Carbondale: Southern Illinois University Press, 2009), 53–54; Barnhart, *loc. cit.;* Lloyd Lewis, *David Glasgow Farragut* (Annapolis: Naval Institute Press, 1943), 107; Deck Logbook of the USS *Carondelet,* July 1–13, 1862, Deck Logbooks of the USS *Carondelet,* May 1862–June 1865 Records of the Bureau of Ships, Record Group 19, U.S. National Archives and Records Service (cited hereafter as *Carondelet* Logbook, with date); *Philadelphia Inquirer,* July 16, 1862; *New Orleans Daily Delta,* July 22, 1862; *Hinds County (MS) Gazette,* December 9, 1874; Robert S. Huffstot, "The Brief, Glorious Career of the C.S.S. *Arkansas,*" *Civil War Times Illustrated* 7 (April 1968), 24; Donald Barnhart, Jr., "Junkyard Ironclad," *Civil War Times Illustrated* 40 (February 2001), 35; Edwin C. Bearss, *Rebel Victory at Vicksburg* (Vicksburg, MS: Centennial Commission, 1963), 240; Raimondo Luraghi, *A History of the Confederate Navy* (Annapolis: Naval Institute Press, 1996), 177; Slagle, *op. cit..,* 256–258, 262–264; Davis, *op. cit.,* 262–263, 267–70. Lt. Brown later confirmed Van Dorn's order that he proceed to Mobile in a letter to Alfred T. Mahan, then writing his first history (Isaac N. Brown to Mahan, May 9, 1883, Confederate States of America, Navy, Confederate Naval Papers, Mississippi River, Area File 5, U.S. Navy Department, Office of Naval Records and Library, Naval Records Collection, Record Group 45, National Archives, Washington, D.C. Ironically, Flag Officer Farragut's July 10 request to return to the Gulf of Mexico brought a positive order to do so from Navy Secretary Welles. It arrived on July 14 — but couldn't be immediately implemented (ORN, I, 18: 675).

6. William Porter (1809–1864), the brother of Cmdr. David Dixon Porter, first joined the USN in 1823. Scalded at Fort Henry in 1862, he recovered to serve in the Natchez, Vicksburg, and Port Hudson campaigns. He would figure prominently in the *Arkansas* story and his *Essex* would, once she completed boiler repairs that kept her idle on July 15, be the bane of the Rebel boat's existence (Mark M. Boatner III. *The Civil War Dictionary* (New York: David McKay, 1959), 662; Dana M. Wegner, "Commodore William D. "Dirty Bill" Porter," *U.S. Naval Institute Proceedings* 103 (February 1977), 40–49). The second flag officer of the Western Flotilla had, like Flag Officer Lynch and Cmdr. John Rodgers, developed an enviable reputation in the antebellum period as a scientific officer. Born in Boston, he earned a degree from Harvard University, becoming superintendent of the Nautical Almanac Office located there. With sea service during the

expedition to capture the filibuster William Walker in Nicaragua and with the South Atlantic Blockading Squadron, Davis was elevated to his post in June 1862, only to be himself succeeded in command of the Mississippi Squadron by David Dixon Porter in October (effective July). He was constantly on duty ashore and afloat, and he would die at his desk as superintendent of the Naval Observatory. Our Davis profile is taken from William B. Cogar, *Dictionary of Admirals of the U.S. Navy*, 2 vols. (Annapolis: Naval Institute Press, 1989), I, 41–43, and Charles Henry Davis, *Life of Charles Henry Davis, Rear Admiral, 1807–1877* (Boston and New York: Houghton, Mifflin, 1899). Engineer Fulton was a frequent contributor to his father's newspaper. This account of the *Arkansas* was reprinted in vol. 5 of *The Rebellion Record: A Diary of American Events*, ed. Frank Moore (New York: G.P. Putnam, 1863; repr., New York: Arno, 1977), 555–556.

7. Hoosier Lt. William Gwin (1832–1863) was regarded as one of the most promising junior officers in the service prior to his death. Transferred west from the USS *Susquehanna*, he commanded the Western Flotilla's timberclad division in early 1862, gaining its greatest laurels. A contemporary of *Arkansas* officer Lt. George Gift at the U.S. Naval Academy, Gwin transferred to the flagboat *Benton*. He would be wounded in action at Haines Bluff on December 27, 1862, and die a week later ("Sketches of the Officers of the Fort Donelson Fleet," *Philadelphia Inquirer*, February 18, 1862; Edward W. Callahan, *List of Officers of the Navy of the United States and of the Marine Corps, from 1775 to 1900, Comprising a Complete Register of All Present and Former Commissioned, Warranted, and Appointed Officers of the United States Navy, and of the Marine Corps, Regular and Volunteer, Compiled from the Official Records of the Navy Department* (New York: L.R. Hamersly, 1901; repr., New York: Haskell House, 1969), 236; Myron J. Smith, Jr., *The Timberclads in the Civil War: The "Lexington," "Conestoga," and "Tyler" on the Western Waters* (Jefferson, NC: McFarland, 2008), 346–347).

8. Lt. Seth Ledyard Phelps (1824–1885) was appointed a midshipman from Ohio in 1841 and prior to the Civil War served primarily in the Atlantic, including a stint aboard the sloop-of-war *St. Mary's* and with the squadron assigned to lay a great cable from the U.S. to the UK. On June 19, the 105th ranking sea service lieutenant received orders from the navy secretary, Gideon Welles, to proceed west to join Cmdr. John Rodgers at Cincinnati. From the time he reached the Queen City well into 1864 when he resigned, Phelps was involved in one significant Western Flotilla/Mississippi Squadron role after another, winning acclaim from all of his superiors. His letters, quoted by Slagle, demonstrated that he was not a fan of certain older officers, especially Henry Walke of the *Carondelet*. After the Civil War, the former Buckeye naval commander was involved with steamship companies and in activities surrounding a possible Nicaraguan canal. He also served as ambassador to Peru (Slagle, *op. cit.*, 8–395; "Sketches of the Officers of the Fort Donelson Fleet," *Philadelphia Inquirer*, February 18, 1862; Callahan, *op. cit.*, 519; Smith, *op. cit.*, p.69).

9. The *Tyler* was one of the three original Western Flotilla gunboats, called "timberclads," converted at Cincinnati from the *A.O. Tyler* in June and July 1861. Displacing 420 tons, she was 180 feet long, with a beam of 45.4 feet and a 6-foot draft. The side-wheeler was powered by two engines and four boilers and was capable of a top speed of 8 mph. Covered all over with various thicknesses of oak, the boat had a crew of 67 and was armed with six 8-inch smoothbores in broadside and a single 32-pdr. sternchaser (Silverstone, *op. cit.*, 159; ORN, II, 1: 227–228; Way, *op. cit.*, 2–3, 461).

10. Constructed at Cincinnati in 1854, the sidewheeler *Queen of the West* was acquired by the War Department in 1862 for conversion into one of the Ellet rams. Unarmored, the 406-ton vessel's two engines were powered by three boilers and her complement of nautical soldiers totaled 120. She was 181 feet long, with a beam of 36 feet and a 6-foot draft. Marshall Legan tells us that, employing timber guards and braces, her boilers were protected by a wall of heavy timber. Timber bulkheads secured by cross braces that ran from stem to stern would permit the entire weight of the vessel to be thrown into any ramming attempt. Relying upon speed, her bow was reinforced back about midships and filled with lumber. Painted black, her name was painted on her paddle-wheel box. The arrangement for the other Ellet rams was similar and neither she nor her sisters were originally armed. During the Battle of Memphis, she was directly responsible for ramming and sinking the Confederate gunboat *General Lovell*. Arriving at the Yazoo, she was given a pair of howitzers for protection against riverbank guerrillas (Way, *op. cit.*, 382; Silverstone, *op. cit.*, 161; Marshall S. Legan, "The Confederate Career of a Union Ram," *Louisiana History* 33 (Summer 2000), 279).

11. The center-wheel Pook-designed Eads gunboat *Carondelet* was the most famous of seven sister vessels constructed at Carondelet, MO, in 1861. First captain Henry Walke's command displaced 512 tons and was 175 feet long, with a 51.2-foot beam and a 6-foot draft. Although her two engines and five boilers allowed her to be rated with a 9 mph top speed, she was, indeed, the slowest of her class. She was protected by a rectangular sloped casemate that was heavily armored in the bow and, like the *Arkansas*, lightly on the quarters and stern. A total of 251 officers and men made up her crew and she was armed with four 8-inch Dahlgren smoothbores, one 42-pdr., six 32-pdrs., and one each 50-pdr. and 30-pdr. rifle (Silverstone, *op. cit.*, 151; ORN, II, 1: 52).

12. "Sketches of the Officers of the Fort Donelson Fleet," *Philadelphia Inquirer*, February 18, 1862; Callahan, *op. cit.*, 594; Lewis R. Hamersly, *The Records of Living Officers of the U.S. Navy and Marine Corps, Compiled from Official Sources*, rev. ed. (Philadelphia: J.B. Lippincott, 1870), 201; Smith, *op. cit.*, 105; Cogar, *op. cit.*, I, 200–201. Walke was transferred to command of the *Sacramento* in 1863 and served on the Atlantic Station, eventually taking a role in the pursuit of the Confederate ocean ironclad *Stonewall*. After the war, he commanded the Mound City naval station and was subsequently named a rear admiral. After his retirement, he wrote his memoirs (*Naval Scenes and Reminiscences of the Civil War in the United States on the Southern and Western Waters During the Years 1861, 1862 and 1863, with the History of That Period Compared and Corrected from Authentic Sources* [New York: F.R. Reed, 1877]) and painted full time, providing illustrations for many of the late 19th century Civil War naval histories. He died in Brooklyn, New York, on March 8, 1896.

13. ORN, I, 18: 636; ORN, I, 19: 4, 6–7, 37–39, 44, 56, 60, 705; ORN, I, 23: 131, 244, 258, 636, 671, 685; OR, I, 15: 32; *Philadelphia Inquirer*, July 22, 1862; *New Orleans Daily Delta*, July 22, 1862; *Baltimore American*, July 25, 1862; *New York Herald*, July 25, 1862; Junius Henri Browne, *Four Years in Secessia: Adventures Within and Beyond the Union Lines* (Hartford, CT: O.D. Case, 1865), 214; Slagle, *op. cit.*, 252; Thomas Williams, "Letters

of General Thomas Williams, 1862," *American Historical Review* 14 (January 1909), 322–323; *Carondelet* Logbook, July 14–15, 1862; James R. Soley, "Naval Operations in the Vicksburg Campaign," *B&L*, III: 555; Barnhart, *op. cit.,* 35–36; Porter, *op. cit.,* 249; Maurice Melton, *The Confederate Ironclads* (New York: A.S. Barnes, 1968), 121–122; Milligan, *loc. cit.*; Silas B. Coleman and Paul Stevens, "A July Morning with the Rebel Ram *Arkansas,*" *U.S. Naval Institute Proceedings* 88 (July 1962), 86; Scharf, *op. cit.,* 309–310; Musciant, *op. cit.,* 249; Davis, *op. cit.,* 262; Flynt, *op. cit.,* 115; Smith, *USS "Carondelet,"* 125–126; Edward W. Bacon, *Double Duty in the Civil War: The Letters of Sailor and Soldier Edward W. Bacon,* ed. George S. Burkhardt. (Carbondale: Southern Illinois University Press, 2009), 58, 62; Hearn, *Ellet's Brigade,* 49–50; Hearn, *Admiral David Glasgow Farragut,* 154–155; Campbell, *op. cit.,* 112–113; Walke, *Naval Scenes,* 303–305; Smith, *op. cit.,* 348–350. Paymaster Coleman of the *Tyler,* also known in the ORN as William, was an eyewitness to the fight with the *Arkansas.* In 1890, the Michigander revealed his unique view of the only major engagement between a timberclad and a Confederate armorclad for the Detroit chapter of the Loyal Legion of the United States. We have noted that version in the bibliography and quote here from a reprint. Incidentally, Coleman was promoted to the rank of acting ensign on October 1, 1862 when the Western Flotilla became the Mississippi Squadron and was named an acting volunteer lieutenant on June 15, 1864. He was honorably discharged on December 12, 1865. Coleman was one of three officers (Fourth Master F.T., Paymaster Silas, and Master's Mate Gilbert L.) by that name aboard the *Tyler* on July 15; it is not known if they were related (Edward W. Callahan, *List of Officers of the Navy of the United States and of the Marine Corps, from 1775 to 1900, Comprising a Complete Register of All Present and Former Commissioned, Warranted, and Appointed Officers of the United States Navy, and of the Marine Corps, Regular and Volunteer, Compiled from the Official Records of the Navy Department* (New York: L.R. Hamersly, 1901; repr., New York: Haskell House, 1969), 123). Having been ordered to return east with most of his mortar fleet, Cmdr. David Dixon Porter was not present when the *Arkansas* made her breakout. Using the reports of others, he wrote of it 20 years later in his *Naval History of the Civil War.*

Seven: Morning (Part I), July 15, 1862: Dawn Fight in the Yazoo

1. Isaac Newton Brown, "The Confederate Gun-Boat *Arkansas,*" in *Battles and Leaders of the Civil War,* ed. Robert V. Johnson and Clarence C. Buell, 4 vols. (New York: Century, 1884–1887, repr., Thomas Yoseloff, 1956), III, 573–574; Charles W. Read, "Reminiscences of the Confederate States Navy," *Southern Historical Society Papers* 1 (May 1876), 352–353; Henry Walke, *Naval Scenes and Reminiscences of the Civil War in the United States on the Southern and Western Waters During the Years 1861, 1862 and 1863, with the History of That Period Compared and Corrected from Authentic Sources* (New York: F.R. Reed, 1877), 304–305; R. Thomas Campbell, *Sea Hawk of the Confederacy* (Shippensburg, PA: Burd Street, 2000), 55–56; George W. Gift, "The Story of the *Arkansas,*" *Southern Historical Society Papers* 8 (1884), 50–51; William N. Still, "The History of the C.S.S. *Arkansas*" (master's thesis, University of Alabama, 1958), 65–66; Myron J. Smith, Jr., *The USS "Carondelet": A Civil War Ironclad on Western Waters* (Jefferson, NC: McFarland, 2010), 127; David Flynt, "Run the Fleet: The Career of the C.S. Ram *Arkansas,*" *The Journal of Mississippi History* 51 (May 1989), 115–116; L.S. Flatau, "A Great Naval Battle," *Confederate Veteran* 25 (October 1917), 458; Dunbar Roland, *The Official and Statistical Register of the State of Mississippi* (Nashville: Brandon, 1908), 849–852; J. Thomas Scharf, *History of the Confederate Navy from Its Organization to the Surrender of Its Last Vessel* (New York: Rodgers and Sherwood, 1887, repr., New York: Fairfax, 1977), 309–312; John D. Milligan, *Gunboats Down the Mississippi* (Annapolis: Naval Institute Press, 1965), 81–82; Chester G. Hearn, *Admiral David Glasgow Farragut: The Civil War Years* (Annapolis: Naval Institute Press, 1998), 154–155; Charles M. Getchell, Jr. "Defender of Inland Waters: The Military Career of Isaac Newton Brown, Commander, Confederate States Navy, 1861–1865" (master's thesis, University of Mississippi, 1978), 60; Robert S. Huffstot, "The Brief, Glorious Career of the C.S.S. *Arkansas,*" *Civil War Times Illustrated* 7 (April 1968), 24.

2. U.S. Navy Department, *Official Records of the Union and Confederate Navies in the War of the Rebellion,* 31 vols. (Washington, D.C.: GPO, 1894–1922), Series I, Vol. 19, 32, 36–38, 68 (cited hereafter as ORN, followed by a comma, the series number in Roman numerals, a comma, the volume number in Arabic, a colon, and the page in Arabic); *Brooklyn Daily Eagle,* July 24, 1862; Brown, *loc. cit.*; Read, *op. cit.,* 353; Silas B. Coleman and Paul Stevens, "A July Morning with the Rebel Ram *Arkansas,*" *U.S. Naval Institute Proceedings* 88 (July 1962), 86; Myron J. Smith, Jr., *The Timberclads in the Civil War: The "Lexington," "Conestoga," and "Tyler" on the Western Waters* (Jefferson, NC: McFarland, 2008), 350–351; Smith, *USS "Carondelet,"* 128–129; Robert G. Hartje, *Van Dorn: The Life and Times of a Confederate General* (Nashville: Vanderbilt University Press, 1967), 201; Campbell, *op. cit.,* 55–57; Gift, *op. cit.,* 50; Still, "The History of the C.S.S. *Arkansas,*" 70–71; Flynt, *op. cit.,* 116–117; Getchell, *loc. cit.*; Scharf, *loc. cit.*; Milligan, *loc. cit.*; David Dixon Porter, *Naval History of the Civil War* (New York: Sherman, 1886; repr., Secaucus, NJ: Castle, 1984), 249; Eliott Callender, "Career of the Confederate Ram *Arkansas,* Given before the Farragut Naval Veterans Association, Chicago," in *Speeches of a Veteran* (Chicago: Blue Sky, 1901; repr., Charleston, SC: BiblioLife, 2009), 49–50. Admiral Porter, writing while the Confederate commander was still alive, admiringly pointed out in his review that the ram was "commanded by Lieutenant Brown, late of the U.S. Navy, whose name will go down in history as one who performed a most gallant and desperate undertaking."

3. ORN, I, 19: 36–38, 68; *St. Louis Daily Missouri Republican,* July 22, 1862; *Chicago Daily Tribune,* July 23, 1862; *Baltimore American,* July 25, 1862; Brown, *loc. cit.*; Gift, *loc. cit.*; Campbell, *op. cit.,* 58–60; Coleman and Stevens, *loc. cit.*; "Stoddard County Confederate Memorial," Missouri Division, Sons of Confederate Veterans Home page, http://www.missouridivision-scv.org/stoddard.htm (accessed January 4, 2010); Walke, *Naval Scenes and Reminiscences,* 206; Milligan, *op. cit.,* 83; Flynt, *op. cit.,* 116–117; Jay Slagle, *Ironclad Captain: Seth Ledyard Phelps and the U.S. Navy* (Kent, OH: Kent State University Press, 1996), 264; Hearn, *Admiral David Glasgow Farragut,* 155; Smith, *The Timberclads, loc. cit.*; Smith, *USS "Carondelet,"* 130; Porter, *loc. cit.*; Ivan Musicant, *Divided Waters: The Naval History of the Civil War* (New York: HarperCollins, 1995), 249–250; Still, "The History

of the C.S.S. *Arkansas,"* 72; Alfred T. Mahan, *The Gulf and Inland Waters,* vol. 3, *Navy in the Civil War* (New York: Scribner's, 1883), 100; for the earlier Walke-Brown relationship, see Samuel Eliot Morison, *"Old Bruin": Commodore Matthew C. Perry, 1794–1858* (Boston: Little, Brown, 1967), 434; Callender, *loc. cit.*; Getchell, *loc. cit.*

4. ORN, I, 19: 36–39, 41, 68, 132; ORN, I, 23: 685–686; U.S. War Department, *The War of the Rebellion: A Compilation of the Official Records of the Union and Confederate Armies,* 128 vols. (Washington, D.C.: GPO, 1880–1901), Series I, Vol. 15: 31–32 (cited hereafter as OR, followed by a comma, the series number in Roman numerals, a comma, the volume number in Arabic, any part number in Arabic, a colon, and the page in Arabic); Isaac N. Brown to Mahan, November 25, 1883, Confederate States of America, Navy, Confederate Naval Papers, Mississippi River, Area File 5, U.S. Navy Department, Office of Naval Records and Library, Naval Records Collection, Record Group 45, National Archives, Washington, D.C.; *Grenada Appeal,* July 16, 23, 1862; *Philadelphia Inquirer,* July 22, 1862; *Chicago Daily Tribune,* July 22–23, 1862; *St. Louis Daily Missouri Republican,* July 22, 1862; *New York Herald,* July 25, 1862; *Philadelphia Inquirer,* July 22, 1862; *Louisville Daily Journal,* July 22, 1862; *New Orleans Daily Delta,* July 22, 1862; *Jackson Mississippian,* July 17, 1862; *Columbus (GA) Daily Enquirer,* July 23, 1862; *Brooklyn Daily Eagle,* July 24, 1862; Read, *op. cit.,* 354; Coleman and Stevens, *op. cit.,* 86, 88; Gift, *op. cit.,* 51–54; Campbell, *op. cit.,* 59–62; Campbell, *Confederate Naval Forces on Western Waters* (Jefferson, NC: McFarland, 2005), 114–119; Brown, *op. cit.,* 572, 574–575; Gift, *op. cit.,* 50–54; Robert S. Huffstot, "The Brief, Glorious Career of the C.S.S. *Arkansas,"* *Civil War Times Illustrated* 7 (April 1968), 24–25; Callender, *op. cit.,* 50–51; Porter, *loc. cit.*; Walke, *op. cit.,* 302–306; James Russell Soley, "Naval Operations in the Vicksburg Campaign," in *Battles and Leaders of the Civil War,* ed. Robert V. Johnson and Clarence C. Buell, 4 vols. (New York: Century, 1884–1887, repr., Thomas Yoseloff, 1956), III, 554–555.; Flynt, *op. cit.,* 118–119; Mahan, *op. cit.,* 100; Flatau, *loc. cit.*; Mary Emerson Branch, "A Story Behind the Story of the *Arkansas* and the *Carondelet,"* *Missouri Historical Review* XXIX (April 1985), 324–325; Slage, *op. cit.,* 265–266; Kevin Carson, "21 Days to Glory: The Saga of the Confederate Ram *Arkansas."* *Sea Classic* 39 (July 2006), 40; Smith, *The Timberclads,* 352–354; Smith, *USS "Carondelet,"* 130–134; Hearn, *Admiral David Glasgow Farragut,* 156; Hearn, *Ellet's Brigade: The Strangest Outfit of All* (Baton Rouge: Louisiana State University Press, 2000), 51; Spencer C. Tucker, *Blue & Gray Navies: The Civil War Afloat.* (Annapolis: U.S. Naval Institute, 2006). p. 211; Getchell, *op. cit.,* 61–64; Jim Miles, *A River Unvexed: A History and Tour Guide of the Campaign for the Mississippi River* (Nashville: Rutledge Hill, 1994), 217; Samuel Carter III, *The Final Fortress: The Campaign for Vicksburg 1862–1863* (New York: St. Martin's, 1980), 69–70; Donald Barnhart, Jr., "Junkyard Ironclad." *Civil War Times Illustrated* 40 (May 2001), 36; Hartje, *loc. cit.*; Charles S. Foltz, ed., *Surgeon of the Seas: The Adventures of Jonathan M. Foltz* (Indianapolis: Bobbs-Merrill, 1931), 247–248; James P. Duffy, *Lincoln's Admiral: The Civil War Campaigns of David Farragut* (Edison, NJ: Castle, 2006), 143–144; Michael B. Ballard, *Vicksburg: The Campaign That Opened the Mississippi* (Chapel Hill: University of North Carolina Press, 2004), 56–57; Musicant, *op. cit.,* 249–250; Milligan, *op. cit.,* 83–84; Junius Henri Browne, *Four Years in Secessia: Adventures Within and Beyond the Union Lines* (Hartford, CT: O.D. Case, 1865), 214–217; Still, "The History of the C.S.S. *Arkansas,"* 74–75; Still, *Iron Afloat: The Story of Confederate Armorclads* (Nashville: Vanderbilt University Press, 1971; repr., Columbia: University of South Carolina Press, 1985), 67–68; Jack D. Coombe, *Thunder Along the Mississippi: The River Battles That Split the Confederacy* (New York: Sarpedon, 1996), 155–156; William H. Parker, *The Confederate Navy,* vol. 12, *Confederate Military History* (Atlanta, GA: Confederate, 1899), 64. Even the acerbic Walke originally admitted that Lt. Gwin sustained him "through the fight in a very gallant and effective manner" (ORN, I, 19: 41). Having enlisted at Lansingburg, NY, on April 24, 1861, Morrison joined the crew of the *Carondelet* on February 15, 1862. Honorably discharged on March 31, 1863, he returned to Brooklyn, New York. His CMH was awarded under General Order 59, June 22, 1865 ("John G. Morrison, Civil War Medal of Honor Recipient," American Civil War Website, http://americancivilwar.com/medal_of_honor6.html [accessed April 9, 2008]).

5. ORN, I, 19: 15; ORN, I, 23: 37–38, 41, 260–263, 268, 270–272; *Carondelet* Logbook, July 15–August 5, 1862; Scott D. Jordan to wife, April 12, 1863, in *Civil War Letters of Scott D. Jordan, Produced for Eleanor Jordan West,* (CD-ROM; Tucson, AZ: Bellnotes.com, 2007), cited hereafter as Jordan Letters, with date; *St. Louis Missouri Daily Democrat,* July 22, 1862; *Cincinnati Times,* July 22, 1862; *Philadelphia Inquirer,* July 22, 25, 1862; *Chicago Daily Tribune,* July 22–23, 1862; *New York Herald,* July 25, 1862; *New Orleans Daily Delta,* July 22, 1862; Gift, *op. cit.,* 53, 55; Foltz, *op. cit.,* 248; Slagle, *op. cit.,* 266; Walke, *op. cit.,* 300–311, 313, 316–317; Porter, *loc. cit.*; Charles H. Davis, Jr., *Life of Charles H. Davis, Rear Admiral, U.S.N.* (Boston: Houghton, Mifflin, 1899), 267–270; Getchell, *op. cit.,* 64–65; A.B. Donaldson to Secretary of the Navy (Charles F. Adams), June 28, 1929 (Files of the U.S. Naval Academy Museum, Annapolis); William D. Puleston, *Mahan* (New Haven, CT: Yale University Press, 1939), 64–65; Mahan, *op. cit.,* 99–100; Mahan, *Admiral Farragut* (New York: D. Appleton, 1895), 191; Smith, *USS "Carondelet,"* 135–140; Musicant, *op. cit.,* 249; William L. Shea and Terrence J. Winschel, *Vicksburg Is the Key: The Struggle for the Mississippi Valley,* Great Campaigns of the Civil War Series (Lincoln: University of Nebraska Press, 2003), 24; George Wright, "USS *Carondelet* vs. CSS *Arkansas,"* Civil War Navies Message Board, http://history-sites.com/cgi-bin/bbs53x/cwnavy/webbbs_config.pl?read=1580, (April 4, 2009).

6. *Pinola* was a $96,000 sister of the *Wissahickon, Sciota,* and *Winona.* Launched at Baltimore, MD, in November 1861, she was commissioned in January 1862. In all other particulars, she was the same (ORN, II, 1: 179; Paul Silverstone, *Warships of the Civil War Navies* (Annapolis: Naval Institute Press, 1989), 49–50).

7. The second largest Federal ship anchored north of Vicksburg, the 2,700 ton *Richmond* was launched at Norfolk, VA, in January 1860 and commissioned 10 months later. With a complement of 260, the sloop-of-war was 225 feet long, with a beam of 42.6 feet and a 17.5-foot draft. Powered by one screw (two engines) and a full suit of sails, her main armament comprised twenty 9-inch Dahlgren SBs, one 80-pdr.Dahlgren rifle, and one 30-pdr. Dahlgren rifle (ORN, II, 1: 192–193; Silverstone, *op. cit.,* 38).

8. Flagship of the West Gulf Coast Blockading Squadron and of Flag Officer Farragut, the 2,900-ton *Hartford* was the largest Union ship to face the *Arkansas.* Launched at Boston in November 1858, she was commissioned in May 1859. With a complement of 310, this

sloop-of-war was also 225 feet long, having a 44-foot beam and a 17-foot draft. Also powered by one screw and a full suit of sails, she was likewise armed with twenty 9-inch Dahlgren SBs and also had two each 20-pdr. Dahlgren rifles and 12-pdr. Dahlgren howitzers (ORN, II, 1: 99; Silverstone, *op. cit.,* 36).

9. *Sciota* was a $96,000 sister of the *Wissahickon, Pinola,* and *Winona.* Launched at Philadelphia in October 1861, she was commissioned that December. In all other particulars, she was the same (ORN, II, 1: 203; Silverstone, *loc. cit.*).

10. One of two sisters anchored above Vicksburg, the 1,488-ton second-class sloop-of-war *Iroquois* was the third largest Federal ship present to fight the *Arkansas.* Launched in April 1859 and commissioned seven months later, the craft was 198.10 feet long, with a beam of 33.10 feet and a 13-foot draft. Powered by one screw and sails, she had a complement of 123 and was armed with two 11-inch Dahlgren SBs, four 32-pdrs., one 50-pdr. Dahlgren rifle, and a 12-pdr. Dahlgren howitzer (ORN, II, 1: 109; Silverstone, *op. cit.,* 39).

11. The 1,032-ton *Oneida,* sister of the *Iroquois,* was launched in November 1861 and commissioned by Cmdr. Lee in February. With dimensions and armament identical to her sister, she had two boilers, one less than the *Iroquois* (ORN, II, 1: 165; Silverstone, *loc. cit.*). An interesting diary kept aboard during the Vicksburg expedition found its way to North Carolina. See *"Oneida" Ship's Diary,* Southern Historical Collection, Wilson Library, University of North Carolina at Chapel Hill.

12. *Winona* was a $101,000 sister of the *Wissahickon, Pinola,* and *Sciota.* Launched at New York City in September 1861, she was commissioned in December. In all other particulars, she was the same (ORN, II, 1: 242; Silverstone, *loc. cit.*).

13. Built by James B. Eads at Carondelet, MO, in 1861, the *Louisville* and *Cincinnati* were "Pook turtle" sisters of the *Carondelet,* which was temporarily out of action up the Yazoo River (ORN, II, 1:129, 58; Silverstone, *op. cit.,* 151–153).

14. Then the most powerful Federal ironclad on the Western waters, the 633-ton *Benton* was converted by Eads from one of his catamaran snagboats at Carondelet at the same time as he was constructing the Pook turtles. Two engines drove a protected stern wheel; however, like the Pooks, the vessel was very slow. With a length of 202 feet, the Benton was 72 feet wide and had a 9-foot draft. Her casemate, unlike the *Arkansas* but like the Pooks, had a sloping side; both it and the pilothouse were covered with 2.5 inches of armor. With a complement of 176, her armament comprised two 9-inch Dahlgren SBs, seven 42-pdr. ex-army rifles, and seven 32-pdrs (ORN, II, 1: 44; Silverstone, *op. cit.,* 155).

15. Also converted, this time from a large ferryboat, the unique center-wheel powered *Essex* was the best protected Federal ironclad with Flag Officer Davis. With a length of 159 feet, a beam of 47.6 feet, and a 6-foot draft, this sometimes controversial craft also had a full casemate covered by 3 inches of iron. With a crew of 134, she was armed with three 9-inch Dahlgren SBs, one 10-inch Dahlgren SB, one 32-pdr., and a 12-pdr. howitzer (ORN, II, 1: 79; Silverstone, *loc. cit.*).

16. The 524-ton ram *Sumter* was lost by Confederate CO Montgomery during the Battle of Memphis. Reconditioned, the side-wheeler had just joined Davis' contingent. Unarmed, she was 182 feet long, with a 28.4-foot beam. (ORN, II, 1: 216; Silverstone, *op. cit.,* 163).

17. ORN, I, 19: 39–40, 44, 56, 71, 132, 705; Brown, *op. cit.,* 575–576; William Y. Dixon, Diary, July 15, 1862, William Y. Dixon Diary, Louisiana and Lower Mississippi Valley Collections, Louisiana State University Library, Baton Rouge; *Chicago Daily Tribune,* July 23, 1862; *Grenada Appeal,* July 16, 23, 1862; *Philadelphia Inquirer,* July 22, 25, 1862; *New York Herald,* July 25, 1862; *New Orleans Daily Delta,* July 22, 1862; *Jackson Mississippian,* July 17, 1862; *Columbus (GA) Daily Enquirer,* July 23, 1862; Gift, *loc. cit.;* Browne, *op. cit.,* 217–219; Read, *op. cit.,* 354; Walke, *op. cit.,* 309–311; Coleman and Stevens, *op. cit.,* 86–88; Coombe, *loc. cit.;* Carter, *op. cit.,* 70–71; Barnhart, *loc. cit.;* Flynt, *op. cit.,* 119–120; Carson, *loc. cit.;* Davis, *op. cit.,* 263; Milligan, *Gunboats Down the Mississippi, op. cit.,* 84–85; Slagle, *op. cit.,* 266–267; Hearn, *Admiral David Glasgow Farragut, loc. cit.;* Hearn, *Ellet's Brigade, op. cit.,* 52; Callender, *loc. cit.;* Harriet Castlen, *Hope Bids Me Onward* (Savannah, GA: Chatham, 1945), 67–68;Charles B. Boynton, *History of the Navy During the Rebellion,* 2 vols. (New York: D. Appleton, 1867–1868), II, 246; Smith, *The Timberclads,* 354–355; Getchell, *op. cit.,* 66–67; Branch, *loc. cit.;* Still, *Iron Afloat,* 68–69; Musicant, *op. cit.,* 250–252; Frank M. Bennett, *The Monitor and the Navy Under Steam* (Boston: Houghton, Mifflin, 1900), 165; Raimondo Luraghi, *A History of the Confederate Navy* (Annapolis: Naval Institute Press, 1996), 177; Stephen R. Davis, "Workhorse of the Western Waters: The Timberclad *Tyler," Civil War Times Illustrated* 44 (February 2005), 40; Scharf, *op. cit.,* 312–315; Bromfield L. Ridley, *Battles and Sketches of the Army of Tennessee* (Mexico, MO: Missouri, 1906), 489. Paymaster Coleman of the *Tyler,* along with many others in the years since, paid high tribute to the *Arkansas,* frankly stating that there was "no pluckier exploit in the war" (Coleman and Stevens, *op. cit.,* 88–89).

Eight: Morning (Part II), July 15, 1862: Running the Gauntlet

1. U.S. Navy Department, *Official Records of the Union and Confederate Navies in the War of the Rebellion,* 31 vols. (Washington, D.C.: GPO, 1894–1922), Series I, Vol. 19: 39–40, 44, 56, 68, 71, 132, 705 (cited hereafter as ORN, followed by a comma, the series number in Roman numerals, a comma, the volume number in Arabic, a colon, and the page in Arabic); U.S. War Department, *The War of the Rebellion: A Compilation of the Official Records of the Union and Confederate Armies,* 128 vols. (Washington, D.C.: GPO, 1880–1901), Series I, Vol. 15: 31–32 (cited hereafter as OR, followed by a comma, the series number in Roman numerals, a comma, the volume number in Arabic, any part number in Arabic, a colon, and the page in Arabic); Isaac Newton Brown, "The Confederate Gun-Boat *Arkansas," Battles and Leaders of the Civil War,* ed. Robert V. Johnson and Clarence C. Buell, 4 vols. (New York: Century, 1884–1887, repr., Thomas Yoseloff, 1956), III, 575–576; James Russell Soley, "Naval Operations in the Vicksburg Campaign," B&L, III, 554–555; *Jackson Mississippian,* July 17, 1862; *Columbus (GA) Daily Enquirer,* July 23, 1862; *Brooklyn Daily Eagle,* July 24, 1862; *Grenada Appeal,* July 16, 23, 1862; *Philadelphia Inquirer,* July 22, 25, 1862; *New York Herald,* July 25, 1862; *Chicago Daily Tribune,* July 22–23, 1862; *New Orleans Daily Delta,* July 22, 1862; *Vicksburg Evening Post,* July 1, 1961; George W. Gift, "The Story of the *Arkansas," Southern Historical Society Papers* 8 (1884), 115–116; Junius Henri Browne, *Four Years in Secessia: Adventures Within and Be-*

yond the Union Lines (Hartford, CT: O.D. Case, 1865), 217–219; Charles W. Read, "Reminiscences of the Confederate States Navy," *Southern Historical Society Papers* 1 (May 1876), 354; Henry Walke, *Naval Scenes and Reminiscences of the Civil War in the United States on the Southern and Western Waters During the Years 1861, 1862 and 1863, with the History of That Period Compared and Corrected from Authentic Sources* (New York: F.R. Reed, 1877), 309–311; Silas B. Coleman and Paul Stevens, "A July Morning with the Rebel Ram *Arkansas*," *U.S. Naval Institute Proceedings* 88 (July 1962), 86–88; Charles M. Getchell, Jr. "Defender of Inland Waters: The Military Career of Isaac Newton Brown, Commander, Confederate States Navy, 1861–1865" (master's thesis, University of Mississippi, 1978), 61–66; David Dixon Porter, *Naval History of the Civil War* (New York: Sherman, 1886; repr., Secaucus, NJ: Castle, 1984), 249; Jack D. Coombe, *Thunder Along the Mississippi: The River Battles That Split the Confederacy* (New York: Sarpedon, 1996), 155–156; Samuel Carter III, *The Final Fortress: The Campaign for Vicksburg 1862–1863* (New York: St. Martin's, 1980), 70–71; Myron J. Smith, Jr., *The Timberclads in the Civil War: The "Lexington," "Conestoga," and "Tyler" on the Western Waters* (Jefferson, NC: McFarland, 2008), 350–356; Donald Barnhart, Jr., "Junkyard Ironclad," *Civil War Times Illustrated* 40 (May 2001), 36 David Flynt, "Run the Fleet: The Career of the C.S. Ram *Arkansas*," *The Journal of Mississippi History* 51 (May 1989), 119–120; Kevin Carson, "21 Days to Glory: The Saga of the Confederate Ram *Arkansas*," *Sea Classics* 39 (July 2006), 40; Charles H. Davis, Jr., *Life of Charles H. Davis, Rear Admiral, U.S.N.* (Boston: Houghton, Mifflin, 1899), 263; John D. Milligan, *Gunboats Down the Mississippi* (Annapolis: Naval Institute Press, 1965), 84–85; Chester G. Hearn, *Ellet's Brigade: The Strangest Outfit of All* (Baton Rouge: Louisiana State University Press, 2000), 52; Hearn, *Admiral David Glasgow Farragut: The Civil War Years* (Annapolis: Naval Institute Press, 1998), 156; Charles B. Boynton, *History of the Navy During the Rebellion*, 2 vols. (New York: D. Appleton, 1867–1868), II, 246; Jay Slagle, *Ironclad Captain: Seth Ledyard Phelps and the U.S. Navy* (Kent, OH: Kent State University Press, 1996), 261–267; Charles M. Getchell, Jr. "Defender of Inland Waters: The Military Career of Isaac Newton Brown, Commander, Confederate States Navy, 1861–1865" (master's thesis, University of Mississippi, 1978), 65–67; Mary Emerson Branch, "A Story Behind the Story of the *Arkansas* and the *Carondelet*," *Missouri Historical Review* 79 (April 1985), 324–325; William N. Still, "The History of the C.S.S. *Arkansas*" (master's thesis, University of Alabama, 1958), 58–80; Still, *Iron Afloat: The Story of Confederate Armorclads* (Nashville: Vanderbilt University Press, 1971; repr., Columbia: University of South Carolina Press, 1985), 68–69; Ivan Musicant, *Divided Waters: The Naval History of the Civil War* (New York: HarperCollins, 1995), 250–252; Alfred T. Mahan, *The Gulf and Inland Waters*, vol. 3, *The Navy in the Civil War* (New York: Scribner's, 1883), 99–100; Stephen R. Davis, "Workhorse of the Western Waters: The Timberclad *Tyler*," *Civil War Times Illustrated* 44 (February 2005), 40; J. Thomas Scharf, *History of the Confederate Navy from Its Organization to the Surrender of Its Last Vessel* (New York: Rodgers and Sherwood, 1887, repr., New York: Fairfax, 1977), 312–315; R. Thomas Campbell, *Sea Hawk of the Confederacy* (Shippensburg, PA: Burd Street, 2000), 55–56; 65–66; Campbell, *Confederate Naval Forces on Western Waters* (Jefferson, NC: McFarland, 2005), 114–119; Robert G. Hartje, *Van Dorn: The Life and Times of a Confederate General* (Nashville: Vanderbilt University Press, 1967), 201; Eliott Callender, "Career of the Confederate Ram *Arkansas*, Given before the Farragut Naval Veterans Association, Chicago," in *Speeches of a Veteran* (Chicago: Blue Sky, 1901; repr., Charleston, SC: BiblioLife, 2009), 48–51.

2. ORN, I, 19: 56, 68, 748; William Y. Dixon, Diary, July 15, 1862, William Y. Dixon Diary, Louisiana and Lower Mississippi Valley Collections, Louisiana State University Library, Baton Rouge; *Grenada Appeal*, July 16, 1862; *Chicago Daily Tribune*, July 23, 1862; *Brooklyn Daily Eagle*, July 24, 1862; *New York Herald*, July 25, 1862; *Baltimore-American*, July 25, 1862; *Vicksburg Evening Post*, July 1, 1961; Brown, *loc. cit.*; Scharf, *op. cit.*, 316, 318; Callender, *op. cit.*, 53–54; Flynt, *loc. cit.*; Smith, *op. cit.*, 356–357; Still, *Iron Afloat*, 68–70; Still, "The History of the C.S.S. *Arkansas*," 84; Gift, *loc. cit.*; Slagle, *op. cit.*, 267; Davis, *op. cit.*; Coleman and Stevens, *op. cit.*, 87, 94; L.S. Flatau, "A Great Naval Battle," *Confederate Veteran* 25 (October 1917), 458–459; Carter, *op. cit.*, 70; Hearn, *Admiral David Glasgow Farragut, op. cit.*, 156–157; Robert G. Hartje, *Van Dorn: The Life and Times of a Confederate General* (Nashville: Vanderbilt University Press, 1967), 201; Charles M. Getchell, Jr. "Defender of Inland Waters: The Military Career of Isaac Newton Brown, Commander, Confederate States Navy, 1861–1865" (master's thesis, University of Mississippi, 1978), 67; Daniel Barnhart, Jr., "Junkyard Ironclad," *Civil War Times Illustrated* 40 (May 2001), 36; Bradley S. Osbon, *Cruise of the U.S. Flagship "Hartford," 1862–1863: Being a Narrative of All Her Operations Since Going into Commission, in 1862, until Her Return to New York in 1863, from the Private Journal of William C. Holton* (New York: L.W. Paine, 1863; repr., Detroit: Gale Archival Editions, 2007), 142; John S. Jackman, *Diary of a Confederate Soldier: John S. Jackman of the Orphan Brigade*, ed. William C. Davis (Columbia: University of South Carolina Press, 1990), 49; Edward W. Bacon, *Double Duty in the Civil War: The Letters of Sailor and Soldier Edward W. Bacon*, ed. George S. Burkhardt (Carbondale: Southern Illinois University Press, 2009), 60.

3. ORN, I, 18: 132, 562; ORN, I, 19: 60, 68, 711; ORN, I, 23: 244; *Philadelphia Inquirer*, July 22, 1862; *New York Times*, July 22, 1862; *Chicago Daily Tribune*, July 23, 1862; *Jackson Mississippian*, July 17, 1862; *Grenada Appeal*, July 23, 1862; *Columbus (GA) Daily Enquirer*, July 23, 1862; *Brooklyn Daily Eagle*, July 24, 1862; *New York Herald*, July 25, 1862; Callender, *op. cit.*, 52; Milligan, *Gunboats Down the Mississippi*, 84; Brown, *loc. cit.*; Scharf, *op. cit.*, 316–319; Gift, *loc. cit.*; Frank M. Bennett, *The Monitor and the Navy Under Steam* (Boston: Houghton, Mifflin, 1900), 165; Raimondo Luraghi, *A History of the Confederate Navy* (Annapolis: Naval Institute Press, 1996), 178; Clarence E. Macartney, *Mr. Lincoln's Admirals* (New York: Funk & Wagnalls, 1956), 56; Bartholomew Diggins, "Recollections of the War Cruise of the USS *Hartford*, January–December 1862," Bartholomew Diggins Papers, 1862–1864, Manuscript Collection, New York Public Library; Osbon, *loc. cit.*; Campbell, *Sea Hawk of the Confederacy*, 64; Flatau, *op. cit.*, 459; Flynt, *op. cit.*, 121; Coleman and Stevens, *op. cit.*, 95; Still, *Iron Afloat*, 69–70; Still, "The History of the C.S.S. *Arkansas*," 85. For the record, the numbers of the Unadilla-class gunboats involved at some point in the *Arkansas* story were *Sciota*, 1; *Winona*, 2; *Kineo*, 3; *Wissachickon*, 4; *Kennebec*, 5; *Pinola*, 6; *Itasca*, 7; *Katahdin*, 8; and *Cayuga*, 9 (ORN, I, 18: 132). Pennsylvanian Crosby was appointed a midshipman in 1838, reaching the rank of lieutenant. in 1853.

Following 1861 adventures in Virginia near Fort Monroe, he commissioned the *Pinola* at Baltimore in early 1862. Later, after she returned downstream past the *Arkansas*, Crosby was transferred to the ocean blockade. Promoted to commander in 1863 and captain in 1868, he was named a commodore in 1874 and rear admiral in 1882. His last active post before voluntarily retiring the following year was command of the Asiatic Station (Lewis R. Hamersly, *Record of the Living Officers of the U.S. Navy and Marine Corps*, 6th ed. (New York: L.R. Hamersly, 1898), 11–12; *New York Times*, June 16, 1899).

4. ORN, I, 19: 68, 133, 244, 747; ORN, 23, 1: 244; Sylvester Doss to Warren D. Crandall, October 8, 1894, Civil War Collection, Missouri Historical Society; *Jackson Mississippian*, July 17, 1862; *Columbus (GA) Daily Enquirer*, July 23, 1862; *Grenada Appeal*, July 23, 1862; *Brooklyn Daily Eagle*, July 24, 1862; *New York Herald*, July 25, 1862; *Baltimore American*, July 25, 1862; Brown, *loc. cit.*; Scharf, *loc. cit.*; Gift, *op. cit.*, 117; Still, *Iron Afloat*; Still, "The History of the C.S.S. *Arkansas*," *op. cit.*, 85–86; Milligan, *Gunboats Down the Mississippi*, 85; Hearn, *Ellet's Brigade*, 52–53; Campbell, *Sea Hawk of the Confederacy*, 65. "Delta," the correspondent for the *New Orleans Daily Delta*, informed his readers — incorrectly — that the *Arkansas* had "struck the gunboat *Winona* right pelt in the boiler" (*New Orleans Daily Delta*, July 22, 1862).

5. ORN, I, 19: 56, 68, 747; *Chicago Daily Tribune*, July 23, 1862; *Brooklyn Daily Eagle*, July 24, 1862; *Baltimore-American*, July 25, 1862; *New York Times*, July 28, 1862; *Hinds County (MS) Gazette*, December 9, 1874; Vicksburg's Old Courthouse Museum, http://www.oldcourthouse.org/history.htm (accessed January 9, 2010); Getchell, *loc. cit.*; Scharf, *op. cit.*, 319–320; Slagle, *op. cit.*, 268; Diggins, *loc. cit.*; Campbell, *Sea Hawk of the Confederacy*, 64–65; Still, *Iron Afloat*,; Still, "The History of the C.S.S. *Arkansas*," 85–86; Milligan, *Gunboats Down the Mississippi*, 84–85; Flatau, *op. cit.*, 259; Brown, *loc. cit.*; Walke, *op. cit.*, 311; Lot D. Young, *Reminiscences of a Soldier of the Orphan Brigade* (Louisville, KY: Courier Journal Press, 1918), 37; Campbell, *Sea Hawk of the Confederacy*, 64–65; Adelaide Stuart Dimitry, "The Queen of the Mississippi," in *War-Time Sketches, Historical and Otherwise* (New Orleans: Louisiana Printing Co. Press, 1911), 13; Callender, *op. cit.*, 54–55.

6. The 1,043-ton ex–Confederate side-wheel cottonclad *General Bragg* was captured by Federal forces during the June Battle off Memphis and reconfigured slightly for Union service. The vessel was 208 feet long, with a beam of 32.8 feet and a 12-foot draft. Armament comprised one each 30-pdr. Parrott rifle and 32-pdr. smoothbore, plus a 23-pdr. rifled howitzer (ORN, II, 1: 91; Paul Silverstone, *Warships of the Civil War Navies* (Annapolis: Naval Institute Press, 1989), 162).

7. ORN, I, 19: 20, 22–23, 68, 133; *Chicago Daily Tribune*, July 23, 1862; *Baltimore-American*, July 25, 1862; Scharf, *op. cit.*, 320; Coleman and Stevens, *op. cit.*, 87–88; Gift, *op. cit.*, 119; Callender, *op. cit.*, 55–56; Slagle, *loc. cit.*; Read, *loc. cit.*; Porter, *loc. cit.*; Still, "The History of the C.S.S. *Arkansas*," 86. Born in Venezuela the son of the American consul, Lt. Reigart B. Lowry (1826–1880) was appointed a midshipman from Pennsylvania in 1840. Serving at sea in most of the period before the Civil War, he served as executive officer of the sloop-of-war Brooklyn during the Battle of New Orleans. Commander of the training ship *Sabine* from 1864 to 1868, during which time he was twice promoted, he became a captain in 1871. Poor health caused his retirement in 1876 (*New York Times*, November 26, 1880).

8. ORN, I, 19: 4, 68, 133; USS *Oneida* Ship's Diary, July 15, 1862, Southern Historical Collection, Wilson Library, University of North Carolina at Chapel Hill; *Chicago Daily Tribune*, July 23, 1862; Gift, *op. cit.*, 117–118; Scharf, *op. cit.*, 319–320; Flynt, *op. cit.*, 122; Bacon, *op. cit.*, 60; Brown, *loc. cit.*; Davis, *op. cit.*, 263; Slagle, *op. cit.*, 268; Campbell, *Sea Hawk of the Confederacy*, 65–66; Flatau, *loc. cit.*; Still, "The History of the C.S.S. *Arkansas*," 86–87; Getchell, *op. cit.*, 67; Tom Hall, "The Bravest Act," quoted in Gordon A. Cotton and Jeff T. Giambrone, *Vicksburg and the War* (Gretna, LA: Pelican, 2004), 30; Hearn, *Admiral David Glasgow Farragut*, 157; Luraghi, *loc. cit.*; Mahan, *Admiral Farragut*, Great Commanders (New York: D. Appleton, 1892; repr., St. Clair Shores, MI: Scholarly Press, 1970), 191; Getchell, *op. cit.*, 67–68, Dimitry, *op. cit.*, 14.

9. ORN, I, 19: 27–32; 56, 64–65, 68; ORN, I, 23: 672; William Y. Dixon, Diary, July 15, 1862, William Y. Dixon Diary, Louisiana and Lower Mississippi Valley Collections, Louisiana State University Library, Baton Rouge; Bacon, *loc. cit.*; *St. Louis Daily Missouri Republican*, July 22, 1862; *New York Times*, July 22, 1862; *Philadelphia Inquirer*, July 22, 1862; *Chicago Daily Tribune*, July 23, 1862; *Jackson Mississippian*, July 27, 1862; *Columbus (GA) Daily Enquirer*, July 23, 1862; *Brooklyn Daily Eagle*, July 24, 1862; *Baltimore-American*, July 25, 1862; Slagle, *op. cit.*, 268–269; Brown, *loc. cit.*; Davis, *op. cit.*, 263–264, 266; *New York Tribune*, July 26, 1862; Read, *loc. cit.*; Flynt, *op. cit.*, 122–123; Gift, *op. cit.*, 118–119; Callender, *op. cit.*, 55–57; Flatau, *loc. cit.*; Smith, *op. cit.*, 357; Still, "The History of the C.S.S. *Arkansas*," 87–88; Coombe, *op. cit.*, 158; Coleman and Stevens, *op. cit.*, 88–89, 95; Campbell, *Sea Hawk of the Confederacy*, 67; Martha Goodwin, "The Ram *Arkansas*," *Confederate Veteran* 18 (July 1920), 263; Getchell, *loc. cit.*; Hartje, *op. cit.*, 202; Milligan, *Gunboats Down the Mississippi*, *loc. cit.*

10. ORN, I, 19: 37–40, 44, 56, 68–71, 686, 705; Brown, *op. cit.*, 575–576; *Grenada Appeal*, July 16, 23, 1862; *St. Louis Missouri Daily Democrat*, July 22, 1862; *Cincinnati Times*, July 22, 1862; *Philadelphia Inquirer*, July 22, 25, 1862; *New York Times*, July 22, 1862; *New Orleans Daily Delta*, July 22, 1862; *Chicago Daily Tribune*, July 23, 1862; *Vicksburg Evening Post*, July 1, 1961; Gift, *loc. cit.*; Browne, *op. cit.*, 217–219; Coleman and Stevens, *op. cit.*, 86–89, 95; Coombe, *op. cit.*, 159; Carter, *op. cit.*, 70–71; Still, *Iron Afloat*, 69–71; Still, "The History of the C.S.S. *Arkansas*," *loc. cit.*; Barnhart, *loc. cit.*; Luraghi, *loc. cit.*; Carson, *loc. cit.*; Davis, *loc. cit.*; Milligan, *Gunboats Down the Mississippi*, *op. cit.*, 84–85; Alfred T. Mahan, *Admiral Farragut* (New York: D. Appleton, 1892), 191–192; Charles B. Boynton, *History of the Navy during the Rebellion*, 2 vols. (New York: D. Appleton, 1867–1868), II, 246; Branch, *loc. cit.*; Harriet Castlen, *Hope Bids Me Onward* (Savannah, GA: Chatham, 1945), 145–148; Musicant, *op. cit.*, 250–252; Scharf, *op. cit.*, 312–315; Campbell, *Confederate Naval Forces on Western Waters*, 120–135; Oliver Wood McClinton, "The Career of the Confederate States Ram *Arkansas*," *Arkansas Historical Quarterly* 7 (Winter 1948), 331. Although there was no "Thanks of Congress" for the Federal officers involved in this particular episode, the highest legislative accolade available to naval men on both sides was awarded to Lt. Isaac Brown. A joint resolution of appreciation would be sent to the daring commander by the Confederate congress on October 2. Brown had been earlier promoted to the rank of commander (ORN, I, 19: 36). Ironically, at least one Federal newspaperman trying to highly praise her captain got his name wrong, identifying him not as Brown, but as

Catesby ap Roger Jones (*Chicago Daily Tribune*, July 23, 1862).

Nine: Surviving Farragut's Charge: Night, July 15, 1862

1. U.S. Navy Department, *Official Records of the Union and Confederate Navies in the War of the Rebellion*, 31 vols. (Washington, D.C.: GPO, 1894–1922), Series I, Vol. 19: 64–65 (cited hereafter as ORN, followed by a comma, the series number in Roman numerals, a comma, the volume number in Arabic, a colon, and the page in Arabic); U.S. War Department, *The War of the Rebellion: A Compilation of the Official Records of the Union and Confederate Armies*, 128 vols. (Washington, D.C.: GPO, 1880–1901), Series I, Vol. 15: 16, 768, 779 (cited hereafter as OR, followed by a comma, the series number in Roman numerals, a comma, the volume number in Arabic, any part number in Arabic, a colon, and the page in Arabic); William Y. Dixon, *Diary*, July 15, 1862, *William Y. Dixon Diary*, Louisiana and Lower Mississippi Valley Collections, Louisiana State University Library, Baton Rouge; John S. Jackman, *Diary of a Confederate Soldier: John S. Jackman of the Orphan Brigade*, ed. William C. Davis (Columbia: University of South Carolina Press, 1990), 49; H. Grady Howell, *To Live and Die in Dixie: A History of the 3rd Mississippi Infantry, C.S.A.* (Madison, MS: Chickasaw Bayou, 1991), 143; *Jackson Mississippian*, July 16, 1862; *Mobile Advertiser and Register*, July 16, 1862; *Richmond Whig*, July 17, 1862; *Grenada Appeal*, July 16, 23, 1862; *St. Louis Missouri Daily Democrat*, July 22, 1862; *Cincinnati Times*, July 22, 1862; *Philadelphia Inquirer*, July 22, 25, 1862; *New York Herald*, July 25, 1862; *Baltimore-American*, July 25, 1862; *New Orleans Daily Delta*, July 22, 1862; Isaac Newton Brown, "The Confederate Gun-Boat Arkansas," in *Battles and Leaders of the Civil War*, ed. Robert V. Johnson and Clarence C. Buell, 4 vols. (New York: Century, 1884–1887, repr., Thomas Yoseloff, 1956), III, 576; Eliott Callender, "Career of the Confederate Ram *Arkansas*, Given before the Farragut Naval Veterans Association, Chicago," in *Speeches of a Veteran* (Chicago: Blue Sky, 1901; repr., Charleston, SC: BiblioLife, 2009), 57; Edward G. Butler to Mary Susan Ker, July 20, 1862, Mary Susan Ker Papers, Southern Historical Collection, Wilson Library, University of North Carolina at Chapel Hill; George W. Gift, "The Story of the *Arkansas*," *Southern Historical Society Papers* 8 (1884), 163; Charles W. Read, "Reminiscences of the Confederate States Navy," *Southern Historical Society Papers* 1 (May 1876), 354–355; William N. Still, "The History of the C.S.S. *Arkansas*" (master's thesis, University of Alabama, 1958), 90–91; Still, *Iron Afloat: The Story of Confederate Armorclads* (Nashville: Vanderbilt University Press, 1971; repr., Columbia: University of South Carolina Press, 1985), 71; Robert G. Hartje, *Van Dorn: The Life and Times of a Confederate General* (Nashville: Vanderbilt University Press, 1967), 202–203; Arthur B. Carter, *The Tarnished Cavalier: Major General Earl Van Dorn* (Knoxville: University of Tennessee Press, 1999), 78; J. Thomas Scharf, *History of the Confederate Navy from Its Organization to the Surrender of Its Last Vessel* (New York: Rodgers and Sherwood, 1887, repr., New York: Fairfax, 1977), 321; Clement Sulivane, "The Arkansas at Vicksburg in 1862," *Confederate Veteran* 25 (November 1917), 490; Henry Walke, *Naval Scenes and Reminiscences of the Civil War in the United States on the Southern and Western Waters During the Years 1861, 1862 and 1863, with the History of That Period Compared and Corrected from Authentic Sources* (New York: F.R. Reed, 1877), 314; Raimondo Luraghi, *A History of the Confederate Navy* (Annapolis: Naval Institute Press, 1996), 178; R. Thomas Campbell, *Sea Hawk of the Confederacy* (Shippensburg, PA: Burd Street, 2000), 67–68; Martha Goodwin, "The Ram *Arkansas*," *Confederate Veteran* 18 (July 1920), 263; L.S. Flatau, "A Great Naval Battle," *Confederate Veteran* 25 (October 1917), 459; James P. Duffy, *Lincoln's Admiral: The Civil War Campaigns of David Farragut* (New York: Castle, 1997), 146. Capt. Sulivane (1838–1920) was a native of Port Gibson, MS, who became a Maryland attorney, practicing there before and after the war ("Capt. Clement Sulivane," Find a Grave, http://www.findagrave.com/cgi-bin/fg.cgi?page=gr&GSln=s&GSmid=46536634&GRid=12872741& [accessed January 20, 2010]). Interestingly, Van Dorn's two July 15 telegraphic reports to Davis and Mallory were immediately sent over to the *Richmond Daily Dispatch*, as well as to Edward Pollard, editor of the *Richmond Examiner*, plus other local newspapers. They were also published in other leading newspapers, such as the *Charleston Daily Courier*. Two days later they appeared in print, virtually unchanged. When he obtained covert copies, perhaps later in the day, U.S. Navy Secretary Gideon Welles was not happy to read of how the 1,200-ton Rebel boat had "attacked the enemy's fleet with impetuous gallantry." A prewar Connecticut newspaperman, he may well have blushed in anger when reading the story-ending tweaking message in the *Dispatch*: "The victory will inspire the people of Vicksburg with renewed confidence and zeal and we hope it will be followed by still more powerful blows. Lessons like this will teach the enemy that his gunboats may be driven from Southern water" (*Richmond Daily Dispatch*, July 17, 1862; *Richmond Daily Examiner*, July 17, 1862; *Charleston (SC) Daily Courier*).

2. New Yorker William B. Renshaw (1816–1863) entered the USN as a midshipman in 1831. Proceeding up through the ranks, he commissioned the gunboat *Westfield* in January 1862, the only vessel he would ever command. Following his sojourn up the Mississippi, he was charged by Rear Adm. Farragut with the blockade of Galveston, TX. When the *Westfield* ran aground on January 1, 1863, he determined to destroy it, but was killed in the premature explosion (Parke Godwin, *The Cyclopedia of Biography: A Record of the Lives of Eminent Persons*, new ed. (New York: G.P. Putnam's Sons, 1878), 262; David G. McComb, *Galveston: A History* (Austin: University of Texas Press, 1986), 77; Edward T. Cotham, Jr., *Battle on the Bay: The Civil War Struggle for Galveston* (Austin: University of Texas Press, 1998), 128–129).

3. Built as a side-wheel New York ferryboat for Cornelius Vanderbilt in 1861, the 822-ton *Westfield* was purchased into Federal service in November, converted into a gunboat at a cost of $27,500, and commissioned in January 1862. With a length of 215 feet, a 35-foot beam, and a draft of 13.6 feet, the craft was armed with one 100-pdr. Parrott rifle, one 9-inch Dahlgren SB, and four 8-inch Dahlgren SBs (ORN, II, 1: 238; Paul Silverstone, *Warships of the Civil War Navies* (Annapolis: Naval Institute Press, 1989), 102).

4. ORN, I, 19: 3, 7, 28–30, 56–57, 69–70, 72–74 133–134, 712, 747–748; ORN, I, 23: 672; OR, I, 15: 31, 1122–1124; *Chicago Daily Tribune*, July 23, 1862; *New York Herald*, July 23, 25, 1862; *Jackson Mississippian*, July 17, 1862; *Columbus (GA) Daily Enquirer*, July 23, 1862; *Baltimore-American*, July 25, 1862; *Brooklyn Daily Eagle*, July 30, 1862; Brown, *op. cit.*, 576–577; Read, *loc. cit.*; Scharf,

op. cit., 321, Still, "The History of the C.S.S. *Arkansas,*" 91–92, 97; Still, *Iron Afloat,* 71–72; Silas B. Coleman and Paul Stevens, "A July Morning with the Rebel Ram *Arkansas," U.S. Naval Institute Proceedings* 88 (July 1962), 95; Edward W. Bacon, *Double Duty in the Civil War: The Letters of Sailor and Soldier Edward W. Bacon,* ed. George S. Burkhardt (Carbondale: Southern Illinois University Press, 2009), 60; W.J. McMurray, *History of the Twentieth Tennessee Volunteer Infantry, C.S.A.* (Nashville: Publication Committee, 1904), 216; Loyall Farragut, *Life and Letters of Admiral D.G. Farragut* (New York: D. Appleton, 1879), 287; Daniel Barnhart, Jr., "Junkyard Ironclad," *Civil War Times Illustrated* 40 (May 2001), 37; Charles M. Getchell, Jr., "Defender of Inland Waters: The Military Career of Isaac Newton Brown, Commander, Confederate States Navy, 1861–1865" (master's thesis, University of Mississippi, 1978), 68; Lot D. Young, *Reminiscences of a Soldier of the Orphan Brigade* (Louisville, KY: Courier Journal Press, 1918), 37–38; Myron J. Smith, Jr., *The Timberclads in the Civil War: The "Lexington," "Conestoga," and "Tyler" on the Western Waters* (Jefferson, NC: McFarland, 2008), 358; Chester G. Hearn, *Admiral David Glasgow Farragut: The Civil War Years* (Annapolis: Naval Institute Press, 1998), 158; Charles H. Davis, Jr., *Life of Charles H. Davis, Rear Admiral, U.S.N.* (Boston: Houghton, Mifflin, 1899), 264; Jay Slagle, *Ironclad Captain: Seth Ledyard Phelps and the U.S. Navy* (Kent, OH: Kent State University Press, 1996), 271–272; Dunbar Roland, *The Official and Statistical Register of the State of Mississippi* (Nashville: Brandon, 1908), 868–869; "The Orphan Brigade at Vicksburg in 1862," First Kentucky "Orphan" Brigade: History, Data, Resources, Other Features, http://www.rootsweb.ancestry.com/~orphanhm/vicksburg.htm (accessed June 25, 2009); Carolyn Elizabeth Whitcomb, *History of the Second Massachusetts Battery (Nims' Battery) of Light Artillery, 1861–1865* (Concord, NH: Rumford, 1912), 30–32; "Pettus Flying Artillery," in Dunbar Roland, *Military History of Mississippi, 1803–1898* (Spartanburg, SC: Reprint Company, 1988), 482–484.

5. It is unknown if these range lights were simply open bonfires set at different heights or employed lanterns. Recently, the term "range light" was defined as "lights that are displayed in pairs to guide ships through a narrow channel. The rear range light will be the taller of the two, with the front range light often at water's edge. When the ship is in the channel, the lights will be in alignment" (Hillsboro Lighthouse Preservation Society, Glossary of Lighthouse Terms, http://www.hillsborolighthouse.org/glossary.html (accessed January 5, 2010).

6. Sailors North and South enjoyed a number of things in common, including the official time of day, which was divided into watches: Noon to 4:00 P.M.; afternoon watch 4:00 P.M. to 6:00 P.M.; first dogwatch 6:00 P.M. to 8:00 P.M.; second dogwatch 8:00 P.M. to midnight; first night watch midnight to 4:00 A.M.; middle watch or mid watch 4:00 to 8:00 A.M.; morning watch 8:00 A.M. to noon; Forenoon watch "dogwatch," *Nautical Terms and Phrases: Their Meaning and Origin,* http://www.history.navy.mil/trivia/trivia03.htm (accessed January 12, 2010).

7. Commander of the unit since its inception as the mortar boat flotilla attached to the Western Flotilla, Capt. Maynadier, a native of Virginia, returned east, to the Army of the Potomac, in the fall of 1862. Breveted a major general, he would command Fort Laramie after the war (Mark M. Boatner III, *The Civil War Dictionary* (New York: David McKay, 1959), 521). There appears to be little if any information on Capt. Pike. Each of Maynadier's mortarboats was supposed to have a crew of 15, many of whom were Mississippi riverboat men who knew the currents (Charles Carleton Coffin, *My Days and Nights on the Battlefield,* 2nd ed. (Boston: Ticknor and Fields, 1864), 249).

8. ORN, I, 19: 3, 8, 57, 133, 712, 748; ORN, I, 23: 672, 681; OR, I, 15: 33; *Brooklyn Daily Eagle,* July 24, 1862; *Mobile Evening News,* July 24, 1862; Gift, *op. cit.,* 160; Still, "The History of the C.S.S. *Arkansas,*" 97–99; Still, *Iron Afloat,* 72; Read, *op. cit.,* 355; Callender, *op. cit.,* 58; Campbell, *Sea Hawk of the Confederacy,* 68; Slagle, *loc. cit.*; Hearn, *Admiral David Glasgow Farragut*; Bradley S. Osbon, *Cruise of the U.S. Flagship "Hartford," 1862–1863: Being a Narrative of All Her Operations Since Going into Commission, in 1862, until Her Return to New York in 1863, from the Private Journal of William C. Holton* (New York: L.W. Paine, 1863; repr., Detroit: Gale Archival, 2007), 142.

9. ORN, I, 19: 8–9, 20–27, 56, 69–70, 72, 134, 705–706, 712–713, 748; ORN, I, 23: 681; I.E. Fiske to James H. Comstock, July 24, 1862, John H. Comstock Papers, Southern Historical Society Collection, Wilson Library, University of North Carolina at Chapel Hill; USS *Oneida* Ship's Diary, July 15, 1862, Southern Historical Collection, Wilson Library, University of North Carolina at Chapel Hill; Isaac Walker to Holly Walker, July 20, 1862, in *The Walker Family of Mississippi, Louisiana, and Texas: A Biographical and Historical Genealogy,* comp. Dorothy Lyons Sutphin (Baytown, TX: 1970), 100; Bacon, *op. cit.,* 61, 64; Jackman, *op. cit.,* 49–50; *Chicago Daily Tribune,* July 22, 1862; *Brooklyn Daily Eagle,* July 24, 1862; *Baltimore-American,* July 25, 1862; Brown, *op. cit.,* 577; Gift, *op. cit.,* 161–165; Read, *op. cit.,* 354–356; Osbon, *loc. cit.*; Thomas R. Campbell, *Confederate Naval Forces on Western Waters* (Jefferson, NC: McFarland, 2005), 129–132; Hearn, *Admiral David Glasgow Farragut, op. cit.,* 158–159; Still, "The History of the C.S.S. *Arkansas,*" 99–101; Charles L. Lewis, *David Glasgow Farragut,* 2 vols. (Annapolis: Naval Institute Press, 1941–1943), II, 113; Alfred T. Mahan, *Admiral Farragut* (New York: D. Appleton, 1892), 192; Farragut, *Life and Letters, loc. cit.*; Getchell, *op. cit.,* 75; Frank M. Bennett, *The Monitor and the Navy Under Steam* (Boston: Houghton, Mifflin, 1900), 165; Milligan, *Gunboats Down the Mississippi,* 86; Slagle, *op. cit.,* 272–273; Tom Hall, "The Bravest Act," quoted in *Vicksburg and the War,* by Gordon A. Cotton and Jeff T. Giambrone (Gretna, LA: Pelican, 2004), 30; Coleman and Stevens, *op. cit.,* 95. By the time these inquiries reached Mathews his fellow Kentucky cannoneers had cleared up the matter of the passwords and had returned to their billets. Needless to say, none were too happy to learn, following what they called "our aquatic expedition," of the mistaken charges. When Mathews explained, the whole thing was dropped. It is unclear, but the six volunteer firemen who had gone aboard with Mathews most likely remained (OR, I, 15: 1123–1124). Who can say if his meeting with Brown convinced Breckenridge to try his hand as a CSN midshipman. In any event, after the war, he served five terms in the U.S. Congress (from Arkansas) in the 1880s and as minister to Russia, 1894–1897 (James Duane Bolin, "Clifton Rodes Breckenridge: 'The Little Arkansas Giant,'" *Arkansas Historical Quarterly* 53 (Winter 1994), 407–427).

Ten: *Arkansas* vs. *Essex*, Round One: July 16–22, 1862

1. Gideon Welles, *Diary of Gideon Welles, Secretary of the Navy Under Lincoln and Johnson*, ed. John T. Morse, Jr., 3 vols. (Boston: Houghton, Mifflin, 1911; repr., New York: W.W. Norton, 1960.), I: 72; Chester G. Hearn, *Admiral David Glasgow Farragut: The Civil War Years* (Annapolis: Naval Institute Press, 1998), 157–159; Thomas R. Campbell, *Confederate Naval Forces on Western Waters* (Jefferson, NC: McFarland, 2005), 129–132; Eliott Callender, "Career of the Confederate Ram *Arkansas*, Given before the Farragut Naval Veterans Association, Chicago," in *Speeches of a Veteran* (Chicago: Blue Sky, 1901; repr., Charleston, SC: BiblioLife, 2009), 49–58; Charles M. Getchell, Jr., "Defender of Inland Waters: The Military Career of Isaac Newton Brown, Commander, Confederate States Navy, 1861–1865" (master's thesis, University of Mississippi, 1978), 71. Henry Walke, captain of the *Carondelet* and an old Brown messmate, was, in fact, quite complimentary of Brown and his achievement. "Our navy officers may well admire the valor of their quondam friend and comrade, Captain I.N. Brown," he wrote in his memoirs (Henry Walke, *Naval Scenes and Reminiscences of the Civil War in the United States on the Southern and Western Waters During the Years 1861, 1862 and 1863, with the History of That Period Compared and Corrected from Authentic Sources* (New York: F.R. Reed, 1877), 321).

2. U.S. Navy Department, *Official Records of the Union and Confederate Navies in the War of the Rebellion*, 31 vols. (Washington, D.C.: GPO, 1894–1922), Series I, Vol. 19: 10, 43 (cited hereafter as ORN, followed by a comma, the series number in Roman numerals, a comma, the volume number in Arabic, a colon, and the page in Arabic); John S. Jackman, *Diary of a Confederate Soldier: John S. Jackman of the Orphan Brigade*, ed. William C. Davis (Columbia: University of South Carolina Press, 1990), 50; *St. Louis Daily Missouri Republican*, July 22, 1862; *Chicago Daily Tribune*, July 23, 1862; *Brooklyn Daily Eagle*, July 24, 1862; *Baltimore-American*, July 25, 1862; Walke, *op. cit.*, 314–315; David Flynt, "Run the Fleet: The Career of the C.S. Ram *Arkansas*," *The Journal of Mississippi History* 51 (May 1989), 125.

3. Henry Erben entered the Navy as a midshipman in 1848. Following his Civil War assignment aboard the *Sumter*, he gave distinguished service commanding the Mississippi River ironclad *St. Louis* and skippering the *Pinola* in the Gulf of Mexico, and with the naval howitzer battery which served with the U.S. Army during the Antietam campaign. He retired as a rear admiral in1894 but returned to duty during the Spanish-American War, commanding the Patrol Fleet which guarded the coast of the United States from Galveston to Bar Harbor (William B. Cogar, *Dictionary of Admirals of the U.S. Navy*, 2 vols. (Annapolis: Naval Institute Press, 1989), I, 56–57).

4. ORN, I, 19: 4, 8–12, 14–15, 57. 134, 706, 713, 749; ORN, I, 23: 681; USS *Oneida* Ship's Diary, July 17, 1862, Southern Historical Collection, Wilson Library, University of North Carolina at Chapel Hill; U.S. War Department, *The War of the Rebellion: A Compilation of the Official Records of the Union and Confederate Armies*, 128 vols. (Washington, D.C.: GPO, 1880–1901), Series I, Vol. 15: 33 (cited hereafter as OR, followed by a comma, the series number in Roman numerals, a comma, the volume number in Arabic, any part number in Arabic, a colon, and the page in Arabic); George Wright to this author, May 10, 2010; *Harper's Weekly*, September 6, 1862; Charles W. Read, "Reminiscences of the Confederate States Navy," *Southern Historical Society Papers* 1 (May 1876), 356–357; Callender, *op. cit.*, 59; Charles Lee Lewis, *David Glasgow Farragut*, 2 vols. (Annapolis: Naval Institute Press, 1941–1943), II, 114–115; Silas B. Coleman and Paul Stevens, "A July Morning with the Rebel Ram *Arkansas*," *U.S. Naval Institute Proceedings* 88 (July 1962), 96; Robert S. Huffstot, "The Brief, Glorious Career of the C.S.S. *Arkansas*," *Civil War Times Illustrated* 7 (April 1968), 25; Hearn, *Admiral David Glasgow Farragut, op. cit.*, 159–160, 199; Charles H. Davis, Jr., *Life of Charles H. Davis, Rear Admiral, U.S.N.* (Boston: Houghton, Mifflin, 1899), 265; Jay Slagle, *Ironclad Captain: Seth Ledyard Phelps and the U.S. Navy* (Kent, OH: Kent State University Press, 1996), p 274; Flynt, *loc. cit.*; R. Thomas Campbell, *Sea Hawk of the Confederacy* (Shippensburg, PA: Burd Street, 2000), 69; J. Thomas Scharf, *History of the Confederate Navy from Its Organization to the Surrender of Its Last Vessel* (New York: Rodgers and Sherwood, 1887, repr., New York: Fairfax, 1977), 326–327; Edwards, Mississippi, "The History of Edwards," Town of Edwards, Mississippi, http://www.townofedwards.com/history.htm (accessed January 30, 2010); William N. Still, "The History of the C.S.S. *Arkansas*" (master's thesis, University of Alabama, 1958), 105; Eugene B. Canfield, *Civil War Naval Ordnance* (Washington, D.C.: Naval History Division, U.S. Navy Department, 1969), 21; ORN, I, 23:104, 280; *St. Louis Missouri Democrat*, February 9, 1862; Scott K. Williams, "St Louis' Ships of Iron: The Ironclads and Monitors of Carondelet (St. Louis), Missouri," Missouri Civil War Museum Home Page, http://www.moissouricivilwarmuseum.org/1ironclads.htm (July 12, 2005). Although these mortar boats would not in any way prove decisive in operation, they were a topic of concern to President Lincoln, whom, it was recorded, paid attention to "the mortar business" (Richard West, Jr., "Lincoln's Hand in Naval Matters," *Civil War History* 4 (June 1958), 181). Washington, MO, artist Gary R. Lucy has posted an outstanding detailed rendering of mortar action in his painting, *The Battle of Island No. 10, 1862*, which was available July 12, 2005, on his home page: http://www.garylucy.com/island.html. Also, on the morning of July 18, Gideon Welles sent RAdm. Farragut permission to "go down river at discretion." The message would be received five days later (ORN, I, 19: 19).

5. ORN, I, 19: 15–16, 44, 134, 706, 713–714, 749; ORN, I, 23: 672, 681; *Mobile Evening News*, July 25, 1862; Read, *op. cit.*, 356–358; Isaac Newton Brown, "The Confederate Gun-Boat *Arkansas*," in *Battles and Leaders of the Civil War*, ed. Robert V. Johnson and Clarence C. Buell, 4 vols. (New York: Century, 1884–1887, repr., Thomas Yoseloff, 1956), III, 577–578; Davis, *op. cit.*, 265–266; George W. Gift, "The Story of the *Arkansas*," *Southern Historical Society Papers* 8 (1884), 168; Read, *op. cit.*, 358; Hearn, *Admiral David Glasgow Farragut*, 160–161; Kate Stone, *Brokenburn: The Journal of Kate Stone, 1861–1868*, ed. John Q. Anderson (Baton Rouge: Louisiana State University Press, 1955; repr., 1995), 133; Thomas Williams, "Letters of General Thomas Williams, 1862," *American Historical Review* 14 (January 1909), 324; Oliver Wood McClinton, "The Career of the Confederate States Ram *Arkansas*," *Arkansas Historical Quarterly* 7 (Winter 1948), 331–332; Hearn, *Ellet's Brigade: The Strangest Outfit of All* (Baton Rouge: Louisiana State University Press, 2000), 54; Still, "The History of the C.S.S. *Arkansas*," 101–102, 104–105. The July 22 attack by the *Essex* and *Queen of the West* prevented Van Dorn from sending his men that day. Unfortunately, however, the

manpower situation did not improve during the next week. As a result of several telegrams from Cmdr. Brown, Navy Secretary Stephen R. Mallory mentioned the matter to President Jefferson Davis. The chief executive, going around Van Dorn, asked John J. Pettus, the governor of Mississippi, for help in recruiting crewmen. That leader agreed, replying that "Captain Brown shall have his crew." It is unlikely that large numbers of men inspired by the Pettus appeal reached the *Arkansas* before she steamed to Baton Rouge (ORN, I, 19: 72; ORN, I, 23: 702; Still, "The History of the C.S.S. *Arkansas*," 103).

6. ORN, I, 19: 16–17, 37, 44, 58, 62, 714; ORN, I, 23: 681; *Memphis Bulletin*, July 29, 1862 quoted in *Chicago Daily Tribune*, August 4, 1862; Hearn, *Ellet's Brigade*, 54–55; Hearn, *Admiral David Glasgow Farragut*, 161; Slagle, *op. cit.*, 275; Dana M. Wegner, "Commodore William D. 'Dirty Bill' Porter," *U.S. Naval Institute Proceedings* 103 (February 1977), 46–47; Still, "The History of the C.S.S. *Arkansas*," 105–107; Still, *Iron Afloat: The Story of Confederate Armorclads* (Nashville: Vanderbilt University Press, 1971; repr., Columbia: University of South Carolina Press, 1985), 75; Flynt, *op. cit.*, 126; John D. Milligan, *Gunboats Down the Mississippi* (Annapolis: Naval Institute Press, 1965), 86–87; Huffstot, *op. cit.*, 26.

7. ORN, I, 19: 17–18, 43, 45–49, 50, 60–63, 69–71, 74, 96–97, 134–135, 320, 706, 714–717, 749; ORN, I, 23: 672, 681; OR, I, 15: 38–39; I.E. Fiske to James H. Comstock, July 24, 1862, John H. Comstock Papers, Southern Historical Society Collection, Wilson Library, University of North Carolina at Chapel Hill; Jackman, *op. cit.*, 51; *Philadelphia Press*, July 28, 1862; *New York Times*, July 31, August 4, August 6, 1862; *Chicago Times*, July 31, August 4, 1862; *Memphis Bulletin*, July 29, 1862, quoted in *Chicago Daily Tribune*, August 4, 1862; *New York Tribune*, July 31, August 4, 1862; *Brooklyn Daily Eagle*, August 2, 15, 1862; Coleman and Stevens, *loc. cit.*; Henry K. Stevens to Sarah F. Stevens, July 27, 1862, quoted in Cythia E. Moseley, "The Naval Career of Henry Kennedy Stevens as Revealed by His Letters, 1839–1863" (master's thesis, University of North Carolina, 1951), 311; Wegner, "Commodore William D. 'Dirty Bill' Porter," 47–48; Still, "The History of the C.S.S. *Arkansas*," 105–111; Still, *Iron Afloat*, 74–75; Milligan, *op. cit.*, 87–89; Flynt, *op. cit.*, 126–129; Spencer Kellogg Brown, "Letter from Spencer Kellogg Brown to Levi Cozzens, 1862," in George G. Smith, ed., *Spencer Kellogg Brown: His Life in Kansas and His Death as a Spy, 1842–1863, as Disclosed in His Diary* (New York: D. Appleton, 1903), 380; Scharf, *op. cit.*, 328–332; Gordon A. Cotton and Jeff T. Giambrone, *Vicksburg and the War* (Gretna, LA: Pelican, 2004), 26–27; Warren D. Crandall and Isaac D. Newell, *History of the Ram Fleet and the Mississippi Marine Brigade* (St. Louis, MO: Buschart Brothers, 1907), 104–105; Edward Porter Thompson, *History of the First Kentucky Brigade* (Cincinnati: Caxton, 1868), 122; Bradley S. Osbon, *Cruise of the U.S. Flagship Hartford, 1862–1863: Being a Narrative of All Her Operations Since Going into Commission, in 1862, until Her Return to New York in 1863, from the Private Journal of William C. Holton* (New York: L.W. Paine, 1863; repr., Detroit: Gale Archival Editions, 2007), 142; Read, *op. cit.*, 357–358; Gift, *op. cit.*, 168–169; Brown, *op. cit.*, 577–578; Davis, *op. cit.*, 266; Hearn, *Ellet's Brigade*, 55–58; Hearn, *Admiral David Glasgow Farragut*, 160–161, 163; Clement Sulivane, "The *Arkansas* at Vicksburg in 1862," *Confederate Veteran* 25 (November 1917), 490–491; Tom Ezell, "Battle Flag of C.S.S. *Arkansas* Found, Placed on Display," in *Capitol Guards: General R.C. Newton Camp, Sons of Confederate Veterans Newsletter*, February 2001, quoted in Civil War Navies Message Board, October 14, 2002, http://history-sites.com/cgi-bin/bbs53x/arcwmb/arch_config.pl?noframes;read=2233 (accessed March 3, 2010); "Flag from the C.S.S. *Arkansas*, August 1862," in *Civil War Naval Flag Display, Welcome to Port Columbus, Georgia: National Civil War Naval Museum*, http://www.portcolumbus.org/exhibits/flagcollection.php (accessed March 3, 2010); Glenn Dedmondt, *The Flags of Civil War Arkansas* (Gretna, LA: Pelican, 2009), 153–154. A number of responses on the message board branded the Skelton episode a fabrication, citing the size and type of flag and numerous other technicalities. Whether true or not, there is no doubt that Skelton was aboard the *Queen* (ORN, I, 19: 47). Maj. Balfour, who fought in Italy as a member of Garibaldi's English Legion, was married to Jean Baptiste Rene Degas, younger sister of the French impressionist painter Edgar Degas. He was killed on October 5, 1862, in the Battle of Davis Bridge, near Corinth, MS (*New York Times*, November 30, 1862; Bob Franks, "The Balfour Family," Issaquena Genealogy and History Project, 2004, http://www.rootsweb.ancestry.com/~msissaq2/balfour.html [accessed February 12, 2010]). The *Tyler*, *Carondelet*, and *Queen of the West* were all sent north for repairs; the ironclad would be out of action until November. For a full history of the *Carondelet*, see my treatment of it, *The USS "Carondelet": A Civil War Ironclad on Western Waters* (Jefferson, NC: McFarland, 2010). Virginia weather reports were known to Western campaigners via the newspapers ("The 17th S.C. Volunteer Infantry at Second Manassas," W.C. Lathan home page http://www.wclathan.com/civil_war/Second_Manassas/17th_at_Second_Manassas.htm [February 22, 2010]).

8. ORN, I, 19: 17–19, 52–55, 62, 75, 81, 96–97, 707, 750; OR, I, 15: 16; Jackman, *op. cit.*, 51–52; Edward W. Bacon, *Double Duty in the Civil War: The Letters of Sailor and Soldier Edward W. Bacon*, ed. George S. Burkhardt. (Carbondale: Southern Illinois University Press, 2009), 64–66; *Memphis Bulletin*, July 29, 1862, quoted in *Chicago Daily Tribune*, August 4, 1862; Davis, *op. cit.*, 266–273; Osbon, *op. cit.*, 143; Lewis, *op. cit.*, 121; Read, *op. cit.*, 358; Still, "The History of the C.S.S. *Arkansas*," 112–115; Spencer Kellogg Brown, "Letter from Spencer Kellogg Brown to Levi Cozzens, 1862," *loc. cit.*; Edwin C. Bearss, *Rebel Victory at Vicksburg* (Little Rock: Vicksburg Civil War Centennial Commemorative Commission, 1963), 281; Michael B. Ballard, *Vicksburg: The Campaign That Opened the Mississippi* (Chapel Hill: University of North Carolina Press, 2004), 62; Read, *op. cit.*, 358; Tom Ezell, "Battle Flag of C.S.S. *Arkansas* Found, Placed on Display," in *Capitol Guards: General R C. Newton Camp, Sons of Confederate Veterans Newsletter*, February 2001, quoted in Civil War Navies Message Board, October 14, 2002, http://history-sites.com/cgi-bin/bbs53x/arcwmb/arch_config.pl?noframes;read=2233 (accessed March 3, 2010); "Flag from the C.S.S. *Arkansas*, August 1862," in "Civil War Naval Flag Display, Welcome to Port Columbus, Georgia": National Civil War Naval Museum, http://www.portcolumbus.org/exhibits/flagcollection.php (accessed March 3, 2010). There have been numerous titles over the past century or so stating that the Confederate ram was the cause of the USN withdrawal. She was, as shown, a "fueling" contributor, but her role in forcing the Federals away was not the deciding one (Still, "The History of the C.S.S. *Arkansas*," 112).

Eleven: *Arkansas* vs. *Essex*, Round Two: Finale Off Baton Rouge, July 23–August 6, 1862

1. Edwin C. Bearss, *Rebel Victory at Vicksburg* (Little Rock: Vicksburg Civil War Centennial Commemorative Commission, 1963), 281; John D. Milligan, *Gunboats Down the Mississippi* (Annapolis: Naval Institute Press, 1965), 89–90; Michael B. Ballard, *Vicksburg: The Campaign That Opened the Mississippi* (Chapel Hill: University of North Carolina Press, 2004), 62; David Flynt, "Run the Fleet: The Career of the C.S. Ram *Arkansas*," *The Journal of Mississippi History,* 51 (May 1989), 129. As noted in the last footnote of the preceding chapter, there have been numerous titles over the past century or so stating that the Confederate ram was the cause of the USN withdrawal. She was, as shown, a "contributor, but her role in forcing the Federals away was not the deciding one (William N. Still, "The History of the C.S.S. *Arkansas*" (master's thesis, University of Alabama, 1958), 112.

2. U.S. Navy Department, *Official Records of the Union and Confederate Navies in the War of the Rebellion,* 31 vols. (Washington, D.C.: GPO, 1894–1922), Series I, Vol. 19: 135 (cited hereafter as ORN, followed by a comma, the series number in Roman numerals, a comma, the volume number in Arabic, a colon, and the page in Arabic); Isaac Newton Brown, "The Confederate Gun-Boat *Arkansas*," in *Battles and Leaders of the Civil War,* ed. Robert V. Johnson and Clarence C. Buell, 4 vols. (New York: Century, 1884–1887, repr., Thomas Yoseloff, 1956), III, 578; George W. Gift, "The Story of the *Arkansas*," *Southern Historical Society Papers* 8 (1884), 207; Charles W. Read, "Reminiscences of the Confederate States Navy," *Southern Historical Society Papers* 1 (May 1876), 358; Flynt, *loc. cit.*; Chester Hearn, *Ellet's Brigade: The Strangest Outfit of All* (Baton Rouge: Louisiana State University Press, 2000), 55–58; Still, "The History of the C.S.S. *Arkansas*," 118. Our timeline on the *Arkansas* officers sent to hospital was provided by acting Master's Mate John Wilson in ORN, I, 19: 134–135.

3. Initially commissioned as a letter-of-marque in May 1861, the side-wheel CSS *William H. Webb*, originally a tugboat, was converted into a wooden ram for use on the Mississippi, Red, and other tributaries. With a length of 195 feet and a beam of 31.5 feet, the vessel was armed with four 12-pdr. howitzers and was reported to be capable of a top speed of 22 knots in smooth water. Under the command of Lt. Read, she would unsuccessfully attempt a breakout from the Mississippi at the end of the war (ORN, II, 1: 271; Frederick Way, Jr., *Way's Packet Directory, 1848–1994: Passenger Steamboats of the Mississippi River System Since the Advent of Photography in Mid-Continent America* (Athens: Ohio University Press, 1983, revised ed.; Athens: Ohio University, 1994), 488).

4. Constructed at Jeffersonville, IN, in 1857, the 330-ton side-wheeler *Music* was originally a Mississippi river towboa0074 that was commissioned as a privateer in 1861. With a length of 172 feet and a beam of 29 feet, she was armed with a pair of 6-pdr. field guns. Before that year was out, she became a fleet tender at New Orleans, but following the fall of the Crescent City to the North, she fled up the Red River, her eventual fate unknown (Paul Silverstone, *Warships of the Civil War Navies* (Annapolis: Naval Institute Press, 1989), 232; Way, *op. cit.,* 334).

5. Gunboat No. 3, the *Kineo*, which Lt. Read and Gift had mistakenly identified as being above Vicksburg on July 15, was a $100,000 "90-day gunboat" of the Unadilla class, built largely of green wood at New York City in late 1861. At 158.4 feet long, with a beam of 28 feet and a 9.6-foot draft, the 507-ton two-masted emergency-made schooner was powered in the river by two engines that took their steam from two boilers. Her principal armament comprised one 11-inch Dahlgren smoothbore, one 20-pdr. Parrott rifle, and two 24-pdr. Dahlgren boat howitzers (ORN, II, 1: 121; Silverstone, *op. cit.,* 49, 52).

6. Built at Bath, ME, the $97,500 Gunboat No. 8, the *Katahdin*, was another sister of the *Kineo*. All of her statistics are the same (ORN, II, 1: 118; Silverstone, *op. cit.,* 49, 52).

7. U.S. War Department, *The War of the Rebellion: A Compilation of the Official Records of the Union and Confederate Armies,* 128 vols. (Washington, D.C.: GPO, 1880–1901), Series I, Vol. 15: 16, 26, 33–34, 76–77, 775–779–781, 785–786, 792, 1124 (cited hereafter as OR, followed by a comma, the series number in Roman numerals, a comma, the volume number in Arabic, a colon, and the page in Arabic); ORN, I, 19: 96–97, 106–107; Arthur B. Carter, *The Tarnished Cavalier: Major General Earl Van Dorn* (Knoxville: University of Tennessee Press, 1999), 81; John Mercer Brooke, *Ironclads and Big Guns of the Confederacy: The Journal and Letters of John M. Brooke,* ed. George M. Brooke, Jr. (Studies in Maritime History; Columbia: University of South Carolina Press, 2002), 106; Milligan, *op. cit.,* 90; Flynt, *loc. cit.*; Henry K. Stevens to Sarah F. Stevens, July 27, 1862, quoted in Cythia E. Moseley, "The Naval Career of Henry Kennedy Stevens as Revealed by His Letters, 1839–1863" (master's thesis, University of North Carolina, 1951), 311; Chester G. Hearn, *Admiral David Glasgow Farragut: The Civil War Years* (Annapolis: Naval Institute Press, 1998), 163–164; Edwin C. Bearss, "The Battle of Baton Rouge," *Louisiana History* 3 (Spring 1962), 77–83, 85, 87, 90–91; Alan G. Gauthreaux, "Lost in the Fog of War," *Civil War Times* 49 (April 2010), 54–57; Richard I. Irwin, "Military Operations in Louisiana in 1862," *B&L*, III, 583. A useful review of upcoming events appears in Thomas B. Richey's *The Battle of Baton Rouge* (College Station, TX: Virtualbookworm.com, 2005).

8. ORN, I, 19: 105–106, 135–136; OR, I, 15: 17; Henry K. Stevens to Sarah F. Stevens, August 2, 1862, quoted in Cythia E. Moseley, "The Naval Career of Henry Kennedy Stevens as Revealed by His Letters, 1839–1863" (master's thesis, University of North Carolina, 1951), 318; George Wright to this author, March 31, 2010; *Jackson Mississippian,* August 10, 1862; Read, *op. cit.,* 358–359; Bearss, *op. cit.,* 88–89; Brown, *op. cit.,* p 579; Gift, *op. cit.,* 207–208; J. Thomas Scharf, *History of the Confederate Navy from Its Organization to the Surrender of Its Last Vessel* (New York: Rodgers and Sherwood, 1887, repr., New York: Fairfax, 1977), 332; Flynt, *op. cit.,* 129–130; Jack D. Coombe, *Thunder Along the Mississippi: The River Battles That Split the Confederacy* (New York: Bantam, 1996), 164; Still, "The History of the C.S.S. *Arkansas*," 118; Still, *Iron Afloat: The Story of Confederate Armorclads* (Nashville: Vanderbilt University Press, 197; repr., Columbia: University of South Carolina Press, 1985), 75–76. It is obvious from Lt. Read's travelogue that either the *Arkansas* had more than one big national flag or Engineer John Skelton of the *Queen of the West* did not steal such a bunting on July 22.

9. Having entered the USN in 1839, Midshipman Ransom was promoted to that rank in 1854. In early 1862, he commissioned the *Kineo* and guided her past the forts at New Orleans in April. He would become at lieutenant

commander in August and a commander in 1863. After the war, he achieved the ranks of captain and commodore, retiring in 1882 (James Grant Wilson and John Fiske, eds., *Appleton's 'Cyclopedia of American Biography*, 7 vols. (New York: D. Appleton, 1888), V, 181).

10. A sister of the *Kineo* and *Kathadin*, the $97,500 Gunboat No. 9, *Cayuga*, was identical to them in all particulars. Built at East Haddam, CT, she was not previously up the Mississippi (ORN, II, 1: 53–54; Silverstone, *op. cit.*, 49, 51).

11. A veteran of the North Pacific Exploring Expedition, Lt. Roe, XO of the *Pensacola* at New Orleans, was, due to the illness of her captain, in command of that ship when she passed the Confederate forts in April. Promoted the day after the *Arkansas* passed through the combined fleets above Vicksburg, he later transferred to the North Atlantic Blockading Squadron. Promoted to commander in 1866, he played a major supporting role for the USN during the exodus of the French from Mexico, winning a letter of commendation from President Andrew Johnson. He became a captain in 1872 and a rear admiral in 1884 (Wilson and Fiske, *op. cit.*, V, 302–303; William B. Cogar, *Dictionary of Admirals of the U.S. Navy*, 2 vols. (Annapolis: Naval Institute Press, 1989), I, 152–153).

12. OR, I, 15: 17, 56, 77–79, 104; ORN, I, 19: 111–112, 114–121, 124, 131, 137, 707, 719, 771; George Wright to this author, March 17, 2010; *Jackson Mississippian*, August 10, 1862; *New York Times*, November 11, 1864; *Harper's Weekly*, September 6, 1862; Bearss, *op. cit.*, 90, 94–95; 99–110, 112–113; Gift, *op. cit.*, 208–210; Read, *op. cit.*, 359–360; Scharf, *op. cit.*, 334–336; Irwin, "Military Operations in Louisiana in 1862," III, 384; Loyall Farragut, *Life and Letters of Admiral D.G. Farragut* (New York: D. Appleton, 1879), 289; Carter, *op. cit.*, 81–82; Still, "The History of the C.S.S. *Arkansas*," 119–122; George Wright to this author, March 17, 2010; Still, *Iron Afloat*; Flynt, *op. cit.*, 130; "John T. Nolan," in *Biographical and Historical Memoires of Louisiana*, 2 vols. (Chicago: Goodspeed, 1892), 280–281; "Sarah Morgan Dawson, 1842–1909)," History Department, University of San Diego, Student Server, history.sandiego.edu/gen/st/~kelliej2/dawson. html (accessed March 3, 2010); Sarah Morgan Dawson, *A Confederate Girl's Diary* (Boston: Houghton, Mifflin, 1913), 144–145; Gauthreaux, *op. cit.*, 57–59; Michael Ballard, *Civil War Mississippi: A Guide* (Jackson: University Press of Mississippi, 2000), 42; Oliver Wood McClinton, "The Career of the Confederate States Ram *Arkansas*," *Arkansas Historical Quarterly* 7 (Winter 1948), 332.

13. ORN, I, 19: 120, 124–125, 131, 135, 771; OR, 17, 2: 241–242; John Grimball to J. Berkeley Grimball, August 13, 1862, quoted in Charles M. Getchell, Jr. "Defender of Inland Waters: The Military Career of Isaac Newton Brown, Commander, Confederate States Navy, 1861–1865" (master's thesis, University of Mississippi, 1978), 79; *Grenada Appeal*, August 6, 1862; *Jackson Mississippian*, August 10, 1862; Read, *op. cit.*, 360–361; Still, "The History of the C.S.S. *Arkansas*," 123–125; Still, *Iron Afloat, loc. cit.*; Flynt, *op. cit.*, 131; Gift, *op. cit.*, 209–210; Bearss, *op. cit.*, 115–116; Brown, *op. cit.*, 572; Coombe, *op. cit.*, 165; Dawson, *op. cit.*, 154; Hearn, *Ellet's Brigade: The Strangest Outfit of All* (Baton Rouge: Louisiana State University Press, 2000), 60; Hearn, *Admiral David Glasgow Farragut*, 165–166; Dana M. Wegner, "Commodore William D. 'Dirty Bill' Porter," *U.S. Naval Institute Proceedings* 103 (February 1977), 48. The *Appeal*'s report on the *Richmond* was incorrect.

14. ORN, I, 19: 118–121, 124–125, 131, 135–136; OR, I, 15: 18, 40; Henry K. Stevens to Clement H. Stevens, September 5, 1862, quoted in Cythia E. Moseley, "The Naval Career of Henry Kennedy Stevens as Revealed by His Letters, 1839–1863" (master's thesis, University of North Carolina, 1951), 318; Spencer Kellogg Brown, "Letter from Spencer Kellogg Brown to Levi Cozzens, 1862," in *Spencer Kellogg Brown, His Life in Kansas and His Death as a Spy, 1842–1863, as Disclosed in His Diary*, ed. George G. Smith (New York: D. Appleton, 1903), 286; *Jackson Mississippian*, August 10, 1862; Read, *op. cit.*, 361; Still, "The History of the C.S.S. *Arkansas*," 125–128; Still, *Iron Afloat, loc. cit.*; Flynt, *op. cit.*, 132; Gift, *op. cit.*, 210–211; Bearss, *op. cit.*, 116–120; Brown, *op. cit.*, 579; Dawson, *op. cit.*, 149–153.

15. ORN, I, 19: 115–117, 119, 124, 130–131, 136; OR, I, 15: 18; Meta Morris Grimball, "Diary Entry, August 19, 1862," in *Meta Morris Grimball Diary, 1860–1866*, Southern Historical Collection, Wilson Library, University of North Carolina at Chapel Hill; *New York Times*, November 11, 1864; *Harper's Weekly*, September 6, 1862; Dawson, *op. cit.*, pp 154–157; Gift, *op. cit.*, 210; Charles P. Roland, "Louisiana Sugar Planters and the Civil War," in Lawrence Lee Hewitt and Arthur W. Bergeron, Jr., *Louisianians in the Civil War* (Columbia: University of Missouri Press, 2002), 19; Eliott Callender, "Career of the Confederate Ram *Arkansas*, Given before the Farragut Naval Veterans Association, Chicago," in *Speeches of a Veteran* (Chicago: Blue Sky, 1901; repr., Charleston, SC: BiblioLife, 2009), 60; Still, "The History of the C.S.S. *Arkansas*," 128–132; Still, *Iron Afloat*, 77; Flynt, *loc. cit.*; Farragut, *The Life of David Glasgow Farragut*, 288–289; Charles L. Lewis, *David Glasgow Farragut*, 2 vols. (Annapolis: Naval Institute Press, 1941–1943), II, 127; Benjamin F. Butler, *Butler's Book* (Boston: A.M. Thayer, 1882), 483–484; Coleman and Stevens, *loc. cit.*; Richard S. West, Jr., *Gideon Welles: Lincoln's Navy Department* (New York: Bobbs-Merrill, 1943), 192; Alfred T. Mahan, *Admiral Farragut* (New York: D. Appleton, 1892; repr., St. Clair Shores, MI: Scholarly Press, 1970.), 194; Loyall Farragut, *Life and Letters of Admiral D.G. Farragut* (New York: D. Appleton, 1879), 289; *New Orleans Picayune*, August 9, 1862; *Jackson Mississippian*, August 10, 1862; *Richmond Dispatch*, August 26; Read, *op. cit.*, 361–362; Bearss, *op. cit.*, 126–128; Moseley, *op. cit.*, 315–317 . These three newspaper articles also appeared in ORN, I, 19. Promoted to the rank of commodore and put out to pasture by a retiring board in the spring of 1863, the colorful and controversial "Dirty Bill" Porter died on May 1, 1864. The following month, the U.S. Congress, under an "*Essex* Bill," awarded the crew of the ironclad $25,000 for the destruction of the *Arkansas* (ORN, I, 19: 117–130; Still, "The History of the C.S.S. *Arkansas*," 131–133; Wegner, *op. cit.*, 48–49).

Epilogue

1. U.S. War Department, *The War of the Rebellion: A Compilation of the Official Records of the Union and Confederate Armies*, 128 vols. (Washington, D.C.: GPO, 1880–1901), Series I, Vol. 15: 18 (cited hereafter as OR, followed by a comma, the series number in Roman numerals, a comma, the volume number in Arabic, any part number in Arabic, a colon, and the page in Arabic); U.S. Navy Department, *Official Records of the Union and Confederate Navies in the War of the Rebellion*, 31 vols. (Washington, D.C.: GPO, 1894–1922), Series II, Vol. 2: 235 (cited hereafter as ORN, followed by a comma, the series number in Roman numerals, a comma, the volume num-

ber in Arabic, a colon, and the page in Arabic); ORN, I, 19: 72; *Richmond Daily Dispatch*, August 14, 1862; *Memphis Bulletin,* August 9, 1862; *Brooklyn Daily Eagle*, August 15, 1862; Adelaide Stuart Dimitry, "The Queen of the Mississippi," in her *War-Time Sketches, Historical and Otherwise* (New Orleans: Louisiana Printing Co. Press, 1911), 15; David Flynt, "Run the Fleet: The Career of the C.S. Ram *Arkansas*," *The Journal of Mississippi History* 51 (May 1989), 132; Alfred T. Mahan, *The Gulf and Inland Waters,* vol. 3, *The Navy in the Civil War* (New York: Scribner's, 1883), 106; Jefferson Davis, *The Rise and Fall of the Confederate Government,* 2 vols. (New York: 1881), II, 244; Eliott Callender, "Career of the Confederate Ram *Arkansas*, Given before the Farragut Naval Veterans Association, Chicago," in *Speeches of a Veteran* (Chicago: Blue Sky, 1901; repr., Charleston, SC: BiblioLife, 2009), 60; William N. Still, "The History of the C.S.S. *Arkansas*" (master's thesis, University of Alabama, 1958), 132–135; Still, *Iron Afloat: The Story of Confederate Armorclads* (Nashville: Vanderbilt University Press, 1971; repr., Columbia: University of South Carolina Press, 1985), 78; Arthur B. Carter, *The Tarnished Cavalier: Major General Earl Van Dorn* (Knoxville: University of Tennessee Press, 1999), 82; Frank E. Vandiver, ed., *The Civil War Diary of General Josiah Gorgas* (Tuscaloosa: University of Alabama Press, 1947), 13; Sarah Woolfolk Wiggins, *The Journals of Josiah Gorgas, 1857–1878* (Tuscaloosa: University of Alabama Press, 1995), 51; John Mercer Brooke, *Ironclads and Big Guns of the Confederacy: The Journal and Letters of John M. Brooke*, ed. George M. Brooke, Jr., Studies in Maritime History (Columbia: University of South Carolina Press, 2002), 108; Jack D. Coombe, *Thunder Along the Mississippi: The River Battles That Split the Confederacy* (New York: Bantam, 1996), 165; Frank E. Smith, *The Yazoo River,* Rivers of America (New York: Rinehart, 1954; repr., Jackson: University Press of Mississippi, 1988), 103; Howard J. Fuller, *Clad in Iron: The American Civil War and the Challenge of British Naval Power* (Westport, CT: Praeger, 2008), 195–196

2. "Search for the Ironclads, November 1981," NUMA: National Underwater and Marine Agency Homepage, http://www.numa.net/expeditions/manassas_louisiana_arkansas.html (accessed March 17, 2010); Clive Cussler and Craig Drago, *The Sea Hunters: True Adventures with Famous Shipwrecks* (New York: Pocket Books, 1996), 130–136; W. Craig Gaines, *Encyclopedia of Civil War Shipwrecks* (Baton Rouge: Louisiana State University Press, 2008), 60; Eliott Callender, "Career of the Confederate Ram *Arkansas*, Given before the Farragut Naval Veterans Association, Chicago," in *Speeches of a Veteran* (Charleston, SC: BiblioLife, 2009), *passim.*

Bibliography

Primary Sources

Bock, William N. Papers. Illinois State Historical Society, Springfield.

Brown, Isaac Newton. *The Autobiography of Isaac Newton Brown*. The Dolph Briscoe Center for American History, University of Texas, Austin.

———. Isaac Newton Brown Papers. Records Relating to Confederate Naval and Marine Personnel. U.S. War Department Collection of Confederate Records. Record Group 109. National Archives. Washington, D.C.

Browne, Symmes. Papers. Ohio Historical Society, Columbus.

Civil War Collection, Missouri Historical Society, St. Louis.

Civil War, Confederate and Federal. Collection. Tennessee State Library and Archives, Nashville.

Civil War Times Illustrated. Collection. U.S. Army Military History Institute, Carlisle Barracks, PA.

Comstock, John H. Papers. Southern Historical Society Collection. Wilson Library, University of North Carolina at Chapel Hill.

Confederate States of America. Congress. *Journal of the Congress of the Confederate States of America, 1861–1865*. 7 vols. Washington, D.C.: GPO, 1904.

———. Navy. Confederate Naval Papers. Mississippi River, Area File 5. U.S. Navy Department, Office of Naval Records and Library. Naval Records Collection. Record Group 45. National Archives, Washington, D.C.

———. Navy. *Register of Officers of the Confederate States Navy, 1861–1865*. Washington, D.C.: GPO, 1931.

———. War Department. *Official Reports of Battles*. Richmond, VA, Enquirer Book & Job Press, 1862.

Crandall, Warren D. Papers. Missouri Historical Society, St. Louis.

Davis, Frederic E. Papers. Emory University, Atlanta.

Diggins, Bartholomew. "Recollections of the War Cruise of the U.S.S. *Hartford*, January–December 1862." Bartholomew Diggins Papers, 1862–1864. Manuscript Collection, New York Public Library, New York City.

Dixon, William Y. Diary. Louisiana and Lower Mississippi Valley Collections, Louisiana State University Libraries, Baton Rouge.

———. Papers. Louisiana and Lower Mississippi Valley Collections, Louisiana State University Libraries, Baton Rouge.

Doak, Henry M. Memoirs. Civil War Collection. Tennessee State Library and Archives, Nashville.

Eads, James B. Papers, Missouri Historical Society, St. Louis.

Ellet, Charles. Ellet Papers, 1827–1926. Transportation History Collection, Special Collections, Clements Library, University of Michigan, Ann Arbor.

Gift, Ellen Shackleford. Papers. Southern Historical Collection. Wilson Library, University of North Carolina at Chapel Hill.

Gift, George W. Papers, 1862–1876. Southern Historical Collection. Wilson Library, University of North Carolina at Chapel Hill.

Grimball, John. Correspondence, 1856–1909. South Carolina Historical Society, Charleston.

———. Family Papers, 1804–1893. South Carolina Historical Society, Charleston.

Grimball, Meta Morris. Diary, 1860–1866. Southern Historical Collection, Wilson Library, University of North Carolina at Chapel Hill.

Johnson, Robert V., and Clarence C. Buell, eds. *Battles and Leaders of the Civil War*. 4 vols. New York: Century, 1884–1887; repr. Thomas Yoseloff, 1956.

Jordan, Scott D. *Civil War Letters of Scott D. Jordan, Produced for Eleanor Jordan West*. CD-ROM. Tucson, AZ: Bellnotes.com, 2007.

Ker, Mary Susan. Papers. Southern Historical Collection. Wilson Library, University of North Carolina at Chapel Hill.

Meigs, Montgomery C. Papers. Manuscript Division. Library of Congress, Washington, D.C.

Oneida, U.S.S. Ship's Diary. Southern Historical Collection. Wilson Library, University of North Carolina at Chapel Hill.

Pennock, Alexander Mosley. Papers. Illinois State Historical Society, Springfield.

Phelps, Seth Ledyard. Papers. Missouri Historical Society, St. Louis.

Porter, David Dixon. Papers. Manuscript Division, Library of Congress, Washington, D.C.

———. Papers. Missouri Historical Society, St. Louis.

Rodgers Family. Papers. Library of Congress, Washington, D.C.

Rodgers, John. Collection. Library of Congress, Washington, D.C.

Ruggles, Daniel. Papers. Special Collections, Hill Memorial Library, Louisiana State University, Baton Rouge.

———. Ruggles Papers, 1862–1865. Archives and Library Division. Mississippi Department of Archives and History, Jackson.

United States. Congress. Joint Committee on the Conduct of the War. *Report: Red River*. 38th Cong., 2nd

sess. Washington, D.C.: GPO, 1864; repr., Greenwood, 1971.
———. Navy Department. *Official Records of the Union and Confederate Navies in the War of the Rebellion* (ORN). 31 vols. Washington, D.C.: GPO, 1894–1922.
———. Navy Department. Bureau of Naval Personnel. Records of the Bureau of Naval Personnel. Record Group 24. National Archives, Washington, D.C.
———. Navy Department. Navy Department Library. ZB Files. Washington, D.C.
———. Navy Department. Office of Naval Records and Library, Naval Records Collection. Record Group 45. National Archives, Washington, D.C.
———. Office of the Quartermaster General. Records of the Office of the Quartermaster General. Record Group 92. National Archives, Washington D.C.
———. Treasury Department. "Controller's Contracts." Treasury Department Collection of Confederate Records. Record Group 365. National Archives, Washington, D.C.
———. War Department. *Atlas to Accompany the Official Records of the War of the Rebellion.* Compiled by Calvin D. Cowles. 3 vols. Washington, D.C.: GPO, 1891–1895.
———. *The War of the Rebellion: A Compilation of the Official Records of the Union and Confederate Armies* (OR). 128 vols. Washington, D.C.: GPO, 1880–1901.
USS *Carondelet*. Logbooks of the USS *Carondelet*, May 1862-June 1865. Records of the Bureau of Ships, Record Group 19. U.S. National Archives, Washington, D.C.
Watson, Theodore. Letters. Newberry Library, Chicago.
Welles, Gideon. Papers. Manuscript Division. Library of Congress, Washington, D.C.

Newspapers

Atlantic Democrat
Boston Morning Journal
Cairo City Weekly Gazette
Charleston Daily Courier
Charleston Mercury
Chicago Daily Post
Chicago Daily Times
Chicago Daily Tribune
Chicago Evening Journal
Cincinnati Daily Commercial
Cincinnati Daily Enquirer
Cincinnati Daily Gazette
Cincinnati Times
Clarksville Chronicle
Cleveland Daily Plain Dealer
Columbus (GA) Daily Enquirer
Columbus (OH) Crisis
Evansville Daily Journal
Florence (AL) Gazette
Frank Leslie's Illustrated Newspaper
Grenada (MS) Appeal
Harper's Weekly
Illinois Weekly State Journal
Indiana Herald
Indianapolis Daily Journal
Indianapolis News
Jackson Mississippian
Little Rock True Democrat
Louisville Courier
Louisville Daily Journal
Macon Daily Telegraph
Macon Weekly Telegraph
Memphis Argus
Memphis Bulletin
Memphis Daily Appeal
Memphis Daily Avalanche
Mobile Daily Advertiser & Register
Mobile Daily Tribune
Mobile Evening News
Nashville Banner
Nashville Daily Patriot
Nashville Daily Union
Nashville Dispatch
Nashville Times
Nashville Union and American
National Intelligencer
New Albany Ledger
New Orleans Daily Crescent
New Orleans Daily Delta
New Orleans Daily Picayune
New Orleans Era
New Orleans Times
New York Herald
New York Times
New York Tribune
New York World
Pine Bluff (MS) Commercial
Richmond Dispatch
St. Louis Daily Missouri Democrat
St. Louis Daily Missouri Republican
Savannah Republican
Vicksburg Evening Post
Vicksburg Sunday Post
Wisconsin State Journal

Internet Sources

Autry, Jaxon B. "William Francis Lynch (1801–1865)." The Latin Library. http://www.thelatinlibrary.com/chron/civilwarnotes/lynch.html (accessed October 29, 2009).
Biographical Directory of the United States Congress, 1774-Present. http://bioguide.congress.gov/scripts/biodisplay.pl?index=B000231 (accessed October 1, 2006).
Branch, Paul. "Armament of Fort Macon." *The Fort Macon Ramparts,* Spring 1996. http://www.clis.com/friends/armament.htm (accessed October 13, 2009).
"Brooke Rifles and Smoothbore Guns." *The Encyclopedia of Civil War Artillery.* http://www.cwartillery.org/ve/brooke.html (accessed October 13, 2009).
"Capt. Clement Sulivane." *Find a Grave.* http://www.findagrave.com/cgi-bin/fg.cgi?page=gr&GSln=s&GSmid=46536634&GRid=12872741& (accessed January 20, 2010).
"Capt. Isaac D. Fulkerson, C.S.N." Fulkerson Organization home page. http://www.fulkerson.org/isaacd.html (accessed October 13, 2009).
"Charles Magill Conrad." *The Political Graveyard: Index to Politicians* http://politicalgraveyard.com/bio/conrad.html. (accessed September 11, 2009).
Clarke, H.C., comp. "*General Directory for the City of Vicksburg* [1860]." Rootsweb.Ancestry.Com. http://homepages.rootsweb.ancestry.com/~holler/dir1860.htm (accessed November 1, 2009).
Clayton, Brian T. *Guide to the John Luke Porter Papers, 1860–1993.* Manuscript Collection, No. 850. East Carolina Manuscript Collection, Special Collections. Joyner Library, East Carolina University, 2003. http://

digital.lib.ecu.edu/special/ead/findingaids/0850/#histnote (accessed August 25, 2009).

"Coastal Ironclads: C.S.S. *Arkansas*." *Civil War Talk*, November 4, 2006. http://civilwartalk.com/Resource_Center/CS/Confederate_Navy/coastal-ironclads-c-s-s-arkansas-a104.html (accessed, September 29, 2009).

Confederate States of America. Navy Department. *Navy Annual Report, 1862*. http://www.csnavy.org/mallory/aug62.htm (accessed November 19, 2009).

"C.S.S. *Arkansas*." Modelmaker.com. http://www.modelshipmaster.com/products/civil_war/index.htm (accessed September 15, 2009).

Cussler, Clive. "*Arkansas*: Locations of the Shipwrecks Found During the 1981 Mississippi River Expedition." NUMA: National Underwater and Marine Agency home page. http://www.numa.net/expeditions/mississippi_river_expedition.html (accessed May 2010).

"Dahlgrens, Brookes, and Parrotts." *Ironclads and Blockade Runners of the Civil War*. http://www.wideopenwest.com/~jenkins/ironclads/ironguns.htm (accessed October 13, 2009).

"Dahlgren Guns and Rifles." The *Encyclopedia of Civil War Artillery*. http://www.cwartillery.org/ve/dahlgrens.html (accessed October 13, 2009).

"David Maney Currin, Sr." *The Political Graveyard: Index to Politicians*. http://politicalgraveyard.com/bio/currencurrin.html (accessed September 11, 2009).

Doyle, Alan. "Ram *Arkansas*/Fort Pickering." *Civil War Navy Message Board*. October 16, 2009. http://history-sites.com/cgi-bin/bbs53x/cwnavy/webbbs_config.pl?read=3516> (accessed October 16, 2009).

Edwards, MS. "The History of Edwards." Town of Edwards, Mississippi. http://www.townofedwards.com/history.htm (accessed January 30, 2010).

"Eliot Callender." "Peoria County Biographies." Rootsweb. http://freepages.history.rootsweb.ancestry.com/~historyconnection/Peoria/Bio/04.htm (accessed April 10, 2010).

"Elisha Whittlesey," *Biographical Directory of the United States Congress, 1774-Present*. http://bioguide.congress.gov/scripts/biodisplay.pl?index=W000431 (accessed January 4, 2010).

Eller, George. "Armor." *World War II in Color*. December 3, 2007. http://www.ww2incolor.com/forum/archive/index.php/t-5644.html (accessed October 6, 2009).

Ewing, Jim. "Liverpool Landing: Mississippi Byways." Yazoo County, MSGenWeb. http://www.rootsweb.ancestry.com/~msyazoo/Liverpool_Landing.htm (accessed January 4, 2010).

Ezell, Tom. "Battle Flag of C.S.S. *Arkansas* Found, Placed on Display." *Capitol Guards: General R.C. Newton Camp, Sons of Confederate Veterans Newsletter*, February 2001, quoted in *Civil War Navies Message Board*. October 14, 2002. http://history-sites.com/cgi-bin/bbs53x/arcwmb/arch_config.pl?noframes;read=2233 (accessed March 3, 2010).

"Flag from the C.S.S. *Arkansas*, August 1862." In *Civil War Naval Flag Display, Welcome to Port Columbus, Georgia*. National Civil War Naval Museum. http://www.portcolumbus.org/exhibits/flagcollection.php (accessed March 3, 2010).

Foenander, Terry. "Charles H. McBlair." *Confederate Naval and Marine Corps Personnel*. http://www.tfoenander.com/csnindex2.htm (accessed October 6, 2009).

Franks, Bob. "The Balfour Family." The Issaquena Genealogy and History Project, 2004. http://www.rootsweb.ancestry.com/~msissaq2/balfour.html (accessed February 12, 2010).

Getchell, Charles M., Jr. "Isaac Newton Brown of Navarro County, Texas." Texas Genealogical Website. http://www.txgenweb6.org/txnavarro/biographies/b/brown_isaac_newton.htm (accessed July 13, 2009).

"Gunpowder." *The Encyclopedia of Civil War Artillery*. http://www.cwartillery.org//glossary/glossarygz.htm (accessed October 13, 2009).

Holmes, Jack D.L. "*Star of the West*." *Handbook of Texas Online*. http://www.tshaonline.org/handbook/online/articles/SS/qts5.html (accessed November 8, 2009).

"James Buchanan Eads." University of Illinois at Urbana-Champaign Riverweb Site. http://www.riverweb.uiuc.edu/TECH/TECH20.htm (September 18, 2006).

Jenkins, Mark F. "Mysteries and Controversies: The Color of the *Arkansas*." In *Ironclads and Blockade Runners of the American Civil War*. http://www.wideopenwest.com/~jenkins/ironclads/mysteries.htm (accessed November 18, 2009).

"Jonathan Hanby Carter, Surry County's Civil War Sailor." *Free State of Patrick: Surry County North Carolina History*. http://www.freestateofpatrick.com/sccwr.htm (accessed October 4, 2009).

"John DeWitt Clinton Atkins." *The Political Graveyard: Index to Politicians*. http://politicalgraveyard.com/bio/athon-atkins.html (accessed September 11, 2009).

"John G. Morrison, Civil War Medal of Honor Recipient." American Civil War Website. http://americancivilwar.com/medal_of_honor6.html (accessed April 9, 2008).

"John J. Pettus," *The Political Graveyard: Index to Politicians*. http://politicalgraveyard.com/bio/pettitt-pezzulo.html (accessed September 11, 2009).

"John Vines Wright." *The Political Graveyard: Index to Politicians*. http://politicalgraveyard.com/bio/wright5.html (accessed September 11, 2009).

Joslin, Jeff. "Leeds & Co., New Orleans." *Old Wood-Working Machines*. http://www.owwm.com/MfgIndex/detail.aspx?id=1490 (accessed September 29, 2009).

Long, Chris and David. *Civil War Battle of Wilson's Creek (Battle of Hills)*. http://www.chrisanddavid.com/wilsonscreek/roles/SOLDIERSMSGL-R.html (accessed December 1, 2009).

McGhee, James. "Units of the Missouri State Guard, 1861–1862." *Confederate Links: Missouri Divisions and Commanders*. http://www.mogenweb.org/mocivwar/confederates.html (accessed December 1, 2009).

Nautical Terms and Phrases: Their Meaning and Origin. http://www.history.navy.mil/trivia/trivia03.htm (accessed January 12, 2010).

New South Associates. C.S.S. *"Georgia": Archival Study*. U.S. Army Corps of Engineers, Contract Number DACW21-99-D-0004, January 31, 2007. http://savharbor.com/Cultural%20Resources/CSS_Georgia_Archival_Study.pdf?CFID=5719029&CFTOKEN=b794a43d13065f5e-928D3131-D60D-557F-44FBC05168261FF4 (accessed May 1, 2010).

"Old Steam Navy: Armament." GlobalSecurity.Org. http://www.globalsecurity.org/military/systems/ship/steam6.htm (accessed November 10, 2009).

"The Origin of the Ranks and Rank Insignia Now Used by the United States Armed Forces, Officers: Lieutenants." *Traditions of the Naval Service*. http://www.history.navy.mil/trivia/triv4-5d.htm, (July 7, 2005).

"The Orphan Brigade at Vicksburg in 1862." In *First Kentucky "Orphan" Brigade: History, Data, Resources, Other Features*. http://www.rootsweb.ancestry.com/~orphanhm/vickburg.htm (accessed June 25, 2009).

Panamerican Consultants and Tidewater Atlantic Research. *In Situ Archaeological Evaluation of the CSS "Georgia," Savannah Harbor, Georgia: Final Report.* U.S. Army Corps of Engineers, Contract Number DACW21–98-D-0019, February 2007. http://sav-harbor.com/Cultural%20Resources/CSS_Georgia_Site_Investigation_Report.pdf (accessed May 1, 2010).

Rector, Charles. "William Pratt 'Buck' Parks." In *The Encyclopedia of Arkansas History and Culture.* http://www.encyclopediaofarkansas.net/encyclopedia/entry-detail.aspx?entryID=1733 (accessed January 23, 2010).

"Richard Cheatham." *Biographical Directory of the United States Congress, 1774-Present.* http://bioguide.congress.gov/scripts/biodisplay.pl?index=C000341 (accessed September 29, 2009).

"Robert Ward Johnson." *The Political Graveyard: Index to Politicians* http://politicalgraveyard.com/bio/johnson7.html (accessed September 11, 2009).

"Rodmans and Confederate Columbiads." In *The Encyclopedia of Civil War Artillery.* http://www.cwartillery.org/ve/rodman.html (accessed October 13, 2009).

Rosen, Michael A. "Historical Aspects and Black Powder Manufacturing." In *The Encyclopedia of Civil War Artillery.* http://www.civilwarartillery.com/disarm/blackpowder.htm (accessed November 20, 2009).

"Sarah Morgan Dawson, 1842–1909)." History Department, University of San Diego, Student Server. history.sandiego.edu/gen/st/~kelliej2/dawson.html (accessed March 3, 2010).

"Search for the Ironclads, November 1981." NUMA: National Underwater and Marine Agency Homepage. http://www.numa.net/expeditions/manassas_louisiana_arkansas.html (accessed March 17, 2010).

South Carolina. "The 17th S.C. Volunteer Infantry at Second Manassas." W.C. Lathan home page. http://www.wclathan.com/civil_war/Second_Manassas/17th_at_Second_Manassas.htm (accessed February 22, 2010).

"*Star of the West.*" In *The Ships List.* http://www.theshipslist.com/ships/descriptions/ShipsSS.html (accessed (November 8, 2009).

"Stephen Russell Mallory." *The Political Graveyard: Index to Politicians.* http://politicalgraveyard.com/bio/mallory.html (accessed September 11, 2009).

"Stoddard County Confederate Memorial." Missouri Division, Sons of Confederate Veterans home page. http://www.missouridivision-scv.org/stoddard.htm (accessed January 4, 2010).

U.S. Navy Department. Naval Historical Center, "Commander Isaac Newton Brown, CSN (1817–1889)." On-Line Library of Selected Images — People — United States. http://www.history.navy.mil/photos/pers-us/uspers-b/in-brwn.htm (accessed March 30, 2007).

Wiener, James G., et al. "Mississippi River." U.S. Geological Survey, Biological Resources Division home page. http://biology.usgs.gov/s+t/SNT/noframe/ms137.htm (accessed August 26, 2006).

Williams, Scott K. "St Louis' Ships of Iron: The Ironclads and Monitors of Carondelet (St. Louis), Missouri." Missouri Civil War Museum home page. http://www.missouricivilwarmuseum.org/1ironclads.htm (accessed July 12, 2005).

Williams, Scott K., and James McGhee. "Missourians Aboard the C.S.S. *Arkansas.*" Sons of Confederate Veterans, Missouri Division. *Missouri Units.* http://www.missouridivision-scv.org/mounits/cssark.htm (accessed December 1, 2009).

Williamson, Thom. Papers of Thom Williamson. Special Collections: Manuscripts, Old Dominion University Libraries, 2008. http://www.lib.odu.edu/special/manuscripts/williamson.htm (accessed August 25, 2009).

Wright, George. "C.S.S. *Arkansas* Engine." In Civil War Navies Message Board, September 2, 2007, May 8 and June 3 2009. http://history-sites.com/mb/cw/cwnavy.cgi?rev=3376; http://history-sites.com/cgi-bin/bbs53x/cwnavy/webbbs_config.pl?read=2321; http://history-sites.com/mb/cw/cwnavy/index.cgi?rev=3383; and <http://history-sites.com/mb/cw/cwnavy/index.cgi?rev=3458 (accessed September 29, October 1, 2009).

_____. "Re: Confederate River Gunboats." Civil War Navies Message Board. http://history-sites.com/mb/cw/cwnavy/index.cgi?read=1948 (accessed November 10, 2006).

_____. "USS *Carondelet* vs. CSS *Arkansas.*" Civil War Navies Message Board. http://history-sites.com/cgi-bin/bbs53x/cwnavy/webbbs_config.pl?read=1580 (accessed April 4, 2009).

Books

Abbott, John S.C. *The History of the Civil War in America.* 2 vols. New York: H. Bill, 1863.

Alden, Carroll Storrs, and Ralph Earle. *Makers of Naval Tradition.* Boston: Ginn, 1925.

Allardice, Bruce S. *More Generals in Gray.* Baton Route: Louisiana State University Press, 1995.

Allen, John W. *Legends and Lore of Southern Illinois.* Carbondale, IL: University Graphics, 1978.

Ambler, Charles Henry. *A History of Transportation in the Ohio Valley.* Glendale, CA: Arthur H. Clark, 1932.

Ambrose, Stephen E. *Halleck: Lincoln's Chief of Staff.* Baton Rouge: Louisiana State University Press, 1962.

Anders, Curt. *Henry Halleck's War: A Fresh Look at Lincoln's Controversial General-in-Chief.* Indianapolis: Guild Press of Indiana, 1999.

Anderson, Bern. *By Sea and by River: The Naval History of the Civil War.* New York: Knopf, 1962.

Andrews, J. Cutler. *The North Reports the Civil War.* Pittsburgh: University of Pittsburgh Press, 1985.

_____. *The South Reports the Civil War.* Pittsburgh: University of Pittsburgh Press, 1985.

Austin, J.P. *The Blue and the Gray: Sketches of a Portion of the Unwritten History of the Great American Civil War.* Atlanta: Franklin, 1899.

Bacon, Benjamin W. *Sinews of War: How Technology, Industry and Transportation Won the Civil War.* Novato, CA: Presidio, 1997.

Bacon, Edward W. *Double Duty in the Civil War: The Letters of Sailor and Soldier Edward W. Bacon.* Edited by George S. Burkhardt. Carbondale: Southern Illinois University Press, 2009.

Ballard, Michael B. *Civil War Mississippi: A Guide.* Jackson: University Press of Mississippi, 2000.

_____. *Vicksburg: The Campaign that Opened the Mississippi.* Chapel Hill: University of North Carolina Press, 2004.

Barrett, Edward. *Gunnery Instruction Simplified for the Volunteer Officers of the U.S. Navy, with Hints for Executive and Other Officers.* New York: D. Van Nostrand, 1863.

Bartols, Barnabas H. *A Treatise on the Marine Boilers of the United States.* Philadelphia: R.W. Barnard, 1851.

Baxter, James P., III. *Introduction of the Ironclad Warship.* Cambridge, MA: Harvard University Press, 1933; repr., Annapolis: U.S. Naval Institute, 2000.

Beale, Howard K., ed. *Diary of Gideon Welles: Secretary of* the Navy under Lincoln and Johnson. 2 vols. New York: W.W. Norton, 1960.

Bearss, Edwin C. *Hardluck Ironclad: The Sinking and Salvage of the Cairo.* Baton Rouge: Louisiana State University, 1966.

_____. *Rebel Victory at Vicksburg.* Vicksburg, MS: Centennial Commission, 1963.

_____. *The Vicksburg Campaign.* 3 vols. Dayton, OH: Morningside Book Shop, 1985–1986.

Bennett, Frank M. *The "Monitor" and the Navy under Steam.* Boston: Houghton, Mifflin, 1900.

_____. *Steam Navy of the United States: A History of the Growth of the Steam Vessel of War in the U.S. Navy, and of the Naval Engineer Corps.* Pittsburgh: Warren, 1896; repr., New York: Greenwood, 1970.

Bennett, Michael J. *Union Jacks: Yankee Sailors in the Civil War.* Chapel Hill: University of North Carolina Press, 2004.

Biographical and Historical Memoirs of Mississippi, Embracing Authentic and Comprehensive Accounts of the Chief Events in the History of the State, and a Record of the Lives of Many of the Most Worthy and Illustrious Families and Individuals. Chicago: Goodspeed, 1891; repr., Spartanburg, SC: Reprint Co., 1978.

Boatner, Mark M., III. *The Civil War Dictionary.* New York: David McKay, 1959.

Boynton, Charles B. *History of the Navy During the Rebellion.* 2 vols. New York: D. Appleton, 1867–1868.

Bradford, Gershom. *The Mariner's Dictionary.* New York: Weathervane, 1970.

Bragg, Marion. *Historic Names and Places on the Lower Mississippi River.* Vicksburg: Mississippi River Commission, 1977.

Brandt, J.D. *Gunnery Catechism, as Applied to the Service of Naval Ordnance.* New York: D. Van Nostrand, 1864.

Brooke, John Mercer. *Ironclads and Big Guns of the Confederacy: The Journal and Letters of John M. Brooke.* Edited by George M. Brooke, Jr. Studies in Maritime History. Columbia: University of South Carolina Press, 2002.

Browne, Henry R., and Symmes E. *From the Fresh Water Navy, 1861–1864: Letters of Acting Master's Mate Henry R. Browne and Acting Ensign Symmes E. Browne.* Edited by John D. Milligan. Naval Letters Series, vol. 3. Annapolis: Naval Institute Press, 1970.

Browne, Junius Henri. *Four Years in Secessia: Adventures Within and Without the Union Lines.* Hartford, CT: O.D. Case, 1865.

Brownlee, Richard S., III. *Gray Ghosts of the Confederacy: Guerrilla Warfare in the West, 1861–1865.* Baton Rouge: Louisiana State University Press, 1958.

Bucy, Carole. *A Path Divided: Tennessee's Civil War Years.* Nashville: Tennessee 200, 1996.

Burton, E. Milby. *The Siege of Charleston, 1861–1865.* Columbia: University of South Carolina Press, 1970.

Brazelton, B.G. *A History of Hardin County, Tennessee.* Nashville: Cumberland Presbyterian Publishing House, 1885.

Callahan, Edward W. *List of Officers of the Navy of the United States and of the Marine Corps, from 1775 to 1900, Comprising a Complete Register of All Present and Former Commissioned, Warranted, and Appointed Officers of the United States Navy, and of the Marine Corps, Regular and Volunteer, Compiled from the Official Records of the Navy Department.* New York: L.R. Hamersly, 1901; repr. New York: Haskell House, 1969.

Calore, Paul. *Naval Campaigns of the Civil War.* Jefferson, NC: McFarland, 2002.

Campbell, R. Thomas. *Confederate Naval Forces on Western Waters: The Defense of the Mississippi River and Its Tributaries.* Jefferson, NC: McFarland, 2005.

_____. *Gray Thunder.* Exploits of the Confederate Navy. New Orleans: Burd Street, 1996.

_____. *Sea Hawk of the Confederacy: Lt. Charles W. Read and the Confederate Navy.* Shippensburg, PA: Burd Street, 2000.

_____. *Southern Thunder.* Exploits of the Confederate Navy. New Orleans: Burd Street, 1996.

Canfield, Eugene B. *Civil War Naval Ordnance.* Washington, D.C.: Naval History Division, U.S. Navy Department, 1969.

Canney, Donald L. *Lincoln's Navy: The Ships, Men and Organization, 1861–65.* London and New York: Conway Maritime Press, 1998.

_____. *The Old Steam Navy.* Vol. 2, *The Ironclads, 1842–1885.* Annapolis: Naval Institute Press, 1993.

Capers, Gerald M. *The Biography of a River Town: Memphis—Its Heroic Age.* Chapel Hill: University of North Carolina Press, 1939.

Carter, Arthur B. *The Tarnished Cavalier: Major General Earl Van Dorn.* Knoxville: University of Tennessee Press, 1999.

Carter, Samuel, III. *The Final Fortress: The Campaign for Vicksburg 1862–1863.* New York: St. Martin's, 1980.

Castlen, Harriet (Gift). *Hope Bids Me Onward.* Savannah, GA: Chatham, 1945.

Catton, Bruce. *The American Heritage Picture History of the Civil War.* New York: American Heritage, 1960.

_____. *The Centennial History of the Civil War.* 3 vols. Garden City, NY: Doubleday, 1961–1965.

_____. *The Coming Fury.* Garden City, NY: Doubleday, 1961.

_____. *Grant Moves South.* Boston: Little, Brown, 1960.

_____. *This Hallowed Ground: The Story of the Union Side of the Civil War.* Garden City, NY: Doubleday, 1956.

Chamberlain, William H., ed. *Sketches of War History, 1861–1865: Papers Prepared for the Ohio Commandry of the Military Order of the Loyal Legion of the United States.* 6 vols. Cincinnati: R Clarke, 1890–1908.

Chappelle, Howard I. *History of the American Sailing Navy.* New York: W.W. Norton, 1935.

_____. *The Search for Speed Under Sail.* New York: W.W. Norton, 1967.

Clarke, Hewitt. *He Saw the Elephant: Confederate Naval Saga of Lt. Charles "Savvy" Read, CSN.* Spring, TX: Lone Star Press, 2000.

Coffin, Charles C. *Drum-beat of the Nation.* New York: Harper, 1888.

_____. *My Days and Nights on the Battlefield: A Book for Boys.* By "Carlton," pseud. 2nd ed. Boston: Ticknor and Fields, 1864.

Cogar, William B. *Dictionary of Admirals of the U.S. Navy.* 2 vols. Annapolis: Naval Institute Press, 1989.

Coggins, Jack. *Arms and Equipment of the Civil War.* Garden City, NY: Doubleday, 1962.

Coleman, Silas B. *A July Morning with the Rebel Ram "Arkansas."* War Papers Read before the Commandery of the State of Michigan, Military Order of the Loyal Legion of the United States, No. 1. Detroit: Winn & Hammond, 1890; repr., *Papers of the Military Order of the Loyal Legion of the United States.* 56 vols. Wilmington, NC: Broadfoot, 1994.

Connelly, Thomas L. *Army of the Heartland: The Army of Tennessee, 1861–1862.* Baton Rouge: Louisiana State University Press, 1967.

Cooling, B. Franklin. *Forts Henry and Donelson: The Key*

to the Confederate Heartland. Knoxville: University of Tennessee Press, 1987.

Coombe, Jack D. *Thunder Along the Mississippi: The River Battles That Split the Confederacy.* New York: Sarpedon, 1996.

Cornish, Dudley Taylor, and Virginia Jeans Laas. *Lincoln's Lee: The Life of Samuel Phillips Lee, United States Navy, 1812–1897.* Lawrence: University Press of Kansas, 1986.

Cotham, Edward T., Jr. *Battle on the Bay: The Civil War Struggle for Galveston.* Austin: University of Texas Press, 1998.

Cotton, Gordon A., and Jeff T. Giambrone. *Vicksburg and the War.* Gretna, LA: Pelican, 2004.

Coulter, E. Merton. *The Civil War and Readjustment in Kentucky.* Chapel Hill: University of North Carolina Press, 1926.

———. *The Confederate States of America.* Baton Rouge: Louisiana State University Press, 1950.

Cozzens, Peter. *The Darkest Days of the War: The Battles of Iuka and Corinth.* Chapel Hill: University of North Carolina Press, 1997.

Crandall, Warren D., and Isaac D. Newell. *History of the Ram Fleet and Mississippi Marine Brigade.* St. Louis, MO: Buschart Brothers, 1907.

Currie, George E. *Warfare Along the Mississippi: The Letters of Lt. George E. Currie.* Edited by Norman E. Clark. Mount Pleasant: Central Michigan University, 1861.

Cussler, Clive, and Craig Dirgo. *The Sea Hunters: Adventures with Famous Shipwrecks.* New York: Simon and Schuster, 1996.

Daniel, Larry J., and Lynn N. Bock, *Island No. 10: Struggle in the Mississippi Valley.* Tuscaloosa: University of Alabama Press, 1996.

Davidson, Donald. *The Tennessee.* Vol. 2, *The New River, Civil War to TVA.* Rivers of America. New York: Rinehart, 1948.

Davis, Charles H. *Charles H. Davis: Life of Charles Henry Davis, Rear Admiral, 1807–1877.* Boston and New York: Houghton, Mifflin, 1899.

Davis, Jefferson. *Jefferson Davis, Constitutionalist: His Letters, Papers, and Speeches.* Edited by Dunbar Rowland. 10 vols. Jackson, MS: Little & Ives, 1923.

———. *Rise and Fall of the Confederate Government.* 2 vols. New York: D. Appleton, 1881.

Davis, William C. *Duel Between the First Ironclads.* Garden City, NY: Doubleday, 1975.

———. *Look Away: A History of the Confederate States of America.* New York: Free Press, 2002.

Dawson, Sarah Morgan. *A Confederate Girl's Diary.* Boston: Houghton, Mifflin, 1913.

DeCell, Harriet, and JoAnne Prichard. *Yazoo: Its Legends and Legacies.* Yazoo City, MS: Yazoo Delta, 1868; repr., 1976.

Dedmondt, Glenn. *The Flags of Civil War Arkansas.* Gretna, LA: Pelican, 2009.

Detzer, David. *Allegiance: Fort Sumter, Charleston, and the Beginning of the Civil War.* New York: Harcourt, 2001.

Dewey, George. *Autobiography of George Dewey: Admiral of the Navy.* New York: Charles Scribner's Sons, 1913.

Dickey, Thomas S., and Peter C. George. *Field Artillery Projectiles of the American Civil War.* Revised and Supplemented 1993 Edition(tm). Mechanicsville, VA: Arsenal Publications II, 1993.

Dictionary of American Naval Fighting Ships. 8 vols. Washington, D.C.: GPO, 1916–1981.

Dorsey, Florence. *Road to the Sea: The Story of James B. Eads and the Mississippi River.* New York: Rinehart, 1947.

Driggs, George W. *Opening the Mississippi; Or, Two Years Campaigning in the Southwest.* Madison, WI: William J. Park, 1864.

Driver, Robert J., Jr. *Confederate Sailors, Marines, and Signalmen from Virginia and Maryland.* Westminster, MD: Heritage Books, 2007.

Drury, Ian, and Tony Gibbons. *The Civil War Military Machine: Weapons and Tactics of the Union and Confederate Armed Forces.* New York: Smithmark, 1993.

Duffy, James P. *Lincoln's Admiral: The Civil War Campaigns of David Farragut.* Edison, NJ: Castle, 2006.

Durkin, Joseph T. *Confederate Navy Chief: Stephen R. Mallory.* Chapel Hill: University of North Carolina Press, 1954; repr., Columbia: University of South Carolina Press, 1987.

Dyer, Frederick H. *A Compendium of the War of the Rebellion.* 3 vols. Des Moines: Dyer, 1908; repr., New York: Thomas Yoseloff, 1959.

Edmondston, Catherine Devereux. *Journal of a Secesh Lady: The Diary of Catherine Ann Devereux Edmondston, 1860–1866.* Edited by Beth G. Crabtree and James Welch Patton. Raleigh, NC: Division of Archives and History, Dept. of Cultural Resources, State of North Carolina, 1979.

Eicher, David J. *The Longest Night: A Military History of the Civil War.* New York: Simon and Schuster, 2001.

Elliott, Robert G. *Gilbert Elliott's Albemarle: Ironclad of the Roanoke.* Shippensburg, PA: White Mane, 1999.

Engle, Stephen D. *Struggle for the Heartland: The Campaigns from Fort Henry to Corinth.* Lincoln: University of Nebraska Press, 2001.

Farragut, Loyall. *Life and Letters of Admiral D.G. Farragut.* New York: D. Appleton, 1879.

Faust, Patricia L. *Historical Times Illustrated Encyclopedia of the Civil War.* New York: Harper Collins, 1986.

Field, Ron and Richard Hook. *The Confederate Army, 1861–1865: Tennessee and North Carolina.* Men-at-Arms. Oxford, England: Osprey, 2007.

Fisk, Harold. *Geological Investigations of the Alluvial Valley of the Lower Mississippi River.* Washington, D.C.: U.S. Army Corps of Engineers, 1944.

Foltz, Charles S. ed. *Surgeon of the Seas: The Adventures of Jonathan M. Foltz.* Indianapolis: Bobbs-Merrill, 1931.

Foote, Shelby. *The Civil War: A Narrative.* 3 vols. New York: Random House, 1958–1974; repr., New York: Vintage, 1986.

Force, Manning F. *From Fort Henry to Corinth.* Campaigns of the Civil War, No. 2. New York: Scribner's, 1882, repr. T.Y. Yoseloff, 1963.

Fowler, William H. *Under Two Flags: The American Navy in the Civil War.* New York: W.W. Norton, 1990.

Fox, Gustavus Vasa. *Confidential Correspondence of Gustavus Vasa Fox, Assistant Secretary of the Navy, 1861–1865.* Edited by Robert Means Thompson and Richard Wainwright. 2 vols. New York: De Vinne, 1918–1919.

Freemon, Frank R. *Gangrene and Glory: Medical Care during the American Civil War.* Urbana: University of Illinois Press, 2001.

Fuller, Howard J. *Clad in Iron: The American Civil War and the Challenge of British Naval Power.* Westport, CT: Praeger, 2008.

Gabel, Christopher R., and the Staff Ride Team. *Staff Ride Handbook for the Vicksburg Campaign, December 1862–July 1863.* Fort Leavenworth, KS: Combat Studies Institute, U.S. Army Command and General Staff College, 2001.

Gaines, W. Craig. *Encyclopedia of Civil War Shipwrecks.* Baton Rouge: Louisiana State University Press, 2008.

Gerteis, Louis S. *Civil War St. Louis.* Lawrence: University Press of Kansas, 2001.

Gibbons, Tony. *Warships and Naval Battles of the Civil War.* New York: Gallery Books, 1989.

Gibson, Charles Dana, with E. Kay Gibson. *Assault and Logistics.* Vol. 1, *Dictionary of Transports and Combat Vessels Steam and Sail Employed by the Union Army, 1861–1868.* Camden, ME: Ensign Press, 1995.

_____. *Assault and Logistics.* Vol. 2, *Union Army Coastal and River Operations, 1861–1866.* Camden, ME: Ensign Press, 1995.

Glazier, Willard. *Battles for the Union.* Hartford, CT: Dustin, Gilman, 1875.

Godwin, Parke. *The Cyclopedia of Biography: A Record of the Lives of Eminent Persons.* New ed. New York: G.P. Putnam's Sons, 1878.

Gorham, George C. *Life and Public Services of Edwin M. Stanton.* 2 vols. Boston and New York: Houghton, Mifflin, 1899.

Gosnell, H. Allen. *Guns on the Western Waters: The Story of the River Gunboats in the Civil War.* Baton Rouge: Louisiana State University Press, 1949; repr., Louisiana State University Press, 1993.

Grant, Ulysses S. *Personal Memoirs of U.S. Grant.* 2 vols. New York: C.L. Webster, 1885–1886; repr. (2 vols. in 1), New York: Penguin, 1999.

_____. *Personal Memoirs of U.S. Grant: A Modern Abridgment.* New York: Premier, 1962.

Green, Francis Vinton. *The Mississippi.* Vol. 8, Campaigns of the Civil War. New York: Charles Scribner's Sons, 1885; repr., The Blue & The Gray, n.d.

Griess, Thomas E., ed. *Atlas for the American Civil War.* West Point Military History Series. Wayne, NJ: Avery, 1986.

Groom, Winston. *Vicksburg 1863.* New York: Alfred A. Knopf, 2009.

Guelzo, Allen C. *The Crisis of the American Republic: A History of the Civil War and Reconstruction.* New York: St. Martin's, 1995.

Hackemer, Kurt. *The U.S. Navy and the Origins of the Military-Industrial Complex, 1847–1883.* Annapolis MD: Naval Institute Press, 2001.

Haites, Erik F., James Mak, and Gary M. Walton, *Western River Transportation: The Era of Early Internal Developments, 1810–1860.* Baltimore: Johns Hopkins University Press, 1975.

Hall, Henry. *Report on the Ship-Building Industry of the United States.* Washington, D.C.: GPO, 1884; repr., New York: Library Editions, 1970.

Hamersly, Lewis B. *The Records of Living Officers of the U.S. Navy and Marine Corps.* Philadelphia: J.B. Lippincott, 1870.

Harris, NiNi. *History of Carondelet.* St. Louis, MO: Southern Commercial Bank, 1991.

Hartjie, Robert C. *Van Dorn: Life and Times of a Confederate General.* Nashville: Vanderbilt University Press, 1967.

Hattaway, Herman, and Archer Jones. *How the North Won: A Military History of the Civil War.* Urbana: University of Illinois Press, 1983.

Haven, Kendall. *Voices of the American Civil War: Stories of Men, Women, and Children Who Lived Through the War Between the States.* Greenwood Village, CO: Libraries Unlimited, 2002.

Hazlett, James C., Edwin Olmstead, and M. Hume Parks. *Field Artillery Weapons of the Civil War.* Rev. ed. Champaign: University of Illinois Press, 2004.

Hearn, Chester G. *Admiral David Dixon Porter: The Civil War Years.* Annapolis: Naval Institute Press, 1996.

_____. *Admiral David Glasgow Farragut: The Civil War Years.* Annapolis: Naval Institute Press, 1998.

_____. *The Capture of New Orleans, 1862.* Baton Rouge: Louisiana State University Press, 1995.

_____. *Ellet's Brigade: The Strangest Outfit of All.* Baton Rouge: Louisiana State University Press, 2000.

_____. *Rebels and Yankees: Naval Battles of the Civil War.* San Diego CA: Thunder Bay Press, 2000.

Hill, Jim Dan. *Sea Dogs of the Sixties.* Minneapolis: University of Minnesota, 1935; repr., New York: A.S. Barnes, 1961.

Hill, Richard, and John Keegan. *War at Sea in the Ironclad Age.* Smithsonian History of Warfare. New York: Harper, 2006.

Hinds, John W. *The Hunt for the Albemarle: Anatomy of a Gunboat War.* Shippensburg, PA: Burd Street, 2001.

_____. *Invasion and Conquest of North Carolina: Anatomy of a Gunboat War.* Shippensburg, PA: Burd Street, 1998.

Hoppin, James M. *The Life of Andrew Hull Foote, Rear Admiral, United States Navy.* New York: Harper and Brothers, 1874.

Horn, Stanley F. *The Army of Tennessee.* Indianapolis: Bobbs-Merrill, 1941.

Hosmer, James K. *A Short History of the Mississippi Valley.* New York: Houghton, Mifflin, 1902.

Howell, H. Grady. *To Live and Die in Dixie: A History of the 3rd Mississippi Infantry, C.S.A.* Madison, MS: Chickasaw Bayou, 1991.

Hubbell, John T., and James W. Geary, eds. *Biographical Dictionary of the Union: Northern Leaders of the Civil War.* Westport, CT: Greenwood, 1995.

Huddleston, Duane, Sammie Rose, and Pat Wood. *Steamboats and Ferries on White River: A Heritage Revisited.* Conway: University of Central Arkansas Press, 1995; repr. Fayetteville: University of Arkansas Press, 1998.

Huling, Edmund J. *Reminiscences of Gunboat Life in the Mississippi Squadron.* Saratoga Springs, NY: Sentinel Print, 1881.

Hunt, Roger D., and Jack R. Brown *Brevet Brigadier Generals in Blue.* Gaithersburg, MD: Olde Soldier, 1997.

Hunter, Louis C. *Steamboats on the Western Waters: An Economic and Technological History.* Cambridge, MA: Harvard University Press, 1949, repr., New York: Dover, 1993.

Jackman, John S. *Diary of a Confederate Soldier: John S. Jackman of the Orphan Brigade.* Edited by William C. Davis. Columbia, SC: University of South Carolina Press, 1990.

Jackson, Rex T. *James B. Eads: The Civil War Ironclads and His Mississippi.* Westminster, MD: Heritage, 2004.

James, Uriah Pierson. *James' River Guide.* Cincinnati: U.P. James, 1866.

Jeter, Katherine Brash, ed. *A Man and His Boat: The Civil War Career and Correspondence of Lt. Jonathan H. Carter.* Lafayette: Center for Louisiana Studies, University of Southwest Louisiana, 1996.

Johnson, Robert E. *Rear Admiral John Rodgers, 1812–1882.* Annapolis: Naval Institute Press, 1967.

Johnson, Timothy D. *Winfield Scott: The Quest for Military Glory.* Lawrence: University Press of Kansas, 1998.

Johnston, William Preston. *The Life of Gen. Albert Sidney Johnston.* New York: D. Appleton, 1878.

Joiner, Gary. *Mr. Lincoln's Brown Water Navy: The Mississippi Squadron.* Lanham, MD: Rowman & Littlefield, 2007.

Jones, Archer. *Confederate Strategy: From Shiloh to Vicksburg.* Baton Rouge: Louisiana State University Press, 1961.

Jones, Robert A. *Confederate Corsair: The Life of Lt. Charles W. "Savez" Read.* Mechanicsburg, PA: Stackpole, 2000.

Joyner, Elizabeth Hoxie. *The U.S.S. "Cairo": History and Artifacts of a Civil War Gunboat.* Jefferson, NC: McFarland, 2006.

Kane, Adam. *The Western River Steamboat.* College Station: Texas A&M University Press, 2004.

Keeler, William F. *Aboard the U.S.S. "Florida," 1863–1865,* Annapolis: Naval Institute Press, 1968.

Kell, John McIntosh. *Recollections of a Naval Life, Including the Cruises of the Confederate States Steamers "Sumter" and "Alabama."* Washington, D.C.: Neal, 1900.

King, William H. *Lessons and Practical Notes on Steam.* Revised by James W. King. New York: D. Van Nostrand, 1864.

Kionka, T.K. *Key Command: Ulysses S. Grant's District of Cairo.* Shades of Blue and Gray Series. Columbia: University of Missouri Press, 2006.

Knight, Edward Henry. *Knight's American Mechanical Dictionary.* 3 vols. Boston: Hurd and Houghton, 1876.

Konstam, Angus, and Tony Bryan. *Confederate Ironclad, 1861–65.* New Vanguard Series 41. Oxford, UK: Osprey, 2001.

_____. *Mississippi River Gunboats of the American Civil War, 1861–1865.* New Vanguard Series 49. London, England: Osprey, 2002.

_____. *Union River Ironclad, 1861–1865.* New Vanguard Series 56. London, England: Osprey, 2002.

Lane, Carl D. *American Paddle Steamboats.* New York: Coward-McCann, 1943.

Lansden, John M. *History of the City of Cairo, Illinois.* Chicago: R.R. Donnelley, 1910.

LaBree, Ben, ed. *The Confederate Soldier in the Civil War, 1861–1865.* Louisville, KY: Courier-Journal Job Printing, 1895.

Levy, U.P. *Manual of Internal Rules and Regulations for Men-of-War.* New York: D. Van Nostrand, 1862.

Lewis, Berkeley R. *Notes on Ammunition of the American Civil War, 1861–1865.* Washington, D.C.: American Ordnance Association, 1959.

Lewis, Charles Lee. *David Glasgow Farragut.* Annapolis: Naval Institute Press, 1943.

Lewis, Gene D. *Charles Ellet, Jr.: The Engineer as Individualist, 1810–1862.* Urbana: University of Illinois Press, 1968.

Lossing Benson J. *Pictorial Field Book of the Civil War: Journeys through the Battlefields in the Wake of Conflict.* 3 vols. Hartford, CT: T. Belknap, 1874; repr. Johns Hopkins University Press, 1997.

Luraghi, Raimondo. *A History of the Confederate Navy.* Translated by Paolo E. Coletta. Annapolis: Naval Institute Press, 1996.

Lynch, William F., *Naval Life; or, Observations Afloat and Ashore: The Midshipman.* New York: Charles Scribner, 1851.

Lytle, William C., comp. *Merchant Steam Vessels of the United States, 1807–1868 "The Lytle List."* Publication No. 6. Mystic, CT: Steamship Historical Society of America, 1952.

Macartney, Clarence Edward. *Mr. Lincoln's Admirals.* New York: Funk and Wagnalls, 1956.

Mahan, Alfred T. *Admiral Farragut.* Great Commanders. New York: D. Appleton, 1892; repr., St. Clair Shores, MI: Scholarly Press, 1970.

_____. *The Gulf and Inland Waters.* Vol. 3, *The Navy in the Civil War.* New York: Scribner's, 1883.

Manucy, Albert. *Artillery Through the Ages.* National Park Service Interpretive Series, no. 3. Washington, D.C.: GPO, 1956.

Martin, Christopher. *Damn the Torpedoes: The Story of America's First Admiral, David Glasgow Farragut.* New York: Abelard Schuman, 1970.

Martin, Richard K., and Daniel L. Schafer. *Jacksonville's Ordeal by Fire: A Civil War History.* Jacksonville: Florida Publishing, 1984.

McCarthy, Mike. *Iron and Steamship Archaeology: Success and Failure of the SS Xantho.* New York: Kluwer Academic, 2000.

McComb, David G. *Galveston: A History.* Austin: University of Texas Press, 1986.

McGrath, Tom, and Doug Ashley. *Historic Structure Report: U.S.S. "Cairo."* Denver: National Park Service, U.S. Department of the Interior, 1981.

McMurray, W.J. *History of the Twentieth Tennessee Volunteer Infantry, C.S.A.* Nashville: Publication Committee, 1904.

McPherson, James M. *Battle Cry of Freedom: The Civil War Era.* New York: Oxford University Press, 1988.

_____. *The Negro's Civil War.* New York: Ballantine, 1991.

Melia, Tamara Moser. *"Damn the Torpedoes": A Short History of U.S. Naval Mine Countermeasures, 1777–1991.* Contributions in Naval History, no. 4. Washington, D.C.: Naval Historical Center, Department of the Navy, 1991.

Melton, Maurice. *The Confederate Ironclads.* New York: Thomas Yoseloff, 1968.

_____. *The Confederate Ironclads.* New York: A.S. Barnes, 1968.

Meriwether, Walter S. *The Paul Jones of the Confederacy: The Brilliant but Forgotten Exploits of Captain Charles W. Read of Mississippi.* New York: F.A. Munsey, 1916.

Merrill, James M. *Battle Flags South: The Story of the Civil War Navies on Western Waters.* Rutherford, NJ: Fairleigh Dickinson University Press, 1970.

_____. *The Rebel Shore: The Story of Union Sea Power in the Civil War.* Boston: Little, Brown, 1957.

Miles, Jim. *A River Unvexed: A History and Tour Guide of the Campaign for the Mississippi River.* Nashville: Rutledge Hill, 1994.

Miller, Charles A., comp. *Official and Political Manual of the State of Tennessee.* Nashville: Marshall & Bruce, 1890.

Miller, David W. *Second Only to Grant: Quartermaster General Montgomery C. Meigs.* Shippensburg, PA: White Mane, 2000.

Miller, Emily Van Dorn. *A Soldier's Honor, with Reminiscences of Major General Earl Van Dorn by His Comrades.* New York: Abbey, 1902.

Miller, Francis Trevelyan, ed. *The Photographic History of the Civil War.* Vol. 6, *The Navies.* New York: Castle, 1911; repr., New York: Thomas Yoseloff, 1957.

Milligan, John D. *Gunboats Down the Mississippi.* Annapolis: Naval Institute Press, 1965.

Mitchell, John L. *Tennessee State Gazetteer and Business Directory for 1860–1861.* Nashville: John L. Mitchell, 1860.

Mitchell, Joseph B., ed. *The Badge of Gallantry: Recollections of Civil War Congressional Medal of Honor Winners.* New York: Macmillan, 1968.

Monaghan, James. *Civil War on the Western Border, 1854–1865*. Boston: Little, Brown, 1955.

Monaghan, Jay. *Swamp Fox of the Confederacy: The Life and Military Services of M. Jeff Thompson*. Tuscaloosa: Confederate, 1956.

Moore, Frank, ed. *The Rebellion Record: A Diary of American Events*. 12 vols. New York: G.P. Putnam, 1861–1863; D. Van Nostrand, 1864–1868; repr., Arno, 1977.

Morgan, James Morris. *Recollections of a Rebel Reefer*. Boston: Houghton, Mifflin, 1917.

Morison, Samuel Eliot. *"Old Bruin": Commodore Matthew C. Perry, 1794–1858*. Boston: Little, Brown, 1967.e

Morrison, John Harrison. *History of New York Ship Yards*. New York: Wm. F. Sametz, 1909.

Mueller, Doris Land. *M. Jeff Thompson: Missouri's Swamp Fox of the Confederacy*. Columbia: University of Missouri Press, 2007.

Murphy, John McLeod. *American Ships and Ship-building*. New York: C.W. Baker, 1860.

Murphy, John McLeod, and W.N. Jeffers. *Nautical Routine and Stowage, with Short Rules in Navigation*. New York: D. Van Nostrand, 1861.

Musicant, Ivan. *Divided Waters: The Naval History of the Civil War*. New York: HarperCollins, 1995.

The Navigator, Containing Directions for Navigating the Monongahela, Allegheny, Ohio and Mississippi Rivers. 8th ed. Pittsburgh: Cramer, Speark and Eichbau, 1814; repr., University of Michigan Press, 1966.

Nevins, Allan. *Fremont: The War for the Union: War The Improvised War*. New York: Charles Scribner's Sons, 1959.

Nichols, James L. *Confederate Engineers*. Tuscaloosa: Confederate, 1957.

Niven, John. *Gideon Welles: Lincoln's Secretary of the Navy*. New York: Oxford University Press, 1973.

Olmstead, Edwin, Wayne E. Stark, and Spencer C. Tucker. *The Big Guns: Civil War Siege, Seacoast and Naval Cannon*. Ontario, Canada, and Bloomfield, New York: Alexandria Bay: Museum Restoration Service, 1997.

Osbon, Bradley S. *Cruise of the U.S. Flagship "Hartford," 1862–1863: Being a Narrative of All Her Operations Since Going into Commission, in 1862, until Her Return to New York in 1863, from the Private Journal of William C. Holton*. New York: L.W. Paine, 1863; repr., Detroit: Gale Archival Editions, 2007.

Owens, Harry P. *Steamboats and the Cotton Economy: River Trade in the Yazoo-Mississippi Delta*. Jackson: University of Mississippi Press, 1990.

Page, Dave. *Ships Versus Shore: Engagements Along Southern Shores and Rivers*. Nashville: Rutledge Hill, 1994.

Park, Carl D. *Ironclad Down: The USS "Merrimack"–CSS "Virginia" from Construction to Destruction*. Annapolis: Naval Institute Press, 2007.

Parker, Foxhall A. *The Naval Howitzer Afloat*. New York: D. Van Nostrand, 1866.

_____. *The Naval Howitzer Ashore*. New York: D. Van Nostrand, 1865.

Parker, William H. *The Confederate Navy*. Confederate Military History, Vol. 12. Atlanta: Confederate, 1899.

_____. *Recollections of a Naval Officer, 1841–1865*. New York: Charles Scribner's Sons, 1883; repr., Annapolis: U.S. Naval Institute Press, 1985.

Parks, Joseph H. *General Leonidas Polk, C.S.A.: The Fighting Bishop*. Baton Rouge: Louisiana State University Press, 1962.

Parrish, T. Michael. *Richard Taylor: Soldier Prince of Dixie*. Chapel Hill: University of North Carolina Press, 1992.

Parrish, Tom Z. *The Saga of the Confederate Ram "Arkansas."* Mississippi Valley Campaign, 1862. Hillsboro, TX: Hill College Press, 1987.

Pearson, Charles E., and Thomas C.C. Birchett. *The History and Archaeology of Two Civil War Steamboats: The Ironclad Gunboat U.S.S. "Eastport" and the Steamer "Ed. F. Dix."* Baton Rouge, LA: Coastal Environments, 2001.

Perry, James M. *A Bohemian Brigade: The Civil War Correspondents, Mostly Rough, Sometimes Ready*. New York: John Wiley, 2000.

Perry, Milton F. *Infernal Machines: The Story of Confederate Submarine and Mine Warfare*. Baton Rouge: Louisiana State University Press, 1965.

Peterson, Harold L. *Notes on Ordnance of the American Civil War, 1861–1865*. Washington, D.C.: American Ordnance Association, 1959.

Plum, William R. *The Military Telegraph during the Civil War in the United States*. 2 vols. Chicago: Jansen, McClurg, 1882.

Polk, William M. *Leonidas Polk: Bishop and General*. 2 vols. New York: Longmans, Green, 1915.

Pollard, E.B. *The Lost Cause: A New Southern History of the War of the Confederates*. New York: E.B. Treat, 1866; repr., New York: Gramercy, 1994.

Porter, David D. *Incidents and Anecdotes of the Civil War*. New York: D. Appleton, 1885; repr., Harrisburg, PA: Archive Society, 1997.

_____. *Naval History of the Civil War*. New York: Sherman, 1886; repr., Secaucus, NJ: Castle, 1984.

Porter, John W.H. *A Record of Events in Norfolk County, Virginia*. Portsmouth, VA: W.A. Fisher, 1892.

Porter, William D. *Defence of Commodore W.D. Porter before the Naval Retiring Board, Convened at Brooklyn Navy Yard, November 1863*. New York: John A. Gray & Green, 1863.

Potter, E.B., and Chester W. Nimitz. *Sea Power: A Naval History*. Englewood Cliffs, NJ: Prentice-Hall, 1960.

Pratt, Fletcher. *The Civil War on Western Waters*. New York: Holt, 1958.

_____. *The Navy, a History: The Story of a Service in Action*. Garden City, NY: Garden City, 1941.

Puleston, William D. *Mahan*. New Haven, CT: Yale University Press, 1939.

Reed, Rowena. *Combined Operations in the Civil War*. Annapolis: Naval Institute Press, 1978; repr., Lincoln: University of Nebraska Press, 1993.

Richard, Allen C., Jr., and Mary Margaret Higgeinbotham Richard. *The Defense of Vicksburg: A Louisiana Chronicle*. Williams-Ford Texas A&M University Military History Series. College Station: Texas A&M University Press, 2003.

Richardson, Albert D. *The Secret Service: The Field, the Dungeon and the Escape*. Hartford, CT: American, 1866.

Richey, Thomas B. *The Battle of Baton Rouge*. College Station, TX: Virtualbookworm.com, 2005.

Ridley, Broomfield L. *Battles and Sketches of the Army of Tennessee*. Mexico: Missouri Printing and Publishing, 1906.

Ringle, Dennis J. *Life in Mr. Lincoln's Navy*. Annapolis: Naval Institute Press, 1998.

Ripley, Warren. *Artillery and Ammunition of the Civil War*. New York: Promontory, 1970.

Roberts, William H. *Civil War Ironclads: The U.S. Navy and Industrial Mobilization*. Baltimore: Johns Hopkins University Press, 2002.

Roe, Francis Asbury. *Naval Duties and Discipline, with*

the Policy and Principles of Naval Organization. New York: D. Van Nostrand, 1865.

Roland, Dunbar. *The Official and Statistical Register of the State of Mississippi.* Nashville: Press of the Brandon Printing Co., 1908.

Roman, Alfred. *Military Operations of General Beauregard.* 2 vols. New York: Harper and Brothers, 1884.

Rombauer, Robert J. *The Union Cause in St. Louis in 1862.* St. Louis: Press of Nixon-Jones Printing Co., 1909.

Rood, Hosea Whitford. *Wisconsin at Vicksburg.* Madison, WI: Wisconsin-Vicksburg Monument Commission, 1914.

Sanders, John. *Memoirs of the Military Resources of the Valley of the Ohio.* Washington, D.C.: C. Alexander, 1845.

Schafer, Louis S. *Confederate Underwater Warfare: An Illustrated History.* Jefferson, NC: McFarland, 1996.

Scharf, J. Thomas. *History of the Confederate Navy from Its Organization to the Surrender of Its Last Vessel.* New York: Rodgers and Sherwood, 1887, repr., New York: Fairfax, 1977.

Shaw, David W. *Sea Wolf of the Confederacy: The Daring Civil War Raids of Naval Lt. Charles W. Read.* Waterville, ME: Thorndike, 2004.

Shea, William L., and Terrence J. Winschel. *Vicksburg Is the Key: The Struggle for the Mississippi Valley.* Great Campaigns of the Civil War Series. Lincoln: University of Nebraska Press, 2003.

Shomette, Donald G. *Shipwrecks of the Civil War: the Encyclopedia of Union and Confederate Naval Losses.* Washington, D.C.: Donic, 1973.

Silverstone, Paul H. *Civil War Navies, 1855–1883.* U.S. Navy Warship Series. New York: Routledge, 2006.

_____. *The Sailing Navy, 1775–1854.* Annapolis: Naval Institute Press, 2001.

_____. *Warships of the Civil War Navies.* Annapolis: Naval Institute Press, 1989.

Simpson, Edward. *A Treatise on Ordnance and Naval Gunnery, Compiled and Arranged as a Text-Book for the U.S. Naval Academy.* 2nd ed. New York: D. Van Nostrand, 1862.

Simson, Jay W. *Naval Strategies of the Civil War: Confederate Innovations and Federal Opportunism.* Nashville: Cumberland House, 2001.

Slagle, Jay. *Ironclad Captain: Seth Ledyard Phelps and the U.S. Navy.* Kent, OH: Kent State University Press, 1996.

Smith, Edward Conrad. *The Borderland in the Civil War.* New York: Macmillan, 1927.

Smith, Frank E. *The Yazoo River.* Rivers of America. New York: Rinehart, 1954; repr., Jackson: University Press of Mississippi, 1988.

Smith, George G., ed. *Spencer Kellogg Brown, His Life in Kansas and His Death as a Spy, 1842–1863, as Disclosed in His Diary.* New York: D. Appleton, 1903.

Smith, Gustavus W. *Confederate War Papers.* New York: Atlantic, 1884.

Smith, Jean Edward. *Grant.* New York: Simon and Schuster, 2001.

Smith, Myron J., Jr. *American Civil War Navies: A Bibliography.* Metuchen, NJ: Scarecrow, 1972.

_____. *Le Roy Fitch: The Civil War Career of a Union River Gunboat Commander.* Jefferson, NC: McFarland, 2007.

_____. *The Timberclads in the Civil War: The "Lexington," "Tyler" and "Conestoga" on the Western Waters, 1861–1865.* Jefferson, NC: McFarland, 2008.

_____. *The USS "Carondelet": A Civil War Ironclad on Western Waters.* Jefferson, NC: McFarland, 2010.

_____. *U.S.S. "Carondelet," 1861–1865.* Manhattan, KA: MA/AH, 1982.

Stern, Philip Van Dorn. *The Confederate Navy: A Pictorial History.* New York: Bonanza, 1962.

Still, William N., Jr., ed. *The Confederate Navy: The Ships, Men, and Organization, 1861–1865.* Annapolis: Naval Institute Press, 1997.

Still, William N., Jr. *Confederate Shipbuilding.* Athens: University of Georgia Press, 1969; repr., Columbia, SC: University of South Carolina Press, 1987.

_____. *Iron Afloat: The Story of Confederate Armorclads.* Nashville: Vanderbilt University Press, 1971; repr., Columbia, SC: University of South Carolina Press, 1985.

Stone, Kate. *Brokenburn: The Journal of Kate Stone, 1861–1868.* Edited by John Q. Anderson. Baton Rouge: Louisiana State University Press, 1955; repr., 1995.

Stotherd, R.H. *Notes on Torpedoes, Offensive and Defensive.* Washington, D.C.: Government Printing Office, 1872.

Street, James. *By Valour and Arms.* New York: Dial, 1944.

Sutphin, Dorothy Lyons, comp. *The Walker Family of Mississippi, Louisiana, and Texas: A Biographical and Historical Genealogy.* Baytown, TX: Private printing, 1970.

Swanberg, W.A. *First Blood: The Story of Fort Sumter.* New York: Charles Scribner's Sons, 1957.

Symonds, Craig L. *The Civil War at Sea.* Santa Barbara, CA: ABC/CLIO, 2009.

_____. *Lincoln and His Admirals: Abraham Lincoln, the U.S. Navy, and the Civil War.* New York: Oxford University Press, 2008.

Taylor, Paul. *Discovering the Civil War in Florida: A Reader and Guide.* Sarasota: Pineapple, 2001.

Thomas, Dean S. *Cannons: Introduction to Civil War Artillery.* Arendtsville, PA: Thomas, 1985.

Thompson, Edward Porter. *History of the First Kentucky Brigade.* Cincinnati: Caxton, 1868.

_____. *History of the Orphan Brigade.* Louisville, KY: Lewis M. Thompson, 1898.

Thompson, M. Jeff. *The Civil War Reminiscences of General M. Jeff Thompson.* Edited by Donal J. Stanton, Goodwin F. Berquist, and Paul C. Bowers. Dayton, OH: Morningside Bookshop, 1988.

Townsend, Edward, *Anecdotes of the Civil War in the United States.* New York: D. Appleton, 1884.

Tucker, Spencer C. *Andrew Foote: Civil War Admiral on Western Waters.* Annapolis: Naval Institute Press, 2000.

_____. *Arming the Fleet: U.S. Navy Ordnance in the Muzzle-Loading Era.* Annapolis: Naval Institute Press, 1988

_____. *Blue & Gray Navies: The Civil War Afloat.* Annapolis: U.S. Naval Institute, 2006.

Turner, George Edgar. *Victory Rode the Rails: The Strategic Place of Railroads in the Civil War.* Indianapolis: Bobbs-Merrill, 1953.

Twain, Mark. *Life on the Mississippi.* New York: Harper & Brothers, 1950.

Underwood, Rodman L. *Stephen Russell Mallory: A Biography of the Confederate Navy Secretary and United States Senator.* Jefferson, NC: McFarland, 2005.

U.S. Navy Department. Naval History Division. *Civil War Naval Chronology, 1861–1865.* 6 vols. in 1. Rev. ed. Washington, D.C.: GPO, 1966.

_____. Navy Department. *Riverine Warfare: The United States Navy's Operations on Inland Waters.* Rev. ed. Washington, D.C.: GPO, 1968.

_____. Office of the Secretary of the Navy. *Report of the Secretary of the Navy.* 6 vols. Washington, D.C.: GPO, 1861–1866.

Vandiver, Frank E., ed. *The Civil War Diary of General*

Josiah Gorgas. Tuscaloosa: University of Alabama Press, 1947.

Van Doren Stern, Philip. *The Confederate Navy: A Pictorial History.* New York: Bonanza, 1961.

Van Doren Stern, Philip, ed. *Soldier Life in the Union and Confederate Armies.* New York: Premier, 1961.

Very, Edward W. *Navies of the World.* New York: John Wiley and Sons, 1880.

Walke, Henry. *Naval Scenes and Reminiscences of the Civil War in the United States on the Southern and Western Waters during the Years 1861, 1862 and 1863, with the History of That Period Compared and Corrected from Authentic Sources.* New York: F.R. Reed, 1877.

Walker, Peter F. *Vicksburg: A People at War, 1860–1865.* Chapel Hill: University of North Carolina Press, 1960.

Warner, Ezra. *Generals in Blue: Lives of Union Commanders.* Baton Rouge: Louisiana State University Press, 1964.

_____. *Generals in Gray: Lives of Confederate Commanders.* Baton Rouge: Louisiana State University Press, 1959.

Wash, W.A. *Camp, Field and Prison Life, Containing Sketches of Service in the South.* St. Louis: Southwestern, 1870.

Way, Frederick, Jr. *Way's Packet Directory, 1848–1994: Passenger Steamboats of the Mississippi River System since the Advent of Photography in Mid-Continent America.* Athens: Ohio University Press, 1983; revised ed., Athens: Ohio University Press, 1994.

Webster's Geographical Dictionary. Rev. ed. Springfield, MA: G. & C. Merriam, 1966.

Webster, William G. *The Army and Navy Pocket Dictionary.* Philadelphia: J.B. Lippincott, 1865.

Weigley, Russell F. *Quartermaster General of the Union Army: A Biography of M.C. Meigs.* New York: Columbia University Press, 1959.

Welcher, Frank J. *The Union Army, 1861–1865: Organization and Operations.* Vol. 3, *The Western Theater.* Bloomington: Indiana University Press, 1993.

Welles, Gideon. *The Diary of Gideon Welles, Secretary of the Navy under Lincoln and Johnson.* Edited by John T. Morse, Jr. 3 vols. Boston: Houghton, Mifflin, 1911; repr., New York: W.W. Norton, 1960.

Wells, Tom H. *The Confederate Navy: A Study in Organization.* Tuscaloosa: University of Alabama Press, 1971.

West, Richard S. *Gideon Welles, Lincoln's Navy Department.* Indianapolis: Bobbs-Merrill, 1943.

_____. *Mr. Lincoln's Navy.* New York: Longman's, Green, 1957.

_____. *The Second Admiral: A Life of David Dixon Porter, 1813–1891.* New York: Coward-McCann, 1937.

Whitcomb, Carolyn Elizabeth. *History of the Second Massachusetts Battery (Nims' Battery) of Light Artillery, 1861–1865.* Concord, NH: Rumford, 1912.

Wideman, John C. *The Sinking of the U.S.S. "Cairo."* Jackson: University Press of Mississippi, 1993.

Wiggins, Sarah Woolfolk. *The Journals of Josiah Gorgas, 1857–1878.* Tuscaloosa: University of Alabama Press, 1995.

Wiley, Bell I. *The Life of Billy Yank, the Common Soldier of the Union.* New York: Bobbs-Merrill, 1952; repr. Baton Rouge: Louisiana State University Press, 1991.

_____. *The Life of Johnny Reb, the Common Soldier of the Confederacy.* New York: Bobbs-Merrill, 1943; repr. Baton Rouge: Louisiana State University Press, 1990.

Wilkie, Franc B. *Pen and Powder.* Boston: Ticknor, 1888.

Williams, T. Harry. *Lincoln and His Generals.* New York: Alfred Knopf, 1952; repr., New York: Vintage, 1962.

_____. *P.G.T. Beauregard.* Baton Rouge: Louisiana State University Press, 1954.

Wills, Charles Wright. *Army Life of an Illinois Soldier.* Compiled by Mary E. Kellogg. Washington, D.C.: Globe, 1906.

Wilson, James Grant, and John Fiske, eds. *Appleton's Cyclopaedia of American Biography.* 5 vols. New York: D. Appleton, 1888.

Winters, John D. *The Civil War in Louisiana.* Baton Rouge: Louisiana State University Press, 1963.

Woodworth, Steven E. *Jefferson Davis and His Generals: The Failure of Confederate Command in the West.* Lawrence: University Press of Kansas, 1990.

_____. *Nothing but Victory: The Army of the Tennessee, 1861–1865.* New York: Alfred A. Knopf, 2005.

Woodworth, Steven E., ed. *Grant's Lieutenants: From Cairo to Vicksburg.* Lawrence: University Press of Kansas, 2001.

Young, John Preston, and A.R. James. *Standard History of Memphis, Tennessee: From a Study of the Original Sources.* Knoxville: H.W., 1912.

Young, Lot D. *Reminiscences of a Soldier of the Orphan Brigade.* Louisville, KY: Courier Journal Press, 1918.

Articles and Essays in Books or Journals

Anderson, Bern. "The Naval Strategy of the Civil War." *Military Affairs* 26 (Spring 1962), 11–21.

Arnold, James R. "Rough Work on the Mississippi." *Naval History* 13, no. 5 (1999), 38–43.

Barnhart, Donald, Jr. "Junkyard Ironclad." *Civil War Times Illustrated* 40 (May 2001), 31–37, 67–68.

Bastian, David F. "Opening of the Mississippi during the Civil War." In *New Aspects of Naval History: Selected Papers from the Fifth Naval History Symposium,* edited by U.S. Navy Academy, Department of History Personnel. Baltimore: Nautical & Aviation, 1985.

Bearss, Edwin C. "A Federal Raid Up the Tennessee River." *The Alabama Review* 17 (October 1964), 261–270.

Blake, W.H. "Coal Barging in Wartime, 1861–1865." *Gulf States Historical Magazine* 1 (May 1903), 409–412.

Blume, Kenneth J. "'Concessions Where Concessions Could Be Made': The Naval Efficiency Boards of 1855–1857." In *New Interpretations in Naval History: Selected Papers form the 14th Naval History Symposium,* edited by Randy Carol Balano and Craig L. Symonds. Annapolis: Naval Institute Press, 2001.

Bogle, Robert V. "Defeat Through Default: Confederate Naval Strategy for the Upper Tennessee and Its Tributaries, 1861–1862." *Tennessee Historical Quarterly* 18 (Spring 1968), 62–71.

Bolin, James Duane. "Clifton Rodes Breckenridge: 'The Little Arkansas Giant.'" *Arkansas Historical Quarterly* 53 (Winter 1994), 407–427.

Branch, Mary Emerson. "Prime Emerson and Steamboat Building in Memphis." *West Tennessee Historical Society Papers* 38 (1984), 69–83.

_____. "The Story Behind the Story of the *Arkansas* and the *Carondelet.*" *Missouri Historical Review* 79 (1985), 313–331.

Brooke, John Mercer. "The *Virginia* or *Merrimac*: Her Real Projector." *Southern Historical Society Papers* 19 (January 1891), 3–5.

Burpo, Robert. "Notes on the First Fleet Engagement in

the Civil War." *American Neptune* 19 (October 1959), 265–273.

Callender, Eliott. "Career of the Confederate Ram *Arkansas*, Given before the Farragut Naval Veterans Association, Chicago." In *Speeches of a Veteran*. Chicago: Blue Sky, 1901; repr., Charleston, SC: BiblioLife, 2009.

Campbell, Donald B. "The Confederate Gunboat *Arkansas*." *U.S. Naval Institute Proceedings* 88 (July 1962), 152–154.

Carr, Margaret Alexander. "Lieutenant Henry Kennedy Stevens, CSN: Warrior of the CSS *Arkansas*." *UDC Magazine* 65 (June-July 2002), 16–17.

Carson, Kevin. "21 Days to Glory: The Saga of the Confederate Ram *Arkansas*." *Sea Classics* 39 (July 2006), 38–41, 58–59.

Castel, Albert. "Earl Van Dorn." *Civil War Times Illustrated* 6 (1967), 38–42.

Catton, Bruce. "Glory Road Began in the West," *Civil War History* 6 (June 1960), 229–237.

Chamberlain, S. "Opening of the Upper Mississippi and the Siege of Vicksburg." *Magazine of Western History* 5 (March 1887), 609–624.

Chandler, Walter. "The Memphis Navy Yard: An Adventure in Internal Improvement." *West Tennessee Historical Papers* 1 (1947), 68–72.

Coggins, Jack. "Civil War Naval Ordnance: Weapons and Equipment." *Civil War Times Illustrated* 4 (November 1964), 16–20.

Coleman, Silas B., and Paul Stevens. "A July Morning with the Rebel Ram Arkansas." *U.S. Naval Institute Proceedings* 88 (July 1962), 84–97.

Cornish, Dudley Taylor, and Virginia Jeans Laas. *Lincoln's Lee: The Life of Samuel Phillips Lee, United States Navy, 1812–1897*. Lawrence: University Press of Kansas, 1986.

Cozzens, Peter. "Roadblock on the Mississippi." *Civil War Times Illustrated* 41 (March 2002), 40–49.

Daniel, Larry J. "The Quinby & Robinson Cannon Foundry at Memphis." *West Tennessee Historical Society Papers* 27 (1973), 18–32.

Davis, Steven R. "Workhorse of the Western Waters: The Timberclad *Tyler*." *Civil War Times Illustrated* 44 (February 2005), 34–40, 80.

Dillon, John F. "The Role of Riverine Warfare in the Civil War." *Naval War College Review* 25 (March-April 1973), 62–63+.

Dimitry, Adelaide Stuart. "The Queen of the Mississippi." In *War-Time Sketches Historical and Otherwise*. New Orleans: Louisiana Printing, 1911.

Dorsett, Phyllis F. "James B. Eads: Navy Shipbuilder, 1861." *U.S. Naval Institute Proceedings* 101 (August 1975), 76–79.

East, Sherrod E. "Montgomery C. Meigs and the Quartermaster Department." *Military Affairs* 25 (Winter 1961–1962), 183–196.

Flatau, Louis S. "A Great Naval Battle." *Confederate Veteran* 25 (October 1917), 458–459.

Flynt, David. "Run the Fleet: The Career of the C.S. Ram *Arkansas*." *Journal of Mississippi History* 51 (May 1989), 107–132.

Gaden, Elmer L., Jr. "Eads and the Navy of the Mississippi." *American Heritage of Invention & Technology* 9 (Spring 1994), 24–31.

Gauthreaux, Alan G. "Lost in the Fog of War." *Civil War Times* 49 (April 2010), 54–59.

Geoghegan, William E. "Study for a Scale Model of the U.S.S. *Carondelet*," *Nautical Research Journal* 17 (Fall and Winter 1970), 147–163, 231–236.

Gift, George W. "The Story of the *Arkansas*." *Southern Historical Society Papers* 8 (January-May 1884), 48–54, 115–119, 163–170, 208.

Gillespie, Michael L. "The Novel Experiment: Cottonclads and Steamboats." *Civil War Times Illustrated* 22 (December 1983), 34–36.

Goodwin, Martha. "The Ram *Arkansas*." *Confederate Veteran* 28 (January-December 1920), 263–264.

Hall, Tom. "The Bravest Act." In *Vicksburg and the War*, by Gordon A. Cotton and Jeff T. Giambrone. Gretna, LA: Pelican, 2004.

Hasegawa, Guy. "Quinine Substitutes in the Confederate Army." *Military Medicine* 172 (June 2007), 650–655.

Hirsch, Charles B. "Gunboat Personnel on the Western Waters." *Mid-America* 34 (April 1952), 73–86.

Hogane, James T. "Reminiscences of the Siege of Vicksburg," *Southern Historical Society Papers* 11 (April-May 1883), 4854–4886.

House, Boyce. "Confederate Navy Hero [Dabney Scales] Put the Flag Back into Place." *Tennessee Historical Quarterly* 19 (June 1960), 172–175.

Huffshot, Robert S. "The Brief, Glorious Career of the C.S.S. *Arkansas*." *Civil War Times Illustrated* 7 (July 1968), 20–27.

_____. "The *Carondelet* and Other 'Pook' Turtles." *Civil War Times Illustrated* 6 (August 1967), 4–11.

Hurst, T.M. "Some Tennessee Historical Notes." *Tennessee Historical Magazine* 7 (April 1921), 134–136.

Jeter, Katherine Brash. "Against All Odds: Lt. Jonathan H. Carter, CSN, and His Ironclad." *Louisiana History* 28 (Summer 1987), 263–288.

Johnson, John. "Story of the Confederate Armored Ram *Arkansas*." *Southern Historical Society Papers* 33 (January-December 1905), 1–15.

Johnson, Kenneth R. "Confederate Defense and Union Gunboats on the Tennessee River." *Alabama Historical Quarterly* 64 (Summer 1968), 39–60.

Legan, Marshall S. "The Confederate Career of a Union Ram [*Queen of the West*]." *Louisiana History* 33 (Summer 2000), 277–300.

Long, E.B. "The Paducah Affair: Bloodless Action That Altered the Civil War in the Mississippi Valley." *Register of the Kentucky Historical Society* 60 (July 1972), 253–276.

_____. "Plum Point Bend: The Forgotten Battle." *Civil War Times Illustrated* 11 (June 1972), 4–11.

Long, John S. "The Gosport Affair." *Journal of Southern History* 23 (May 1957), 155–172.

"Major General William Giles Harding." In *Norwich University, 1819–1911: Her History, Her Graduates, Her Roll of Honor*, compiled by William A. Ellis. 3 vols. Montpelier, VT: Capital City, 1911.

Maness, Lonnie E. "Fort Pillow under Confederate and Union Control." *West Tennessee Historical Society Papers* 38 (1984), 84–98.

Mangum, Ronald S. "The Vicksburg Campaign: A Study in Joint Operations." *Parameters* 21 (Autumn 1991), 74–86.

McCammack, Brian. "Competence, Power, and the Nostalgic Romance of Piloting in Mark Twain's *Life on the Mississippi*." *Southern Literary Journal* XXXVIII (March 2006), 1–18.

McClinton, Oliver Wood. "The Career of the Confederate States Ram *Arkansas*." *Arkansas Historical Quarterly* 7 (Winter 1948), 329–333.

McGlone, John E., III. "*The Lost Corps: The Confederate States Marines*." *U.S. Naval Institute Proceedings* 99 (November 1972), 69–73.

Melville, Philip. "*Carondelet* Runs the Gauntlet." *American Heritage* 10 (October 1959), 65–77.

Merrill, James M. "Cairo, Illinois: Strategic Civil War River Port." *Journal of the Illinois State Historical Society* 76 (Winter 1983), 242–257.

_____. "Union Shipbuilding on Western Waters during the Civil War." *Smithsonian Journal of History* 3 (Winter 1968–1969), 17–44.

Miller, Milford M. "Evansville Steamboats during the Civil War," *Indiana Magazine of History* 37 (December 1941), 359–381.

Milligan, John D. "Charles Ellet and His Naval Steam Ram. *Civil War History* 9 (1963), 121–132.

_____. "The First American Ironclads: The Evolution of a Design." *Missouri Historical Society Bulletin* 22 (October 1965), 3–13

_____. "From Theory to Application: The Emergence of the American Ironclad War Vessel." *Military Affairs* 48 (July 1984), 126–132.

_____. "Navy Life on the Mississippi River." *Civil War Times Illustrated* 33 (May-June 1994), 16, 66–73.

Milligan, John D., ed. "The Dark and the Light Side of the River War." *Civil War Times Illustrated* 9 (December 1970), 12–19.

Mullen, Jay C. "Pope's New Madrid and Island No. 10 Campaign." *Missouri Historical Review* 49 (April 1965), 325–343.

_____. "The Turning of Columbus." *Register of the Kentucky Historical Society* 64 (July 1966), 209–225.

Nash, Howard P. "Island No. 10." *Civil War Times Illustrated* 5 (December 1966), 42–50.

"Neil S. Brown." In *Tennessee: The Volunteer State, 1769–1923*, by John Trotwood Moore and Austin P. Foster. 2 vols. Chicago: S.J. Clarke, 1923.

Newcomer, Lee N. "The Battle of Memphis, 1862." *West Tennessee Historical Society Papers* 12 (1958), 41–57.

Parent, Edward D. "A Conjectural Model of C.S.S. *Arkansas*." *Seaways' Ships in Scale* 13 (September-October 2002), 32–38.

_____. "The New *Arkansas* Kit by Old Steam Navy." *Seaways' Ships in Scale* 17 (May-June 2006), 48–53.

Parks, William M. "Building a Warship in the Southern Confederacy." *U.S. Naval Institute Proceedings* 49 (August 1923), 1299–1307.

Perret, Geoffrey. "Anaconda: The Plan That Never Was." *North and South* 6 (May 2003), 36–43.

"Pettus Flying Artillery." In *Military History of Mississippi, 1803–1898*, by Dunbar Roland. Spartanburg, SC: Reprint Company, 1988.

Pirtle, John B. "The Defense of Vicksburg and the Battle of Baton Rouge." *Confederate Veteran* 32 (June 1924), 264–266.

Read, Charles W. "Reminiscences of the Confederate States Navy." *Southern Historical Society Papers* 1 (May 1876), 331–362.

Reid, Brian Holden. "Rationality and Irrationality in Union Strategy, April 1861–March 1862." *War in History* 1 (March 1994), 25–29.

Riggs, David F. "Sailors of the U.S.S. *Cairo*: Anatomy of a Gunboat Crew." *Civil War History* 28 (September 1982), 266–273.

Roberts, John C., and Richard H. Webber. "Gunboats in the River War, 1861–1865." *U.S. Naval Institute Proceedings* 91 (March 1965), 83–100.

Roland, Charles P. "Louisiana Sugar Planters and the Civil War." In *Louisianians in the Civil War*, by Lawrence Lee Hewitt and Arthur W. Bergeron, Jr. Columbia: University of Missouri Press, 2002.

Rose, F.P. "The Confederate Ram *Arkansas*." *Arkansas Historical Quarterly* 12 (Winter 1953), 333–339.

Sawyer, William D. "The Western River Engine." *Steamboat Bill* 35 (1978), 71–80.

Sessions, James O.H. "Diary of James Oliver Hazard Perry Sessions of Rileby Plantation, on the Yazoo, January 1, 1862-June 1872." *Journal of Mississippi History* 39 (August 1977), 239–254.

Smith, Myron J., Jr. "The Final Fate of the U.S.S. *Carondelet*." *Nautical Research Journal* 20 (January 1974), 50–58.

Still, William N., Jr. "The Common Sailor—The Civil War's Uncommon Man: Part I, Yankee Blue Jackets." *Civil War Times Illustrated* 23 (February 1985), 25–39.

_____. "Confederate Behemoth: The C.S.S. *Louisiana*." *Civil War Times Illustrated* 16 (November 1977), 20–25.

_____. "Confederate Naval Strategy: The Ironclad." *Journal of Southern History* 27 (August 1961), 330–343.

_____. "Confederate Shipbuilding in Mississippi." *Journal of Mississippi History* 30 (Fall 1968), 291–303.

Stucky, Scott W. "Joint Operations in the Civil War." *Joint Forces Quarterly*, no. 6 (Autumn-Winter 1994–1995), 92–105.

Suhr, Robert C. "Converted River Steamers Dubbed 'Timberclads' Gave the Union Navy an Important Presence on Southern Waters." *America's Civil War* 11 (July 1998), 20–25.

_____. ""Personality: Charles Henry Davis' Brilliant U.S. Navy Career Was Interrupted, Not Enhanced, by the Civil War." *Military History* 21 (January-February 2005), 74–75.

Sulivane, Clement. "The *Arkansas* at Vicksburg in 1862." *Confederate Veteran* 25 (November 1917), 490–491.

Trexler, H.A. "The Confederate Navy Department and the Fall of New Orleans." *Southwest Review* 19 (Autumn 1933), 88–102.

Tucker, Spencer C. "Capturing the Confederacy's Western Waters." *Naval History* 20 (June 2006), 16–23.

_____. "Timberclads Attack Up the Tennessee." *Naval History* 16 (February 2001), 27–29.

United States. Naval Historical Foundation. "River Navies in the Civil War." *Military Affairs* 18 (Spring 1954), 29–32.

"The Walke Family of Lower Norfolk County, Virginia." *The Virginia Magazine of History and Biography* 5 (October 1897), 149–150.

Waterman, George C. "Notable Naval Events of the War." *Confederate Veteran* 6 (January 1891), 59–62, 170–173.

Watts, Tim J. "The *Arkansas*." In *Encyclopedia of the Civil War: A Political, Social, and Military History*, edited by David Stephen Heidler, Jeanne T. Heidler, and David J. Cole. New York: W.W. Norton, 2000.

Webber, Richard, and John C. Roberts. "James B. Eads: Master Builder." *The Navy* 8 (March 1965), 23–25.

Wegner, Dana S. "Commodore William D. 'Dirty Bill' Porter." *U.S. Naval Institute Proceedings* 103 (February 1977), 40–47.

_____. "Little Egypt's Naval Station." *U.S. Naval Institute Proceedings* 98 (March 1972), 74–76.

_____. "S.X.: The Federal Gunboat *Essex*." *Nautical Research Journal* 19 (Spring 1972), 49–51.

Weigley, Russel F. "Montgomery C. Meigs: A Personality Profile." *Civil War Times Illustrated* 3 (November 1964), 42–48.

West, Richard, Jr. "Lincoln's Hand in Naval Matters." *Civil War History* 4 (June 1958), 175–181.

White, Lonnie J. "Federal Operations at New Madrid and

Island No. 10." *West Tennessee Historical Society Papers* 17 (1963), 47–67.

Whitesell, Robert D. "Military and Naval Activity between Cairo and Columbus." *Register of the Kentucky Historical Society* 61 (April 1963), 107–121.

Williams, Thomas. "Letters of General Thomas Williams, 1862." *American Historical Review* 14 (January 1909), 309–328.

Unpublished Sources

Barr, Alwyn. "Confederate Artillery in the Trans-Mississippi." Master's thesis, University of Texas, 1961.

Chapman, Jesse L. "The Ellet Family and Riverine Warfare in the West, 1861–1865." Master's thesis, Old Dominion University, 1985.

Getchll, Charles M., Jr. "Defender of Inland Waters: The Military Career of Isaac Newton Brown, Commander, Confederate States Navy, 1861–1865." Master's thesis, University of Mississippi, 1978.

Holcombe, Robert. "The Evolution of Confederate Ironclad Design." Master's thesis, East Carolina University, 1993.

Moseley, Cynthia E. "The Naval Career of Henry Kennedy Stevens as Revealed in His Letters, 1839–1863." Master's thesis, University of North Carolina, 1951.

Neill, John Hamilton, Jr. "Shipbuilding in Confederate New Orleans." Master's thesis, Tulane University, 1940.

Parker, Theodore R. "The Federal Gunboat Flotilla on the Western Waters during Its Administration by the War Department to October 1, 1862." PhD diss., University of Pittsburgh, 1939.

Polser, Aubrey Henry. "The Administration of the United States Navy, 1861–1865." PhD diss., University of Nebraska, 1975.

Smith, Myron J., Jr. "A Construction and Recruiting History of the U.S. Steam Gunboat *Carondelet*, 1861–1862." Master's thesis, Shippensburg State University, 1969.

Still, William N. "The History of the C.S.S. *Arkansas*," Master's thesis, University of Alabama, 1958.

Whisenant, Johnny H. "Samuel Phillips Lee, U.S.N.: Commander, Mississippi Squadron, October 19, 1864–August 14, 1865." Master's thesis, Kansas State College of Pittsburg, 1968.

Wright, Aubrey Gardner. "Henry Walke, 1809–1896: Romantic Painter and Naval Hero." Master's thesis, George Washington University, 1971.

Wright, Homer. "Naval Career of Charles W. Read, 1856–1890." Master's thesis, Auburn University, 1965.

Correspondence/Interviews

Cussler, Clive. Telephone Interview with the author. May 6, 1981.

McKibben, Joyce A. Reference Librarian, University of Memphis, "Re: Ask a Librarian: John T. Shirley." Message via e-mail to the author, June 29, 2009.

Meagher, David. Letters to the author, May 2, 4–5, 7, 12–13, 20, 23, 28, 2010.

Ticer, Sarah. Reference Intern, Dolph Briscoe Center for American History, "Re: Ask a Question: Isaac Newton Brown." Message via e-mail to the author, August 14, 2009.

Wright, George. Letters to the author. March 17, 31, 2010.

Other Sources

Meagher, David. "C.S.S. *Arkansas*." Chart. N.p.: 1995.

Index

Numbers in ***bold italics*** indicate pages with photographs.

Abram B. Reading Foundry (Vicksburg foundry) 98, 106
Alabama, C.S. sloop 14
Albemarle (C.S. ironclad) 109
Alden, U.S. Cmdr. John 185–186, 208, 213, 219, 224, 232–233, 237, 239, 242; *see also* Richmond (U.S. sloop)
Allen, C.S. Pvt. Caleb 214, 253; *see also* Kentucky, CS regiments (Infantry, 6th)
Allen, U.S. Master's Mate/messenger E.J. 209
Altona (steamer) 25–26; *see also* Emerson, C.S. contractor/steamboat builder Primus
"Anaconda Plan" (1861) 17, 20; *see also* Scott, U.S. Lt. Gen. Winfield
Anderson, U.S. Maj. Robert 14; *see also* Fort Sumter (SC)
Arkansas (C.S. ironclad ram): armament 54, 74, 77, 101–103; armor 43–45, 65, 74, 78, 80–82, 97–99, 235, 268, 281; Battle in the Yazoo (July 15, 1862) 151–177 (*see also Carondelet* [U.S. ironclad]; *Queen of the West* [U.S. ram]; *Tyler* [U.S. timberclad]); "breakout" down the Yazoo to the Mississippi (July 14, 1862) 142–150; bulkheads 99–100; casemate 35–36, 52, 59, 74, 96–99; construction 38–56, 59–61, 65–66, 74–75, 78, 80–***84***, 90, 96–119, 125; crew recruitment 116–117, 123–124, 135, 138, 214–215, 240–243, 265, 274; design 32–37, 42, 50–52, 74, 96; destruction (August 6, 1862) 286–***291*** (*see also* impact of loss); dimensions 50–52, 69–70; Dowdey profile drawing 121; engines/machinery/propulsion 35, 45, 52, 60–61, 74, 77, 107–112, 122, 179, 268, 273–279, 282–283, 285–286; escape from Memphis to Yazoo River 65–66, 71, 74, 77–81; gun carriages 104–106; gunnery drill 139–140, 216; illustrations ***68***, ***84***; loss, impact of 295–297 (*see also* destruction [August 6, 1862]); meager profile drawing 120; Milliken profile drawing ***68***; *New York Tribune* profile drawing 147; officer assignments 117–119; ordnance stores and gunpowder 106, 143, 151; paint scheme and color 100, 220; pilothouse 59–60, 100, 117; ram 51–52, ***54***, "running the gauntlet" of Union ships (July 15, 1862) 143, 178–***189***, 190–200, ***201–202***, 203; Scales profile drawing ***68***; shakedown cruise 119–120, 122–125, 127–129, 132, 135–136, 140 (*see also* Liverpool Landing, MS); Skerrett profile drawing 121; U.S. Fleet passage downriver under the guns of Vicksburg vs. CSS *Arkansas* (July 15-16, 1862) 204–230; vs. U.S. ram *Queen of the West* at Vicksburg (July 22, 1862) 231–266; vs. USS *Essex* at Baton Rouge (July 23–August 6, 1862) 267–293; vs. USS *Essex* at Vicksburg (July 22, 1862) 231–***248***, 249–266, 286; wreck site 297
Atkins, C.S. Rep. John DeWitt Clinton 29, 33
Autry, C.S. Col. Jason L. 83

Bacon, U.S. Captain's Clerk Edward W. 135, 139, 146, 180, 194, 200, 208, 219, 221; *see also Iroquois* (U.S. sloop)
Bacon, Kate *see* U.S. Captain's Clerk Edward W. Bacon
Bacot, C.S. Midshipman Richard H. 75, 274, 277, 287; *see also Arkansas* (C.S. ironclad ram)
Balfour, C.S. Maj. Joseph Davis 253–254; *see also* Porter, U.S. Cmdr. William D. ("Dirty Bill")
Barbot, C.S. Lt. Alphonso 87, 92, ***113***, 138, 160, 198, 235, 240; *see also Arkansas* (C.S. ironclad ram)
Bartlett, U.S. Lt. E.W. 126
Bates, U.S. Attorney Gen. Edward 17
Baton Rouge, LA 80–81, 267–293; *see also Arkansas* (C.S. ironclad ram); *Essex* (U.S. ironclad)
Battle in the Yazoo (July 15, 1862) 151–177; *see also Arkansas* (C.S. ironclad ram); *Carondelet* (U.S. ironclad); *Queen of the West* (U.S. ram); *Tyler* (U.S. timberclad)
Beaman, *St. Louis Daily Missouri Democrat* correspondent George W. 236
Beauregard, C.S. Gen. P.G.T. 10, 12–14, 67, 69–70, 75, 77, 83, 86, 88–***89***, 91–93, 113; *see also* Fort Sumter (SC)
Bell, U.S. Cmdr./Fleet Capt. Henry H. 83, 113, 209, 211, 213, 220–221, 223, 225, 230, 232, 237–238, 240, 245, 251, 260, 263, 279; *see also* Brooklyn (U.S. sloop); Farragut, U.S. RAdm. David G.
Belmont, MO, Battle of (1861) 148; *see also* Grant, U.S. Maj. Gen. Ulysses S.; Walke, U.S. Cmdr. Henry
Ben McCulloch (steamer) 106
Bentley, *Philadelphia Inquirer* correspondent Henry 51–52, 66, 79, 108, 122, 130, 137, 180, 202
Benton (U.S. ironclad) 137, 145–146, 149, 169, 176–177, 180, 186, 190, 195, 196–***197***, 198–199, 210, 212, 215–216, 233–234, 240–241, 243–246, 262–263; *see also* Davis, U.S. RAdm. Henry H.; Phelps, U.S. Lt. Cmdr./Acting Fleet Capt. S. Ledyard; "running the gauntlet" (July 15, 1862)
Bishop, U.S. Lt. Joshua 190; *see*

343

also General Bragg (U.S. gunboat)
Blackmore, Plantation owner Lizzie McFarland 91; *see also* Brown, C.S. Lt. Isaac Newton
B.M. Runyan (steamer) 59; *see also* Miller, Capt. James
Bodman, *Chicago Daily Tribune* correspondent Albert H. 136, 162, 172, 180, 183, 202, 226
Brady, C.S. Pilot James 117, 164–165, 168, 183–185, 196, 198, 223, 279, 285, 292–293; *see also Arkansas* (C.S. ironclad ram); Baton Rouge, LA; "running the gauntlet" (July 15, 1862); Yazoo River, Battle in the (July 15, 1862)
Bragg, C.S. Gen. Braxton 115, 269
Breckenridge, C.S. general's aide Clifton Rodes 229; *see also* Breckenridge, C.S. Brig. Gen. John C.
Breckenridge, C.S. Maj. Gen. John C. 115, 133, 189, 206, 229, 269–**271**, 273–274, 276–277, 279, 281–282, 284, 290, 292–293, 296; *see also* Baton Rouge, LA
Brennand, U.S. First Master Edward E. 231, 249; *see also Carondelet* (U.S. ironclad)
Brierly, Capt. Tom 29; *see also Ferdinand Kennet*, C.S. steamer
Brooke, C.S. Lt. John Mercer 12, 21–**22**, 23–24, 28, 31–33, 43, 269, 296; *see also Arkansas*, impact of loss; *Virginia* (C.S. ironclad);
Brooklyn (U.S. sloop) 185, 209–210, 215, 217, 220–221, 223, 225, 232, 236, 238, 246, 251, **256**, 262–263, 279–280, 291; *see also* U.S. Fleet passage downriver under the guns of Vicksburg vs. CSS *Arkansas* (July 15-16, 1862)
Broome, USMC Capt. John 224; *see also Hartford* (U.S. sloop)
Brown, Eliza 88; *see also* Brown, C.S. Lt. Isaac Newton
Brown, C.S. Third Assistant Engineer Eugene 118, 272, 274, 276–277, 282–283, 285–286; *see also Arkansas*, engines/machinery/propulsion; Baton Rouge, LA
Brown, C.S. Lt. (later Cmdr.) Isaac Newton 31–32, **34**, 45, 53, 56–63, 65–66, 73, 76, 85–92, 95–97, 99–102, 105–107, 111, 113–124, 127–129, 132, 135–138, 140–144, 147; 153–179, 182, 184–185, 187, 189, 192–193, 195–198, 200, 205–209, 211, 213–214, 216–217, 220–223, 225–226, 229, 233, 235, 238–243, 249–250, 253–254, 257–263, 265–266, 268–269, 271–275, 285–286, 292–294; *see also Arkansas* (C.S. ironclad ram); Baton Rouge, LA; *Eastport* (C.S. ironclad); Fort Pillow, TN; Liverpool Landing, MS; McBlair, C.S. Cmdr. Charles H.; "running the gauntlet" (July 15, 1862); USS *Essex* vs. CSS *Arkansas* at Vicksburg (July 22, 1862); U.S. Fleet passage downriver under the guns of Vicksburg vs. CSS *Arkansas* (July 15-16, 1862); Yazoo River, Battle in the (July 15, 1862)
Brown, U.S. steamboat line proprietor Capt. Joseph 25; *see also Altona*, U.S. steamer
Brown, U.S. TN Gov. Neil S. 53
Brown, U.S. Fourth Master Spencer Kellogg 245, 252–253, 255, 263, 265, 288–289; *see also Essex* (U.S. ironclad)
Browne, *New York Tribune* correspondent Junius Henri 150, 155, 202, 265
Bulloch, C.S. Cmdr. James D. 295; *see also Arkansas*, impact of loss
Butler, U.S. Maj. Gen. Benjamin 84, 234, 271, 274–275, 280–281, 289, 293; *see also* Baton Rouge, LA
Butler, C.S. Pvt. Edward 204; *see also* Louisiana, CS regiments (Artillery, 1st)

Cable, Capt. John 28; *see also John Walsh*, C.S. steamer
Cahill, U.S. Col. Thomas 280–281; *see also* Baton Rouge, LA
Calhoun (C.S. gunboat) 53
Callender, U.S. Master's Mate Eliot 134, 136–137, 155, 164, 167, 174, 179, 181, 183, 187, 196, 198–199, 215, 234, 289, 297; *see also Cincinnati* (U.S. ironclad)
Camp Moore, LA 115, 132, 207, 269, 293; *see also* Breckenridge, C.S. Maj. Gen. John C.; Ruggles, C.S. Brig. Gen. Daniel
Capitol (C.S. auxiliary steamer) 74, 78–82, **84**, 91, 96–98, 101, 119, 122, 125; *see also* Arkansas (C.S. ironclad ram)
Carondelet (U.S. ironclad) 46, 115, 136, 142, 146–147, 150–**153**, 154–**163**, 164–179, 202, 211, 231, 234, 249, 255, 260, 268, 281, 285, 296; *see also Arkansas* (C.S. ironclad ram); Walke, U.S. Cmdr. Henry; Yazoo River, Battle in the (July 15, 1862)
Carondelet (MO) Marine Railway and Drydock 26, 28–29, **49**; *see also* U.S. contractor Eads, James B.; Emerson, C.S. contractor/steamboat builder Primus

Carter, C.S. Lt. Jonathan Hanby 31, 48, 58, 63, 93, 95, 127–128, 297; *see also General Polk* (C.S. gunboat); Liverpool Landing, MS; *Missouri* (C.S. ironclad)
Cayuga (U.S. gunboat) **278**, 282, 284, 288
C.E. Hillman (steamer) 59
Champion (steamer) 189, 208; *see also* "running the gauntlet" (July 15, 1862)
Charleston (C.S. ironclad) 92; *see also* Brown, C.S. Lt. Isaac Newton
Cheatham, Nashville mayor Richard B. 53, 56–59, 64, 67
Cincinnati (U.S. ironclad) 82, 155, 157, 176, 181, 183, 187, 196, 198–199, 215–216, 234, 243, 246, 289; *see also* Callender, U.S. Master's Mate Eliot; Plum Point Bend, Battle of (1862)
City, C.S. Chief Engineer George 75, 118, 120, 178, 198, 220, 223, 235, 237, 268, 272, 274–275, 296; *see also Arkansas* (C.S. ironclad ram)
City Series (U.S.) gunboats 20–33, 120, 296; *see also* Eads, U.S. contractor James B.; Foote, U.S. RAdm. Andrew H.; Lenthall, U.S. naval architect John; Meigs, U.S. quartermaster gen. Montgomery C.; names of specific vessels, e.g. *Carondelet* (U.S. ironclad); Pook, U.S. Naval Constructor Samuel M.; Rodgers, U.S. Cmdr. John, II
Clark, C.S. Brig. Gen. Charles 270, 278; *see also* Baton Rouge, LA
Cobb, C.S. Capt. Robert S. 113; *see also* Cobb's Battery; Kentucky, CS regiments (Artillery, 1st [Cobb's Battery])
Cobb's Battery 113, 182, 204, 214, 229, 281; *see also* Cobb, C.S. Capt. Robert S.; Kentucky, CS regiments (Artillery, 1st [Cobb's Battery]); Mathews, C.S. Lt. Robert Ballard
Coleman, U.S. Paymaster Silas B. 156–158, 168, 175, 177, 179, 180, 196; *see also Tyler* (U.S. timberclad); Yazoo River, Battle in the (July 15, 1862)
Columbus (KY) 39–41, 53, 56
Combined U.S. Fleet, Passage by *see* "running the gauntlet" (July 15, 1862)
Conestoga (U.S. timberclad) 20, 24, 39, 48, 62–64; *see also Eastport* (C.S. ironclad)
Confederate River Defense Force 49, 61–62, 72, 73, 75, 82, 93–94; *see also* Fort Pillow, TN; Montgomery, C.S. Com. J.E.; New Orleans, Battle of (1862)

Index

Confederate States Marine Corps 118
Conrad, C.S. rep. Charles N. 18, **35**, 36, 65–66
Cook, C.S. Midshipman H.S. 75; *see also Arkansas* (C.S. ironclad ram)
Copper, Tin, and Sheet-Iron Manufactory (Memphis metal factory) 45
Corinth, MS, Battle of (1862) 91–92; *see also* Halleck, U.S. Maj. Gen. Henry W.
Cowan, C.S. Capt. James J. 204; *see also* Mississippi, C.S. regiments (Artillery, 1st Light)
Cox, Plantation mistress Mrs. W. 206, 235, 240; *see also* Hodges, C.S. Pilot John
Crimean War 12
Crosby, U.S. Lt. Pierce 185; *see also Pinola* (U.S. gunboat)
Currin, C.S. Rep. David M. 29, 33, 36
Curtis, C.S. Quartermaster's Mate 194; *see also Arkansas* (C.S. ironclad ram)
Cussler, U.S. novelist and explorer Clive 297; *see also Arkansas*, wreck site

Davis, U.S. RAdm. Charles H. 20, 64, 77, 84, 100, 113–114, 126, 132–133, 137, 141–**144**, 145–146, 148–149, 151, 173–174, 176, 179, 195, 198–199, 201, 203–204, 208, 210–212, 215–216, 218–220, 222, 231–234, 237, 239–241, 243–246, 249, 255, 257, 260, 262, 264–267, 292; *see also Benton* (U.S. ironclad); "running the gauntlet" (July 15, 1862)
Davis, U.S. Yeoman Edward S. 264; *see also Iroquois* (U.S. sloop)
Davis, C.S. President Jefferson 9–**10**, 12, 14, 36, 56, 67, 88, 113, 115, 123, 136, 141, 143, 204, 207, 253, 261, 265, 267, 272, 290, 295
Davis, U.S. Third Assistant Engineer Oscar S. 159; *see also* "running the gauntlet" (July 15, 1862); *Tyler* (U.S. timberclad); Yazoo River, Battle in the (July 15, 1862)
De Camp, U.S. Cmdr. John 132, 222, 232; *see also Wissahickon* (U.S. gunboat)
Deming, U.S. Pilot John 155, 231, 249; *see also Carondelet* (U.S. ironclad)
Diggins, U.S. Seaman Bartholomew 183; *see also Hartford* (U.S. sloop)
Dills, C.S. Pvt. William 214; *see also* Kentucky, CS regiments (Infantry, 3rd)

Dismukes, C.S. Capt. Paul T. 123; *see also* Tennessee, CS regiments (Artillery, 1st Heavy)
Dixon, C.S. Pvt William Y. 130, 177, 180, 199, 205; *see also* Louisiana, CS regiments (Infantry, 4th)
Doak, C.S. Gunner Henry Melvil 92; *see also Charleston* (C.S. ironclad)
Dolan, C.S. Third Assistant Engineer James 118; *see also Arkansas* (C.S. ironclad ram)
Donaldson, U.S. Carpenter Oliver 172; *see also Carondelet* (U.S. ironclad); Yazoo River, Battle in the (July 15, 1862)
Donelson, C.S. TN attorney general Daniel S. 48; *see also* Fort Donelson
Doss, U.S. Pvt. Sylvester 186; *see also Lancaster* (U.S. ram)
Dun, U.S. Second Master Martin 62; *see also Lexington* (U.S. timberclad)
Dupuy, C.S. Third Assistant Engineer John 118; *see also Arkansas* (C.S. ironclad ram)

Eads, U.S. contractor James B. 17–**18**, 20, 24, 26, 33, 36, 46, 52, 54, 57–58, 109, 120; *see also* City Series (U.S.) gunboats
Eastport (C.S. ironclad) 49–50, 52–53, 55–59, 61–65, 92, 124, 185; *see also* Brown, C.S. Lt. (later Cmdr.) Isaac Newton
Eaton, C.S. Quartermaster's Mate 193; *see also Arkansas* (C.S. ironclad ram); "running the gauntlet" (July 15, 1862)
Ed Howard (steamer) *see General Polk* (C.S. gunboat)
Edwards, C.S. Capt. William 262; *see also* South Carolina, CS regiments (Infantry, 17th)
Elizabeth City, NC, Battle of (1862) 73; *see also* Lynch, C.S. Flag Officer/Capt. William F.
Ellet, U.S. Lt. Col. Alfred 114, 123, 125–**126**, 127–129, 132, 141–142, 146, 149, 175–176, 182, 198, 240–241, 243, 245–246, 249, 257–259, 261–262, 264, 266–267; *see also Queen of the West* (U.S. ram)
Ellet, U.S. engineer/Col. Charles, Jr. 70–**72**, 114
Ellet, U.S. Medical Officer Charles Rivers 114, 123, 125–129, 142, 183
Ellet, U.S. Corporal Edward C. 245; *see also* Illinois, U.S. regiments (Infantry, 59th)
Emerson, C.S. contractor/steamboat builder Primus 25–26, 28–29, 33, 38, 41–42, 46, 50, 52–53, 57, 59, 63, 65, 71, 78,

80–81, 90, 93; *see also Altona* (steamer); *Arkansas* (C.S. ironclad); *Tennessee I* (C.S. ironclad)
Erben, U.S. Lt. Henry 232, 245, 255–256; *see also Sumter* (U.S. gunboat)
Essex (U.S. ironclad) 118, 142, **149**, 176, 183, 190, 196, 232–234, 240, 243–**247**, 249–250, 252–256, 259–260, 262, 264–265, 267–268, 271, 273, 277–279, 281–282, 284–291; *see also* Marbles as *Essex* ammunition; Porter, U.S. Cmdr. William D. ("Dirty Bill"); vs. CSS *Arkansas* at Baton Rouge (July 23–August 6, 1862) 267–293; vs. CSS *Arkansas* at Vicksburg (July 22, 1862) 231–**248**, 249–266

Fairfax, C.S. Cmdr. Archibald B. 23
Fanny (U.S. steamer) 73; *see also* Lynch, C.S. Flag Officer/Capt. William F.
Farragut, U.S. RAdm. David G. 62, 75, 80, 83–**85**, 87–88, 112, 115, 125–126, 132, 137–139, 142–143, 146–147, 149, 151, 173, 176–179, 183–185, 195, 198–204, 208–212, 215–218, 222, 230, 232–234, 237–238, 240, 243, 245–246, 255–256, 259, 262, 264–269, 273–274, 276–277, 280, 291–292; *see also Hartford* (U.S. sloop); New Orleans, Battle of (1862); "running the gauntlet" (July 15, 1862); U.S. Fleet passage downriver under the guns of Vicksburg vs. CSS *Arkansas* (July 15–16, 1862); U.S. Fleet passage upriver under the guns of Vicksburg (June 28, 1862); Vicksburg, MS
Ferdinand Kennet (steamer) 29; *see also* Brierly, Capt. Tom
Fireship defense *see* Liverpool Landing, MS
Fiske, U.S. Lt. E.A. 149; *see also* Massachusetts, U.S. regiments (Infantry, 13th)
Flag-saving heroism (Scales) 193
Flatau, C.S. Sgt. Louis S. 154, 164, 179, 184, 193, 204, 206; *see also* Mississippi, C.S. regiments (Artillery, 1st Light)
Foote, U.S. RAdm. Andrew H. 62, 88, 114, 120, 177; *see also* City Series (U.S.) gunboats; Fort Donelson, TN; Fort Henry, TN; Island No. 10 (Mississippi River)
Fort Donelson (TN) 47–48, 64, 142
Fort Henry (TN) 47–48, 62, 64, 145
Fort Pickering (TN) 38–**39**, 42, 45–47, 50, 52, 56–57, 59, 65,

69, 74, 79–80, 93; *see also* Emerson, C.S. contractor/steamboat builder Primus
Fort Pillow (TN) 30–31, 33, 41, 47, 53, 71, 73, 78, 82, 87, 92, 137; *see also* Plum Point Bend, Battle of (1862)
Fort Randolph (TN) 30, 33, 93
Fort Sumter (SC) 9, 12; *see also* Beauregard, C.S. Gen. P.G.T.; Hamilton, C.S. Lt. John; Trapier, C.S. Maj. J.H.
Fort Sumter (SC) Floating Battery 12–13, **14**, **15**, 17, 21, 28, 32; *see also* Hamilton, C.S. Lt. John; Trapier, C.S. Maj. J.H.; Yates, C.S. Col. Joseph A.
Fox, U.S. Assistant Navy Secretary Gustavus V. 16
Fulkerson, C.S. Capt. Isaac D. 93, 122; *see also General Earl Van Dorn* (C.S. gunboat)
Fulton (U.S. ram) 127, 132
Fulton, *Baltimore American* publisher Charles C. 145, 180, 224; *see also* Fulton, U.S. Third Assistant Engineer John K.
Fulton, U.S. Third Assistant Engineer John K. 145, 156, 180–181, 186–187, 189, 224, 232; *see also Hartford* (U.S. sloop)

Gallagher, Capt. T.M. (steamboat owner) 64; *see also James Woods* (steamer); *John Walsh* (steamer)
Gaty, U.S. naval architect Sam 25
General Beauregard (C.S. ram) 72; *see also* Hurt, C.S. Capt. J.H.
General Bragg (U.S. gunboat) 169, 190, **192**, 243, 246; *see also* Bishop, U.S. Lt. Joshua; "running the gauntlet" (July 15, 1862)
General Earl Van Dorn (C.S. gunboat) 93–94, 122, 127–128; *see also* Fulkerson, C.S. Capt. Isaac D.; Liverpool Landing, MS
General Polk (C.S. gunboat) 48–49, 57, 63, 93–95, 124, 127–128, 132; *see also* Carter, C.S. Lt. Jonathan Hanby; Liverpool Landing, MS; Stone, C.S. Lt. Sardine G., Jr.
Georgia (C.S. ironclad) 44
Gettis, C.S. Third Assistant Engineer James 118; *see also Arkansas* (C.S. ironclad ram)
Gift, C.S. Lt. George 42, 51, 87, 92, 97, 104–105, 108, 117, 119, 129, 140–142, 145, 154–156, 158–160, 162, 164–165, 167–168, 172, 179, 182–184, 193–194, 198, 200, 214–216, 220–224, 226, 229, 235, 242, 246, 250–251, 253–254, 258–262, 268, 272–274, 278–280, 284–285, 287; *see also Arkansas* (C.S. ironclad ram); Baton Rouge, LA; "running the gauntlet" (July 15, 1862); U.S. Fleet passage downriver under the guns of Vicksburg vs. CSS *Arkansas* (July 15-16, 1862)
Gilmore, C.S. Pilot William 117, 164–165, 183, 194, 216, 223, 230; *see also Arkansas* (C.S. ironclad ram); "running the gauntlet" (July 15, 1862); U.S. Fleet passage downriver under the guns of Vicksburg vs. CSS *Arkansas* (July 15-16, 1862); Yazoo River, Battle in the (July 15, 1862)
Gloire (French ironclad) 18–**19**; *see also Warrior*, HMS
Gorgas, C.S. Col. (later Brig. Gen.) Josiah 295; *see also Arkansas*, impact of loss
Gosport Navy Yard (VA) 13, **16**, 22–23, 31; *see also Virginia*, C.S. ironclad
Gracey, C.S. Capt. Frank P. 214; *see also* Cobb's Battery; Kentucky, CS regiments (Artillery, 1st [Cobb's Battery])
Grampus (C.S. ersatz gunboat) 29–30, 40; *see also* Miller, Capt. Marshall ("Marsh")
Grandpre, C.S. Capt. Pierre 128, 142; *see also* Liverpool Landing, MS; Louisiana, CS regiments (Artillery, 8th)
Grant, U.S. Maj. Gen. Ulysses S. 39, 41, 48, 55, 62, 71, 148, 296
Great Western (steamer) 189, 208; *see also* "running the gauntlet" (July 15, 1862)
Greenwood, MS 79–81, 85–88, 90; *see also Arkansas*, construction
Grimball, C.S. Lt. John ("Jack") 75–**76**, 95, 117, 129, 140, 144, 160, 162, 165, 192, 198, 235, 250, 273, 285, 287, 293; *see also Arkansas* (C.S. ironclad ram)
Grimme, Sawmill proprietor Frank 77, 96
Grimme's Mill, MS (Yazoo City sawmill) 77
Gross, Peter (co-owner) *see* Copper, Tin, and Sheet-Iron Manufactory (Memphis metal factory)
Gusley, USMC Pvt. Henry C. 280, 292; *see also* Baton Rouge, LA; *Westfield* (U.S. gunboat)
Guthrie, C.S. Lt. John Julius 69–71, 74, 85–86, 88, 90, 92, 117; *see also Arkansas* (C.S. ironclad)
Gwathmey, C.S. Lt. Washington 27; *see also Jackson*, C.S. gunboat
Gwin, U.S. Lt. William 146–147, 149–**157**, 158–177, 180, 211; *see also Arkansas* (C.S. ironclad ram); *Tyler* (U.S. timberclad); Yazoo River, Battle in the (July 15, 1862)

Hall, C.S. Pvt. Tom 223; *see also* Gilmore, C.S. Pilot William
Halleck, U.S. Maj. Gen. Henry W. 70–71, 74, 86, 91
Hamilton, C.S. Lt. John 12–14; *see also* Fort Sumter (SC); Fort Sumter (SC) Floating Battery
Harding, C.S. Maj. Gen. William Giles 53
Harris, C.S. TN Gov. Isham G. 41, 48, 53
Harris, C.S. Capt. Samuel S. 135, 138, 207; *see also* Missouri, C.S. State Guard
Hartford (U.S. sloop) 84, **86**, 112–113, 122, 138, 148, 150, 156, 176–**181**, 183, 185–186, 189–190, 208, 212, 215, 217–218, 222–**225**, 226, 230, 232–233, 238, 243, 246, 256, 260, 264, 280, 291; *see also* Farragut, U.S. RAdm. David G.; "running the gauntlet" (July 15, 1862); U.S. Fleet passage downriver under the guns of Vicksburg vs. CSS *Arkansas* (July 15-16, 1862); U.S. Fleet passage upriver under the guns of Vicksburg (June 28, 1862); Wainwright, U.S. Cmdr. Richard
Hartford City (steamer) 91
Haynes, C.S. Col. Milton A. 56
Haynes' Bluff, MS 145, 152
H.D. Connell (Memphis sawmill) 42
Henry, C.S. TN Sen. Gustavus A. 48; *see also* Fort Henry
Hewitt, U.S. ironmaster Abram S. 18
Hiner, U.S. Pilot David 159, 175; *see also Tyler* (U.S. timberclad); Yazoo River, Battle in the (July 15, 1862)
Hodges, Pilot John 91, 117, 156, 164, 183, 198, 206; *see also Arkansas* (C.S. ironclad ram); Cox, plantation mistress Mrs. W.; Yazoo River, Battle in the (July 15, 1862)
Hollins, C.S. Com. George 31–33, **34**, 37, 46, 49, 53–54, 71, 296
Holton, C.S. Yeoman William C. 179, 181, 224, 246; *see also Hartford* (U.S. sloop)
Hood, U.S. Seaman Thomas Jefferson 159; *see also Tyler* (U.S. timberclad); Yazoo River, Battle in the (July 15, 1862)
Hoole, C.S. Capt. James L. 214; *see also* Mississippi, C.S. regiments (Artillery, Pettus Flying Artillery/Hudson's Battery)
Hudson's Battery *see* Mississippi, C.S. regiments (Artillery, Pettus Flying Artillery/Hudson's Battery)
Huger, C.S. Lt. T.E. 184; *see also* New Orleans, Battle of (1862)

Hunter, U.S. Lt. James M. 149–177, 246, 258, 265; *see also* *Queen of the West* (U.S. ram); Yazoo River, Battle in the (July 15, 1862)
Hurt, C.S. Capt. J.H. 72; *see also* *General Beauregard* (C.S. ram)

Illinois, U.S. regiments: Infantry 7th 142; 59th 245; 63rd 245
Ironclad Board (U.S.) 20–21
Iroquois (U.S. sloop) 80, 135, 139, 146, 176, 180, 193–194, 200, 208, 215, 218–222, **226**, 264; *see also* Palmer, U.S. Cmdr. James; "running the gauntlet" (July 15, 1862); U.S. Fleet passage downriver under the guns of Vicksburg vs. CSS *Arkansas* (July 15-16, 1862); U.S. Fleet passage upriver under the guns of Vicksburg (June 28, 1862)
Irwin, U.S. Lt. Col. Richard 280; *see also* Baton Rouge, LA
Island No. 10 (Mississippi River) 67, 71, 137; *see also* New Madrid, MO

J.A. Cotton (C.S. gunboat) *see* Stevens, C.S. Lt. Henry K.
Jackman, C.S. Pvt. John S. 134, 182, 205, 220, 226, 229, 231, 254, 265; *see also* Kentucky, CS regiments (Infantry, 5th [later 9th])
Jackson (C.S. gunboat) 27, 40
Jackson (U.S. gunboat) 280
Jackson, C.S. Third Assistant Engineer William 235; *see also* *Arkansas* (C.S. ironclad ram)
James Johnson (steamer) 59, 64
James Laughlin (steamer) 29; *see also* Shirley, C.S. contractor James T.
James Woods (steamer) 59, 64
J.H. Dickey (steamer) 181, 186–187, 208; *see also* "running the gauntlet" (July 15, 1862)
John Walsh (steamer) 28; *see also* Cable, Capt. George
Johnson, C.S. Sen. Robert Ward 29, 33
Johnston, C.S. Gen. Albert Sidney 57

Katahdin (U.S. gunboat) 269, **278**, 282, 284, 286, 289; *see also* Baton Rouge, LA; Roe, U.S. Lt. Cmdr. Francis A.
Keeling, C.S. Capt. Franklin 94; *see also* *Paul Jones* (C.S. auxiliary steamer)
Kentucky, CS regiments: Artillery: 1st (Cobb's Battery) 113, 182, 204, 214, 281; Infantry: 3rd 214, 241, 250; 4th 188, 210; 5th (later 9th) 134, 182, 205, 220, 226, 229, 231, 254, 265; 6th 214, 253
Kinburn, Battle of (1855) 12; *see also* Crimean War
Kineo (U.S. gunboat) 183, 269, 277–279, 281, 284, 289, 292; *see also* Baton Rouge, LA; Ransom, U.S. Lt. George M.; "running the gauntlet" (July 15, 1862)
K.J. and B.J. Winn (Memphis sawmill) 42
Knapp, A.J. (co-owner) *see* Quinby & Robinson (Memphis foundry)
Knox, *New York Herald* correspondent Frank 152

Lancaster (U.S. ram) 122–123, 125, 127, 129–**130**, 142, 145, 185–**187**; *see also* "running the gauntlet" (July 15, 1862)
Lee, C.S. Gen. Robert E. 31
Lee, U.S. Cmdr. Samuel Phillips 81, 83, 222–223; *see also* *Oneida* (U.S. gunboat); "running the gauntlet" (July 15, 1862); U.S. Fleet passage downriver under the guns of Vicksburg vs. CSS *Arkansas* (July 15-16, 1862); Vicksburg, MS
Lee, C.S. Maj. Gen. Stephen D. 188; *see also* Warren County Courthouse
Leeds, Charles J. *see* Leeds and Company (New Orleans foundry)
Leeds and Company (New Orleans foundry) 110
Lenthall, U.S. naval architect John 20–21, 26
Lewis, U.S. Fireman William 212; *see also* *Benton* (U.S. ironclad)
Lexington (U.S. timberclad) 20, 24, 39, 62, 64, 114
Lincoln, U.S. President Abraham 13, 16–17, 33
Livermore Foundry & Machine Company (Memphis foundry) 45
Liverpool Landing, MS 79, 91–92, 94–95, 119, 122–125, 127–129, 135–136, 139; *see also* Ellet, U.S. Lt. Col. Alfred; Pinkney, C.S. Cmdr. Robert F.
Livingston (C.S. gunboat) 93–95, 127–128, 132; *see also* Liverpool Landing, MS
Lockett, C.S. engineer/Maj. Samuel H. 83, 130, 133; *see also* Vicksburg, MS
Louisiana (C.S. ironclad) 54, 75, 110, 191; *see also* New Orleans, Battle of (1862); Tift, C.S. contractors Asa and Nelson
Louisiana, CS regiments: Artillery: 1st 85, 124, 204; 8th 85, 128, 221; Infantry: 4th 130, 177, 180, 199, 205; 20th 133; 27th 85, 133, 226; 28th 124
Louisville (U.S. ironclad) 176, 196, 215–216, 243, 246, 260
Lounsberry, U.S. Master's Mate George 224; *see also* *Hartford* (U.S. sloop)
Lovell, C.S. Maj. Gen. Mansfield 76–**77**, 83, 88, 91, 113, 116–117; *see also* New Orleans, Battle of (1862); Vicksburg, MS
Lowry, U.S. Lt. Reigart B. 190–191, 227, 229; *see also* *Sciota* (U.S. gunboat)
Lynch, C.S. Flag Officer/Capt. William F. 72–73, 87, 95, 119, 123, 127, 141, 195, 213, 229, 241–242, 263, 273–275, 293; *see also* *Arkansas* (C.S. ironclad ram); Baton Rouge, LA; Brown, C.S. Lt. Isaac Newton
Lynn, U.S. Capt. John W. 149, 159; *see also* *Tyler* (U.S. timberclad); Yazoo River, Battle in the (July 15, 1862)

Mackall, C.S. Brig. Gen. William 67; *see also* Island No. 10 (Mississippi River)
Magnolia (steamer) 80–81; *see also* *Arkansas* (C.S. ironclad ram)
Magoffin, KY C.S. Gov. Beriah 40
Malaria risk 115–116, 234–235, 264
Mallory, C.S. Navy Secretary Stephen R. 10–**11**, 13–14, 17–18, 21–23, 31–34, 36, 43, 47–49, 54, 56–58, 61, 63, 65–66, 71–72, 77, 79, 86–87, 90, 119, 207, 258, 295, 297; *see also* *Arkansas* (C.S. ironclad ram); Shirley, C.S. contractor Capt. John T.; *Virginia* (C.S. ironclad)
Manassas (C.S. ironclad) 138; *see also* New Orleans, Battle of (1862)
Marbles as *Essex* ammunition 245, 250–252
Martin, C.S. Lt. John L. 135, 138; *see also* Missouri, C.S. State Guard
Massachusetts, U.S. regiments: Artillery, 2nd Light (Nims) 213; Infantry, 13th 146, 149, 215; *see also* *Queen of the West* (U.S. ram)
Mathews, C.S. Lt. Robert Ballard 214, 216, 224, 229; *see also* Cobb's Battery; Kentucky, CS regiments (Artillery, 1st [Cobb's Battery])
Maury, C.S. Cmdr. Matthew Fontaine 63
Maynadier, U.S. Capt. Henry E. 216–217, 233–234, 237–239, 244, 261, 265; *see also* mortarboats (U.S.)
McBlair, C.S. Cmdr. Charles H. 64, 69–71, 74–75, 77–82, 85–

86, 89–93, 95, 101, 117, 124; see also *Arkansas* (C.S. ironclad); Brown, C.S. Lt. Isaac Newton
McClellan, U.S. Maj. Gen. George B. 17, 20, 24, 26–27
McCowan, C.S. Brig. Gen. John P. 67; see also Island No. 10 (Mississippi River)
McDonald, C.S. Capt. Robert 135, 138; see also Missouri, C.S. State Guard
McDonald's Battery see Missouri, C.S. State Guard
McDowell, C.S. Capt. Drake 135; see also Missouri, C.S. State Guard
McDowell Battery see Missouri, C.S. State Guard
Meigs, U.S. quartermaster gen. Montgomery C. 26, 28, 30, 32–33; see also City Series (U.S.) gunboats
Memphis, Battle of (1862) 93–94, 113, 232; see also Confederate River Defense Force; Davis, U.S. RAdm. Charles H.; Ellet, U.S. engineer/Col. Charles, Jr.
Merrimack (U.S. frigate) see *Virginia* (C.S. ironclad)
Miller, Capt. James 59; see also *B.M. Runyan* (steamer)
Miller, Capt. Marshall ("Marsh") 29–30; see also *Grampus* (C.S. ersatz gunboat)
Milliken, C.S. Acting Master Samuel 51, 68, 92, 118; see also *Arkansas* (C.S. ironclad ram)
Mingo (U.S. ram) 245
Minton, C.S. Pvt. Smith 158; see also Yazoo River, Battle in the (July 15, 1862)
Minton, C.S. Pvt. Stephen 158; see also Yazoo River, Battle in the (July 15, 1862)
Mississippi (C.S. ironclad) 54, 62, 75, 113, 191; see also New Orleans, Battle of (1862); Tift, C.S. contractors Asa and Nelson
Mississippi, C.S. regiments: Artillery 1st Light 154, 179, 184, 193, 204, 206; 12th Light 137; Pettus Flying Artillery/Hudson's Battery 214, 281
Missouri (C.S. ironclad) 297
Missouri, C.S. State Guard 135, 207
Mobile (C.S. gunboat) 91
Monarch (U.S. ram) 123, 125–127, 129–**130**
Monitor (U.S. ironclad) 23, 65; see also *Virginia* (C.S. ironclad)
Montgomery, C.S. Pilot James 117; see also *Arkansas* (C.S. ironclad ram)
Montgomery, C.S. Com. J.E. 49, 61, 72, 82, 86, 93, 116–117, 123, 296; see also Confederate River Defense Force

Morfit, C.S. Assistant Surgeon Dr. Charles M. 119; see also *Arkansas* (C.S. ironclad ram)
Morgan, Miriam see Diarist Sarah Morgan
Morgan, Diarist Sarah 280, 284–285, 287–288, 292; see also Baton Rouge, LA
Morrison, U.S. Coxswain John G. 166; see also *Carondelet* (U.S. ironclad); Yazoo River, Battle in the (July 15, 1862)
mortarboats (U.S.) 209–210, 213, 216–217, 220, 233–234, 237–239, 244–246, 261, 265; see also *Arkansas* (C.S. ironclad ram); Maynadier, U.S. Capt Henry E.; Pike, U.S. Capt. E.B.; Porter, U.S. Cmdr. David Dixon; Renshaw, U.S. Cmdr. William B.; Vicksburg, MS
Mound City (U.S. ironclad) 82, 94, 157; see also Plum Point Bend, Battle of (1862)
Murray, C.S. contractor E.C. 37
Music (C.S. steamer) 269, 277, 279, 288, 290

Napoleon III, French Emperor 12; see also Crimean War
Nashville (C.S. gunboat) 93; see also Emerson, C.S. contractor/steamboat builder Primus
New Madrid (MO) 30–31, 40–41, 67; see also Island No. 10 (Mississippi River)
New Orleans, Battle of (1862) 75, 138, 191; see also Farragut, U.S. RAdm. David G.; *Louisiana* (C.S. ironclad); *Manassas* (C.S. ironclad); *Mississippi* (C.S. ironclad)
Nichols, U.S. Lt. Edward T. ("Bricktop") 226–227; see also *Winona* (U.S. gunboat)
Nims, U.S. Capt. Ormand F. 213, 219; see also Massachusetts, U.S. regiments (Artillery, 2nd Light [Nims])
Nims' Battery see Massachusetts, U.S. regiments (Artillery, 2nd Light [Nims]); Nims, U.S. Capt. Ormand F.
Nolan, Plantation owner Dr. John T. 280; see also Baton Rouge, LA
Nolan, Lilly see Nolan, Plantation owner Dr. John T.
Norman, C.S. Capt. H.T. 123; see also Tennessee, CS regiments (Artillery, 1st Heavy)

"Oh! Louisa and the babes," memorable quote 238
Old River see Yazoo River, Battle in the (July 15, 1862)
Oneida (U.S. gunboat) 176, 215, 218, 220, 222–223, **227**, 237; see also "running the gauntlet" (July 15, 1862); U.S. Fleet passage downriver under the guns of Vicksburg vs. CSS *Arkansas* (July 15–16, 1862); U.S. Fleet passage upriver under the guns of Vicksburg (June 28, 1862)
"Orphan Brigade" see Breckenridge, C.S. Brig. Gen. John C.; Kentucky, CS regiments (Infantry, 3rd, 4th, 5th [later 9th]) 6th

Paducah, KY 40–41
Palmer, U.S. Cmdr. James 219, 221–222; see also *Iroquois* (U.S. sloop)
Parker, C.S. Capt. William 23
Parks, C.S. Capt. William P. 123–124; see also Tennessee, CS regiments (Artillery, 1st Heavy)
Parsons, C.S. Lt. John D. 135, 138; see also Missouri, C.S. State Guard
Passage downriver under the guns of Vicksburg: US vs. CSS *Arkansas* (July 15–16, 1862) 204–230
Passage upriver under the guns of Vicksburg: U.S. (June 28, 1862) **133–134**
Paul Jones (C.S. auxiliary steamer) 94–95; see also Keeling, C.S. Capt. Franklin
Pensacola, FL 147–148; see also Walke, U.S. Cmdr. Henry
Perry, C.S. Seaman William Perry 230; see also *Arkansas* (C.S. ironclad ram)
Peters, U.S. Gunner Herman 155, 160, 164, 175; see also *Tyler* (U.S. timberclad); Yazoo River, Battle in the (July 15, 1862)
Pettus, C.S. MS Gov. John J. 80, 115, 123, 261
Pettus Flying Artillery/Hudson's Battery see Mississippi, C.S. regiments (Artillery, Pettus Flying Artillery/Hudson's Battery)
Phelps, U.S. Lt. Cmdr./Acting Fleet Capt. Seth Ledyard 100, 114, 146, 148, 169, 177, 180, 186, 190, 195–198–199, 212, 218, 238–239, 245, 252, 262; see also *Benton* (U.S. ironclad); *Eastport* (C.S. ironclad); *Tyler* (U.S. timberclad)
Philbrick, U.S. Carpenter's Mate William 149; see also *Essex* (U.S. ironclad)
Phillips, C.S. Acting Master John L. 92, 118, 143; see also *Arkansas* (C.S. ironclad ram)
Pike, U.S. Capt. E.B. 216, 219, 233–234, 241
Pillow, C.S. Maj. Gen. Gideon J. **27**, 30, 40

Pinkney, C.S. Cmdr. Robert F. 71, 87, 93, 95, 101, 115, 119, 122, 124, 127–129, 138; *see also* Fort Randolph, TN; Liverpool Landing, MS

Pinola (U.S. gunboat) 176, 183–185, 191, 215, 245; *see also* "running the gauntlet" (July 15, 1862); U.S. Fleet passage downriver under the guns of Vicksburg vs. CSS *Arkansas* (July 15-16, 1862); U.S. Fleet passage upriver under the guns of Vicksburg (June 28, 1862)

Plum Point Bend, Battle of (1862) 82, **94**, 157; *see also Cincinnati* (U.S. ironclad); Confederate River Defense Force; Fort Pillow, TN; *Mound City* (U.S. ironclad)

Polk (C.S. gunboat) *see General Polk* (C.S. gunboat)

Polk, C.S. Maj. Gen. Leonidas 30–31, 33, 40–41, 45, 47–50, 54–**58**, 62–63, 65, 70

Pook, U.S. Naval Constructor Samuel M. 20–21, 27–28, 30, 32; *see also* City Series (U.S.) gunboats

Pope, U.S. Maj. Gen. John 67, 71, 74, 91; *see also* Island No. 10 (Mississippi River)

Port Hudson, LA 293

Porter, U.S. Cmdr. (later RAdm.) David Dixon 63, 112, 130–131, 167, 209, 292

Porter, C.S. naval constructor John Luke 12, 22–23, 32, **35**, 50–52

Porter, U.S. Cmdr. William D. ("Dirty Bill") 145, 183, 232, 238, 243–**244**, 245–246, 249–251, 253–255, 257, 265, 267, 271, 273, 276, 280, 282, 284, 286, 288, 290–292; *see also Essex* (U.S. ironclad)

Postlethwaite, C.S. Capt. John P. 123; *see also* Tennessee, CS regiments (Artillery, 1st Heavy)

Preston, C.S. Brig. Gen. William 206, 214; *see also Arkansas*, crew recruitment

Queen of Memphis (tugboat) 94

Queen of the West (U.S. ram) 118, 146, 149, 151–178, 186, 211, 240, 243, 245–246, 249–250, 255–**257**, 258–262, 265, 267–268, 285–286; vs. CSS *Arkansas* at Vicksburg (July 22, 1862) 231–266, 286; vs. CSS *Arkansas* in Battle of the Yazoo River (July 15, 1862) 151–**171**, 172–177; *see also Arkansas* (C.S. ironclad ram); Ellet, U.S. Lt. Col. Alfred; Hunter, U.S. Lt. James M.; Yazoo River, Battle in the (July 15, 1862)

Quinby, William T. (co-owner) *see* Quinby & Robinson (Memphis foundry)

Quinby & Robinson (Memphis foundry) 45, 97

Raft defense *see* Liverpool Landing, MS

"Ram fever" 70–71, 139–140, 145

Randolph, C.S. War Secretary George W. 117, 262

Ransom, U.S. Lt. George M. 277, 279, 289; *see also Kineo* (U.S. gunboat)

Read, C.S. Lt. Charles W. 76, 87, 92–93, 95, 102, **113**, 117, 127, 129, 137–138, 140–141, 143, 153–154, 167–168, 176, 183, 185, 192, 198, 206, 211, 222, 233, 235–236, 238, 241–242, 250, 253–254, 259, 265–268, **270**, 272–275, 277, 281, 284–288, 292–293; *see also Arkansas* (C.S. ironclad ram)

Red Rover (U.S. hospital boat) 169, 173

Reilly, U.S. Capt. Thomas 142; *see also Lancaster* (U.S. ram)

Renshaw, U.S. Cmdr. William B. 209–**210**, 213, 217, 220, 233, 245–246, 256, 261; *see also* mortarboats (U.S.); *Westfield* (U.S. gunboat)

Richardson, C.S. Capt. E.S. 135; *see also* Missouri, C.S. State Guard

Richardson Artillery *see* Missouri, C.S. State Guard

Richmond (C.S. fictitious ironclad ram) 284; *see also Star of the West* (C.S. auxiliary steamer)

Richmond (U.S. sloop) 80, 176, 180–181, 185–**188**, 213, 215, 219, 223, 224–225, **228**, 232, 236–237, 239, 242, 246, 256; *see also* Alden, U.S. Cmdr. James; "running the gauntlet" (July 15, 1862); U.S. Fleet passage downriver under the guns of Vicksburg vs. CSS *Arkansas* (July 15-16, 1862); U.S. Fleet passage upriver under the guns of Vicksburg (June 28, 1862)

Richmond, C. (co-owner) *see* Copper, Tin, and Sheet-Iron Manufactory (Memphis metal factory)

Robinson, William A. (co-owner) *see* Quinby & Robinson (Memphis foundry)

Rodgers, U.S. Cmdr. John, II 20, 24, 27–28, 39, 88; *see also* City Series (U.S.) gunboats

Roe, U.S. Lt. Cmdr. Francis A. 279, 282, 284, 286, 289–290, 292; *see also Katahdin* (U.S. gunboat)

Rudloff Ridge *see* Liverpool Landing, MS

Ruggles, C.S. Brig. Gen. Daniel 86–88, 91–93, 95, 115–117, 120, 123–124, 132, 135, 207, 269–270, 293; *see also* Brown, C.S. Lt. (later Cmdr.) Isaac Newton

"running the gauntlet" (July 15, 1862) 143, 178–**189**, 190–200, **201–202**, 203, 216; *see also Arkansas* (C.S. ironclad ram); Brown, C.S. Lt. (later Cmdr.) Isaac Newton

St. Mary (C.S. gunboat) 127, 140, 142–143, 145

St. Philip (C.S. gunboat) *see Star of the West* (C.S. auxiliary steamer)

Satartia, MS 79, 114, 127, 129, 142–143

Scales, C.S. Midshipman Dabney M. 51, 68, 75–**76**, 80–81, 118, 160, 193–194, 198, 214, 216, 224, 236, 249–250, 257, 260, 274, 287; *see also Arkansas* (C.S. ironclad ram); flag-saving heroism (Scales)

Sciota (U.S. gunboat) 176, 190–191, 215, 227, 229; *see also* "running the gauntlet" (July 15, 1862); U.S. Fleet passage downriver under the guns of Vicksburg vs. CSS *Arkansas* (July 15-16, 1862); U.S. Fleet passage upriver under the guns of Vicksburg (June 28, 1862)

Scott, U.S. Lt. Gen. Winfield 17, 20–21, 26; *see also* "Anaconda Plan" (1861)

Sebastian, U.S. Pilot John 175; *see also Tyler* (U.S. timberclad); Yazoo River, Battle in the (July 15, 1862)

Selma (C.S. gunboat) 53

Sessions, Plantation owner/diarist James Oliver Hazard Perry 91

Shacklett, Pilot James 91, 118, 120, 129, 142, 152, 164; *see also Arkansas* (C.S. ironclad ram); Yazoo River, Battle in the (July 15, 1862)

Shaw, U.S. First Master Edward 175; *see also Tyler* (U.S. timberclad); Yazoo River, Battle in the (July 15, 1862)

Shiloh, Battle of (1862) 71

Shirley, C.S. contractor Capt. John T. 29, 31–36, 38–39, 41–42, 45–48, 50, 52, 54–59, 63, 65, 70–71, 75, 77–78, 80–81, 89–90, 97, 104, 107, 109, 119–120, 176, 266; *see also Arkansas* (C.S. ironclad); *James Laughlin* U.S. (steamer); *Tennessee I* (C.S. ironclad)

Sidney C. Jones (U.S. mortar schooner) 209–210; *see also* Renshaw, U.S. Cmdr. William B.

Skelton, U.S. Fourth Assistant Engineer John P. 259, 265–266; *see also Queen of the West* (U.S. ram)
S.M. Coates (Memphis foundry) 45
Smith, C.S. Brig. Gen. Martin Luther ("M.L.") 76, 83–85, 88–*89*, 113, 117, 123, 133, 206; *see also* Vicksburg, MS
South Carolina, CS regiments: Infantry 17th 262; *see also* Edwards, C.S. Capt. William
Stanton, U.S. War Secretary Edwin 70–71, 114, 259, 280; *see also* Ellet, U.S. Lt. Col. Alfred; Ellet, U.S. engineer/Col. Charles, Jr.
Star of the West (C.S. auxiliary steamer) 91, *102*, 122, 125, 138, 140, 284; *see also* C.S. fictitious ironclad ram *Richmond*
Stephenson, C.S. Capt. John A. 62; *see also* Confederate River Defense Force
Stevens, C.S. Lt. Henry K. 71, 74, 79, 85, 89–92, 105, 113, 116–117, 119, 138–140, 154–155, 158, 164, 167, 176, 179, 182, 189, 194, 198, 201, 208, 213, 220, 223, 229, 235, 238, 241–242, 249–250, 253, 260, 263, 268, 270, 272–274, 276, 278–279, 281–282, 284–289, 293; *see also Arkansas* (C.S. ironclad ram); Baton Rouge, LA
Stevens, U.S. engineer Robert L. 10–11; *see also* Stevens' Floating Battery
Stevens, Sarah F. 105; *see also* Stevens, C.S. Lt. Henry K.
Stevens Floating Battery 10–*13*
Stone, Diarist Kate 125, 239
Stone, C.S.Lt. Sardine, Jr. 93, 95; *see also General Polk* (C.S. gunboat)
Street, Mississippi writer James 106
Street, Hungerford & Company (Memphis foundry) 45
Submarine No. , (snag boat) 24, 29; *see also Benton* (U.S. ironclad); Eads, U.S. contractor James B.
Sulivane, C.S. Capt. Clement 205–206, 253–254; *see also* Porter, U.S. Cmdr. William D. ("Dirty Bill"); Van Dorn, C.S. Maj. Gen. Earl
Sumter (U.S. gunboat) 176, 196, 215, 222, 232, 234, 244–245, 255, 260, 264, 268, 278, 281, 284–285, 288, 292; *see also* Erben, U.S. Lt. Henry; *Essex*, U.S. vs. CSS *Arkansas* (July 22, 1862); "running the gauntlet" (July 15, 1862); U.S. Fleet passage downriver under the guns of Vicksburg (July 15/16, 1862); U.S. Fleet passage upriver under the guns of Vicksburg (June 28, 1862)
Swallow (U.S. ersatz gunboat) 27
Switzerland (U.S. ram) 241, 245–246

Talbott, C.S. Midshipman Daniel 118, 274, 287–289; *see also Arkansas* (C.S. ironclad ram)
Taylor see *Tyler* (U.S. timberclad)
Taylor, C.S. Paymaster Richard 119; *see also Arkansas* (C.S. ironclad ram)
Tennessee, CS regiments: Artillery: 1st Heavy 123–124, 199, 212, 219, 274; Infantry: 20th 213
Tennessee I (C.S. ironclad ram) 36, 38, 42, 50, 54, 57, 65, 69, 75, 77–78, 80, 82, 93, 107, 296; *see also Arkansas* (C.S. ironclad ram)
Tennessee II (C.S. ironclad) 109
Thompson, U.S. Seaman Edward Porter 253; *see also Essex* (U.S. ironclad)
Thompson, C.S. Brig. Gen. M. Jeff 72, *75*, 82, 87, 92–93, 116–117, 123, 135, 138; *see also Arkansas,* crew recruitment
Thompson Gravel Company, LA 297; *see also Arkansas,* wreck site
Tift, C.S. contractors Asa and Nelson 36–37, 54; *see also Louisiana* (C.S. ironclad); *Mississippi* (C.S. ironclad); New Orleans, Battle of (1862)
Totten, U.S. Brig. Gen. Joseph G. 20–21, 26
Trapier, C.S. Maj. J.H. 12–14; *see also* Fort Sumter (SC); Fort Sumter (SC) Floating Battery
Travers, C.S.Gunner Thomas 96, 105–106, 117, 235, 272, 274, 287; *see also Arkansas* (C.S. ironclad ram)
Tredegar Iron Works (VA) 9, *44*, 101
Tyler (U.S. timberclad) 20, 24, 28, 39, 62–64, 88, 114, 146–147, 149–*152*, 153–180, 182, 190, 196, 200, 211, 285; *see also Arkansas* (C.S. ironclad ram); *Eastport* (C.S. ironclad); Gwin, U.S. Lt. William; Phelps, U.S. Lt. Cmdr. S. Ledyard; "running the gauntlet" (July 15, 1862); Yazoo River, Battle in the (July 15, 1862)
Tyler, C.S. Midshipman Clarence W. 75, 118, 193, 198, 235, 272; *see also Arkansas* (C.S. ironclad ram); Brown, C.S. Lt. (later Cmdr.) Isaac Newton

Underwood, Memphis city marshal William 29; *see also* Shirley, C.S. contractor John T.
U.S. Fleet passage downriver under the guns of Vicksburg vs. CSS *Arkansas* (July 15-16, 1862) 204–230
U.S. Fleet passage upriver under the guns of Vicksburg (June 28, 1862) *133–134*

Van Dorn (C.S. gunboat) *see General Earl Van Dorn* (C.S. gunboat),
Van Dorn, C.S. Maj. Gen. Earl 42, 88, 91, *97*, 115, 119, 123–124, 136–138, 141, 143, 168, 178, 188, 204–206, 208, 236, 240, 242–243, 253, 261, 265–267, 269–273, 275, 288–290, 295–296; *see also Arkansas* (C.S. ironclad ram); Baton Rouge, LA; Vicksburg, MS; Warren County (MS) Courthouse
Vicksburg, MS 76, *78*, 80–81, 83–85, 87–88, 93, 112–116, 119, 123, 130–132, 135, 137–138, 141–142, 153–154, 182, 188–*217*, 230, 236–266, *263*, 265–267, 269, 296; *see also* mortarboats (U.S.); "running the gauntlet (July 15, 1862); U.S. Fleet passage downriver under the guns of Vicksburg vs. CSS *Arkansas* (July 15-16, 1862); U.S. Fleet passage upriver under the guns of Vicksburg (June 28, 1862); Warren County Courthouse
Virginia (C.S. ironclad) 14, 21–23, 28, 34–35, 37, *43*, 54, 61, 65, 70, 83, 107, 114, 119, 288, 297; *see also Monitor* (U.S. ironclad)

Wainwright, U.S. Cmdr. Richard 190, 208, 224; *see also Hartford* (U.S. sloop)
Walke, U.S. Cmdr. Henry 31, 52, 115, 136, 146–148, 151–*158*, 159–177, 179, 205, 234, 255, 260; *see also Arkansas* (C.S. ironclad ram); *Carondelet* (U.S. ironclad); Yazoo River, Battle in the (July 15, 1862)
Walker, C.S. Pvt. Isaac A. 226; *see also* Louisiana, CS regiments (Infantry, 27th)
Walker, U.S. Second Assistant Engineer James M. 159; *see also Tyler* (U.S. timberclad); Yazoo River, Battle in the (July 15, 1862)
Walker, C.S. War Secretary Leroy P. 27, 41, 47
Warren, U.S. Pvt. William 126
Warren County (MS) Courthouse 188–189, *191*; *see also* "running the gauntlet" (July 15, 1862); Vicksburg, MS
Warrior (British ironclad) 18–*19*; *see also Gloire* (French ironclad)
Washington, C.S. Surgeon Dr. H.W.M. 75, 119, 139, 194, 207,

Index

223, 235, 238, 240; *see also Arkansas* (C.S. ironclad ram)
Webb (C.S. gunboat) 269, 277, 279, 289–290
Webb, St. Louis *Daily Missouri Republican* correspondent William E. 51, 96, 99, 136, 159, 165, 231–232
Weggener, C.S. military tailor John H. 56
Welles, U.S. Navy Secretary Gideon 16, 18, 20, 70, 88, 112, 132, 137–138, 173, **196**, 203, 231–232, 237, 252, 262, 290–291; *see also* Davis, U.S. RAdm. Charles H.; Farragut, U.S. RAdm. David G.
Western Foundry *see* Quinby & Robinson (Memphis foundry)
Westfield (U.S. gunboat) 209, **211**, 213, 220, 245, 280, 291–292; *see also* Gusley, USMC Pvt. Henry C.; Renshaw, U.S. Cmdr. William B.
Wharton, C.S.Lt. Arthur Dickson ("A.D.") 75, 95, 118, 138, 140, 160, 167, 189, 194, 198, 235, 287; *see also Arkansas* (C.S. ironclad ram)
Wilkie, *New York Times* correspondent Franc B. ("Galway") 79
Williams, U.S. Brig. Gen. Thomas 84–86, 112, 115–116, 143–**144**, 146–147, 177, 179, 209, 213, 215, 234, 236, 239, 241, 264–265, 267–270, 277–278; *see also* Baton Rouge, LA; Vicksburg, MS
Williamson, CS chief engineer William P. 22–23; *see also Virginia* (C.S. ironclad)
Wilson, C.S. Master's Mate John A. 75, 102, 118, 120, 141, 155, 172, 186, 191, 194, 198, 214, 221, 235, 261, 268, 272, 274, 286–287; *see also Arkansas* (C.S. ironclad ram)
Winona (U.S. gunboat) **148**, 176, 195, 215, 226–227; *see also* Nichols, U.S. Lt. Edward T. ("Bricktop"); "running the gauntlet" (July 15, 1862); U.S. Fleet passage downriver under the guns of Vicksburg vs. CSS *Arkansas* (July 15-16, 1862); U.S. Fleet passage upriver under the guns of Vicksburg (June 28, 1862)
Wisconsin, U.S. regiments: Infantry 4th 149, 159, 175; *see also Tyler* (U.S. timberclad); Yazoo River, Battle in the (July 15, 1862)
Wise, C.S. Brig. Gen. Henry 73; *see also* Lynch, C.S. Flag Officer/Capt. William F.
Wissahickon (U.S. gunboat) 132, 176, 195, 215, 218, 222, 232; *see also* De Camp, U.S. Cmdr. John; "running the gauntlet" (July 15, 1862); U.S. Fleet passage downriver under the guns of Vicksburg vs. CSS *Arkansas* (July 15-16, 1862); U.S. Fleet passage upriver under the guns of Vicksburg (June 28, 1862)
Withers, C.S. Col. William Temple 137–138; *see also* Mississippi, C.S.regiments (Artillery, 12th Light); Read, C.S. Lt. Charles W.
W.L. and J.B. Griffing (Memphis sawmill) 42
Woltering, J.W. (co-owner) *see* Copper, Tin, and Sheet-Iron Manufactory (Memphis metal factory)
Wood, Capt. Elijah 49; *see also Eastport* (C.S. ironclad)
Woodward, C.S. Pvt. W. 214; *see also* Kentucky, CS regiments (Infantry, 3rd)
Wright, C.S. Rep. John Vines 29, 33
Wybrant, U.S. Chief Engineer John 186; *see also Lancaster* (U.S. ram)

Yankee (C.S. gunboat) *see Jackson* (C.S. gunboat)
Yates, C.S. Col. Joseph A. 12–13; *see also* Fort Sumter (SC) Floating Battery
Yazoo City, MS 77, 79–80, **83**, 87, 90–91, 95–110, 114–120, 124, 135, 140–141; *see also Arkansas*, construction
Yazoo River, Battle in the (July 15, 1862) 151–**171**, 172–177; *see also Arkansas* (C.S. ironclad ram); *Carondelet* (U.S. ironclad); *Queen of the West* (U.S. ram); *Tyler* (U.S. timberclad)
Young, C.S. Lt. Lot D. 188, 210; *see also* Kentucky, CS regiments (Infantry, 4th)